The
INTERNATIONAL CRITICAL COMMENTARY
on the Holy Scriptures of the Old and New Testaments

GENERAL EDITORS

G. I. DAVIES, F.B.A.
Professor of Old Testament Studies in the University of Cambridge
Fellow of Fitzwilliam College

AND

C. M. TUCKETT, Ph.D.
Professor of New Testament Studies in the University of Oxford
Fellow of Pembroke College

CONSULTING EDITORS

J. A. EMERTON, F.B.A.
Emeritus Regius Professor of Hebrew in the University of Cambridge
Fellow of St John's College, Cambridge
Honorary Canon of St George's Cathedral, Jerusalem

AND

C. E. B. CRANFIELD, F.B.A.
Emeritus Professor of Theology in the University of Durham

FORMERLY UNDER THE EDITORSHIP OF

S. R. DRIVER
A. PLUMMER
C. A. BRIGGS

LAMENTATIONS

A CRITICAL AND EXEGETICAL COMMENTARY

ON

LAMENTATIONS

BY

R. B. SALTERS

Hon. Reader in Hebrew, University of St Andrews

t&t clark

T&T Clark International
A Continuum Imprint

The Tower Building
11 York Road
London SE1 7NX

80 Maiden Lane,
New York, NY 10038
USA

www.continuumbooks.com

© R. B. Salters, 2010

All rights reserved. No part of this publication may be reproduced or transmitted in any form or by any means, electronic or mechanical, including photocopying, recording, or any information storage or retrieval system, without prior permission in writing from the publishers.

British Library Cataloguing-in-publication Data
A catalogue record for this book is available at the British Library

ISBN: 978 0 567 57651 4

The NewJerusalem and TranslitLS fonts used to print this work are available from Linguist's Software, Inc., PO Box 580, Edmonds, WA 98020-0580 USA. Tel (425) 775-1130. www.linguistsoftware.com

The Helena font used to print this work is available from OakTree Software, Inc., 498 Palm Springs Drive, Suite 100, Altamonte Springs, FL 32701 USA. Tel (407) 339-5855. www.accordancebible.com

Typeset and copy-edited by Forthcoming Publications Ltd
www.forthcomingpublications.com

Printed and bound in Great Britain by the MPG Books Group

For Audrey

Sine qua non

CONTENTS

General Editors' Preface	viii
Preface	ix
Bibliography	xi
Editions Cited	xxix
Abbreviations	xxxi
INTRODUCTION	1
Shape of the Commentary	1
Title	2
Place in the Canon	3
Authorship	4
Date and Place of Composition	7
Origin	9
Genre	11
Mesopotamian Links	13
Poetry	15
Alphabetic Acrostics	17
Text and Versions	21
Prefaces in the Septuagint and Vulgate	21
Hebrew	22
Tetragrammaton	23
Qumran	23
Greek	24
Syriac	24
Aramaic	25
Latin	26
Theology	26

COMMENTARY

CHAPTER 1	30
CHAPTER 2	107
CHAPTER 3	185
CHAPTER 4	282
CHAPTER 5	339

GENERAL EDITORS' PREFACE

Much scholarly work has been done on the Bible since the publication of the first volumes of the International Critical Commentary in the 1890s. New linguistic, textual, historical and archaeological evidence has become available, and there have been changes and developments in methods of study. In the twenty-first century there will be as great a need as ever, and perhaps a greater need, for the kind of commentary that the International Critical Commentary seeks to supply. The series has long had a special place among works in English on the Bible, because it has sought to bring together all the relevant aids to exegesis, linguistic and textual no less than archaeological, historical, literary and theological, to help the reader to understand the meaning of the books of the Old and New Testaments. In the confidence that such a series meets a need, the publishers and the editors are commissioning new commentaries on all the books of the Bible. The work of preparing a commentary on such a scale cannot but be slow, and developments in the past half-century have made the commentator's task yet more difficult than before, but it is hoped that the remaining volumes will appear without too great intervals between them. No attempt has been made to secure a uniform theological or critical approach to the problems of the various books, and scholars have been selected for their scholarship and not for their adherence to any school of thought. It is hoped that the new volumes will attain the high standards set in the past, and that they will make a significant contribution to the understanding of the books of the Bible.

G. I. D.
C. M. T.

PREFACE

There was no commentary on Lamentations in the first series of ICC, although it had been assigned at an early stage to C. A. Briggs, one of the first editors. He died in 1913 before it saw the light of day; and the death of S. R. Driver, another early editor, in 1914, followed by the First World War, may have led to a hiatus during which no re-assignment was made. The absence of such a commentary may have contributed to the comparative neglect of Lamentations in the first half of the 20th century. There has, however, been considerable increase of interest in the book in recent years, and a number of commentaries, monographs and articles have appeared.

The ICC editors do not attempt to secure 'a uniform theological or critical approach'. Previous writers in the series have, however, usually tended to wrestle with the complexities of the Masoretic text; and this has been my aim in this volume. In addition, I have tried to sketch the history of exegesis where it seemed appropriate to do so.

Working on the volume has been a most rewarding experience, and I would like to thank Professor John Emerton (a former editor of the ICC series) for his invitation to write the commentary. Professor Graham Davies, ICC's present Old Testament editor, read my entire typescript and made many very pertinent suggestions on exegesis and presentation. Duncan Burns, my copy-editor, applied his invaluable technical skills and attention to detail to my text and thereby greatly enhanced the final product; and the genial and helpful communications with Anna Turton and Dominic Mattos of T&T Clark International have meant a lot. I am indebted to them all.

During the several years of preparation I have had considerable help and direction from library staff in various institutions: the Universities of St Andrews, Edinburgh, Cambridge and Amsterdam, and the National Library of Scotland, the British Library and Princeton Theological Seminary. I am most grateful to all concerned for their expertise and gracious accessibility. I am glad to acknowledge financial support from the British Academy, The Carnegie Trust, the Honeyman Foundation and the Leverhulme Trust. Finally, for her constant support and encouragement, I wish to thank my wife, Audrey, to whom this volume is dedicated.

R. B. S.
St Andrews, September 2010

BIBLIOGRAPHY

COMMENTARIES

Berlin, A., *Lamentations: A Commentary* (Louisville, 2002).
Blayney, B., *Jeremiah and Lamentations: A New Translation with Notes Critical, Philological and Explanatory* (Oxford, 1784).
Broughton, H., *The Lamentations of Ieremy* (Amsterdam, 1608).
Budde, C., *Die Klagelieder* (KHCAT 17; Freiburg, 1898^a).
Calvin, J., *Commentaries on the Book of the Prophet Jeremiah and the Lamentations* (Edinburgh, 1855).
Dobbs-Allsopp, F. W., *Lamentations* (Louisville, 2001).
Dyserinck, J., 'De Klaagliederen', *ThT* 26 (1892), 359-80.
Ewald, H., *Die Psalmen und die Klaglieder* (Göttingen, 1866).
Fuerst, W. J., *The Books of Ruth, Esther, Ecclesiastes, The Song of Songs, Lamentations* (CBC; Cambridge, 1975).
Gerstenberger, E. S., *Psalms, Part 2, and Lamentations* (FOTL 1; Grand Rapids, 2001).
Goldman, S., 'Lamentations: Introduction and Commentary', in A. Cohen (ed.), *The Five Megilloth* (Hindhead, 1946), 66-102.
Gordis, R., 'A Commentary on the Text of Lamentations', in *The Seventy-Fifth Anniversary Volume of the Jewish Quarterly Review* (Philadelphia, 1967), 267-86.
———'Commentary on the Text of Lamentations', Part 2, *JQR* NS 58 (1967–68), 14-33.
———*The Song of Songs and Lamentations* (New York, 1974^a).
Gottlieb, H., *A Study on the Text of Lamentations* (Acta Jutlandica XLVIII; Theology Series 12; Århus, 1978).
Gottwald, N. K., *Studies in the Book of Lamentations* (SBT 14; London, 1954).
Haller, M., 'Die Klagelieder', in M. Haller and K. Galling, *Die fünf Megilloth* (HAT I:18; Tübingen, 1940), 91-113.
Henderson, E., *The Book of the Prophet Jeremiah and that of the Lamentations* (London, 1851).
Hillers, D. R., *Lamentations* (AB 7a; Garden City, 1972).
———*Lamentations* (AB 7a; 2nd edn; Garden City, 1992).
Houbigant, C. F., *Notae criticae in universos Veteris Testamenti libros* (Frankfurt/Main, 1777).
House, P. R., *Lamentations* (WBC 23B; Nashville, 2004).

Hugo de S. Victore, *In threnos Ieremiae* (MPL 175), 255-22.
Joyce, P. M., 'Lamentations', in J. Barton and J. Muddiman (eds.), *The Oxford Bible Commentary* (Oxford, 2001), 528-33.
Kaiser, O., *Klagelieder*, in H. Ringgren *et al.*, *Sprüche, Prediger, Das Hohe Lied, Klagelieder, Das Buch Esther* (ATD 16; 3rd edn; Göttingen, 1981), 291-386.
Kalkar, C. A. H., *Lamentationes Critice et Exegetice Illustratae* (Hafniae, 1836).
Keil, C. F., *The Lamentations of Jeremiah*, in vol. II of *The Prophecies of Jeremiah* (being the translation of *Der Prophet Jeremia und die Klagelieder*, Leipzig, 1872) (Edinburgh, 1874).
Kraus, H.-J., *Klagelieder* (BKAT 20; Neukirchen–Vluyn, 1960).
Löhr, M., *Die Klagelieder des Jeremia* (Göttingen, 1894).
——*Die Klagelieder des Jeremia* (Göttingen, 1906).
Meek, T. J., 'The Book of Lamentations', in *The Interpreter's Bible*, vol. VI (New York, 1956), 1-38.
Michaelis, J. D., *Observationes Philologicae et Criticae in Ieremiae Vaticinium et Threnos* (Göttingen, 1793).
Moskowitz, Y. Z., 'Lamentations', (in Hebrew), in *Five Megillot* (Jerusalem, 1990).
Nägelsbach, C. W. E., *The Lamentations of Jeremiah* (Edinburgh, 1871).
O'Connor, K. M., 'Lamentations', in C. A. Newsom and S. H. Ringe (eds.), *The Women's Bible Commentary* (London/Louisville, 1992), 178-82.
——'Lamentations', in *NIB* vol. VI (2001), 1011-72.
Oettli, S., *Die poetischen Hagiographen: Buch Hiob, Prediger Salomo, Hohelied und Klagelieder* (Nördlingen, 1889).
Peake, A. S., *Jeremiah and Lamentations*, vol. II (Edinburgh, 1912).
Perles, F., 'איכה', in A. Kahana (ed.), חמש מגלות (Tel Aviv, 1930), 97-123.
Plöger, O., *Die Klagelieder* (HAT 1/18; Tübingen, 1969), 127-64.
Provan, I. W., *Lamentations* (New Century Bible Commentary; London, 1991a).
Radbertus, P., *Pascasii Radberti: Expositio in Lamentationes Hieremiae Libri Quinque* (cura et studio Bedae Paulus; CCCM 85; Turnholt, 1988).
Re'emi, S. P., 'The Theology of Hope: A Commentary on the Book of Lamentations', in *God's People in Crisis* (ITC; Edinburgh, 1984), 73-134.
Renkema, J., *Lamentations* (Historical Commentary on the Old Testament; Leuven, 1998).
Ricciotti, G., *Le Lamentazioni de Geremia* (Rome, 1924).
Rozenberg, A. J., *The Five Megilloth*, vol. II (New York, 1992).
Rudolph, W., *Die Klagelieder* (KAT 16/3; Leipzig, 1939).
——*Die Klagelieder* (KAT 17; Stuttgart, 1962).
Salters, R. B., *Jonah and Lamentations* (OTG; Sheffield, 1994).
Schäfer, R., 'איכה', in Megilloth, *BHQ* (Stuttgart, 2004).
Schönfelder, J. M., *Die Klagelieder des Jeremias nach rabbinischer Auslegung* (Munich, 1887).

Schneedorfer, L. A., *Die Klagelieder des Propheten Jeremia* (Prag, 1876).
Streane, A. W., *Jeremiah and Lamentations* (CBSC; Cambridge, 1913).
Thenius, O., *Die Klagelieder* (Leipzig, 1855).
Theodoret, *In threnos* (MPG 81), 779-806.
Vermigli, Peter Martyr, *Commentary on the Lamentations of the Prophet Jeremiah* (trans. and ed with Introduction and Notes by D. Shute; Sixteenth-Century Essays and Studies 55; Kirksville, 2002).
Westermann, C., *Die Klagelieder: Forschungsgeschichte und Auslegung* (Neukirchen–Vluyn, 1990).
——*Lamentations: Issues and Interpretation* (Edinburgh, 1994).
Wiesmann, H., *Die Klagelieder: Übersetzt und erklärt* (Frankfurt, 1954).

ARTICLES AND OTHER STUDIES

Abelesz, A., *Die syrische Übersetzung der Klagelieder und ihr Verhältnis zu Targum und LXX* (Privigye, 1895).
Albertz, R., *Israel in Exile: The History and Literature of the Sixth Century B.C.E.* (Atlanta, 2003).
Albrecht, K., 'Die sogenannten Sonderbarkeiten des masoretischen Textes', *ZAW* 39 (1921), 160-69.
Albrektson, B., *Studies in the Text and Theology of the Book of Lamentations* (STL 21; Lund, 1963).
Alexander, P. S., 'The Textual Tradition of Targum Lamentations', *AbrN* 24 (1986), 1-26.
Allegro, J. M., 'The Meaning of the Phrase *šeṭūm hāʿayin* in Num. xxiv 3, 15', *VT* 3 (1953), 78-79.
Allegro, J. M., and A. Anderson, *Qumran Cave 4, I (4Q158–4Q186)* (DJD 5; Oxford, 1968), 75-77.
Anderson, D., 'Medieval Jewish Exegesis of the Book of Lamentations' (unpublished thesis, University of St Andrews, 2004).
Anderson, G. W., 'נצח', *TDOT* vol. IX (1998), 529-33.
Avineri, I. *Heikal Rashi* (Hebrew) (Jerusalem, 1985).
Baars, W., 'A Palestinian Syriac Text of the Book of Lamentations', *VT* 10 (1960), 224-27.
Banitt, M. (ed.), *Le Glossaire de Leipzig*, vol. III (Jerusalem, 2001).
Barnes, W. E., 'Ancient Corrections in the Text of the Old Testament (*Tikkun Sopherim*)', *JTS* 1 (1899–1900), 387-414.
Barr, J., *Comparative Philology and the Text of the Old Testament* (Oxford, 1968).
——*The Variable Spellings of the Hebrew Bible* (The Schweich Lectures of the British Academy, 1986; Oxford, 1989).
Barth, J., *Etymologische Studien zum semitischen insbesondere zum hebräischen Lexicon* (Leipzig, 1893).
Barthélemy, J. D., *Les devanciers d'Aquila* (VTSup 10; Leiden, 1963).
——*Critique Textuelle de l'Ancien Testament* (OBO 50/2; Göttingen, 1986).

Bartlett, J. R., *Edom and the Edomites* (JSOTSup 77; Sheffield, 1989).
Barton, J., *Oracles of God: Perceptions of Ancient Prophecy in Israel after the Exile* (London, 1986).
Bauer, H., and P. Leander, *Historische Grammatik der Hebräische Sprache des Alten Testaments* (Hildesheim, 1965).
Baumann, A., 'דמם', *TDOT* vol. III (1978), 262-65.
Bayno, R. (ed.), *Compendium Michlol* (Paris, 1554).
Beer, G., 'Klagelieder 5.9', *ZAW* 15 (1895), 285.
Bergler, S., 'Threni V - Nur ein Alphabetisierendes Lied? Versuch einer Deutung', *VT* 27 (1977), 304-20.
Berlin, A., 'Introduction to Hebrew Poetry', in *NIB*, vol. IV (1996), 301-15.
———*The Dynamics of Parallelism* (Grand Rapids, 2008).
Beyse, K.-M., 'עצם', *TDOT* vol. XI (2001), 304-309.
Bickell, G., *Carmina Veteris Testamenti metrice: Notas criticas et dissertationem de re metrica Hebraeorum adjecit* (Oeniponte, 1882).
———'Kritische Bearbeitung der Klagelieder', *WZKM* 8 (1894), 101-21.
Bleek, J., *An Introduction to the Old Testament*, vol. II (London, 1869).
Bloch, J., 'The Printed Texts of the Peshitta Old Testament', *AJSL* 37 (1921), 136-44.
Boase, E., *The Fulfilment of Doom? The Dialogic Interaction between the Book of Lamentations and the Pre-Exilic/Early Exilic Prophetic Literature* (JSOTSup 437; London, 2006).
Bodenheimer, F. S., *Animal Life in Palestine* (Jerusalem, 1935).
Bogaert, P.-M., 'Septante', in *DBSup* vol. XII (1928–), 536-692.
Böhmer, J., 'Ein alphabetisch-akrostisches Rätsel', *ZAW* 28 (1908), 53-57.
Böttcher, F., *Neue exegetisch-kritische Aehrenlese zum Alten Testamente* (Abtheilung 3; Leipzig, 1863).
Bouzard, W. C., *We Have Heard with Our Ears, O God: Sources of the Communal Laments in the Psalms* (SBLDS 159; Atlanta, 1997).
Brady, C. M. M., *The Rabbinic Targum of Lamentations: Vindicating God* (Leiden, 2003).
Brandscheit, R., *Gotteszorn und Menschenlied: Die Gerichtsklage des leidenden Gerechten in Klgl 3* (Trierer Theol. Studien 41; Trier, 1983).
Brenner, A., *Colour Terms in the Old Testament* (JSOTSup 21; Sheffield, 1982).
Brockelmann, C., *Lexicon Syriacum* (2nd edn; Berlin, 1928).
Brown, F., S. R. Driver, and C. A. Briggs, *A Hebrew and English Lexicon of the Old Testament with an Appendix Containing the Biblical Aramaic* (Oxford, 1968).
Brug, J., 'Biblical Acrostics and Their Relationship to Other Ancient Near Eastern Acrostics', in W. W. Hallo et al. (eds.), *Scripture in Context*, vol. III (Lewiston, 1990), 283-304.
Brunet, G., *Les Lamentations contre Jérémie* (Paris, 1968).
Budde, C., 'Das hebräische Klagelied', *ZAW* 2 (1882), 1-52.
———'Zum hebräischen Klagelied', *ZAW* 11 (1891), 234-47.
———'Zum hebräischen Klagelied', *ZAW* 12 (1892), 261-75.

───'Poetry (Hebrew)', in *HDB* vol. IV (1898ᵇ), 2-13.
───'Zum Kina-Verse', *ZAW* NS 11 (1934), 306-308.
Buhl, F., *Canon and Text of the Old Testament* (Edinburgh, 1892).
───*Geschichte der Edomiter* (Leipzig, 1893).
Cannon, W. W., 'The Authorship of Lamentations', *BS* 81 (1924), 42-58.
Cappel, L., *Critica Sacra*, auxit G. J. L. Vogel and J. G. Scharfenburg. 3 vols. (Halle, 1775–86).
Cheyne, T. K., 'Lamentations', in T. K. Cheyne and J. S. Black (eds.), *Encyclopaedia Biblica*, vol. III (London, 1902), cols. 2696-2706.
Clines, D. J. A., 'Was there an *ʾbl* II "be dry" in Classical Hebrew?', *VT* 42 (1992), 1-10.
───(ed.), *The Dictionary of Classical Hebrew* (Sheffield, 1993–).
───'Lamentations', in J. D. G. Dunn and J. W. Rogerson (eds.), *Eerdmans Commentary on the Bible* (2003), 617-22.
Cohen, A., 'Lamentations 4:9', *AJSL* 27 (1910–11), 190-91.
Cowley, A. E., *Aramaic Papyri of the Fifth Century B.C.* (Oxford, 1923).
Cross, F. M., 'The History of the Biblical Text in the Light of Discoveries in the Judaean Desert', *HTR* 57 (1964), 281-99.
───'Newly Found Inscriptions in Old Canaanite and Early Phoenician Scripts', *BASOR* 238 (1980), 1-20.
───'Studies in the Structure of Hebrew Verse: The Prosody of Lamentations 1:1-22', in C. L. Meyers and M. O'Connor (eds.), *The Word of the Lord Shall Go Forth: Essays in Honor of D. N Freedman in Celebration of His Sixtieth Birthday* (Winona Lake, 1983), 129-55.
───'4QLam', in Eugene C. Ulrich et al., *Qumran Cave 4.XI: Psalms to Chronicles* (DJD 16; Oxford, 2000), 229-37.
Cross, F. M., and D. N. Freedman, 'The Song of Miriam', *JNES* 14 (1955), 248-49.
Dahood, M., 'Textual Problems in Isaia', *CBQ* 22 (1960), 400-409.
───'Ugaritic Studies and the Bible', *Gregorianum* 43 (1962), 55-79.
───'Review of B. Albrektson *Studies in the Text and Theology of the Book of Lamentations*', *Bib* 44 (1963), 547-49.
───'Hebrew–Ugaritic Lexicography III', *Bib* 41 (1965), 311-32.
───'G. R. Driver and the Enclitic *mem* in Phoenician', *Bib* 49 (1968), 89-90.
───'Hebrew–Ugaritic Lexicography VIII', *Bib* 51 (1970), 391-404.
───'New Readings in Lamentations', *Bib* 59 (1978), 174-97.
Daiches, S., 'Lamentations ii. 13', *ExpTim* 28 (1917), 189.
Davidson, A. B., *Hebrew Syntax* (Edinburgh, 1901).
Davies, G. I., *Ancient Hebrew Inscriptions* (Cambridge, 1991).
De Boer, P. A. H., 'An Inquiry into the Meaning of the Term משא', *OTS* 5 (1948), 197-214.
De Hoop, R., 'Lamentations: The Qinah-Metre Questioned', in M. C. A. Korpel and J. M. Oesch (eds.), *Delimitation Criticism* (Assen, 2000), 80-104.

De Savignac, J., 'Theologie Pharaonique et Messianisme d'Israel', *VT* 7 (1957), 82-90.
De Vaux, R., *Ancient Israel: Its Life and Institutions* (London, 1961).
Delitzsch, F., *A System of Biblical Psychology* (Edinburgh, 1867).
——*Die Lese- und Schreibfehler im Alten Testament nebst den dem Schrifttexte einverleibten Randnoten klassifiziert* (Berlin/Leipzig, 1920).
Derousseaux, L., *La crainte de Dieu dans l'AT: Royauté, Alliance, Sagesse dans les royaumes d'Israël et de Juda; recherches d'exégèse et d'histoire sur la racine yârê'* (LD 63; Paris, 1970).
Dhorme, E., *La Bible, L'Ancien Testament, II* (Bruges, 1959).
Dicou, B., *Edom, Israel's Brother and Antagonist: The Role of Edom in Biblical Prophecy and Story* (JSOTSup 169; Sheffield, 1994).
Dines, J. M., *The Septuagint* (London and New York, 2004).
Diringer, D., *The Alphabet: A Key to the History of Mankind*, vols. I and II (3rd edn; London, 1968).
——'The Alphabet—Letters Used as Numbers', in *EncJud* vol. II (1971), 743.
Dobbs-Allsopp, F. W., 'The Syntagma of *bat* Followed by a Geographical Name in the Hebrew Bible: A Reconsideration of its Meaning and Grammar', *CBQ* 57 (1995), 451-70.
——'Tragedy, Tradition, and Theology in the Book of Lamentations', *JSOT* 74 (1997), 29-60.
——'Linguistic Evidence for the Date of Lamentations', *JANES* 26 (1998), 1-36.
——'Darwinism, Genre Theory, and City Laments', *JAOS* 120 (2000), 625-30.
——'Lamentations from Sundry Angles: A Retrospective', in N. C. Lee and C. Mandolfo (eds.), *Lamentations in Ancient and Contemporary Cultural Contexts* (SBLSS 43; Atlanta, 2008).
Dobbs-Allsopp, F. W., and T. Linafelt, 'The Rape of Zion in Thr 1, 10', *ZAW* 113 (2001), 79-81.
Döderlein, J. Ch., 'Zu den Hexaplen des Origens', *Repertorium fur biblische und morgenländische Litteratur* 6 (1780), 195-207.
Dornseiff, F., *Das Alphabet in Mystik und Magie* (Leipzig, 1922).
Driver, G. R., 'Some Hebrew Words', *JTS* 29 (1928), 391-96.
——'Studies in the Vocabulary of the Old Testament III', *JTS* 32 (1931), 361-66
——'Studies in the Vocabulary of the Old Testament IV', *JTS* 33 (1932), 38-47.
——'Notes on the Text of Lamentations', *ZAW* 52 (1934), 308-309.
——'Studies in the Vocabulary of the Old Testament VIII', *JTS* 36 (1935), 293-301.
——'Hebrew Studies', *JRAS* (1948), 164-76.
——'Hebrew Notes on "Song of Songs" and "Lamentations"', in W. Baumgartner, O. Eissfeldt, K. Elliger, and L. Rost (eds.), *Festschrift Alfred Bertholet* (Tübingen, 1950), 134-46.

———'Some Hebrew Medical Expressions', *ZAW* 65 (1953), 255-62.
———'Abbreviations in the Massoretic Text', *Textus* 1 (1960), 112-15.
———'The Resurrection of Marine and Terrestrial Creatures', *JSS* 7 (1962), 12-20.
———'Once Again Abbreviations', *Textus* 4 (1964), 76-94.
Driver, S. R., *A Treatise on the Use of the Tenses in Hebrew* (Oxford, 1892).
———*An Introduction to the Literature of the Old Testament* (9th edn; Edinburgh, 1913ᵃ).
———*Notes on the Hebrew Text and Topography of the Books of Samuel* (Oxford, 1913ᵇ).
Driver, S. R., and G. B. Gray, *A Critical and Exegetical Commentary on the Book of Job* (Edinburgh, 1921).
Ehrlich, A. B., *Randglossen zur hebräischen Bibel. Textkritisches, Sprachliches und Sachliches*, vol. VII (Leipzig, 1914).
Eissfeldt, O., *The Old Testament: An Introduction* (Oxford, 1965).
Eitan, I., 'Hebrew and Semitic Particles', *AJSL* 45 (1928), 197-211.
Elliger, K., *Deuterojesaja*, I Teilband (BKAT 11/1; Neukirchen–Vluyn, 1978).
Emerton, J. A. (ed.), *The Peshitta of the Wisdom of Solomon* (Leiden, 1959).
———'The Meaning of אבני קדש in Lamentations 4:1', *ZAW* 79 (1967), 233-36.
Fensham, F. C., 'The Semantic Field of *kly* in Ugaritic', *JNSL* 7 (1979), 27-30.
Ferris, P. W., *The Genre of Communal Lament in the Bible and the Ancient Near East* (SBLDS 127; Atlanta, 1992).
Fitzgerald, A., 'Hebrew *yd* = "Love" and "Beloved"', *CBQ* 29 (1967), 368-74.
———'*BTWLT* and *BT* as Titles for Capital Cities', *CBQ* 37 (1975), 167-83.
Fleischer, G., 'ראש II', in *TDOT* vol. XIII (2004), 262-64.
Fohrer, G., *History of Israelite Religion* (London, 1973).
Follis, E. R., 'Zion, Daughter of', *ABD* 6 (1992), 1103.
Freedman, D. N., 'Acrostics and Metrics in Hebrew Poetry', in *Pottery, Poetry and Prophecy: Studies in Early Hebrew Poetry* (Winona Lake, 1980), 51-76.
———'Acrostic Poems in the Hebrew Bible: Alphabetic and Otherwise', *CBQ* 48 (1986), 408-31.
Freedman, H., and M. Simon (eds.), *Midrash Rabbah*, vol. VII (London, 1939).
Freehof, S. B., 'Note on Lam. 1.14', *JQR* 38 (1947/48), 343-44.
Frensdorff, S., *Das Buch Ochlah W'ochlah (Massora)* (Hannover, 1864).
———*Die Massora Magna* (Hannover and Leipzig, 1876).
Friedrich, J., and W. Röllig (eds.), *Phönizische-Punische Grammatik* (AnOr 55; Rome, 1999).
Fries, S. A., 'Parallele zwischen den Klageliedern Cap. IV, V und der Maccabäerzeit', *ZAW* 13 (1893), 110-24.
Fuhs, H. F., 'ירא', in *TDOT* vol. VI (1990), 290-315.

———'ראה', in *TDOT* vol. XIII (2004), 208-42.
Gadd, C. J., 'The Second Lamentation for Ur', in D. W. Thomas and W. D. McHardy (eds.), *Hebrew and Semitic Studies* (Oxford, 1963), 59-71.
Galambush, J., *Jerusalem in the Book of Ezekiel: The City as Yahweh's Wife* (SBLDS 130; Atlanta, 1992).
Garr, W. R., 'The *Qinah*: A Study of Poetic Meter, Syntax and Style', *ZAW* 95 (1983), 54-75.
Gaster, T. H., *Myth, Legend and Custom in the Old Testament* (New York, 1969).
Gerlach, E., *Die Klagelieder Jeremiä* (Berlin, 1868).
Gerstenberger, E. S., *Psalms, Part 1, with an Introduction to Cultic Poetry* (FOTL 14; Grand Rapids, 1988).
Gerstenberger, E. S., and W. Schrage, *Suffering* (Nashville, 1980).
Gesenius, W., *Thesaurus Philologicus Criticus Linguae Hebraeae et Chaldaeae Veteris Testamenti*, I-III (Leipzig, 1835–53).
Gibson, J. C. L., *Davidson's Introductory Hebrew Grammar—Syntax* (Edinburgh, 1994).
Ginsburg, C. D., *The Massoreth Ha-Massoreth of Elias Levita* (London, 1867).
———*Introduction to the Masoretico-Critical Edition of the Hebrew Bible* (New York, 1966).
———*The Massorah: Translated into English with a Critical and Exegetical Commentary,* vol. IV (Vienna, 1897–1905).
Goldingay, J., and D. Payne, *Isaiah 40–55*, vol. II (ICC; London, 2006).
Goldziher, I., 'Ethische Deutungen', *ZAW* 31 (1911), 73.
Gordis, R., 'A Note on Lamentations ii 13', *JTS* 34 (1933), 162-63.
———*The Biblical Text in the Making: A Study of the Kethib–Qere* (New York, 1971).
———'The Conclusion of the Book of Lamentations (5:22)', *JBL* 93 (1974ᵇ), 289-93.
Gordon, C. H., *Ugaritic Textbook* (AnOr 38; Rome, 1965).
Gosling, F. A., 'An Open Question relating to the Hebrew Root נלה', *ZAH* 11 (1998), 125-32.
Gous, I. G. P., 'Lamentations 5 and the Translation of Verse 22', *OTE* 3 (1990), 287-302.
———'A Survey of Research on the Book of Lamentations', *OTE* 5 (1992), 184-205.
Gradwohl, R., *Die Farben im Alten Testament* (BZAW 83; Berlin, 1963).
Gressmann, H., 'Die literarische Analyse Deuterojesajas', *ZAW* 34 (1914), 254-97.
Grotius, H., *Annotata ad Vetus Testamentum*, vol. I (1644), 549-58.
Guillaume, A., 'A Note on Lamentations IV 9', *ALUOS* 4 (1962–63), 47-48.
———'Hebrew and Arabic Lexicography IV', *AbrN* 4 (1963–64), 1-18.
Gunkel, H., *What Remains of the Old Testament* (New York, 1928).
Gunkel, H., and J. Begrich, *Einleitung in die Psalmen* (Göttingen, 1933).
Gurewicz, S. B., 'The Problem of Lamentations iii', *ABR* 8 (1960), 19-23.

Gwaltney, W. C., 'The Biblical Book of Lamentations in the Context of Near Eastern Lament Literature', in W. W. Hallo (ed.), *Scripture in Context*. Vol. II, *More Essays on the Comparative Method* (Winona Lake, 1983), 191-212.
Hallo, W. W., 'Lamentations and Prayers in Sumer and Akkad', in J. Sasson (ed.), *Civilizations of the Ancient Near East* (4 vols.; New York, 1995), vol. III, 1871-81.
Haran, M., 'The Disappearance of the Ark', *IEJ* 13 (1963), 46-58.
Hardt, H. van der, *Threnos quos vulgus Jeremiae tribuit...* (Helmstadii, 1712).
Harrison, R. K., *Introduction to the Old Testament* (London, 1970).
Hatch, E., and H. A. Redpath, *Concordance to the Septuagint and Other Greek Versions of the Old Testament* (2 vols.; Graz, 1975).
Haupt, P., 'A New Hebrew Particle', *JHUC* 13 (1894), 107-108.
———'The Hebrew Stem Nahal, To Rest', *AJSL* 22 (1905), 195-206.
———'Some Assyrian Etymologies', *AJSL* 26 (1909), 1-26.
Hausmann, J., 'סלח', *TDOT* vol. X (1999), 258-65.
———'רנן', *TDOT* vol. XIII (2004), 515-22.
Helfmeyer, F. J., 'כלה', *TDOT* vol. VII (1995), 157-64.
Hertzberg, H. W., *I and II Samuel* (London, 1964).
Hoffmann, G., 'Ergänzungen und Berichtigungen zu Hiob', *ZAW* 49 (1931), 141-45.
Hoftijzer, J., and K. Jongeling, *Dictionary of the North-West Semitic Inscriptions* (2 vols.; Leiden, 1995).
Holladay, W. L., *The Root Šûbh in the Old Testament* (Leiden, 1958).
Honeyman, A. M., 'The Pottery Vessels of the Old Testament', *PEQ* (1939), 76–90.
———'Magôr mis-sabib and Jeremiah's Pun', *VT* 4 (1954), 424-26.
Horgan, M. P., 'A Lament over Jerusalem ("4Q179")', *JSS* 18 (1973), 222-34.
Hummel, H. D., 'Enclitic *mem* in Early Northwest Semitic, Especially in Hebrew', *JBL* 76 (1957), 85-107.
Hunter, J., *Faces of a Lamenting City: The Development and Coherence of the Book of Lamentations* (Berlin, 1996).
Illman, K.-J., 'מות', *TDOT* vol. VIII (1997), 185-201.
Jacob, B., 'Das hebräische Sprachgut im Christlich-Palästinischen', *ZAW* 22 (1902), 83-113.
———'Erkärung einiger Hiob-Stellen', *ZAW* 32 (1912), 278-87.
Jahnow, H., *Das hebräische Leichenlied im Rahmen der Völkerdichtung* (BZAW 36; Berlin, 1923).
Jastrow, M., *A Dictionary of the Targumim, the Talmud Babli and Yerushalmi, and the Midrashic Literature* (New York, 1950).
Jenni, E., and C. Westermann, *Theological Lexicon of the Old Testament* (3 vols.; Peabody, 1997).
Jepsen, A., 'Gnade und Barmherzikeit im AT', *KuD* 7 (1961), 261-71.

Jeremias, A., *Das Alte Testament im Lichte des Alten Orients* (Leipzig, 1930).
Johnson, B., 'Form and Message in Lamentations', *ZAW* 97 (1985), 58-73.
Joüon, P., 'Etudes de Philologie Sémitique', *Mélanges de la Faculté Orientale* 6 (1913), 16-211.
——*Grammaire de l'Hébreu Biblique* (Rome, 1923).
Joüon, P., and T. Muraoka, *A Grammar of Biblical Hebrew* (Subsidia Biblica 14; 2 vols.; Rome, 2005).
Joyce, P. M., 'Lamentations and the Grief Process: A Psychological Reading', *BibInt* 1/3 (1993), 304-20.
——'Sitting Loose to History: Reading the Book of Lamentations Without Primary Reference to its Original Historical Setting', in E. Ball (ed.), *In Search of Wisdom: Essays in Old Testament Interpretation in Honour of Ronald E. Clements* (JSOTSup 300; Sheffield, 1999), 246-62.
Kaiser, B. B., 'Poet as "Female Impersonator": The Image of Daughter Zion as Speaker in Biblical Poems of Suffering', *JR* 67 (1987), 164-82.
Kartveit, M., 'Sions dotter', *Tidsskrift for Teologi og Kirke* 1–2 (2001), 97-112.
Keel, O., *The Symbolism of the Biblical World: Ancient Near Eastern Iconography and the Book of Psalms* (New York, 1978).
Kellermann, D., 'סבל', in *TDOT* vol. X (1999), 139-44.
Kelso, J. A., *Die Klagelieder: Der masoretische Text und die Versionen* (Leipzig, 1901).
Kinnier Wilson, J. V., 'Hebrew and Akkadian Philological Notes', *JSS* 7 (1962), 173-83.
Klein, J., 'Lamentation over the Destruction of Sumer and Ur (1.166)', in W. W. Hallo (ed.), *The Context of Scripture*, vol. I (Canonical Compositions from the Biblical World; Leiden, 1997), 535-39.
Knox, R. A., *The Holy Bible* (London, 1955).
Köhler, L., *Hebrew Man* (London, 1956).
Kopf, L., 'Arabische Etymologien und Parallelen zum Bibelwörterbuch', *VT* 8 (1958), 161-215.
Korpel, M. C. A., and J. M. Oesch (eds.), *Delimitation Criticism* (Assen, 2000).
Kramer, S. N., 'Lamentation over the Destruction of Ur', *ANET* (1955), 455-63.
——'Sumerian Literature and the Bible', in *Studia Biblica et Orientalia* III, *Oriens Antiquus* (AnBib 12; Rome, 1959).
Kraus, H.-J., *Psalms 60–150: A Continental Commentary* (Minneapolis, 1993).
Kronholm, T., 'סמך', *TDOT* vol. X (1999), 236-54.
Kugel, J. L., *The Idea of Biblical Poetry* (New Haven, 1981).
Lachs, S. T., 'The Date of Lamentations V', *JQR* NS 57 (1966–67), 46-56.
Lambdin, T. O., 'Egyptian Loan Words in the Old Testament', *JAOS* 73 (1953), 145-55.
Lambert, W. G., *Babylonian Wisdom Literature* (Oxford, 1960).

Lanahan, W. F., 'The Speaking Voice in the Book of Lamentations', *JBL* 93 (1974), 41-49.
Landy, F., 'Lamentations', in R. Alter and F. Kermode (eds.), *The Literary Guide to the Bible* (London, 1987), 329-34.
Lee, A. C. C., 'Book of Lamentations', in *NIDB* vol. III (2008), 565-68.
———'Engaging Lamentations and *The Lament for the South*: A Cross-Textual Reading', in Lee and Mandolfo (eds.), *Lamentations in Ancient and Contemporary Cultural Contexts*, 125-38.
Lee, N. C., *The Singers of Lamentations: Cities under Siege, from Ur to Jerusalem to Sarajevo* (Leiden, 2002).
Lee, N. C., and C. Mandolfo (eds.), *Lamentations in Ancient and Contemporary Cultural Contexts* (SBLSS 43; Atlanta, 2008).
Levin, C., 'Klagelieder Jeremias', in *RGG*[4] (2001), 1394-96.
Liebreich, L. J., 'Notes on the Greek Version of Symmachus', *JBL* 63 (1944), 397-403.
Linafelt, T., *Surviving Lamentations* (Chicago, 2000).
———'The Refusal of a Conclusion in the Book of Lamentations', *JBL* 120 (2001), 340-43.
———'Surviving Lamentations (One More Time)', in Lee and Mandolfo (eds.), *Lamentations in Ancient and Contemporary Cultural Contexts*, 57-63.
Lindblom, J., *Prophecy in Ancient Israel* (Oxford, 1962).
Lipiński, E., 'נחל נחלה', in *TDOT* vol. IX (1998), 319-35.
———'נקם', in *TDOT* vol. X (1999), 1-9.
———'נתן', in *TDOT* vol. X (1999), i-iv, 90-107.
Lockshin, M. I., *Rashbam's Commentary on Exodus: An Annotated Translation* (Atlanta, 1997).
Lohfink, N., 'Enthielten die im Alten Testament bezeugten Klageriten eine Phase des Schweigens?', *VT* 12 (1962), 260-77.
Löhr, M. 'Threni III und die jeremianische Autorschaft des Buch der Klagelieder', *ZAW* 24 (1904[a]), 1-16.
———'Der Sprachgebrauch des Buches der Klagelieder', *ZAW* 24 (1904[b]), 31-50.
———'Sind Thr IV und V makkabäisch?', *ZAW* 24 (1904[c]), 51-59.
———'Alphabetische und alphabetisierende Lieder im Alten Testament', *ZAW* 25 (1905), 173-98.
Löhse, E., *Die Texte aus Qumran* (Darmstadt and Munich, 1981).
Lowth, R., *Isaiah: A New Translation; with a Preliminary Dissertation, and Notes Critical, Philological, and Explanatory* (Edinburgh, 1807).
———*De sacra poesi Hebraeorum: praelectiones academicae Oxonii habitae* (Oxford, 1821).
Lundbom, J. R., *Jeremiah 1-20* (AB 21a; New York, 1999).
Lust, J., et al., *A Greek–English Lexicon of the Septuagint* (2 vols.; Stuttgart, 1992, 1996).
Macintosh, A. A., *Hosea* (ICC; Edinburgh, 1997).
Malamat, A., 'Mari and the Bible', *JAOS* 82 (1962), 143-50.

Marcus, R., 'Alphabetic Acrostics in the Hellenistic and Roman Periods', *JNES* 6 (1947), 109-15.
Margalith, O., 'Samson's Foxes', *VT* 35 (1985), 224-29.
Martin, J. D., *Davidson's Introductory Hebrew Grammar* (27th edn; Edinburgh, 1993).
Mayes, A. D. H., and R. B. Salters (eds.), *Covenant as Context: Essays in Honour of E. W. Nicholson* (Oxford, 2003),
McCarthy, C., *The Tiqqune Sopherim and Other Theological Corrections in the Masoretic Text of the Old Testament* (OBO 36; Göttingen, 1981).
McDaniel, T. F., 'Philological Studies in Lamentations I–II', *Bib* 49 (1968), 27-53, 199-220.
———'The Alleged Sumerian Influence upon Lamentations', *VT* 18 (1968), 198-209.
McKane, W., Review of D. B. Hillers *Lamentations*, *JSS* 19 (1974), 97-105.
———*Jeremiah*, vol. I (ICC; Edinburgh, 1986).
———*Jeremiah*, vol. I (ICC; Edinburgh, 1996).
———*Micah: Introduction and Commentary* (Edinburgh, 1998).
Meinhold, J., 'Threni 2, 13', *ZAW* 15 (1895), 286.
Michaelis, J. D., *Deutsche Übersetzung des Alten Testaments* (Göttingen, 1773–88).
Middlemas, J., *The Troubles of Templeless Judah* (Oxford, 2005).
———*The Templeless Age* (Louisville, 2007).
Miller, P. D., *They Cried to the Lord: The Form and Theology of Biblical Prayer* (Minneapolis, 1994).
Mintz, A., *Ḥurban: Responses to Catastrophe in Hebrew Literature* (New York, 1984).
Moscati, S., *Introduction to the Comparative Grammar of the Semitic Languages* (Wiesbaden, 1964).
Mowinckel, S., 'The Verb *śiᵃḥ* and the Nouns *śiᵃḥ*, *śiḥā*', *ST* 15 (1961), 2-10.
———*The Psalms in Israel's Worship* (Oxford, 1962).
Mulder, M. J., 'פחת', *TDOT* vol. XI (2001), 526-28.
Müller, H.-P., 'מָשָׁא', *TDOT* vol. IX (1998), 20-24.
———'פחד', *TDOT* vol. XI (2001), 517-26.
Munch, P. A., 'Die Alphabetische Akrostichie in der jüdischen Psalmendictung', *ZDMG* 90 (1936), 703-10.
Muraoka, T., *Emphatic Words and Structures in Biblical Hebrew* (Jerusalem, 1985).
———*A Greek–English Lexicon of the Septuagint* (Louvain, 1993).
Naveh, J., 'Dated Coins of Alexander Janneus', *IEJ* 18 (1968), 20-25.
———'The Scripts in Palestine and Transjordan in the Iron Age', in J. A. Sanders (ed.), *Near Eastern Archaeology in the Twentieth Century— Essays in Honor of Nelson Glueck* (New York, 1970), 277-81.
———'The Ostracon from ʿIzbet Sartah', *IEJ* 28 (1978), 31-35.
Neusner, J., *Israel after Calamity: The Book of Lamentations* (Valley Forge, 1995).

Nicholson, E. W., *God and his People: Covenant and Theology in the Old Testament* (Oxford, 1986).
Nöldeke, T., *Compendious Syriac Grammar* (trans. J. A. Crichton; London, 1904).
Nötscher, F., 'Heisst *kābôd* auch "Seele"?', *VT* 2 (1952), 358-62.
O'Connor, K. M., *Lamentations and the Tears of the World* (Maryknoll, 2002).
Olyan, S. M., *Biblical Mourning: Ritual and Social Dimensions* (Oxford, 2002).
Pabst, H., 'Eine Sammlung von Klagen in den Qumranfunden (4Q179)', in *Qumran: Sa Piété, sa théologie et son milieu* (BETL 46; Louvain, 1978), 137-49.
Pagnini, S., אוֹצַר לְשׁוֹן הַקֹּדֶשׁ *Hoc est Thesaurus Linguae Sanctae...* (Lugduni, 1577).
Payne Smith, J. A., *A Compendious Syriac Dictionary Founded upon the Thesaurus Syriacus of R. Payne Smith* (Oxford, 1903).
Payne Smith, R., *Thesaurus Syriacus* (2 vols.; Oxford, 1901).
Peiser, F. E., 'Miscellen', *ZAW* 17 (1897), 350-51.
Perles, F., 'A Miscellany of Lexical and Textual Notes on the Bible', *JQR* NS 2 (1911/12), 97-132.
——'Was bedeutet כמות Threni 1,20?', *OLZ* 23 (1920), cols. 157-58.
——*Analekten zur Textkritik des Alten Testament* (Leipzig, 1922).
Peters, N., *Hebräische Text des Buches Ecclesiasticus* (Freiburg, 1902).
Pfeiffer, R. H., *Introduction to the Old Testament* (2nd edn; New York, 1948).
Pham, X. H. T., *Mourning in the Ancient Near East and the Hebrew Bible* (JSOTSup 302; Sheffield, 1999).
Porteous, N. W., 'Jerusalem—Zion: The Growth of a Symbol', in A. Kuschke (ed.), *Verbannung and Heimkehr* (Tübingen, 1961), 235-52.
Praetorius, F., 'Threni I 12, 14. II 6, 13. III 5, 16', *ZAW* 15 (1895), 143-46.
Provan, I. W., 'Past, Present and Future in Lamentations III 52-66: The Case for a Precative Perfect Re-examined', *VT* 41 (1991ᵇ), 164-75.
Pseudo-Jerome, *In Lamentationes Jeremiae* (MPL 28), 827-32.
Rabin, C., 'The Ancient Versions and the Indefinite Subject', *Textus* 2 (1962), 60-76.
Reider, J., *An Index to Aquila* (completed and revised by N. Turner; VTSup 12; Leiden, 1966).
Reimer, D. J., 'Good Grief? A Psychological Reading of Lamentations', *ZAW* 114 (2001), 542-59.
——'An Overlooked Term in Old Testament Theology—Perhaps', in Mayes and Salters (eds.), *Covenant as Context*, 325-46.
Reindl, J., 'נצב/יצב', in *TDOT* vol. IX (1998), 519-29.
Rendtorff, R., *The Covenant Formula* (Edinburgh, 1998).
Reyburn, W. D., *A Handbook on Lamentations* (New York, 1992).
Ringgren, H., 'זנח', in *TDOT* vol. IV (1980), 105-106.
——'מרר', in *TDOT* vol. IX (1998), 15-19.

———'עשׂה', in *TDOT* vol. XI (2001), 387-404.
Roberts, B. J., *The Old Testament Text and Versions: The Hebrew Text in Transmission and the History of the Ancient Versions* (Cardiff, 1951).
Roberts, J. J. M., 'Zion in the Theology of the Davidic–Solomonic Empire', in T. Ishida (ed.), *Studies in the Period of David and Solomon* (Winona Lake, 1982), 93-108.
Robertson, E., 'The Apple of the Eye in the Masoretic Text', *JTS* 38 (1937), 56-59.
Robinson, H. W., 'The Hebrew Concept of Corporate Personality', in P. Volz et al. (eds.), *Werden und Wesen des Alten Testaments* (BZAW 66; Berlin, 1936).
Robinson, T. H., 'Notes on the Text of Lamentations', *ZAW* 51 (1933), 255-59.
———'Once More on the Text of Lamentations', *ZAW* 52 (1934), 309-10.
———'Anacrusis in Hebrew Poetry', in *Werden und Wesen des Alten Testaments* (BZAW 66; 1936), 37-40.
Rosenfeld, A. (ed.), *Tisha B'Av Compendium* (New York, 1986).
Rössler, O., 'Die Präfixkonjugation Qal der Verba I^{ae} Nûn im Althebräischen und das Problem der sogenannten Tempora', *ZAW* 74 (1962), 125-41.
Rudolph, W., 'Der Text der Klagelieder', *ZAW* 56 (1938), 101-22.
Saebø, M., 'Who is "The Man" in Lamentations 3?', in G. Auld (ed.), *Understanding Poets and Prophets: Essays in Honour of George Wishart Anderson* (Sheffield, 1993), 294-306.
Sakenfeld, K. Doob (ed.), *The New Interpreter's Dictionary of the Bible* (3 vols.; Nashville, 2008).
Salters, R. B., 'The Mediaeval French Glosses of Rashbam on Qoheleth and Song of Songs', in *Studia Biblica* (JSOTSup 11; Sheffield, 1979), 249-52.
———'Lamentations 1:3—Light from the History of Exegesis', in P. R. Davies and J. D. Martin (eds.), *A Word in Season* (JSOTSup 42; Sheffield, 1986), 73-89.
———'The Sceptic in the Old Testament', *OTE* 2 (1989), 96-105.
———'Searching for Pattern in Lamentations', *OTE* 11 (1998), 93-104.
———'Using Rashi, Ibn Ezra and Joseph Kara on Lamentations', *JNSL* 25 (1999), 201-13.
———'Structure and Implication in Lamentations 1?', *SJOT* 14 (2000), 293-300.
———'The Unity of Lamentations', *IBS* 23 (2001), 101-10.
———'Yahweh and His People in Lamentations', in Mayes and Salters (eds.), *Covenant as Context*, 347-69.
———'The Text of Lam II 9a', *VT* 54 (2004), 273-76.
———'Text and Exegesis in Lamentations 4:21-22', in *Shai le-Sara Japhet: Studies in the Bible, its Exegesis and its Language* (Jerusalem, 2007), 327-37.

Sawyer, J. F. A., 'שָׁוְא šāwʾ Trug', in E. Jenni and C. Westermann (eds.), *Theologisches Handwörterbuch zum Alten Testament* (Band 2; Munich, 1976), 882-83.
Scharbert, J., 'אלה', in *TDOT* vol. I (1977), 261-66.
Schick, G., 'The Stems *dûm* and *damâm* in Hebrew', *JBL* 32 (1913), 219-43.
Schleusner, J. F., 'Curae Criticae et Exegeticae in Threnos Ieremiae', in *Repertorium fur biblische und morgenlandische Litteratur* (12 Teil; Leipzig, 1783), 1-57.
Schmitt, J. J., 'The Virgin of Israel: Referent and Use of the Phrase in Amos and Jeremiah', *CBQ* 53 (1991), 365-87.
Schüpphaus, J., 'בלע', in *TDOT* vol. II (1975), 136-39.
Segal, M. H., *A Grammar of Mishnaic Hebrew* (Oxford, 1958).
Segert, S., *Grammar of Phoenician and Punic* (Munich, 1976).
Seow, C. L., 'A Textual Note on Lamentations 1:20', *CBQ* 47 (1985), 416-19.
Seybold, K., 'לענה', in *TDOT* vol. VIII (1997), 14-16.
———'משח', in *TDOT* vol. IX (1998), 43-54.
Shea, W. H., 'The *qinah* Structure of the Book of Lamentations', *Bib* 60 (1979), 103-107.
Shute, D., 'Peter Martyr and the Rabbinic Bible in the Interpretation of Lamentations' (unpublished dissertation, McGill University, Montreal, 1995).
Simian-Yofre, H., 'נחם', in *TDOT* vol. IX (1998), 340-55.
———'עוד', in *TDOT* vol. X (1999), 495-515.
Simon, U., *Four Approaches to the Book of Psalms* (Albany, 1991).
Sjöberg, Å. W., and E. Bergmann, *The Collection of the Sumerian Temple Hymns* (Texts from Cuneiform Sources 3; New York, 1969).
Smalley, B., *The Study of the Bible in the Middle Ages* (3rd edn; Oxford, 1983).
Smend, R., 'Über das Ich der Psalmen', *ZAW* 8 (1888), 49-147.
Smith, W. Robertson, 'Lamentations', in *Encylopedia Britannica* (9th edn; 1882), 240-43.
Soll, W., 'Acrostic', in *ABD* vol. I (1992), 58-60.
Sommer, B. D., *A Prophet Reads Scripture: Allusion in Isaiah 40–66* (Stanford, 1998).
Stade, B., *Lehrbuch der hebräischen Grammatik* (Leipzig, 1879).
Stenmans, P., 'כבד', in *TDOT* vol. VII (1995), 17-22.
Stinespring, W. F., 'Zion, Daughter of', in *IDBSup* (1976), 985.
Stoebe, H. J., 'Die Bedeutung des Wortes *ḥsd* im AT', *VT* 2 (1952), 244-54.
Strugnell, J., 'Notes en marge du Volume V des *Discoveries in the Judaean Desert of Jordan*', *RevQ* 7 (1970), 250-52.
Thomas, D. W., ' "A Drop of a Bucket"? Some Observations on the Hebrew Text of Isaiah 40.15', in M. Black and G. Fohrer (eds.), *In Memoriam Paul Kahle* (BZAW 103; Berlin, 1968), 215-21.
Thompson, J. A., 'Israel's "Lovers"', *VT* 27 (1977), 475-81.

Tigay, J. H., 'Book of Lamentations', in *EncJud* vol. X (1972), 1368-75.
———*The JPS Torah Commentary: Deuteronomy* (Philadelphia and Jerusalem, 1996).
Tomback, R. S., *A Comparative Semitic Lexicon of the Phoenician and Punic Languages* (Missoula, 1978).
Torczyner, H., 'Anmerkungen zum Hebräischen', *ZDMG* 66 (1912), 389-409.
Tov, E., *Textual Criticism of the Hebrew Bible* (Assen and Maastricht, 1992).
Tristram, H. B., *The Natural History of the Bible* (London, 1880).
Tsevat, M., 'חלק', in *TDOT* vol. IV (1980), 447-51.
Tyer, C. L., 'Yoke', in *ABD* vol. VI (1982), 1026-27.
Vermes, G., *Post-biblical Jewish Studies* (Studies in Judaism in Late Antiquity 8; Leiden, 1975).
Von Soden, W., *Akkadisches Handwörterbuch* (Wiesbaden, 1965–81).
Wagner, S., 'יגה', in *TDOT* vol. V (1986), 380-84.
Waltke, B. K., and M. O'Connor, *An Introduction to Biblical Hebrew Syntax* (Winona Lake, 1989).
Wambacq, B. N., *L'Epithète divine Jahve Seba'ot: Etude philologique, historique et exégetique* (Paris, 1947).
Wanke, G., 'אוי und הוי', *ZAW* 78 (1966), 215-18.
Waschke, G., 'קוה', in *TDOT* vol. XII (2003), 564-73.
Watson, W. G. E., 'Archaic Elements in the Language of Chronicles', *Bib* 53 (1972), 191-207.
———*Classical Hebrew Poetry* (JSOTSup 26; Sheffield, 1984).
Weil, G. E. (ed.), *Massorah Gedolah* (Rome, 1971).
———'Qere-kethibh', in *IDBS* (1976), 716-23.
Weinfeld, M., 'ברית', in *TDOT* vol. II (1972), 253-79.
Weitzman, M. P., *The Syriac Version of the Old Testament* (Cambridge, 1999).
Wernberg-Møller, P., Review of B. Albrektson, *Studies in the Text and Theology of the Book of Lamentations*, *JSS* 10 (1965), 103-11.
Westermann, C., *Praise and Lament in the Psalms* (Edinburgh, 1981).
Willey, P. T., *Remember the Former Things: The Recollection of Previous Texts in Second Isaiah* (SBLDS 161; Atlanta, 1997).
Williamson, H. G. M., 'Laments at the Destroyed Temple', *BRev* (1990), 12-17, 44.
———*Isaiah 1–5* (ICC; London, 2006).
Wolfenson, L. B., 'Implications of the Place of Ruth in Editions, Manuscripts, and Canon of the Old Testament', *HUCA* 1 (1924), 151-78.
Wolff, H. W., *Dodekaphropheton 2, Joel und Amos* (BKAT 14/2; Neukirchen–Vluyn, 1969).
Wright, W., *A Grammar of the Arabic Language* (Cambridge, 1967).
Würthwein, E., *The Text of the Old Testament: An Introduction to the Biblia Hebraica* (2nd edn; Grand Rapids, 1995).
Wutz, F., 'Untersuchungen zu den Klageliedern', *Klerusblatt* 11 (1930), 185-87, 202-206.

———Die Transkriptionen von der Septuaginta bis zu Hieronymus (BWAT NF 9/1-2; Stuttgart, 1933).
Yaron, R., 'The Meaning of זנח', VT 13 (1963), 237-39.
Young, E. J., *An Introduction to the Old Testament* (London, 1960).
Young, G. D., 'Ugaritic Prosody', *JNES* 9 (1950), 124-33.
Ziegler, J. (ed.), *Ieremias, Baruch, Threni, Epistula Ieremiae*, vol. XV of *Septuaginta: Vetus Testamentum Graecum* (1957, 1976), 467-94.
Zobel, H.-J., 'הוי', in *TDOT* vol. III (1978), 359-64.
———'חסד', in *TDOT* vol. V (1986[a]), 44-64.
———'יהודה', in *TDOT* vol. V (1986[b]), 482-99.
———'עליון', in *TDOT* vol. XI (2001), 121-39.
Zorrell, F., 'Isaiae cohortatio ad poenitentiam (caput 1)', *VD* 6 (1926), 65-79.

EDITIONS CITED

MASORETIC TEXT

A. Alt and O. Eissfeldt (eds.), *Biblia Hebraica* (3rd edn; 1937) (*BHK*).
K. Elliger and W. Rudolph (eds.), *Biblia Hebraica Stuttgartensia* (1977) (*BHS*).
R. Schäfer (ed.), *Biblia Hebraica quinta editione* (2004) (*BHQ*).
B. Kennicott (ed.), *Vetus Testamentum Hebraicum cum variis lectionibus* (2 vols.; Oxford, 1776–80).
G. B. de Rossi, *Variae lectiones Vetus Testamentum* (Parmae, 1784–99).

THE SEPTUAGINT

H. B. Swete (ed.), *The Old Testament According to the Septuagint* (3 vols.; Cambridge, 1902).
J. Ziegler (ed.), *Ieremias, Baruch, Threni, Epistula Ieremiae* . Vol. 15 of *Septuaginta: Vetus Testamentum Graecum* (1957).

THE MINOR GREEK VERSIONS (AQUILA AND SYMMACHUS)

M. Ceriani (ed.), *Codex Syro-hexaplaris Ambrosianus* (Milan, 1874).
F. Field, *Origenis Hexaplorum quae supersunt* (2 vols.; Oxford, 1867).
J. Ziegler (ed.), *Ieremias, Baruch, Threni, Epistula Ieremiae*. Vol. 15 of *Septuaginta: Vetus Testamentum Graecum* (1957).

THE OLD LATIN

P. Sabatier, *Bibliorum Sacrorum latinae versiones antiquae: seu, Vetus Italica, et caeterae quaecunque in codicibus mss. & antiquorum libris reperiri potuerunt: quae cum Vulgata latina, & cum textu graeco comparantur* (Paris, 1751).

THE VULGATE

R. Weber, *Biblia Sacra Iuxta Vulgatam Versionem* (Stuttgart, 1969).

THE PESHITTA

A. M. Ceriani (ed.), *Translatio-Syra Pescitto Veteris Testamenti* (Milan, 1876–83).
B. Albrektson, *Studies in the Text and Theology of the Book of Lamentations* (STL 21; Lund, 1963).
S. Lee (ed.), *Vetus Testamentum Syriace* (London, 1823).

THE TARGUM

P. de Lagarde, *Hagiographa Chaldaice* (1873), 170-79.
E. Levine, *The Aramaic Version of Lamentations* (New York, 1976).
A. van der Heide, *The Yemenite Tradition of the Targum of Lamentations: Critical Text and Analysis of the Variant Readings* (1981).
P. S. Alexander, *The Targum of Lamentations* (The Aramaic Bible 17B; Collegeville, 2008).

TALMUD

L. Goldschmidt, *Der Babylonische Talmud* (Berlin, 1897–1935).
I. Epstein (ed.), *The Babylonian Talmud Translated into English* (London, 1938–61).
M. Schwab, *Le Talmud de Jérusalem* (Paris, 1885).

MIDRASH

A. Cohen (trans.), *Midrash Rabbah* (London, 1939).
J. Nacht, *Tobia ben Elieser's Commentar zu Threni (Lekach Tob)* (Berlin, 1895).
A. W. Greenup, *The Commentary of R. Tobia b. Elieser on Echah* (London, 1908).

MEDIAEVAL RABBINIC COMMENTARIES

R. Solomon ben Isaac, מקראות גדולות (Warsaw, 1860–69) (Rashi).
R. Abraham Ibn Ezra, מקראות גדולות (Warsaw, 1860–69) (IE[1]).
────── [מקראות גדולות] פי" הטעמים לראב"ע (Warsaw, 1860–69) (IE[2]).
R. Joseph Kara, פי" ר" יוסף קרא על מגלת איכה (ed. S. Buber; Breslau, 1901).

ABBREVIATIONS

AB	Anchor Bible
ABD	D. N. Freedman (ed.), *The Anchor Bible Dictionary* (6 vols.; New York, 1992)
ABR	*Australian Biblical Review*
AbrN	*Abr-Nahrain*
AJSL	*American Journal of Semitic Languages and Literature*
AnBib	Analecta Biblica
ANET	J.B. Pritchard (ed.), *Ancient Near Eastern Texts Relating to the Old Testament* (3rd edn; Princeton, 1969)
AnOr	Analecta orientalia
AO	*Der Alte Orient*
Aq	Aquila
ATD	Das Alte Testament Deutsch
AV	Authorized Version
BASOR	*Bulletin of the American Schools of Oriental Research*
BDB	F. Brown, S. R. Driver and C. A. Briggs, *A Hebrew and English Lexicon of the Old Testament* (Oxford, 1907)
BETL	Bibliotheca Ephemeridum Theologicarum Lovaniensium
BHK	R. Kittel (ed.), *Biblia Hebraica* (3rd edn; Stuttgart, 1937)
BHQ	*Biblia Hebraica Quinta, (Megilloth)* (Stuttgart, 2004)
BHS	W. Rudolph and H. P. Rüger (eds.), *Biblia Hebraica Stuttgartensia* (Stuttgart, 1967–77)
Bib	*Biblica*
BibInt	*Biblical Interpretation*
BKAT	Biblischer Kommentar: Altes Testament
BL	H. Bauer and P. Leander, *Historische Grammatik der Hebräischen Sprache des Alten Testaments* (Hildesheim, 1965)
BRev	*Bible Review*
BT	*The Bible Translator*
BWAT	*Beiträge zur Wissenschaft vom Alten Testament*
BZAW	Beihefte zur Zeitschrift für die alttestamentliche Wissenschaft
CAD	I. J. Gelb *et al.* (eds.), *The Assyrian Dictionary of the Oriental Institute of the University of Chicago* (Chicago, 1956–)
CBC	Cambridge Bible Commentary

CBQ	*Catholic Biblical Quarterly*
CBSC	Cambridge Bible for Schools and Colleges
CCCM	Corpus Christianorum: Continuatio mediaevalis (Tunhout, 1969–)
cf.	compare
ch(s).	chapter(s)
CTA	A. Herdner (ed.), *Corpus des tablettes en cunéiformes alphabétiques découvertes à Ras Shamra-Ugarit de 1929 à 1939.*
DBSup	L. Pirot and A. Robert (eds.), *Dictionnaire de la Bible, Supplément* (Paris, 1928–)
DCH	D. J. A. Clines (ed.), *The Dictionary of Classical Hebrew* (Sheffield, 1993–)
DISO	Ch. F. Jean and J. Hoftijzer (eds.), *Dictionnaire des inscriptions sémitiques de l'ouest* (Leiden, 1965)
DJD	Discoveries in the Judean Desert
DOTT	D. W. Thomas (ed.), *Documents from Old Testament Times* (London, 1958)
ed(s).	editor(s)
EncJud	*Encyclopaedia Judaica* (16 vols. Jerusalem, 1972)
ESV	English Standard Version
ExpTim	*Expository Times*
FOTL	The Forms of Old Testament Literature
GK	E. Kautzsch (ed.) and A. E. Cowley (trans.), *Gesenius' Hebrew Grammar* (2nd edn; Oxford, 1910)
GN	Geographical name
GNB	Good News Bible
HALOT	L. Koehler, W. Baumgartner, and J. J. Stamm, *The Hebrew and Aramaic Lexicon of the Old Testament* (trans. and ed. under the supervision of M. E. J. Richardson; 4 vols.; Leiden, 1994–99)
HAT	Handbuch zum Alten Testament
HDB	F. C. Grant and H. H. Rowley (eds.), *Hastings' Dictionary of the Bible* (New York, 1963)
HKAT	Handkommentar zum Alten Testament
HTR	*Harvard Theological Review*
HUCA	*Hebrew Union College Annual*
IB	*Interpreter's Bible*
IBS	Irish Biblical Studies
ICC	International Critical Commentary
IDB	G. A. Buttrick (ed.), *The Interpreter's Dictionary of the Bible* (4 vols.; Nashville, 1962)
IDBSup	K. Crim (ed.), *The Interpreter's Dictionary of the Bible: Supplementary Volume* (Nashville, 1976)
Int	*Interpretation*
ITC	*International Theological Commentary*
JANES	*Journal of the Ancient Near Eastern Society*

JAOS	*Journal of the American Oriental Society*
JB	Jerusalem Bible
JM	P. Joüon and T. Muraoka, *A Grammar of Biblical Hebrew* (Subsidia biblica 14; 2 vols.; Rome, 1993)
JNSL	*Journal of Northwest Semitic Languages*
JPS	New Jewish Publication Society Translation
JQR	*Jewish Quarterly Review*
JR	*Journal of Religion*
JSOT	*Journal for the Study of the Old Testament*
JSOTSup	*Journal for the Study of the Old Testament*, Supplement Series
JSPSup	*Journal for the Study of the Pseudepigrapha*, Supplement Series
JSS	*Journal of Semitic Studies*
JTS	*Journal of Theological Studies*
K	*Kethib*
KAT	Kommentar zum Alten Testament
KBL	L. Koehler and W. Baumgartner, *Lexicon in Veteris Testamenti libros* (2nd edn; Leiden, 1958)
KHCAT	*Kurzer Hand-Commentar zum Alten Testament*
KuD	Kerygma und Dogma
LD	Lectio divina
LSJ	H. G. Liddell, R. Scott, and H. S. Jones, *A Greek–English Lexicon* (9th edn with revised supplement; Oxford, 1996)
LXX	Septuagint
MPG	J.-P. Migne (ed.), Patrologia graeca
MPL	J.-P. Migne (ed.), Patrologia latina
MS(S)	Manuscript(s)
MT	The Masoretic Text
NEB	New English Bible
NF	neue Folge
NIB	*The New Interpreter's Bible*
NIV	New International Version
NJPS	New Jewish Publication Society Translation
NRSV	New Revised Standard Version
NS	New Series
NTT	*Norsk Teologisk Tidsskrift*
OBO	Orbis Biblicus et Orientalis
OL	Old Latin
OLZ	*Orientalistische Literaturzeitung*
OTE	*Old Testament Essays*
OTG	Old Testament Guides
OTL	Old Testament Library
OTS	*Oudtestamentische Studiën*
P	Peshitta
p.	person
pl.	plural

prb. rdg.	probable reading
Q	*Qere*
REB	Revised English Bible
RevQ	*Revue de Qumran*
RGG	*Die Religion in Geschichte und Gegenwart* (4th edn; Tübingen, 1998–)
RSV	Revised Standard Version
RV	Revised Version
s.	singular
SBLDS	Society of Biblical Literature Dissertation Series
SBLSS	Society of Biblical Literature Symposium Series
SBT	Studies in Biblical Theology
SH	Syrohexapla
SJOT	*Scandinavian Journal of the Old Testament*
ST	*Studia theologica*
STL	Studia Theologica Lundensia
Sym	Symmachus
T	Targum
TA	*Tel Aviv*
TDOT	G. J. Botterweck and H. Ringgren (eds.), *Theological Dictionary of the Old Testament* (trans. J. T. Willis, G. W. Bromiley, and D. E. Green; 15 vols.; Grand Rapids, 1974–)
THAT	E. Jenni and C. Westermann (eds.), *Theologisches Handwörterbuch zum Alten Testament* (2 vols.; Munich, 1971–76)
ThT	Theologisch tijdschrift
v(v).	verse(s)
VT	*Vetus Testamentum*
VTSup	Supplements to *Vetus Testamentum*
WBC	Word Biblical Commentary
WZKM	*Wiener Zeitschrift für die Kunde des Morgenlandes*
ZAH	*Zeitschrift für Althebräistik*
ZAW	*Zeitschrift für die alttestamentliche Wissenschaft*
ZDMG	*Zeitschrift der deutschen morgenländischen Gesellschaft*

INTRODUCTION

Shape of the Commentary

After dealing with introductory matters such as title, date, origin etc., I come to the commentary proper. The commentary is in four sections. I begin with an introductory piece to each chapter—a brief survey of its structure, style and characteristics. Secondly, I offer my translation of the chapter in hand. Although presented *before* the exegetical commentary begins, it is an expression of my findings in the textual and exegetical matters that follow. While I have tried to reproduce a few poetic features, such as chiasmus and assonance, I have not, by any means, aimed at literary excellence. In an ideal world the aim would be to reproduce (in English etc.) a poetic equivalent, but this is hardly possible. Beauty of form and image in any literary work is necessarily lost in translation, though it may be imitated to some extent. The same can be said of meaning.[1] Dobbs-Allsopp (2008, 24) calls for poetic renderings of biblical poems and he cites John Donne's English rendering of Lamentations as an example of what he yearns for. But what he envisages is virtually impossible.[2] While Donne's piece is poetically impressive, it is often wide of the exegetical mark. I am not convinced that Hebrew scholars, even with a literary expert at their very elbow, are capable of this. They are, after all, not known for their felicitous and sensitive vocabulary or style even when free from the constraints of translating the ancient text. What is important in a serious academic work is vocabulary which embodies exegesis. I have, therefore, aimed at clarity in expressing the exegetical issues involved in each passage.

The third part comprises notes on the Masoretic Text (MT) and the ancient Versions in order to establish the text on which I propose to base my argument. When there is no significant material questioning the received text, this section is empty, and MT stands. Occasionally the Versions raise textual issues, and it is possible that the *Vorlagen* of the ancient translators differed from the prototype of MT, though, more often than not, the latter lies behind the various renderings.

---

[1] Fitzgerald's rendering of the Rubaiyat of Omar Khayyam is a treasured work of art, but the precise exegesis of the original quatrains is not always represented in Fitzgerald's poetry, which often strays from the original.
[2] A glance at Knox's translation (see below, *Alphabetic Acrostics*), which aims merely to reproduce the alphabetic element, should bring such aspirations down to earth.

In the fourth section I launch into the exegetical commentary. I take the text verse by verse, citing Hebrew words and phrases and offering an explanation of disputed passages. This section also involves the Versions (insofar as they reflect the exegetical decisions made by the translators) and, when it is thought appropriate, the history of interpretation up to recent commentaries.

The reader will notice that the mediaeval Jewish exegetes—Rashi, Ibn Ezra and Joseph Kara—are cited in the commentary from time to time. There being no critical editions, I have relied on *Mikraoth Gedoloth* for the commentaries of Rashi and Ibn Ezra (designated IE¹) and on the publication by Buber of Kara's commentary. In addition, I refer to IE². This represents what is traditionally thought to be a second composition by Ibn Ezra and appears, in *Mikraoth Gedoloth*, alongside Ibn Ezra's first commentary under the heading פי" הטעמים לראב"ע. The authenticity of the latter has been questioned by Shute (1995, 25-35; 2001, xxv),³ but I am not persuaded. The fact that IE¹ stuck his neck out against prevailing opinion vis-à-vis the interpretation of the suffix at 3.1—T, Rashi, Kara, MR and MLT all assume that the referent there is God—and that IE² is in agreement with IE¹, even using similar language, leads me to be cautious in this regard.

Title

Hebrew MSS usually entitle the book איכה (Alas!)—i.e. by the first word of ch. 1, a custom seen also in Genesis (בראשית), Exodus (שמות) etc. The name 'Lamentations' is an English rendering of the Vulgate *Lamentationes*, which, in turn, is a translation either⁴ of the early Jewish title (*b. Bat.* 14b)⁵ קִינוֹת or of the Septuagint's title θρῆνοι. Jerome, in his *Prologus Galeatus* and in the prologue to his translation, has: *Incipiunt Threni, i.e. lamentationes, quae Cynoth hebraice inscribuntur*. The fact that these 'titles' are in the plural shows that the book, although only 154 verses in length, was seen as a collection of items/units, in the same way as the title of the book of Psalms (תהלים, ψαλμοί, *Psalmi*) suggests a plurality of recognisable units.⁶

The Peshitta title (most MSS; cf. Albrektson, 36f.) ܐܘܠܝܬܐ ܕܐܪܡܝܐ ܢܒܝܐ *'wlyth d'rmy' nby'* is also in the plural. The Peshitta goes further

---

³ The Ibn Ezra scholar Uriel Simon maintains that it *is* authentic in spite of what Shute says, so we must await further research on Ibn Ezra commentaries before concluding to the contrary. Alexander (2008, 63) is also sceptical.
⁴ It is difficult to say which came first—the Hebrew קינות or the Greek θρῆνοι.
⁵ We find it also referred to as מגלת קינות (*y. Šab.* 16.15.c) and ספר קינות (*b. Ḥag.* 8b).
⁶ Contrast the title of the book 'Song of Songs' which, though comprised of several sections, has a title in the singular. Chapter divisions are a late development (cf. Würthwein 1995, 21, 98), but the alphabetic acrostics (see *Acrostics*) employed by the authors of Lamentations ensured that the book was viewed as five items.

and identifies the units as the work of the prophet Jeremiah (see *Authorship*); indeed, the Syriac MSS tend to number the first four as ܐܘܠܝܬܐ ܩܕܡܝܬܐ *'wlyth qdmyt'*, ܐܘܠܝܬܐ ܕܬܪܬܝܢ *'wlyth dtrtyn*, ܐܘܠܝܬܐ ܕܬܠܬ *'wlyth dtlt*, ܐܘܠܝܬܐ ܕܐܪܒܥ *'wlyth d'rbʿ*; and the final one bears the title ܨܠܘܬܐ ܕܐܪܡܝܐ *ṣlwth d'rmy'* 'the prayer of Jeremiah'.

Renkema (33) objects to 'Lamentations' as a translation of קִינוֹת in that the noun קִינָה is specifically a dirge, a lament for the dead. What he really objects to, however, is the title קִינוֹת itself, because, for him (cf. also Clines, 617), 'dirges' does not adequately describe the contents of the book (see *Genre*); indeed, the noun קִינָה does not appear in any of the poems, although the metre 3:2, sometimes referred to as קִינָה-metre, is largely maintained in chs. 1–4. He is right in his observation that the reason for the title lies in the tradition that Jeremiah is the author of the book and that he is associated with a collection known as הַקִּינוֹת (2 Chron 35.25). This passage reads: 'Jeremiah also uttered a lament for Josiah, and all the singing men and singing women have spoken of Josiah in their laments to this day. They made these a custom in Israel; they are recorded in the Laments (הַקִּינוֹת)'. After Josephus (*Ant.* x.5.1) refers to the death of Josiah, he says, 'But all the people mourned greatly for him, lamenting and grieving on his account many days; and Jeremiah the prophet composed an elegy to lament him, which is extant till this time also'. It may be[7] that Josephus regarded our book, Lamentations, as containing Jeremiah's lament for Josiah. Certainly, Jerome was of this opinion as we gather from his commentary on Zech 12.11. In fact Josephus may have been referring to *another* document entitled הַקִּינוֹת—a document no longer extant, for it is difficult to detect any reference to the death of Josiah in our 'Lamentations'. Renkema's (further) objection—to איכה as a title because that word belongs to the genre 'dirge'—is groundless in that it is simply the first word of the book and is really meant as a marker rather than a title.

Place in the Canon

Unlike some other items in the Megilloth—Ecclesiastes, Song of Songs, Esther—the canonical status of Lamentations does not seem to have been in question. This may be because of its early association with the prophet Jeremiah. Indeed, although Jerome notes that in some circles the book is to be found among the Hagiographa or Writings (the third section of the Hebrew Bible, the other two being Torah and Prophets), Jerome himself regards it as part of the book of Jeremiah; and Josephus appears to treat both books as one. In the Septuagint (LXX) translation, Lamentations stands immediately after Jeremiah, and it is that placing which carried over via the Vulgate into the Authorized Version and most modern

---

[7] Cf. Robertson Smith (242).

English translations. The exceptions are the Jewish translations (cf. JPS) whose translators follow the Hebrew grouping. In the Hebrew tradition Lamentations is found in the Writings, not in the Prophets; however, within that section its position varies. In the Babylonian Talmud, in a passage which appears to deal with chronological order, we read: 'the order of the writings is Ruth, Psalms, Job, Proverbs, Ecclesiastes, Song of Songs, Lamentations, Daniel, Esther, Ezra and Chronicles' (*b. B. Bat.* 14b). In the latter passage the five scrolls (Megillot) are not placed together but scattered throughout the section, and Lamentations comes well down the list. But elsewhere, in editions of the Hebrew Bible and in Hebrew manuscripts, books are grouped according to Jewish liturgical practice. The books known as the five scrolls, which were traditionally linked with the five major Jewish festivals, are there grouped together. But there was no fixed tradition. Even in printed Jewish Bibles there was no uniformity in grouping the books: occasionally we find the Megillot between the Torah and the Prophets, while at other times each of the five Megillot has been inserted after a book of the Torah. These practices presumably reflect liturgical interests. In some manuscripts and printed Bibles the order seems to be controlled by the order in which the major Jewish festivals occur; hence there is a strong tradition which runs: Song of Songs (Passover), Ruth (Weeks), Lamentations (Ninth of Ab), Ecclesiastes (Sukkoth), Esther (Purim). The modern editions of the Hebrew Bible (*BHK, BHS, BHQ*) follow more or less the order of the eleventh-century manuscript—Codex Leningradensis. This lists the Megillot in what was thought to be a chronological order: Ruth, Song of Songs (the young Solomon), Ecclesiastes (the old Solomon), Lamentations and Esther. There is, therefore, no 'correct' or original order. Indeed, although we may make observations as to the place Lamentations finds itself in one or other codex, the idea of order was probably meaningless in the pre-codex era when works existed as separate scrolls.

Authorship

The Coverdale Bible (1535) and the Authorized Version (1611) both entitle the book 'The Lamentations of Jeremiah', and subsequent commentators were inclined to take Jeremian authorship for granted. Blaney's 1784 commentary is entitled *The Lamentations of Jeremiah*, and in the introduction the author does not feel the need to discuss authorship. In German scholarship, this consensus was beginning to change by the middle of the nineteenth century,[8] and Nägelsbach (1871,[9] 13) confidently

---

[8] Kalkar (57ff.) is sceptical, Thenius (120ff.) thinks that Jeremiah wrote only chs. 2 and 4, while Ewald (326) rejects Jeremian authorship entirely and attributes the book to 'Barûkh oder ein anderer'. It would seem, therefore, that the first questioning of Jeremian authorship—by von der Hardt (1712, [7])—had, to some extent, fallen on deaf ears or had not been taken seriously, in that a full century had elapsed before the question was raised

declares '...I know not how the conclusion can be escaped, that Jeremiah could not have written the Lamentations'. At the same time, the traditional position was strenuously upheld by Bleek (102f.), Keil and others, and Keil devoted several pages (339-50) to defence of Jeremian authorship. The latter viewpoint was maintained in English-speaking scholarship, and Streane (1881, 358) declared '...we conclude that Jeremiah was beyond question the writer of the Book'. Robertson Smith (1882, 241-43), Cheyne (2704f.) and S. R Driver (1913ª, 461-65) eventually inclined to the views of Ewald and Nägelsbach, but English translations appearing as late as 1952 (RSV—'The Lamentations of Jeremiah') continued to assume Jeremian authorship, though more recent ones (NEB, JB, NRSV, NIV) are content with the title 'Lamentations'. If the latter are right in distancing themselves from connections with Jeremiah, how did that link come about and in what circumstances?

There is no doubt that the tradition is ancient. The LXX's superscription (q.v.) runs: 'When Israel was taken captive, and Jerusalem made desolate, Jeremiah sat weeping and lamented with this lamentation over Jerusalem and said...' If, as seems likely, the translation into Greek took place before the end of the second century BCE, it follows that already[10] at that time there was a strong tradition that Jeremiah was the author of Lamentations; and Lamentations is placed immediately after the book of Jeremiah in the LXX. The Peshitta entitles the book 'The Lamentations of Jeremiah', the Targum begins 'Jeremiah the prophet and high priest said...' and the Vulgate begins with a superscription very similar to that of the LXX. The Church Fathers follow this tradition, which is also found in the Babylonian Talmud: 'Jeremiah wrote the book of his name, Kings and Lamentations' (*b. B. Bat.* 15a). Rashi and Kara both accept this position,[11] and Luther and Calvin refer to 'The Lamentations of Jeremiah'. So, in the history of the book's interpretation there has been a substantial body of opinion which has held to Jeremian authorship. The view that Jeremiah was not the author is comparatively recent.

It should be noted that the Hebrew text of Lamentations has no superscription and makes no mention of Jeremiah; and in the Hebrew Bible the book stands in the Megilloth and is not juxtaposed with Jeremiah. Since it is difficult to imagine Jeremiah's name having been *omitted* in transmission—the name is more likely to have been added—it is likely that the Hebrew text preserves the more original tradition. How, then, did the book

---

again. Von der Hardt had suggested that the five chapters had been written by Daniel, Shadrach, Meshach, Abednego and Jehoiachin respectively. Nägelsbach (7) refers to von der Hardt as 'learned and whimsical'; cf. also Keil (340).

[9] The German original is dated 1868.

[10] It is usually thought that the Greek style in the superscription suggests that the latter is an actual translation from Hebrew and not simply added in the Greek transmission of the text. If that is so, it pushes the tradition back even further.

[11] IE¹ is critical of the tradition and, at 3.1, appears to distance himself from it; cf. Simon (185).

come to be linked with Jeremiah? It is likely that the origin of the tradition lies in 2 Chron 35.25: 'And Jeremiah lamented for Josiah; and all the singing men and singing women spoke of Josiah in their laments, unto this day; and they made them an ordinance in Israel; and, behold, they are written in the Laments[12] (הקינות)'. Furthermore, although the term 'Yahweh's anointed' in Lam 4.20 probably alludes to King Zedekiah, it was interpreted by early commentators as referring to Josiah; and this would have consolidated the link with Jeremiah. If this was the origin of the tradition, it probably arose in the time when it was thought important 'to father anonymous literature on some conspicuous personality' (Peake, 293). In the Pseudepigraphic literature, the names of Adam and Eve, Solomon etc. were associated with works with a view to enhancing their standing. Moses, the lawgiver, becomes the source of all Israelite law, David the author of all the Psalms. The association with Jeremiah will have been strengthened by the tone of passages such as Jer 8.18-22; 9; 14; 15, which are to some degree reminiscent of Lamentations; and some have argued that passages such as Lam 3.14, 53-56 fit neatly with or, indeed, refer back to, incidents in Jeremiah's life (cf. Jer 20.7; 38.6-8). Driver (1913[a], 461) felt that these similarities may in fact have been the origin of the tradition. It may have been thought that Lamentations must have been written by someone who had experienced the fall of Jerusalem and the subsequent hardships, and that the prophet Jeremiah, who had been present at that time and who had agonised over the imminent collapse of Judah, was the most probable author.[13]

One argument in favour of the Jeremian link is that the disaster is presented in both books as the result of national sin (compare Lam 1.5 with Jer 26). This is an important observation, but it is not conclusive. We may suppose from this comparison that the author of Lamentations was following in the footsteps of, or was in agreement with, Jeremiah on this point but we may perhaps go no further than that. Again, there is the observation that the sympathetic outpouring of emotion on behalf of the nation, which is clear in Lamentations, is also found in Jeremiah (cf. Jer 14 and 15). Thirdly, some scholars have drawn attention to similarities of expression in both books. Thus the phrase 'eyes flow down with tears' (1.16; 2.11; 3.48-49) is echoed in Jeremiah (9.1, 18; 13.17; 14.17); the phrase 'terror on every side' (2.22) is found in Jeremiah (6.25); and the reference to the 'sins of the prophets and priests' (2.14; 4.13) is shared with Jeremiah (2.8; 5.31; 14.13f.; 23.11). On the other hand, some are

---

[12] The Catholic Biblical Association of America translation actually renders the last word 'Lamentations', thereby linking this passage with the book in the Hebrew Bible!

[13] As late as 1954, Wiesmann (54-84) argued strongly in favour of Jeremian authorship. Conservative scholarship was reluctant to abandon the traditional position; however, Young (1960, 364) admits that we cannot really know who the author was, although he feels that Jeremiah is the likely author, and Harrison (1970, 1069) rejects Jeremian authorship.

convinced that evidence points in the opposite direction—that Jeremiah could not have written Lamentations. The fact that the latter has a vocabulary which differs from that of Jeremiah, is inconclusive, for it might be argued that Jeremiah is prophecy while Lamentations is psalmody. But the evidence from the contents of the book is more convincing. At Jer 2.18 Jeremiah is scathing about Egypt, at 2.36 he expects Egypt to be hostile to Judah, while at Lam 4.17 the author expresses expectation of help from Egypt; and this leads us to conclude that the latter passage could hardly have been written by Jeremiah. Again, if Lam 4.19f. refers to the flight of Zedekiah and entourage, described in 2 Kgs 25.4f., it would seem that the author was in the royal party, whereas Jer 38.28 implies that Jeremiah was in custody at that time. It would seem, therefore, that it is difficult to hold to the tradition that Jeremiah wrote Lamentations;[14] but if not Jeremiah, who did write the book? Was there in fact only one author?

Some of the arguments adduced against Jeremian authorship lead one to consider the possibility that Lamentations was not written by a single author. The fact that the order of the alphabet assumed in ch. 1 is different from that in chs. 2, 3 and 4 raises the possibility that the authorship of the first chapter differed from that of chs. 2, 3 and 4. The fact that ch. 5 is the only poem which is not an acrostic, has a different metre and form from chs. 1–4, and that ch. 3 differs in genre from the other chapters has a bearing on the debate. Furthermore, if the view of Rudolph (1962, 209)—that ch. 1 was written just after 597 BCE and not after the fall of Jerusalem in 586 BCE—could be sustained, the case for single authorship is further weakened. Finally, if we abandon Jeremiah authorship, we might ask why we should think in terms of a single author for a collection of poems which make no claims as regards authorship. If the book of Psalms, once thought to be the work of David, can be thought of as a collection of poems by various writers, why not the collection we call Lamentations?

Date and Place of Composition

While Jeremiah was considered to be the author of Lamentations, there was little or no debate as to the date of the poems—they had been written shortly after Jerusalem's fall (cf. LXX superscription)—but ever since Jeremian authorship was rejected or seriously questioned there have been various suggestions as to date, ranging from confident precise dating[15] to

---

[14] In ancient times the question of authorship was not investigated as it is today. For many, it was not important; and we know very little about the authorship of any of the books in the Hebrew Bible.

[15] For example, Bleek (102f.) was confident that the poems were written 'in the interval between the surrender of the city and its destruction, during which time Jeremiah remained in Jerusalem (Jer xxxix. 14)'. And Keil (350) is in no doubt that Jeremiah completed the work 'in the interval between the destruction of Jerusalem and his involuntary departure to Egypt'.

sheer agnosticism.[16] Many scholars are still inclined to the view that Lamentations was written not long after the fall of Jerusalem (cf. House 302f.). Certainly it would seem that 586 BCE is the *terminus a quo* in that the poems' concentration, for the most part, has to do with the terrible events of the aftermath of the city's destruction.[17] But the view that the poems were written soon after the fall of Jerusalem was not always dependent on the Jeremian link. It was argued that the poetry was too vivid to have been penned by someone other than an eyewitness. This view is not now generally pressed. Provan (12) argues that 'the "freshness" and "vividness" of a poem may have more to tell us about the creativity and imagination of the author than about when he lived'; and Hallo (1872) draws attention to several laments commemorating the fall of the Third Dynasty of Ur written 'in such vivid terms that they suggest the reaction of eyewitnesses' but are known to have been composed over fifty years after the event! These observations, coupled with the abandonment of Jeremian authorship, lead on to the possibility that there was more than one author, and that, if so, the authors could have composed their poems over a wide period.[18] There is more dispute over the *terminus ad quem*. Some scholars would argue that, since Deutero-Isaiah (normally dated 550–539 BCE) appears to lean on the text of Lamentations to some extent, 539 should be the cut-off point; but opinions differ. Some assume a different date for each poem;[19] and Lachs (46-56) would date ch. 5 as late as the Maccabean period.[20] Some of the arguments for the dating of the poems—especially the precise dating—lack hard evidence and are unconvincing, but with Dobbs-Allsopp's study of the linguistic evidence one is on firmer ground.[21] Dobbs-Allsopp concludes that the language of the poems is not as late as the late postexilic and Maccabean periods. It has closest affinities with the language of Ezekiel and so should probably be dated in the sixth century. His final paragraph (36) suggests a *terminus ad quem* as 520 BCE, but he adds 'or even somewhat later'; and in the final footnote he draws back, preferring to date the poems earlier rather than later in the period 587–520.

---

[16] Cf. Provan (11), who states: '...it is not clear that, even if we were to accept the consensus view as to the historical events (i.e. the events surrounding the fall of the Judaean state in the early sixth century B.C.) to which they [the poems] allude, we should be able to say very much about when they were *composed*'.

[17] Rudolph (1962, 209f.) argued that ch. 1 was composed shortly after 597 BCE, but most commentators are unconvinced.

[18] The comments of Provan and Hallo do not, of course, rule out the possibility that eyewitnesses were involved in the composition of Lamentations.

[19] For example, Pfeiffer (723) dates chs. 2 and 4 c. 560, ch. 1 between 520 and 444, ch. 5 before 520, and ch. 3 c. 4th–3rd century.

[20] See Dobbs-Allsopp (1998, 2-11) for a critique of past attempts at dating Lamentations.

[21] Dobbs-Allsopp regards the instinct of M. Löhr (1904^b) to date the book by grappling with the vocabulary and syntax as sound, but the latter's method is found wanting in some respects.

We can say very little about the provenance of the poems. It is generally held that they were composed in Judah.[22] The several references to Judah, Jerusalem and Zion, and the complete absence of any specific reference to Babylon, point in the same direction.

Origin

In Lamentations we are dealing with a short document—one of the shortest in the Hebrew Bible—and to refer to it as a book is misleading. Such terminology sets us thinking in terms of name/title, bulk, authorship, structure etc. In the Leningrad Codex, Lamentations follows Qoheleth and precedes Esther, none of which are introduced either by name/title or marker, the only indicator (that we are ending one section and beginning a new one) being that the final verse is followed by a note indicating the number of verses which comprise that part of the Writings. In the case of Lamentations, the note is 154.[23]

The alphabetic structures (see *Acrostics*) point to five separate entities/divisions: (1) 22 verses, (2) 22 verses, (3) 66 verses, (4) 22 verses, and (5) 22 verses. If we accept that Jeremiah cannot have been the author of the whole corpus (see *Authorship*), then the question arises as to whether there may have been more than one author,[24] and that the document may comprise a collection. The latter seems the most reasonable position to take. It is true that Lamentations seems, at first glance, to be homogeneous—alphabetic structures, similar language throughout etc., but it does not follow that the units were written by the same person, any more than that similar psalms were written by the same pen. It may simply mean that (as with the psalms) a similar focus has led to a degree of imitation, as I have argued elsewhere.[25] It seems to me that these poems were composed in connection with the commemoration of the destruction of Jerusalem and the temple in 586 BCE; that is to say, the purpose of the compositions was liturgical. The commemoration of the destruction of the first temple (along with that of the destruction of the second temple in 70 CE) takes

---

[22] Ewald (326) believed that Lamentations originated in Egypt, but his opinion has not commanded support.

[23] The division of the biblical text into chapters is comparatively late, originating with Stephen Langton (1150–1228) who divided the Vulgate into chapters (Würthwein, 20f.). The system was adopted in Hebrew MSS in the 14th century. While the divisions arrived at may have been debateable or controversial at times, the division of Lamentations was not: because of the alphabetic acrostics (see below) it must have been the easiest of all biblical documents to divide.

[24] Scholars differ on this: some—e.g. Gottwald (28-30), Rudolph (1962, 196-99) and House (303)—still hold to the view that only one author was involved.

[25] Salters (2001, especially 108-10). It is difficult to imagine why someone, having finished a sophisticated alphabetic acrostic poem concerning the aftermath of the fall of Jerusalem, would begin again and pen another alphabetic acrostic on the same theme! One might just, perhaps, accept the possibility that the author of one of the poems 1 to 4 could have supplemented it with the more prayerful fifth poem.

place in the Jewish community on the 9th of Ab. That it is an ancient custom is confirmed by references to it in rabbinic writings: *y. Šab.* 16.15c; *Lev. R.* 15.4. It would seem strange if the commemoration should have begun as late as Talmudic times; it is more likely that mourning and lamenting the destruction of the temple and of Jerusalem will have begun shortly after 586 BCE in some form or other. Jeremiah 41.5 reads: 'Eighty men arrived from Shechem and Shiloh and Samaria, with their beards shaved and their clothes torn and their bodies gashed, bringing grain offerings and incense to present at the temple of the Lord'. That this event took place shortly after the destruction of Jerusalem is clear from the context; and McKane (1996, 1019) stresses that the mourning of these pilgrims was because of the destruction of the temple[26] and that they 'were taking their offerings to the sacred site of the ruined temple'. If these northerners felt drawn to the site, how much more would surviving Judahites continue to view that temple mount with reverence and, if and when the occupying forces permitted, begin to worship again in that place? Zechariah 7.3-5 (dated c. 518 BCE) refers to mourning and fasting in the fifth month (Ab) and implies that this had been customary for the previous seventy years; and 2 Kgs 25.8 and Jer 52.12-14 confirm that the destruction of Jerusalem took place in the fifth month. It seems likely, therefore—though we do not have any hard evidence—that those who remained in Jerusalem engaged in some rudimentary form of commemoration from an early stage.

Central to the commemoration in the Jewish community is the reading of Lamentations, after which there are many prayers which have accumulated over the centuries.[27] These prayers receive their inspiration from the text of Lamentations. In particular, the alphabetic structures seem to appeal to author after author, so that, for example, we have one where a first line begins with a letter of the alphabet, as in Lamentations, and much more sophisticated ones where, for example, every stanza begins with the word איכה, the first strophe of the first stanza has five occurrences of א, the second strophe has six occurrences of ב; the first strophe of the second stanza has five occurrences of ג, the second strophe has occurrences of ד, etc. What has happened is that the material for the commemoration has grown over the centuries, some of the vocabulary has been re-used, and the alphabetic acrostic has been imitated and intensified to a greater or lesser degree. Although we cannot prove it, this quasi-imitation was probably at work in the growth of Lamentations. The first author chose to structure his piece as an alphabetic acrostic and to compose in the unbalanced (3:2) rhythm; and the other authors followed in similar vein. The fifth poem is a (concluding) prayer and, though not in 3:2 rhythm, is alphabetical in that it has twenty-two lines.[28]

---

[26] Later, Isa 61.3 looks back on 'those who mourn in Zion' (אֲבֵלֵי צִיּוֹן).

[27] See A. Rosenfeld, *Tisha B'Ab Compendium*, 1986.

[28] It is likely that the lengthy section—vv. 2-18—is an expansion, so that the number 22 (lines) is achieved. If so, this would be a further example of imitation.

We must, however, realise that the compositions that have come down to us are not, as they stand, the raw reactions to the events of 586 BCE. Westermann (104) is right when he points out that 'the acrostic form cannot have been a feature of this material at its early stage'.[29] There is no doubt that the survivors of the catastrophe will have reacted immediately with horror and grief. Many expressions of misery, affliction and sad reflections will have escaped the lips of these people who now struggled to come to terms with the loss of their city, their temple, their family and their way of life. These utterances—and there would be a multitude and a growing number of them—would be shared and repeated to such an extent that, when the community of survivors came to remember and to commemorate the calamity of 586, the now familiar phrases and vocabulary would be employed by those (the poets) who gave voice to the feelings of the people. Westermann (102) seems to believe that the poems existed and served as community songs before they were subjected to re-shaping as acrostics. I would have thought that the compositions, as we have them, are the end result of, perhaps, years of commemorating the fall of Jerusalem, during which time the vivid and poignant descriptions of misery were preserved and became the raw material for special and artistic endeavour. It is likely that in the efforts to refine the material for the commemoration of the catastrophe some compositions were deemed better than others. It is possible that Pss 74 and 79 were at some stage employed in the commemoration (Kraus 1993, 97, 134), but were rejected when a final decision on the collection was made regarding style, quality etc.

Genre

In the history of interpretation scholars have differed somewhat as to the genre of the material in Lamentations.[30] Are we dealing with plaintive laments, or should we detect another genre here? Even on a first encounter, one finds that Lamentations reminds us of some of the lament elements in the book of Psalms. Early in the 20th century, Gunkel (1933) analysed the psalms according to their respective types (*Gattungen*).[31] The type of psalm which most readily comes to mind for Lamentations is the communal lament,[32] in that the initial impression conveyed by the text is of a grief-stricken community; indeed, the fifth poem conforms quite

---

[29] He might have added that the 3:2 rhythm may also have been absent at this stage.
[30] See Westermann (1994, 24-85) for a survey of opinion; cf. also N. C. Lee (1-37) for some recent observations.
[31] It was discovered that there are five main categories: hymns, communal laments, royal psalms, individual laments and individual thanksgiving psalms, in addition to less common types such as entrance liturgies and pilgrimage psalms, and others which appear to display various forms (what Gunkel called mixed poems). It was observed that these types are not confined, in the Hebrew Bible, to the book of Psalms, but are to be found elsewhere, for instance in Lamentations.
[32] On the communal lament, see Ferris (1992, especially 89-92).

closely to those psalms in the Psalter which are usually placed in this category, such as Pss 74, 79 and 89. Communal laments appear to have been composed and recited on occasions of national disaster, military or natural, and also to *commemorate* such events. It is usual, in these laments, for the people to complain to God about their plight and to plead with him for relief or deliverance. Although ch. 5 is closest in shape to the other psalms of communal lament in the book of Psalms, all five poems have that flavour. The other four chapters of Lamentations fall into the category of 'mixed poems', since they exhibit or draw on elements from at least two recognizable types: the individual lament and the communal lament; but there is also a considerable element of what we may call the קינה, the funeral song (see *Title*). The funeral song or dirge is, in its simplest form, the utterance of the bereaved at the bier or at the burial of the deceased. It probably varied considerably from one community to another in the ancient Near East,[33] only later taking on fixed forms; but it has, as essential elements, cries of shocked despair (in Hebrew איכה, איך, אה, אההּ), the statement of death, the name of the deceased, the contrast between 'then' and 'now', and the call to weep. In the Hebrew Bible the funeral dirge is uncommon. References are made to it, as when Abraham mourns the death of Sarah (Gen 23.2); and occasionally we get a fragment of such a dirge, as when David mourns the death of Abner (2 Sam 3.33-34). The fullest example is the passage in 2 Sam 1.17-27 where David mourns for Saul and Jonathan: 'Alas, the mighty are fallen...! Beloved and lovely were Saul and Jonathan... Daughters of Israel, weep for Saul... I grieve for you, my brother Jonathan; you were most dear to me.' In the course of time the dirge came to be applied, metaphorically, to the demise of communities—cities and tribes—their downfall being interpreted as death. In the Hebrew Bible this device is seen in Amos: 'Fallen, no more to rise, is the maiden Israel; forsaken on her land, with none to raise her up' (Amos 5.2; cf. Jer 9.20-21), although in the hands of the prophet the form is used *before* the fall in order to shock the audience. The funeral song is profane[34] and focuses on death and misery. By contrast, the lament proper, although it *may* have death as its occasion, concentrates on life, and is often in the form of a prayer to God, confessing sins, expressing trust and pleading for help (e.g. Ps 79).

In the history of interpretation, most scholars designate Lam 5 as a communal lament; and ch. 3 is considered to be of mixed genre, mainly of individual lament and communal lament. When it comes to chs. 1, 2 and 4 there is some disagreement. Jahnow (118), Eissfeldt (501-503), Plöger (128f.) and Hillers[1] (xxviif.), classified chs. 1, 2 and 4 of Lamentations as modified dirges, while Westermann (88), vehemently opposed to such a designation, sees all three as clear communal laments. Driven

---

[33] On mourning rites in the ancient Near East, see Pham (16-35), Olyan (28-61).
[34] Even in the literary form of the dirge (2 Sam 1.17-27; Amos 5.2) this is evident: there is no religious context, no prayer, no mention of God.

by form-critical considerations—preventing him also from viewing the alphabetic acrostics in any positive way—Westermann argues that the addressing of (and references to) Yahweh in chs. 1, 2 and 4 rule out the designation 'dirge'. This approach lands Westermann in the uncomfortable situation of having to explain the very unusual shape of his 'communal laments'. We must note that whereas the dirge and the lament are distinct genres, they do have something in common: they are both reactions to tragedy/misfortune. One is natural and concentrates on the tragedy itself and its effects; the other, interpreting misfortune as accessible to the deity, seeks escape from the tragedy and craves divine restoration. While the two could and did exist side by side, there was bound to be some overlap eventually; and this is what is happening in Lam 1, 2 and 4. In the case of these chapters, we have unique poetic creations, beginning in the style of the dirge and heavy with dirge-like motifs, but which not only focus on the awful situation but which place it in the context of Yahwistic faith. What separates the poems of Lamentations from all other compositions in the Hebrew Bible is that the focus, from the beginning, is on the greatest catastrophe ever to hit the people of Yahweh—the fall of Jerusalem and the destruction of the temple in 586. We cannot emphasise this too much. Even the present day Jewish community, being so far removed in time from this event, cannot appreciate it fully. It had to do with the devastation of a confident people, the loss of statehood, the collapse of the economy, the destruction of social structures, the relocation of many families, the removal of religious props, the dashing of theological positions. These compositions were contributions to the commemoration ceremonies sometime after 586 BCE. They are unique. Other set-backs in pre-exilic Judah gave rise to dirges and to communal laments, but nothing, perhaps, was thought to be adequate to capture the mood which would have followed 586 BCE. Clearly, special efforts were called for. An 'ordinary' communal lament would not suffice. This commemoration demanded the special powers of the Poet Laureate, as it were (Salters 2000, 298). Berlin (25f.), who recognizes that the form is unique, designates it the Jerusalem lament and lists a few other examples: Pss 7, 79 and 137.[35]

Mesopotamian Links

The argument that Lamentations is related to the city lament literature of Mesopotamia is a difficult one to control, and scholars are very much divided on the matter. From the 1950s onwards there has been great interest in establishing connections between the literature of Mesopotamia and

---

[35] Alluding to Pss 46, 48, 50, 76, 84, 87 and 122, which she terms 'odes to Zion', Berlin suggests that Ps 137 'transforms the Zion song into the Jerusalem lament, or, more properly, in Ps 137 we see the demise of the Zion songs and the birth of Jerusalem laments. The Jerusalem laments are the antithesis of Zion songs: they are the songs for the lost Zion. Lamentations is the Jerusalem lament par excellence.'

the Hebrew Bible; so Kramer[36] (1955) writes: 'There is little doubt that it was the Sumerian poets who originated and developed the "lamentation" genre—there are Sumerian examples dating possibly from as early as the Third Dynasty of Ur...and that the Biblical Book of lamentations, as well as the "burden" laments of the prophets, represent a profoundly moving transformation of the more formal and conventional Mesopotamian prototypes'. This enthusiasm continues with Kraus (1968, 9-11), Gwaltney (1983), Bouzard (201), Joyce (2001, 529) and especially Dobbs-Allsopp (2002, 6-12). McDaniel (1968, 198-209) was sceptical of direct influence, as were Tigay[37] (1972, 1375), Ferris (174), Rudolph (9), Eissfeldt (504) and Gordis (127f.), all of whom have been reluctant to come down on the side of Kraus, Kramer etc.[38] Dobbs-Allsopp, however, is not asking us to believe that there was a direct borrowing from Mesopotamia. He argues that the genre 'city lament' was present in Israel several centuries before the fall of Jerusalem, that it is found in the prophetic literature and in the Psalms (1993, 97-156) and had already become an Israelite genre by 586 BCE. Hillers, who had earlier been sceptical (1972, xxix) of the connection, changes his mind (1992, 32-39) somewhat and now argues that the resemblances between the Mesopotamian laments and Lamentations are evidence of 'some kind of connection'; and he suggests that there may have been a city-lament tradition within Israel as far back as the earliest prophetic writings, although he admits that he is trying to reconstruct 'a dinosaur out of bits of fossil'. I agree with McDaniel that the literary dependence of Lamentations on the Sumerian laments cannot be demonstrated (cf. Westermann, 19). Nevertheless, the similarities cannot be denied or ignored. Both in Palestine and in Mesopotamia the destruction of a city made such an impression that aspects of the experience drove poets to produce commemorative compositions; and in both cases the context was religious (cf. Westermann, 20f.). I do not think it is enough to say that similar circumstances lead to similar products. Israel lived in the ancient Near East. The Fertile Crescent invited and saw the movement of peoples between Palestine and Mesopotamia. Israel's own traditions speak of her origins in Ur (Gen 11.31), and she shared something of the creation and flood stories with her eastern neighbours; and although the people of Yahweh sought eventually to distance themselves from the polytheistic culture which surrounded them, they were part and parcel of that ancient world. As Gerstenberger (2001, 469) says '...Israel had been living in a common Near Eastern cultural sphere for centuries before the exile. Therefore generic affinity of lamenting songs and customs is to be expected and beyond question.' I agree to some extent; but I remain

---

[36] Cf. also Gadd (1963, 61).

[37] Tigay (1972, 1375) observes: 'Numerous parallels in subject matter—hunger, destruction of city and temple, pillage, flight, captivity, wailing can reflect simply similar experiences in time of destruction rather than a literary relationship'.

[38] For a survey of opinion, see Dobbs-Allsopp (1993, 2-10).

unconvinced on the question of the city lament genre in Israel. The prevalence of the dirge and of the communal and individual lament are enough to explain why the poets of Lamentations were driven to react and to compose as they did (see *Origin*).[39]

Poetry

While the poems which comprise Lamentations differ from one another in structure and intensity, many of the poetic features which we encounter there are found throughout the Hebrew Bible.[40] A glance at the opening chapter of Jeremiah in the RSV and NEB demonstrates that scholars are not always in agreement as to the distinction between poetry and prose, but in Lamentations there is no dispute: Lamentations is poetry from start to finish. Why poetry? If the background to these poems is the fall of Jerusalem and its aftermath, why were the survivors not content to describe the awful situation in prose, naming Babylon and various prominent personages—Nebuchadnezzar, Nebuzaradan, Zedekiah, Jeremiah, Hananiah—the kind of information which is supplied, in part, by Jer 52 and 2 Kgs 25?[41] The answer to this question is at least two-fold. To begin with, these compositions were made for the liturgy at the commemoration of the great disaster, which liturgy assumed the horrors as described in Jer 52 and 2 Kgs 25. As Hillers[2] (4f.) observes: 'Lamentations was meant to serve the survivors of the catastrophe simply as an *expression* of the horror and grief they felt. People live on best after calamity, not by utterly repressing their grief and shock, but by facing it, and by measuring its dimensions... The fact that Lamentations is verse begins to find its explanation here. Poetic form serves to set off the words of a text from ordinary words, to remind us by its very artificiality that we are not dealing with reality directly, but as shaped and structured by human invention and skill. To face an utterly chaotic experience of loss, ruin, and guilt, even in memory and retelling, may be devastating. The same experiences reworked into a sculpture, or a painting, or a poem, may enable survivors, and their descendants, to remember and contemplate their loss—not coolly, not without emotion—but without unbearable and measureless grief.' The second, and related, reason is that poetic language—imagery, repetition etc. drawn from the dirge, the lament psalms and the prophetic traditions—is more powerful than mere narrative, and stays with the hearers/readers; and the openness of poetry, where no specific names appear, allows that literature to apply to varied and different experiences of the

---

[39] Berlin (26-30) has raised some interesting challenges to the arguments of Kraus and Dobbs-Allsopp which should be taken into consideration in future research.

[40] For a description of Hebrew poetry in general, see Berlin (1996, 301-315); cf. also Watson (1984) and Kugel (1981)

[41] Details of this nature are hidden in Lamentations. The author of ch. 4 gets close to divulging names such as Egypt (v. 17) and Zedekiah (v. 20) and, in fact, does name Edom (vv. 21f.).

same events and even to subsequent experiences of communal adversity.[42] On beginning to read the poems, one is immediately struck by the vividness of the imagery[43] which the poets employ in their compositions—the image of Jerusalem as a weeping female figure, comfortless and betrayed; the portrayal of Judah as a fugitive; the personification of Sword and Death and of Zion's roads, walls and gates; the likening of leaders to pursued deer; the casting of Yahweh as a hostile archer and as a bear lying in wait. Like other poets in the Hebrew Bible, the authors of Lamentations, in particular chs. 1–4, indulge in artistic convention such as repetition, assonance, chiasmus etc.[44]

Perhaps the most conspicuous feature of Hebrew poetry is parallelism, a phenomenon observable in other ancient Near Eastern poetry—Egyptian, Canaanite, Akkadian and Aramaic.[45] It may be described as the balancing of one half-line (stich) with the following one. It is immediately observable in Ps 34.1: 'I will bless the Lord at all times//His praise shall continually be in my mouth'.[46] While the latter illustrates a balance of thought, scholars have noticed that these half-lines are often balanced by their length, thereby creating a certain rhythm. The question of metre in Hebrew poetry is a vexed one, and the statement by Gordon (1965, 131 n. 2), 'Perhaps the most important fact to bear in mind is that the poets of the ancient Near East…did not know of exact meter', is not hopeful of ever detecting any; indeed, Kugel (301) and Berlin (1996, 308) conclude that the quest for Hebrew metre should be abandoned.[47] Nevertheless, the rhythm engendered by parallelism is noticeable. In spite of the fact that precise metre is absent, scholars often describe a line of poetry as comprising three stresses for each stich, sometimes four, sometimes two. This perceived balance is often broken, and so we find 3:4, 4:3, 3:2, 2:3 and so

---

[42] The inclusion, in the festival of the 9th of Ab, of the second fall of Jerusalem in 70 CE, is a specific example of this. On the question of ceremonial poetry, see Gerstenberger (1988, 1-22).

[43] The imagery is taken from human life and from the natural world, and few instances are difficult to understand. Noticeable is the lack of allusion to Jerusalem's institutions and history. Even in the very positive middle section of ch. 3 there is no reference to the exodus, the entry into Canaan, the giving of the Torah or to the various festivals. The only historical reference is to Sodom, at 4.6. Westermann (106) thinks that this shows that the 'songs of Lamentations arose among simple folk', but this seems to me a strange conclusion to draw. The poems are of a high quality. The absence of imagery from history would seem to be because the institutions had all been swept away by the enemy, and the poets were feeling their way in the vacuum left behind.

[44] See Watson (222-348).

[45] Cf. Eissfeldt (58); on parallelism in Hebrew, see Berlin (2008).

[46] Less common is when the second half-line is the opposite of the first, as in Prov 14.5: 'A faithful witness does not lie//but a false witness breathes out lies'; and a further variation is when the second half-line takes further the idea of the first and completes it, as in Ps 2.6: 'I have set my king on Zion//my holy hill'.

[47] This lack of confidence leads Gordis (121) to warn against text-critical issues being settled on the basis of metrical considerations.

on. Indeed, as Watson (98) observes, 'no single poem is consistently written in one metrical pattern'. As far as Lamentations is concerned, the rhythm that predominates is (the unbalanced) 3:2. Although it may have been noticed earlier, it was Budde (1882, cf. also 1898[b]) who drew attention to the fact that throughout Lam 1–4 the poetic rhythm 3:2 stood out as the basic one. He further argued that we ought to acknowledge this as the pattern of the traditional Hebrew lament for the dead and, consequently, gave it the name קינה[48] (*qinah*) verse. Scholars continue to use this term to denote the limping rhythm, though not all accept the whole of Budde's argument.[49] Indeed, there are many lines in Lam 1–4 which do not follow this pattern—for example, 1.6a, 8a; 2.17c; 4.1a, 8b; furthermore, the rhythm is not found only in Lamentations or in dirges. The authors of Isa 1.10-12; 40.9-11 and Song 1.9-11 employ this rhythm,[50] but the latter are not dirges by any stretch of the imagination. Again, the composition at 2 Sam 1.17-27, a famous dirge for Saul and Jonathan, is not composed in this rhythm. Budde's argument was that the lack of balance (3:2) conveyed itself to the reader and hearer alike. The limping effect suggested that something was wrong, and it had developed in the context of death and grief where the mourners, in particular the professional and official mourners, wished to convey in word and action but also in the *shape* of their utterances, that adversity was at hand. Budde may be right, but the presence of the rhythm in passages which have no connection with adversity, and its absence in the classic dirge for Saul and Jonathan, renders his theory suspect. It may be that the unbalanced rhythm developed from the balanced form and was thought to be an attractive variation, but was then hijacked by the professional mourners as a style that could enhance the effect that they were aiming at.[51]

Alphabetic Acrostics

An acrostic is a feature in poetry whereby the initial letter of a/each line is chosen by the poet to begin to constitute a name or a statement or an alphabetic sequence. The earliest examples are Babylonian (c. 1000 BCE), where the device is employed to suggest names or make statements (cf. Soll, 58). In the Old Testament the feature is in the form of alphabetic sequence and is found in several psalms (Pss 9–10, 25, 34, 37, 111, 112, 119, 145), in Nah 1.2-8, in Prov 31.10-31, and in Lam 1–4; and is also present in the Hebrew text of Sir 51.13-30. Readers of the Hebrew text of Lamentations will notice that the poems are closely related to the Hebrew alphabet. Each verse of chs. 1, 2 and 4 begins with a letter of the alphabet

---

[48] The Hebrew word for dirge.
[49] For a negative view, see de Hoop (80-104).
[50] See Watson (98) for other passages.
[51] On the poetry of Lamentations, see Gordis (117-24), Westermann (105-108), Hillers[2] (15-31), Dobbs-Allsopp (5-20), Berlin (2-7).

in sequence, while in ch. 3 each of the first three lines begins with א, the second three with ב, and so on. Chapter 5 is different. This is not an acrostic, but it is 'alphabetic' in that it consists of 22 verses (the number of letters in the Hebrew alphabet). Chapter 1 differs from chs. 2, 3 and 4 in that it follows the order of the alphabet which has come down to us, with ע (v. 16) before פ (v. 17),[52] whereas chs. 2, 3 and 4 have the verses beginning with פ before those beginning with ע.[53] That this reflects a fluidity in the alphabetic order seems likely.[54] It is also a consideration when reflecting on authorship and the integrity of the book.

Readers of the English translation in, say, AV, RSV, or REB may be unaware that they are looking at alphabetic acrostics.[55] This is because the phenomenon is not apparent in translation unless the translator tries to imitate it. This is sometimes attempted, and one may get a flavour of the phenomenon by consulting the translations of Lam 3.1-6 by Ewald (337):

1. Ah ich der mann der elend sah—durch seines grimmes ruthe!
2. Ah mich führte und leitete er—in trübnis, nicht in licht!
3. Auf mich nur kehrt er wiederholt—alle tage seine hand.
4. Beschädigte mir fleisch und haut—zerbrach meine gebeine,
5. Bauete rings um mich her—gift und mühsal auf,
6. Brachte mich in finsternisse—wie uralte todte.

or Knox (1251):[56]

1. Ah, what straits have I not known, under the avenging rod!
2. Asked I for light, into deeper shadow the Lord's guidance led me;

---

[52] At 4QLam the order differs from MT in ch. 1: the פ verse comes before the ע verse. In the light of the contents of the passage it would seem that the Qumran scribe made his text conform to the order in chs. 2, 3 and 4.

[53] In this connection we should note that the person who placed Ἄλεφ, Βήθ etc. above the verse units of the LXX^{אA} (cf. Swete, vol. III, 360) is unlikely to have been the translator, for the Ἄιν has been placed above the Φή verse and vice versa in these three chapters. B. *Sanhedrin* 104b offers a reason for the anomaly: 'Because of the Spies who spoke with their mouths (פה) what they had not seen with their eyes (עין)'; so also MR and Rashi at Lam 2.16; but this need not detain us.

[54] Grotius (549), in the 17th century wondered if this was the explanation: that the Chaldean order was פ–ע and the Hebrew order ע–פ. Grotius imagines that Jeremiah began with the Hebrew order but changed under the influence of his captors (*Chaldaeorum subditus*)! The *Vorlage* of the LXX of Prov 31 seems to have had the order פ–ע, while scholars believe that the original order at Ps 34 was פ–ע; and the order is found in the abecedaries of Kuntillet ʿAjrūd and in an ostracon at ʿIzbet Ṣarṭah (cf. Cross, 1980, 13). While the order that has come down to us existed at Ugarit (15th century BCE) and was the dominant order, flexibility in this regard need only have been ruled out when the letters of the alphabet were also employed to denote numbers, and this was probably only introduced (from the Greeks) in the second century BCE, on Hasmonean coins; cf. Diringer (1971, 743), Naveh (20-25).

[55] LXX and V have transliterated Hebrew letters at the head of every verse; and this is found in the translations of Wycliffe, Coverdale, Challoner, Douai and, more recently, JB, NJB and in JPS (where actual Hebrew letters appear).

[56] Keil (355 n. 1) was not entirely successful in another attempt.

3. Always upon me, none other, falls endlessly the blow.
4. Broken this frame, under the wrinkled skin, the sunk flesh.
5. Bitterness of despair fills my prospect, walled in on every side;
6. Buried in darkness, and, like the dead, interminably.

The question arises as to the reason for the employment of this feature in these poems. Why did the poets take the trouble to express themselves in this way? One suggestion is that the purpose of the form was to teach the alphabet.[57] Luther called Ps 119 'the golden ABC'. The suggestion has few adherents. For one thing, this is not children's literature, nor is it for unschooled and ignorant adults. It is quite sophisticated poetry. Secondly, the alphabet is really only discernible visually. Listening to the poems (with the possible exception of ch. 3), one would be hard pressed to recognise the device; it is only when one looks at the text that one is aware of it. In the case of ch. 3 it is more obvious in that every three lines begin with the same letter. It might be argued that the origin of the sequence (the abecedary) was indeed to teach the alphabet to children, but this was not the purpose of these poems. Another suggestion is that the acrostic was an endeavour to control magical power. It is common knowledge that certain language forms—particular phrases and words, spells and exorcisms—have been widely used in various cultures to ensure that evil was kept at bay and that blessings were received; and there may have been a belief that the letters of the alphabet had a special divine power.[58] To employ them in sequence would, therefore, lend power to one's composition. However, there is no evidence that the people of Israel or Judah of this period held such beliefs, although they are to be found on the outskirts of mediaeval Judaism. But the fact that we have transliterated Hebrew letters placed above text units in the LXX makes one wonder if it was felt, at a very early stage, that they were thought to have some mystical significance. The fact that Tallis, in setting Lam 1.1-5 to music in the sixteenth century, devoted no fewer than sixteen bars to the singing of the word *aleph* may point in the same direction. But these responses or interpretations probably misrepresent the original intention.

Another theory is that the acrostic was used as an aid to memory. One might be better able to memorise a poem or list if one had the help of a sequence of letters. This is, on the surface, a plausible theory, but this may be because we ourselves have used sequence as a memory aid. The problem here is that the 22 letters are used six times in the book to introduce verses, so those reciting the text are not helped much if they cannot remember which of the six ⊃s, say, they are presently at! Of course, if Lamentations is not a literary unit, and the poems were composed separately, the mnemonic theory seems more credible. The *individual* poems might have been composed in the acrostic manner to aid memory. It was

---
[57] See Munch (703-10).
[58] Cf. Radbertus (7f.), Jeremias (665).

only when they were brought together that the alphabetic confusion would have arisen!

Another theory, originating with de Wette (530-32), is that the purpose of the acrostic was to convey completeness in the expression of grief. This view has been picked up and expressed differently by a number of commentators. The last word, the ultimate in confession or in lament, can only be achieved if all the letters in the Hebrew alphabet are used; and the tidiness of the acrostic serves to emphasise this. There is a passage in the Talmud (*b. Šab.* 55a) which speaks of 'the people who fulfil the Torah from א to ת', and Gottwald (30-32) uses this to back *his* argument. The authors of Lamentations 'wanted to bring about a complete cleansing of the conscience through a total confession of sin'. However, there is a weakness here. If the author had complete confession in mind, why did he not list the sins committed? As I have argued elsewhere (1994, 90f.), if what Gottwald claims is correct we should have expected lists of sins and acts of rebellion, but apart from the allusion to prophets and priests shedding the blood of the righteous (4.13), the very few references to sins are couched in such *general* terms that it might be deduced that the poet was not conscious of specific wrongdoing.[59] In a recent article, taking a psychological approach to Lamentations, Joyce (1993, 316) puts forward the suggestion that the acrostic form and the generally disciplined handling of metre may reflect an attempt to establish some order in the immediate reaction in Israel to radical loss of meaning. There may be something in what Joyce says here; but, without trying to minimise the effect of the fall of Jerusalem on the people of Jerusalem and Judah, we should note that the alphabetic acrostic in the Hebrew Bible is not confined to poems of disaster or crisis. That is not to say that the purpose of the acrostic is always the same, but one would need to explain the reason for its existence in, say, Prov 31. One might point out, in this connection, that Lam 3, arguably the least intense of the poems, exhibits the strongest alphabetic structure.

The most likely possibility is that the acrostic is simply an artistic device[60] (like the sonnet in English literature) and one which was imitated by the authors of Pss 34, 119 etc. We may note that the device is confined to *poetic* material, an area where authors were inclined to show their ability in features such as parallelism (synonymous, antithetic, staircase), onomatopoeia, assonance, pun, metaphor and rhythm. That the poet had to be skilful in couching his thoughts in the straitjacket of the acrostic form goes without saying (contrast Knox's tortuous and constipated attempt at

---

[59] Tigay (1972, 1369) observes: 'Lamentations is strikingly uncommunicative concerning the nature of Israel's sins. One searches the book almost in vain for the mention of a specific sin. Idolatry is not mentioned. Nowhere do we hear of the sins for which classical prophecy threatened destruction: social injustice, oppression of the weaker classes, bribery, and so on'.

[60] Westermann (1994, 99) describes it as pedantic.

reproducing the phenomenon in English translation!). The poems are a collection for the commemoration of the most momentous event in the history of the people of Judah (see *Genre*). The author of the first poem to appear showed his ability by his lyric composition, by choosing a particular rhythm, and by opting for the alphabetic framework; and this influenced the subsequent contributions. While the various theories are worthy of consideration, what influences me to embrace the 'artistic' theory is that the mediaevalists (Rashi, Kara and Ibn Ezra) say nothing about the device in their exegetical comments.[61] This is particularly pertinent in Ibn Ezra's case in that he was a noted poet in his day and occasionally composed alphabetic acrostics! It seems to me that his silence on the matter suggests that he took for granted that his readers would understand that the acrostic was a device to show the skill and dexterity of the poet, and nothing more. Lamentations subsequently came to be associated with the alphabetic sequence feature and, later, for the commemoration ceremonies, prayers and poems were written, obviously inspired by this feature and which exhibit intense alphabetic concentration (cf. Salters 2001, 108).

Text and Versions

Prefaces in Septuagint and Vulgate

While the other Versions (P and T) merely include Jeremiah's name in the title[62] of their translations (see *Authorship*), LXX and V have (almost identical) short preambles which seem at first sight to nail the authorship and date of the text which follows. LXX prefixes the following to 1.1:

Καὶ ἐγένετο μετὰ τὸ αἰχμαλωτισθῆναι τὸν Ἰσραὴλ καὶ Ἱερουσαλὴμ ἐρημωθῆναι ἐκάθισεν Ἱερεμίας κλαίων καὶ ἐθρήνησε τὸν θρῆνον τοῦτον ἐπὶ Ἱερουσαλὴμ καὶ εἶπεν

V has:

Factum est postquam in captiuitatem redactus est israel et ierusalem deserta est sedit ieremias propheta flens et planxit lamentatione hac in ierusalem et amaro animo suspirans et eiulans dixit

The words *amaro animo suspirans et eiulans* are a plus in V.

Scholars agree that the Greek and Latin appear to have been translated from Hebrew,[63] perhaps (in the case of LXX):

ויהי אחר שבית ישראל וירושלם מחרבה וישב ירמיהו בוכה ויקונן
הקינה הזאת על ירושלם ויאמר

---

[61] Rashi does acknowledge (1.1) that chs. 1–4 are acrostics but does not make any further comment; cf. Salters (1999, 204).
[62] T simply begins אמר ירמיהו.
[63] Cf., for example, Peake (292).

No serious commentator has claimed that this preface, in either form, is original; rather, the view in general is that it was introduced to link the books of Jeremiah and Lamentations. No form of it appears in any Hebrew MS, and there is no suggestion of it at the beginning of P and T. It was rejected as 'text' by Wycliffe, Geneva Bible, AV and in Luther's translation; and Calvin does not discuss its presence. Douai does include the V form of it in translation, and we find the same represented in Coverdale, Great Bible, Bishops' Bible and Challoner. A translation of the LXX form appears as a footnote in JB and NJB, but other translations generally ignore it.

It should be noted that while the LXX title is θρῆνοι, i.e. a plurality of a particular genre θρῆνος, the preface seems to designate what follows as τὸν θρῆνον τοῦτον. It is unlikely that the author of the preface was thinking only of ch. 1: it is more likely that, in the absence of text divisions, he had the whole 'book' in mind; but it would seem, therefore, that the author of the preface was not responsible for the title.[64]

Hebrew

Compared to some other biblical books, one might say that the Hebrew text of Lamentations is in a good state of preservation (cf. Kraus, 6, and Rudolph 1962, 189). We may come to this conclusion for a number of reasons and on a number of counts. There are not many passages where the Hebrew is unintelligible and where the exegete is driven to despair. The alphabetic acrostic pattern, characteristic of chs. 1–4, is sustained throughout; i.e. the full alphabet is represented;[65] and one might say that ch. 5, though not an acrostic, is alphabetic in that it consists of twenty-two lines (see *Acrostics*, above). Again, the poetic rhythm chosen by the poets of chs. 1–4, *viz* 3:2—is, for the most part, maintained (see *Poetry*, below).

The base text for this commentary is the MT used by *BHK*, *BHS* and *BHQ*, *viz* the Leningrad Codex B 19a. We have to remind ourselves that the latter represents the Ben Asher form of the Masoretic tradition, which became the accepted form of the text over against other Masoretic forms,[66] mainly due to its espousal by Maimonides and David Kimchi in mediaeval times. We must not, therefore, regard it as absolute or sacrosanct and use it to the exclusion of other witnesses.[67] Hence, attention is also given to variant readings in many Hebrew MSS[68] and to the variants suggested by the ancient Versions. In addition, the Hebrew fragments found at Qumran are taken into consideration.

---

[64] It is precisely the same in V: the preface speaks of *lamentationem hanc*, while the title in V is *Lamentationes*.

[65] Cf. incomplete acrostics in Psalms and Nahum.

[66] Cf. Tov (22f.). On the question of the formation of MT, see Tov (21-79).

[67] Indications that the Masoretes were aware of problems in transmission are found in the their notes and apparatus: *Kethib/Qere*, *Sebirin*, *Inverted Nuns*, *Suspended Letters*, *and Corrections of the Scribes*.

[68] See Kennicott and De Rossi (Editions Cited).

Tetragrammaton

There are thirty-two occurrences of the tetragrammaton (יהוה) in MT of Lamentations—1.5, 9, 11, 12, 17, 18, 20; 2.6, 7, 8, 9, 17, 20, 22; 3.18, 22, 24, 25, 26, 40, 50, 55, 59, 61, 64, 66; 4.11, 16, 20; 5.1, 19, 21. אדני occurs fourteen times—1.14, 15 (twice); 2.1, 2, 5, 7, 18, 19, 20; 3.31, 36, 37, 58. Nineteen of the thirty-two יהוה occurrences have no (אדני) variation in the manuscript tradition, whereas יהוה appears somewhere in the tradition for all of the fourteen אדני occurrences. On no occasion is אדני maintained throughout. As the actual pronunciation of the divine name יהוה (Yahweh) came to be avoided, over time, in reading and in worship, and was replaced, in pronunciation, with the word אדני ($^a d\bar{o}n\bar{a}y$ Lord), scribes sometimes substituted the term אדני for יהוה in the actual transmission of the text. We see this at 1.14, where MT reads אדני, and many MSS[Ken] and 4QLam read יהוה. It is unlikely that the text before the Qumran scribe read אדני and that he changed it to יהוה. The MT scribe (or one further back in the transmission), encountering יהוה in the text he was copying, repeated $^a d\bar{o}n\bar{a}y$ to himself and wrote the same; cf. also at 1.18 where the Qumran scribe did it again.[69] While it is possible that the original composition included both words, appearing variously throughout the document, it is more likely that יהוה was used throughout and that אדני crept into the transmitted text in the manner suggested above. In any case, neither the meaning nor the rhythm is affected in any of the passages involved.

Qumran

Several fragments of the text of Lamentations are among the DSS discoveries. Cave 3 has a manuscript (designated 3QLam[a])[70] which contains fragments of Lam 1.10-12 and 3.53-62; cave 4 has the manuscript 4QLam[a] which contains Lam 1.1-18;[71] and cave 5 has fragments of two manuscripts: 5QLam[a] which contains Lam 4.5-8, 11-16, 19–22; 5.3-13, 16-17; and 5QLam[b] which contains 4.17-19.[72] These manuscripts and fragments are usually dated to the first century BCE. In addition to the actual text of Lamentations, poems quoting and alluding to Lamentations appear in other Qumran texts, e.g. 4Q179[73] and 4Q501.[74] The most extensive manuscript, 4QLam[a], differs from MT in several places.[75] The Qumran scribe is often careless—erasures, omissions, additions, dittography, wrong word-division etc.—and Cross (2000, 229) reckons that the copy was not for public use. While Cross accepts more than I would, a few

---

[69] Cf. Gerstenberger (485) who thinks that the change to אדני may be deliberate.
[70] See DJD III, 95.
[71] See DJD XVI, 229-37.
[72] See DJD III, 174-77 and 177-78.
[73] See DJD V, 75-77; Allegro misleadingly entitles this 'Lamentations'; cf. also Strugnell (1970), Horgan (1973) and Pabst (1978).
[74] See DJD VII, 79f.
[75] Cross (1983 and 2000) has made a detailed study of this text; cf. also Hillers[2] (41-47) who also presents a collation of MT and this manuscript (47f.).

readings do seem to be superior to MT, and occasionally there is agreement with LXX and P over against MT. Reference is made to these differences in the commentary.

Greek

The LXX is generally regarded as the oldest translation of the Hebrew and, for this reason alone, is valuable from the text-critical point of view. The LXX translator of Lamentations took his task very seriously, aiming, it seems, to represent in Greek every detail of his Hebrew *Vorlage*.[76] The result was a document in inelegant Greek, obviously translated from Hebrew but providing the text-critic with important data.[77] The base text here is the edition by Ziegler (1957/1976, 467-94). For the most part, the LXX supports MT, though it does deviate from the Hebrew in places. The latter consist mostly in the addition of a pronoun or the occasional free rendering and usually does not presuppose a different Hebrew text.

For the minor Greek Versions—Symmachus and Aquila—I have relied on the marginal readings in Syriac in the Syrohexapla. These have been converted into Greek in Field (1875) and in Ziegler's apparatus. Strangely, Theodotion is not cited in these marginal readings. Barthélemy had pointed out (1963, 33) that in our 'Septuagint' (at 1.8; 2.9; 3.8; 4.3, 15, 21), καί γε[78] is used for the Hebrew וגם, and Schäfer (19*) wonders if the 'Septuagint' is really the text of Theodotion; cf. Tov (145).

Syriac

The Syriac translation (Peshitta) was made (probably in Edessa or Adiabene) as early as the first or second century CE.[79] While the edition of the Peshitta by Lee (1823) reproduced the text of the London Polyglott (1657), the Leiden edition currently being published, is based on Codex Ambrosianus (A), published by Ceriani in 1876. Although the text of Albrektson's edition of Lamentations is, in his words, an eclectic text, it disagrees with A in only a very few passages. In this commentary I have, for the most part, followed A and have taken account of Albrektson's wisdom and expertise.[80] The Syriac translation is a careful rendering[81] of

---

[76] As a translation it is quite different from that of Jeremiah; and Bogaert (642) observes that it was made independently of the LXX of Jeremiah and much later.
[77] Contra Cross (1983, 136), who dismisses the LXX of Lamentations as 'of relatively little use'; but see Schäfer (19*), who states 'Although the Greek version of Lamentations is not a "good translation", it is valuable for textual criticism, because the *verbatim* translation technique makes it comparatively easy to determine the consonantal text of a Hebrew *Vorlage*...'
[78] An explanation of this phenomenon is found in Tov (145). It is thought that the Greek text of Lamentations belongs to the so-called *kaige* recension/group, a type of Greek text which has deliberately been brought into line with the emerging MT; cf. Dines (83f.) and Alexander (2008, 46f.).
[79] Cf. Weitzman (1f.).
[80] On the Peshitta of Lamentations, see Albrektson (210-13).
[81] Weitzman (26).

a Hebrew text very close to MT. Unlike the translator of the LXX, the Syriac translator was concerned to provide an intelligible and clear text. He took the liberty, on very many occasions, to add a copula or a suffix where, we presume, he felt the meaning could be helped, but the lack of suffix and (especially) copula in the Hebrew were intentional on the part of the author—giving, perhaps, a certain sobbing effect—and this is not sustained in the Syriac rendering. His additions are not usually significant and like the copula and the suffixes, they amount to explanatory renderings. As Albrektson (210) observes: 'he explains matters which are perfectly clear from the context and which the Hebrew poet in an effort to produce a reserved and laconic form has omitted'; and this tendency sometimes results in a free rendering. The translator is concerned with clarity but appears not to be interested in the poetic nature of the Hebrew composition before him. For example, faced with two Hebrew synonyms in parallel stichs, he will render both by the same Syriac word. This may reflect poor vocabulary (Albrektson, 211) but it may be that the translator simply lacked sensitivity. These tendencies mean that the Version is limited as far as textual criticism is concerned, though its value from an exegetical point of view remains important. While there are lively connections between the LXX and the Peshitta in several Old Testament books, this is not the case in Lamentations (Weitzman, 68), and Albrektson (212) concludes 'that it seems quite clear that P cannot possibly be dependent on LXX in Lam.'.

Aramaic

The date of the Aramaic translation (Targum) is considered to be late fifth or early sixth century CE, and its provenance is thought to be the Galilee.[82] There are two branches of the Targum tradition: the Western Text (WT) and the Yemenite Text (YT). Both have a common ancestor, but WT is older and is closer to the original than YT. The *textus receptus* of T (WT) goes back to the first Bomberg Bible (Venice, 1517) and this is reproduced in מקראות גדולות (Warsaw 1860–69) and in Lagarde (unpointed). YT is the base for the edition by van der Heide (1981). The latter, in describing the two versions, refers to YT as 'a definitely different and apparently revised version, the text of which is somewhat inferior to the Western Text' (Heide 1981, 3, 23-26). I have, for the most part, stayed with WT as in מקראות גדולות.[83] While WT is longer than YT, both exhibit a paraphrasing tendency in translation method, though this is modest in comparison to the Targum of, say, Qoheleth. But T's translation is uneven. At 1.1 the Hebrew consists of 14 words while T 'expands' into 77

---

[82] See Alexander (2008, 87-90). For any study of the Targum of Lamentations, Alexander should be consulted.
[83] The Sperber edition (1968) of YT has been found to be unreliable in that, *inter alia*, the editor supplements YT with text from the second Bomberg Rabbinic Bible; see Alexander (2008, 3) and Heide (1981, 52*-55*).

words; and this is more or less the picture until the end of ch. 2, though the latter's paraphrasing is noticeably more subdued. The rendering in ch. 3 is different, being less a paraphrase and more a bona fide translation, while ch. 4 begins to expand again, though not on the same scale as in the first two chapters; and ch. 5 is also quite modest in its paraphrasing. When T attempts simply to translate it is not without value as a text-critical tool. In the paraphrasing mode its chief value is in the realm of exegesis. Occasionally, the 'extra' material is to be found in the Midrash (MLT and MR).

Latin

(a) The *Old Latin* Version exists only in fragmentary form. It is, in any case, limited from the point of view of textual criticism of the Hebrew, in that it is thought to be a translation of the LXX. From what exists, it is often clearly a rendering of the Greek, but occasionally it maintains an independent stance. I have relied on Sabatier's *Bibliorum Sacrorum latinae versiones antiquae : seu, Vetus Italica, et caeterae quaecunque in codicibus mss. & antiquorum libris reperiri potuerunt : quae cum Vulgata latina, & cum textu graeco comparantur* (1743).

(b) The *Vulgate*, translated in Bethlehem (393–406 CE), is a stylish and readable translation. Jerome will have had the OL available, though his avowed aim was to translate from the Hebrew (*Hebraica veritas*). Although he claims to have had a Jewish teacher (*hebraeus meus*), it is often claimed that his knowledge of Hebrew was not of a high standard. V usually agrees with the consonantal text of MT, although Jerome occasionally takes a different line regarding the vocalisation of the text; and he was not above forcing a Christological interpretation on an innocent passage. The edition I have used is R. Weber, *Biblia Sacra Iuxta Vulgatam Versionem* (1969).

The variations in the Hebrew MSS, the slight differences suggested by the *Vorlagen* of the Versions and the suspected scribal errors in transmission confirm the suspicion that our MT may not represent the original composition in every detail. Having said that, I have found myself accepting the reading of MT in the vast majority of problematic cases. Unlike some earlier commentators—Ehrlich (1914), Delitzsch (1920) and Perles (1930)—I have resorted to emendation and conjecture in only a very few instances.

Theology

Reflecting earlier on theological thought in Lamentations (Salters 1994, 108-20), I took the view that all the poems were the work of a single author, a position held by many commentators, and, consequently, gave an overall assessment of the poetic corpus. I have, subsequently, come to the conclusion that the poems did not come from the same pen (see above:

Author, Genre). In my introduction to each poem and in the commentary I discuss some of the theological features of the particular poem, drawing attention to the different emphases of each author and piece.[84]

The historical background to these poems is very important and needs to be emphasised and kept in mind in the exegesis of any passage and in the interpretation of the corpus.[85] The fall of Jerusalem constitutes a major watershed in the history of the people of Judah. The loss of statehood was in itself momentous but with it came the loss of the Davidic line; and the deportation of many important sections of the surviving population, including the leading figures, left a gaping hole in the fabric of society. The destruction of the temple meant the cessation of the normal practices in the worship of Yahweh. The dreaded enemy was in the ascendancy, and the people had become the laughing-stock of their neighbours. In this situation, with people fleeing across borders and striving to stay alive for lack of food, many of those remaining must have been stunned, to say the least. Those who, before the fall, had been half-hearted in their loyalty to Yahweh, would point out that Yahweh had been unable to keep his promise of protection. Some may have considered Josiah's reform to have been dangerous, an offence to other deities. Now, perhaps, was the time to seek approval of these gods or to pay homage to the Babylonian gods who had recently demonstrated superiority. According to Fohrer (309f.), there appears to have been a resurgence of the practice of magic and astrology post-586; and the belief in the inviolability of Zion (Jer 7 and 26) is likely to have been silenced for good. What, now, was the point in being loyal to Yahweh?

Yet, in the midst of all the doom and gloom, with faith in Yahweh at an all time low, there appears a thread of hope. Among the various factions there existed another element among the survivors, probably few in number—those still loyal to Yahweh. Their loyalty did not die; indeed, it gave rise to these poems.[86] What we witness in Lamentations is faith rising, Phoenix-like, from the ashes of doom and gloom, for the authors of these verses demonstrate a dogged loyalty to Yahweh. That is the first theological observation.

Another feature is that all five poems agree that the catastrophe must be interpreted as Yahweh's punishment for sin (1.5; 2.14; 3.42; 4.13; 5.16). The poets had inherited the Deuteronomistic theology of reward and punishment: if Israel obeyed God's law they would have peace and prosperity; if, on the other hand, they disobeyed, they would experience adversity. That, I think, is taken for granted in Lamentations; indeed, in the first poem, Jerusalem declares that Yahweh was in the right (1.18). It

---

[84] For a survey of views on theology in Lamentations, see House (316-23).
[85] Chapter 3 is probably the latest of the poems (see above, *Date*), and its inclusion in the collection suggests that the suffering of the people continued long after the fall of the city.
[86] Dobbs-Allsopp (2002, 47) seems to argue that the very quality of composition—rhythm, style, creative vocabulary etc.—amounts to an element of hope.

is, however, erroneous to think that this is why the poems were written, for although the authors do make it clear that the sins committed by the people were being punished by Yahweh—referring to the various words for sin: פשע (1.5 etc.), חטא (1.8 etc.), עון (2.14)—they do not labour the point. Dobbs-Allsopp (2002, 37) is right when he says that while we find genuine acknowledgment of sin in Lamentations, '...that is not the whole story, or even the most important part of the story'.

The third feature is that Yahweh is depicted as the lord of history. Our first observation was that the poets were loyal to their God, Yahweh, but what one senses in the corpus is that this God is not just the deity of the now defunct state of Judah but is a deity above and beyond the people of Judah. This is found elsewhere in the Hebrew Bible, though normally in a situation where the state is intact. It says something of the faith of the poets that, in the face of disintegration and great suffering, this view of God could persist. We may not be in the realm of explicit monotheism—we have to wait until Deutero-Isaiah for that—but it is there in embryonic form. Westermann (1994, 223) points out that the concept '...encompasses other peoples only insofar as the activities of those other peoples—such as the Assyrians, Babylonians, or Edomites—affect Israel'. Nevertheless, the poets stand their ground on this issue, probably in the face of much scepticism. There may be a trace of the view that the Babylonian gods were stronger than Yahweh or even that the Babylonians showed themselves superior, but the poets are at pains to stress that no other power was at work in the events which came together in the fall of Jerusalem and the destruction of the temple. This is emphasised in 2.1-9, a passage which may have been intended to counter any residual belief in the power of Babylon and its gods, and which leaves no doubt that Yahweh was the only protagonist on the scene. It is further demonstrated in the passages where the poets call on Yahweh to bring destruction on the enemies and in the invective against Edom (4.21-22).

The commemoration of the fall of Jerusalem and the destruction of the temple for which the poems were written concerns itself, in the main, with the terrible sufferings which the people of Yahweh have experienced at the hands of Yahweh. The references to the disaster as punishment are vastly outnumbered by the descriptions of affliction. A brief glance at the poems leaves the impression that they are chiefly about intense suffering. This suffering is presented to Yahweh, not only in the passages where he is actually addressed (1.9c, 11c, 12-22; 2.20-22; 3.1-18; 5.1-18) but, by virtue of the corpus's creation as commemoration, in the descriptions of horror and destitution which are found throughout the chapters. The idea must be that Yahweh must be confronted with the affliction he has caused, not only in the fall of Jerusalem but in the ongoing misery of the Babylonian yoke. Yahweh, it is assumed, will ultimately be unable to ignore the presentation; the pouring out of the heart before Yahweh must somehow reach and soften the heart of the God the authors still regard as their own.

In this connection we should note that the call for restoration is almost completely absent in the corpus. In his treatment of ch. 1, Westermann (119) interprets this silence as due to the shock of the catastrophe being so deep as to forestall its articulation. When it does appear (5.21) it is still rather muted and in general terms.[87] But it is there and, together with the whole corpus, the assumption is that Yahweh, whose throne is for ever, is a God of mercy, something that the author of ch. 3 feels needs to be stressed.

---

[87] It is only with the later commemorative literature that the call for restoration becomes specific in terms of city, temple and dynasty; see Rosenfeld (9 *et passim*).

CHAPTER 1

Introductory

We do not know which of the five poems was the first to be written,[1] but ch. 1 is, perhaps, the most striking, and it may be for this reason that it is placed at the beginning of the group. Kraus (22) declares that there is simply no structure in ch. 1. Renkema (1988, 294-320; cf. 1998, 85) is of the opinion that there is a clear structure. Both these views are contrary, and most commentators, though not all in agreement, find a position between the extremes. We may understand how Kraus came to the conclusion that there is no structure to the chapter. Lamentations 1 lacks a clear logic and obvious development. The author appears to snatch at various images to describe horrific scenes, thereby producing *non sequiturs* even within individual verses (cf., e.g., vv. 5c and 18c); and sudden voice changes (cf. vv. 9c, 10, 12, 17) may suggest a lack of integration.[2] But this first chapter does have a structure/shape, albeit not as sharp as would satisfy Kraus, nor as elaborate as Renkema perceives. We may begin by observing that the poem divides roughly in two: vv. 1-11 and vv. 12-22. The first section is mostly in the third person, the second mostly in the first person. The first speaker appears to be a lamenter, the second seems to be the city of Jerusalem. These two sections are skilfully dovetailed, forming a unity of composition. Not just held together by the alphabetic acrostic (see *Introduction: Acrostics*), the two are like two interlocking fists—distinct yet inextricably bound together. Both sections are in similar poetic form, the theology is consistent and the vocabulary is distinct; and the background in each case appears to be the fall of the city of Jerusalem. The fragment at v. 9c, addressing Yahweh, which interrupts the first speaker seems, at first, to be stray and anomalous, but we should note that the first speaker picks up (from the interruption) the idea of the enemy in the ascendancy and continues in the same vein, so that one could say that the fragment at v. 9c, in the first person, is enclosed thematically in the first section. Moreover, the form of the cry is similar to the one at v. 11c and, again, at v. 20. Again, while the section vv. 12-22 is mostly in the

---

[1] Rudolph (1962, 193) claimed that ch. 1 was the first to be written, but he argues that it was composed not after 586 but between 597 and 586 BCE (see *Introduction: Date*).
[2] Had the alphabetic acrostic been absent there would have been a plethora of suggestions among scholars as to how corruption had set in.

first person, the interruption at v. 17 is hardly intrusive. It shows that the first speaker is still around and now comes back in the same vein. That this is the same voice as in vv. 1-11 is shown by the identical subject matter, *viz* Jerusalem and her plight, and the similarity of language (cf. v. 2, v. 8 and v. 10). Finally, the personified Jerusalem is depicted in v. 2 as weeping copiously, without a comforter, and v. 16 appears to supply confirmation of this, when the city says: 'This is why I weep...tears stream from my eyes...a comforter is far from me'. These features in themselves serve to demonstrate that we do not have a haphazard construction held together by an acrostic pattern.

In interpreting Lamentations I have stressed the need to take cognizance of the fact that the fall of Jerusalem in 586 BCE was the greatest calamity in the history of the people of Yahweh (see *Introduction*) and that this is at least part of the reason that the composition is unlike any other in the Hebrew Bible. The movement from third person to first person is striking and, as Rudolph (1962, 209) observes, gives the composition a certain dramatic touch. I have argued (2000, 298) that the description of the disaster in vv. 1-11 is followed by the victim's own story in vv. 12-22 in much the same way as a television or radio reporter from, let us say, a war zone tells his/her audience of the awful circumstances and then introduces a victim of the violence who then speaks for himself/herself. The whole report is thereby given life, no matter how inarticulate the victim. That, I think, is the psychology behind the structure: maximum effect is thus obtained. But there may be something else here. In his work on the Psalms, Mowinckel (1962, 5f.) encouraged us to interpret mixed style in terms of cultic movement and drama; and Rudolph (*op. cit. ibid.*) has suggested that that this poem, with its different speakers, was meant to be performed. The dramatic effect would have been there had there been a clear break between third person and first person, but the text as it stands offers further dramatic elements. Jerusalem, the city, is depicted as destitute and weeping (v. 2). As the description nears its end, the agony of the personified city finds expression in two short cries to Yahweh—v. 9c and v. 11c—which interrupt the description of her misery and which convey an urgency on the part of the weeping figure. The latter cannot contain herself (as she listens to and identifies with the description of misery), and the first speaker finally stands aside and gives her the floor, as it were, in v. 12. These fragmentary cries are like off-stage noises in a drama that are part of the plot.

The aforementioned *non-sequiturs* and disjointed features should not be explained simply as the result of the author drawing together stray phrases; but they need to be explained. The fact that the alphabetic acrostic is maintained through to the final verse suggests that the author intended such features as he shaped his poem. The second speaker, the personified city, calls out to passers-by, to Yahweh, to nations intermittently; and even within verses (e.g. vv. 14, 16, 18) there can be a break in the flow of thought. Verses do not appear in any particular order; indeed, we could place vv. 12-19 in almost any order without serious loss of effect. The author, I believe (2000, 299f.), is drawing on his knowledge of human nature and of the keening[3] of his day. That keening reflected and is inextricably bound up with the disorientation of the bereaved. In the shock of any bereavement, the bereaved are inclined to give way to expressions of grief, to describe their own sadness and pain at the loss of the deceased, to contrast the present with the good old days of the past. The expressions may, at times, seem connected, but more often than not, although quite understandable and lucid in themselves, they do not hang together as a balanced statement.[4] This, then, is the reason for the apparent lack of flow and logic in vv. 12-22. The author is trying to convey in the drama the disturbed mind of the weeping figure casting around for ways of expressing her grief, admitting her faults. Looking for comfort, until she finally gathers her thoughts and, in vv. 20-22, in a slightly more coherent passage, calls for reprisals on the enemy who has been responsible for her plight. And the same can be said of vv. 1-11. That is why some scholars speak of the dirge here (see *Introduction*). The tragic reversal element is highlighted from v. 1 onwards. The subject may vary—Jerusalem, Judah, priests, maidens, leaders, people—but this only adds to the disorientation which the author is trying to convey.

Amidst the dirge-like elements the poet gives his interpretation of the disaster and reveals his theological thinking. First of all, the fact that Yahweh is addressed at all points to the author's allegiance to this deity. Again, it is clear that the destruction of Judah has not entirely brought his faith in Yahweh to an end. Yahweh is still the God of the suffering people. The poet knows that the fall of Jerusalem could be interpreted in more than one way. One might simply conclude that the enemy was more powerful than Zion's defences. It was a fact, and statements such as 'her adversaries have become her masters' (v. 5), 'her foes gloat' (v. 7), 'the enemy is victorious' (v. 16) show that it was undisputed. But the interpretation which the author espouses is that Yahweh was somehow in control of the enemy (cf. vv. 12, 14f., 17, 21f.). This interpretation was necessary if Yahwism was to survive. If all that could be said of the fall of Jerusalem was that the enemy was superior, then the conclusion would have to be that Yahweh was either powerless or unconcerned. The author did not accept that Yahweh was powerless, and it must have been difficult, in these circumstances, for him or any Judahite to believe that he was concerned for these suffering people. However, the cries to Yahweh at vv. 9c, 11c and 20-22 are based on a belief that Yahweh could not ignore the misery and distress of his people. The tradition which the poet had inherited and which he clings to comes from Israel's classic relationship with Yahweh (Exod 3.7f.), and it is on this basis that these cries are made.

---

[3] Keening skills are alluded to in Jer 9.16-21; cf. McKane (1986, 208-12).
[4] Cf. Joyce (1993, 304-20).

And yet there is a tentativeness about these cries, a certain lack of confidence, especially in vv. 9c, 11c. Westermann (1994, 137) notes that there is no prayer for restoration—something that usually appears in the communal laments in the Psalms. It is as if the poet, believing in Yahweh's power, is not so sure that Yahweh was concerned enough to act. Better, simply, to draw attention to the misery and suffering and to hope. But the traditional call for vengeance on the enemies is made in more confident language (vv. 21f.). Perhaps this is because the basis on which these calls were made in pre-exilic times remains the same, namely the doctrine of reward and punishment. Evil deeds merit punishment, so if Jerusalem has been punished for her evil deeds, so should the cruel adversaries. Surely, thinks the poet, that principle stands even if all else may have fallen.

Translation

1. Alas! The city, once populous, sits alone;
   Once the Lady among nations, now like a widow;
   Now enslaved who was Princess among provinces.

2. She weeps bitterly throughout the night, her cheeks wet with tears;
   No one to comfort her among all who loved her;
   Friends have all betrayed her, becoming her enemies.

3. Judah has departed from affliction and harsh service,
   She sits among the nations but finds no rest;
   All her pursuers run her to ground in narrow places.

4. The roads to Zion mourn for lack of festival pilgrims
   All her gates are appalled, her priests moan,
   Her maidens grieve; and she herself is wretched.

5. Her foes have become her masters, her enemies prosper
   For Yahweh has made her suffer for her many transgressions
   Her children are gone into captivity before the foe.

6. From Zion[5] has departed all her splendour.
   All her leaders have become like deer, they find no pasture;
   And they run on, exhausted, before the pursuer.

7. In her affliction and trouble, Jerusalem recalls
   All the precious things she once had,[6]
   As the foes gloat, they mock her downfall.

8. Jerusalem has sinned so she has become filthy.
   All who respected her now despise her, for they have seen her pudenda.
   Even she groans and turns away.

---

[5] Heb. reads *daughter Zion*; see note.
[6] Prb. rdg. Heb. adds: *when her people fell into the hand of the foe, and there was no one to help her.*

9. Her unclearness is seen in her skirts; she had given no thought to her future.
    She fell dramatically and no one comforts her.
    See, O Yahweh, my affliction, for the enemy has triumphed.

10. The foe has laid hands on all her desirable things.
    She has seen, entering her sanctuary, nations
    Of whom you commanded: 'They must not enter your assembly'.

11. All her people are groaning as they search for bread.
    They trade their personal treasures for food to keep themselves alive.
    See, O Yahweh, and take note for I am despised.

12. Come,[7] all you passers-by—look and see
    If there is any pain like the pain brought upon me,
    Which Yahweh inflicted on his day of fierce anger.

13. From on high he sent fire, he brought it down into my bones.
    He has spread a net for my feet, he has turned me back;
    He has left me stupefied and faint all day long.

14. Tied on[8] is the yoke of my sins, by his hand it is fastened.
    His yoke is upon my neck, it saps my strength.
    Yahweh has handed me over to those I cannot withstand.

15. Yahweh cast aside my mighty men within me;
    He summoned an assembly to crush my young men.
    Yahweh trod, as in a wine-press, Maid Judah.

16. For these things I weep; my eyes, my eyes run with water;
    For a comforter is far from me, one to revive my spirits.
    My children are devastated, for the enemy has prevailed.

17. Zion spreads out her hands, but there is no one to comfort her.
    Concerning Jacob, Yahweh has commanded his neighbours to be his foes.
    Jerusalem has become a filthy thing among them.

18. Yahweh was in the right, for I had rebelled against his command.
    Hear, all you peoples, and see my suffering;
    My young women and men have gone into captivity.

19. I have called to my lovers, they have abandoned me.
    My priests and my elders expire in the city
    While they seek for food to stay alive.

20. See, O Yahweh, how distressed I am, within I am in torment,
    My heart is upside down, for I have wantonly rebelled.
    The sword bereaves outdoors, as Death indoors.

---

[7] *Come* prb. rdg. Heb. reads *Not unto you.*
[8] *Tied on* prb. rdg. Heb. reads *obscure.*

21. Hear,[9] how I groan, I have no one to comfort me.
    All my foes have heard of my misfortune; they rejoice that you have done it.
    May you bring the day you promised that they may be like me.

22. Let all their evil doing come before you; and deal with them
    As you have with me for all my transgressions;
    For my groans are many, and my heart is faint.

Commentary

1.1

Text and Versions

LXX καὶ ἐγένετο μετὰ τὸ αἰχμαλωτισθῆναι τὸν Ισραηλ καὶ Ιερουσαλημ ἐρημωθῆναι ἐκάθισεν Ιερεμιας κλαίων καὶ ἐθρήνησεν τὸν θρῆνον τοῦτον ἐπὶ Ιερουσαλημ καὶ εἶπεν

V *et factum est postquam in captivitatem reductus est israel et jerusalem deserta est sedit jeremias propheta et planxit lamentatione hac in jerusalem et amaro animo suspirans et eiulans dixit*

This is a minus in MT and P. Although they read as though translated from Hebrew, these (very similar) prologues have arisen with the claim of Jeremiah authorship. MT is preferred (see Introduction).

The *athnaḥ*, placed after כְּאַלְמָנָה by the Masoretes, should be placed after עַם.[10] This gives proper parallelism in all three lines. If the Masoretic punctuation is followed (so T, cf. House 2004, 331), the balance in the first line is lost.

* * *

אֵיכָה—The word with which the poet begins is generally thought to be an emphatic form of אֵיךְ and is found elsewhere at Deut 1.12; 7.17; Isa 1.21 (1QIs^a reads אֵיךְ); Jer 48.18 etc., and in this book (1.1; 2.1; 4.1, 2). Jahnow (1923, 136) argues that it conveys desperation and may have been a common beginning to a lament. However, many laments do not begin this way, hence it may just have seemed particularly appropriate to this poet to begin to express the horror which follows. While the word can have an interrogative force (Deut 12.30; Jer 8.8), it probably has more of an exclamatory function here—Alas! Although not repeated with each line, the force of אֵיכָה continues throughout the verse (cf. Calvin). Robinson (1936, 37-40; cf. *BHK, BHS*) argues that אֵיכָה is unstressed and stands separate from the first stich, but in this he is not normally followed (cf. Westermann 1994, 112; *BHQ*).

יָשְׁבָה—Qal perfect 3rd f. s. because 'city' is feminine. The perfect is to be understood in the sense of the present (GK 106). The contrasting dirge-like images which follow make it probable that the poet here contrasts the present state of affairs (or at least, the image he wishes to convey) with the

[9] *Hear* prb. rdg. Heb. reads *They have heard*.
[10] Schleusner (1), cf. Rosenberg (2).

past. The verb can have the meaning 'dwell' (Ps 133.1) or 'remain' (Gen 24.55)—and according to SH margin, Sym understood it as 'remain' (ἔμεινεν)[11]—but the poet goes on to paint a picture of a grieving female figure; and sitting (on the ground) characterized ancient mourners (cf. Isa 47.1; Ezek 26.16).

בָּדָד—'Alone, solitary'. Although a noun meaning 'isolation', it is in the adverbial accusative position (GK 118n). The word is construed with יָשַׁב in Lev 13.46; Jer 15.17; Lam 3.28. Rashi interprets 'bereft of inhabitants'. It may go a bit too far in that the poet later makes reference to priests and maidens on the scene (v. 4), but his aim may have been to conjure up an image of desolateness (cf. Isa 27.10 regarding the isolation of a besieged city) in contrast with the grandiose past which he goes on to describe. This is the first of several examples of the poet's tendency to exaggerate.

הָעִיר רַבָּתִי עָם—It is at this point that the contrast comes into focus and the subject of יָשְׁבָה is mentioned. The city[12] (= Jerusalem[13]), once full of people, sits alone. A passage that comes to mind here (cf. Kara), Isa 1.21, also begins with אֵיכָה, deals with contrasts and also contains an old case ending, מְלֵאֲתִי מִשְׁפָּט.

כְּאַלְמָנָה—The poet increases the pathos by the very use of the word 'widow'. The latter's status in society was, along with the orphan, rock bottom—lacking security, with a precarious future, and vulnerable. The presence of the word here led to problems in exegesis. MR is exercised by the implication of widowhood—in the light of Hosea's imagery of Yahweh as the husband of Israel (Hos 2) might not widowhood imply the death of God?—and steers the reader to Jer 51.5, where it is stated that neither Israel nor Judah has been widowed by God: the widowhood consists of the loss of the ten tribes. Rashi also is concerned, picking up a comment from *b. Sanh.* 104a: she is not really a widow; rather, she is like a woman whose husband goes abroad but who intends to return to her. IE[2], on the other hand, is unconcerned. He sees it as it was intended by the author, *viz* as imagery: Not only does she sit alone facing the death of her children (עָם), but like a widow she cannot hope for further children.

The forms רַבָּתִי (twice) and שָׂרָתִי bear the old case ending *yod compaginis* (GK 90l; BL 526 l). By the use of these archaic forms, the poet is trying to emphasise the contrasts that he is drawing between the present,

---

[11] Sym may have considered the combination of √ישב with בדד as suggesting security (cf. Num 23.9; Deut 33.28), or had not accepted that a city could 'sit'; indeed, there may be an allusion to *former* security here, cf. Dobbs-Allsopp (2002, 54).

[12] Weitzman (181f.) points out that the Syriac translator shows sensitivity in his rendering of the word for city: 'the mighty Jerusalem of the past is called ܡܕܝܢܬܐ (Lam. 1:1), but in its ruined state it is called ܩܪܝܬܐ (Lam. 2:12, 15; 5:11)'.

[13] Jerusalem is not specified by name until v. 7, though Zion—used interchangeably with Jerusalem (see 2.6-8)—is mentioned at v. 4.

tragic situation and the glorious past (cf. Isa 1.21). Rashi refers to this ending as superfluous, and Kara emphatically implies that the exegesis in not affected by it—רבתי עם פתרונו רבת עם. While we do not have an exact equivalent of רבתי עם in the Hebrew Bible, there is the construction רבת בנים = 'with many children' (1 Sam 2.5) which supports the interpretation that it is an adjective f. s. construct of רב 'much, many'. The city, once teeming with people (much/great of people), sits alone. In the history of exegesis, this is how רַבָּתִי has been understood—LXX, V, F, T, Rashi, Kara, Vermigli (2002, 11), Calvin, Luther, AV, Rudolph (1962, 204), JB, NRSV, NEB, Westermann (1994, 109), Berlin (2002, 41), BDB, *HALOT*.

McDaniel (1968b, 29-31; cf. Gottlieb 1978, 11), maintains that רַבָּתִי should be understood as the feminine of the word for 'ruler', רב, and that רבת in the sense of 'lady' or 'mistress' is often found as a divine epithet in Phoenician, Ugaritic and Punic. His translation is 'Mistress of the people'. But this interpretation is difficult to accommodate in the first line, where, as Hillers[2] (64) notes, it would destroy the contrast with בדד. There is a play on words here. The first רַבָּתִי has to do with quantity (people), while the second is concerned with greatness and status. Hence, the contrast in the second line is between the city's *status* past and present.

רַבָּתִי בַגּוֹיִם—Although one may take this phrase as a construct followed by a preposition (see GK 130a)—cf. V *domina gentium*—the parallelism of lines two and three demands that we take רַבָּתִי בַגּוֹיִם and שָׂרָתִי בַּמְּדִינוֹת in the same way, i.e. as nouns in the absolute state. And it is here that McDaniel's suggestion may be accepted: Lady among the nations... Princess among the provinces. The author, who is given to hyperbole, imagines that Jerusalem was prominent among nations; cf. the psalmist's allusion to Zion at Ps 48.3 'the joy of all the earth' and Lam 2.15. He may have had in mind here the heyday of the Davidic empire, in which case the nations referred to will have been Moab, Edom, Ammon etc. After the reign of Solomon, with the secession of the northern tribes followed by the rise of Damascus and the dominance of Assyria, Babylonia and Persia, Jerusalem and Judah were anything but prominent.

שָׂרָתִי בַּמְּדִינוֹת—The term שרה is f. of שר, which may denote 'chief, ruler, prince' (BDB 978), and is usually translated 'princess'. Apart from this passage, it usually appears in the plural and refers to Solomon's wives (1 Kgs 11.3), to ladies attending Sisera's mother (Judg 5.29), to companions of kings (Isa 49.23) and to wives of nobles (Est 1.18).

The term מְדִינוֹת is often translated 'provinces'. מדינה is a f. noun[14] from the root דין 'to judge' and has the idea of the *area* where judging/administrating takes place. In 1 Kgs 20.14f., 17, 19 the plural appears to refer to districts in the northern kingdom ruled by שרים. In Ezek 19.8 the reference

---

[14] In Arabic, later Aramaic and Syriac the noun means 'city', though in earlier but apparently not Old) Aramaic the meaning 'province' is found (DNWS 597) and in Biblical Aramaic (Ezra 5.8; 6.2; Dan 2.48f.).

is to a province of the Babylonian empire. At Est 1.1 there is a reference to 127 provinces (of the Persian empire); and Neh 1.3 speaks of Palestine as a province of the same empire. The author, having placed himself in the aftermath of 586 BCE, may be thinking here of the provinces of the Assyrian and Babylonian empires and imagining that Jerusalem was the top dog among them all. He employs exaggerated language to make his point that the glorious past is just that.

הָיְתָה לָמַס—The construction היה ל (= has become) is also found in Isa 1.21. The etymology of מַס is uncertain. It is probably a loan-word (cf. *massu* = corvée worker in Akkadian; CAD, Vol. 10, part I, 327). It functions as a collective m. noun and usually refers to 'a band of forced labourers' or 'forced service' (cf. Gen 49.15; Josh 16.10; Judg 1.30). In Est 10.1 it may mean 'tribute'. Common in the ancient Near East, a defeated state or a subjugated people or grouping could expect such an imposition (Deut 20.11; Isa 31.8). Although, in the tradition, Israel had experienced forced labour in Egypt (cf. the term שָׂרֵי מִסִּים in Exod 1.11, usually translated 'taskmasters') before the settlement in Palestine, it does not seem to have been organised within the community before the monarchy. It was fully developed under Solomon (1 Kgs 5.27) and was considered to have been the cause of the secession of the northern tribes under Jeroboam (1 Kgs 12.4-16). LXX, V, OL, P and T translate here in terms of tribute, but if the poem was written after 586 BCE then the emphasis will be on slavery or forced labour (cf. Luther, Budde 1898[a], 79; Rudolph 1962, 204; Westermann 1994, 109; NIV, NEB). With the mention of 'forced labour', the poet will have touched a sensitive spot in the psyche of his readers/hearers. They had risen to superlative status in the land flowing with milk and honey and they had exchanged it for ignominy and slavery, as in pre-exodus days.

This verse has been carefully and sensitively constructed; indeed, it is the most artistic in the poem, and one gets the impression (after reading through to v. 22) that the author wanted to begin with a flourish. He maintains parallelism throughout the three lines. Each reference to the glorious past is furnished with an archaic form giving emphasis to the contrast. The first two lines are linked by the repetition of רבתי, with a play on words; and the second and third are in chiastic formation: a:b/b:a.

1.2

Text and Versions

MT בָּכוֹ תִבְכֶּה; some MSS[Ken] בכה תבכה; P ܒܟܐ *bkt*. P is the only Version which does not represent the infin. abs. Since the acrostic demands an initial ב, and the following impf. תִבְכֶּה is witnessed to in Hebrew MSS and the Versions, MT is not in question. Cf. Albrektson (1963, 56). The position of the letters בכה in the Qumran fragmentary text (see Cross 1983, 134) suggests that one form of the infin. abs. is original. There is no need to emend to בכה, as does Cross (*op. cit.* 136). The older orthography is frequent in ל"ה verbs (GK 75n).

MT בַּלַּיְלָה; SH has a marginal reading, ܒܟܐ ܒܟܠ ܠܠܝܐ *bky' bkl lly'* 'weeping throughout the night', but this is probably an exegetical expansion.

MT לֶחֱיָהּ; two MSS^Ken לחייה; the plural לחייה may have been the *Vorlage* of LXX, P, V, T; but the likelihood is that both the Versions and the MSS are interpreting the singular used distributively. MT should be retained. The plural 'tears' found in LXX, V, OL, P and T should be seen as natural expansion.[15]

* * *

The f. s. verbal forms and suffixes underline the image, continued from the first verse, of the city as a female figure sitting alone. While the past and present are vividly contrasted in v. 1, v. 2 has mainly to do with the present, though the past is certainly alluded to later in the verse. The picture here is of the female figure weeping bitterly. The imperfect תִּבְכֶּה is to be understood as frequentative. The reference to the night has been variously interpreted. Rashi suggests, tentatively, that it was because the Temple was burned at night. Kara suggests that the reference emphasises the solitariness of the figure, for at night there would be no one to comfort her. Kara also implies that the preposition בְ means 'throughout the night'; so also Nägelsbach (1871, 41; cf. Dahood 1978, 174f.) who garners, in support, quotes from the Mesha Inscription (14-15), the Hadad Inscription (24) and Lam 2.19, where the preposition בְ must mean 'throughout'. This is also the import of the SH marginal reading (see above). The pathos is heightened by this observation. At night, when one may expect respite in sleep, this solitary figure is weeping. Hillers (1992, 66) notes that in Ugaritic poetry the verbs *bkh* and *dm'* often appear in parallel, *bkh* always coming first (cf. Jer 13.17). Here the verb בכה is followed by a verbless statement with the noun דִּמְעָתָהּ as subject. 'Her tears (are) on her cheeks' is probably meant to allude to continuous weeping, cf. Rashi (מתוך שהיא בוכה תמיד). By using the emphatic statement about weeping, followed by the verbless clause, the poet is able to convey the meaning that the female figure/city weeps copiously and continually.[16]

אֵין־לָהּ מְנַחֵם—This phrase, with slightly different word order, is employed in vv. 9, 17, 21. What might seem superfluous and repetitious to a modern Western ear/eye is used by the poet to emphasise a point (cf. Eccl 4.1 where the phrase וְאֵין לָהֶם מְנַחֵם occurs twice), namely, that the weeping figure is without a comforter. The root נחם in the Piel can have a stronger meaning than 'sympathise/comfort': it can carry the added nuance of 'strengthen/encourage'(cf. *HALOT* and Simian-Yofre 1998, 351f.). It may

---

[15] P and OL make the same adjustment at v. 10 (ܐܝܕܘܗܝ *'ydwh* and *manus suas* for ידו). P and T both expand further by introducing a verb: her tears *run down* her cheeks; cf. modern translations (NEB, NIV, ESV) of MT.
[16] The phrase 'in the night' is variously interpreted in T and midrash (MR and MLT; cf. also Renkema 1998, 101f.). T's elaborate paraphrase identifies the night as being that of the 9th of Ab when the Temple had been destroyed by Nebuchadnezzar. That night Israel wept bitterly.

be that, if this lament was used liturgically during the years following the fall of Jerusalem, the prophet of the exile was picking up the theme with his נַחֲמוּ נַחֲמוּ עַמִּי (Isa 40.1). The poet intensifies the isolation by referring to the absence of 'all who loved her'. The female figure might have expected someone to comfort her among her lovers/friends, but she is on her own. Personal abandonment in any circumstances and for whatever reasons is hurtful but when it is by those closest it is particularly bitter. This is an element sometimes found in laments (cf. Ps 38.12 [11]). Renkema (1998, 105: 'Such behaviour might be expected from outsiders or strangers but from lovers it is unthinkable') appears to be unacquainted with the adage 'A friend in need is a friend to be avoided'!

'All who loved her': the verb אהב 'to love' is used of love of man to God (Deut 6.5), of God to man (Deut 4.37) but also of love between men and women (Gen 24.7) and even love of neighbour (Lev 19.18). The active participle can mean 'lover' or 'friend' (1 Kgs 5.15; Est 5.10) and at Ps 38.12 (cf. Ps 88.19) it appears as here in parallel with רֵעַ. The latter term is from the root רעה 'to associate with' and can refer to a neighbour or an associate. The poet is not making a distinction between the two here.[17] The preposition מִן in מִכָּל־אֹהֲבֶיהָ is partitive (GK 119w). Just as we are meant to identify 'the city' as Jerusalem in v. 1, so we are meant to sense what the poet means by 'her friends/neighbours' here. This is the line taken by most commentators, though it should be noted that in midrash and in the mediaeval Jewish commentators, where one might think such identification might be thoroughly explored, this is not done.[18] The interpretation of these terms may be found in the historical situation following 586 BCE. They probably refer to the surrounding nations[19] on whom Jerusalem had relied when Zedekiah rebelled against Babylon. The alliance she thought she had made with Egypt, Syria, Moab and Ammon came to nothing when the invasion came. There was no one to comfort or strengthen/support her. Realising that the rebellion against Nebuchadnezzar was a lost cause, these nations would have tried to minimise their part in the alliance in order to avoid maximum retribution. At 2 Kgs 24.2, Nebuchadnezzar organised some of these neighbours against Judah in her final days. They had joined the enemy ranks. JPS spells it out in translation: 'All her allies have betrayed her'.

√בגד—בָּגְדוּ בָהּ construed with בּ means 'to betray'. At 1.19, where the poet speaks of the absence of 'comforters', it is stated that 'my friends מְאַהֲבַי deceived me רִמּוּנִי'. The sense of both verbs is similar. Here the meaning is backed up with the final words of the verse; hence NEB translates 'all

---

[17] P uses ܪܚܡܝܗ rḥmyh for both terms, while Rashi (cf. also Jer 3.1) equates them both.
[18] Kara is perhaps an exception. Targum seems to identify 'her lovers' as 'her idols which she loved to follow after'. This is an interpretation which may be deduced from the prophet Hosea (2.7ff.). At Jer 3.1 T and Kimḥi take the imagery to refer to both idolatry and the making of foreign alliances.
[19] On the political overtones of the verb 'to love', see Thompson (1977, 475-81).

her friends turned traitor'. There is little doubt that 'her friends' would have a double meaning for the reader/hearer. The poet may speak of the unreliability of alliances with other nations, but at the same time the prophetic warnings about false gods will have come to mind.

1.3

Text and Versions

MT מֵעֹנִי...עֲבֹדָה—so also P, V and T; LXX ἀπὸ ταπεινώσεως αὐτῆς...δουλείας αὐτῆς. The appearance of αὐτῆς probably does not imply a different Hebrew text (contra *BHK*). It may be a corruption in the Greek tradition—original δουλείας αὐτή (αὐτή translating היא which follows) adjusted to δουλείας αὐτῆς by a scribe, and this influenced a later scribe to add αὐτῆς after ταπεινώσεως (so Albrektson, 57); or the Greek translator may have simply vocalised עָבְדָהּ, and a later hand supplied a balancing suffix to ταπεινώσεως.

MT היא—so also P and T. LXX and V omit. The explanation here may be that the Greek and Latin translators thought the pronoun unnecessary in translation (so Schäfer, *BHQ* 113*); cf. AV, NRSV etc. which do not specifically represent היא.

* * *

There are several exegetical problems in this verse.[20] Is it, as in vv. 1f., a description of a present situation, or is the poet referring to the past? Or could both be alluded to? What is the syntax of the first line? Who are the nations? What does the hunting imagery refer to? In this passage we encounter a number of verbs in the perfect. Should they all be taken as declarative perfects (cf. v. 1) and so translated by the English present/ present perfect? On the question of the verbal tenses, I have interpreted the perfects as in the first two verses, where the poet appears to be describing the present condition of the female figure.[21] Present circumstances seem to be operating also in vv. 4ff.

גָּלְתָה יְהוּדָה מֵעֹנִי וּמֵרֹב עֲבֹדָה—The subject throughout the verse is 'Judah'. By this term is meant the people of Judah, as is clear from the rest of the verse. As in vv. 1f., where the city is personified, so here the people are depicted as a female figure,[22] the subject of the verbs גלתה, ישבה and מצאה. The main difficulty lies in the first line and, in particular, in the meaning of the construction גלה מן.[23] In the Hebrew Bible the verb גלה 'uncover',

---

[20] I have discussed some of these elsewhere (Salters 1986, 73-89).
[21] Rudolph (1962, 211f.) and Hillers[2] (66) argue that this verse refers to conditions *before* the fall of Jerusalem, but Provan (38f.) rightly points out that to adopt such a position is to loose the contrast which was established in vv. 1f. The verb ישבה in vv. 1 and 3 is unlikely to refer to different periods.
[22] Normally construed as m. s., the term יְהוּדָה is found as f. s. at Isa 7.6; Jer 23.6 etc. On 'Judah', see Zobel (1986[b]). The name Judah appears at 1.15; 2.2, 5; 5.11.
[23] We should note here that Kara seems to take גלה as separate from the preposition, and Houbigant (1753, 367, 369) argues that the first statement is simply 'Migravit Juda'; but it is the difficult construction which forces these scholars into this unlikely position.

when used intransitively, as here, can mean 'go into exile, depart'.[24] Since the Hiphil can mean either 'force into exile' or 'take into exile', and the nouns גּוֹלָה and גָּלוּת came to focus on the Babylonian captivity, there has been a tendency among some translators and commentators to interpret גָּלְתָה יְהוּדָה as referring to the captivity in Babylon. Hence, LXX[25] μετῳ-κίσθη, Coverdale 'is taken prisoner', Luther 'ist gefangen', AV 'is gone into captivity', Rudolph (1962, 204) 'Weggeführt ist', Berlin (41) 'was exiled'. However, the verb is *not* in the passive in spite of the LXX rendering, hence the aforementioned obsession with the Babylonian deportation is misplaced and misleading. V *migravit Iuda* is reproduced by Calvin who comments: 'Interpreters apply this, but in my view improperly, to the captivity of the people; on the contrary, the Prophet means that the Jews had been scattered... The real meaning...is that the Jews had migrated, that is, had left their own country and fled to other countries...' Douai translates the Vulgate 'Juda hath removed her dwelling place'.

In the Hebrew Bible the construction גלה מן occurs eleven times apart from this passage: 1 Sam 4.21, 22; 2 Kgs 17.23; 25.21; Isa 5.13; Jer 52.27; Ezek 12.3; Hos 10.5; Amos 7.11, 17; Mic 1.16. In all but the last passage the מן is local (GK 119v). In Isa 5.13 it is causal (GK 119z). The fact that the majority of instances favour the מן local leads us to interpret in this way;[26] yet in the history of exegesis, the causal has found support. Hence V *propter adflictionem et multitudinem servitutis*; so also T, MR, Rashi,[27] Kara, AV, Blayney (149), cf. RSV, RV; but it is usually rejected by modern interpreters: Levine (83), Albrektson (57), Kraus (16), Hillers[2] (66), though see Gottwald (7), JPS and ESV where it is still maintained. The issues are inextricably linked. If the Babylonian captivity is envisaged, then the causal מן is problematic, for how can Judah be taken captive *because of* affliction etc.? It is for this reason that the 'causal מן camp' divided. It was argued (MR, MLT) that Judah was punished by the captivity *because* she was guilty of sin (cf. 1.5 etc.), and these sins are alluded to in the terms עני and עבדה. Various sins are listed which have a connection with the roots ענה and עבד, where Judah is accused of afflicting (ענה) the poor or of idolatry (עבודת כוכבים). This interpretation is found in T and, more recently, Henderson (7) who cites Jer 34 in support. In the same vein is Dahood (1978, 175) who emends the text to read מעוני (from עון 'iniquity', taking the suffix as 3rd f. s. as in Phoenician) 'because of her iniquity'.[28] When this adjustment is made, עבדה 'assumes the pejorative sense of serving other gods'. He translates: 'Judah went into exile for her iniquity and for the diversity of her worship'. The other 'causal' interpreters accept that Judah fled into exile because of conditions (affliction

---

[24] On the possibility of there being two (גלה) roots see Gosling (1998).
[25] LXX (confirmed by SH) leads the way here in giving a passive sense to the verb.
[26] P may be as ambiguous as MT, but LXX interprets it as local, and so does IE[2].
[27] Rashi's comments are unclear in that he begins with the local (מארצה) but goes on to include the causal.
[28] He notes that LXX reads '*her* humiliation'.

and harsh service) at home under the Babylonian regime; so Rashi. If we understand that Judah is fleeing the country, then the 'movement from' and the 'reason for' are closely related; indeed, we may note that a temporal interpretation of מִן is not in serious conflict either. Hence, Calvin's *prae afflictione et prae magnitudine servitutis*, which is reflected in Broughton (1608 *ad loc*) 'Judah leaveth country after affliction...', in JB, Hillers[2] (61) and Fuerst (217); cf. Albrektson (57). Yet the poet may be thinking in terms of 'out of the frying pan into the fire', in which case the מִן local serves us best.

But having concluded that the Babylonian exile is being alluded to, especially with the terms 'affliction' and 'hard service', some translators have concluded that what we have here is what Gordis (153f.) calls 'the *mem* of condition'. Luther had translated 'Juda ist gefangen im Elend und schweren Dienst', Moffatt 'To an exile of sad slavery has Judah departed', Meek (7) takes the view that מִן 'has to do with the consequence instead of the cause; hence it means "to suffer"' and NEB renders 'Judah went into the misery of exile and endless servitude'. Gordis translates 'Judah is in exile, in a state of poverty and oppression', but his biblical examples of this *mem* are unconvincing.

הִיא יָשְׁבָה בַגּוֹיִם לֹא מָצְאָה מָנוֹחַ—'She sits among the nations, she finds no rest'. The people of Yahweh are promised 'rest' on entering the holy land (Deut 3.20; 12.9), but Deut 4.27 threatens the settlers in Canaan, if they disobey Yahweh 'Yahweh will scatter you...among the nations (בַּגּוֹיִם)'; cf. also Jer 9.15. Deuteronomy 28.64ff. is particularly apropos here: 'Yahweh will scatter you...and among these nations (בַגּוֹיִם) you shall find no ease, and there shall be no rest (מָנוֹחַ) for the sole of your foot...' The poet is picking up the prophetic threat and is describing the plight of the exiles in those terms. The Mosaic threats have now been realised. Judaeans have fled to other countries—Moab, Ammon, Edom, Egypt etc.—in the hope of finding conditions less intolerable than those obtaining in Palestine, but in vain.[29]

כָּל־רֹדְפֶיהָ הִשִּׂיגוּהָ בֵּין הַמְּצָרִים—In the final line Judah is represented only by the suffixes on רֹדְפֶיהָ and הִשִּׂיגוּהָ, the subject being רֹדְפֶיהָ. In view of the occurrence of the verb √נשׂג Hiphil 'to reach, overtake', the verb רדף (which can mean either 'pursue' or 'persecute') probably means 'pursue' here; cf. several passages where one verb follows the other: Gen 44.4; Exod 14.9; 15.9; Jer 39.5; 52.8 etc. That is to say, the poet employs hunting imagery here, and it is important to retain this imagery in translation if not in exegesis. The people of Judah are depicted as fugitives. The

---

[29] Those who interpret גלה as referring to the captivity in Babylon have difficulty with the second line of the verse. It is possible to interpret יָשְׁבָה בַגּוֹיִם as referring, poetically, to life in Babylon, but if people are taken captive they can scarcely expect to find rest in captivity.

pursuers may be the Babylonian army or a combination of the latter and the erstwhile 'lovers' (v. 2), and the scene is the aftermath of the fall of Jerusalem.

The crux in this line is the phrase בֵּין הַמְּצָרִים. The noun מֵצַר is uncommon in the Hebrew Bible (here and at Pss 116.3; 118.5). This is the only instance of the plural and the only one where it combines with the preposition בֵּין.[30] It derives from √צרר I 'bind, be narrow, restricted'. BDB (865) gives the meaning 'straits, distress', *HALOT* 'distress', *DCH* 'distress, narrow place, confinement'. While LXX (also Sym) ἀνὰ μέσον τῶν θλιβόντων (oppressors) seems to have vocalised as a participle from √צרר III 'to show hostility towards', V *inter angustias* (and probably P[31]) maintains the hunting image. That there were several interpretations in vogue in the early period is seen in the T paraphrase where there is a double translation of the phrase: כד היא מתחבאה בין תחומיא ואעיקו לה. Neither of these corresponds with that of V. The first may correspond with that of LXX, but the second, בין תחומיא, assumes that מֵצַר can mean 'boundary, border'—a meaning which it comes to have in post-biblical Hebrew (cf. Jastrow, 828, and see Kara[32]). Rashi is aware of this interpretation among others, but he begins his comment by taking it to mean narrow places, referring to height on both sides with no way of escape. His third interpretation comes from the midrash (MR, MLT) which takes הַמְּצָרִים as the 'distresses' between 17th Tammuz and 9th Ab.[33] Vermigli (16) holds to the 'narrow places' interpretation, as does Calvin—'it is one of the greatest of evils to fall into the hands of enemies, and to be taken by them when we are enclosed as it were between two walls, or in a narrow passage'. Several translations have understood מֵצַר as 'distress'—thus Luther, Moffatt, RSV, NRSV, REB, ESV, NIV—but this is to miss the imagery of the poet. Better are the renderings of Rudolph (1962, 204), Provan (39), Hillers² (67), JPS, NJB, House (334). We should note a further twist in the history of exegesis. Joüon (1913, 209) believes that the Masoretes got the vocalisation wrong and that it should read הַמִּצְרִים 'The Egyptians'. This, he feels, identifies the גוים mentioned earlier in the passage: 'Notre "lamentation" suppose la situation historique décrite dans Jér 4.11ff.: les Judéens réfugiés en Egypte sont menacés, par le prophète, du *glaive* et d'autres fléaux (vv. 12, 27). Lamentations 1.3 parle des Judéens qui ne pouvant supporter la misère qui suivit la ruine de Jérusalem préfèrent s'exiler en Egypte: "Juda s'est exilee pour fuir l'oppression et l'excés de

---

[30] At Qumran (1QHa 13.31) we have the reading וישינוני במצרים לאין מנוס.
[31] P ܒܝܬ ܐܘܠܨܢܐ *byt ʾwlṣnʾ* has the singular, but should probably be written with *seyame* as in one MS.
[32] Kara adds 'because they were wanderers and fugitives near their neighbours'; cf. also Hugo of St Victor: 'Coarctatus undique locum evadendi invenire non potuit; fugiens Chaldaeos, incidit in Aegyptios; et cum ab Aegyptiis fugeret, occurrit Assyriis'.
[33] See Salters (1986, 83f.). The first date was thought to be the day on which the walls of Jerusalem were breached, and the second the day on which the temple was destroyed.

la servitude; elle s'est établie parmi les nations, mais sans y trouver le repos; tous ses persécuteurs l'ont atteinte chez les Egyptiens".'

After the vivid description of the city as a distressed and shattered female figure (vv. 1f.), the poet focuses on the people of Judah. This may seem to be a change of subject, but it is merely a widening of perspective—taking in the whole fallen state and explaining, to some extent, why the once populous city is alone, and alluding to circumstances which provide background to v. 4. The people of Judah are also personified as a female figure—escaping, restless, run to ground. If the final line of v. 1 harks back to slavery in Egypt, the final word in v. 3 may have conjured up the same image. A further connection with v. 1 is seen in that the same verb 'sits' is used of both the city and Judah—Jerusalem alone, Judah restless. Furthermore, the several epithets attributed to the city in v. 1 are paralleled in the various aspects of Judah's situation. Again, as in the first verse, the poet indulges in hyperbole.

It may be that the various statements in v. 3 have been picked up from the plethora of sentiments and descriptions expressed by many in the aftermath of the fall of Jerusalem and Judah, but the poet's 'selection' is his own observation of what has taken place, and he skilfully weaves the elements together in such a way that his readers will conclude that the ancient threats of Yahweh have been realised (Deut 4.27; 28.64f.; Jer 9.15 etc.). Quite apart from the many who were taken forcibly to Babylon and about which the author will go on to speak, some were unable to bear the Babylonian yoke and fled the country, to Moab, to Ammon, to Egypt, or to Edom in the hope of finding a more tolerable regime. Rumour had it that those who successfully escaped the Babylonian authorities were unable to settle in the country of their choice. Reports were rife that many were run to ground as they made their run for it.

1.4

Text and Versions
MT נּוּגוֹת; LXX ἀγόμεναι; OL *abductae*; V *squalidae*; Aq διωκόμεναι; Sym αἰχμάλωται; P ܡܚܒܚܐ *mmkkn*; T ספדן.

* * *

In this verse we are back with the city, this time identified as Zion (= Jerusalem). The f. s. suffixes throughout emphasise this.[34] The picture here is of another aspect of the desolation.

דַּרְכֵי צִיּוֹן—This is probably not a reference to the streets *within* Jerusalem, as suggested by LXX, OL, V, T, AV, RV, Vermigli (17), Douai, JPS,

---

[34] Kara seems to take the suffixes as referring to Judah, 'for example, (the gates) of Jerusalem, Nob and Gibeon'.

Cross (137) and Berlin (41), but the roads leading *to* Jerusalem (so Luther, Rudolph (1962, 204), NEB, NJB, NRSV; cf. today דרך שכם = the road to Shechem, or closer to home, Portsmouth Road = the road in the south of London in the direction of Portsmouth. Probably the reference is to the roads leading up to (and in the vicinity of) Jerusalem.

אֲבֵלוֹת—The f. pl. of the adj. 'mourning'. The noun דרך is usually m.[35] It is construed here as f. possibly because the poet, in personifying the roads, has in mind the groups of females that characterised the mourning scene in his day (cf. Jer 9.16 [17]). The roads to Zion are personified much as the gates of Zion are in Isa 3.26 'All her gates shall lament and mourn...'

מִבְּלִי—The preposition מן (causative) combined with the poetic form of the adverb of negation בל (BDB 115).

בָּאֵי מוֹעֵד—Literally 'festival comers' (GK 116h). Rashi takes this to mean 'pilgrims' (עולי רגלים). The second stich may be understood as 'from lack of festival comers'. The suggestion that the original text read מבאי מועד (*BHK*), presumably based on metrical considerations, is unnecessary and unsupported.[36] IE[1] thinks that מוֹעֵד is a specific reference to Temple visitors, quoting Ps 74.4,[37] but it is probable that festivals in general are meant (cf. 2.7, 22, and House, 350). That there was a complete cessation of the cult after 586 BCE is uncertain (cf. Jer 41.4f.; McKane 1996, 1019; De Vaux, 337, 387), but the poet is given to hyperbole.

כָּל־שְׁעָרֶיהָ שׁוֹמֵמִין—The ין ending, usually found in the latest parts of the Hebrew Bible, though it does appear in some of the older poetic parts (GK 87e), is found also at 4.3, although the *Qere* there is ים. A few MSS[Ken] do have the latter reading here, and Cross (1983, 138) emends thereto, citing v. 16 and suggesting that MT is the result of a scribal error; but the fact that we find two spellings in the same poem may simply reflect a measure of fluidity in spelling at the time of writing.[38] The sense is not affected. The root שמם is a difficult one in Hebrew. It may have the meaning 'be desolate', 'be deserted', or 'be appalled', the context being the cue. LXX ἠφανισμέναι 'are ruined' is too strong here, as is V *destructae*, but P ܟ̈ܐܒ *ṣdyn* 'be worn out, deserted, lonely' (also T) is closer to what is required. The personification in the poetry is sustained if, in addition to the roads mourning, the gates show emotion—they are appalled/disconsolate; cf. Jer 14.2 and especially Isa 3.26 where Zion's gates mourn and lament. IE[2] and Kara think that the reference to gates is to the area where the elders of

---

[35] BDB 202. IE[1] notes that the words בית, מקום and דרך appear as m. and f.
[36] 4QLam testifies to מבלי.
[37] Cf. Lam 2.6 where the term seems to be equated with שׁ and must refer to the Temple.
[38] In the Moabite inscription the only m. pl. ending is *–n*, while in Phoenician it is always *–im*. Cf. Segal (1958, 126).

Israel would congregate, but it is more likely that the author envisages the actual gateways just as he pictures the actual roads. The roads leading up to Jerusalem would have thronged with pilgrims at festival time, and the gates would have witnessed and served the same crowds coming and going. In the absence of pilgrims, they look forlorn, and the debris of war on the roads and the damaged gates gave the poet the impression that they were appalled and disconsolate. The suggestion by *BHS* of 'all her porters' (vocalising שֹׁעֲרֶיהָ) is presumably dictated by the presence of human beings in the next two clauses, but it is has no support in MSS or Versions; besides, the combination of roads and gates followed by priests and maidens affords a better balance. 'All her gates' refers to every city entrance.

'Her priests...her maidens'. Having led us up the roads to the city and through the gates, the poet continues his focus on the lack of cultic activity by referring to the effect on some of those remaining within the city. The Jerusalem priesthood was devastated by the Babylonian invasion. The head priest and several other leading Temple staff were executed (2 Kgs 25.18-21 = Jer 52.24-27; 39.6); and many were taken into exile. Lamentations refers to some priests dying (1.19) or having been killed (2.20), but, judging from this passage and at 4.16, the assumption is that some priests remained and survived. The poet refers to them moaning (Niphal participle of אנח).[39] According to IE², the reason for the moaning was because they now lacked firstfruits and tithes. It may seem strange that maidens are mentioned along with priests, but it is likely that this is a reference to girls who took part in dancing at the festivals (cf. Judg 21.19-21; Jer 31.13).

נוּגוֹת—This unusual form[40] (see GK 69t, 27n) is usually taken as Niphal partl. f. pl. from יגה I. The only other occurrence of it is at Zeph 3.18. The root occurs also at Lam 1.5, 12; 3.32f. In the Niphal it seems to mean 'grieve' (BDB) or 'worry' (*HALOT*). It seems likely that LXX (ἀγόμεναι) has understood the term as from the root נהג 'to lead', i.e. either the *Vorlage* read נהגות or MT was taken as an apocopated form of נהגות.[41] Perhaps the translator was influenced by what he thought might happen to young women after conflict. LXX is followed by Aq, Sym and OL, but the other Versions are attempting to translate a Niphal partl. Of יגה I.[42] Ewald (327) adopts the LXX reading, as do *BHK, BHS*, RSV, Cross (138). Rashi, IE¹ and Kara all understand the form as Niphal of יגה, and this is how the majority of commentators take it. Translations vary. Luther (jämmerlich), Rudolph (1962, 204, bekümmert), NIV (grieve), NJB (grief-stricken), JPS (unhappy).[43]

---

[39] The verb occurs also at 1.4, 8, 11, 21.
[40] Cf. Driver (1950, 136); Gottlieb (12).
[41] So Albrektson (58); *BHQ* (113*).
[42] V *squalidae* can mean 'dirty' but may also mean 'gloomy'.
[43] As Barthélemy (863) observes, Ewald's emendation is unattractive because the parallelism is lost.

The Targumic paraphrase explains that they (the maidens) are mournful because they have stopped going on the 15th of Ab and on the Day of Atonement to dance the dances.

וְהִיא מַר לָהּ—Literally either 'And, as for herself, bitterness/wretchedness is hers' (if we take מַר to be a substantive: cf. BDB), or 'And, as for her, it is wretched[44] for her' (taking מַר to be Qal perfect from the root מרר). The verse ends with this brief clause. The subject is Zion, mentioned at the beginning of the verse and in the suffixes throughout. The poet, having alluded to the feelings of the roads, gates, priests and maidens, looks back—forming an *inclusio*—at the lonely figure (v. 1) and senses that she herself has feelings. Although the city has been described earlier in the poem—alone, weeping—the poet has not alluded to the depth of her feelings; but here, with a light touch, coincidentally perhaps with the second stich of the 'qinah' line, she is depicted as wretched.

1.5

Text and Versions
MT הוֹגָהּ followed by LXX^AR, P and T; LXX^B ἐταπείνωσεν; V *locutus est super eam* following Aq and Sym. It is supposed (*BHK*) that the original LXX translator did not identify the accusative (suffix) here. Even if this was so, the consonantal text in the *Vorlage* would have been the same as MT.

* * *

Zion's enemies have not been far from the mind of the poet throughout vv. 1-4, but now, in the first line of v. 5, they are centre stage. The humiliation and misery being experienced by Zion is the result of the enemy being now in the driving-seat. In the second line, it is as if the poet recalls his theological position: it may be that the enemy is Zion's master, but it is Yahweh who is ultimately in control and who is active in all this suffering and for a very good reason—Zion's transgressions. Then, in the final line—somewhat loosely connected to the foregoing—the author perhaps picks up what must be for the female figure (v. 1) a heart-rending sight: her children driven away captive.

צָרֶיהָ...אֹיְבֶיהָ—Thenius (130) interprets צָרֶיהָ as those adversaries (the Babylonians) who are now in charge, and אֹיְבֶיהָ as those neighbours who were enemies of Judah, while Brunet (8) takes the former to refer to the Babylonians and the neighbouring countries, and the latter as the *internal* enemies, e.g. the pro-Babylonian party of Gedaliah. However, the interplay between the two terms in the Hebrew Bible generally and the further

---

[44] The usual translation 'bitter' is misleading, carrying the element of resentfulness. The idea here is akin to that at Ezek 27.31; Amos 8.10, or at Prov 31.6, where the expression מרי נפש parallels אובד and where the idea is one of extreme distress.

use of איב at 1.9 would suggest that the poet is not making a fine distinction between the two here. We are dealing with a poetic description of a complete upset. This is not to say that there were not elements in the downfall of Judah that benefited in different ways; and the author would have been aware of this. But one cannot press exegesis too far in what is, apparently, synonymous parallelism. Hillers[2] (84) draws attention to MR, which connects this passage with Deut 28.13—'the Lord will make you the head (הראש) and not the tail…if you listen to the commandments of the Lord your God…'; cf. the obverse at v. 44. It is likely that the poet had these words or this tradition in mind and has concluded that, Yahweh's covenant with his people having been broken (cf. v. 5b), the curse had come upon the people of Judah, and that the adversaries had assumed the role of ראש.

שָׁלוּ—Qal perfect, 3rd c. pl. from √שלה 'to prosper' or 'be at ease'. The meaning here is probably 'prosper', as in LXX εὐθηνοῦσαν and V *locupletati*, rather than 'be at ease' (contr. JPS, Cross, cf. T). The first part of the verse uses words which speak of success—the first time in the poem where something positive is said—but it is the success of the enemy at the expense of Judah; hence, though it is ostensibly different, it is really the other side of the coin of what has been described in vv. 1-4.

כִּי־יְהוָה הוֹגָה—Cross (1983, 139) has understood כי as adversative, but the majority of commentators interpret it as a causative conjunction (GK 158b) following the lead of LXX, P, V and T. The reason that the adversaries have risen to the top and are prospering is because Yahweh was punishing his people for their rebelliousness. This notion anticipates what is made clear at v. 8. This is the first time in the poem that Yahweh is mentioned, and it is the first allusion to the reason for all the suffering and distress described in vv. 1-4. The fact that the enemy is in control demands an explanation: it is the violation of the covenant with Yahweh which is at the bottom of it all; cf. Isa 1.2.

הוֹגָה—from √יגה I 'to suffer': Hiphil perfect, 3rd p. m. s. + suffix 3rd p. f. s. V (so also Aq) derived this from √הגה I 'to muse, speak' but the result is unsatisfactory.[45] The Hiphil of √יגה echoes v. 4, where the root has already been employed; and Rashi, IE[1] and Kara stress this fact.

Budde (1898[a], 80) regards the second line as too short and suggests reading כי יהוה הוא הוגה, while Bickell (1894, 105) imagines that the original line read כי יהוה הונה הוגה, i.e. he 'restores' an infin. abs. which has dropped out through haplography. Although there is no Versional support for either of these ingenious proposals, Budde's suggestion is the more attractive, though most commentators follow MT.

---

[45] Hence, Douai 'the Lord has spoken against her'. Knox has disregarded Jerome here and has consulted the Hebrew: 'the Lord has brought doom on her'.

פְּשָׁעֶיהָ—'her transgressions, rebellions'. Albrektson (59) notes that P (ܢܘ̈ܚܬܗ݁ *ḥṭhyh*) misses the nuance of the Hebrew, while LXX (τῶν ἀσεβειῶν αὐτῆς) does not (cf. also T). It is deliberate rebellion against Yahweh, not just sin or iniquity, that is being highlighted here.

שְׁבִי—At 1.18, we have the construction הָלְכוּ בַשֶּׁבִי where שְׁבִי has the meaning 'state of captivity', and LXX in both passages has ἐν αἰχμαλωσίᾳ. It is clear that the translator understood both passages in the same way. Whether he had בַשֶּׁבִי in his *Vorlage* is not clear: he may simply have interpreted as though the ב were present, cf. 2 Kgs 22.9, where בֵּית יְהוָה must have the same meaning as בְּבֵית יְהוָה (v. 8). This is the understanding of v. 5c in P and T also (both representing a ב). V *captivi* appears to take שְׁבִי as a collective (= captives) (cf. BDB 985), in an accusative position (GK 118q), 'as captives'; and this is the exegesis of REB 'taken captive', cf. RSV, Westermann (109), Kraus (16), Rudolph (1962, 204), NIV. It should be noted that the construction הלך שבי is found only here in the Hebrew Bible. In other passages, the preposition ב is employed: Isa 46.2; Amos 9.4. The Amos passage reads יֵלְכוּ בַשֶּׁבִי לִפְנֵי אֹיְבֵיהֶם, which is so close to our passage that if we are not to emend the text to בַשֶּׁבִי our exegesis must be as per 2 Kgs 22.9.[46]

עוֹלָלֶיהָ—The noun עולל is either from √עול II 'to suckle' (*HALOT*) or √עלל II (BDB), meaning 'child'. We find it used several times in Lamentations (2.11, 19, 20; 4.4), though not elsewhere in this chapter. In the Hebrew Bible it is sometimes in parallel with בחורים (Jer 6.11) or בנים (Ps 17.14), but everywhere it appears to denote the young, the child or the youth. LXX, P and V simply translate 'children',[47] and it is not easy to determine the precise meaning in this context. It may be that the nation's youth (T) are in the poet's mind here, and he is thinking of the extent of Judah's affliction/suffering mentioned in the second line.[48] Her youths, the hope for the future, have gone into captivity before the foe. This reflects the custom of the victor driving[49] the captives, on foot, back to the home country, like cattle.

---

[46] This is noticed by Kara, who supplies the preposition in exegesis. IE¹ observes: בחסרון בית כמו הנמצא בית יהוה (2 Chron 34.30).
[47] Kara glosses it with הנערים (boys, youth), while IE¹ comments שאין להם און, i.e. 'the innocent'.
[48] It may be, as Provan (41) points out, that the term is a reference to Judaeans in general rather than the young people in particular, though this is less likely.
[49] The fact that the captives travel in front of the foe has led to translations such as NEB 'driven away captive by the enemy'.

1.6

Text and Versions
MT וַיֵּצֵא—so also P, V, T and some LXX MSS; LXX^B καὶ ἐξήρθη.
BHK (so also *BHS* and *BHQ*) reckons that the Greek translator vocalised וַיֻּצָּא. Albrektson (59) considers ἐξήρθη to be a scribal error for ἐξῆλθεν; in any case, MT is not in question.
MT (*Kethib*) מִן־בַּת; MT (*Qere*) מִבַּת—so also 4QLam + several MSS^{Ken}. The more unusual מִן־בַּת (GK 102b) is to be preferred (*BHQ*). The sense is not affected.
MT כְּאַיָּלִים—so also P and T; LXX ὡς κριοί; V *velut arietes*, LXX and V have vocalised the same consonantal text: כְּאֵילִים. MT is preferable.
MT בְלֹא—so also LXX, P and T; 4QLam בלי; Cross (1983, 139) wants to emend to בלי, noting '...It is not easy to see how an original בלא would have been corrupted to בלי'. Exegetically, there is nothing to choose between the two. It is true that בלא occurs at 4.14, but בלי occurs in this poem, v. 4!

* * *

The connection of this verse with the preceding one is not simply the *waw*-consecutive (the acrostic demands an initial ו).[50] Verse 5 had concluded with the forced departure of Zion's children 'before the foe'. This is presented as a poignant example of the suffering which Yahweh has brought upon the city, but it reminds the poet of further deprivation: a further forced exodus. He thinks of the leaders, attempting to escape the clutches of the invading enemy, being hunted down like wild deer, increasingly weak. The phrase 'before the pursuer' at the end of the verse echoes 'before the foe' at the end of v. 5, though the scene is different (contra JPS).

בַּת־צִיּוֹן—This phrase, which the AV translates as 'daughter of Zion',[51] is found seven times in Lamentations (1.6; 2.1, 4, 8, 10, 18; 4.22), twelve times in the Prophets (Isa 1.8; 10.32 [*Qere*]; 62.11; Jer 4.31; 6.2, 23; Mic 1.13; 4.10, 13; Zeph 3.14; Zech 2.14; 9.9), once in Psalms (9.15)[52] and once in 2 Kgs (19.21). In addition, in Lamentations, we find similar and related expressions—בת יהודה (2.2, 5), בת ירושלים (2.13, 15), בת עמי (2.11; 3.48; 4.3, 6, 10), בתולת בת ציון (2.13) and בתולת בת יהודה (1.15). All these passages are poetic pieces.[53] The phrases do *not* appear in prose,

---

[50] In fact, when an initial ו is required, throughout the book—1.6; 2.6; 3.16, 17, 18; 4.6—the *waw*-consecutive is used. The choice of the alphabetic acrostic style forces the hand of the poet somewhat in that there are very few Hebrew forms beginning with ו. However, the authors of these poems do use the *waw*-consecutive a further 23 times; and Hillers[2] (67f.) is of the opinion that, since earlier poets seem to eschew this construction, this reflects a change in poetic style by the sixth century BCE.
[51] For a succinct discussion of this expression, see Williamson (2006, 67-71); cf. also Stinespring (1965), Schmitt (1991, 365-87), Kartveit (2001, 97-112).
[52] Another (incomplete) alphabetic acrostic poem.
[53] The Kings passage, which actually reads בתולת בת ציון and is parallel to בת ירושלים, is part of a poetic section (vv. 21-28) within dense prose narrative.

suggesting that they are poetic terms.⁵⁴ Follis (1103) is probably correct in her observation that the phrases are poetic personifications of the city of Jerusalem and its inhabitants. The origin of the expression is shrouded in mystery. Dobbs-Allsopp (1995, 452-55) draws attention to the fact that, in Akkadian, a goddess is sometimes referred to as *mārat* GN, i.e. daughter of GN (= Geographical Name). In this she is understood to be a citizen of the city where her shrine was located;⁵⁵ and Dobbs-Allsopp argues that this is the origin of the terminology, though he acknowledges that, in the hands of the biblical writers, the idea of a goddess has long gone, and the phrase has become a 'purely literary phenomenon'. There may be something in what Dobbs-Allsopp says in this regard—and his thesis deserves consideration and further study—but problems arise (for this argument) when other phrases involving a country/people are involved—בת אדום, בת מצרים, and, in particular, the phrase בת עמי.⁵⁶ In the Bible, when someone addresses a male of lower rank, the term is often 'my son' (Prov 1.8, 10; 2.1; Eccl 12.12; cf. also 2 Tim 2.1; Phlm 10; Heb 12.5). In the book of Ruth, Naomi and Boaz both address Ruth as 'my daughter' (2.2, 8, 22; 3.1, 10, 11, 16, 18) even though she was not the actual daughter of either. She was, however, a widow—someone without status in society. At 3.1, Naomi is concerned about Ruth's status, and it is not until the final chapter that she acquires a standing in the community. The word 'daughter', juxtaposed with 'Zion' etc., therefore, may have originally conveyed an element of vulnerability and concern. This is roughly the position taken by Stinespring (985); cf. also Kartveit (97-112).

The rendering, in translation, of these phrases has always seemed unsatisfactory. For example, 'daughter of Zion' (so AV, RV, RSV, NIV, NEB, NJV, ESV), though familiar,⁵⁷ is ambiguous and misleading; and 'daughter Zion' (Rudolph, Kraus, NRSV, Renkema, Westermann), while less ambiguous, is still not really intelligible. JPS 'Fair Zion' and Berlin 'Dear Zion' read better, but the occurrence of the phrase בת אדום at 4.21f. forces the translations 'Fair Edom' and 'Dear Edom', which, even if we view the passage as ironic, sound ridiculous, given the sentiments of the passage. The poets' intentions can hardly be captured in translation and it is best to side with Moffatt and Hillers and translate simply 'Zion' (also

---

⁵⁴ Further examples occur elsewhere: בתולת ישראל (Amos 5.2; Deut 22.19; Jer 31.21), בתולת (Isa 37.22), בתולת בת ציון (Isa 47.1), בתולת בת בבל (Jer 46.11), בתולת בת מצרים, בת צידון (Isa 23.12).

⁵⁵ Dobbs-Allsopp, therefore, sees the form as a genitive of location.

⁵⁶ See Williamson (*op. cit.* 68); Berlin (11f.). Berlin cautiously rejects the explanation: 'we refer to countries or cities as female without the implication that this usage derives from the city as a goddess. *Bat-ʿammî* is a personification of the people just as *bat-ṣiyyôn* is a personification of the city. Both phrases have the same grammar, and the best explanation of that grammar remains the appositional genitive. The same holds true for *bĕtûlat yiśrāʾēl* (Amos 5.2; Jer 31.2, 4) and *bĕtûlat bat X.*'

⁵⁷ Williamson (*op. cit.* 67) retains it for this very reason!

'Jerusalem', 'Judah', 'Edom'.[58] In the case of בת עמי, AV, NRSV, ESV, Rudolph and Kraus render 'the daughter of my people'—again, obscure and misleading; and Renkema has 'my daughter, my people', NJB 'my young people', JPS 'my poor people', Steinspring 'my beloved people' or 'my unfortunate people' and Berlin 'my Dear People'. While 'my unfortunate people' may be closest to the poets' meaning, it is best, with Moffatt, NIV, Hillers, NEB and REB, to settle for 'my people', for the reason given above. As Hillers[2] (31) remarks vis-à-vis the several phrases, 'no thoroughly idiomatic English equivalents are available'.

הֲדָרָהּ—An abstract noun 'her splendour'. The passage which comes to mind here is 1 Sam 4.21f., גָּלָה כָבוֹד מִיִּשְׂרָאֵל, where the term is not הדר but כבוד, and where the allusion is to the capture of the Ark of God. Two other passages (Ezek 10.18 and Hos 10.5) echo the language used here, but they do not help to nail the meaning. It is unclear what is meant by this term. It is possible that it is a reference to the plundering of the city's wealth, in terms of silver and gold. The image is, perhaps, still that of the woman now deprived of her comeliness. It has gone. It may be that the exegesis is supplied by the next line, namely 'her leaders' (JPS), and Dahood (176) actually translates הֲדָרָהּ 'her nobility'; but this is to disregard the poetry of the line, which has to do with the image of the female figure.[59] The departure of this splendour is then seen in terms of the leaders being hunted by the enemy so that they resemble harts or deer[60] (REB). Hunted deer which[61] find no pasture are liable to get weaker; and the image continues (for the subject is still the deer, not the leaders) as the animals are described as 'without strength' but still fleeing before the pursuer/hunter. Dahood (176), reading 'they collapsed exhausted in front of the hunter', argues that the verb הלך 'carries the nuance of Arabic *halaka* "to pass away"'. If that were the case, then because of similarity of language, we would surely have to translate in v. 5: 'her children have collapsed like captives before the foe'! In v. 5, the description is of the cruel foe driving the young into captivity, and in this verse it is an image of the hunter chasing the weakening deer; but the interpretation of the image is of the leaders being seriously hunted down.

שָׂרֶיהָ—The term שׂר (found also, in Lamentations, at 2.2, 9; 5.12) is translated 'prince' by AV, NRSV, NIV, NJB, REB etc., but this is misleading. In the Hebrew Bible שׂר often denotes a captain, leader or ruler (BDB 978), whereas the English word 'prince' often refers to a male member of

---

[58] Stinespring is critical: 'Most of the standard grammars explain this matter correctly, though the translators with few exceptions have paid no attention, preferring instead the simplistic notion that the construct state must always be followed in translation by the word "of" introducing a possessive genitive.'
[59] IE[1] suggests 'her royalty' (מלכות).
[60] LXX and V 'rams' (see above) is not suitable in the hunting scenario.
[61] IE[1] notes that we must supply the relative pronoun (אשר), suppressed in poetry.

a royal family. The LXX (οἱ ἄρχοντες αὐτῆς) and V (*principes eius*) renderings (= rulers) get the right note here (cf. also JB, Provan, 41) 'leaders'. House's (332) 'officials' is also a possible rendering. Presumably, the capture of the leaders was not a simple operation since they would make a supreme effort to avoid the clutches of the enemy, even escaping into the countryside. The forced exile of these leaders to Babylon was subsequent to their capture. The two verses (5 and 6) use similar vocabulary, but the phrases לִפְנֵי־צָר and לִפְנֵי רוֹדֵף refer to different scenarios: the one envisages the orderly transfer of young captives, the other of the relentless enemy efforts to secure the leaders of the vanquished people.[62]

1.7

Text and Versions

MT זָכְרָה יְרוּשָׁלַם—so also LXX, P, V and T; 4QLam זכורה יהוה. MT is preferred. 4QLam's reading may be the result of a scribe interpreting the text he was copying, a text which read זכרה י'. 4QLam differs from MT to such an extent that many scholars are loath to adopt its variants. Beginning, not with 3rd f. s. perfect, but with the imperative + the tetragrammaton: 'Remember, O Yahweh', it then mixes 1st p. pl. with 3rd p. f. s. in such a way that one has to conclude that corruption is deep and radical.[63]

MT יְמֵי עָנְיָהּ וּמְרוּדֶיהָ—so also LXX, P, V and T; 4QLam omits. MT is preferred.

MT וּמְרוּדֶיהָ—LXX καὶ ἀπωσμῶν αὐτῆς; Aq καὶ ἀποστασιῶν(αὐτῆς); P ܘܡܪܘܕܘܬܗ *wmrdwth*; V *et praevaricationis* (*omnium desiderabilium suorum*).

MT צָרִים—so also V and T; LXX οἱ ἐχθροὶ αὐτῆς—so also P and 4QLam. The suffix reflected in LXX and P might be due to interpreting the stark Hebrew,[64] but 4QLam makes it more likely that their *Vorlagen* had the suffix. Cross (141) adopts the Scroll reading, and this may be correct.

MT מִשְׁבַּתֶּהָ; many MSS[Ken] משבתיה—reflected in Masoretic pointing; 4QLam משבריה; LXX[B] κατοικεσίᾳ αὐτῆς; LXX[A] μετοικεσίᾳ αὐτῆς; Aq καθέδρᾳ (αὐτῆς); Sym (κατεγέλασαν) τῆς καταργήσεως αὐτῆς; V *sabbata eius*; P ܬܒܪܗ *tbrh*. The plural, hinted at by the Masoretes, is found in V and 4QLam but not in the other witnesses. Most scholars accept the difficult MT, though Ehrlich (31) prefers to point מִשְׁבַּתָּה.

* * *

[62] Westermann (110, 112), casting around for a solution to the longer than usual v. 7, finds a candidate in the second line, which he suggests has fallen out of v. 6. While the tension is removed from v. 7, he has now overburdened v. 6! Furthermore, the introduction of the v. 7 material seriously affects the imagery of v. 6: הַדְּרָהּ now finds its exegesis in the introduced material, *viz.* the desirable things (מַחֲמָדֶיהָ); and the departure of the leaders comes awkwardly after this. Besides, as it stands, v. 6 makes good sense.

[63] Cross (140f.), however, is so enamoured with the new discovery that he is less then critical in his handling of it. He adopts the imperative + יהוה, which he feels corresponds to other addresses to the deity in the poem; but at vv. 9, 11 and 20-22 the cries are uttered in the first person (the city speaking), while at v. 7 (if we read the imperative) the cry to God is on behalf of the city or people by another voice. Cross's choice here is unfortunate. He is followed by Schäfer (*BHQ*).

[64] Cf. NJB, ESV, House (332) who, without emendation, render as though the suffix were present.

In this verse the poet imagines the personified city reflecting as she sits alone (v. 1), weeping bitterly (v. 2) and generally suffering. She recalls the precious things which had long been in her possession, now lost. The tragic reversal is expressed in terms of possessions. It is said that, in adversity, one's memories of the good life add significantly to one's agony and sorrow.[65] And this is further emphasised by the gloating of the foes and their mocking at her downfall.

Because the other verses in this poem are of a uniform length, the presence here of an extra line has led many scholars and commentators to conclude that the original verse must have consisted of material of a similar length to the other verses in the poem and that the extra line is the result of interpolation or expansion by a later hand. There is no help from the Versions here, as all presuppose the extra material; and 4QLam, though differing significantly from MT, appears to represent enough of the wording to lead us to conclude that it is roughly the transmission of a text containing the same bulk as MT. Scholars are divided on this issue. A few scholars defend the four-line verse. Gordis (154) warns that 'deletions on metric grounds are increasingly recognised as methodologically unsound' and points out that the *qinah* rhythm is maintained in the pattern 4:3|3:2| 3:2. Freedman (378ff.) points out that the vocabulary of whatever we would delete is characteristic of Lamentations, while the contrast between the past glory and the present misery is an important theme of the first poem. But Freedman's translation, 'Jerusalem remembers the days of her affliction and homelessness—all the precious possessions which were hers from ancient times—when her people fell...', simply will not do, and merely points up the problem. *BHK* and *BHS* suggest deleting line 2. The verse might then be translated: 'Jerusalem remembers the days of her affliction and restlessness when her people fell into the hands of her adversaries...' The deletion produces a smooth syntax, and the verse can take its place among the other three-line verses in the poem. This is the approach taken by JB, NEB, Ewald (327 fn.), Kraus (16), Westermann (110), Plöger (133f.), Wiesmann (110), Bruno (72, 217). The idea here is that Jerusalem looks back bitterly at her time of affliction, the time of her fall. One might argue that the extra material (כל...קדם) is really an interpretative gloss on the ambiguous phrase כל הדרה (v. 6), which, originating as a marginal gloss, was subsequently incorporated into the text. But since the poet has been describing affliction in the extreme, the question arises as to the present situation: Is Jerusalem not *presently* distressed? Are we not dealing with the weeping and distressed city? Consequently, there are those who prefer to delete line 3: 'when her people fell into the hands of the foe, and there was no one to help her'; so Rudolph (1962, 206), Albrektson (62), Gottlieb (13). One might argue that these words are an interpretative gloss on the phrase ימי...ומרודיה (first line). Meek (9),

---

[65] Dante (*Inferno* V.121).

followed cautiously by Hillers[2] (68f.), decides that since the deletion of either line leaves an *intelligible* text, the verse contains two variant readings, two different text-forms of which MT is a conflation. But, as Albrektson (63) remarks, 'this is hardly more than a new label on the old problem. The very "variant" after all presupposes that the textual tradition has resulted in two readings of which only one could have been written by the author, and we are still left with the problem which of these variants is original and which is secondary.' Schäfer (114*) prefers to omit (with 4QLam) the phrase ימי...ומרודיה.

Freedman notes that at 2.19, where we have another four-line verse, it may be doing violence to the verse by deleting, as most do, line 4. He observes (380), 'The fact that the same deviation, one four-line stanza in a poem of three-line stanzas, occurs in both poems, suggests the possibility that it is a deliberate device'. The latter cannot be entirely ruled out. The metre, which is adhered to throughout the poem, appears to have been selected by the author as the vehicle in which his thought is best conveyed. That metre has, as a characteristic, an unbalanced line. Could it be that, by adding a line in one of the stanzas, the poet was signalling another imbalance, as it were? The fact that we find it again at 2.19 should make for caution; and Freedman draws attention to 4.15, which has two lines appreciably longer than all the others in the poem. While it may not be surprising that NIV and JPS translate the text as it stands, it is interesting to note that REB reverses the decision of NEB to delete line 2, while NRSV resists the tendency to shorten the verse. While we may try to elucidate MT as it stands, I am inclined to the view that line 3 is secondary, that it constitutes an explanation of the adverbial accusative phrase ימי...ומרודיה. If this is the case, we must conclude that it is an erroneous explanation in that the days of her affliction refer to her present suffering and not to the time when she fell into the hands of the enemy.

יְמֵי עָנְיָהּ וּמְרוּדֶיהָ—P's rendering shows that the translator took this phrase, along with the second line, as direct accusative[66] (note ܘܟܠܗܝܢ *wklhyn* later in the verse). T also seems to have understood the text this way (Alexander 2008, 115); so also Rashi, Vermigli (27), Ewald (328), Westermann (110). IE[1] believes that this is *not* the accusative of זכרה, quoting Exod 20.11 (כִּי שֵׁשֶׁת־יָמִים עָשָׂה יְהוָה) to show a parallel passage where the preposition ב has to be understood; and MLT, Kara, Calvin, AV, Perles (1930, 100), Gordis (130), RSV, JPS, NIV, REB follow this exegesis;[67] that is to say, the phrase is an adverbial accusative of time (GK 118k). The poet imagines the city remembering her precious things, but in an adverse context—while she is suffering, and that makes it all the more galling. Kara notes that it is natural, when one is afflicted, to recall the former good times, quoting Job 29.2, 4 in support (cf. also Keil, 364; Berlin, 46).

---

[66] Albrektson, Abelesz, Wiesmann and Kelso do not appear to notice this.
[67] There is no need to 'restore' to בִּימֵי (so Houbigant, 477) or to מִימֵי (so Blayney, 307).

מְרוּדֶיהָ—a word found only here, in 3.19 (singular) and Isa 58.7 (plural). It is linked here with עָנְיָהּ, as it is in 3.19. Kimḥi (Roots) handles the term under two roots—under √מרד the meaning is 'misery/humiliation', but under √רוד the meaning he gives is 'wandering'. This confusion is reflected in the history of exegesis.[68] LXX 'her rejection' may mean that the Greek translator was uncertain, for it is difficult to understand this rendering. Wiesmann (110) suggests that the translator had read מדוחיה because מדוחים is rendered in LXX by ἐξώσματα at 2.14, while Albrektson (60) explains the rendering as the result of the mixing up of ד and ר where the root was thought to be דרא/דרה from the Arabic 'to reject, repel'. Aq seems to have taken the word as from מרד 'to rebel' (so Kelso, 11, who reconstructs מֹרְדֶיהָ; cf. also *BHK*), and it may be that this root explains LXX also. P could mean 'her chastisement' which would mean that the translator understood the root as רדה 'to chastise, dominate', although, as Albrektson (61) points out, it is possible to take the Syriac as from מרד. V's 'and perversion (of all her desirable things)' appears to have understood the word as in the construct state—מרודי—and from the root מרד. T was probably uncertain as to the origin of the word and translates twice—ומרדא...מדורה. MR also interprets as from מרד, though the passage is seen as a reference to Jerusalem's rebellions against God. The comment of IE[1]—that the מ is a root letter—would suggest that he understood the root to be מרד. When Rashi says that the basic meaning is 'pain' (צער) and quotes Judg 11.37 and Ps 55.3—two difficult passages where the root is ירד 'to descend—he is struggling; but his instinct (that the context calls for such a meaning) is correct.

Gesenius (1269b) came down on the side of √רוד; and it is now common to identify the word with √רוד 'to wander, be without home' (cf. Isa 58.7), and to understand it as an abstract plural (cf. חיים, נעורים), meaning 'homelessness' or 'wandering'—so BDB, Nägelsbach (45), Ehrlich (31), Rudolph (1962, 206), Albrektson (60), Gottwald (7), NEB, NIV, NRSV, *DCH*, *HALOT*, Barthélemy (866), Renkema (127). Hillers[2] (69) regards עָנְיָהּ וּמְרוּדֶיהָ as a hendiadys—'when she was banished in misery', though he does not explain how he gets 'banished' from מְרוּדֶיהָ.

The phrase must refer to the period that the author has been describing (with perfect tenses) in the previous verses. At v. 3 Judah departs from affliction and harsh service, and it is natural to think of a meaning not far removed from that. 'Homelessness/wandering', as referring to the city is difficult, and this is why translators and commentators have struggled to accommodate it.[69] Provan (43) points out that 'wandering' is inappropriate

---

[68] On the various renderings here and at Lam 3.19 and Isa 58.7, see Barthélemy (864ff.). Commentators even offer a different interpretation when they come to 3.19; thus, Vermigli (122) there translates 'trouble' but at 1.7 'wandering'. And Calvin concludes, at 1.7, that the meaning is either 'exile' or 'want', but at 3.19 translates 'trouble', though he is aware of other views.

[69] REB's 'restlessness' for NEB's 'wandering' probably reflects this unease.

here in that 'elsewhere in the poem it is always the people, not the city, who are on the move. Zion remains behind to mourn'. The only way Provan can accommodate the derivation from √רוד is to see here a distinction between the city and her people—the affliction of the city and the homelessness of her people. He translates (taking the form as a passive participle) 'Jerusalem remembers in the days of her affliction and her homeless ones...' He may be right, but it seems to me that the poet is speaking only of Jerusalem and that we are meant to understand here two terms which are predicated of the female figure herself—sitting, weeping, now reflecting—and that we need an interpretation which does not do violence to that imagery. The tragic reversal, begun at v. 1, saw the lonely, demoted, abandoned, enslaved and suffering figure weeping. Here the poet encompasses those experiences with his phrase יְמֵי עָנְיָהּ וּמְרוּדֶיהָ. The Versions struggled with מְרוּדֶיהָ, but their attempts are in the same category as that of Rashi (pain) who seems to derive the term from √ירד; and Blayney (307) makes the same derivation (her abasement), though without reference to Rashi. Other commentators and translators not convinced that 'homelessness' fits here are AV (miseries), Calvin (*penuriae*), Keil (persecutions), RSV 'bitterness'[70] Plöger (Mühsal), Westermann (Ängste), Kaiser (Ängste), JB (distress), JPS (sorrow), Berlin (trouble). Perhaps Meek (9) is correct in claiming that the word is an abstract plural noun from √רדד 'to subdue' (related to √רדה meaning 'oppression'). The verb is used at Isa 45.1 for the actions of Cyrus at Yahweh's direction. Zion is surely subjugated.

מַחֲמַדֶּיהָ—As pointed, this word מחמוד is distinguished from מחמד, which occurs at vv. 10, 11 (*Qere*) and 2.4, though Stade (§ 273a) argues that all instances are from מחמד. The latter means 'desirable thing' or 'desire', and the former must have a similar meaning (see BDB 327). It may be that this is a reference to desirable things in general (LXX πάντα τὰ ἐπιθυμήματα αὐτῆς)—anything is better than the present scenario—but it may refer to particular former possessions of the city; cf. T כל רגונה, Thenius (130) 'Kostbarkeiten', REB 'treasures'. Jerusalem recalls the good things she had in the good old days. The repetition of 'days' points up the contrast. She had been in possession of those things when the foe captured her people and she was without help (וְאֵין עוֹזֵר לָהּ). There may be an allusion here to v. 2, where it was stressed that among all her lovers there was no one to comfort her; but it may be the specific failure (in 586 BCE) of Egypt to come to her aid, mentioned in Ezek 29.1-16; 30.20-26; 31.1-18; cf. 2 Kgs 18.21; Jer 46.17; Lam 4.17.

---

[70] RSV 'bitterness' is based on an emendation of MT—reading מְרוֹרֶיהָ, also suggested by BHS, from √מרר 'be bitter'; cf. 3.15; possibly relying on Calmet, but see Barthélemy (865) who traces it back to Châteillon (1555).

רָאוּהָ צָרִים שָׂחֲקוּ—The idea of enemies gloating over the adversity of opponents is a common one in the Hebrew Bible (Ps 54.9).[71] The author has already mentioned צרים in v. 5. They not only topple her: they now stand and laugh at the result. They rub her nose in it. The construction here is that of a temporal clause, 'when they saw her/as they looked on', followed by the main clause (GK 164).

מִשְׁבַּתֶּהָ—BL 490 z. This is another *hapax legomenon*, and it has occasioned some confusion and speculation. LXX^B 'her habitation' shows that the translator[72] derived it from √ישב 'to dwell'. This root is reflected also in Aq 'settlement'. In the minds of the translators the scenario may have been the enemies mocking what was left of Jerusalem. Sym 'her abolition, cessation' is an indication that the translator derived it from √שבת 'to cease', and the image here is similar, if not stronger—her ruin. V, 'her Sabbaths', though quite different, is also based on this root. The idea here would be that the enemies mocked any attempt at Sabbath observance by their captives. The latter rendering may owe something to Jerome's contact with rabbis, as this is an interpretation found in MR; and Rashi is acquainted with it, though he interprets it with regard to the cessation of various festivals. Kara, too, derives the word from √שבת. P's 'her ruin, breakdown' is thought by Rudolph (1938, 102) and Albrektson (61) to rest on the same root, but *BHK* (cf. *BHQ*) may be right in presupposing √שבר, while 4QLam's reading makes this more likely.[73] At Hos 1.4 we have the threat '…and I will put an end to (וְהִשְׁבַּתִּי) the kingdom of the house of Israel', while at Jer 31.36 we get the prediction that 'the offspring of Israel will cease to be a nation (יִשְׁבְּתוּ מִהְיוֹת גּוֹי) before me'.

1.8
Text and Versions

MT חֲמָא—so also LXX, P, V and T; 4QLam חמוא; Ehrlich (31) suggested that it should be vocalised as for infin. abs.—חָמֹא, cf. also *BHS*; and Cross (141) is persuaded that this is the correct reading. MT is preferred.

MT לְנִידָה; 20 Heb MSS^{Ken} לנדה; 4QLam לנוד; LXX εἰς σάλον; V *instabilis*; P ܢܕܬ *ndt'*; Aq εἰς κεχωρισμένην; Sym σίκχος ἀνάστατον; T לטלטיל.

* * *

In this verse the image of the female figure is maintained, but there is a change of emphasis. Up to this point the poet paints a picture of tragic reversal. Here the tragic downfall is linked to the fact that Jerusalem has sinned (cf. v. 5). The poet's reasoning is, simply, that the great catastrophe

---
[71] Cf. also the Moabite Stone, lines 4 and 7.
[72] The reading of LXX^A, 'her captivity', may be an (inner Greek) scribal error; cf. Rudolph (1938, 102).
[73] We should note that שבר at Amos 6.6 is rendered ܬܒܪ *tbr'* by P.

is the result of evil doing. He does not spell out a single example of this evil doing; indeed, although it would have been natural to have mentioned Yahweh's part in this—and v. 5 shows that this is what he believed—he refrains from doing so. It is as if he wants his readers here to think of the logical consequences of sin. Yahweh may be behind it all, but there is a certain logic about the process: sin leads to ignominy. The description is of a debased woman. Enemies can be expected to gloat and mock at her downfall, but even those who respected her now despise her; and, under the gaze of them all, she groans and turns away.

חָטְאָה חֵטְא—Jerusalem is again the subject of this verse. In v. 5 the author tells us that Yahweh afflicted Jerusalem (or Judah?) because of her many crimes/transgressions. Here a different noun, חֵטְא, meaning 'sin', is used with the cognate verb—the root חטא is used at 3.39; 5.7, 16. The construction (internal accusative [GK 117p]) is often taken to convey emphasis—that Jerusalem sinned *greatly* (so T, AV, NRSV etc.), though emphasis is usually expressed either by the infin. abs. or by adding an adjective (גדול) to the noun (Gen 27.34; Jonah 1.16; 4.1).[74] The point here is not the greatness of Jerusalem's sin but the fact that she has gone wrong and that this has led to her being despised etc.

לְנִידָה—נידה is another *hapax legomenon*, often taken as a variant form of נדה (v. 17), 'filthy rag'. LXX 'restless', V 'unstable', T 'wanderer' all derive from √נוד 'to move to and fro'. The exegesis of T probably has to do with the exile, and this may explain the renderings of LXX and V. MR also interprets in terms of 'wanderer'. On the face of it, and with the apparent support of the 4QLam reading, we should perhaps be looking to the root נוד to explain the term. However, P and Aq appear to derive from √נדד or √נדה I, while Sym's double rendering appears undecided. The early translators, therefore, struggle with the term.

Rashi comments לנידה. לגולה לשון נע ונד—clearly in the same camp as T and MR, cf. also Berlin 'banished' (42); but IE[1], whilst agreeing that the root is נוד, takes a different line. Quoting Ps 44.15, מנוד ראש 'shaking of the head', he glosses נידה with לעג 'mocking'; that is, he suggests that Jerusalem became a target for derision.[75] Pagnini[76] *in derisionem* follows this line, while Vermigli (29-31) is undecided between derision and exile. Calvin struggles: *in migrationem (vel, commotionem) facta est (hoc est, reddita fuit instabilis)*, but he concludes that exile is meant here. Luther 'wie ein unrein Weib' is satisfied that the term is a variant (*plene*) spelling of נדה (v. 17), and this is the view that has most adherents—RV, Keil

---

[74] The sense of the construction וַיָּצָם דָּוִד צוֹם in 2 Sam 12.16 is not that David fasted *intensely*, merely that he fasted.
[75] Ibn Ezra is followed by Rudolph (1962, 204), Hillers[2] (70), Wiesmann (111), Meek (10), Gordis (130), JPS, NRSV.
[76] Quoted by Shute (29). The latter points out that, in his Thesaurus, Pagnini defines the term as *in commotionem demigrationem*, which is closer to Rashi.

CHAPTER 1   61

(365), Thenius (132), Kraus (21), RSV, NJB, NIV, NEB, Gottwald (8), Provan (44), Haller (96), Kaiser (308), Renkema (133f.), House (354). For one thing, the idea of Jerusalem as 'wanderer' or even 'an exile' does violence to the context. For another, the idea of an object of scorn is not well-founded (Albrektson, 63), for the noun ראש is probably needed to make this meaning possible. Provan (44) argues: 'The idea of the city's impurity does accord well, however, both with the immediate and wider context... In the immediate context, we find two other terms, *ʿerwāh* nakedness and *ṭumʾāh* uncleanness, which are used elsewhere in the *OT*, often closely associated with *niddāh* in statements about ritual cleanness and uncleanness.' By 'filthy rag', REB alludes to the menstrual rag, and this picture is enhanced in the lines which follow.

כָּל־מְכַבְּדֶיהָ—The use of the participle is, on the face of it, ambiguous; but this is a reference to those who had *previously* honoured her (cf. v. 2), as Kara is careful to point out. The picture is of an individual who has fallen from grace and whose present plight is now reflected in the complete turnaround of erstwhile supporters. It is a reference to those who had acknowledged the great reputation of Jerusalem, as a power. They are probably the surrounding states: Egyptians, Philistines, Ammonites, Moabites, Edomites etc. They now despise her.

עֶרְוָתָהּ—This noun, from √ערה 'be naked, bare', is often translated 'nakedness'; but the word means 'pudenda, genitals'. Being seen naked, especially the exposure of the genitals, was such a horror and disgrace in the ancient Near East that it is scarcely imaginable to the modern West. If a woman was guilty of a sexual misdemeanour, she could be stripped naked (Ezek 16.35-39), and the ensuing disgrace was so great as to be left undescribed. The reluctance to spell out the blunt fact is reflected not only in the bland LXX ἀσχημοσύνην αὐτῆς[77] 'her shame' and V *ignominiam eius* 'her disgrace', but possibly in T בדקתה—translated 'nakedness' by Levine (64) and Brady (156) and 'shortcomings' by Jastrow (141);[78] cf. also AV, NIV, JB, NEB, NRSV 'nakedness', Bishop's 'filthiness', Luther's 'Blöße', JPS's 'have seen her disgraced'.[79] The image is of a woman whose genitals has been seen and so is utterly disgraced. Those who had once respected her can do so no longer. This line is underlining what has been said about her being treated as a filthy rag.

גַּם־הִיא נֶאֶנְחָה—The picture of the disgraced woman continues. McDaniel (31f.) finds the traditional interpretation of the particle גם 'also' to be

---

[77] LSJ notes that this is a euphemism for αἰδοῖον 'pudenda' in Lev 18.7 etc.
[78] Alexander (2008, 116), while questioning Jastrow's translation, observes that the Aramaic word, from √בדק 'to split' involves 'an explicit physical reference to the female genitalia'.
[79] Calvin is undecided: *turpitudinem (vel foeditatem) ejus*.

unacceptable and argues for the meaning 'aloud' on the basis of the occasional use in Ugaritic of the adverb *gm*. He is followed by Hillers[2] (62). But the argument for taking this line of reasoning is weak. Gottlieb (14) points out that גם is used in the same way at Gen 32.19; Ps 52.7 and Job 13.16, where one could not possibly argue for it as an adverb; hence it is best to reject McDaniel here. Whether גם is to be taken in the sense of 'furthermore, and' or as an adversative 'but, yet' (GK 160b; Ps 129.2)—so Westermann (110), Rudolph (1962, 204), Kraus (21)—is another question. It would seem more natural to view the particle either as an intensifying element 'yea, she' or 'she herself' (AV) or as introducing a further aspect of the disgraced woman: 'She herself moans'.

וַתָּשָׁב אָחוֹר—This final cryptic statement is interpreted variously. Although *waw*-consecutive, it is clearly an extension of the image of the moaning woman and should probably be taken in the same tense—see Gibson §78, Waltke (555). From line 1b onward, the description has been of how others were treating her. Now, the poet looks to the woman's response. Her reaction was inevitable (NEB paraphrases: 'What could she do but sigh and turn away?'). There is no question of the woman being 'frustrated' (Hillers[2], 62) or 'defeated' (Cross, 141). This is a case of shame and disgrace, cf. Ezek 23.18. IE[2] כאשר ראו ערותה נאנחה והשיבה פניה לאחור מפני הכלמה.

Hence the poet provides another image of Jerusalem. Having depicted her (v. 1) like a widow, desolate and without children, he now conjures up the image of the guilty harlot (so Kara): disgraced and covered in shame. And the picture continues in the next verse.

1.9

Text and Versions

MT בְּשׁוּלֶיהָ—so also P and T; LXX πρὸς ποδῶν αὐτῆς; V *in pedibus eius*; OL *ante pedes ejus*. Apparent deviation is probably due to difficulty with the Hebrew שׁוּל, as can be seen from the renderings of LXX and V at Exod 28.33, 34; 39.24-26; Isa 6.1; Jer 13.22, 26; Nah 3.5.

MT וַתֵּרֶד פְּלָאִים; LXX καὶ κατεβίβασεν ὑπέρογκα; P ܘܐܬܬܚܬܬ ܐܕܫܘܐ *wnḥtt tšbwḥth*; V *deposita est vehementer*; Sym και κατήχθη. Differences are due to the difficult Hebrew construction. LXX may have vocalised וַתֵּרֶד while Sym and V may have read וַתּוּרַד.

MT עָנְיִי—followed by LXX, Aq, P, V and T; OL *humilitatem ejus*. BHK, BHS and NEB follow OL, but MT is to be preferred (cf. REB), not only on the basis of the Versions, but also on the grounds that we have a similar construction at vv. 11 and 20. We should note that at v. 11c OL again makes the 1st p. s. conform to the context.

* * *

The image of the unclean woman continues into v. 9. The impurity just mentioned cannot be hidden. The exposed woman may rearrange her clothing, but the stains from her activity⁸⁰ are evident on her skirts.⁸¹ Just as a woman's sexual activity may have physical, observable results, in that her clothes are stained, so too the city displays the results of her sins.

לֹא זָכְרָה אַחֲרִיתָהּ—The second half of the line, therefore, is not such a *non-sequitur* as Hillers supposes. The picture may be of the woman who, caught up in her sinful activity, forgets the outcome, forgets that the effects of her sins are still visible. She had forgotten what was to follow. The writer puts it negatively—'she did not remember'—to heighten the negative effect. He had used the verb earlier (v. 7) to convey Jerusalem's agony of recalling the past. Here the implication is that if Jerusalem had remembered (in the context of the covenant) what might result from her sins, the present state of affairs might not have taken place. אַחֲרִיתָהּ = 'her future'. The outcome is not just inevitable in the way that stepping into water results in wet feet. Behind this term lies the author's belief that Yahweh's judgment would follow the sins committed. Gordis (155) argues for the meaning 'her offspring/children', but this is unlikely in the light of Isa 47.7, where Babylon is accused of not remembering the end result of her behaviour. The language is very similar, and the phrase there is in parallel with לֹא־שַׂמְתְּ אֵלֶּה עַל־לִבֵּךְ. Jerusalem thought that she was above the law, as it were, and would survive, come what may.

Hillers² (71) draws attention to the shortness of the second line and wonders whether a verb has been lost at the beginning of the line, which was followed by the *waw*-consecutive וַתֵּרֶד 'the kind of coordinate construction common in the book'. Hillers tentatively suggests 'she has fallen' = נפלה, which would restore length to the line. It should be noted that there is no Versional support for a missing verb; and the author does not appear to be a slave to the kind of coordinate construction which Hillers observes; cf. 1.6 וַיֵּצֵא. It might be argued that the structure of the line has the effect of sharpening the meaning of the following וַתֵּרֶד פְּלָאִים and the additional אֵין מְנַחֵם לָהּ.

וַתֵּרֶד פְּלָאִים—The LXX translator's interpretation is occasioned by the unusual function of פְּלָאִים. It is the only place in the Hebrew Bible where it may function as an adverbial accusative. Because the term is otherwise used as a noun, the LXX took the bold step of vocalising Hiphil (וַתֹּרֶד) and

---

⁸⁰ The fixation with menstrual blood, rather than the stains of sexual activity, leads scholars astray here. Thus Rashi says that the stains are those of דם נדותה. But menstruation does not constitute a sin. The stains reveal what has happened (v. 8). The woman has engaged loosely in sexual activity (see Kara) and has been consigned to the category of the despised. B. Kaiser (175f.) holds that the figure is of a menstruant, while Pham (75) thinks that the stains are the dirt of the ground where the female figure sits. Both are mistaken.

⁸¹ Renkema's (136) observation that it is strange to speak of the clothing of the naked woman merely shows that *ʿerwâ* does not mean nudity. See Ezek 16.37-39.

making פְּלָאִים the object. P 'and her glory is low' found a different solution to the problem, making פְּלָאִים the subject of the verb and adding a suffix. V 'she is wonderfully cast down' gives the lead in taking פְּלָאִים as an adverbial accusative, while T testifies to MT's vocalisation and, though elaborating somewhat, does suggest that פְּלָאִים was taken adverbially.

Rashi seems to take the *waw* as 'therefore' and to take פְּלָאִים as adverbial accusative. Her descent was astonishing in that what happened to Jerusalem had not happened to any other city. IE¹, too, cryptically (ירדה ירידה) indicates that the unusual construction is for emphasis; and Kara agrees, citing Deut 28.59, where the Hiphil of פלא is used. The construction, however, is unusual. Provan (46) points out that, since פלא is often used of God's great acts of judgment and redemption in the Old Testament, the implication here is still 'that Jerusalem's fall is not only extraordinary (in that it was unexpected, perhaps, or in its extent), but also an act of God's judgement'.

√ירד 'to come/go down' is used occasionally in the Hebrew Bible (Isa 47.1; Ezek 30.6) of the humiliation and punishment of people; and the Isaiah passage is a particularly good parallel in that Babylon is personified there (as is Jerusalem here). And in Deut 20.20 the verb is used of the subduing of a city. The language of the second stich in this line is typical (cf. vv. 2, 16, 17, 21) of the author. He has used it (v. 2) to emphasise the aloneness of the female figure weeping in the night. Here it adds poignancy to the tragedy which is the fall of Jerusalem.

The final line is unusual in that it addresses Yahweh, and the speaker is Jerusalem herself (see *Introduction*). The language of address is echoed[82] at v. 11c, which is another surprising cry by the city (cf. 2.20); but its position here is arresting. As discussed above, the unexpected appearance of the 1st p. s. here probably led to the OL rendering '*her* humiliation'; cf. *BHQ*. עָנְיִי will surely have the same meaning as in v. 7. In the light of the remainder of the verse, the emphasis will be on her lowly estate over against the confident stance of the enemy. But the call to Yahweh is significant here. As Westermann (130) observes, this cry could 'just as well stand in one of the many psalms of lament in the Psalter'. It is ironic, too, that the call is to Yahweh who has been depicted (v. 5, cf. v. 8) as the one who has brought about the disaster of her fall. There is no one to comfort her: she is at her wit's end. To whom can she turn? There is only one who can help, namely, the author of her affliction. The final stich refers to the triumph of the enemy. There is an intended contrast here between the 'humiliation' of the one who cries out and the superior stance of the foe. The success of one's enemy is never attractive, but the success here has been at the expense of the city. Hence כִּי has an explanatory function. The cry, however, assumes that Yahweh is in control. It also

---

[82] Indeed, T appears to represent the actual wording of v. 11c here, rather than v. 9c!

assumes that Yahweh can be approached in distressful circumstances (cf. Renkema, 141).
Up to this point Yahweh, although mentioned at v. 5, has not been addressed, and vv. 1-9b are almost pure dirge. But with this cry to Yahweh the poet takes the first steps to indicate that he is in the business of creating a plaintive lament. It is further underlined at v. 11c and in the verses which follow. The abrupt nature of v. 9c and v. 11c has a certain dramatic effect as another speaker is suddenly introduced.

1.10

Text and Versions
MT יָדוֹ—followed by LXX, V and T; P ܐܝܕܘܗܝ, *'ydwhy*—so also OL. *BHK* suggests that P and OL read ידיו, but it is more likely that this is a question of interpretation, cf. *BHQ*.

* * *

This is the only place in the Hebrew Bible where 'to stretch out (פרשׂ) the hand' has a hostile/negative sense.[83] The hand of the enemy/foe was mentioned in v. 7 in the sense of power/control, and it is this same power or control that is being exercised here vis-à-vis Jerusalem's precious things. It is, therefore, going too far, as does Ehrlich (32), to declare this 'unhebräisch'. We are dealing here with poetry, and the poet is being innovative (see *Introduction*). The adversary here is probably the same as in v. 7, *viz* Babylon, and T spells this out by naming Nebuchadnezzar. Rashi identifies צָר as Ammon and Moab, as does MR, but this is to allow the allusion in the latter part of the verse to influence the first line.
This verse refers to the enemy plundering of Jerusalem's treasures and to the foe entering her sanctuary in violation of a sacred edict forbidding such trespass. While the verse opens in the style of v. 9ab (i.e. in third person), thereby isolating v. 9c as an interjection breaking through the fabric of the passage, as it were, the imprecise allusion to a law forbidding Moabites and Ammonites from entering the temple (Deut 23.4) in v. 10c, is presented in complicated fashion. The poet purports to describe Jerusalem witnessing the enemy intrusion, but switches to 2nd p. m. s., addressing Yahweh (though the name is not mentioned).

פָּרַשׂ יָדוֹ—It may be that Jerusalem's desperate plea (v. 9c) conjures up the image of hands spread out in prayer. The verb פרשׂ with יד usually denotes an attitude of pleading (as at 1.17; cf. 1 Kgs 8.38; Ps 143.6; Isa 1.15). Here, as Pham (79) observes, '...the phrase פרשׂ יד על, "to stretch the hand over/for", ironically depicts the greed of the foes eager to gather up everything, not leaving anything left over'.

---

[83] When the verb שלח is construed with יד the sense is often hostile, cf. BDB 1018b.

Mintz (25) sees in this passage an allusion to rape; indeed, he casts his exegetical net to include the imagery in vv. 8f. also. In this he is followed by Dobbs-Allsopp and Linafelt (77-81), cf. Berlin (55). Mintz may be right when he says '...what began as unwitting, voluntary promiscuity, suddenly turned into unwished for, forcible defilement'—certainly Jerusalem was violated in the conquest—but the poet is concerned to link Jerusalem's sin with what follows; and she is depicted (v. 8f.) as a debased woman. That is the further image—on top of that of the bereft female and toppled princess. To be raped is rarely reprehensible, hence the image of the raped woman would be weak. It may be that we should look for elucidation in the nature of Zion's sin. The prophets Hosea and Jeremiah refer to the apostasy of Israel and Judah in terms of punishable faithlessness and adultery (Hos 3.1; Jer 3.9).

מַחֲמַדֶּיהָ—'Her precious things' probably alludes to anything of value that they could get their hands on, though Rudolph (1962, 213) and Hillers[2] (87) think that temple treasures only are being referred to, citing 2 Kgs 25.13-17. The latter passage plus 2 Chron 36.19 might suggest a more restricted interpretation of the term, though indiscriminate looting was possibly on the cards. It may be, as Renkema (143) observes, that the Babylonian soldiers regarded booty in battle as earning their 'salary', in which case the reference may be to wholesale plundering coming after the lean period of the siege of Jerusalem. According to Levine (64), T takes מַחֲמַדֶּיהָ to refer to 'desirable people',[84] while Rashi expands on a MR suggestion that the aim of the enemy was to seize and destroy the books of the Law because of the injunction (Deut 23.4) that an Ammonite or a Moabite shall not enter the sanctuary. Presumably, silver and gold were taken as read, but the Ammonites and Moabites were keen to destroy the document which prohibited them from entering the temple!

כִּי—Although LXX (γὰρ) and V (*quia*) have translated כִּי as conjunction (so also AV, RV), T (אַף) and P identify this as a particle of emphasis (so also RSV, NIV, NRSV, NJB). There is no causal connection between the first and second lines. However, the mention of מַחֲמַדֶּיהָ of the first line has brought to mind the temple of Yahweh in Jerusalem, and now the poet thinks of another outrage—pagans entering the house of Yahweh.

רָאֲתָה—LXX, P, T, OL and V reflect MT, but Albrektson (65) suggests (rightly) that P ܘܡܐ ܚܙܝܬ *whzyt* may be either 1st p. s. or 2nd p. m. s. If this is so, then P has either taken v. 10b as a continuation of Jerusalem's words of v. 9c (though very unlikely in the light of v. 10a), or (vocalising רָאָתָה) has been influenced by the 2nd p. m. s. צִוִּיתָה later in the verse and sees

---

[84] Presumably the reference (in T) to the sword has influenced Levine here, but Brady (156) translates רגונהא as 'her lovely things'. The translator may have had in mind Hos 9.16 גַּם כִּי יֵלֵדוּן וְהֵמַתִּי מַחֲמַדֵּי בִטְנָם where the reference is to children (Macintosh, 378); cf. Alexander (2008, 117 n. 44).

v. 10b as the beginning of the poet's address to Yahweh; and, in consequence of this interpretation, has changed the suffix on מקדש to 2nd p. m. s. It is, however, Jerusalem who witnessed the heathen entering the sanctuary. While מקדש can refer to any Israelite shrine (e.g. Josh 24.26) or even to heathen sanctuaries (Isa 16.12), the author uses the term here to mean the temple of Yahweh in Jerusalem. That this is the case is shown by the use of the same term at 2.7, and also by the words which follow, for there is an allusion to a tradition enshrined in Deut 23.4: לֹא־יָבֹא עַמּוֹנִי וּמוֹאָבִי בִּקְהַל יְהוָה גַּם דּוֹר עֲשִׂירִי לֹא־יָבֹא לָהֶם בִּקְהַל יְהוָה עַד־עוֹלָם The prohibition, as it stands, refers only to Ammonites and Moabites, and that is why MR, Rashi, IE[2] and Kara have such a fixation with Ammon and Moab at this point. While the text refers only to גוים, MR suggests that Ammonites and Moabites entered along with the nations. Hillers[2] (87) remarks 'Since the Babylonians (Chaldeans) were the ones who entered the temple, and since there is no evidence that Moabites and Ammonites figured in the destruction of Jerusalem at this time, it is evident that the Deuteronomic command has been broadened, if only by poetic license, to cover the "heathen", גוים, in general'.

We are reminded of Ps 79.1, where the phrase באו גוים occurs and which probably points to the same event. There, the author is addressing God. He does not say that the heathen have entered 'the temple' or 'our sanctuary' but '*your* heritage'. It is as if the author is appealing to God to do something about it. In like manner here the poet, who might have simply said 'whom God has prohibited from entering the congregation', turns around and appears to say to God: 'It is true that we have sinned and have deserved the punishment, but here is something which not only outrages us but must surely be of particular concern to you, O God; after all, it *is* your assembly'. It should also be noted that, when the poet considers the prohibition, he does not quote verbatim; indeed, he adapts the wording to suit his poetic line.[85]

אֲשֶׁר צִוִּיתָה—The final line is difficult. It is possible to take לֹא־יָבֹאוּ בַקָּהָל לָךְ as speech of Yahweh, in which case the suffix on ל will refer to Jerusalem. The referent of the relative pronoun is גוים, and the verb באו is plural to agree with this, though it is singular in Deut 23.4; see Renkema (145f.).

בְקָהָל לָךְ—All the Versions translate as 'your assembly', and no one appears to have any problem with this construction until the 20th century.[86] While we might have expected בקהלך, the construction in MT is reproduced in T, and may have been the style which developed in later Hebrew (e.g. בקהל שלך; cf. GK 129h).

---

[85] Cf. also Ezek 44.8f. which, although the terminology differs, is a strong prohibition forbidding all foreigners from entering the sanctuary.
[86] Ehrlich (32) suggests deleting the entire phrase and reading 'צויתה mit Mappik'; but that would make for a more awkward construction.

1.11

Text and Versions
MT מְבַקְשִׁים; Schäfer (*BHQ* 115*) is not convinced that a *dageš* exists in MT (as in *BHK* and *BHS*) and notes that it is absent in M^L34 and M^Y—which is what we might expect—see Bomberg, BDB (134), Martin (1993, 106).
MT (*Kethib*) מַחֲמוֹדֵיהֶם; MT (*Qere*) מַחֲמַדֵּיהֶם—so also several MSS^Ken; LXX τὰ ἐπιθυμήματα αὐτῆς—so also 1MS^Ken and 4 QLam; P ܪܓܬܗܘܢ *rgthwn*; V *pretiosa quaeque*.
MT הָיִיתִי—so also LXX^A, P, V and T; LXX^B ἐγενήθη. The latter is probably a scribal error within the Greek textual tradition (cf. Rudolph 1938, 102; Albrektson, 66), though *BHK* is inclined to emend. The fact that LXX has '*her* treasures' earlier in the verse might suggest that the predominance of 3rd p. f. s. suffixes has influenced the rendering here. MT has support from a similar first person interjection beginning similarly at v. 9c (see *Introduction*).

* * *

This verse resembles v. 9 in that the poet allows the city to interrupt and cry out to Yahweh in the final line, and in similar fashion. But it differs from vv. 1-10 in two respects: (a) it alludes to severe shortage of food, and (b) it is the people, not the personified city, who are centre stage. The author, in the previous verses, had concentrated on images of the city—weeping, suffering etc. Behind the various vignettes, however, there lay the stark reality of severe famine. This state of affairs had existed for some time before the actual fall of Jerusalem. Although there would have been considerable stockpiling of foodstuffs when a siege was expected, and with it hope of ultimate survival, this siege lasted nearly two years, and starvation resulted in the death of many in Jerusalem.[87] 2 Kings 25.2ff. merely sums up the situation—'the famine was severe in the city, and there was no food for the people'. Narrative accounts of famine often contain gruesome stories[88] of the lengths to which victims will go to track down anything that might remotely serve as nourishment in order to stay alive. No doubt the writer of 2 Kgs 25.2ff. knew of such tales, but he is not an eye-witness and is content to summarise.[89] Our poet, however, hears the groans of the victims and observes that, when the starving are driven to it, they will barter anything for food, even dearly loved items; and as he makes this observation, the personified city comes through the fabric once more with a desperate call to Yahweh.

---

[87] See Renkema (147-50) for a fuller description of the starving inhabitants of Jerusalem. Many from the villages and towns of Judah will have sought refuge within the walls of Jerusalem, and they too required to be fed and watered.
[88] Examples within Lamentations are 2.12, 20; 4.4f., 10.
[89] The author of 2 Chron 36, writing much later, does not so much as mention the famine or any shortage of food in his account.

כָּל־עַמָּהּ—Here, for the first time in the poem, the survivors, as a whole, are mentioned. The famine conditions resulting from the devastation are affecting everyone, high and low. It is also the first time that famine is referred to.[90] The 3rd f. s. suffix refers to Jerusalem, though the inhabitants of Judah could also be said to be Jerusalem's people. The word 'all' is used in this poem some sixteen times, reflecting the author's tendency to hyperbole. This is not to say that the feature he describes was not widespread.

נֶאֱנָחִים—The verb אנח is not common in the Hebrew Bible, yet it occurs five times in this poem. One cannot deduce anything from the use of the Niphal here (contra Renkema, 148), in that the root only occurs in the Niphal. The meaning here is stronger and more serious than 'sigh' (AV, Luther, Calvin, JPS). T expands to אניחן מכפנא, which shows that the translator stresses that the sound made has to do with severe hunger—better 'moan' or 'groan' (RSV, NEB). The picture here is of a general and desperate search for food. The long siege would have put severe strain upon Jerusalem's resources, and 2 Kgs 25.3 indicates that famine was severe in the city just prior to the capitulation (cf. also Jer 32.24; 37.21; 38.9; 52.6). The participles נֶאֱנָחִים מְבַקְשִׁים together without copula are meant to paint a picture of an ongoing search accompanied by moans. As Renkema (148) points out, we must not assume that things were better once the town had been invaded, and the siege brought to an end. Many who had resided outside Jerusalem had taken refuge within the city prior to the siege; and farm produce in the Jerusalem neighbourhood would probably have been mopped up during the siege, by the Babylonian soldiers. Nevertheless, contact now with the outside world would have raised the hopes of the starving masses, and the desperate search was a daily activity.

נָתְנוּ...בְּאֹכֶל—The ב is ב-*pretii* (GK 119p)—'in exchange for food'. The *Qere* מַחֲמַדֵּיהֶם is the form we have in v. 10, although in that passage the enemy appears to have laid claim to same; and the *Qere* reading may in fact be a harmonising of the text. The *Kethib* may be vocalised מַחֲמוֹדֵיהֶם i.e. from מַחְמוֹד (see BDB 327), but Ehrlich (32) and Rudolph (1938, 102) suggest reading מֵחֲמוּדֵיהֶם, i.e. the passive participle of חמד with a partitive מִן: = 'some of their desired/desirable things'.[91] In the light of v. 10, it would seem that *Qere* is the correct reading, though whereas in v. 10 it is the treasures of the city, here it is things treasured by the individual inhabitants.[92] Westermann (132) observes that this wholesale bartering for

---

[90] Though Westermann (131) feels that the passage originally belonged with vv. 1-6.
[91] Alexander (2008, 118 n. 47) observes that this would be a weaker interpretation: 'giving only some of one's precious things hardly smacks of desperation'.
[92] LXX and 4QLam 'her treasures' have been influenced by the previous verse, where the treasures are those of the city or temple. Here, we are on a different level, *viz* that of the ordinary folk (כָּל עַמָּהּ).

food rings true of a community in dire straits. One's dearest possessions mean nothing except insofar as they can procure food to survive. Hillers[2] (62) and Gordis (157) take the term to refer to 'dear children'. It is true that, at Hos 9.16 and Lam 2.4, the term does appear to refer to humans, but it should be noted that in each case the word is in construct with another—womb (Hos 9.16), eye (Lam 2.4). It is not enough to argue that the bartering of one's children for food adds poignancy to the horrific situation. The fact that the same term appears in v. 10 should point us in the same direction; besides, it might be asked, just what advantage was there to the party supplying the food if all he gets in return is another starving mouth to feed! Berlin (56f.), aware of this problem, still thinks that 'children' is meant here—not that they were bartered for food, but that they were given away to someone who would feed them in exchange for their labour: 'in order to keep the *children* alive'. However, the ב-*pretii* in the phrase באכל militates against such an interpretation.

לְהָשִׁיב נָפֶשׁ—'to keep themselves alive' (JPS), cf. similar phrasing at vv. 16, 19.[93] The final line is akin to v. 9c (see *Introduction*). The city bursts in on the poet to plead with Yahweh. Behind this plea lies the belief that the dire straits experienced by the inhabitants are Yahweh's doing. To whom else can she go? At v. 9c she refers to her humiliation over against the enemy's exaltation. Here, there is an emphasis on grabbing Yahweh's attention, using the same verb ראה and reinforcing it with the emphatic והביטה '(look) and take note'. While the previous cry referred to the enemy's triumph, the motif in this verse is 'dishonour', already alluded to at v. 8.

זוֹלֵלָה—We have already had the root זלל in v. 8 where the Hiphil appears to mean 'despise, count as worthless'. This is the Qal participle f. s. LXX translates 'dishonoured', and V 'vile'. T renders גרגרניתא, which Jastrow (265) gives as 'glutton, bibber'. Levine (98) explains that this refers to 'the excesses to which the people would go in search of food'. In the context of famine, this would seem strange in the extreme, unless one were to take it ironically.[94] The root is uncommon in the Hebrew Bible. On the basis of Jer 15.19, where זולל is represented as the opposite of יקר 'precious', one might render 'worthless', whereas in passages such as Deut 21.20 and Prov 23.20, where the term is linked with סבא√, the meaning is more akin to what the Targum finds for the passage. Although Rashi does not comment, IE[1] glosses it with a cryptic quote from Deut 21.20, which puts him in the same camp as T. And IE[2] comments '...after she had given every precious thing for food she was like a glutton, for she

---

[93] Renkema's (149) translation 'to restore their vigour' reflects an image of healthy individuals who are in need of a pick-me-up!
[94] In this regard JPS translates 'abject' but has a footnote '*Or (ironically) What a glutton; cf Prov 23.20-21*'. In the latter passage זֹלֵלִי בָשָׂר is parallel to סֹבְאֵי־יָיִן.

would give all that was asked of her to satisfy her desire'.⁹⁵ Kara, on the other hand, focuses on √זול, which in Aramaic and later Hebrew means 'to be cheap, worthless': '...for the nations of the world call me cheap'. And MLT follows Kara here. Luther 'schnöde' and Calvin '*vilis (aut, contempta)*' set the pattern for later renderings—AV, RSV, NJB, NEB, NIV. The mindset here may be: Take note, Yahweh, that I am despised by the nations, for my ignominy is your disgrace.

1.12

Text and Versions

The ל (in MT), with which this verse must begin if the alphabetic acrostic is to be maintained, is slightly smaller than normal—לוא.⁹⁶ This *may* indicate some hesitation (as to the genuineness of the text at this point) on the part of a scribe or the Masoretes in the transmission of the text (cf. Albrektson, 67), though there may have been some other reason for this.⁹⁷

MT לוֹא אֲלֵיכֶם—followed by P; 4QLam [י' אליכן לוא; LXX οὐ πρὸς ὑμᾶς—so also Sym (Ms Marchalianus); many LXXᴹˢˢ οἱ πρὸς ὑμᾶς; V *O vos omnes*; Sym (SH) ܐܘ ܐܢܬܘܢ = ὦ ὑμεῖς; T לכון אשבעית.⁹⁸ Because the Versions and manuscript evidence, despite the differences, seem to reflect the consonantal MT, we have to say that if there is corruption here it must have occurred before the translations were made. We should probably delete the phrase and read לכו (Praetorius, 143).

MT אֲשֶׁר הוֹגָה יְהוָה; 4QLam, LXX, P and T add explanatory 1st p. s. suffix; 4QLam אשר הוגירני]יהוה involves a Hiphil form of √ינר 'to fear', not otherwise attested in Hiphil. MT is preferred; cf. Schäfer (117*).

* * *

In the first half of the poem the bulk of the material consists of descriptions of the city's sufferings and of allusions to the causes. In addition to the poet's pause, in v. 10, to address Yahweh briefly, we find the voice of the personified city bursting in at v. 9c and v. 11c, pleading with Yahweh to take note of her plight. At v. 12 we begin a section where Jerusalem takes the stage and addresses passers-by, not Yahweh, but alluding to the suffering that has already been referred to by the first speaker. Her first words imply that her pain is unparalleled, and Yahweh is depicted as the one who has caused it. At the same time, the poet reveals that this action

---

⁹⁵ This line of thought is also followed by Vermigli (38): '...I have become a glutton in this famine. For gluttons are so taken captive by the vice of palate and stomach that they give whatever is demanded of them in taverns and delicatessens for wine or sweet and delicious food.'
⁹⁶ A list of some thirty-three words containing a small letter is found in the *massorah finalis* and also in the *massorah marginalis* at Lev 1.1; see Ginsburg (1867, 231), Rudolph (207).
⁹⁷ We should note that, of the 41 instances of the negative particle in Lamentations, this is the only occasion where it is written *plene*.
⁹⁸ 'I adjure you' may be an attempt, on T's part, to make sense of the text. T adds further words—זורו הכא—'turn aside here'; cf. Alexander (2008, 119).

on Yahweh's part constitutes the arrival of the 'Day of Yahweh' (Zeph 1.14ff.), a time when Yahweh would come against his people in judgment.⁹⁹

לוֹא אֲלֵיכֶם—Almost all modern commentators struggle with the meaning of the first stich. It is ironic that the opening phrase, which causes the greatest difficulties, has been picked up and utilised confidently in subsequent literature with meanings which may have nothing to do with the original intention. Thus, the ancient Jewish exclamation לא עליכם¹⁰⁰ has the meaning 'may it never happen to you!' And AV rendering 'Is it nothing to you…?' was picked up by Steiner in his *Crucifixion* for an aria where the subject matter is far removed from our text. It may not be surprising to find MR reflecting the (wish) interpretation given above. There, Israel says to the nations: 'May this not happen to you that has happened to me'.¹⁰¹ Rashi, too, although taking quite a different line as a whole, holds to the same interpretation of the phrase; and IE¹ and Kara are in the same camp.¹⁰² The meaning has become so fixed in Jewish parlance that JPS reproduces it for this passage, although there is a footnote to the effect that the meaning of the Hebrew is uncertain. It is equally true that the translation 'is it nothing to you?' has so captured the minds of Christian interpreters who apply it to the crucifixion, that it too persists even today (RV, RSV, NRSV, NIV); and this is so in spite of the fact that commentators are doubtful if this meaning may be wrung from the phrase.¹⁰³ However, we should resist coming to a conclusion as to the meaning of the opening words until we consider the other parts of the verse and/or line. The imperatives—הַבִּיטוּ וּרְאוּ are in the opposite order to which they appear in v. 11c but the same as in 5.1, but whereas in 1.11c and 5.1 the addressee is Yahweh, here, in v. 12, the addressees are כָּל־עֹבְרֵי דֶרֶךְ. The latter expression occurs also at Pss 80.13; 89.42 and in Lam 5.15. Albrektson (68f.) agonises over the meaning of this, but it is clear that it describes 'passers-by'—in this case, passers-by as witnesses. The sedentary figure (v. 1) calls out to anyone within earshot. From v. 12 until the end of the poem, it is the personified city who speaks (with an inter-

---

⁹⁹ See Renkema (102ff.).
¹⁰⁰ This differs only slightly from the phrase in this verse: לוֹא אֲלֵיכֶם has become לא עֲלֵיכֶם.
¹⁰¹ עלי דאתא עליכון ייתי לא. But even if this is the meaning of the phrase, it could not be maintained that Israel is addressing the nations here. The speaker at v. 21 (part of the same speech which begins here in v. 12) requests that the enemies should experience similar sufferings!
¹⁰² The lemma in Buber's edition of Kara mistakenly reads לא עליכם; and this is true also with Perles (1930, 102). Gordis (157) seems not to have noticed (or has ignored) the difference.
¹⁰³ Barthélemy (869) notes that Salmon ben Yeruiḥam also interprets it as a question. N.B. GK 150 lists several passages where (in the absence of the interrogative particle) a question is a likely interpretation, but Lam 1.12. is not cited.

ruption at v. 17 by the first speaker), she whose plight has been described, in the third person, in vv. 1-11. The image of the female figure—weeping, having lovers, sinning—is maintained, although just as vv. 1-11 the poet moves in and out of the imagery; that is to say, at one time one may picture the female figure weeping (vv. 2, 16), having lovers (vv. 2, 19), suffering (vv. 5, 12), sinning (vv. 5, 18), but at other times the female figure fades somewhat and the image is applied: her sanctuary (v. 10), her people (v. 11), my priests (v. 19), her gates (v. 4). The picture at v. 12 seems to begin with the suffering female figure, seen by those who pass by; and she asks them to consider whether they have ever witnessed 'pain' like she is experiencing.

A notable attempt at understanding MT לוֹא אֲלֵיכֶם כָּל־עֹבְרֵי דֶרֶךְ is Albrektson (66-69), who translates '(This is) not for (= nothing which concerns) ordinary people, this does not happen to everybody'. But though he has some guarded support for his suggestion (Gottlieb, 15-17), it is not convincing. We must concede that the text as it stands has foundered, albeit before the Versions were made.

If the addressees are the target of the two imperatives, it is natural to think of the previous words as hailing them or otherwise introducing them (rather than making a separate statement). That is why the emendation of Praetorius (143) is the one which is often adopted in commentaries.[104] He deletes the initial words and replaces them with לְכוּ. This form, followed by אִם, is found at Isa 1.18, and the emended text may be translated 'Come, all you passers-by, look and see if...'

JB 'All you who pass this way...' has taken its cue from V. The fact that the two imperatives echo v. 11c should not be ignored here. There may be no significance in the reverse order, but it should be noted that while the addressee has changed, the speaker is still the distressed female figure—the personification of Jerusalem. The latter had burst forth into the third person description of her plight at v. 9c and v. 11c without apparent answer from Yahweh. Now, at the beginning of this section, she turns to anyone who will hear, the passers-by, with the request that they verify what she is convinced of, *viz* that her desperate situation is without parallel and reminding them that Yahweh is the author of it all. The repetition of the two verbs emphasises her frantic search for contact with anyone who will hear. If anyone needs a comforter it is Jerusalem.

אֲשֶׁר עוֹלַל לִי—The relative pronoun אֲשֶׁר refers to מַכְאֹבִי 'my pain'. The root עלל emphasises the negative aspect of the experience in that it seems to have the meaning (in Poel) 'to deal severely (with)'. This root in uncommon in the Hebrew Bible but it occurs in Lamentations (1.12, 22; 2.20; 3.51); indeed, all the Poel occurrences are in Lamentations. The Masoretes have vocalised the occurrence in 1.12 as Poal, i.e. the passive of the Poel. If this is the correct pointing it is the only instance of the Poal

---

[104] So, Kraus (23), Rudolph (1962, 205), Westermann (113), Hillers[2] (71).

of this verb in the Hebrew Bible. The fact that LXX and T render in the passive would suggest a strong tradition to read the text in this way.[105] Hence, although a unique form, MT is probably the correct reading. The view taken by Levine (99) and Hillers² (72), that the original was probably Poel and was altered to Poal to avoid ascribing to Yahweh the responsibility for pain, seems to me to fly in the face of the rest of the verse and the second half of this poem, where Yahweh is specifically depicted as the author of the disaster. The poet, depicting the unusual nature of the pain, wants to stress that it was not fortuitous, that it had been dealt out to the speaker specifically, and that it was Yahweh, her God, who was behind it all: it is not just that my pain is unusually severe. It has been intended specifically for me and, what's more, it is my God that has inflicted it. The emphasis is obtained by the second use of the relative pronoun.[106]

הוֹגָה—This verb appeared at v. 4 (Niphal), and at v. 5, where the Hiphil form, as here, has Yahweh as subject. LXX's double translation φθεγξάμενος ἐν ἐμοὶ ἐταπείνωσέν με κύριος reflects uncertainty surrounding the Hebrew root; and one of the renderings (based on the root הגה 'to utter, speak') is reflected in Sym ἀνεκάλεσε κύριος and V *ut locutus est Dominus*.[107]

בְּיוֹם חֲרוֹן אַפּוֹ—'on his day of fierce anger'. The suffix on אַפּוֹ applies to the entire phrase. The speaker wants to stress that this disaster was Yahweh at his most vehement. The poet may have in mind the concept 'day of Yahweh' (cf. Renkema, 158).[108]

So, at the beginning of this extended soliloquy the female figure, described in vv. 1-11 as bereft, alone and in distress, immediately picks up on the previous picture by saying the same thing, but in the 1st p. s. The verb יגה (v. 5) in the Hiphil is used again to give emphasis to the image of a figure in dire straits and insisting that Yahweh has caused it (as in v. 5). It is not just passive experience: Yahweh is actively engaged against her.

---

[105] P translates in the active, i.e. reading the Poel, but introduces 'the Lord' as subject, while V, although active, is otherwise corrupt, deriving it from another (denominative) root 'to glean'.

[106] The second אֲשֶׁר *may* refer to the suffix in לִי (Rudolph 1938, 103), in which case one may translate '...dealt to me whom Yahweh has made suffer...', but this is less satisfactory.

[107] See Schäfer (116f.*).

[108] For the people of Yahweh the 'day of Yahweh' was a time in the future when Yahweh would defeat his enemies (= the people's enemies). He had shown his might in the past, and the defeat of the Midianites (Judg 7.19-22) was later referred to as the day of Midian (Isa 9.3; cf. 10.26). The concept led to a false sense of security in Israel, and Amos (5.18-20) turned it on its head by declaring that the day of Yahweh would be the opposite of what the people expected: darkness and not light! The latter reference and interpretation is picked up by Isaiah (13.9, 13).

1.13

Text and Versions

MT מִמָּרוֹם—so also P, V and T; LXX ἐξ ὕψους αὐτοῦ; the *Vorlage* of LXX may have had מִמְּרֹמוֹ, or even מְרֹמוֹ. MT is preferred.

MT וַיִּרְדֶּנָּה; LXX κατήγαγεν αὐτό; SH ܐܚܬܗ *w^eḥth* plus ܠܗ *'ly* in margin; P ܐܚܬܢܝ *w^eḥtny*; V *et erudivit me*; Aq ἐλικμησεν αὐτα; Sym κατεπαιδευσεμε. 4QLam (*ויורידנ*:); T וכבש יתהון. The *waw*(-consecutive), absent from LXX (though evident in SH), is vouched for in P, V, T and 4QLam. The *Vorlage* of LXX may have read הוֹרִידָהּ (so *BHK*) or יוֹרִדֶנָּה (*BHQ*). Suffix 1st p. s. (P, V, Sym and probably 4QLam) occasioned by context; we should read יוֹרִדֶנָּה.

* * *

The author of the disaster, as seen from the point of view of Jerusalem, has been introduced (v. 12) in no uncertain terms. The poet now depicts the female figure, describing her experiences in terms of Yahweh's actions; hence there is no need to spell out the subject of the verb 'sent'. The idea of Yahweh sending fire is found in Amos 1.4, 7, 10 etc. It is not clear what is meant by sending fire into the bones, but the imagery of being caught in a net and being turned around are attempts on the part of the author to convey a picture of total desolation—stunned and faint all day long.

מִמָּרוֹם שָׁלַח־אֵשׁ בְּעַצְמֹתַי—The poet is not speaking of actual fire, but of an experience so painful that it seems like fire in the bones. The latter were thought to be the organs which particularly felt pain.[109]

וַיִּרְדֶּנָּה—The Masoretes vocalised as if from √רדה I 'to tread, dominate', with a 3rd f. s. suffix.[110] The subject, according to Rashi is אֵשׁ. He is aware of another interpretation—taking the form as from √רדה II 'to scrape', cf. Judg 14.9; the meaning would be 'it (or he?) scraped and dragged the marrow from it (= bone?)'. IE¹, too, takes 'fire' to be the subject,[111] pointing out that אֵשׁ (usually feminine) can be masculine (Job 20.26). He cites Lev 25.53, which would indicate that his interpretation is 'it mastered them'. Kara, also, makes it clear that אֵשׁ is the subject; and he employs √שלט 'to be master of' to interpret the verbal form, citing Judg 5.13 (where the root is debatable, cf. AV and NRSV). These mediaeval exegetes were not in the business of questioning the Masoretic text, and their

---

[109] T renders מִמָּרוֹם 'from heaven'—not a different Hebrew *Vorlage* but the translator's interpretation, cf. Keil (370). T, thinking of what 'bones' might mean vis-à-vis a city, renders 'into my strong cities' (and, of course, √עצם = 'be strong'), but the poet will have wanted his readers to think primarily of the human frame; cf. Calvin, Keil (371).

[110] Rashi unpicks the form as וירד אותה which he says means 'he broke it', the singular suffix referring to the plural bones, one by one!

[111] Berlin (46) misreads Ibn Ezra here, believing that he understood the *suffix* to refer back to 'fire'.

wrestling with the syntax is quite unrelated to that of earlier would-be translators, faced with unpointed *Vorlagen*. Hence, LXX translates as though from √ירד 'to go down'. Kelso (16) claimed that Sym and V 'and chastised me' were based on the verb √יהר (cf. also *BHK*[112]), and both reflect 1st p. s. suffix. P and 4QLam (probably) 'and brought me down' follow LXX as to root but are in accordance with Sym and V as to suffix; and Aq 'he scattered them' appears to agree with LXX as to subject, and with T as to suffix.[113] Clearly, the early interpreters were confused. But Luther and Calvin take their cue from the mediaeval Jewish exegetes, and this is further reflected, according to Shute (41),[114] in Pagnini and Münster, and in AV, RV. Schleusner (6f.), Michaelis (1773–88, 413) and Blayney (308) together raise the possibility of considering the LXX reading and, since then, a number of commentators and translators have taken a similar line.[115]

There remain those who retain the Masoretic reading, though not all are in agreement. Driver (1935, 297f.) first of all argued for the meaning 'run' for √רדה and he translated: '...and it ran through them'.[116] Then (1950, 137), making no mention of his earlier plea (nor of AV, Keil, 370f.), with which he hardly differs, he renders: 'he sent fire into my bones and it overcame them'. He is followed by Albrektson (72), Barthélemy (870f.) and House (335).[117]

The Versions take Yahweh to be the subject of all the verbs in the verse, although a change of subject (to 'fire') would not be out of the question (cf. Amos 1.4, 7, 10 etc. and especially Ps 78.45). However, a change of subject combined with אֵשׁ construed as masculine and the plural עַצְמֹתַי construed as singular[118] makes for difficult and tortuous Hebrew poetry. It is best to take our cue from LXX. The consonantal text וירדנה probably read (originally) יורדנה (simple metathasis of י and ו) and was vocalised יוֹרִדֶנָּה. The use of an imperfect form following a perfect but continuing the past tense is not a problem, as can be seen in the very next verse. Schäfer (118*) draws attention to the parallelism which is restored by this emendation: 'יוֹרִדֶנָּה is not only a perfect parallel with מִמָּרוֹם שָׁלַח

---

[112] Though see Ziegler (471) and *BHQ*: Sym and V may have derived the form from the Aramaic/Syriac √rdʾ which can mean 'to chastise'.
[113] Kelso (16) thinks that Aq may have read תָרֶנָּה, but it is likely that the Aq reading (ܪܕܐ drʾ) in SH is incorrect and should read ܪܕܐ rdʾ; see Ziegler (471) and *BHQ*.
[114] It should be noted that Vermigli (41f.) is aware of other interpretations, including one which is based on taking the form to be from √ירד.
[115] Dyserinck (364), Ehrlich (33), Kaiser (309), Westermann (113), Rudolph (1962, 207), Dahood (1978, 176f.), Provan (49), Berlin (46), Schäfer (*BHQ*, 117*), RSV, NJB, NIV, ESV, JPS.
[116] Reflected in NEB and REB translations.
[117] Meek (12f.) differs in that he believes the subject to be Yahweh, but he feels the need to transpose the final two words of the stich, וַיִּרְדֶּנָּה בְּעַצְמֹתַי, which he translates '...and trampled it into my bones'. Gordis (131, 157) renders 'From above he has sent fire into my bones and crushed them'.
[118] Although this is not serious in itself, cf. GK 145e.

at the beginning of the verse, but also solves the syntactical or stylistic problems and produces a well balanced parallelism: "from on high he sent fire, into my bones he made it descend"'.

פָּרַשׂ רֶשֶׁת לְרַגְלַי—The poet employs hunting imagery to convey what life at Yahweh's hands has felt like. It has seemed at times like he was setting and hiding a net at ground level in order to catch an animal. With a variety of images, the poet gives the impression that there was no escaping Yahweh's attention; cf. 3.1-6.

הֱשִׁיבַנִי אָחוֹר—'He turned me back'. The phrase is used (Ps 44.11; Isa 44.25) for negative reversal. Renkema (162) is incorrect to see here a connection with the sending of fire. The poet employs imagery from various quarters to convey a picture of a victim at the mercy of one who is in complete control. The idea is of a figure disorientated by being stopped and turned in her tracks, as an army facing a superior force.[119]

נְתָנַנִי שֹׁמֵמָה—נתן in the sense of 'render, make'. The active participle שֹׁמֵמָה (from √שׁמם 'be desolate, stunned') rather than the adjective שְׁמֵמָה, conveys the image of a troubled, trembling figure; cf. Tamar at 2 Sam 13.20.

דָּוָה—'Unwell, ill, sick'. Hillers[2] (72) is correct to question the suggestion by B. B. Kaiser (1987, 164-82) and echoed by Levine (100) and Provan (50) that the two terms—שֹׁמֵמָה and דָּוָה describe the menstrual state of the female figure. These terms are employed to complete the vignette of the distressed figure, buffeted by Yahweh—bones racked with Yahweh's fire, feet entangled in Yahweh's net, completely discomfited at Yahweh's hands, so that she is rendered trembling and sick continually (כָּל־הַיּוֹם).

1.14

Text and Versions
MT נִשְׂקַד עַל פְּשָׁעַי בְּיָדוֹ; LXX ἐγρηγορήθη ἐπὶ τὰ ἀσεβήματά μου ἐν χερσίν μου; V *vigilavit iugum iniquitatum mearum in manu eius*; P ܐܬܬܥܝܪ ܥܠ ܚܛܗܝ ܒܐܝܕܘܗܝ; T אתיקר ניר מרורי בידיה; 4QLam נקשרה על פשעי בידו; *'tt'yrw 'ly ḥṭhy wb'ydwhyy*; T אתיקר ניר מרורי בידיה is probably the original reading.

MT יִשְׂתָּרְגוּ—so also LXX, P and V; 4QLam וישתרג; the singular יִשְׂתָּרֵג is probably the original reading.

MT עָלוּ עַל־צַוָּארִי—so also LXX, V and T; P ܥܠܘ ܥܠ ܨܘܪܝ *nyrwhy 'l ṣwry*, Sym ὁ ζυγὸς αὐτοῦ ἐπὶ τὸν τράχηλόν μου; 4QLam עולו על צ[וארי]; I read עֻלּוֹ (for עָלוּ).

MT אֲדֹנָי; 4QLam יהוה; the Tetragrammaton is probably original.

* * *

In this verse Jerusalem acknowledges that her present suffering is directly linked with her past sins (cf. v. 5). The result is unbearable, as if those sins

---
[119] Cf. Ps 44.11 and T 'He has hurled me back in fright before my enemies'; see also Kara.

were a yoke of a beast of burden bound to her neck by Yahweh himself and weighing her down. Then, in another vaguely related image, she sees herself, a much weakened victim, having been handed over by Yahweh, to her powerful captors (cf. vv. 5, 9).

The beginning of two translations illustrate the divergence among scholars as to the text and exegesis of this passage:

> The yoke of my sin branches out like an almond tree in His hand; they (the branches) ramify and grow up over my neck. (Freehof, 344)

> Watch is kept over my steps. They are entangled by his hand. His yoke is on my neck. (Hillers², 62)

נִשְׂקַד—This verse has its share of problems, often inter-related. The first word is a *hapax legomenon* and is doubly difficult[120] in that the root שׂקד does not appear to exist in other Semitic languages. Albrektson (74) is ultra-cautious in defending MT and thinks (as did Ewald, 329) that the meaning of שׂקד has been lost and perhaps was a technical term for the putting on of a yoke. The Versions struggled here. LXX, V and P have all read from √שׁקד, though P has a plural form.[121] This means that the *Vorlage* of LXX and of V was נִשְׁקַד,[122] which, although a recognisable root, is also, in fact, a unique form. T 'is heavy' may have read נקשׁה. 4QLam 'was bound' is different again. Clearly, the early exegesis of this verse had a rough ride. MR and MLT are both aware of the possibility of reading נשׁקד, and so is Kara. Rashi and IE¹ point out (in different ways) that this is a *hapax legomenon*. Rashi relates it to the Aramaic מסקדא 'a goad' and declares it to be like *pointrent* in Old French, i.e. 'marked': 'My transgressions were marked by the hand of the Holy One, blessed be he, for a remembrance'. IE¹ suggests 'extended or hastened'—mere guesswork, it seems. Rosenberg (8) divulges other mediaeval suggestions: 'appeared', 'clung', 'was bound'. The latter appears to originate with Kimḥi who explains נִשְׂקַד as נקשׁר או נתחבר and may be a guess from the context. Calvin rejects Jerome's reading (of שׁ for שׂ) and renders *ligatum est*, probably under the influence of Kimḥi. Luther (sind erwachet) seems to prefer Jerome here, but Vermigli (42) goes back to Kimḥi, though he does not mention him.[123] Calvin's rendering seems to have been the basis for AV 'is bound'. Michaelis (1773–88, 142) favours the reading of נשׁקד, and several later scholars follow suit, though the exegesis is often different:

---

[120] Hence, there have been several conjectures as to the original reading: Böttcher (202, נעקד), Bickell (106, נשקדו), Löhr (1894, 4, נשׁקף), Praetorius (1895, 143f., נקשׁה), Ehrlich (33, נקשׁרו) etc.
[121] שׂ and שׁ were originally (and still in unpointed texts) represented by only one form—ש—but the Masoretes distinguished between them by the diacritical point—שׁ (š) and שׂ (ś); cf. GK 6i.
[122] The alphabetic acrostic requires an initial *nun*.
[123] In his commentary, he refers, obliquely, to his source. This is identified by Shute (43) as Pagnini and Münster. Kimḥi is mentioned by Houbigant (478), and he reads נקשׁרו, which Ehrlich later adopts.

Bickell (106), Blayney (308), Perles (1930, 102), Gordis (158), Hillers[2] (73), Wiesmann (118), Meek (13), Gottlieb (18), *BHK*, NJB, *HALOT*.
Those who prefer the rendering 'bound/was bound' can be divided into different camps: those who feel that the text, as it stands, yields this meaning—Calvin, AV, Gottwald (8), JPS, Renkema (163), House (333), NIV, NRSV, ESV, and those who regard the original text as from √קשר—Houbigant (478), Oettli (206), Ehrlich (33); thus NEB assumes the corruption[124] of MT and emends to נקשר. The reading of 4QLam, *viz* נקשרה,[125] convinces Cross—and I think that he is right—that נקשר is original and that MT has arisen from an early metathesis and the confusion of ר and ד; but see Schäfer (118*). T's 'is heavy' stands alone among the Versions. It may presuppose the reading נקשה, and Praetorius (144) suggests we read נִקְשָׁה. He translates 'schwer gemacht ist das Joch meiner Sünden', and this has been taken up by Budde (1898ª, 82), Kraus (23), Plöger (134), Westermann (113) and JB. Rudolph (1962, 207), who regards פְּשָׁעַי as the subject, reads the plural נִקְשׁוּ. His suggestion is followed by Haller (98).
The decision on the first word affects other choices that need to be made in the rest of the verse. The Masoretes have vocalised עֹל 'yoke' (contra LXX and P), and the full phrase עֹל פְּשָׁעַי = 'the yoke of my transgressions' becomes the subject of the verb. After his description of Yahweh's treatment of Jerusalem in v. 13, the author is thinking of the punishment *resulting* from transgressions and experienced as a burden. As בְּיָדוֹ belongs with the second stich, the first is cryptic: the yoke of my transgressions is tied in place. In this way the poet introduces the image of the beast of burden.

בְּיָדוֹ יִשְׂתָּרְגוּ—The verb שׂרג is uncommon in the Hebrew Bible (only here and at Job 40.17), though the root occurs in the words for twig (Gen 40.10; Joel 1.7) and descendant (1 Chron 1.26). The Pual (in Job) means 'to be intertwined, tied'. Here, the Hithpael must have something of the same meaning. The plural would refer back to פְּשָׁעַי, which is awkward. It is better to read the singular, with 4QLam: 'It is tied on by his hand'. The poet does not want to play down Yahweh's role in the action. The punishment comes from him.

עָלוּ עַל־צַוָּארִי הִכְשִׁיל כֹּחִי—I read עָלוֹ (for עָלוּ) as in 4QLam/Sym (cf. P): 'His yoke is upon my neck'. This helps to clarify the following clause: the subject of הִכְשִׁיל is probably 'his yoke'—it saps my strength.[126]

---

[124] See Brockington (217), though no mention is made of 4QLam. REB follows NEB.
[125] The Qumran reading is f., which must have arisen because of the context in which the city speaks; cf. Cross (1983, 146).
[126] It is possible to interpret 'he (Yahweh) saps my strength', but Yahweh is introduced in the final line, which suggests that the poet wants to dwell on his image of the heavy burden on the neck.

80   LAMENTATIONS

נְתָנַנִי אֲדֹנָי בִּידֵי לֹא־אוּכַל קוּם—On נְתָנַנִי, see v. 13c. The elliptical syntax of
the following words is similar to that in Exod 4.13 בְּיַד־תִּשְׁלָח = 'by the
hand of (the one) you will send', cf. GK 130d.

The final line continues the image of the abused beast of burden. Yahweh,
the owner, who has harnessed the beast, hands it over to another party, a
more aggressive party and one so powerful that the beast cannot cope (is
unable to stand up). The reality for Jerusalem is that her sins are so great
that they cannot be ignored, and they fetch appropriate punishment.
Yahweh, the one in control at all times, has handed her into the control of
the Babylonians.

1.15

Text and Versions
MT סִלָּה; LXX ἐξῆρεν; V *abstulit*; P ܟܒܫ *kbš*; T כבש.

MT בְּקִרְבִּי—so also P and T; LXX ἐκ μέσου μου—so also V. MT is to be preferred;
LXX and V adjust on the basis of their rendering of the verb. Wiesmann's (115, 118)
vocalisation, בְּקָרְבִי 'in meinem Kampf', is unnecessary.

MT אֲדֹנָי (lines 1 and 3); several MSS[Ken] יהוה; 4QLam אדני (line 1), יהוה (line 3);
preferred reading in both instances is יהוה.

* * *

The author has the city declare that Yahweh has devastated her. The
imagery, though quite different from that in v. 14, is traditional, as is the
vocabulary. The first two lines are words of Jerusalem, in the 1st p. s. The
third line may be the words of the 'narrator', the speaker of vv. 1-11,
interrupting a speech which continues from v. 12 and who interrupts
further at v. 17. Yahweh is depicted as a warrior of Goliath dimensions
casting aside the best soldiery that Jerusalem had to offer in her defence
of the city. He is then seen in a more civilised role as having arranged for
the crushing of the young men, the city's future strength. Finally, with
imagery taken from the harvest time, Yahweh is seen as treading Judah
out of existence, as one treads grapes in a wine-press. The entire verse,
therefore, turns Israel's traditional language upside down. Yahweh might
have been expected to act *for* Jerusalem, but he appears here to be on the
side of the enemy.

סִלָּה—There are only two occurrences of √סלה I in the Hebrew Bible—the
Qal in Ps 119.118 and the Piel here. The meaning is uncertain. It may be
equivalent to Aramaic/Syriac 'to despise, reject', though Gordis (158)
points out that both T and P do not employ this 'equivalence' in their
renderings. Rashi, who takes it to mean 'trampled', רמס, seems to derive
the term from סלל which means 'cast up', in that he cites Isa 62.10;[127] and
this may point to P's derivation also[128] and to T's.

---

[127] It may be that Rashi understood סלל as meaning 'to tread'.
[128] Although Kelso (18) thinks that P read סלף.

IE[1] also explains the word in this way, again citing Isa 62.10 and pointing out the verb דרך later in the verse; and Kara employs the verbs דוש and רמס to make a similar point. It would seem, therefore, that in the absence of certainty we should, perhaps, note that LXX 'he has cut off' and V 'he has taken away' are guesses and that P and T preserve an understanding of the word which better fits the rest of the verse.[129] The image, then, would be of Yahweh, as warrior supreme, trampling the best of Jerusalem's fighting men. Again, there is the shock that Yahweh, who was expected to fight for Israel (2 Chron 20.29; 32.8), not only allows the mighty men to be set at nought, but is himself active in the crushing of them. Vermigli (47) follows Rashi here, as do Calvin *calcavit* and Luther 'hat zertreten' and AV 'has trodden under foot' (cf. Blayney, 151).

A more recent tendency is to explain סָלָה from √סלה II, which occurs only in the Pual 'weigh, balance, pay' (Job 28.16) with the idea 'to give a negative judgment'. This is the exegesis behind Rudolph (1962, 205) 'als wertlos behandelte', NEB 'treated with scorn', House (333; cf. Provan, 51) 'Like an enemy commander, God has weighed up the opposition and found them of no account'.[130] Yet another slant on this is seen in the renderings of Kraus (22), Kaiser (309), Haller (98), NIV, NJB, JPS, NRSV—'rejected', presumably on the basis of Aramaic/Syriac 'despise'. However, if this line is taken, the meaning of the entire phrase is less than clear. What does it mean for Yahweh to scorn (or, indeed, reject) the mighty men of Jerusalem in her midst? Does not the rest of the verse demand a more aggressive role for Yahweh? As Hillers[2] (74) says, 'the phrase "in my midst" seems to demand a verb describing a physical action'. The answer to this lack of aggression may be found in the nuance of the Aphel of סלא 'to throw away'.[131] The best soldiers ('my mighty men') Jerusalem could muster were thrust aside in disdain by the Babylonians when they broke into the city. The phrase בְּקִרְבִּי 'in my midst', in the mouth of the personified city, suggests that this took place in Jerusalem. Yahweh is depicted as performing the task because he is behind it all.

Hillers translates 'heaped up' which sees here a root סלה equal in sense to סלל 'to heap up'. Hillers cites Jer 50.26 at this point and depicts Yahweh piling up, like sheaves, the mighty men of Jerusalem. This exegesis is followed by Renkema (168), but he presses too hard for a 'harvest' interpretation of the entire verse.

קָרָא עָלַי מוֹעֵד לִשְׁבֹּר בַּחוּרָי—Yahweh's active aggression continues in this clause, though there is some dispute as to the precise meaning. מוֹעֵד can

---

[129] LXX and V both read the preposition מן for ב in the second stich probably to accommodate their take on סלה.
[130] A variation on this understanding of the root sees Cross (147) taking the idea of 'to pay' as 'to pay tribute, dedicate as an offering', leaning on Old South Arabic; but his translation 'he made an offering of...' appears forced and has no followers.
[131] Cf. also Akk š/salû 'to hurl away'. See von Soden (1152) and *HALOT*.

mean 'appointed time, place, meeting'. The verb קרא means 'to call, announce'; and the combination קרא על could mean 'proclaim against' (1 Kgs 13.4; Jonah 1.3), 'proclaim concerning' (Jer 49.29). The unusual thing about this clause is that it is Yahweh who is the subject of the verb. God may call unto someone (1 Sam 3.4), or announce something via his prophets (Zech 7.7). Men may call out to God against an enemy (Deut 15.9; 24.15) or may announce a fast (1 Kgs 21.9, 12); but here it looks as though Yahweh is doing the announcing or convoking of the מוֹעֵד, and it is against his own people. The author employs the terminology of the religious life of Israel (cf. Jer 25.29) to produce shock in his 'audience'. The idea here seems to be an announcement of negative action against Jerusalem by her own God: either 'an assembly' (= the enemy, so P), or 'an appointed time' (so LXX, V, Calvin) for action. The conquest by Babylon was 'by appointment', not by chance and not even because the Babylonians decided on it; and one of the purposes was to crush the city's young men. The destruction of both the mighty men and the young men constitutes the removal of the city's defence and potential. Rashi and Kara both interpret the clause as referring to 'an assignment of troops', and this may have given rise to Dyserinck (364) suggesting the vocalisation מוֹעָד 'een leger'. According to Brockington (217), NEB has vocalised מֹעָד—a rare form found elsewhere only at Isa 14.31 where it may mean 'place of soldier in army' (BDB 418). NEB renders 'he marshalled rank on rank against me'. This is roughly the line taken by NJB 'he has summoned a host' and NIV 'he has summoned an army', though they do not admit to reading a different vocalisation and are probably stretching the meaning of 'assembly' in the context of aggression. The poet probably has in mind the Babylonian invasion which destroyed resistance, but to render as per NEB, NJB and NIV is perhaps exegetical forcing. The author has used מוֹעֵד at v. 4 where it must mean 'appointed feast'. May it not mean here that that happy fixed occasion has now been replaced by an unhappy one, organised by the one who would have been honoured in the former? Renkema (169) sees harvest imagery from this and the following motive clause: 'He proclaimed a time of harvest for me to thresh my young men', but his efforts seem forced. Although Yahweh is the subject of √שבר in Isa 14.25; Jer 17.18; 19.11; 43.38, and of √רעע in Ps 2.9, there he is depicted as crushing the nations. Hence the strangeness of Yahweh announcing an appointed time/assembly against Jerusalem is further emphasised by depicting him as the very one who has crushed her brightest and best.

The final line does draw on harvest imagery. The poet may have had Isa 63.1f. in mind—cf. Rashi, Kara, Ehrlich (34) and Gordis (158)—where the treading of grapes image is employed to convey slaughter. LXX (cf. also V) 'The Lord has trodden a wine-press for the virgin daughter of Jerusalem' misses the imagery here and illustrates the literal approach of the translator. The construction employs גת as an adverbial accusative (GK 118q)—so AV, RSV, JPS, Rudolph (1962, 205), Kraus (22), NRSV: 'as in a wine-press'.¹³² The target of the treading, then, is בְּתוּלַת בַּת־יְהוּדָה, the object marker being לְ (GK 117n), occasionally found in Ethiopic and common in Aramaic.

בְּתוּלַת בַּת־יְהוּדָה—This genitive construction¹³³ is a further example of *genitivus explicativus* (GK 128k), 'the maid daughter Judah', cf. Amos 5.2. The translation 'virgin daughter of Judah'—LXX, RSV, NIV, NEB, NJB—misses the force of this genitive. The fuller phrase¹³⁴ may have originally *emphasised* vulnerability. בתולה need not mean virgin but a young marriageable woman—a vulnerable member of a family; and בת, as we have seen (1.6), carries that nuance too. It is probably a mistake to see here an allusion to Judah's inviolability,¹³⁵ though T's (paraphrastic) rendering seems to have fixed on the 'virgin' element of the phrase: 'They (nations) polluted the maiden house of Judah until the blood of their virginity flowed like wine from the press...' Rashi's comment—'he trampled the women to extract their blood in the way that one treads grapes for wine'—may also allude to the blood of the violated virgin; but this, I think, is misreading the passage.

Again, Yahweh has taken the active role. He it is who 'treads the grapes' as in Isa 63.3f. and Joel 4.13; but whereas in the latter passages his target is the nations, here it is his own people. Hence, the author, although utilising traditional terminology, turns on its head the idea that Yahweh sides with his people against their enemies. Kara takes the phrase בת יהודה as 'the people of Judah'.¹³⁶ The poet declares that Yahweh, the traditional guarantor, has become the opposition and has turned the tradition upside down. If this line is in the mouth of Jerusalem—a possible interpretation¹³⁷—then it is the only point where the city looks beyond its walls. In any case, there is a reference here to the fall of the state of Judah.

1.16

Text and Versions

The alphabetic order in MT is ע followed by פ. In 4QLam the order is reversed and conforms to that in chs. 2, 3 and 4 in MT (see *Introduction*).

MT עֵינִי עֵינִי; some MSS^Ken עיני—so also LXX and V; P ܥܝܢܝ *w'yny*; T עיניי—so also OL; some T MSS עיני ותרחין; Sym ὁ ὀφθαλμός ἀδιαλείπτως; 4QLam עיני (בכו). MT is preferred.

---

¹³² Hillers² (63) prefers to take בת as accusative and the לְ as the לְ of possession. He renders: 'The Lord trod the wine-press of the young lady Judah'.
¹³³ On בת יהודה, see on בת ציון at 1.6.
¹³⁴ Cf. 2.13, where בתולת בת ציון is in parallel with הבת ירושלם.
¹³⁵ Cf. the same construction regarding Sidon at Isa 23.12, Babylon at Isa 47.1 and Egypt at Jer 46.11. See Goldingay and Payne (2006, 92f.).
¹³⁶ The remark by Renkema (171)—'Rashi is of the opinion that בתולה refers to Jerusalem itself as the daughter of daughter Judah'—is strange and is not based on his commentary in מקראות גדולות.
¹³⁷ Clearly seen in RSV, NIV, ESV, Hillers² (63) etc.

* * *

If we accept the verse order in MT, then this verse concludes the first part of the speech by Jerusalem, begun at v. 12. Jerusalem resumes after v. 17. The city looks back at what she has uttered and declares that her continuous weeping is caused by what has happened to her. She avoids mentioning Yahweh's hand in it all, though that has been apparent in every verse (12-15). This is an inward-looking self-pitying exercise, and the pain she feels is unrelieved in that there is no one to comfort her (cf. v. 9). Then, like the mother she is, she describes her inhabitants as devastated, for the power of the enemy has stunned them.

The repetition of words (even phrases) is not uncommon in the Hebrew Bible and is usually interpreted either as due to considerations of style or for emphasis; indeed, at 4.15 the form סורו is repeated.[138] In the latter passage, however, the Versions follow suit, while in this passage Versional support is weak. Consequently a number of commentators[139] have suggested deleting one עֵינִי.

When Hillers[2] (75), in referring to the 4QLam reading, speaks of a 'welcome confirmation of an old conjecture' it is begging the question. We cannot say for certain that the *Vorlage* of LXX and V had only one עֵינִי, but even if they did, one might have been lost, in transmission, through haplography (Gottlieb, 19); and the same could be said regarding 4QLam. Besides, in 4QLam we are dealing with a plural[140] that is the subject of בכו (another variation), not the subject of יָרְדָה. On the other hand, a number of scholars[141] feel that MT should be retained. It is the *lectio difficilior* and it does have a certain poignancy: 'My eyes, my eyes flow'. We should note, however, that those who retain MT are divided as to how to translate the passage. Thus AV 'mine eye, mine eye runneth down with water' and NRSV 'my eyes flow with tears' both translate MT; and translation concerns may also underlie the differences in the Versions.

Several scholars are not content with the simple deletion of עֵינִי. McDaniel (32f.), based on an earlier remark by Dahood, emends to עין עיני 'the fount of my eye (runs down with water)'. This has not commanded support (cf. Gottlieb, 19); indeed, even Dahood himself (1978, 178f.)

---

[138] Cf. also Deut 16.20; Isa 21.9; 51.9, 17; 52.1; Ps 68.13
[139] So Houbigant (477), Dyserinck (365), Löhr (1906, 7), Bickell (107) Kelso (19), Rudolph (1962, 208), Haller (98), Kaiser (309), Wiesmann (121), Albrektson (77), Westermann (113), Hillers[2] (75), *BHK*, *BHS*. In these suggestions there is the added concern as to the length of the line here.
[140] The pl. in P (not recognised by Hillers) and T may simply reflect that these Versions recognised the Hebrew custom of referring to one of a pair but meaning both (cf. Ps 88.10); on the other hand, it may have been their way of handling a double עֵינִי. We may note that Luther renders 'meine beiden Augen'!
[141] Keil (373), Gottlieb (19), Gordis (159), Renkema (172), Provan (52), Barthélemy (878), Berlin (44), House (336), Schäfer (119*).

appears to have abandoned it in favour of another conjecture: reading *'ōnî* ('my sorrow') for MT אֲנִי. He renders 'over these my sorrow, /my weeping eye, /my eye running with tears', but the latter state is worse than the first.[142] Brockington (217) reveals that the NEB translators read the first עֵינִי as עָנְיִי, 'for these things I weep over my plight, my eyes run with tears', but while this is followed in REB, the tendency is either to accept MT or simply to delete one עֵינִי.[143]

עַל־אֵלֶּה, therefore, refers back to vv. 12-15 where the city has described sufferings, alluded to in the third person in vv. 1-11. She was depicted there as weeping bitterly (v. 2), bereft of comforter and betrayed by friend. The weeping is emphasised here, not by the infin. abs. and the reference to tears on her cheeks, but by the repetition[144] of עֵינִי (if indeed this is not a case of dittography!), by the combination of √ירד with מִיִם, and by the employment of two active participles בוֹכִיָּה[145] and יֹרְדָה. Just as the weeping prompted the idea of a comforter at v. 2, so too, at this point, the poet stresses that loneliness by referring to the stark absence of someone who might comfort or revive her spirits. The suggestion by Renkema (172f.) that there is an important distinction here between רָחַק מְנַחֵם and אֵין מְנַחֵם (v. 2) is unconvincing. מֵשִׁיב נַפְשִׁי is in apposition to מְנַחֵם, and both are governed by רָחַק.

שׁוֹמֵמִים—A difficult word to translate (see on vv. 4, 13). AV, RSV, REB translate 'desolate', NIV 'destitute', NJB 'shattered', JPS 'forlorn', NEB 'an example of desolation'. Hillers[2] (75) notes that it is an adjective usually used of cities, less often of people, as here (בָּנַי); cf. also 2 Sam 13.20; Isa 54.1. P's translation ܫܩܡܝܢ *šqmyn* 'sycamores, figs' seems strange. At 1.4 the same word is rendered ܨܕܝܢ *ṣdyn* (cf. T here) and one would have expected something similar here. Brockelmann (1928, *ad loc.*: 'exhausted') and Payne Smith (1903, 594: 'sad') seem to be guesses from context.[146] Albrektson (77) opines 'perhaps, after all, the most likely explanation is that the translator misread שׁ(ו)מֵמִים as שִׁקְמִים and translated accordingly'.

[142] If MT had read עַל־אֵלֶּה עָנְיִי, many scholars would have deleted the latter word or else emended to אֲנִי.
[143] Cross (1983, 148f.) is the most radical on this passage. Regarding MT as corrupt, and suspicious of עַל־אֵלֶּה, he settles for עיני בכיה עיני ירדה מים 'My eye weeps,/My eye runs with tears.' But see Hillers[2] (75).
[144] Rashi (followed by Kara) interprets the repetition as indicating that there was no relief, while Sym 'without ceasing' interprets similarly; and, at Jer 4.19, Kimḥi explains repetition as stylistic on the part of lamenters. This latter passage, where the word מֵעַי 'my bowels' is repeated, disproves the claim by Westermann (113) that emphasis is only meaningful in the case of verbal forms; cf. also Ps 22.2; 2 Kgs 2.12; 13.14.
[145] On the form of the active participle here (= בוֹכָה), see GK 75v.
[146] Abelesz (33) rules out the possibility of a scribal error from ܫܡܝܢ *šmyn* in that the root *šmm* does not occur in Syriac. He wonders if the translator's *Vorlage* had a smudged מ which led him to think in terms of 'Frucht, die schon zum Abpflücken ist'; and he raises the possibility that the translator was influenced by the harvest imagery of v. 15.

The city, having described her plight (vv. 12-15) is now inward-looking. עַל־אֵלֶּה, supplies the formal reasons for her weeping, but then, as is the case with distressed people, other reasons flood into her mind. Those tears might have been abated had someone been around to comfort and raise her spirits; and, finally, as a mother, she mentions her children who have become shattered. The translation 'sons' (LXX, NEB, Rudolph) is too narrow. She is not thinking of the mighty men and the young men of v. 15: she is the mother of all the inhabitants of Jerusalem. It is better, therefore, to render 'my children' with AV, JPS, NRSV, Kraus (22) and Westermann (111). בני has been taken by IE[1] to refer to her people who have gone into exile, but this interpretation is, again, too narrow.

כִּי גָבַר אוֹיֵב—'For the enemy has prevailed'. This final stich virtually repeats the idea already expressed at vv. 9c, 13c, 14c, cf. v. 5a. That theme of the victorious enemy is one which keeps raising its head in various ways. The fact that Jerusalem was invaded is implied in the references to her forced labour (v. 1), migration (v. 3), her being hunted (v. 6), the power of the foe (v. 7) and in the pain expressed in vv. 12-15. This bitter fact shatters the inhabitants of Jerusalem, for their whole world is turned upside down.

1.17

Text and Versions

MT בְּיָדֶיהָ—so also 4QLam; LXX χεῖρας αὐτῆς—so also OL, V, P and T. This is not an indication that the Versions had a text where ב was not represented (implied by *BHK*). At 1.10, the construction פרש (Qal) with the accusative יד is used, but there the meaning was of the enemy reaching for the treasures of Jerusalem. Here the picture is of Zion spreading out her hands either in desperation to those who pass by (v. 12), to anyone who can help, or to Yahweh in prayer (REB, cf. Ps 143.6). Renkema (176f.) thinks that both meanings may be intended. The Versions, therefore, interpret correctly. This is the ב of instrument (GK 119q) which introduces the object;[147] cf. also Josh 8.18; Jer 18.6; Job 16.4. MT is not in doubt.

MT לָהּ—so also LXX, P, V and T; 4QLam לה מכול אוהביה צדיק אתה יהוה; the scroll reading has additional material incorporated from vv. 2 and 18. MT is preferable.

MT צִוָּה יְהוָה—so also LXX, P, V and T; 4QLam צפה אדוני; Cross (Studies, 147) opts for צפה יהוה, as does Schäfer (*BHQ*, 119*) who vocalises צִפָּה. MT is preferable.

MT לְנִדָּה בֵּינֵיהֶם—so also LXX, P, V; five MSS[Ken] לנידה ביניהם; 4QLam לנדוח בניהמה; 4QLam is clearly corrupt. The suggestion בעיניהם (*BHS*), though more idiomatic, is a mere conjecture.[148] MT is preferred.

---

[147] The phenomenon occurs in Rabbinic Hebrew and in Arabic. Rashi explains the construction by quoting Isa 25.11 (ופרש ידיו), while IE[1] notes that the ב is superfluous as in Ps 80.6 וַתַּשְׁקֵמוֹ בִּדְמָעוֹת. Calvin translates *in manibus suis (id est, manus suas)*.

[148] It is adopted by Rudolph (1938, 104), Kaiser (310), Westermann (113). Renkema (179) 'in their eyes' *seems* to have followed this (cf. also Kraus, 22), but neither admit to it! There is nothing awkward about בֵּינֵיהֶם. It appears at 1 Sam 17.3; 26.13; 2 Sam 14.6; Job 41.8. The sense is not affected, and I suspect that Renkema and Kraus were offering a free translation of MT here.

* * *

From v. 12, Zion has been speaking, having burst in earlier during the 'narration' (vv. 1-11) at vv. 9c and 11c. The speech continues to the end of the poem, but here, at v. 17, the original speaker returns, and in the same vein, to offer a comment on what the city has been saying. He picks up her plea to passers-by (v. 12) and her observation that no comforter is near, and concludes that she gets no response whatever. Perhaps he thinks that Yahweh might be the ideal comforter, for his next statement has Yahweh as subject but behaving in a very uncomforting manner! As though he was thinking that the passers-by could be the neighbouring nations, he explains that Yahweh had mobilised these neighbours against her. Far from being thought of in a favourable light, Jerusalem is now regarded by them as something to be shunned.

פֵּרְשָׂה—The vast majority in the history of interpretation has taken this to be from פרשׂ 'to spread', but the homonym פרס has given rise to the interpretation, found in Rashi (as an addendum) and Kara, that the meaning is 'to break'. The origin of this interpretation may be Lam 4.4, where פרשׂ has this meaning. While it is not Rashi's own interpretation, he includes it in such a way that one suspects that there was strong support for it;[149] indeed, Kara embraces it, not even mentioning the meaning 'to spread', and draws support from Isa 58.7 and Jer 16.7. IE[1] assumes the meaning to be 'to spread' as does T. The fact that there is no *waw* connecting the first two stichs emphasises the contrast (cf. 1.2, 9, 21) between the pleading Zion and the lack of response.[150] The juxtaposition of these suggests that the picture is of the female figure entreating the passers-by (v. 12).[151] The fact that we have the idea of 'no comforter' repeated five times in this chapter—vv. 2, 9, 16, 17, 21—(but nowhere else in the book) suggests that the poet wishes to stress the image of the aloneness of the figure: she is forsaken by all. Whether he is also hinting at Yahweh's unwillingness to comfort is debateable, though Renkema (177) argues for this; cf. NEB's 'in prayer' and Dobbs-Allsopp (70).

אֵין מְנַחֵם לָהּ—Cf. vv. 2, 9 and 21. We should note that the ל has been taken as an object marker by LXX and V.

צִוָּה יְהוָה לְיַעֲקֹב סְבִיבָיו צָרָיו—The Versions struggled with this passage. LXX 'The Lord has commanded regarding Jacob; his oppressors are

---

[149] Calvin is aware of it but rejects it.
[150] It is natural, in translation, to supply some connecting particle, such as 'and' (P, T, AV), or 'but' (NRSV, NEB). LXX and V resist this, as do also RV, JPS, Rudolph (1962, 205), Berlin (44), but the contrast is sharper when the clauses are left side by side.
[151] Calvin: 'These clauses ought to be read together; that is, that Sion expanded her hands, and yet no one responded to alleviate her sorrow by consolation'.

round about him' has read the line as though a pause was required after לְיַעֲקֹב; and this is how P read the line, though a copula has been introduced to facilitate this. T is very paraphrastic here but its starting point is similar to LXX and P. V reads the line in its entirety, as did the Masoretes. Nevertheless, as Kelso (20) notes, the underlying text is the same in all the Versions. Albrektson (78) observes that צָרָיו is governed by צִוָּה. סְבִיבָיו can mean (a) 'round about him', as in Pss 50.3; 97.2, or (b) 'those around him', as in Jer 48.17, 39; Pss 76.12; 89.8. Both translations are possible and both are reflected in the Versions. MR assumes the latter, but Rashi the former: 'He commanded concerning (עַל) Jacob that his foes should be round about him'; and he goes on to explain, quoting *b. Kid.* 72a, that 'this took place even in Babylonia and Assyria in exile, for Babylon and Assyria exiled their enemies, Ammon and Moab, and settled them beside them'. There is still no consensus on this. While AV is ambiguous, RV, NIV, NRSV, Gottwald (9), Rudolph (1962, 205), Kaiser (309), Westermann (111), Kraus (22), Renkema (177) follow (b), whereas NEB, REB, JPS, NJB, Luther, Hillers[2] (63) have followed (a).

Already in v. 2 neighbours have become enemies, though in that passage it is a mere observation of fact. Here the same voice picks up the city's theological reflection (vv. 12-16) that Yahweh is behind all the suffering and adds theological colour to the discussion. Yahweh, the covenant God, the protecting God, is the commander of the enemies all around Jacob. Such a thought has been alluded to at v. 5, but this is much more graphic: it is almost as though the poet has been informed by the city's speech (vv. 12-16). Indeed, the picture of Jerusalem pleading with passers-by (v. 12) is echoed by the first line of v. 17, and this line puts, in a nutshell, the declaration of the city that Yahweh controls the enemies, the adversity. While disagreeing with Renkema's (177f.) translation here, I think he is correct in pointing out the significance of what is being said. Renkema shows how the Moabite Stone provides a theological explanation for a similar situation. The inscription interprets the Moabite defeat, at the hands of Israel, as being the consequence of Chemosh's anger with his people: he has allowed them to be defeated. He stood back from it. Taken this way, Chemosh's power was not in question, whereas the defeat of a nation could easily call in question the power of the main (or protecting) deity of that nation. But here the idea is a far-reaching one. Yahweh is not just standing back, allowing the foe to attack—and one could interpret v. 2 in this way—he is actually the commander-in-chief of the allied enemies. That is what is so shocking about this line. Jeremiah may have believed that Yahweh would not, willy nilly, *protect* Jerusalem, but he did not explicitly envisage that Yahweh would take over the command of all Jerusalem's enemies. This is the first and only use of the term 'Jacob' in the poem (cf. 2.2f.). Whether or not there is significance in its appearance here is debateable. The poet began the verse with Zion as subject, and this was continuing the image of the abandoned, friendless, comfortless woman. In the final line of this verse Jerusalem is again the subject; but in the second line the poet mentions 'Jacob'. If the poet had substituted 'Zion' or 'Jerusalem' for 'Jacob' here would anything have been lost? Does he revert to (a synonym for) Israel here because Yahweh is known and thought of as the God of Israel/Jacob, and the God of Jacob was thought to be a refuge (Pss 46.8, 12) for his people? Kraus (32f.) notes that 'Jacob' is used in exilic and postexilic times for all Israel, all of God's people, and so views its use here as of all Judah, surrounded by the hostile neighbours, with Zion/Jerusalem being *pars pro toto*.

The poet has stated in the first line that there is no one to comfort Zion. In the second, he offers a theological rationale for this state of affairs—Yahweh is in control of her foes; and in the final line the poet suggests a non-theological reason for it all—she is now regarded by her hostile neighbours as something to be shunned, a filthy item.

נִדָּה—The form נִידָה is probably a variant spelling; see on v. 8. LXX εἰς ἀποκαθημένην, V *quasi polluta menstruis*, T לאתתא מרחקא and probably P ܢܕܬ *ndtʾ* understand this to be a reference to a 'menstruous woman' or some such abomination;[152] so also Rashi (לריחוק לבוז), IE[2], Vermigli (51f.), Calvin (*facta est Jerusalem in abominationem inter ipsos [vel, tanquam immunda, vel, menstruata,* נדה*, enim vocatur mulier menstruata apud Mosen]*), Luther 'wie ein unrein Weib'; so also AV, Rudolph (1962, 208). Berlin (58f.) argues strongly for this position and translates 'Jerusalem has become a menstruating woman among them', the implication being that, since Lev 18.19 forbids approaching a woman in her menstrual impurity, none of Judah's neighbours (erstwhile lovers) would want to have sexual relations with her. Others, while not denying the connections with menstruation, are inclined to take the term to mean something unclean and to be shunned, hence RV 'an unclean thing', Gottwald (9) 'filthy', Westermann (111) 'an object of loathing', NEB 'a filthy rag', REB 'an unclean thing to be shunned', cf. also Gordis (132), NIV, RSV, NRSV, JPS.

In allowing the first speaker to intervene at this point, the poet maintains the drama[153] of the poem and carefully weaves the themes and vocabulary of the first speech with that of Zion's in vv. 12-16.

---

[152] The root is נדד 'to retreat, wander'. The f. noun נִדָּה has the meaning 'impurity'—referring either to ceremonial impurity (Lev 20.21), especially of menstruation (Ezek 18.6), or figuratively, to immorality (Ezra 9.11).

[153] Gerstenberger (481) suggests that the 'intrusion' may be related to liturgical considerations.

1.18

Text and Versions
MT יְהוָה; 4QLam א[דוני]. MT is to be preferred.
MT (*Kethib*) כָּל־עַמִּים; MT (*Qere*) כָל־הָעַמִּים—so also several MSS[Ken], LXX[L]. MT (*Kethib*) is preferred, in that it is a form which appears more in poetry (cf. GK 127c [a]).

* * *

The first person speech of Zion continues after the third person 'interruption' in v. 17; but it is not just a continuation of vv. 12-16. There, Zion declares her pain to be inimitable and states that Yahweh has been the protagonist. The third person emphasises the origin of her pain and anguish, depicting Yahweh as in command of her enemies. Now, Zion responds to the interruption itself by admitting her part in the disaster. If there had been any debate as to the cause of Yahweh's anger—and there was no allusion to it in vv. 12-16—it now becomes clear. Zion has rebelled against his command, and Yahweh is in the right. The speech in the third person has (vv. 5, 7) already mentioned the fact that her punishment was due to sin, but most of the chapter has concentrated on the calamity itself and on the pain of it all.

Scholars point out that the term צַדִּיק derives from the legal context (cf. Jer 12.1) and conveys the idea that Yahweh is justified in what he has done. The translation 'the Lord is righteous' (AV, RV, NIV), therefore, misses the point. The court verdict is that Yahweh is in the right—so Luther 'gerecht', Kraus (22) and most translations—implying that Zion is in the wrong; and the following clause is the basis for the verdict, *viz*. 'for I rebelled against his commands'.

MR's comments on this verse are confined to the first line. The statement is lifted out of context and attributed to Josiah. The comments reflect the theodicy debate in Ancient Israel where the wicked king Manasseh lived to a ripe old age, whereas the good king, Josiah, died young. The story in 2 Kings is presented in a matter-of-fact manner, whereas in the account in 2 Chron 35 the writer is attempting to answer the question 'Why did good king Josiah die young?'. His answer is: because Josiah actually disobeyed God: 'and hearkened not unto the words of Necho from the mouth of God' (2 Chron 35.22). That tradition attracted the words of Lam 1.18a to the extent that MR credits Josiah with uttering them to Jeremiah (cf. also MLT) on his deathbed. T, too, interprets these words in terms of Josiah's demise. In both MR and T, Josiah is depicted as arguing that Moses had declared (Lev 26.6) that 'the sword shall not go through your land' and that was the reason for Josiah's attempt at stopping Neco's march past Megiddo. However, according to MR, Moses was referring to a loyal Israel, whereas Josiah's generation were idolaters (and so the promise would not hold); and, according to T, Josiah did not seek

God's will before intervening. One should note here that Rashi, Kara, IE[1] and IE[2] do not comment on this passage.

מָרִיתִי—From √מרה 'be rebellious', often with respect to God.[154] This verb, which occurs again at v. 21, is construed with פֶּה[155] at Num 20.24; 27.14; 1 Sam 12.15; 1 Kgs 13.21, 26 with the idea of wilful disobedience. No specific command is mentioned. Calvin suggests that this was a reference to the teaching of the prophets 'for when the word of God was proclaimed by the mouth of these prophets, it was despised as an empty sound'. This is the view taken also by Kraus (33) and Kaiser (322). Renkema (181) notes that 'the expression is always used for resistance to a particular command given in a particular situation, but never with respect to commandments which have eternal validity. For this reason the text here must refer exclusively to daughter Zion's resistance to the preaching of the prophets who had warned her about the consequences of her behaviour and had announced YHWH's judgement upon it'.

The confession wrung out of Jerusalem has, of course, been hovering in the background. It is there at vv. 5 and 9, in the third person description, and it is hinted at in v. 14 while Zion describes her experience of being swamped by Yahweh. But this is it with no holds barred, fortissimo. Hillers[2] (90) thinks that from this point there is a progressive turning towards Yahweh, and Westermann (136) says that this line 'intimates a significant "nevertheless"'. There is certainly something different here, but it may be going too far to say that Zion is turning towards Yahweh. We must remember that she cried out to Yahweh at v. 9c and at v. 11c, though there is no specific confession of sin at those points. We may say that, qualitatively, the attitude to Yahweh is now on a firmer footing (Prov 28.13), but Zion is not actively addressing Yahweh in this verse and it is not until vv. 20-22 that this takes place.

שִׁמְעוּ־נָא—This is the first instance of the root שמע in the poem; and it is in the imperative. The precative נא (GK 110d), which was absent with the imperatives at vv. 9 and 11, may not be significant, but it does appear to add poignancy. Often, for example in the Psalms, the imperative of this verb is used to address Yahweh: here it is directed at 'the peoples', by which the poet means the neighbouring peoples.

The fact that, at v. 12, passers-by are asked to 'look' and here the peoples are asked to 'hear' probably has no significance (contra Renkema, 182), for the peoples are also asked to 'look'. The poet has found it

---

[154] LXX παρεπίκρανα 'provoked' understood the form to be from √מרר 'be bitter', and P ܡܪܡܪܬ mrmrt derives from the same root (contra Kelso, 20); so, too, V *provocavi*. Jerome tries to make sense by adding the words *ad iracundiam* 'to wrath'.

[155] The word פה may mean 'mouth' but also 'command', i.e. what comes from the mouth, cf. 1 Chron 12.24 (see BDB). LXX τὸ στόμα αὐτοῦ 'his mouth', V *os eius* have translated in literal fashion; Sym τῷ λογῳ αὐτου; T מימריה 'his word' are close to the poet's meaning, while P ܠܗ *lh* 'him' translates freely.

difficult to maintain absolutely the image of the abandoned woman, just as he allowed the picture of the hunter and the hunted to slip at v. 6. At 1.12 he depicted Zion calling on passers-by—a street scene. Here, the image is substantially the same, only the passers-by are identified as the peoples. We are really back with 1.12 when the passers-by were asked to witness Zion's agony.[156] Provan (53) may be right in suggesting that the peoples are being invited to learn from Zion's mistake, but it is more likely that Zion is asking for sympathy.

The connection between the first and second lines of this verse is not easy to detect, and it may be that the poet intends to convey in verse what people do in times of bereavement and disaster: they make dirge-like utterances about what is important to them at the moment, but the utterances may not necessarily connect in a logical way.[157] Her pain here seems to be defined as the exile of her maidens and her young men. One gets the impression that, from this point on to the end of v. 22, there is a harking back to the rest of the poem. For example, the call to the peoples and the pain (cf. v. 12), the reference to maidens (cf. v. 4), young men (cf. v. 15); and the phrase הָלְכוּ בַשְּׁבִי is an echo of הָלְכוּ שְׁבִי (v. 5).

At v. 5 we read of the children (עוֹלָלֶיהָ) being taken into exile. Here, the categories are maidens and young men—still the young people, but the emphasis seems to be on the youth of the nation, those on whom the nation depends for its future. The emphasis on the youth reflects mother Zion's concern for her children's fate. One is reminded of the use of hyperbole in the poem. The young men are crushed in v. 15, the maidens made to suffer at v. 4; here, both groups have gone into captivity. What we have here are impressions gathered by the poet for the purpose of this poem (Westermann, 100-104) constituting the lament itself. One may not, in poetry, take the image too far, or take the superlative as fact.

1.19

Text and Versions
MT נַפְשָׁם—so also V and T; LXX ψυχὰς αὐτῶν καὶ οὐχ εὗρον—so also P; the obelisk in SH shows that the words καὶ οὐχ εὗρον were not in the Hebrew to which Origen had access. MT is preferred. The extra words are occasioned by misinterpretation of כִּי.

* * *

Up to this point in her speech Jerusalem has sought sympathy from passers-by (v. 12) and peoples (v. 18), but has not made concrete overtures for help. Here Zion intimates that she had endeavoured to secure help, but that these efforts had been fruitless; indeed, worse than fruitless in that those whom she had approached had actually deceived/turned their back on her. Then, in a manner reminiscent of v. 18, she changes the

---

[156] The same form, מַכְאֹבִי, is used in both passages.
[157] See Salters (2000, 299).

subject and picks up the theme of famine (though this may have been one reason that she had sought help), referred to at v. 11. In the latter passage all the people were suffering through lack of food; here, Zion seems concerned only for her priests and elders. But whereas at v. 11 the people are said to groan as they look for food, here Zion says that the priests and elders are perishing. It is not clear why she singles out her priests and elders, but the theme of tragic reversal is perhaps emphasised when leading citizens, who had once fared reasonably well, are now dying of starvation.

קָרָאתִי לַמְאַהֲבַי—Here, Zion indicates that she had called out to/summoned her lovers/friends, presumably for help, but without success. On the use of a participle with suffix sporting the definite article, see GK 116f. The 'lovers' here remind us of v. 2, though in that passage it is the Qal participle that is used. Whether there is any significance in the use of the Piel here is debateable, but the image of the suffering female figure is perhaps emphasised.[158] Does the author intend us to make the identification of the 'lovers' here—in which case we should perhaps think (as does NIV 'allies') of the alliances which Jerusalem/Judah had made with other nations[159]—or should we simply keep in mind the female figure abandoned by lovers (AV, RV, RSV, REB, NJB, NRSV)? Rashi feels that the Piel carries the aspect of pretence,[160] 'those who make themselves appear as lovers (אוהבים)', while IE¹ says in effect that the meaning of the Piel form (as opposed to the Qal) is 'those who want me to love them', and IE² paraphrases 'I called to strangers, my neighbours, that they should give me counsel...' Kara, as usual, makes the identification straightaway: 'those with whom I associated (דבק) for friendship, as for example, the Assyrians and the Babylonians'. MR (cf. also MLT), on the basis of 2.14 where the prophets are said to have seen empty and deluded visions, takes מְאַהֲבַי to refer to the false prophets who made Jerusalem love idol-worship, i.e. giving the Piel a causative sense.

רמה—הֵמָּה רִמּוּנִי II Piel, 'abandon, betray'. The usual rendering is 'they deceived me' (AV) or 'they played me false' (JPS), but the meaning 'abandon' may suit best here (*HALOT*). The sequence of verbs in this line may suggest that the action of the second is a *response* to the first, but the poet may have thought that the abandonment preceded the calling out:

---

[158] Although the Qal may denote Judah's adulterous love (Jer 2.25; Isa 57.8), nearly all the instances of the Piel (except Zech 13.6) in Hos 2.7, 9, 12, 14; Ezek 23.5, 9; Jer 22.20, 22 have to do with Judah's metaphorical lovers.
[159] T renders 'I called to my friends among the nations, those with whom I had established treaties...' Although T is thinking here of the first fall of Jerusalem, in that Nebuchadnezzar is mentioned, it goes on to apply this to the second fall of the city, mentioning the Romans and Titus; that is to say, there is a double application of this first line.
[160] Cf. also Gordis (159), Perles (1930, 103f.).

'they had abandoned me'. The absence of a *waw*[161] and the presence of the (pleonastic) pronoun help to sharpen the contrast between love and betrayal. The natural application of this line is the situation where Judah sought help from Egypt (cf. 4.17) and others either in the run up to the fall of Jerusalem, in which case one might translate 'I had called to my lovers', or during the siege, the fall and the aftermath, in which case one might translate 'I have called upon...'

כֹּהֲנַי וּזְקֵנַי בָּעִיר גָּוָעוּ—At v. 4 there is a reference to priests groaning, in the context of the cessation of cultic activity. In this passage they are grouped with the elders and, with them, represent an important section of society. When the poet uses the phrase 'my priests and my elders' he does not mean every single priest and elder. The phrase 'in the city' may carry the meaning 'publicly, before all' (so Gordis, 159; cf. 'en pleine ville' Barthélemy, 879). In Amos 7.17, where Amos declares that Amaziah's wife will be a harlot in the city, the same phrase carries this meaning. It is not a question of in the city rather than in the countryside, but in the city as opposed to in their homes. It is meant to emphasise the manner of the death of the priests and elders.[162] The meaning of √גוע is not entirely clear. At Gen 25.8 וַיִּגְוַע וַיָּמָת אַבְרָהָם, where it is construed with the verb 'to die', it seems to mean something other than simply 'to die', and REB renders 'breathed his last'. Driver (1962, 15ff.) shows that the verb originally meant 'gasp for breath' (cf. Ps 88.16 עָנִי אֲנִי וְגֹוֵעַ מִנֹּעַר where it cannot mean 'die' or 'expired') and came to mean 'breathe one's last'.[163] In this passage and in most instances, most scholars render 'perished/expired'. The root in Arabic *can* mean 'be empty/hungry', and this is the basis for NEB's 'went hungry', but this has not commanded support, and the revision (REB) rejects it.[164] It gives the impression that the priests and elders were just looking for another meal!

כִּי־בִקְשׁוּ אֹכֶל לָמוֹ וְיָשִׁיבוּ אֶת־נַפְשָׁם—The final line furnishes a comment on the expiration of priest and elder but, apart from the awkward syntax, it is

---

[161] There is a tendency to supply a connecting particle, as LXX δὲ, V *et*, P ܐ, T ו, Luther 'aber', AV, NRSV 'but'. McDaniel (33f.) suggests that המה is equivalent to the Ugaritic *hm*, a demonstrative particle like Hebrew הנה. But while the pronoun is not grammatically necessary in the passage, its presence serves to point up the contrast and, as Hillers[2] (76) suggests, it may have seemed metrically desirable to include it here; cf. also at v. 8 (היא) and v. 21 (אתה). Gottlieb (20) refers also to Pss 48.6, 15; 74.13ff. Calvin, NEB and NJB resist the temptation to supply a contrasting particle.

[162] P's rendering (of בעיר), ܒܓܘܝ *bgwy* 'within me' (some MSS) seems to reflect the translator's awareness that it is the city that is speaking here; but see Albrektson (79f.) for alternative explanation. Abelesz (33) thinks that P's *Vorlage* read בקרבי; cf. v. 15 and P's translation there.

[163] 'גוע in relation to death properly describes the sounds preceding death or accompanying the process of death and even the process of dying but never the state of death' (Driver, *ibid.*).

[164] Cf. also Barthélemy (879), Provan (53).

rather prosaic and is rather long. The Versions do not offer a shorter line; indeed, there is an addition in LXX and P: 'and they did not find (any)'. If MT is retained[165]—and most modern commentators are reluctant to emend here—we must understand the ו + the imperfect וְיָשִׁיבוּ coming after a perfect as introducing a final clause 'that they might...'; cf. 2 Kgs 19.25; Isa 25.9 (see JM 116c). The idea is similar to that of v. 11b (q.v.). לָמוֹ is poetic for לָהֶם (GK 103f).

At first glance one thinks that the extra words in LXX and P are a gloss on the existing MT in that the latter merely tells us that priests and elders expired while they had sought sustenance. The extra words, then, explain that the search was fruitless. The fact that the words are not attested in V or T perhaps suggests that their *Vorlagen* conformed to the MT tradition. This is the view taken by AV, Luther, RSV, REB, NJB, JPS, NIV, Hillers[2] (76), Kaiser (310), Westermann (111). But other proposals have been made. Budde (1882, 267) deletes the final words of the line in favour of ולא מצאו and in this he is followed by Bickell (107), Dyserinck (365), Löhr (1894, 5, though cf. 1906, 8), *BHK*, Kraus (23), Haller (98), Cross (1983, 149f.). Ehrlich (34) suggests וַיַּשִּׁיאוּ (for וְיָשִׁיבוּ), i.e. from √נשא II Hiphil 'deceive'. It is found (with similar construction) in Jer 37.9 אַל־תַּשִּׁאוּ נַפְשֹׁתֵיכֶם 'do not deceive yourselves'. Rudolph (1962, 205, 208) accepts this conjecture and translates 'aber Enttäuschung erfuhren'. The problem arose early in the transmission of the text when a scribe understood כי as 'because' and then realised that the following words did not amount to a reason for the expiration of the priests and elders. His addition of ולא מצאו eventually appeared in the *Vorlagen* of LXX and P, each of whom understood כי in the same way.[166] If כי is understood as 'when, while' (GK 164d; cf. Gen 6.1; Judg 1.28), the problem does not exist (Keil, 375).[167]

Zion is rejected and abandoned, famine is rife in her streets where prominent citizens are dying of hunger. The scenario is bleak. Appeals for human help fall on deaf ears. Where can she turn to?

1.20

Text and Versions
MT מָרוּ מָרִיתִי; LXX παραπικραίνουσα παρεπίκρανα; P (and SH) ܡܡܪܡܪܘ ܡܪܡܪܬ *mmrmrw mrmrt*, V *amaritudine plena sum*; T ארום מעבר עברית על גזירת מימרא דיי; LXX, P and V are based on misunderstanding of the Hebrew text.

---

[165] Rudolph (1962, 208) wonders why the construction להשיב was not used, as in v. 11.
[166] V and T also understood כי as 'because', but their *Vorlagen* did not include the extra words; and their subsequent translations are problematic.
[167] Barthélemy (879), while rejecting the plus of LXX and P, maintains that כי means 'because'. He argues 'Le כּי initial de 19b ne vise pas à expliquer pourquoi ils se meurent (ce qui requerrait la mention de l'échec de la tentative), mais à expliquer pourquoi c'est en pleine ville qu'ils se meurent: ils ont dû sortir de chez eux pour essayer de trouver de la nourriture.'

MT בְּבַיִת כַּמָּוֶת; LXX ὥσπερ θάνατος ἐν οἴκῳ; P ܡܘܬܐ ܒܒܝܬܐ wdbbyt' mwt';
V et domi mors similis est; OL (frag.) et ab intus mors. LXX may have altered the word
order in order to make sense. It is possible, though far from certain, that P read a text
which omitted the כ (see Albrektson, 81f.), and OL, though fragmentary, may hint in that
direction, but the כ is attested in LXX and V; and in the T paraphrase it is clearly present.

* * *

The opening words of this verse remind us of the final words of vv. 9 and
11—vv. 9c, 11c and 20a begin 'See, O Yahweh'—and draw attention to
the fact that in Zion's first person speech, which began at v. 12, she has
not yet formally addressed Yahweh. Now, at this late stage in the poem,
she turns to Yahweh, and vv. 20-22 consist entirely of address to Yahweh.
The imagery with which the verse begins is of someone (Zion, the female
figure) in great physical and mental distress. The request is for Yahweh
to take notice of this distress; and Zion acknowledges that she has been
rebellious. In the final line she sums up the dire straits she finds herself in
by using terminology relating to death in the streets and at home.

This verse has caused problems for exegetes and translators. The main
stumbling block has been the final line, especially the phrase בְּבַיִת כַּמָּוֶת,
but also מָרוֹ מָרִיתִי in the second line; and the elucidation of these passages
involves the rest of the verse. I have argued elsewhere[168] that apparent
non-sequiturs in the utterances of the bereaved may be the norm and that
lack of cohesion in these (stylised) poetic laments may well be original—
allusions to the distressful conditions being described. That is to say, we
may do violence to the text by insisting on logical development and
connections. Having said that, we must, nevertheless, find meaning in the
individual components of a phrase or line.

רְאֵה—The imperative 'see', as with vv. 9c, 11c, requests Yahweh to pay
attention to the distress being experienced by Zion. As in Pss 18.7; 66.14;
107.6, 13, 19, 28; 106.44 where the speaker calls on Yahweh from a situation of distress, so Zion is here depicted as being in distress[169] and calling
on her God who has a record of responding in such circumstances. That is
to say, Zion puts herself in the traditional pose by employing the language
of the liturgy.

כִּי־צַר־לִי—Either 'that I am in distress' or 'for I am in distress' or 'how
distressed I am'.

מֵעַי חֳמַרְמָרוּ—This phrase occurs (words in reverse order) at 2.11 and the
verbal form at Job 16.16. There is some doubt as to the root.[170] It is likely

---

[168] Salters (2000, 299).
[169] The noun צר from √צרר I occurs only here in Lamentations.
[170] BDB lists four different חמר roots, while *HALOT* lists five.

that it is related to the Arabic noun *ḥamīr* 'leaven'. In the Hebrew Bible, the Qal of √חמר I (BDB 330) means 'to foam' (Pss 46.4; 75.9). At Sir 4.2 the Hiphil תחמיר seems to mean 'disturb'. The conjugation here is unusual—Pealal (see GK 55e)—and probably means 'be in ferment/be troubled'.[171] The subject of the verb is 'my bowels'—the seat of the emotions in the Hebrew Bible; but the translation 'my bowels are in ferment' (cf. AV, NRSV, REB etc.) is inadequate. Better to 'translate' into modern English idiom—'my heart is in anguish' (JPS), or 'I am in torment within' (NIV).

נֶהְפַּךְ לִבִּי בְּקִרְבִּי—One is initially tempted to see both מעים and לב, in this verse, as parts of Zion's body which are experiencing suffering and pain in the same way as the bones (v. 13). That is to say, it is possible to view the agony of v. 20 as the continuation of the pain referred to in vv. 12ff. But there is something different about this verse, and it is not just that Yahweh is being addressed (after all, Zion addresses Yahweh at vv. 9c, 11c): it is partly that Zion has now plucked up the courage to sustain her invocation of Yahweh. If we take מעים 'bowels' to be equivalent to 'heart', then לב which has a wide semantic range and has often been translated 'heart' (cf. AV, NRSV, REB), may refer to the mind or will. The occurrence of the construction at Hos 11.8 נֶהְפַּךְ עָלַי לִבִּי which is parallel with the phrase יַחַד נִכְמְרוּ נִחוּמָי and which seems to indicate a change of attitude (cf. also Exod 14.5 where we have the words וַיֵּהָפֵךְ לְבַב פַּרְעֹה where the idea involves a change of mind, would suggest that we may be dealing here with confession/repentance. At v. 18 Zion acknowledged that she had rebelled and that Yahweh was in the right, but at that point she did not show any remorse. Now she declares that she has turned the corner, so to speak, is upset and is determined to change. MR's comment (cf. also MLT) on נחפך is 'Why? Because I have grievously rebelled', which seems to take the passage as indicating repentance, and IE[2] הייתי צועקה לשם ומתודה 'And I cried out to God and confessed (when I saw the sword of the enemy bereaving)', which appears to take the first two lines as a cry of confession on Zion's part. If it is acknowledged that Zion is finally in a mood of repentance, then the following words כִּי מָרוֹ מָרִיתִי cease to be problematic for exegetes. Zion calls on Yahweh to look at her distressed state, which involves a state of contrition and acknowledges that she has wantonly rebelled. At v. 18 she admits rebellion. Here, repentance and confession combine to complete the picture and provide Yahweh with a new situation: now he can come to the rescue.

כִּי מָרוֹ מָרִיתִי—The Versions represent the infin. abs.[172] emphasis, and the traditional translation has been '...I have been very rebellious'. Seow

---

[171] LXX ἐταράχθη, V *conturbatus est*, P ܐܬܕܠܚ and T אדנגרו. IE[1] glosses with עכורים, Kara with רותחו.
[172] Note that the Inf. Abs. מָרוֹ is similar in form to בְּכוֹ at v. 2.

(416-19) expresses surprise that 'the majority of commentators do not note the readings of the versions' and he goes on to advocate that the root מרר should undergird our interpretation of this passage. It is true that Jerome probably bases his rendering on √מרר,[173] and LXX and P are in the same camp, but T clearly interprets as from √מרה. Furthermore, at v. 18, P mistakenly translated מריתי as from √מרר—a meaning which it *cannot* have there; hence, P's rendering must not be pressed into any argument on this passage; and since LXX, at v. 18 and v. 20, employs the same Greek verb in translating מריתי, it seems as if V is the only Version which has real value in any textual argument.[174] The choice of √מרר is a natural one given that Zion at v. 4 has been described as devastated (מר), and it is in keeping with the previous sentiments of the Zion speech which began at v. 12; and especially so if one does not recognise here that Zion has had a change of heart/mind. While RSV, NJB and NIV show signs of taking this latter line of exegesis, it is JPS which emphatically conveys the confession of Zion (albeit in a rather free translation): 'I know how wrong I was to disobey'.

מִחוּץ שִׁכְּלָה־חֶרֶב בַּבַּיִת כַּמָּוֶת—The final line reminds one of words in Deut 32.25 מִחוּץ תְּשַׁכֶּל־חֶרֶב וּמֵחֲדָרִים אֵימָה; cf. also Ezek 7.15; Jer 14.18. Hillers[2] (77) refers to lines from 'Lamentation over the Destruction of Sumer and Ur' (*ANET*, 618, lines 403f.): 'Ur…inside it we die of famine/Outside we are killed by the weapons of the Elamites'. In all these passages the writers are describing desperate affliction. It is as though the message is that there is nowhere to turn for relief: inside is as bad as outside. And that must be what is meant here. Perhaps this idea underlies the reason for Zion's turning in confession to Yahweh. There is no one to turn to except Yahweh. Yahweh has caused all her pain and so she repents of her rebellion. IE[2] has seen this connection: 'I cried out and confessed when I saw the sword of the enemy making orphans in the street…'

The cryptic בַּבַּיִת כַּמָּוֶת is an ancient crux. LXX reverses the word order (while otherwise supporting MT), which may be an attempt to squeeze meaning from the text, though 'as death at home' requires some elucidation. P 'and that which is in the house of death' is a free rendering and may mean 'and death (bereaves) that which is in the house'. Several emendations have been suggested. Ehrlich (34) suggests reading אך מות 'lauter Pest', taking אך as an asseverative (cf. BDB 36). Dyserinck (365) cites a suggestion by J. G. De Hoop Scheffer—בבית תך מות, thought worthy of consideration by *BHK* but dismissed by Budde (1898ᵃ, 84).[175]

---

[173] Not on מלאתי, as *BHK* claims.
[174] Cf. Pham (48), who concludes that Versional evidence does not warrant emendation of MT.
[175] Dyserinck does not disclose his source. It seems that de Hoop Scheffer did not publish his suggestions on Lamentations, but conveyed them privately to Dyserinck, who quotes him on several occasions. Budde and *BHK* probably rely on Dyserinck's commentary here. Two letters on Lamentations from de Hoop Scheffer to Dyserinck are preserved in the library of the University of Amsterdam (Public Services Special Collections).

Perles (1920, 157f.; 1922, 57; 1930, 104),[176] observing that in Deut 32.25 we have a synonym of 'sword', suggested reading כָּמוּת = Akk. *kamûtu* 'captivity', and in this he is followed by Wiesmann (122f.), Rudolph (1962, 208) and *BHS*, though 'captivity' hardly fits the context.[177] Hillers[2] (77) reads כפן 'hunger' (an Aramaism, cf. Job 5.22; 30.3) for כמות and translates (63) 'inside it was famine'. Others follow LXX's rearrangement of the words (Meek, cf. *BHK*), or delete the כ (Schleusner, 12; Haller, 98; Kraus, 23; Plöger, 134; *BHK*), reading המות for כמות (Oettli, 207, Kaiser, 310). Cross (1983, 150), leaning on Deut 32.25, and without reference to Perles, chooses to read בבית אימות 'inside there was terror'.

The interpretation represented by AV—'abroad the sword bereaveth, at home there is as death'—is how it has been taken by several translators; cf. Calvin *domi tanquam mors*, RSV, NRSV, NJB, ESV. If MT is retained—and the majority of translations presuppose it—one solution is that pressed by Gordis (1943, 177f.; 1974a, 159), namely, that we have here an example of the asseverative כ and that we should translate 'inside is death itself';[178] cf. also McDaniel (210f.), Dahood (1978, 179), Westermann (114), Renkema (192), Gottlieb (20), Berlin (47). NIV's 'inside, there is only death' may be a free rendering but may rest on the latter interpretation; and P's translation *may* have originated from this observation.

Most of these renderings take the second stich as an independent statement. Another slant on this passage is in the realm of syntax—to view the verb שִׁכְּלָה as doing double duty (cf. Renkema, 192): Just as the sword causes me[179] bereavement in the streets, so death causes me bereavement indoors. The LXX adjustment of the word order may have been to facilitate this interpretation which is found in Luther, Michaelis (1773–88, 143), Plöger (134), Moffatt, NEB, REB. This may necessitate interpreting מות as death personified, as in Jer 9.20 'Death has come up into our windows,/it has entered our palaces,/to cut off children from the streets/and young men from the squares'; cf. also Ps 18.6; Hos 13.14; or one may see 'death' as a synonym for 'suffering' (Exod 10.17; Sir 40.9), as Ehrlich (34) 'die Pest', Moffatt, NEB, REB, Gordis (133) 'plague' have done.[180]

---

[176] Perles had, earlier (1911, 128) suggested that the word אימות had dropped out and that the original read בבית אימות כמות, which, presumably, he would have translated 'inside terrors like death'.
[177] It is true that the Chronicler saw the outcome of the fall of Jerusalem in black and white terms—people were either killed or taken captive—but we know that this was not the case as this poem, in fact, bears witness.
[178] On p. 133 of his commentary, however, his translation is 'within, it is the plague'!
[179] The LXX translator, reminding us that Zion is still speaking, includes the 1st p. s. accusative pronoun here.
[180] The comment of IE[2] reveals that his instinct is that famine is what was causing bereavement indoors, but his cryptic comment ובבית רעב כמות leaves us in the dark as to his understanding of the construction. On the final phrase, Vermigli (59) comments: 'Some interpret "a dead body". As for myself, I think that it means not just one thing, but many

There remains the exegesis of the phrases מִחוּץ and בַּבָּיִת. Pham (48) draws attention to Ezek 7.15 (cf. Jer 14.18) where בחוץ is defined by בשׂדה 'in the countryside', and מבית by בעיר 'in the city'. Pham's observation draws attention to the scenario envisaged by the poet, and her interpretation must remain a possibility; but the poem as a whole has mostly concentrated on the tragic scene within the city, and this consideration makes her exegesis less probable.

Zion recognises that there is no escape outside or in; one is between a rock and a hard place. Death seems to await everyone. The element of hyperbole should be noted again here, for if Zion's people in the streets had all been killed and those inside had met with death, there would have been no one to lament.

1.21

Text and Versions
MT שָׁמְעוּ—so also V; LXX ἀκούσατε δή; P ܫܡܥ *šm‘*; T שמעו אומיא. Read שְׁמַע.
MT הֲבֵאתָ—so also LXX, V and T; P ܐܬܐ *’yt’*. MT is preferred.

* * *

The final two verses of this poem continue Zion's direct address to Yahweh begun at v. 20. Text-critics, translators and exegetes differ on the wording of this verse and on its meaning. The final occurrence of the phrase 'I have no comforter' appears in the first line. There is a further reference to enemies gloating at Zion's plight; and the verse ends with Zion's plea for retribution on her foes (cf. Ps 143.12), a plea which continues into v. 22.

שָׁמְעוּ—LXX probably read the same consonantal text as the Masoretes but understood the form as a pl. imper.—שָׁמְעוּ. Since no subject for שָׁמְעוּ is supplied until the second line, when שָׁמְעוּ appears again, and since Yahweh has been addressed at the beginning of the previous verse and is addressed later in this verse, שָׁמְעוּ is somewhat suspect. However, LXX is also suspect in that there are no (plural) addressees in the vicinity.[181] P's singular imperative possibly preserves the original text here. Yahweh has been asked to look (v. 20): now he is being asked to listen. Many

---

troubles: hunger, siege, rebellion, shouting, tears, din of battle, a continuous fear that the city will be taken, and imagining the future.'

[181] It is likely that the LXX translator reckoned that the addressees here are the same as at v. 18. There, the addressees are כל עמים. Note the Greek extra particle δή. The LXX, elsewhere in Lamentations, uses this to represent the Hebrew נא (1.18; 5.16); indeed, ἀκούσατε δή usually renders שִׁמְעוּ־נָא (Mic 3.1; 6.1; Isa 7.13; Jer 5.21; Ezek 18.25; Lam 1.18).

commentators[182] follow this reading in spite of the fact that V and T follow MT. Albrektson (83) argues strongly for the retention of MT. He is not convinced that P read שמע, and in this he is followed by Gottlieb (20f.)[183] and Kaiser (310). Albrektson dismisses the argument by Rudolph that MT is tautological and argues that in a poetic text such as Lamentations this argument should not carry weight, pointing out that at 2.5 the verb בלע is repeated in lines 1 and 2. It is true that repetition is a device employed by poets to emphasise or underline what is being said (cf. Eccl 4.1 where an entire phrase וְאֵין לָהֶם מְנַחֵם is repeated), but the difference in this verse is that no subject appears with the first שמעו, whereas at 2.5 בלע is followed immediately by the subject (so also at 3.59f.). Nevertheless, many follow MT here.[184] In opting for שָׁמְעוּ, we have to admit that the *Vorlagen* of LXX, V and T read שמעו. We may account for what we presume to be a corrupt reading in those *Vorlagen* as having arisen under the influence of שמעו in the second line. The imperative 'hear' is followed by a construction (כִּי נֶאֱנָחָה אָנִי) similar to what follows the imperative 'see' at v. 20. The unique address to Yahweh which began in that verse is sustained: 'Hear, how I groan'.

אֵין מְנַחֵם לִי—While the author has used this phrase (or a form of it) at vv. 2, 9, 16, 17, this is the first time that Zion herself (finally) admits to Yahweh that she is without a comforter. Renkema (193) may be right in his view that by this statement Yahweh is implicitly called upon to be Zion's comforter, but I think that he interprets in the light of Isa 40.1. There the prophet picks up the language of Lamentations for his message of deliverance.

כָּל־אֹיְבַי שָׁמְעוּ רָעָתִי שָׂשׂוּ כִּי אַתָּה עָשִׂיתָ—The second line is the longest in the poem and, in the eyes of several commentators, is considered suspect. Bickell (1894, 108) deletes כָּל־אֹיְבַי as a gloss; so also *BHK* and Cross (151). This would certainly give a better-balanced line, and the phrase can be accounted for as having been a marginal gloss (copied into the text in transmission) identifying the subject of שמעו. But if the enemies are not mentioned at this point they get no specific mention at all; and this leaves plural verbs and suffixes unexplained in vv. 21f. Another note in *BHK* suggests that some scholars delete שָׂשׂוּ or אַתָּה. That שָׂשׂוּ might have have been a gloss is possible. It could be regarded as epexegetical—an expansion of the statement 'my enemies have heard of my plight', perhaps in the

---

[182] Cf. Budde (1898a, 84), Abelesz (34), Rudolph (1962, 208), Gottwald (9), Kraus (23), Westermann (114), Hillers² (77), Renkema (193), Pham (48), *BHS*, RSV, NJB, NEB; cf. also Gordis (133), who translates with an imperative but without comment!

[183] Gottlieb backs up his argument by pointing out that there is considerable orthographic inconsistency in the Syriac MSS of the Bible, where the forms ܡܠܝ and ܡܠܝ̈ are sometimes used at random; and he advises against relying on P.

[184] Cf. Provan (55), Kaiser (310), Meek (15), Berlin (44), House (334), REB, NIV, JPS, NRSV.

light of 2.16f. But this is a remote possibility in that the final words of the line (כִּי אַתָּה עָשִׂיתָ) would not follow smoothly after רָעָתִי. And if אַתָּה were to be deleted it would be difficult to account for its appearance in MT. Pham (48) tackles the problem by regarding שמעו 'as a dittography from the preceding line and to read ששו ברעתי איבי כל, "all my enemies rejoiced at the evil done to me". The ב before רעתי may have dropped out due to haplography.'
    Hillers[2] (77f.) wonders if the line is a conflation of variants:
1. All my enemies—*heard of my trouble*—that you had done it.
2. All my enemies—*rejoiced*—that you had done it.

However, our knowledge of Hebrew poetry is insufficient to say with certainty that this line is too long. The sentiments expressed here are in line with 2.16f., *viz*. the enemies' satisfaction regarding the downfall of the city. Zion has known of this mocking (v. 7) and here she emphasises that aspect of her fall.

הֵבֵאתָ יוֹם־קָרָאתָ וְיִהְיוּ כָמוֹנִי—The difficulties in the verse do not diminish as we enter the last line. Several scholars come to textual and exegetical conclusions based on the connection between vv. 21 and 22.[185] P's imperative 'bring' may mean the Syriac translator read הבא (or הבא את cf. *BHK*). As there is no doubt about the Syriac here, the imperative reading of P at the beginning of the verse appears to be confirmed. P has taken both to be addressing Yahweh. On the strength of P, many emend the text.[186] In fact, the P *Vorlage* may not have been (את) הבא. The Syriac translator, having begun with the imperative 'hear', may have interpreted הבאת as an optative (so Abelesz, 34). It is interesting to note that several translators opt for the imperative without referring at all to P. Among these is Hillers[2] (78), who explains his 'Oh bring on...' as interpreting MT as 'a case wherein the perfect is used to express a wish or request, a use that seems to be attested elsewhere in the book; cf. 4:22 and especially 3:55-66 passim, where perfects alternate with imperatives and other expressions of volitive ideas'. This stance is found in NIV 'May you bring', Gordis (160), NRSV.[187]

---

[185] Budde (1892, 267f.), deciding that it was all too complicated, recreates two 'new' verses from the various elements in the existing text and ends up with: 21cα-22bβ' / 22aα-21cβ' / 22bα-22aβ. But this is textual criticism going too far and is pure conjecture; indeed, Budde later (1898ª, 84f.) adopts a softer approach.
[186] RSV, NJB, Rudolph (1962, 208), Kraus (23), Westermann (114) all read with P. Brockington (217) explains NEB 'but hasten...' as based on a reading הבא or והבאת, the latter (*waw*-consecutive with the perfect = imperative) being possible because NEB has accepted the imperative at the beginning of the verse (GK 112r), though this is syntactically clumsy because of the intervening material.
[187] The use of the perfect as optative is common in Arabic but not so common in Hebrew. It is to be found at 1 Sam 24.15, and a comparison of the 1 Chron 17.27 with the parallel passage 2 Sam 7.29 demonstrates that it exists in Hebrew; cf. Joüon (2005, §112k). It

A factor in all of this is the phrase יוֹם־קָרָאתָ. Albrektson (84) wonders if this clause 'the day which you promised' (suppressed relative pronoun אשר) could apply to the destruction of the enemies: 'For it is a (or perhaps even *the*) fundamental idea...especially in this chapter that the present calamities are Yhwh's punishment for Israel's transgressions,...and in the light of this leading theme, and of such passages as 1.12...and 1.15...it is *a priori* likely that יום קראת in v. 21 refers to the judgment upon Israel, not to that upon the enemies. This is a strong argument for retaining MT's reading "thou hast brought"...' Albrektson has a point, and we must not lose sight of the fact that V and T, in addition to LXX, represent the verb הבאת in the past tense. Kara interprets in this way, referring to Nebuchadnezzar and the destruction of Jerusalem. Calvin, too, sees it as referring to the calamity experienced by Jerusalem and proclaimed (קרא) by the prophets ahead of time, and this is the exegesis of Meek (15), JPS, Kaiser (310) and Provan (56).

LXX has misunderstood the construction יום קראת and, having construed יום with הבאת, begins again with קראת and 'supplies' the term καιρόν, which may represent מועד as in the construction at 1.15. The difference with V *adduxisti diem consolationis* is that although representing the perfect הבאת, it has interpreted יום קראת as the time of judgment for the enemies and has translated freely: 'you have brought about a day of consolation, (and they will be like me)'.

Rashi's comment, 'Oh that you had brought upon them the appointed day which you proclaimed against me', acknowledges that the terminology alludes to Zion's punishment, but appears also to interpret הבאת as a precative. IE[1] states that the word לו is lacking before הבאת, which would make the passage amount to a wish that God had brought the day of judgment upon the enemies. So IE[2] says that it is possible that we should interpret as to the future: 'May the day come that you proclaimed through the prophets, that it will happen to them as it has happened to me'.

וְיִהְיוּ כָמוֹנִי—LXX καὶ ἐγένοντο ὅμοιοι ἐμοί 'they are become like me' makes little sense in the context, but this is probably because the translator misunderstood יום קראת. Whether the *Vorlage* was היו (*BHK*) is debateable. It may be that the translator vocalised *waw*-consecutive וַיְּהְיוּ (see Albrektson, 85). *BHK* also suggests that Aq and Sym had a *Vorlage* והיו, but the SH marginal note ܐ.ܣ ܩܣܘ cannot be interpreted so precisely.

Although T takes הבאת as referring to the past, alluding to Zion's day of reckoning, the translator looks again at the phrase יום קראת and applies it now to the enemies: 'So may you deal with them that they may become desolate like me'; that is to say, T reflects both approaches to the passage. Kara is similar. Having interpreted יום קראת as the invasion by Babylon, he comments: 'And now O Lord, bring upon them that day of punishment

should be noted that AV and RV seem to have taken the perfect as a prophetic perfect (cf. also MLT, and Freedman's translation of MR) 'Thou wilt bring the day'.

which you have promised to come upon them'. He then adds, in case we should be in any doubt: 'as if to say—As I am desolate so let them be desolate'.[188]

It is sometimes hard to keep in mind that we are dealing here with poetry, but there is something here that raises the possibility that the author may not have been so rigidly focussed. The word רָעָה is used here and at v. 22—the only two instances of the singular in the poems. They are juxtaposed here but they have different meanings. In v. 21 רָעָתִי = my plight, in v. 22 רָעָתָם = their evil (deeds). That is to say, there is a play on the word רָעָה. This play is lost in English translation, though LXX and V have attempted to convey it in Greek and Latin. There is a possibility that the author, in using הֵבֵאתָ יוֹם־קָרָאתָ, was thinking of *both* concepts of the day of Yahweh—the traditional one and the 'Amos' version. Yahweh had brought about his day, Amos fashion, in that Jerusalem had been destroyed, but the traditional day—the day in which Yahweh would prove victorious over his enemies—would certainly come to pass; and the enemies would come to ruin, like Jerusalem.

There is a sense in which line 3a, 'you have brought about the day you promised', does double duty. It is epexegetical of line 2b, 'that you have done it', and it serves to introduce 3b in that the concept of the day of Yahweh, traditionally the crushing of Israel's enemies, and though experienced by Israel herself, must still apply to them.

1.22

Text and Versions
MT לִי—so also V, P, T, SH; LXX omits; LXX reading may be due to haplography (see Albrektson, 85) or, less likely, as implied (Schäfer, *BHQ*).

* * *

The latter sentiments of v. 21 are taken further here; indeed, vv. 21-22, unlike many juxtaposed verses in the poem, clearly belong together. The previous verse raised the question of the 'day of Yahweh', a day when the

---

[188] Barthélemy (881) notes that we are left with a choice in this final line: (a) O Lord, you have already brought upon Israel the day that you have announced, i.e. the day of exile, as scripture says (Deut 31.17). And now, that they may become like me. (b) It has come upon them the day which you have announced, and they shall become like me, as you promised (Isa 6.34; Zech 3.8). (c) Bring on these enemies all the plagues that you have threatened and reduce them to impotence as I am, in that they are busy rejoicing while the Israelites who are with them are unhappy (cf. 1 Kgs 3.26). The difficulty with the first option is that the final stich is very isolated and abrupt (cf. Gottlieb, 21f.), even if v. 22 does carry on the theme. We have to read 'but let them be like me', i.e. a *waw*-adversative with the jussive. The second option allows a more smooth entry into the final stich in that the enemies are already the subject being discussed and they will end up as Zion has ended up. The third seems more in keeping with v. 22, but the use of the perfect as an imperative is unusual.

heathen enemies of Israel, who were also Yahweh's enemies, would get their due reward. Zion, having mentioned earlier that Yahweh was behind all her misfortunes and identified that with the 'day of Yahweh', seizes on the concept, as she remembers it, and asks Yahweh to implement his promises/threats. Renkema (197-99) is incorrect in saying that this prayer is not a prayer of vengeance and that its true intention is Zion's own liberation. True, it is not simply a prayer for vengeance, but it does arise from hurt feelings. The reflection that her enemies laughed at her plight sparked off this prayer. Zion, realising that her disaster was the result of her evil ways, now cannot bear the thought of the hated enemies gloating. They appear to be at ease (v. 5) and have triumphed (v. 9). They seem to have Yahweh on their side; indeed, Yahweh directed their operations (v. 17). But that promised day originally applied to these enemies; so Zion leans on this strong tradition that the evil nations, the enemies of Zion and Yahweh should meet their come-uppance.

תָּבֹא כָל־רָעָתָם לְפָנֶיךָ—The idea of evil doings coming before Yahweh has an echo at Jonah 1.2, where, speaking of the evil (רעה) of the Ninevites, Yahweh says: כִּי־עָלְתָה רָעָתָם לְפָנָי. The image is of a judge at court to whom reports have been handed. תָּבֹא is to be taken as a jussive, following on from v. 21. The term רעה, used in this poem for the first time at v. 21 where it means calamity/disaster/plight, is used again in this verse to refer to the wickedness/evil of the enemies. There is, clearly, a play on the word here which is not discernible in English translation.[189]

The balance between רָעָתִי and רָעָתָם, however, is only symbolic: the real balance is between כָּל־רָעָתָם and כָּל־פִּשְׁעֵי; and Zion is asking Yahweh for fair play: I have suffered for my rebellious/sinful ways, so why not my enemies for theirs? The poet spells it out in line 1b and line 2ab. Two jussives are followed by an imperative וְעוֹלֵל.

וְעוֹלֵל—Poel imperative from עלל I (see on v. 12). LXX translated the Poal (v. 12) with ἐγενήθη, but here the Poel, by a rare verb ἐπιφύλλισον, which seems to mean 'to glean grapes'.[190] BDB (760) lists a few passages where this meaning (from a denominative verb עלל 'to glean') obtains (e.g. Jer 6.9), but it is unsuitable here.[191] Albrektson (85) notes that P ܒܒܝܫܬܝ *trp*

---

[189] P ܒܒܝܫܬܝ, *bbyšty* / ܒܒܝܫܘܬܗܘܢ *byšwthwn* and T בישתא / בשותהום convey this in translation; and even the non-Semitic Versions—LXX τὰ κακά μου / ἡ κακία αὐτῶν and V *malum meum / malum eorum*—manage to achieve something of the original pun.
[190] At the second occurrence of the verb in this verse, LXX renders עוֹלֵלְתָּ by ἐποίησαν ἐπιφυλλίδα '(as) they made a gleaning', where the third person plural must be taken as referring to the enemies. The Greek text is possibly a corruption which has resulted from uncertainty and debate—ποιέω and ἐπιφυλλίζω might reflect two possible solutions to the difficult Hebrew.
[191] It should be noted that V *et devindemia eos sicut vindemiasti me* 'and make vintage of them as you have made vintage of me' is not necessarily leaning upon LXX here, in that

'treat roughly' is close to the meaning in this passage, though P uses ܚܒܠ
ʿbd for the same root at v. 12. Rashi glosses with ופעול למו 'and do to
them'; so also Kara. IE² paraphrases the entire clause with עשׂה להם בעבור
רעתם כאשר עשׂית לי. The comments of IE¹ show that he linked the verb
with the root of עֲלִלוֹת (= deeds) in 1 Sam 2.3.

דַּוָּי—Ehrlich (35) points out that this adjective occurs at Jer 8.18 and Isa
1.5 in connection with לב and he thinks that the term must signify a particular weakness or illness of the 'heart'. If we allow that לב does not refer
to the heart but to 'mind' or 'inner self', then the final line may be indicating that Zion's condition has two aspects: outwardly, she is constantly
groaning, and inwardly, she is ill: 'For my groans are many, and my mind
is sick'.

The final words remind Yahweh that his treatment of Zion has left her
desperate and, as with the phrase כִּי־צַר־לִי (v. 20), are a final attempt to
move Yahweh to action. כִּי is not recognised as asseverative by any of the
ancient Versions. There is a causal connection between the last line and
the two previous ones. So AV, RV, NRSV, NEB, JPS, Hillers² (64),
Westermann (112), Gottwald (9), Kaiser (310), Renkema (200). Some do
take it as emphatic—Rudolph (1962, 206), Kraus (22), JB, NIV—but an
emphatic כִּי here isolates the entire line and weakens the connection
between Zion's prayer and her state of mind.

The poet, as he nears the end, intentionally alludes to themes already
dealt with, a device which brings home to the hearer/reader the importance
of those elements. Thus v. 12 comes back at v. 18; v. 8 gets an echo at vv.
21f.; v. 2 is alluded to at v. 19; v. 1 is mentioned again at v. 19; v. 4 comes
again at v. 18; v. 11 is repeated at v. 19. Hillers² (91) likens this 'echoing'
to that of 'a composer's restatement, at the end of a movement, of the
themes with which it began'.

---

at v. 12 V renders *vindemiavit me*, independently of LXX. MR 'cut off their gleanings as
you have cut off my gleanings' preserves this interpretation.

CHAPTER 2

Introductory

We do not know if this second poem was the second to be composed. If it was, then the author intentionally copied some of the features of the first one. It begins in the same way with the exclamation 'Alas!', and like the first chapter it is an alphabetic acrostic[1] of 66 lines composed in similar rhythmic poetry; and the depiction of Zion as a female figure is repeated. Furthermore, the tragic reversal element shines through, and the dirge-like atmosphere is strong.

The structure of this poem is perhaps easier to detect than in ch. 1. Having said that, we should note that not all are in agreement. Hence the different subdivisions of Johnson (1-10, 11-22), Hillers (1-9a, 9b-17, 18-19, 20-22), Dobbs-Allsopp (1-8, 9-12, 13-19, 20-22), Berlin (1-10, 11-19, 20-22).

Verses 1-8: In this sustained passage the speaker describes Yahweh's angry assault on Judah and Jerusalem. While the author of ch. 1 made it clear that the hand of Yahweh was involved in the suffering and the devastation, the author of this second poem paints a picture of Yahweh in violent action against his people. Whereas in ch. 1 we had 'the enemy has become master', 'the enemy has triumphed', no such sentiments appear in ch. 2. Indeed, apart from v. 16, which speaks of the enemy jeering, the references to the enemy in ch. 2 (vv. 3, 17, 22) involve Yahweh, graphically, in total control, withdrawing his protecting hand as the enemy approached, handing over to the enemy, letting the enemy rejoice, summoning the enemy and filling them with pride. The sub-text seems to be 'The fall of Jerusalem was not a Babylonian triumph, either military or theological: it was a conquest by Yahweh himself'. Hence, Yahweh is the subject of verbs which show him on the rampage: 'beclouds', 'has thrown down', 'paid no heed' (v. 1), 'engulfed', 'has torn down', 'flattened', 'defiled' (v. 2), 'cut down', 'withdrawn (his protection)', 'blazed' (v. 3), 'strung (his bow)', 'killed', 'poured out (his fury)' (v. 4), 'engulfed', 'destroyed', 'multiplied (mourning)' (v. 5), 'cut down', 'destroyed',

---

[1] The alphabetic order is slightly different: ch. 1 has the traditional order (with the ע before the פ), while this chapter has the פ before the ע. This suggests a different author (see *Introduction: Acrostics*).

'erased', 'spurned' (v. 6), 'repudiated', 'disowned', 'handed over' (v. 7), 'planned (to destroy)', 'measured up', 'caused to mourn' (v. 8). There is hardly a passage in the Hebrew Bible to compare, in intensity, with this opening section.

Verses 9-10: In this brief passage the poet stands back, as it were, and takes a look at the effects of Yahweh's onslaught: the city gates and bars are no more, Judah's leaders are in exile, the cult is not functioning and the scene is one of mourning and desolation.

Verses 11-19: We noticed in ch. 1 that the voice of the lamenter gave way to a sustained passage where the speaker was the personified Zion. In this section the poet himself appears to burst in with his own feelings of grief, almost as though in response to the scene in v. 10. Identifying himself as one of the ruined people, he is moved by the sight of children dying of hunger (vv. 11-12). He then addresses Zion and acknowledges that her terrible circumstances are incomparable (v. 13, cf. 1.12). Up to this point in the poem nothing has been said regarding the reason for Yahweh's attack on Zion, but the poet now alludes to her guilt and to the failure of her prophets to expose this guilt. The implication is that the disaster could have been averted had the prophets of Judah functioned properly (v. 14). The author reflects further on the ignominy which Zion now experiences in addition to the suffering. Those who witness the devastation are depicted as jeering at the fall of Jerusalem in tragic reversal terms (v. 15); and her enemies, by which the author may mean local enemies—Edom, Moab, Ammon—are seen as gloating (v. 16). At v. 17 the poet picks up the thought of v. 8 and stresses that what Zion has experienced was not an unfortunate accident. Yahweh had planned it from of old (cf. Lev 26). This image of the aggressive Yahweh, further embellished by the description of him demolishing without pity (cf. vv. 2, 21), paints a gruesome picture, though it is in keeping with Jer 13.14. We may wonder if the merciless action of Yahweh, coupled with his destruction of temple, altar etc., could be interpreted as Yahweh permanently casting off his people, but the poet apparently does not think so. If that had been his interpretation he would not have written this poem. He *was*, however, observing that Yahweh's relationship with his people did not consist of the paraphernalia of the cult, albeit dedicated to him (cf. Jer 7.22), for he himself had destroyed them. They were not of the essence: they had merely been the props. The faith of the poet is shown in that, although he has spoken of Yahweh's aggression and lack of compassion, he encourages Zion to pray and plead with Yahweh; indeed, he urges Zion to pull out all the stops (of noise and tears) in this exercise. Perhaps it was a case of 'To whom shall we go?' (John 6.68). Perhaps the alternative to a serious approach to the prime mover in the destruction of Zion was despair.[2] There is no suggestion that Zion had suffered unjustly, but the

---

[2] Cf. Jonah 3.9 where the king of Nineveh, after having decreed a fast and repentance, says: 'Perhaps God will relent and turn from his fierce anger'.

poet feels that if Yahweh is to be moved at all it may be that the sigh starving, innocent children, the weakest members of society, will be the trigger (vv. 18, 19).

Verses 20-22: The final verses constitute the prayer of Zion, although we must surely interpret this as the prayer of the poet and, in the commemoration of the 9th of Ab, the prayer of the community. In addition to calling on Yahweh to take note (cf. 1.9c, 11c), there is a clear element of accusation here. The question 'Should women be driven to eating their own children?' appears to accuse Yahweh of going too far in his aggressive attacks. The reference to the slaughter of priest and prophet in Yahweh's temple reminds us of 1.10. Lying behind this appeal is the belief that the temple was not just dedicated to Yahweh but Yahweh's very own; hence, Yahweh is reminded (cf. Ps 79.1) that the slaughter of the cultic personnel took place in *his* sanctuary; and the sub-text is: that slaughter was *your* work, O Yahweh! (v. 20). There is no sub-text in the language that follows. The day of Yahweh is referred to twice (vv. 21, 22; cf. v. 1)—that is acknowledged—but 'you killed, you slaughtered mercilessly' (v. 21 line 3) could not be more blunt or direct. The fact that, before these words, there is a reference to the sight of Zion's slaughtered inhabitants (lines 1 and 2), puts the ball firmly in Yahweh's court. The intensity fades a little in the final verse (cf. 1.22). There is a dirge-like sadness about the final line as Zion bewails the destruction of her children at the hands of the enemy, but in the preceding lines Yahweh is accused of having invited the enemy to the scene as though to a party.

Translation

1. Alas! Yahweh beclouds Zion in anger.
   He has thrown down, heaven to earth, the glory of Israel
   And has paid no heed to his footstool in his day of anger.

2. Yahweh has engulfed, without pity, all Jacob's settlements.
   In fury he has torn down, he has flattened Judah's strongholds;
   He has defiled the kingdom and its princes.

3. He has cut down the entire might of Israel.
   He has withdrawn his right hand in the face of the foe
   And has blazed in Jacob like flaming fire which rages all around.

4. He strung his bow like an enemy, right hand in place,
   And he killed, like a foe, all who delighted the eye.
   In the tent of Zion he poured out his fury like fire.

5. Yahweh became like an enemy; he engulfed Israel,
   Engulfed all her mansions, destroyed her strongholds;
   And he multiplied mourning and moaning in Judah.

LAMENTATIONS

'n his booth as in a garden, destroyed his meeting place.
ased the memory of festival and sabbath in Zion;
nger, he spurned king and priest.

ıudiated his own altar, disowned his sanctuary;
ιιc handed over to the enemy the walls of its mansions;
They raised a clamour, in the house of Yahweh, as on a festival.

8. Yahweh had planned to destroy the wall of Zion;
He had measured up and went ahead with destruction.
He caused wall and rampart to mourn, together they languish.

9. Her gates have sunk into the ground, her bars vanished;[3]
Her king and rulers are among the nations; instruction is no more;
And her prophets receive no vision from Yahweh.

10. The elders of Zion sit upon the ground in silence,
They put earth on their heads, they gird themselves with sackcloth;
The maidens of Jerusalem bow their heads to the ground.

11. My eyes are worn out with tears, within I am in torment;
My very grief is poured out on the ground for the ruin of my people,
While infants and babes faint in the city's squares.

12. They cry to their mothers 'Where is there food and drink?'
As they faint like wounded men in the city's squares,
As their life runs out in their mothers' arms.

13. To what can I compare you or liken you, O Jerusalem?
What can I match with you to comfort you, Maid Zion?
For your ruin is great, like the sea—who can heal you?

14. The visions that your prophets had were false whitewash;
They did not expose your guilt so as to change your fortunes;
They offered you false and seductive oracles.

15. All those who pass by clap hands at you;
They whistle and shake their heads in horror at Jerusalem:
'Is this the city that was called "Perfection of Beauty", "Joy of all the Earth"?'

16. All your enemies openly rail against you.
They whistle, grind their teeth, they cry, 'We have destroyed her',
'Surely, this is the day we've waited for', 'We've achieved it',
'We've witnessed it'.

17. Yahweh did what he planned to do; he carried out the threat
That he decreed long ago; he demolished mercilessly.
He made your enemy rejoice, he promoted the might of your foes.

18. Cry out from the heart to Yahweh, O wall of Zion;
Let your tears flow down like a torrent, day and night;
Give yourself no respite, your eyes no rest.

---

[3] *Her bars vanished* prb. rdg. Heb. reads *he has broken and shattered her bars*.

19. Rise up, cry aloud in the night as the watches begin;
    Pour out your heart like water in the presence of Yahweh,
    Lift up your hands to him for the lives of your children.[4]

20. See, O Yahweh, and take note! Whom have you treated like this?
    Should women eat their own fruit, their new-born children?
    Should priest and prophet be killed in Yahweh's sanctuary?

21. Young and old are lying around in public places,
    My maidens and my young men have fallen by the sword.
    On your day of anger, you killed, you slaughtered mercilessly.

22. You summoned, as if for a festival, my attackers[5] on every side,
    And, on the day of Yahweh's wrath, no one escaped or survived.
    Those whom I bore and reared my enemy destroyed.

Commentary

2.1

Text and Versions
MT יָעִיב; LXX ἐγνόφωσεν; Aq ἐπάχυνεν; Sym συνεσκότασεν; There is no need to emend the text to read הֵעִיב (so Budde, 85, *BHK*) on the grounds that the other verbs in the verse are in the perfect. The imperfect may allude to the continued state, conveyed by the verb, within which הִשְׁלִיךְ and לֹא זָכַר are to be understood. LXX's reading may be the result of harmonising.

MT אַפּוֹ—so also LXX and V; LXX^Mss ὀργῆς θυμοῦ αὐτοῦ—so also P and T. The variation seems like a copying of בְּיוֹם חֲרוֹן אַפּוֹ at 1.12;[6] but MT is to be preferred, cf. Schäfer (*BHQ*).

* * *

The first verse of this poem begins a section (vv. 1-7) where Yahweh is depicted as active against his own people. Yahweh's anger is mentioned twice in v. 1 and several times throughout the poem and is the motivation for and explanation of his drastic actions towards what he had created—all the glory that was Israel.

אֵיכָה יָעִיב בְּאַפּוֹ אֲדֹנָי אֶת־בַּת־צִיּוֹן—The second chapter begins, as did the first, with the exclamatory and negative אֵיכָה. The meaning of יָעִיב is in doubt (cf. NRSV, NIV), as the verb (possibly the Hiphil of עוב) is a *hapax legomenon*. Traditionally, it has been understood as a denominative verb 'to becloud' from עָב 'cloud' and related to the Syriac ܥܒ *ʿwb* (Aphel 'to overcloud') and Arabic *ʿyb* 'be hidden'. So, LXX, P, Sym and V. Aq has taken an independent line, deriving the form as a Hiphil from עבה 'be

---

[4] *Your children* prb. rdg. Heb. adds *who faint with hunger at every street corner*.
[5] *My attackers* prb. rdg. meaning of Heb. uncertain.
[6] Alexander (2008, 127) explains T's rendering: '...the phrase has become so stylized in Tg. Aram. that it can be used to represent *ʾppo* on its own, as here'.

thick, fat' (Hiphil 'to make gross'). T is different again: יקוץ 'detest, despise' suggests that the translator may have derived the form before him as from the Arabic root ʿyb 'blame, revile'. These differences of opinion reflect an uneasiness with the basic meaning; and this is seen to be the case also in MR, where יעיב, in addition to being derived from עב 'cloud', is also said to mean 'condemned' (on the basis that חייבא is sometimes pronounced עייבא) or 'pained' (on the basis that כיבא is sometimes pronounced עייבא).

Rashi's comment is brief. He glosses the form with יאפיל 'darken', a verb which is unattested in Biblical Hebrew, though cognate nouns and adjectives appear there; and he quotes 1 Kgs 18.45, וְהַשָּׁמַיִם הִתְקַדְּרוּ עָבִים 'and the heavens grew black with clouds'. Kara merely glosses the form with יחשיך and indicates that the basis of his exegesis is the word עבים. MLT is in the same vein and sees a connection with 3.44, 'you have covered yourself with a cloud'. IE¹, however, while acknowledging that this exegesis exists, says that the correct interpretation is יגביה עד עב.[7] Calvin is aware of this interpretation, though he does not mention Ibn Ezra by name, and he takes it to imply that Lord is depicted as raising the daughter of Zion up in order to dash her down with greater force; but Calvin prefers the 'beclouded' exegesis.

One reason for the differences of opinion is the feeling that the notion of Yahweh 'beclouding' the Daughter of Zion[8] seems unsatisfactory in the context. Michaelis (1773–88, 417f.), perhaps leaning on T, has suggested that this *hapax* is to be interpreted on the basis of the Arabic ʿyb, and he translates *opprobrio adfecit*, pointing out that the noun ܚܣܕܐ 'yb' in Syriac has the meaning 'shame'.[9] This lead has been followed by Ehrlich ('beschimpft' [35]), Rudolph (1962, 218), Kaiser (324), Meek (16), and is reflected in some translations—NRSV ('humiliated'), JPS ('shamed'), NIV footnote ('treated with contempt'). McDaniel (34f.) and Hillers[2] (96f.) take a slightly different line by suggesting a root יעב 'treat with contempt', a root which may well lie behind תועבה (cf. *HALOT* which suggests יעב).[10]

Considerable support exists for the 'beclouded' interpretation—AV, Luther, RSV, NJB, NEB, NIV, Westermann (140), Gordis (161), Kraus (36), Renkema (215f.), Albrektson (85f.). Albrektson makes out a good case for the retention of this exegesis: 'The expression may be chosen here

---

[7] It is difficult to be certain as to the meaning here. I think he means that the passage does *not* mean 'he darkened' but 'he raised her cloudwards'. IE² points out that the Lord has raised up the Daughter of Zion in order to cast her down from a high place.

[8] On the term בַּת־צִיּוֹן, see on 1.6.

[9] Earlier, in his German translation (1773–88), Michaelis had rendered 'umwölkt'.

[10] McDaniel suggests reading הועיב, i.e. the Hiphil, with the same meaning as the Hiphil of the denominative verb תעב—'make abominable'. Hillers suggests vocalising יֹעִיב; and both refer to Ps 106.40, 'And the anger of the Lord...and he treated with contempt וַיְתָעֵב his inheritance'.

in conscious contrast to the idea of the cloud as the sign of Yahweh's merciful presence…: as Yhwh formerly descended to Zion in the cloud and filled the temple with his glory, so he now overclouds the daughter of Zion—in his anger'. It should be kept in mind that the text under discussion is poetry, and that allusions such as Albrektson refers to are quite possible. Without the phrase בְּאַפּוֹ 'in his anger', the verb might have conveyed the benign protection of God, but the presence of בְּאַפּוֹ suddenly turns the picture in the opposite direction; and the poet may have chosen the words so as to convey the assonance of עב and אף. That the anger of Yahweh is important for the understanding of this poem (Provan, 60) is seen in the fact that the concept is alluded to twice in v. 1, and in vv. 2, 3, 4, 6, 21, 22. Westermann (149) remarks that there is hardly any other place in the Old Testament with so much concentration on the wrath of God.

The second line of v. 1 depicts Yahweh in action against his people. If the first verb, in the imperfect, describes the ongoing general state of affairs, הִשְׁלִיךְ in the perfect and the following לֹא זכר together serve to describe the effect of יעיב באפו. In the Hebrew Bible, Yahweh is often the subject of הִשְׁלִיךְ. In Neh 9.11, he is depicted as flinging the Egyptians into the Sea of Reeds; at 2 Kgs 24.20, the writer uses the same verb to describe Yahweh's rejection of Jerusalem and Judah in 586 BCE, while in Ps 102.11 the psalmist experiences Yahweh's personal rejection, depicting Yahweh as picking him up and casting him aside.[11] In this line Yahweh has cast down תִּפְאֶרֶת יִשְׂרָאֵל from the heavens to earth. Westermann (144) rightly notes that there is no mythological allusion here: it is merely an expression for a complete reversal.

תִּפְאֶרֶת יִשְׂרָאֵל—The word תִּפְאֶרֶת (f. noun from √פאר I Piel 'to beautify') is used in the Hebrew Bible for finery (Isa 52.1), the greatness of a king (Est 1.4), an attribute of Yahweh (Ps 71.8). Here, the meaning may be the 'fame/honour of Israel' (cf. BDB 802), and the poet may be reflecting on Israel's great past. This would be in keeping with the contrast motif of the dirge, which typically focuses on the good old days and would echo the sentiments of 1.1. Occasionally, the term can refer to boasting (e.g. of nations, Isa 13.19), and it is possible that this is a reference to the boasting of Israel, now destroyed by Yahweh; but this is less likely. Michaelis (1773–88, 418) and Meek (16) have suggested that this is a reference to the city of Jerusalem; and Isa 13.19, which speaks of Babylon as תִּפְאֶרֶת גְּאוֹן כַּשְׂדִּים, offers some support for this. MLT identifies it with the temple and quotes Isa 64.10 in support: בֵּית קָדְשֵׁנוּ וְתִפְאַרְתֵּנוּ. Renkema (219) seems also to make this identification.[12]

---

[11] Possibly the passage which inspired IE[1]'s comments, cf. n. 1.
[12] Although at v. 6 the author is clearly speaking of the Jerusalem temple, it is possible that the phrase may also refer to it.

While there may be some ambiguity here, it is perhaps best to interpret this as a reference to Israel's illustrious past. The force of the poet's איכה 'Alas!' extends throughout the verse: he is astonished that Yahweh could take such measures against his people. Just as in 1.1, the poet is struck by the great reversal experienced by the people (although at 1.1 it is mere description), here the emphasis is on Yahweh's role in it all. Furthermore, the occurrence of the name Israel in this line should not go unnoticed. 'Israel' occurs only three times in Lamentations—all three in this chapter (at vv. 1, 3 and 5). Since it is Judah which has been vanquished, Israel the old northern state having been wiped out a century or so ago, the poet must be using the term to refer to the people of Yahweh. If this is the case, then תִּפְאֶרֶת יִשְׂרָאֵל will refer to the people's famous past. It is less likely that the phrase could apply to Jerusalem or the temple.

וְלֹא־זָכַר—To translate this 'he did not remember' is to miss some of the import of the words. It is not a reference to a lapse in memory on God's part, but an active ignoring; hence, while AV, RSV, NRSV, NIV, ESV, JB, NEB, JPS still retain this rendering, some try to sharpen the terminology: Hillers 'he had no regard', REB 'with scant regard for', NJB 'without regard for', Meek 'has given no heed'.

הֲדֹם־רַגְלָיו—'His footstool'. The term is always combined with רגלים. IE[1] defines it as כסא קטן לרגלים. In Isa 66.1 we find 'Yahweh says: Heaven is my throne and the earth my footstool'; in Ps 99.5 the psalmist cries 'worship at his footstool'; in Ps 132.7 we get 'let us enter his dwelling, let us worship at his footstool'. In 1 Chron 28.22 we have '…a house, a resting place for the Ark of the covenant of Yahweh which might serve as a footstool for our God'. Finally, Ps 110.1 reads 'I shall make your enemies your footstool'. Clearly, the phrase can be used in different ways. In Isa 66.1 and Ps 110.1 the reference is general and has to do with the status of 'Yahweh' and 'my lord', but in the Psalms and in 1 Chron 28.2 the reference seems to be cultic in nature. The T paraphrase of Lam 2.1 spells it out, 'his temple, his footstool'. MLT, which had interpreted תִּפְאֶרֶת יִשְׂרָאֵל as the temple, takes 'footstool' to mean the same thing, as does MR; and this is how Rashi and Kara understand it. Hence, the early interpretation of 'footstool' is the temple in Jerusalem. There does not appear to be any dispute about it. Calvin accepts this interpretation without question, and it is still a view that is strongly held (see footnotes in JB, NJB, JPS). However, Nägelsbach (71) suggests that the expression refers to the Ark of the covenant, and he is followed by Kraus (42)[13] and Albrektson (86). While there is no doubt that the temple was destroyed in 587 BCE (2 Kgs 25.9), there is some doubt as to the existence of the Ark at that time.

---

[13] 'הדם רגליו ist die Lade, die im AT der Zeuge und Bürge der Ehrwählung des heiligen Ortes und der Gegenwart Jahwes ist (Pss 99.5; 132.7; 1 Chron 28.2).'

Certainly, there is no reference in the Kings account to its having been either burnt or taken off as booty to Babylon. Indeed, it is possible to interpret Jer 3.16 as implying that it no longer existed, and Haran (46-58) has argued that Manasseh had destroyed the Ark and had put in its place an image of Asherah. Hillers[2] (97) is also critical of Albrektson and Kraus for their identification of the Ark as the footstool; yet, as Renkema (221) points out, it is hard to imagine that, had the Ark been lost at an earlier stage of Israel's history, some reference to its demise would not have appeared; and he argues 'the most reasonable suggestion continues to be that the ark remained in Jerusalem until its downfall in 587'. Yet another identification is Zion itself. Michaelis (1773–88, 418) and *HALOT* interpret thus, and indeed, NEB (cf. also REB) translates 'and did not remember that Zion was his footstool'. There is no doubt that the Ark's presence in the Holy of Holies rendered the latter holy ground; indeed, the temple's sanctity and the city's holy character derive from the presence of the Ark there. Hence, while it may be that the Ark was originally thought to be Yahweh's footstool, the concept may have expanded to include the temple and, indeed, the city.

בְּיוֹם אַפּוֹ—Cf. Zeph 2.3 (בְּיוֹם אַף־יְהוָה). Renkema (221) notes that this is 'a further reminder of the day of Yahweh (cf. 1.12) which has now become a reality for Israel', cf. Kraus (42). One thing is certain: whatever the various components of v. 1 mean, it is Yahweh's anger (mentioned twice in this verse) which has motivated his terrible actions. The God who had promoted Israel's glory is the one who has destroyed it; he has ignored his special relationship. Well might the poet cry, איכה!

One is struck by the violence that characterises Yahweh's actions vis-à-vis his people here. The author of ch. 1 certainly believed that Yahweh had caused the downfall of Zion and that her pain could be traced to Yahweh's anger (1.12) but he was seemingly content to describe the effects of the conquest and its aftermath on the people and their city. Here (at 2.1) and in subsequent verses the scenario is very different, and the images are quite graphic.

2.2

Text and Versions

MT (*Kethib*) לֹא—so also LXX; MT (*Qere*) וְלֹא—so also V, P and T; MT (*Kethib*) is preferred; cf. *BHQ* (119*).

MT חִלֵּל מַמְלָכָה—so also V and T; LXX ἐβεβήλωσεν βασιλέα αὐτῆς; P ܩܛܝܠܝ ܡܠܟܝܗ *qṭylyh mlkyh*. LXX may have had a *Vorlage* which read חלל מלכה, and one could explain this as being the result of haplography (Gottlieb, 23). Explaining P is more difficult: it could be that the translator had a text where word division was not clear and where the first מ of ממלכה seemed to him to belong with חלל, meaning that he read the word was חֲלָלִם. His translation, 'her slain' (Albrektson, 88; cf. Abelesz 34), may have been occasioned by the suffix on שריה and what looked like another suffix on מלכה. All three terms,[14] then, were the object of the verb הִגִּיעַ. Bickell (108) preferred to read with LXX, and he is followed by Löhr (1906, 10), Ehrlich (35), Hillers[2] (97), Gottlieb (23f.). In favour of the LXX reading is the occurrence, at v. 9, of the words 'her king and her princes'. In this case, one might explain the extra מ in MT as the result of dittography;[15] cf. *BHQ* (120*). MT is preferred.

* * *

The poet continues the picture of Yahweh in aggressive mood, active against his people. Again, the phrases and the verbs, with Yahweh as subject, are chosen to convey the idea that Yahweh himself was the cause of the disaster; and the phrase 'in his wrath', making a conscious link with 'in his anger' (v. 1), adds colour to the imagery in this verse.

בִּלַּע—This verb in the Qal has the meaning 'to swallow' (Jonah 2.1), but may also have the figurative meaning 'to demolish, destroy'. In the Piel the meaning is 'to devour, engulf'. The fact that the verb is employed five times in the chapter (vv. 2, 5 [twice], 8, 16), though not at all in the other poems, is interesting. The poet is trying to emphasise the completeness and speed of the devastation caused by Yahweh. LXX κατεπόντισεν is a strange rendering: καταπόντιζω has the meaning 'throw into the sea' or 'plunge/drown in the sea'. P ܛܒܥ *tbʿ* in the Pael means 'to plunge, dip'. The Syriac ܒܠܥ *bly* means 'to swallow', but does not seem to have a figurative meaning—hence the Syriac translator, realising that ܒܠܥ would be inadequate, turned to LXX and followed the approximate meaning of the Greek. Neither Version, however, captures the sense of בלע. V *praecipitavit* 'has destroyed' gets closer to the sense of the Hebrew (contra Kelso, 23).[16] T שיצי (Shaphel of יצא) 'complete, make an end of, destroy' has avoided using the Aramaic בלע 'swallow', probably for the same reason as P. The rendering 'to swallow', though followed by AV, RV, NIV, is inadequate here, as sensed by Luther 'vertilget', NRSV 'destroyed'; cf. also Rudolph (1962, 206), Hillers[2] (93), Kraus (36), Kaiser (324), JB, JPS. The phrase לֹא חָמַל, though (literally) 'he did not spare', is equivalent to an adverbial accusative of manner (GK 156f).[17] The direct accusative of בלע is כל נאות יעקב.

נְאוֹת—There is some confusion as to the meaning of נְאוֹת. LXX, reading τὰ ὡραῖα 'beautiful things', identified the word as the pl. of נאוה 'delightful'.

---

[14] P 'her kings' is probably a free translation, in keeping with the other plurals.
[15] Although one should be very wary about 'detecting', in the mediaeval Jewish exegetes, a reading which does not tally with MT, the text of IE[2] in *Mikraoth Gedoloth*, appears to point to the reading מלכה rather than ממלכה. There, we read והשפיל המבצרים וחלל מלכה שהיו דרים מגדל וארמון. We should note that the absence of ושריה and the presence of the plural היו, would suggest, at least, that ושריה should be restored before שהיו in the IE[2] text.
[16] But Douai erroneously translates V 'cast down headlong'; so also Coverdale.
[17] The phrase is also found at 2.17, 21; 3.43, and Yahweh is the subject each time.

Perhaps the translator was influenced by v. 1, where the phrase תִּפְאֶרֶת יִשְׂרָאֵל is the victim of Yahweh's anger. T עִידִית and V *speciosa* also appear to have made the same connection with נָאוֹה. P ܕܝܪܗ *dyrh* is the only Version which clearly takes the word as from נוה 'stopping place, settlement', from √נוה 'to wander'.[18] The word may also refer to 'grazing place'—Renkema (222), Westermann (151); but 'settlements' is, perhaps, more appropriate in this context. At vv. 5 and 8, the verb בלע is used with 'buildings' as object. This was noticed by Rashi, whose exegesis is 'houses of Jacob', and IE[1], who points out that א here is in place of ו, quoting Amos 1.2 and Zeph 2.6 in support. It is not clear why the poet uses the term 'Jacob' here, unless, as in v. 1, he is thinking of the people of Yahweh in general and wants to stress this. The settlements may refer to any habitations; and כל is employed to convey the totality of the demolition.

The second and third lines add to the picture of the angry Yahweh.

הָרַס בְּעֶבְרָתוֹ מִבְצְרֵי בַת־יְהוּדָה—The verb הרס is frequently used in contexts of violence and demolition—against altar (Judg 6.25), city (Isa 14.17), house (Prov 14.1), men (Exod 15.7). It occurs only twice in Lamentations: here and at v. 17. Here, the object is מבצרים,[19] and the 'strongholds, fortifications' mentioned again at v. 5. While casual (or even permanent) settlements throughout the country[20] were an easy prey to the invader, the fortified positions would present some difficulties. However, they too had been torn down, and Yahweh is credited with being the aggressor. In v. 1, the poet stresses Yahweh's mood in his attack on Zion. The emphasis continues here, not only by the phrase 'without mercy', but in a variation of באפו *viz* בעברתו. This phrase is used also at 3.1. עברה means 'fury' and is sometimes used in parallel with אף (e.g. Amos 1.11); but it frequently carries the idea of overflowing or excessive anger (BDB 720) and is construed with אף in Job 40.11 in the phrase עֶבְרוֹת אַפֶּךָ 'your outbursts of anger'. Hence, one might conclude that the poet was trying to raise the temperature of the scene, as it were. It should be noted that no reason is given for Yahweh's outburst.

הִגִּיעַ לָאָרֶץ—The Hiphil of √נגע (touch) 'cause to touch, apply' seems suddenly quite gentle after the foregoing lines, but the combination with לָאָרֶץ has the effect of making it a more vigorous action.[21] The Masoretes have placed an *athnaḥ* at לָאָרֶץ, which is awkward. They have understood

---

[18] Cf. Malamat (146f.). In addition to the meaning 'settlements' in MR, one finds also a (personal) interpretation from נאוה: נאותיו של יעקב 'celebrities of Jacob'; and in MLT where the phrase is interpreted 'students of wise men'.
[19] The P translator has the singular here, as he had in the first line. He may have been thinking of the single fortified city, Jerusalem; cf. Albrektson (87).
[20] On בת יהודה, see on בת ציון (1.6).
[21] LXX ἐκόλλησεν εἰς τὴν γῆν 'glued to the ground' is strange; cf. Albrektson (88).

the action as further treatment of the strongholds of Judah; and this is how T, V (probably[22]), MR, Rashi, Luther, Calvin, AV, RV, Keil (383) have interpreted. However, IE[2] and most translators and commentators read *against* the Masoretic punctuation—cf. Rudolph (1938, 105), 'הִגִּיעַ לָאָרֶץ gehört aus rhythmischen Gründen auf die 3. Zeile'; that is to say, most translators read with the *athnaḥ* at יהודה. If the rest of the verse has been correctly preserved, הִגִּיעַ לָאָרֶץ must then be seen as an idiom for 'bringing down' in a *figurative* sense (though cf. Isa 25.12; Ezek 13.14): the kingdom and its rulers, intact until the fall of Jerusalem, have been brought down. Babylon appeared to have been responsible for this, but it is Yahweh who is credited with it. However, Keil's (383) explanation that הִגִּיעַ לָאָרֶץ is epexegetical of הרס (i.e. supporting the Masoretes) should not be dismissed lightly. He argues that it should not be read with what succeeds: 'For neither does חִלֵּל need any strengthening, nor does לָאָרֶץ הִגִּיעַ suitably apply to the kingdom and its princes'. It is true that, if we read with the punctuation, the rhythm is adversely affected, but the fact that הִגִּיעַ לָאָרֶץ is not used figuratively elsewhere is in Keil's favour.

The meaning of the second stich in the third line must be associated with Isa 43.28, where Yahweh says 'I desecrated (וָאֲחַלֵּל) the princes of the sanctuary (שָׂרֵי קֹדֶשׁ)', and with Isa 47.6, where Yahweh speaks of desecrating (חִלַּלְתִּי) his inheritance and of handing them over to Babylon. In both of these passages the invasion of Judah by Babylon is interpreted as Yahweh himself polluting or desecrating.[23] Lamentations 2.2 may be the source for the Isaiah passages. While either LXX or MT may be the original, MT 'the kingdom and its princes' is probably a better fit with the Isaiah passages. The language used implies the breaking of the special relationship between Yahweh and his people. The verb, which has the basic meaning 'to untie' (*HALOT*), has to do with the profanation of the holy—the treating as profane that which is sacred. The conquest of Judah means that Yahweh no longer regards Zion as a holy entity (cf. גּוֹי קָדוֹשׁ, Exod 19.6; עַם קדוֹשׁ, Deut 14.2): 'After such devastation daughter Zion is now outlawed. She can no longer rely on YHWH. He has cut his connections with her' (Renkema, 226).

The author wants to emphasise the devastation that has been caused by the invasion—settlements and strongholds alike have been levelled. The very angry Yahweh is depicted as the ruthless aggressor bent on utter destruction. No reason is given for the attack other than he is angry (one has to wait until v. 14 for a veiled reference to Zion's iniquity). The final statement on the sacred status of Israel as a holy people (cf. Exod 19.6; Deut 14.2) sounds a tragic note. Yahweh appears to have put an end to this.

---

[22] V is slightly ambiguous, but is translated by Coverdale, Douai and Knox in this way.
[23] At Ps 79.1 it is the heathen invaders who are said to contaminate (טמא) the temple, but the author of Lam 2 might have interpreted that action as Yahweh's doing.

2.3

Text and Versions

MT בָּחֳרִי־אָף; LXX ἐν ὀργῇ θυμοῦ αὐτοῦ—so also P. Some MSS of V and T agree with MT, and some with LXX. The variation is natural. It is likely that MT is original and that the possessive has been influenced by the suffix (אַפּוֹ) at v. 1, cf. *BHQ*. We may note that Luther, AV, NEB, NJB translate as though the suffix were present, but no mention is made of emendation.

MT אָכְלָה סָבִיב; LXX καὶ κατέφαγεν πάντα τὰ κύκλῳ; V *devorantis in gyro*; P ܐܟܠܬ ܐܝܕܘܗܝ *'klt 'ydwhy*; T אכלת חזור חזור. V and T probably had the same *Vorlage* as the Masoretes, but V vocalised the form as a participle, *viz* אֹכְלָה. The LXX translator is usually very literal and so may have had a different *Vorlage*. Bickell (108) and Kelso (24) take the view that כֹּל (= πάντα) is original here, but it is likely that the Greek translator read the last three consonants of אכלה twice—אכלה כל הסביב—so Albrektson (90) and Schäfer (*BHQ*, 120*). P ܐܝܕܘܗܝ *'ydwhy* does not make sense and is probably a corruption of ܚܕܪܘܗܝ *ḥdrwhy* (cf. P on Jer 50.32) 'his surroundings'—so Abelesz (8), *BHK*, Rudolph (1938, 106), Albrektson (90f.), *BHQ*—which would be a free rendering of סביב. MT is preferred.

* * *

In this verse the poet appears to focus on the reason Judah was unable to defend herself. Yahweh, again the protagonist, was active in removing her defences and refrained from offering protection against the enemy. Yahweh's aggression against the people is such that he is likened to an all-consuming fire.

גָּדַע בָּחֳרִי־אָף—The verb √גדע (Qal) often means 'cut down, cut off' (cf. Arabic *jada'a*) and probably carries with it the idea of mutilation; that is to say, it is not used in a positive context. It is used in parallel with √שבר 'break' in Jer 48.25; 50.23. The usage here is close to that at Amos 3.14, where it is used of hacking off the horns of an altar, and at Ps 75.11, where the horns of the wicked will be cut off. Again, Yahweh's mood is stressed by the phrase בָּחֳרִי־אָף, which is akin to בחרון אף (cf. 2 Chron 28.13). Renkema (226) observes that there is a difference in the contextual use of both terms: חרון (1.12) is found only as describing divine wrath, whereas חרי usually describes human anger: 'Yahweh's anger is presented with a more anthropomorphic colouring in the present colon and thereby becomes more humanly conceivable. For this reason the 3m sg suffix is unnecessary with אָף...'

כֹּל קֶרֶן יִשְׂרָאֵל—The noun קֶרֶן (cf. also v. 17) may refer to the horn of an animal (e.g. a ram, Gen 22.13), which could be used as a wind-instrument (Josh 6.5) or an oil-container (1 Sam 16.1). It may also refer to the (horn-like) projections of an altar (Amos 3.14; Jer 17.1). However, quite often in the Hebrew Bible it is used figuratively. At Deut 33.17 and Ps 18.3 it is a symbol of strength, while at 1 Sam 2.1, 10 it may include an element of dignity as well as strength. At Ps 75.5, 'to raise the horn', seems to carry the idea of arrogance (REB). It is not clear what precise sense is intended here. While LXX, P and V leave the image intact, T[24] יקרא ישראל 'glory of Israel' has decided that the imagery must be spelled out, though 'glory' may be going too far, in that תפארת ישראל (v. 1), very close in concept, has already been mentioned. Since 'every horn of Israel' is simply obscure in a culture/language where the imagery is not found,[25] it is best to avoid the literal rendering as in RSV 'all the might of Israel'; cf. also JPS, ESV, NJB, NRSV, Kaiser (325), Westermann (141), Kraus (36). NEB (REB) 'the horn of Israel's pride' is an attempt to retain something of the original imagery, but the result is not sufficiently transparent. The decision as to whether the clause refers to 'strength' or 'pride' depends to some extent on the context. The second line has to do with Yahweh declining to protect the people against the enemy, while the third depicts him as consuming the land. The first line, then, probably refers to the removing of the people's defensive and attacking strength, rather than their pride; cf. Keil (496).[26]

הֵשִׁיב אָחוֹר יְמִינוֹ—LXX ἀπέστρεψεν ὀπίσω 'he turned back' is too literal a rendering. The background to this language is the idea that Yahweh, the God of Israel, was her protector and deliverer, and there are a number of passages where Yahweh's right hand is credited with achieving victory for his people and with protecting them (Exod 15.6; Pss 20.7; 98.1; 108.7). However, the exact opposite is the case here. Yahweh did not intervene in face of the enemy. His right hand, which could make all the difference, had been withdrawn, and Israel had been left powerless and defenceless (cf. MLT). T paraphrases 'He withdrew his right hand and did not help his people...' The notion of holding back the (right) hand is found at Ps 74.11—לָמָּה תָשִׁיב יָדְךָ. Blayney (311f.), Nägelsbach (74) and Hillers[2] (98) take the suffix on יְמִינוֹ to refer to Israel—it is Israel's strength (paralleling כל קרן ישראל) which Yahweh turned back; but this is to fly in the face of biblical evidence (Ps 74.11) and the context. Yahweh is the protagonist throughout this verse, and it is most natural to understand the suffix as referring to him.[27]

---

[24] T draws on MR here, where ten horns are referred to: of Abraham, of Isaac, of Joseph, of Moses, of the Torah, of the priesthood, of the Levites, of prophecy, of the Temple, and of Israel. When it comes to the horn of Israel, the reference is to Ps 148.14. The Midrash speaks of these horns being set upon the head of Israel in such a way that they appear as honour or glory.

[25] Though many retain it—Luther, Calvin, AV, Vermigli (74), RV, NIV, JB, Rudolph (1962, 216), Hillers[2] (93), Renkema (226), Berlin (62).

[26] IE[2] makes a cryptic note to the effect that the phrase כל קרן ישראל means both kingdoms (Israel and Judah). Ahlström's (95) suggestion that 'horn' represents the king in this passage has little support, though NIV's footnote entertains it; cf. Albrektson (89f.).

[27] Rashi had interpreted as Yahweh himself withdrawing from the waging of war on behalf of his children. Kara, quoting Exod 15.6, points out that God's right hand which until now had been a protecting cover over Israel, now stands against her; as if to say: he had withdrawn his hand from helping them as it was taught in the past.

מִפְּנֵי אוֹיֵב—Literally 'from before the enemy'. LXX ἀπὸ προσώπου ἐχθροῦ 'from the face of the enemy' is, again, quite literal, as is V *a facie inimici*. The prepositional phrase מִפְּנֵי could mean 'from the presence of', 'from before' or 'because of' (BDB 818). The idea here is of the advancing enemy which Israel now faces without the aid of Yahweh's protection. The translation should reflect this—thus Luther 'da der Feind kam' and NEB 'as the enemy came on', cf. Rudolph (1962, 216).

וַיִּבְעַר בְּיַעֲקֹב כְּאֵשׁ לֶהָבָה—This is the first *waw* consecutive of the poem. LXX καὶ ἀνῆψεν ἐν Ιακωβ ὡς πῦρ φλόγα appears to have taken בער as transitive, with להבה as the object. Although √בער in the Qal is usually intransitive, Ps 83.15 is a passage where it appears to be transitive; hence we cannot assume that LXX read a Piel here (see Albrektson, 90). But the action here is not of Yahweh setting fire to the countryside, a concept which would be shocking enough: it is a picture of Yahweh himself depicted as a fire blazing all around him. The poet has credited Yahweh with devastation in the previous verses. In this final line of verse 3, the poet produces 'a daring and climactic image', as Renkema (228) puts it. The fire which consumed all around is none other than Yahweh himself! Although the third line is a bit long, it should not necessarily lead to deletion.[28] While the text is quite intelligible without להבה, the fact that in Isa 4.5 we get the same combination (אֵשׁ להבה) and in Ps 105.32 we find אֵשׁ להבות should prevent us from being too hasty here. The poet usually keeps to the 3:2 metre, but he is not rigid; and the Versions represent להבה.

אָכְלָה סָבִיב—As it stands in MT, the perfect tense of √אכל presupposes a (suppressed) relative pronoun (אשר). V *devorantis* has vocalised the form as a participle, *viz* אֹכְלָה, thus obviating the need for the relative pronoun. LXX καὶ κατέφαγεν has vocalised as per MT, has not assumed a suppressed pronoun, but has added καὶ to make the link.

Yahweh is depicted as increasingly violent and hostile in his rage against Judah. He is seen as a ruthless warrior hacking away all Judah's might, offering no protection from the enemy aggression and, indeed, in the most violent imagery yet, appears equivalent to a blazing and consuming fire.

2.4

Text and Versions
MT נִצָּב—LXX ἐστερέωσεν; cf. also P, V and T; unpointed *Vorlagen* and difficult syntax led to the treatment of the form as finite verb to parallel דרך in the first stich. MT is preferred.
MT כִּצָר וַיַּהֲרֹג—so LXX, P, V and T; the transposition of these words—כִּצָּר וַיַּהֲרֹג—makes for good sense and is probably the original reading.

[28] Ehrlich (35) deletes כאש, while Löhr (1893, 6) and Hillers² (98) delete להבה.

MT עֵינִי—so also V and T; LXX ὀφθαλμῶν μου; P ܥܝܢܝ 'yn'.
It may be that LXX's *Vorlage* read עיני, but Zion is not the speaker here, hence MT is superior. P's plural 'eyes' is a natural interpretation, not untypical of P.

* * *

The poet perceives Yahweh's actions as those of an enemy. In the previous verse Yahweh is depicted as withdrawing his help as the enemy closed in, thereby leaving Israel naked and vulnerable. While one might construe Yahweh's actions in vv. 1-3 and 6-9 as those of the enemy, it is only in vv. 4f. that the poet allows himself to articulate what he feels to be the case: Yahweh is like an enemy! We should note that the anger of God continues to be emphasised. Yahweh is not mentioned by name in v. 3 or v. 4, but it is clear that he is the subject of all the verbs; and vv. 3f. are further linked by the occurrence of the nouns 'right hand', 'enemy' and 'fire' in both verses. Nevertheless, the verse is fraught with problems—in punctuation, in syntax and in exegesis—and has attracted several critical comments.

דָּרַךְ קַשְׁתּוֹ—The image is of a hunter/archer preparing to attack by stringing[29] his bow. This, it seems, was done by placing the foot against the base of the bow whilst bending it so as to engage the string.[30] The image is found again at 3.12, and at Ps 7.13; Jer 9.2; 46.9; 50.14, 29; 51.3. At v. 3 one image was of Yahweh as a warrior wielding a great sword; here the poet imagines him representing the invader's archers.

כְּאוֹיֵב—T, MR and MLT are concerned that Yahweh is not seen as the enemy itself but that he is acting *like* an enemy.[31] Here, and v. 5, are the only passages in the Hebrew Bible where the phrase occurs. Renkema (229) is correct when he observes that the poet hesitates to call Yahweh the enemy. If Yahweh were the enemy '...in the absolute sense of the word then there would be no more point in turning to him for help'.[32]

---

[29] P employs the verb ܡܠܐ *ml'* to translate (as also at 3.12, though at Ps 7.13 the verb is ܡܬܚ *mth* 'stretch'). According to Payne Smith (1903, 274), ܡܠܐ *ml'* can mean 'to draw (a bow)', a meaning which seems to go beyond the Hebrew and beyond LXX ἐνέτεινεν and may refer to the actual fitting (i.e. filling the bow) of an arrow to the bow. T מתח 'stretch', depicts Yahweh as the archer with his bow ready to be discharged and goes on to specify that Yahweh 'shot arrows at me (עלי)'. Here the Targumist gives the impression that the speaker is Zion, though there is no suggestion of this in the Hebrew; cf. LXX 'my eyes' later in the verse. V *tetendit* is more ambiguous.
[30] Rashi carefully explains the image and the reason for the use of the verb דרך.
[31] In this regard, we may note that T has understood the suffix on ימינו to refer to Nebuchadnezzar: 'He stood ready at the right of Nebuchadnezzar and helped him'. This kind of allusion is frequent in Midrash and, in fact, MR makes reference to Pharaoh and Haman in this context.
[32] Gordis (161f.) and Berlin (62, 66) regard the כ on כְּאוֹיֵב and כְּצָר as the preposition 'like' but at v. 5 take the כ to be asseverative, while Dobbs-Allsopp (2002, 83) regards the כ in

נִצָּב יְמִינוֹ כְּצָר—The second stich and the following words are problematic, and several emendations have been suggested. That there was some confusion as to syntax in the early stages of exegesis is seen from the appearance of *zaqeph qaton* on adjacent forms, *viz* וַיַּהֲרֹג and כְּצָר. According to the punctuation, כְּצָר should be read, syntactically, with נִצָּב יְמִינוֹ, but if כְּצָר is placed at the end of line 1, then line 2 is rather short, and line 1 rather long. Accordingly, *BHK* and *BHS* (but not *BHQ*) place כְּצָר with line 2. One should not, however, press arguments based on metre too far, and LXX, P, V and T read according to the Masoretic punctuation. If we set aside metrical considerations, there is a certain balance obtained: He has strung his bow like an enemy//His right hand is set like a foe, cf. RSV, JB, JPS, NRSV. A grammatical objection to this is that יָמִין is f. while נצב is m., though IE¹ points out that at Exod 15.6[33] יָמִין is construed as m. It is perhaps because of grammatical propriety that LXX, P and V take נצב to be a finite verb[34] with יָמִין as the object,[35] translating 'he steadied his right hand like a foe'. The exegesis here would be that Yahweh, as archer, not only had prepared his bow for attack but was ready to discharge, with his right hand in position on the bow-string. The trouble with this is that נִצָּב (vocalised as Niphal participle by the Masoretes) is not a transitive verb and, unless we emend to Hiphil הִצִּיב, or go with Perles, the sense is not there. If we retain MT, we acknowledge that יָמִין is construed here as masculine, and we may translate 'his right hand (was) in position', that is, he is ready to shoot; cf. Kraus (37) '"aufgerichtet ist seine Rechte', d.h.: sie ist schußbereit erhoben'.[36] Albrektson (91), quoting Isa 3.13, נִצָּב לָרִיב יְהוָה, argues that נצב means 'stand ready' and translates 'standing ready with his right hand'—יְמִינוֹ being taken as an accusative of manner (GK 118m); and he is followed by Renkema (230); cf. Reindl (528). The advantage of this interpretation is that נִצָּב now refers to Yahweh, and the gender issue no longer exists. Torczyner (403) had suggested that the original reading was חֵץ בִּימִינוֹ 'arrow in his right hand'—so also Kaiser (325) and Westermann (144)—and this is picked up by Rudolph (1938, 106) who reads חִצָּו בִּימִינוֹ 'his arrows in his right hand'. Hillers² (98) takes another line. In Judg 3.22, the form הַנִּצָּב must mean 'hilt/handle' (LXX λαβη; cf. BDB 662), and Hillers supposes that a *beth* has dropped out of the text through haplography. He reads נִצָּב בִּימִינוֹ and translates 'the sword

---

each case as the preposition, but as a theological addition to prevent Yahweh being regarded as an actual enemy.

[33] The text reads יְמִינְךָ יְהוָה נֶאְדָּרִי בַּכֹּחַ יְמִינְךָ יְהוָה תִּרְעַץ אוֹיֵב, where יָמִין is construed first as m. (נֶאְדָּרִי) and then as f. (תִּרְעַץ). Rashbam argues that נֶאְדָּרִי here refers not to יָמִין but to Yahweh. (Lockshin, 154).

[34] Perles (1911/12, 128) suggests pointing נִצֵּב (as Piel), comp. Arabic *naṣṣaba* used of the horse pricking up the ears'. Gottlieb (26) thinks that this may well explain the renderings in the Versions.

[35] Kelso (25) thinks that these Versions read a Hiphil—הִצִּיב, and one should note here that at 3.12 the Hiphil of נצב is used in a similar context.

[36] This is substantially the line taken by IE¹, Kara, RSV, NRSV, NIV, Gottwald (10).

hilt was in his right hand'. However, this latter suggestion conflicts with the imagery of the hostile archer. The picture of Yahweh with sword in hand was offered in the previous verse.

Considerations of metre have led some scholars to delete certain elements from the text. Thus Löhr (1893, 6) deletes ימינו, and Budde (1898a, 86) deletes כצר. Gordis (161), while more cautious, has suggested some rearrangement, namely,

דרך קשתו כאויב נצב כצר
ויהרג ימינו כל מחמדי עין

and translates (135), 'He bends his bow like an enemy, poised like a foe./ His right hand has slain all our handsome men.'[37] Certainly, some explanation is called for. Watson (1984, 332-35) raises the question of enjambment, which may help to explain some aspects of this passage, in particular the awkward position of כצר. Retaining MT, we may translate 'standing ready with his right hand like a foe'.

Several translators feel that כצר belongs with ויהרג yet the sequence כצר ויהרג is awkward Hebrew (and the double use of *zakeph qaton* suggests that the Masoretes were aware of this); hence, the words are transposed by *BHK, BHS*, Kraus (37), Meek (17), Rudolph (1938, 106)—see also NIV, NJB—in spite of the fact that there is no textual or Versional support for such a measure. Hillers[1] (37), who concludes that the corruption in this passage is deep and real, thinks that a verb has dropped out after כצר and suggests הִכָּה (Hiphil of √נכה). His translation is 'like a foe, he smote and slew all those...' Having introduced the idea of the sword in the previous line, it is the sword which is used to smite and to kill. Both Westermann (144) and Kaiser (325) accept the Hillers suggestion, while Renkema (232), though finding the idea of a missing verb attractive, feels that the verb ירה (often used for the shooting of arrows, e.g. Exod 19.13) has an advantage over הכה in that its absence may be explained as a combination of *aberratio oculi* and *metathesis*. He points out that ירה carries on the image of the archer. However, it should be noted that Renkema merely raises this as a better alternative. He prefers MT and explains כצר as the end of the poetic line running into line two (enjambment). Albrektson (92) observes that, without vocalisation, כצר looks like a verb in the perfect. There being no verb כצר, he wonders if the original reading was בצר 'cut off', which would fit well with the following ויהרג.[38] There are no easy solutions to the problem, but the awkwardness of this passage is best tackled by taking MT's Niphal participle to refer to the right hand (his right hand in place) and by conceding that כְּצָר, which belongs *after* וַיַּהֲרֹג, had been transferred, in the course of transmission, to

---

[37] NEB (cf. REB) may owe something to Gordis here, but Brockington does not acknowledge this.

[38] He points out that this reading is found in a Hebrew MS (cf. Kennicott *ad loc*) and while it may be a scribal error there, it does draw attention to the common confusion between ב and כ in Hebrew texts, the basis of his suggestion.

its present position because of the balance with כאויב. The latter belongs with the verb denoting the stringing of the bow, while כְּצָר belongs with the verb denoting 'killing': נִצָּב יְמִינוֹ וַיַּהֲרֹג כְּצָר.

כֹּל מַחֲמַדֵּי־עָיִן—As object of the verb הרג, it is most natural to think of the phrase as referring to people, perhaps the fine specimens of Zion. Although הרג usually has humans or beasts as its object, it can mean 'ruin, destroy' in passages such as Job 5.2 and Prov 1.32; and it may be that early in the history of the interpretation of this passage there was felt that some ambiguity existed here. T, although a paraphrase, appears to have preserved both possibilities: 'He slew every young man and everything beautiful to see',[39] while V's *et occidit omne quod pulchrum erat visu* is, perhaps, ambiguous.[40] However, most translators tend to favour the human slaughter interpretation: Luther, Calvin, AV, RSV, NIV, NJB, JPS.

בְּאֹהֶל בַּת־צִיּוֹן—The first stich of line 3 is sometimes taken as referring to the place where the slaughter took place, although the *athnaḥ* suggests otherwise. LXX and P have read it this way; also Calvin, AV, RSV, NRSV. T (and possibly V, though see Douai) renders according to the Masoretic punctuation. *BHK* tentatively suggests transposing the stichoi of line 3; and, certainly, a transposition would remove the ambiguity. Luther renders as though he had made the adjustment himself, and the translations of NEB, REB, JPS and NIV follow in his footsteps. But there seems no need for actual transposition (cf. Kaiser, 325 n. 9). It is perfectly acceptable Hebrew, and all the Versions vouch for the present order.

בְּאֹהֶל בַּת־צִיּוֹן שָׁפַךְ כָּאֵשׁ חֲמָתוֹ—Is the poet referring to the temple in Jerusalem or simply to Jerusalem? The temple is called אֹהֶל in Pss 15.1; 27.5; 61.5; 78.60, but Jerusalem is also called אֹהֶל at Isa 33.20; 54.2 (cf. Jer 10.20). In Pss 27.5 and 61.5 the reference is to Yahweh's refuge and not specifically to the temple. In these passages it is not Yahweh's tent but the tent/dwelling-place of Zion, hence it is likely that Jerusalem is meant here. This is not to say that the temple is excluded, but the passage echoes the final words of Ezek 9.8 where Yahweh is said to have poured out his fury on Jerusalem. Those taking it as the temple are T, Ewald (332), Kaiser (334), JPS 'the Tent of Fair Zion'; but most commentators take it to be a reference to Jerusalem. The poetic idea of wrath being poured out is found at 4.11; Hos 5.10; Jer 6.11. In the Hosea passage, the prophet likens it to poured-out water, while here it is 'like fire' picking up the terminology of v. 3a. On the phrase בַּת־צִיּוֹן, see on 1.6.

---

[39] Indeed, Blayney (312), following Lowth (1807, xxxixf.), suggests restoring כל נער on the basis of T, claiming that the metre demands it.
[40] Coverdale renders it: 'and every thing that was pleasant to see he hath smitten down', but see Douai.

The connection between the archery and the fire may be the image of the flaming arrows of the Babylonian army raining down on the city and setting it ablaze (2 Kgs 25.9). The poet asks his readers to consider that experience as the work of Yahweh, the expression of his wrath; and here we must note this further reference to Yahweh's anger pouring out his wrath upon the city. The poet exaggerates to make his point, a point which is already mind-stretching in that Yahweh is the subject of הרג. The idea that Yahweh is responsible for the atrocities has already been absorbed in previous verses. Does the poet refer to the Babylonian slaughter or to starvation, alluded to in 1.19? While הרג may be employed with inanimate objects (Ps 78.47), it is never elsewhere used with buildings as object, a view entertained by Renkema (233). The fact that this line follows one where the image is of the archer preparing to strike should rule out the idea of an inanimate interpretation of כֹּל מַחֲמַדֵּי־עָיִן. The poet has inherited a tradition where Yahweh was known to have slain in judgment (Gen 20.4; Exod 4.23; Amos 2.3), but the expectation was that the enemies of Israel would be the target. Hosea (6.5) had used the verb figuratively to speak of Yahweh attacking his people by means of the prophets, but this is not figurative language (cf. v. 21), though there is some hyperbole here.

The images in this verse are dire and stark. Yahweh is the hostile archer who kills Zion's fine specimens. That right hand of his, which might have been expected to protect Zion, but which was withdrawn as the enemy approached (v. 3), is depicted as being actually involved in her downfall. Yahweh's fury is like fire poured out upon the city.

2.5

Text and Versions

MT אַרְמְנוֹתֶיהָ—so also LXX, P and T; Sym τὰ βασίλεια αὐτῆς; Sym repeats this rendering at v. 7. MT is not in doubt.

MT תַּאֲנִיָּה וַאֲנִיָּה—so also Aq and T; LXX ταπεινουμένην καὶ τεταπεινωμένην; V *humiliatum et humiliatam*; P ܪܘܒܐ ܘܐܒܠܐ *twny' w'wlyt'*; Sym κατώδυνον καὶ ὀδυνωμένην. It is difficult to say if the *Vorlagen* of the Versions differed from MT. The unusual words occur again only at Isa 29.2 where P and V render as Aq and T here. MT is preferred; see below.

* * *

This is the first verse in ch. 2 which does not describe Yahweh's actions as performed in anger, but the mood is no less intense. Yahweh is again depicted as having behaved as an enemy, engulfing (the verb is employed twice) palaces and strongholds and actively increasing mourning and moaning.

The verse is firmly bound to what precedes by the depiction of Yahweh as enemy and by the repetition of בלע (v. 2) and 'Israel' (v. 3). The verb שחת, confined in Lamentations to this chapter, is used in vv. 5, 6 and 8.

This is in keeping with the intensity of the Babylonian invasion, conceived here as Yahweh's doing. IE² takes the overwhelming of Israel here to refer to the exile of the northern kingdom, after which Judah was in lament. This interpretation may have originated with MR and MLT, where the exile of the ten tribes is also alluded to.

הָיָה אֲדֹנָי כְּאוֹיֵב—Again, MR and MLT are careful to point out that Yahweh is not the enemy but that he became *like* an enemy. In this way, the concept of a malicious Yahweh is avoided. Yahweh may be acting with extreme violence against his people, and he may have aided the Babylonian invaders, but it cannot be said that he is the enemy of Israel. The poet clearly believes that the divine action has a meaning, however obscure. Whether 'he became like an enemy' means something significantly different from 'he strung his bow like an enemy' is not clear. Perhaps the poet simply wants to underline what he has said in v. 4, but perhaps, having raised the enemy-like actions of Yahweh, he wants to make it clear that one may conclude that Yahweh became like an enemy in every respect. This is the reason for the following actions.

Albrektson (93) notes that P omits the preposition 'like' here. Since P *does* represent the preposition in v. 4, Albrektson thinks that P may have read לאויב. Gordis (162)[41] holds that the *qaph* is the asseverative *qaph* and that the meaning is 'Yahweh has become the enemy'. If this is so, it might account for the absence of the preposition in P; but the fact that it is represented in the other Versions and that it is interpreted there as a preposition makes this view doubtful.[42] The construction is similar to היתה כאלמנה in 1.1.

בִּלַּע יִשְׂרָאֵל—In v. 2 the poet refers to Yahweh demolishing the 'habitations of Jacob'. When he now says that Yahweh has demolished Israel he is making the stark point that the covenant people, Israel, have been destroyed by Yahweh, the God of Israel. He employs the verb again as he specifies the destruction of palaces and strongholds. There is, therefore, some repetition here, as the strongholds are already mentioned (v. 2) as having been torn down.

בִּלַּע כָּל־אַרְמְנוֹתֶיהָ—MLT gives the meaning of ארמון as פלטרין i.e. 'palace'. Although it appears frequently in the prophetic literature, the word only occurs in Lamentations here and at v. 7. In both instances it is in the plural with f. s. suffix. 'Palaces' (P, T, Luther, Calvin, AV, RSV, NIV, NRSV, ESV) may be too strong a word with which to translate this term (cf. also

---

[41] So also Berlin (66), Hillers² (93), Pham (98); cf. Dobbs-Allsopp's explanation (2002, 83f.).
[42] The juxtaposition with כאויב and כצר (v. 4), where even Gordis translates the כ as a preposition, argues against the asseverative *qaph* here in v. 5; besides, 'he became an enemy' in Hebrew is more likely to be היה לאויב.

JPS 'citadels'). LXX τὰς βάρεις αὐτῆς may mean 'her mansions', V *moenia eius* could be translated 'her dwellings'. REB's 'mansions', which may include royal residences as well as other fine buildings (cf. Jer 52.13), may be the best rendering. The question of the suffixes on אַרְמְנוֹתֶיהָ and מִבְצָרָיו is a vexed one. Have they the same referent, *viz* Israel, or does the poet have Jerusalem in mind when he speaks of אַרְמְנוֹתֶיהָ and Israel when he thinks of מִבְצָרָיו?[43] The tendency has been to emend the text to read ארמנותיו, bringing it into line with מבצריו—so Budde (87), Löhr (1906, 11), Ehrlich (36), Meek (18), *BHK*)—or to read ארמנותו השחת—so Wutz (1933, 204), followed by Rudolph (1938, 106), Kaiser (325) and *BHS*.[44] LXX and P, however, appear to have read a text identical with MT, while the grammar of Latin does not allow us to draw any conclusion from V *eius...eius*. Schäfer (*BHQ*, 120*) is probably correct in maintaining that the *lectio difiicilior* must not be altered here. Keil (497) had argued for the retention of MT. 'The interchange of the suffixes יה and יו is accounted for on the ground that, when the writer was thinking of the citadels, the city hovers before his mind; and when he regarded the fortresses, the people of Israel similarly presented themselves. The same interchange is found in Hos 8.14; the assumption of a textual error, therefore, together with the conjectures based on that assumption, is shown to be untenable.' Whether Keil is correct or whether it is simply a stylistic variation (cf. Gottlieb, 27) it is difficult to say, but Kraus (37) and Westermann (144), Albrektson (93), Renkema (236), Hillers[2] (93) do not emend, though only the latter two represent the difference in their translations. Hence, we may deduce from other translations which do not claim to be based on an emendation, but which have the same personal possessive pronoun—JB ('her' twice), NEB ('their' twice), NJB, RSV, NRSV ('its' twice)—that 'her...his' would be infelicitous in a translation.

וַיֶּרֶב בְּבַת־יְהוּדָה—Because the unvocalised text is ambiguous (וירב could be Qal or Hiphil) Rashi and, to a lesser extent, IE[1] and Kara, are concerned to draw attention to the pointing beneath the *yod*, which shows (i.e. interpreted by the Masoretes) that it is a Hiphil form. Judah[45] had experienced the richness of Yahweh's grace to them. He had multiplied them as a nation and had increased their prosperity (Gen 15.1; 16.10; 26.4; Deut 1.10; 7.13; Isa 51.2), but the same Yahweh who has now become like an enemy and—still the subject of this verb—increases adversity. The only increasing Yahweh does in this poem (or in any of the other four) is negative!

תַּאֲנִיָּה וַאֲנִיָּה—Both words are f. nouns from √אנה I 'to mourn, lament'. They occur only here and at Isa 29.2. They appear to have been lifted from Isa

---

[43] Cf. Hillers[2] (93) 'her citadels...his fortresses'.
[44] Michaelis (1773–88, 419) reads ארמנות יה which he takes to mean 'shrines of Yahweh'.
[45] On בת יהודה, see on בת ציון (1.6).

29.2. Indeed, MR Proem 26 appears to take the Isaiah passage as the prediction of what the poet is describing here. MLT explains the terms with לשון עצב ולשון אנינות while Rashi glosses them with צער ויללה. It may be that in mediaeval times there was some doubt as to the meaning of the words, for IE¹ also shows an interest by pointing out that the *taw* of the form תַּאֲנִיָּה is a nominal prefix and that it is from the same root as ואנו in the passage ואנו ואבלו Isa 3.26; and Kara glosses the phrase with אנינות ואבילות which is much the same as the rendering in T. The poet employs the phrase here because of the paronomasia of the two words (cf. תֹהוּ וָבֹהוּ, Gen 1.2; שְׁמָמָה וּמְשַׁמָּה, Ezek 35.3) and because of onomatopoeia. These two factors serve to highlight and emphasise what the poet is trying to say in this third line. The bitter wailing that one has heard was stirred up by Yahweh, the God which we had come to know as the comforter in such circumstances. Further evidence of uncertainty about this phrase is seen in the Versions. LXX ταπεινουμένην καὶ τεταπεινωμένην 'the afflicted and the humbled', while reproducing the paronomasia, appears to have taken the root to be ענה rather than אנה;[46] and this is true also of V *humiliatum*[47] *et humiliatam*.[48] At Isa 29.2 P translates the phrase correctly as 'mourning and lamentation', but here the first word is translated by 'story/byword', which cannot be right. It seems as though the translator made a ham-fisted attempt at transliteration!

The theme of tragic reversal is clear. Yahweh, who ought to have fought for Israel, was on the side of the enemy; he engulfed rather than protected Israel, he reduced the fine building to rubble. The only positive-sounding verb—רבה 'increase/make many'—where he is the subject, applies to the sounds of sadness.

2.6

Text and Versions

MT כַּנֶּן—so also P, V and T; LXX ὡς ἄμπελον. MT is preferred.

MT(L) שָׁכוֹ; some 20 MSS^Ken סכו; LXX τὸ σκήνωμα αὐτοῦ; P ܡܛܠܬܗ *mṭlth*; V *tentorium suum*; T בית מקדשיה. Whether or not the Versions read שכו or סכו is difficult to say. *BHK* assumes that LXX read משכנו (presumably on the grounds that, in LXX, σκήνη often translates משכן), but it is possible that the Greek translator had the same text as the Masoretes. V, P and T may have read סכו, or they may have read שכו and taken it as a variant spelling (cf. Eccl 1.17 שכלות for סכלות; GK 6k). P's f. suffix may be explained as the Syriac translator's desire to mitigate the shocking idea that Yahweh destroyed his own sanctuary (Albrektson, 97).

---

[46] LXX at 5.11 has ἐταπείνωσαν for עָנוּ.
[47] At Isa 53.4 V translates מְעֻנֶּה with *humiliatum*. The paronomasia is lost in Douai '...the afflicted, both men and women', though Knox attempts to retain it with 'weeps man, weeps maid, with cowed spirits'. Knox acknowledges that the Latin has missed the sense of the Hebrew.
[48] It is interesting to note that LXX on Isa 29.2 translates ἰσχὺς καὶ τὸ πλοῦτος 'strength and riches', while V has *tristis et maerens* 'sadness and mourning'.

MT מֶלֶךְ וְכֹהֵן—so also V; LXX βασιλέα καὶ ἱερέα καὶ ἄρχοντα; P ܡܠܟܐ ܘܟܗܢܐ *mlk' wkhn'*; T מלכא וכהנא רבא; *BHK* suggests that LXX had a text which read וָשָׂר. If so, then the reading is inferior to MT on several grounds: (a) the extra element produces too long a leg in the 3:2 metre, and (b) there is no textual support for it.

* * *

While vv. 1-5 appear to deal with the devastation of the land and people, vv. 6f. have to do with the destruction of the temple in Jerusalem. Although Jer 52.13 documents that destruction by the Babylonians, the poet interprets it as the action of Yahweh.[49] Again, the anger of Yahweh is mentioned. It is Yahweh who was responsible for the cessation of sabbath observance and festival keeping. He even spurned king and priest. While this passage is very important in the poem, the text and meaning are not always clear.

To begin with, the LXX translation of ויחמס—καὶ διεπέτασεν 'and he scattered'. According to HR, this verb translates פרש ('spread out'), פטר ('set free') and שטח ('spread'). Only here in the LXX does it represent חמס. Unless one were able to interpret 'spread out' in a negative fashion, the LXX rendering seems out of place in a list of actions by Yahweh which are noticeably violent (בלע, הרס, גדע, הרג, שחת). For that reason alone the LXX reading is suspect. P and T 'uproot' are sufficiently aggressive in the context. That V *et dissipavit* has captured the sense of MT is not altogether clear. As well as 'destroy' (so Douai), *dissipo* can mean 'scatter, spread, disperse'; and since V does not translate חמס elsewhere with *dissipo*, it might be deduced that Jerome has been influenced here by LXX.

Rashi takes חמס in the sense of 'to cut' (לשון כריתה), citing Job 15.33 and Jer 13.22. IE[1] glosses with חשׂף 'strip', citing Jer 13.22 in support, while Kara glosses with ויגל 'and he exposed'; cf. also IE[2]. It is clear that חמס, in the present context, presented a challenge to the early interpreters. The situation was not helped by the immediate context, for the next two words pose further problems of interpretation.[50]

כַּגַּן שֻׂכּוֹ—BDB lists four roots שׂכך, none of which are common in the Hebrew Bible; and שׂךְ (שׂכך II) is a *hapax legomenon*. BDB (968) hints that this may be a variant spelling of סֹךְ (סכך II see BDB 697) meaning 'booth'. The nouns סֹךְ (m.) or סֻכָּה (f.) can mean a temporary shelter (army, harvest, cf. also Jonah 4.5) or lair, but is used at Pss 27.5 and 76.3 as poetic for the temple of Yahweh. It is also used at Amos 9.11 of the house (dynasty) of David. Here, in a context where Yahweh is destroying

---

[49] Cf. 2 Kgs 24.2 where the original Hebrew (cf. LXX καὶ ἀπέστειλεν αὐτῷ) read וישלח בו, the subject being Neuchadnezzar, and was changed in the course of transmission to וישלח יהוה בו because it was felt that Yahweh had been in charge of the assault.
[50] And many commentators regard the text as corrupt.

buildings and strongholds, it may refer to the temple in Jerusalem. This seems to be how it is taken in the Versions, MR, MLT. Rashi glosses the word with מעונתו 'his dwelling' (a term which is parallel to סכו at Ps 76.3). IE¹ and IE² actually cite סכו (instead of שכו), and IE² identifies this as מקום הדביר 'the Holy of Holies'.

כְּגַּן—'Like a garden'. LXX 'like a vine' may have had a *Vorlage* reading כגפן.[51] Driver (1964, 80) wonders if גן might be an abbreviation for גפן, while McDaniel (37) thinks that a ב has dropped out of MT and that כנפן should be restored.[52] The situation is not so corrupt as is sometimes claimed. Deuteronomy 11.10 has the phrase כגן ירק, which REB translates 'as in a vegetable garden', that is, the translators recognised that after the כ, the preposition ב has been omitted and is implied (cf. JM 133h, and BDB 455a). If we read the phrase not as 'as a garden' but 'as in a garden', then the entire statement can be rendered 'he has torn down his booth as in a garden', meaning 'he has torn down his booth as one tears down a booth in a garden' (so Albrektson, 95). Rashi 'and he cut down his dwelling as they cut the vegetables of a garden' is close to that of Albrektson.

There are those who remain unconvinced that שכו = סכו = 'his booth'. Blayney (312) translates 'as it were the garden of his own hedging', taking שכו to be an infinitive with suffix from √שׂוּךְ 'to hedge'. He feels that the concept reflects the passage in Isa 5.2, 5 where Yahweh had fenced and hedged about his vineyard. McDaniel (36ff.) argues more tortuously, following LXX to some extent but emending to בגפן where the ב has the force of 'from'; and he takes שכו to be a noun שׂוֹךְ 'branch' (as at Judg 9.49). His translation then is: 'And he has stripped from the vine its branches'.

שִׁחֵת מוֹעֲדוֹ—The verb שחת occurs in vv. 5, 6 and 8 of this chapter but nowhere else in Lamentations. Regarding מוֹעֲדוֹ, LXX ἑορτὴν αὐτοῦ takes מועד to mean 'festival', as does P.[53] V *tabernaculum suum* and T אתר מזומן לכפרא על עמיה 'the place appointed for his people's atonement' take the line that the parallelism with the first stich calls for something less abstract; and MLT בית המקדש is in no doubt that this is a reference to the temple.[54] Rashi identifies it as בית קדשי הקדשים 'the Holy of Holies', citing Exod 25.22 where Yahweh says: 'I will meet (ונועדתי) you there'. IE¹ comments briefly כמו באי מועד, i.e. a reference to 1.4 where he has already explained מועד as referring to מקדש.

---

[51] N.B. at Job 15.33 חמס is construed with גפן.
[52] Budde (1898ᵃ, 87) suggested that the original read כגנב 'like a thief'. This suggestion has the advantage of supplying a parallel to כצר,כאויב of vv. 4f., but it is not one that has commanded support.
[53] On P ܕܥܕܗ̇ *'d'dyh* 'her festivals', see Albrektson (97).
[54] Cf. Alexander (2008, 130 n. 20).

It is true, מועד most often means 'festival' or 'appointed time'. It is also true that the other occurrence of מועד in this verse has to mean 'festival, appointed time'; and it is argued that a writer would hardly mean different things by the same term. While this is arresting and while one ought not to dismiss lightly the uncertainty reflected in the Versions, the clinching argument must be from context. The verb requires a more material object, and parallelism points to an equivalent of 'his booth'. If our interpretation of the first stich of line 1 is correct, we have here a case of synonymous parallelism חמס // שחת and שכו // מועדו. That is to say, מועדו should be seen as an equivalent to שכו, namely, a *place* of meeting (= tabernacle) rather than a *time* of assembly; cf. Ps 74.4, 8.[55]

The poet, in making these oblique references to the temple, is also alluding to what the temple stood for. The basic meaning of the term 'booth' is 'shelter, protection', which is what is afforded a Yahweh-worshipper and is what is mentioned in Ps 27.5. That protection has gone, and its removal is the work of the one who had sponsored and provided it. The term 'meeting place' alludes to where Yahweh was wont to meet his people, cf. Exod 25.22. The possibility of meeting Yahweh is no more, and that lack is the work of the one who had made it possible in the first place. Hence, the קינה element of contrast, though veiled, is present here, in the allusion to former protection and former meeting with Yahweh, now gone.

שִׁכַּח יְהוָה—This is the only occurrence of the Piel of this verb. Unvocalised, it could easily be read as a Qal, which is what LXX ἐπελάθετο κύριος did, producing the awkward statement that Yahweh forgot[56] festival and Sabbath. None of the other Versions follow LXX: P ܐܢܫܝ 'ṭ'y, V *oblivioni tradidit* and Sym ἐπιλελῆσθαι ἐποίησε all read a causative here.[57] Yahweh is, then, credited with having caused festival and Sabbath to be forgotten in Zion. It is not that he has caused memory loss in Jerusalem! The verb 'forget' is the opposite of 'remember' (cf. the note on לא זכר at v. 1, and see Deut 9.7), and the poet may have had in mind here the commandment: 'Remember the Sabbath Day...' (Exod 20.8, i.e. observance of festival and Sabbath). The poet declares that Yahweh is the cause of the present lack of observance. The destruction of the place of worship in Zion resulted in the cessation of cultic activity and public festival, and when the poet mentions festival and Sabbath this is what he is referring to. If Yahweh was the one who removed the temple, he can be said to have brought these religious observances to an end. The use of the singular

---

[55] This is how it is taken by AV, NJB, REB, RSV, NIV JPS, Calvin, Luther, Ehrlich (36), Kaiser (325), Gordis (135), Renkema (239), Berlin (66).
[56] Blayney (312) reads the Qal of שכח and wonders why translators read the causative. For him, the meaning is that Yahweh 'holds those services no longer in esteem but slights and disregards them'.
[57] T's paraphrase could also be based on the Piel.

'festival and Sabbath' is meant to convey generality, as P renders and Calvin notes.

מֶלֶךְ וְכֹהֵן—The P translator rendered in the plural 'kings and priests' probably for the same reason he rendered מוֹעֵד in the plural, i.e. he interpreted the Hebrew as collectives (Abelesz, 35). The early exegetes were uncertain how to take the reference. MR takes the (singular) 'king' to refer to Zedekiah and the (singular) 'priest' to refer to Seraiah (so also MLT), while T 'High Priest' also sought a narrow interpretation.

While line 2 speaks of the cessation of festival and sabbath, line 3 has to do with the personnel connected with the cult itself. It might be argued that line one is declarative—Yahweh has removed the place of worship—while lines 2 and 3 spell out the consequences and implications. The priests were not the only official personnel of the cult. The Jerusalem temple was a royal shrine, and the priests were in the king's employ (cf. 1 Kgs 2.27, 35). In fact, the king was responsible for the sanctuary and its upkeep (2 Kgs 12.4-8; 22.3-7). In addition, the king had a sacral role (cf. 2 Sam 6; 1 Kgs 8; 2 Kgs 23). Hence, the linking of king and priest here is significant: they represent the cultic personnel. When the poet says that Yahweh rejected king and priest the verb used (נאץ) means 'to spurn'. He wants to stress that Yahweh despised his own staff, as it were, in addition to removing his own place of abode. Nor is it done in the cool hour. The poet uses a new word here (זעם 'indignation') in conjunction with אף 'anger'. These words are not construed together elsewhere in the Hebrew Bible, although they are in parallel at Isa 10.5, 25; 30.27. The poet here wants to convey the mood in which Yahweh carries out the actions in this verse. He was not only hostile: he was intensely angry.

2.7

Text and Versions

MT נִאֵץ; LXX ἀπετίναξεν; P ܐܣܠܝ *'sly*; Aq κατηράσατο; Sym εἰς κατάραν ἐποίησε; V *maledixit*; T בעט. LXX may have read נער 'cast off'—so Döderlein (197), Kelso (26), Rudolph (1938, 107), *BHK, BHQ*.

MT הִסְגִּיר—so also P, V, T and Sym; LXX συνέτριψεν; Aq συνέκλεισεν. LXX and Aq misunderstood syntax (see below). MT is preferred.

* * *

The uncharacteristic actions of Yahweh continue in this verse. If there was any doubt, in v. 6, that the cult was the object of Yahweh's destructive behaviour it is dispelled in v. 7, where his negative attitude towards the sanctuary in Zion is sharply drawn. It was Yahweh who handed Zion over to the enemy, and the noise of pagan celebrations in the temple resembled that of a festival of old.

The verbs נאץ (v. 6), and זנח and נאר (v. 7) are very close in meaning. They all have Yahweh as subject, and the impression is given that the poet is casting around for verbs which will emphasise each other and which will portray Yahweh in utterly negative fashion, spurning all that he had formerly supported. In so doing, the author allows the contrast with the past to be heard. Verses 6 and 7 are further held together by the mention of the temple's destruction and by further allusions to Yahweh distancing himself from the cult. There are echoes here of Amos 5.21 'I hate, I despise your feasts' and Isa 1.14 'I loathe your new moons and festivals'.

נאר—This is a very uncommon verb in the Hebrew Bible, occurring only here and at Ps 89.40. In the latter context (vv. 39f.) the verb is parallel to חלל (Piel) 'defile, profane' and associated with זנח (as here) and מאס. Hence, its meaning may be adduced from these contexts (BDB 611).[58] Rashi glosses with ביטל 'abolish, abrogate', IE[1] with עזב או שנא 'forsook or forgot', and this demonstrates that the early translators and commentators were uncertain of the verb and interpreted in the light of the context. NEB seems to have opted for Driver's suggestion, 'laid a curse…', but REB has pulled back from this position with 'abandoned' (so also NIV). Others draw their conclusions from the context—disdained (JPS), disowned (NRSV), has come to loathe (JB).

מִזְבְּחוֹ…מִקְדָּשׁוֹ—Yahweh's altar must be that referred to at 1 Kgs 8.22; 2 Kgs 18.22, while מקדש must refer to the temple, as at 2 Chron 2.8; Ps 96.6. The repudiation of his own altar and his own sanctuary—which to some will have been the very essence of Yahweh worship—may have seemed inconceivable to a Yahweh devotee, but the poet wants to shock; and so he presents Yahweh in masochistic mood, removing the very means whereby he was worshipped in Zion.

הִסְגִּיר—√סגר in the Qal means 'to shut', but the Hiphil means 'to hand over, deliver'. It is construed with ביד 'into the hand of' at Josh 20.5; 1 Sam 23.11f., 20; 30.15; Ps 31.9 and here. LXX συνέτριψεν[59] 'broke' and Aq συνέκλεισεν 'besieged' probably do not represent another Hebrew text but, as Albrektson (99f.) points out, are based on a misunderstanding of the phrase ביד. LXX and Aq took this to mean 'by the hand of, by means of (the enemy)', not 'into the hand of' (cf. 1.14; 5.12). The Greek translator having made that mistake, Albrektson argues, 'the object חוֹמֹת אַרְמְנוֹתֶיהָ demanded a verb meaning "destroy, crush" etc.'. Aq, perhaps influenced by LXX interpretation of ביד, interpreted the basic meaning of

---

[58] *HALOT* ('repudiate') speculates that it may be related to Arabic *nwr* 'to insult', while Driver (1950, 138) thinks it may be a by-form of ארר 'to curse', which is how Aq, Sym and V seem to have taken it. It is possible that it relates to Akkadian *nāru* 'to kill'.
[59] As LXX employs this verb to translate שבר at 1.15; 2.9; 3.4, it is sometimes argued that the LXX *Vorlage* here may have been שִׁבֵּר (so *BHK*) or even הִשְׁבִּיר (so Kelso, 27).

the verb 'shut' to refer to shutting in/besieging. This latter interpretation is not out of the question, but the fact that P, V, T and Sym take the verb to mean 'delivered/handed over', and בְּיַד as meaning 'into the hand of' is an argument against it.

חוֹמֹת אַרְמְנוֹתֶיהָ—The f. suffix must refer back to Zion in v. 6 because מִקְדָּשׁ and מִזְבֵּחַ are masculine. The fact that אַרְמְנוֹתֶיהָ has been mentioned earlier in the poem as having been demolished, coupled with the f. s. suffix, has led some scholars to regard the passage with suspicion in spite of the fact that LXX, V, P and T render roughly as at v. 5.[60] Budde (1898[a], 87) and Löhr (1894, 7f.) were early sceptics, Löhr deleting the entire phrase and Budde reading instead ארון בריתו 'his covenant ark', while more recently Rudolph (1938, 107), followed by Kraus (38) and *BHS*, emend the text to חֶמְדַּת אוֹצְרוֹתֶיהָ 'the costliest of her treasures'. Those who retain MT (and most translations seem reluctant to abandon it)—Keil (379), Kaiser (325), Renkema (248), Provan (67), Hillers[2] (94), Westermann (141), Albrektson (100)—are not all in agreement as to what is meant by the phrase. IE[2] considered that the whole phrase referred to the temple; so also Keil (389), Nägelsbach (79). There is something to be said for an interpretation which associates this term with the complex of buildings which included the temple, in that the final line refers to the house of Yahweh. It would be strange if the poet, alluding to the temple in line 1 and mentioning it clearly in line 3, should have gone off on a complete tangent in line 2. It is also possible that the noise referred to in line 3 was the enemy's shout of triumph at having breached the walls of the heart of Zion, namely, the house of Yahweh.

קוֹל נָתְנוּ—Although there is no plural subject in the vicinity, it is possible that the poet is unpacking the term אוֹיֵב here, and we are to understand that the invaders of the temple are the subject of נתנו. This is how it has been understood by LXX, V, Rashi (האויבים), IE[2] (הצרים), AV, Luther, Calvin, JPS, Renkema (249), Westermann (141). Others—RSV, Gottwald (10), NRSV, JB, Rudolph (1962, 216), Kraus (36)—have taken נתנו to be an impersonal passive (GK 144g), 'a clamour was raised' (NRSV). The problem with this is that the resultant *translation* is not clear. נתן קול usually means 'to make a loud noise'. When Yahweh is subject it can refer to thunder (Exod 9.23), but with a human being it may be weeping (Gen 45.2), shouting (Jer 22.20) and can also denote an army cry (Jer 4.16). In this passage the meaning may be close to the army cry, a cry of triumph; so NEB 'shouts of victory'; cf. Ps 74.4 where the verb שאג 'roar' is used for the same occasion.

---

[60] Although V uses a different word at v. 5 (*moenia*; here, *turrium*), it is probable that Jerome's *Vorlage* was as MT.

כְּיוֹם מוֹעֵד—LXX, P, V, IE² etc. recognise that כיום is equivalent to כביום, cf. 1.20; 2.22; Isa 30.29. T paraphrases 'like the shout of the people in the house of Israel praying in it on the day of Passover', which is probably meant to refer to some significant volume. The important point to note here is that the enemy, whom Yahweh has admitted to the sanctuary, has raised cries of celebration[61] which compare with what the poet associates with יום מועד (cf. v. 22). In Hos 9.5, we have the term יום מועד parallel to יום חג יהוה, and the latter probably refers to the autumn pilgrim festival. This festival was not confined to a single day, hence יום in the Hosea passage may mean 'time, period of time' (Macintosh, 347). The poet, at 2.7, may of course be thinking of the noise on any day during the festival. The recollection of the joyful noise of a great throng in the temple is poignant here, for the noise the poet refers to is that of the heathen in the very house of Yahweh at the focal point of Israel's worship. By contrast, the people of Yahweh have abandoned the festivals (1.4; 2.6). Yahweh's masochism had reached an all-time low. The author, at 1.10, refers to the heathen entering the temple contrary to Yahweh's own ruling. Here, it seems that Yahweh either does not care about his former ban or is actively encouraging the violation of it. As Calvin says, the statement is as if to say 'that the Chaldeans had fought under the authority and banner of God'.

As the poet nears the end of this section he speaks of the devastation in terms of the cult, the cultic personnel and the very centre of cultic activity. While the people of Yahweh could absorb defeat—even the loss of statehood, the destruction of their homes and fine buildings etc.—and understand it as punishment, the fact that Yahweh had actually repudiated and disowned the worship in his own house and had arranged, in its place, for the heathen to enter and celebrate, must have taken the rug from under even the most pious Yahwist.

2.8

Text and Versions
MT חָשַׁב—so also P, V and T; LXX καὶ ἐπέστρεψεν; SH ܐܗܦܟ *'hpk*; SH margin ܐܬܚܫܒ *'thšb*. Döderlein (1780, 198) argues that LXX read הֵשִׁב while *BHK* and *BHS* claim that LXX read הֵשִׁיב. In view of the καὶ (though SH does not represent this), Albrektson (100) thinks they read וַיָּשֶׁב. MT is preferred.

MT לֹא; V *et non*—so also P and T. It may be that the *Vorlagen* of V, P, and T did represent the copula, in which case it may have been a case of dittography of the letter ו with which the previous word ends. However, it is more likely that the translators felt the need to link the two actions in this line. (cf. P at v. 5 and *Kethib/Qere* difference at v. 2).

---

[61] Rashi comments 'for they (Israelites) used to rejoice and sing inside it (temple) with a loud voice, so the enemies made a joyful noise when it was destroyed'. He, therefore, understands the noise to be celebratory; so also IE². V *sicut in die sollemni*, AV 'solemn feast' are in danger of missing the point here. Moffatt 'as in an orgy' may be going too far in the other direction, but Knox 'like shout of holiday' is closer to the import of the Hebrew.

וַיְאַבֶּל MT—so also P; LXX καὶ ἐπένθησεν—so also V and T. The consonantal text is ambiguous, but MT (Hiphil pointing) is preferable (contra Alexander, 132 n. 28).

* * *

The author in this verse is concerned to depict Yahweh acting with such premeditated precision that the end result could be said to have been one of his goals. He planned the destruction of Zion's walls. Having decided to go ahead with the demolition, he showed no signs of hesitation or holding back. The poet then surveys the scene of devastation, where the defences are down, and he imagines the very remains themselves mourning and lamenting; and this too is the work of Yahweh.

חָשַׁב יְהוָה לְהַשְׁחִית—Although there is nothing sinister in the construction חשב plus infinitive, it is almost always found in contexts where the planning is for negative or evil consequences (e.g. 1 Sam 18.25; Prov 24.8; Jer 23.27; 36.3). Could the fall of Jerusalem have been a mere side effect of Yahweh's anger? This is a question which may have been asked in the debate following the destruction of the city; and the answer is clearly negative. This was not just a by-product of Yahweh's anger. It was premeditated.

חוֹמַת בַּת־צִיּוֹן—P vocalises חוֹמֹת i.e. plural. It may be that the translator felt that the singular could refer to a particular construction and not apply to the walls surrounding the city (*pars pro toto*). The destruction of these walls left the city and its people vulnerable and undefended. Renkema (252) notes: 'The wall of Jerusalem, however, did not only possess a profane, strategic value, it was simultaneously the visible symbol of faith in Jerusalem. The protective power of Zion's fortifications was not guaranteed by the quality of its stones nor the height or thickness of its walls but by YHWH's presence alone.' On the phrase בַּת־צִיּוֹן, see on 1.6.

נָטָה קָו—Yahweh's intentions are spelled out here. The poet depicts Yahweh as a skilled craftsman—a demolition expert—going about his work (cf. Isa 44.13; Job 38.5). In Jer 31.38f. and Zech 1.16 the words are used in the context of the rebuilding of Jerusalem, but in 2 Kgs 21.13 (cf. Isa 28.17; 34.11) they refer to the destruction of Jerusalem (cf. Amos 7.7-9). It is probable that the statement in Kings is related to this passage. Yahweh had said, via the prophets, that he would use, against Jerusalem, the measuring line of Samaria and the plummet of the house of Ahab. The phrase, therefore, probably carries the idea of making a mathematical judgment about an object. In the case of Jerusalem the idea is that, just as Samaria was found to be 'out of line' with Yahweh's demands, so it is with Jerusalem.

Rashi, who senses that the term is neutral in itself, comments: קו של משפט, and IE¹ has the same concern, adding the word תהו (a cryptic quote from Isa 34.11 where we get the phrase קו תהו). Kara is unequivocal: 'He stretched over them the judgment measure'.

לֹא־הֵשִׁיב יָדוֹ מִבַּלֵּעַ—Literally 'he did not bring back his hand from engulfing'. The image of Yahweh as engineer, making decisions, changes to that of a workman who, without compunction, pursues his task. At v. 3 Yahweh is depicted as withdrawing his right hand of protection at the enemy's attack. Here, using similar terminology, the meaning seems to be that Yahweh did not restrain himself as he demolished[62] the wall.

וַיַּאֲבֶל—Since LXX, V and T chose to vocalise as Qal, the picture which emerges is of the rampart (and wall) mourning; that is to say, the statement of these Versions does not continue the actions of Yahweh but describes the *result* of those actions in lines 1 and 2. MT, in adopting a Hiphil reading, depicts Yahweh still in action, causing the rampart and wall to mourn. LXX (cf. also V) takes חל as subject of ויאבל and then construes וחומה as the subject of אמללו (which LXX reads as a singular, though cf. LXX^A which retains the plural—ἠσθένησαν). P also took ויאבל as Hiphil but, whereas in MT חל וחומה are construed together as object, P takes חל as object and construes וחומה as subject of אמללו. P's way of obtaining number agreement was to take וחומה as plural (*pars pro toto*); and, as often with P in Lamentations, adds a suffix—ܫܘܪܝܗ *šwryh*—'her walls'.

חֵל—According to BDB (298), the noun חֵל (also written חֵיל in Nah 3.8) denotes 'rampart' or 'fortress'. At Isa 26.1 and here, the word[63] combines with חומה/חומות. LXX takes חל to be τὸ προτείχισμα 'the outer wall' and חומה as τεῖχος 'the wall'. MR (cf. also MLT and Rashi) interprets חל as חומה קטנה and חומה as חומה גדולה. IE¹ quotes 2 Sam 20.15 where the word denotes 'the area around the wall (חומה)'.

אֻמְלָלוּ—This is the rare conjugation, Pulal,[64] of √אמל 'be weak' (cf. Akk. *ummulu* 'be sad'). It is usually translated 'languish' (BDB 51). This is the only verb in the verse which does not have Yahweh as subject. This concluding clause describes the effect that Yahweh's action has had on the rampart and wall. The penultimate clause states that Yahweh had caused wall and rampart to mourn (אבל). This latter root was used at 1.4 where the roads to Zion were said to mourn. It is often used with an inanimate

---

[62] בלע has been used at v. 2 and v. 5 (twice) and occurs again at v. 16 but is confined, in Lamentations, to ch. 2, hence it serves as a connecting word or theme.
[63] There is some confusion as to terminology here because another noun חיל can mean 'strength', 'wealth' or 'army'; and P, again supplying the f. s. suffix, translates ܚܝܠܗ *ḥylh* 'her forces', though this need not detain us.
[64] GK 55d.

subject, so the surprise is not that the walls mourn but that Yahweh is the cause of the mourning.[65] Again, אמל, which is often parallel to אבל, can take an inanimate subject; so both rampart and wall are depicted as languishing together. The Versions show a measure of uncertainty—LXX ('weak'), P ('desolate'), V ('destroyed'), T ('crumbled'), Sym ('fell'), though they are all convinced of a negative tone. Of the mediaeval Jewish commentators, Kara is the only one who comments. He cites Nah 1.4 and 1 Sam 2.5 where the verb occurs and claims that it has the meaning 'to cease' in the sense 'to cease to function'. However, the fact that אמל is often in parallel with אבל (Isa 24.4; 33.9; Jer 14.2; Hos 4.3; Joel 1.10) would suggest that the meaning is akin to אבל 'mourn'. The poet has attempted to paint a picture of rampart and wall in such a dilapidated condition that they themselves appear to lament.

Yahweh's violent actions are not extended in this verse; rather, the poet reminds his readers that, before the violence took place, Yahweh was, architect-like, planning it all, in the cool hour.

2.9

Text and Versions

MT אִבַּד וְשִׁבַּר בְּרִיחֶיהָ...טָבְעוּ—so also LXX, V and T; P ܐܒܕܘ ܘܬܒܪܘ ܣܘܟܪܝܗ ܛܒܥܘ... *tbʿw...ʾwbdw wtbrw swkryh*. The P translator, finding the change from plural to singular awkward, decided that the first verb was probably causative and that the subject of all three verbs was probably the enemies. Conjecture: טָבְעוּ בָאָרֶץ שְׁעָרֶיהָ אָבְדוּ בְרִיחֶיהָ; see below, cf. Salters (2004, 273-76).

* * *

There is a clear connection with v. 8 in that at v. 8c the rampart and wall are said to languish and v. 9 begins with the gates and bars disappearing. Walls, gates and bars are mentioned together at 2 Chron 8.5; 14.6. The author has made it clear that the mourning and languishing of these (inanimate) things is the result of Yahweh's actions. Consequently, when he goes on to refer to gates sinking and bars vanishing it is understood to be the result of further action by Yahweh. The theme continues in the second and third lines. The poet, who has made it clear that Zion has no physical defences left, proceeds to list several other features of Zion's life which have been removed. Zion had been ruled by the Davidic dynasty for centuries, but her last king, Zedekiah, and princes are now said to be 'among the nations', which must refer to the exile in Babylon, an allusion to Jer 52.8-11, thus indicating that the control of the country had passed to Babylon, and the very personnel associated with that former control had disappeared. In addition to the removal of the rulers, the author mentions that instruction is no more. This is a clear allusion to priestly activity:

---

[65] On the root אבל, see Clines (1992, 1-10).

תורה is not the Law, but refers to cultic activity and life, which was the domain of the priests, cf. NJB, NRSV, REB (and see below). The final line has to do with the silence of the prophetic voice. The statement that the prophets did not find a vision from Yahweh might mean a lack of faith on the part of the prophets but, more likely, that Yahweh had withheld his message from the prophets (which is how T puts it). Although Yahweh is not the subject of any verbs in this verse (given the restoration of line 1), there is no question but that the author believes that Yahweh is behind the various aspects of calamity described here; and it is not without significance that he concludes with the name Yahweh.

טָבְעוּ בָאָרֶץ שְׁעָרֶיהָ—Although Yahweh appears in this verse, the proliferation of f. s. suffixes remind one of the victim in all this—Zion. The change of subject is clearly indicated—'her gates'—but the subject is also very much associated with the subject matter of v. 8c, *viz* rampart and wall mourning and languishing. This latter scene expands in the mind of the poet, and he pictures the gates of Zion surrounded by the rubble of the crumbling walls. It is as if the gates themselves had sunk into the ground. Hence, we can say that the final statement of v. 8, where the walls languished, is continued by the observation that the gates of Zion sank into the ground.

אִבַּד וְשִׁבַּר בְּרִיחֶיהָ—Although the Versions testify to both verbs, scholars have long suspected that the original text contained only one. One reason for this is that the second stich of the first line is longer than normal, and that one verb would suffice. Budde (1882, 9) wanted to delete ושבר (cf. *BHK*, Kaiser, 326), while Löhr (1894, 8) suggested deleting ו אבד on the grounds that when bars are said to be broken in the Hebrew Bible the verb is usually שבר (cf. Amos 1.5; Ps 107.16; Isa 45.2). While it may be going too far to say that 'אִבַּד וְשִׁבַּר בְּרִיחֶיהָ is not only metrically too long but is logically contradictory or redundant' (Gordis, 162), several modern commentators are uneasy with MT. Gordis rejects the idea that the second verb is a gloss on the first and suggests that 'the two verbs are a conflate, representing variants of manuscripts which were both preserved in a very early state of Proto-masoretic activity'; so also, Gottlieb (30) and Hillers[2] (99f.). If MT is retained—and it is by Keil (500), Kraus (38), Rudolph (1962, 216), Westermann (141), Provan (68), Renkema (256), Berlin (63), House (371)—the text reads awkwardly,[66] quite apart from the length of the second stich. Verse 8 has ended with the poetic description of rampart and wall languishing together, and v. 9 continues with the picture of the sunken gates. Then we get two verbs whose subject is not specified but which must be Yahweh, the subject of several verbs in v. 8. As Yahweh is not the subject thereafter in vv. 9, 10, 11, 12 and 13, this is a reversion

---

[66] IE[1] feels the need to point out that the subject of אבד ושבר is found in the previous verse; cf. also Gerlach (64).

to the style of vv. 2-8. Coming after the statement that the gates are sunk, these two verbs fit poorly in the passage. Should they be translated as pluperfects? If Yahweh shattered the bars of the gates, he did it before the gates sank into the ground! Hence, if we retain MT, we must translate 'he had ruined and shattered her bars'.

I have argued elsewhere (Salters 2004, 273-76) that the present text is corrupt and that it has been since before the Versions were made. Bickell (1894, 109) had suggested[67] reading אבדו בריחיה, and he is partly supported by Budde (1898[a], 88). This conjecture seems to have been ignored by later scholars as it does not appear in BHK, BHS or BHQ. MT may be accounted for if we take the original reading to be אבדו בריחיה 'her bars vanished' (along with her gates). The text was incorrectly copied אבדו ברבריחיה (dittography of בר), and a correction was later made by inserting ש after the ו because a scribe associated שבר with bars (Isa 45.2). The restored text is smoother in every way. The whole line is now a continuous observation on the lines of the final clause of v. 8; and there is a certain assonance with the verbs טבעו/אבדו.

מַלְכָּהּ וְשָׂרֶיהָ בַגּוֹיִם—LXX (also V) thought that the two nouns were further accusatives of the verbs אָבַד וְשֻׁבַּר, rather than the subject of the next clause, as P, Sym and T have correctly understood. In addition to the disappearance of the gates and bars, the defences of Zion, the poet recalls the disappearance of the leaders—king and princes/rulers—captured and in exile (cf. Lam 4.20 and 2 Kgs 25.7; Ezek 12.10-13). While the phrase בַגּוֹיִם can be ambiguous in some passages, here it must surely mean 'exile', as IE[2] claims: 'When the gates sank, the king went into exile'.

אֵין תּוֹרָה—The location of this phrase in line 2 has led to some misunderstanding. The Masoretic punctuation seems to connect the words with what precedes. Because LXX misunderstood the first stich, connecting it with line 1, the translator read אֵין תּוֹרָה as a separate statement; so also P. It is difficult to tell how V construed these words, though Douai translates 'her king and her princes are among the Gentiles: the law is no more...', that is to say, V has been read as beginning a separate statement with אֵין תּוֹרָה. But T's paraphrase makes a connection: '...among the nations, for they had not kept the words of the Torah...' MR makes a similar connection: 'if someone tells you that there is Torah among the nations, do not believe it; because it is written "her king and her princes are among the nations where Torah is no more"' (cf. also MLT); and, according to SH margin, Sym translated '...among the nations which have no law' (cf. Morgenstern, 107). Furthermore, Rashi's comment on אין תורה is 'There is no one among them who gives instruction', where 'them' refers to the king and princes who are in exile. IE[2] refers to the king 'without a copy

---

[67] Bickell (109) also makes the strange suggestion of placing ושבר before נביאיה and deleting גם, but it is difficult see what he can possibly mean by this.

of the Torah', while Kara comments 'it is as if to say they were not able to engage in Torah study in exile because of affliction and heavy service'.[68] The mediaeval commentators were clearly influenced by the Masoretic punctuation. So also Luther '...da sie das Gesetz nicht üben können' and Vermigli (84). Calvin's comments, however, show that he saw no connection between the king in exile and אין תורה and he is critical of the Targumist for twisting the words of the passage. He sees אין תורה as another in the list of signs that God had forsaken his people. AV, perhaps influenced by Calvin, does not link the two parts of line 2, and it is common among subsequent commentators and translators to ignore the Masoretic punctuation—Keil (500), Albrektson (103f.), Westermann (145), Provan (69), Gottlieb (30f.), Renkema (259), Hillers[2] (105), Rudolph (1938, 107), JPS. As Gottlieb (30) says, 'The text is not concerned with the situation of the exiles, but with those who remain in the land who must go without king and prince, the (priestly) instruction and the prophetic revelation'. As mentioned above, תורה refers *not* to Torah/ Pentateuch, but to instruction by the priests[69] on the practical matters of behaviour and relationship with Yahweh—1 Sam 3.1; Ps 74.9; Ezek 7.26; Mic 3.6; Hag 2.10-13. The poet does not say that there are no priests (cf. v. 20), but that instruction from them is no more: they have ceased to function. It is interesting to note in this connection the manner in which this term is handled in the translations. LXX νόμος, V *lex*, P ܢܡܘܣ *nmws'* are all fairly neutral renderings, though T אורייתא interprets as Torah. This neutrality is struck in translations such as AV, RSV, NIV, NEB, but JB 'the Law' appears to agree with T, and this produced a reaction in later translations such as NJB 'there is no instruction', NRSV 'guidance is no more' and (even more strongly) REB 'there is no direction from priests'.

לֹא־מָצְאוּ חָזוֹן מֵיְהוָה—The implication here is that the prophets have attempted, in vain, to receive messages from Yahweh. The חזון appears to have been the standard means of communication between Yahweh and the prophetic figures (cf. Isa 1.1; Amos 1.1 etc.). It is not as though the prophets were consulting other deities, which might have been the natural thing to do after such a set-back as the fall of Jerusalem. The prophets alluded to here are genuinely trying to make contact with Yahweh, but to no avail. T paraphrases 'the spirit of prophecy from the Lord was withheld from the prophets'.

The great features and symbols of Zion's former life have disappeared— gates and bars, the king and rulers, priestly instruction and prophetic vision.

---

[68] Alluding to the terminology of 1.3.
[69] Cf. de Vaux (1961, 206-209).

2.10

Text and Versions
MT יֵשְׁבוּ; LXX ἐκάθισαν—so also P, V, OL and a Cairo Genizah MS; T יתבין.
MT יִדְּמוּ; LXX ἐσιώπησαν—so also V and OL; P ܢܫܬܩܘ *wštqw*; T שתקין.
Both verbs have been interpreted as perfects by all the Versions except T (participles). The latter may offer support for MT's imperfects, cf. Schäfer, *BHQ* 121*. It is perhaps understandable, in the case of the first verb, in view of the context (other verbs in vv. 8, 9, 10, 11 are all perfects); and *BHK* considers it as a possible reading. But the second verb looks unambiguously like an imperfect form. It is *possible* that both verbs originally stood as perfects, that the *Vorlagen* of the Versions read דמו...ישבו and that the Masoretes' text read ידמו, which had to be vocalised as imperfect, forcing them to bring the vowels of ישבו into line. Most commentators accept MT.[70]

MT רֹאשָׁן בְּתוּלֹת יְרוּשָׁלִָם—so also P, V, T, Aq and Sym; LXX ἀρχηγοὺς παρθένους ἐν Ιερουσαλημ; OL *principes, virgines Jerusalem*. It may be that LXX had a different Hebrew text. Two MSS^Ken have the variant ראשם, and Albrektson (104) wonders if this form (pointed רָאשָׁם) underlay the LXX. The suggestion of Kelso (29) that ראשן was read as an Aramaising plural is also possible. (ראשן is a variant reading of ראשם, earlier in the verse, by three MSS^Ken). See Schäfer *BHQ* 121*.

* * *

In the previous verse the poet described the various features of the disaster of the fall of Jerusalem. In this verse he turns his focus on the effect of these calamities on the people of Zion. Among those left behind, after king and leaders had been deported, were the priests and prophets, but they failed to function as before. And the rest of the population, represented here by elders and maidens, are to be seen engaged in lament.

יֵשְׁבוּ לָאָרֶץ—The *lamed* here carries the idea of 'down to' (the ground); cf. v. 2; Isa 3.26. The sitting on the ground was a traditional way of expressing grief and humiliation (cf. Josh 7.6; 2 Sam 13.31; Ezek 26.16; Job 2.12; Isa 47.1), the ground symbolising the low estate.

יִדְּמוּ—On the form יִדְּמוּ, see BL, 433f, GK 67g. Although the Versions understand the verb here to be דמם I 'to be silent' (BDB 198) and most commentators and translators have accepted this, there is some dispute as to whether the root might be דמם II 'wail, lament'. In 1909, Haupt (4ff.) argued, alluding to Akkadian *damâmu* 'mourn, moan' that there was no Hebrew root דמם 'be silent', only דמם 'mutter, moan', while Schick (240) took a similar line, translating our passage 'there sat on the ground moaning maid Zion's elders'. Dahood (1960, 402) comes to the same conclusion, on the basis of Ugaritic *dmm* 'mourn'; and McDaniel (39) concurs.[71] Dahood comments 'Silence seems to have played very little part

---

[70] Renkema remarks 'If one were to read perfects here then the elders would be given a place in the sequence king, princes, priests and prophets. The difference with the king and the princes, however, is that the elders are still present in the city…'
[71] Cf. Berlin (63), NEB.

in mourning ceremonies, while weeping and screaming in excessive degree were a marked feature of Oriental rites of lamentation' but, as Gottlieb (31f.) points out, 'there is no suggestion that the behaviour described has a ritual character in particular'; and he sides with Lohfink (276), who shows from passages such as Job 2.11ff.; Ezra 9.3ff. that silence did indeed have a place in lament. At Job 2.12 the three friends do raise their voices in mourning with Job, but then, at v. 13, they become silent: 'They sat with him on the ground seven days and seven nights, and no one spoke a word to him, for they saw that his suffering was very great'. The occurrence of the verb at v. 18, where it cannot possibly mean 'moan' would seem to argue in favour of the meaning assigned to it by the Versions. If MT is followed, יִדְּמוּ may have an auxiliary role, almost as an adverb 'silently'; cf. GK 120a, so Kaiser (326), Westermann (145), Rudolph (1962, 219), JB, RSV, REB, JPS, but the juxtaposition of the two verbs, without the copula, has a certain sharpness to it—LXX, V, Calvin, Luther, AV, Keil (493), Renkema (263).

זִקְנֵי בַת־צִיּוֹן—The main leadership having either gone into exile or ceasing to function, the heads of the families left behind react as one would expect. Elders were an important element in society, involved in court-sittings and offering advice (1 Kgs 12.6f.). They are the subject of the first two lines. Provan (70) thinks the reference to the silence of the elders 'may be understood in the light of the previous verse. Like those others who provided leadership and dispensed wisdom, they have nothing to say. They are fully occupied with their grieving'; cf. Pham (129f.). On the phrase בַת־צִיּוֹן, see on 1.6.

הֶעֱלוּ עָפָר עַל־רֹאשָׁם—As a further sign of extreme grief and distress, they cover their heads with earth (lit. put up soil/dust on their heads); cf. the same construction at Josh 7.6 and Ezek 27.30. This custom may have something to do with a present desire to be buried, but it may simply be another aspect of dishevelment which was also achieved by the tearing of one's garments (Job 2.12).

חָגְרוּ שַׂקִּים—Cf. 2 Sam 3.31; 1 Kgs 20.32; Isa 15.3; Jer 4.8; 49.3. The verb חגר expresses the idea of putting clothing round one's body, especially the loins.

שַׂקִּים—The same word is used of a bag for holding grain/foodstuffs at Gen 42.35. Coarse cloth made from hair of goats or camels, it served as mourning garb and was worn next to the skin (2 Kgs 6.30). It is used in the singular (שַׂק Isa 15.3) as well as the plural, as here. It is an adverbial accusative here (GK 117y): with sackcloth.

הוֹרִידוּ לָאָרֶץ רֹאשָׁן בְּתוּלֹת יְרוּשָׁלָיִם—Because the subject of the previous four verbs in the verse are the elders, the LXX translator decided that 'elders' was also the subject of this final verb[72] and, since this is transitive, the object must lie in the final words. The result was confusion: 'They have brought down to the ground the chief maidens in Jerusalem'!

בְּתוּלֹת יְרוּשָׁלָיִם—The subject of line 3 is the Jerusalem maidens. They are mentioned, along with priests, at 1.4, where it is said that they were afflicted, at 1.18 along with young men, said to have gone into captivity, at 2.21, where, along with young men, they have been slain, and at 5.11, where they have been raped. It is obvious that the poets are not referring to all the maidens in any one passage. Women, especially unmarried women, were the most vulnerable of society, especially in the event of violence or invasion. Perhaps the poet, by grouping them with the elders here, points to both ends of the social spectrum: the elders who are the least vulnerable and the maidens who are the most vulnerable. By doing so he means that all the people are stunned and are lamenting.

Although the wearing of sackcloth, the sitting on the ground and the putting of soil on the head are all mourning customs found elsewhere in the Hebrew Bible, the description in the third line is nowhere exactly paralleled. V *abiecerunt* may mean 'hung down' (cf. AV, RV and JB), but whether Jerome has caught the meaning of the Hebrew is difficult to say. RSV, NRSV, NIV and REB refer to 'bowing the head towards the ground'. At 1.4 the maidens are said to be 'afflicted', but the meaning is not precise. However, it would seem from the context that we are dealing with a characteristic of Jerusalem society in the event of disaster. In sitting silently on the ground, putting soil on the head, wearing sackcloth, hanging the head, the poet is alluding to the extremes of lamenting here. He is not describing prayer of any kind (contra Renkema, 266f.). In these verses (vv. 9f.), the poet, who is finishing off a section on Yahweh's attack on Zion and its immediate effect, describes it in human terms: king and rulers gone, priests and prophets not functioning, and elders and maidens (= the top and bottom rungs of the remaining social ladder) responding to it all as in a disaster, which it was. The reversal element is poignant here, for the elders might have been expected to display strength of morale, while the maidens were perhaps associated with happier times (Zech 9.17).

2.11

Text and Versions
MT מֵעַי—so also Sym, P, V, OL and T; LXX ἡ καρδία μου. As LXX, at 1.20, translates the same word as ἡ κοιλία μου, the LXX reading may be accounted for as an inner Greek error (καρδία for κοιλία).[73]

---

[72] So also OL. The fact that the subject comes late in the construction leads to this error; cf. also LXX of Eccl 1.6 due to the late introduction of the subject רוח.

MT כְּבֵדִי—so also Aq, V, OL and T; LXX ἡ δόξα μου—so also P. Error on the part of LXX and P in vocalising כְּבֹדִי. MT is preferable.

* * *

Up to this point in the poem the author has described the plight of Zion, attributing it all to the anger of Yahweh who has acted like an enemy. The poetic description of Zion's devastation and misery has been achieved without author involvement: the poet remains in the background. But just as in ch. 1 the poet's own feelings burst through the fabric, as it were (v. 17), so here, in this poem, the poet shows how he feels; but this time he is quite open about it. It is as though he cannot contain himself, but it was one thing to describe the destruction of walls, temple, altar etc. It is quite another to observe the removal of the leadership, the silencing of priest and prophet and the mourning of the people (elders and maidens); and when he thought on the starvation of children, he alludes to the effect it is having on him. The fact that the speaker is not identified in the text led IE[2] to interpret the 1st p. s. in the light of the immediate context: 'Each one of the elders says "my eyes..."' when they remember the days of famine in Zion.' MR, MLT, Rashi and Kara are silent on this matter, but Calvin identifies the speaker as the author, as do Vermigli (88), Blayney (313), Keil (501), Rudolph (1962, 224), Lanahan (44), Kaiser (336), Provan (70) and most moderns.[74]

כָּלוּ בַדְּמָעוֹת עֵינַי—The verb כלה, in the Qal, is found also at 4.17, where it is also construed with 'eyes'. The same combination is found at Ps 119.82, 123. LXX ἐξέλιπον 'fail', the same verb as used to translate כלה at Lam 4.17; Ps 119.82, 123, and גוע at Lam 1.19. P ܚܫܟ ḥšk 'become dim', V *defecerunt*, T ספקו (cf. Levine, 115), Aq ἐτελέσθησαν and Sym ἀνηλώθησαν ὑπὸ δακρύων are all feeling their way with the sense of the passage. The poet is saying either that his eyes are worn out with crying (JB, RSV, NIV, Hillers[2], 94) or that his vision is significantly affected because of tears in his eyes (NEB, REB, Renkema, 268f.).

חֳמַרְמְרוּ מֵעַי—The same expression was used at 1.20 (q.v.), though the words are in reverse order.

---

[73] So *BHK*, Rudolph (1938, 107) and Albrektson (105). The latter points out that at Ps 40.9 the same variation occurs in LXX: Cod. A and S read κοιλίας whereas Cod. B has καρδίας. This raises the possibility that ἡ καρδία μου here may be what Wiesmann (150) calls a synecdochic rendering. The argument against this is the strictly literal approach of the LXX translator of Lamentations.
[74] Renkema (268) thinks, with Wiesmann (151) and Pham (105), that the speaker is Zion, as in the second half of ch. 1, but the speech, which begins at v. 11, *addresses* Zion at v. 13, and this rules out such an identification.

נִשְׁפַּךְ לָאָרֶץ כְּבֵדִי—'My liver is poured out on the ground'. The poet continues with yet another physical symptom of his extreme grief. Although the image may not be one with which we can easily identify, there is some evidence that in the ancient Near East the liver was associated with the emotions (cf. Aramaic √כבד 'be angry') on a par with the heart. Hence, in Ugaritic (*CTA* 3.B.25f.): *tgdd. kbdh. bṣhq // ymlu. lbh. bšmḫt // kbd. ʾnt. tšyt* 'her liver swelled up with gladness // her heart was replete with joy // the liver of Anat with triumph'; cf. also Akkadian. Stenmans (22) claims that several instances of *kābôd* in the Hebrew Bible should be emended to *kābēd*: Gen 49.6; Pss 7.6; 16.9; 30.13; 57.9; 108.2, and that these references have to do with the seat of the emotions. The idea of the liver being poured out on the ground has puzzled commentators and translators. The idea may be that the author's grief has had such an effect that his violent vomiting of bile is what is being referred to here. It may have seemed as if his very liver must have poured forth (Blayney, 313f.). AV 'my liver is poured upon the earth' makes no attempt at interpretation—cf. also RV, JB, Luther, Calvin, Keil (493). Some translators, however, decided to make the interpretation in translation, thus RSV renders 'my heart is poured out in grief', JPS 'my being melts away', Renkema (269) 'My spirit is torn asunder', NJB 'my heart plummets', while NEB, REB, NRSV have been content to leave the interpretation to the commentators.

עַל־שֶׁבֶר בַּת־עַמִּי—This second stich of the second line summarises the reason for the aforementioned physical symptoms. While בַּת־עַמִּי, meaning 'my people' occurs at Jer 4.11 in the mouth of Yahweh (cf. also Jer 6.14), at Jer 8.21 the phrase is in the mouth of Jeremiah. The same language is employed here, this time in the mouth of the poet, who associates himself closely with the fate of his own people. While שבר can mean 'break' or 'crushing' (BDB 991) of something physical, such as a pot (Isa 30.14), it is often used of the breaking or wounding of people. Thus, Jeremiah speaks of שבר גדול (4.6) referring to the great invasion from the north, but he also uses the term with reference to the dire state of health of the nation (6.14; cf. 8.11). That the poet had the language of Jeremiah in mind here is very likely, in that he uses the very phrase that we find in Jeremiah—עַל־שֶׁבֶר בַּת־עַמִּי. He is referring not to the meaning that Jeremiah had in mind at 6.14, but to the שבר גדול of Jer 4.6, to the aftermath of 586 BCE. He may be implying that the catastrophe that he had witnessed was predicted.

בֵּעָטֵף עוֹלֵל וְיוֹנֵק בִּרְחֹבוֹת קִרְיָה—The verb √עטף III is found also at v. 12 and at v. 19. MT is prep. בּ + Niphal infin. const. (with elided ה)[75] introducing a temporal clause[76] (GK 114e). GK 511 queries the Masoretic vocalisation

---

[75] IE¹ draws attention to the elision of the ה and cites another example at Ezek 26.15.
[76] The construction (בּ + infin. const.) could be taken as causal—AV, RV, RSV, NRSV, NIV, ESV, Keil (493), Renkema (271)—but the basic reason for the distress has already

(cf. also Joüon, 51 b; BDB 742; *BHK*) as Niphal and suggests that the Qal infin. is sufficient, i.e. בַּעֲטֹף. If the Masoretes are correct, then this is the only instance of the Niphal of עטף√ in the Hebrew Bible, and it raises the question of its possible meaning. The meaning of the Qal ('be feeble, faint'),[77] however, appears to fit the context.[78] The poet's distress is over the ruin of his people, and his unusual physical symptoms, exaggerated for effect, take place while the children and infants are fainting in public. עוֹלֵל occurs at 1.5 (q.v.), 2.19f. and 4.4. יוֹנֵק, the Qal act. part. of ינק√ 'to suck', is used as a substantive, 'suckling, infant'. It occurs also at 4.4 where it combines with עוֹלֵל; cf. also Ps 8.3; Jer 44.7; Joel 2.16.

בִּרְחֹבוֹת קִרְיָה—The term רְחֹב occurs here, at v. 12 and at 4.18. It is f. noun from רחב√ 'be or grow wide' and means 'open area/public place'. In the following verse the phrase is בִּרְחֹבוֹת עִיר. Whether this is just a synonymous expression or whether קִרְיָה refers to settlements other than Jerusalem is difficult to say: probably the former, as most commentators render.

The poet waxes lyrical in his allusions as to how the tragic circumstances have affected him physically. His devastation is couched in imagery unfamiliar to one from Western culture. It is poetic hyperbole for excessive weeping, inner turmoil and overt sickness. And he follows this with a stark allusion to the dire effects of famine in Zion. A common sight is of little children languishing in public places.

2.12

Text and Versions

MT דָּגָן וָיָיִן—so also LXX, V and T; P ܒܗܒܘܪܐ ܘܒܚܡܪܐ ܘܒܡܫܚܐ *'bwr' whmr' wmšḥ'*. Albrektson (106) is probably correct in surmising that P's rendering is not just an addition of a word, but the standard Syriac rendering of the phrase הַדָּגָן וְהַתִּירוֹשׁ וְהַיִּצְהָר at Deut 11.14; Hos 2.10; Joel 1.10.

* * *

Verses 11 and 12 are closely related; indeed, v. 12 continues the picture begun at v. 11c. The subject is the young children, alluded to in the (four) 3rd p. pl. suffixes. Verse 11c seems to suggest that the children were alone in the public places, but v. 12 fills out the scene as the children are depicted with their mothers in the same location.

---

been given as the crushing of the people. LXX, V, T (P ܒܕ ܐܬ̈ܛܪܦܘ *kd 'ṭṭrpw* is ambiguous), Luther, Calvin, Vermigli (89), NJB, JPS, NEB, REB, Hillers[2] (4), Kraus (36), Westermann (142), Rudolph (1962, 217), Berlin (63) understand it to be temporal.

[77] Rashi glosses with Old French *pasmer* 'to faint'.
[78] The meaning of the Niphal may be close to that of Qal, but chosen to convey the idea that the fainting/languishing was not of the infants' choosing.

יֹאמְרוּ—LXX translates this with an aorist (εἶπαν) but if the poet's grief in v. 11 coincided with the plight of the children, then he is enlarging that picture by alluding to the cries of the children to their mothers, and so we should think of this imperfect as a frequentative: 'they say/keep saying'. The rest of the line is direct speech: 'Where is corn and wine?'

אַיֵּה דָּגָן וָיָיִן—This is the only place in the Hebrew Bible where 'corn' and 'wine' are combined, the more usual expression being לחם ויין (Gen 14.18). Elsewhere in Lamentations the normal word for food is לחם (1.11; 4.4; 5.6, 9) or אֹכֶל (1.11, 19).

Scholars have had some difficulty understanding this passage in that it seems strange for children who are starving to ask for corn and wine. It would be more natural for them to ask for bread and water. While we might interpret דגן to mean the source of basic food, 'wine' on the lips of children is another matter.[79] Budde (1892, 269), followed by Löhr (1893, 9) considered that the first line of v. 12 is unnaturally balanced: that the first stich is too short and the second too long. It is also suggested that wine for children is unthinkable. Budde's suggestion is that the words אֵין לָנוּ have dropped out after יאמרו, and that ויין should be deleted: the line would then read—לאמתם יאמרו אי לנו איה דגן. Another suggestion, by Ehrlich (37), followed by Gottwald (11) and Pham (132), is that ויין is a scribal error for וָאָיִן 'but there is none'. Kraus (38) is prepared, with Haller (100), *BHK* and JB, only to delete ויין, while Rudolph (1962, 219f.) prefers retaining MT. Of the modern translations, only JB 'where is the bread?' and NJB 'where is some food?' appear to emend here,[80] though several (RSV, REB, JPS, NIV, Westermann, 142), render 'bread[81] and wine'. In an observation quite detached from the 'children' issue, Albrektson (106) draws attention to the assonance of דָּגָן וָיָיִן where the long 'a' is juxtaposed four times and thinks that the poet may have chosen the combination for the sake of euphony.[82] Renkema (273f.) picks this up but suggests that, given that we are dealing with direct speech, 'it seems more reasonable to imagine that the poets were in fact imitating child talk, the repeated a-sound being primary in infancy, no matter what the language'. Renkema goes on to argue that the young children would always be with their

---

[79] It is interesting to observe that neither MR nor MLT show any unease with children requesting wine, nor does T make any attempt to sidestep the issue; and Rashi and Kara make no comment. IE², who points out that mothers are mentioned, and not fathers, because it is the mothers who give suck, says nothing about the request for wine. One midrash (*lechem dim'ah*) explains that the children were thinking about the past and reminiscing that at one time they had many delicacies. That is, when they were fainting in the streets they would recall the time when they had eaten corn and wine; cf. 1.7. We should, perhaps, note that, whereas at 4.4 the children ask (שָׁאַל) for bread, here it says they said (אמר) 'Where is corn and wine?' Calvin, however, is exercised by the request of the children and wonders if older children are being referred to here.
[80] JB's footnote acknowledges the deletion of 'and wine', but NJB does not footnote this.
[81] At Ps 78.24 the word דגן is used as poetic for לחם: דְּגַן־שָׁמַיִם 'the corn of heaven'.
[82] The same assonance is obtained with דָּגָן וָמַיִם.

mother when she was baking bread and would know that corn was the first stage of baking, hence their cry; and in wine-producing countries, children drink wine at an early age. Berlin (72) points out that 'What *dāgān* and *yayin* have in common, as opposed to *tîrôš* and *leḥem*, is that both grain and wine can be stored for long periods, while bread and juice spoil quickly. I interpret the children's request as meaning "Are there any remnants of stored-up food?"' While there may be something in what Berlin says, it is hardly likely that starving children would think in these terms and less likely that their cries would consist of anything other than the basic 'Give us something to eat and drink!' We must remember that, although the cry is couched in direct speech, we are dealing with Hebrew poetry (cf. Hos 14.8). 'Corn and wine' may seem a little strange to the Western mind of the 21st century CE, but the frantic casting around for emendations appears to have abated; hence, commentaries such as Provan, Dobbs-Allsopp and House do not discuss the aforementioned problems.

כֶּחָלָל—Literally 'like a wounded person'. The def. art. denotes the class, i.e. 'like wounded men' (NEB). The construction here of the prep. + infin. const. occurs at v. 11c and v. 12b and c. At v. 12b the poet employs the same verb עטף as in v. 11c, though now in the Hithpael, and in v. 12c another Hithpael, this time of a root שׁפך, used in v. 11.

בְּהִשְׁתַּפֵּךְ נַפְשָׁם—The final line is variously interpreted. LXX ψυχὰς αὐτῶν 'their souls' gives the impression that the children were dying; cf. also V. P and T are ambiguous. Luther and Calvin continue to hold that the construction שׁפך נפשׁ means 'to expire', as do AV, JB, NRSV, NIV, Keil (502), Rudolph (1962, 217), Westermann (142), Kaiser (326), Driver (1953, 262). However, Provan (71f.) has drawn attention to the use of this terminology in other passages, where the meaning is other than dying. At Job 30.16, where the Hithpael of שׁפך is used in combination with נפשׁ, the sense is of personal suffering (or giving voice to suffering). The Qal of שׁפך is used, again with נפשׁ, at 1 Sam 1.15 where Hannah, responding to Eli's accusation, declares that he has misinterpreted her behaviour, which was in fact her pouring out her נפשׁ before Yahweh. The combination appears also at Ps 42.5, where the author seems to speak merely of lamenting his present situation; and in Ps 102.1, the superscription, where the root עטף also occurs, we read that it is a prayer of someone who is 'afflicted, when he is faint and pours out his שׂיח before Yahweh'. These passages are important for the understanding of the present passage. None of them can refer to death, nor are they merely describing suffering or affliction. To pour out one's נפשׁ may not be exactly the same as to pour out one's שׂיח, but it would seem that what is common to the above passages is the giving voice to affliction. If this is so, then the aforementioned children are probably crying/screaming with hunger in the arms of their mothers. The prep. אל (BDB 39, 3), rather than ב, may allude to their faces turned towards/buried in their mothers' bosoms. That the poet was differentiating between the עולל and the יונק is quite possible. Having introduced the categories, עולל and יונק, the two circumstantial clauses may refer each to one of the two categories—12b referring to the עולל in the street, and 12c to the יונק in the arms of the mother.

חֵיק—This word is used of men (Num 11.12) and women (Ruth 4.16) where it denotes the fold of a garment at chest level. It may also refer to the breast of a woman (Prov 5.20). But expressions such as אִישׁ חֵיקָהּ (Deut 28.56), which must mean the man whom she embraces, i.e. her husband (REB), should warn against being too precise here. Hence, the translations 'lap' (Kraus, 36; Renkema, 276; Rudolph 1962, 217; Hillers[2], 94) and 'breast' (Kaiser, 326; JB) are too narrow; and in any case may rule out the עולל. It is better to see here a picture of mothers embracing their offspring/children; cf. NIV 'in their mothers' arms'.

Renkema (273) notes the double occurrence of 'their mothers' in this verse, holding that this is not a mere repetition but 'a quite intentional and meaningful inclusion: ...The mothers are mentioned at the beginning and the end and thus they embrace (in literary terms) their weakening children and dying infants.' Renkema may be reading too much into this verse, but it is certain that the repetition of 'their mothers' and the mention of children and infants (v. 11c and the subject of v. 12) create a vivid and heart-rending picture of the hopeless victims of famine, a picture which touched the heart of the poet (cf. v. 11).

2.13

Text and Versions

MT מָה־אֲעִידֵךְ; LXX τί μαρτυρήσω σοι; P ܐܟܘܬܟܝ ܡܢ ’shdky; V cui conparabo te; OL quid testabor tibi; SH ܐܟܘܬܟܝ ܠܟܝ ܡܢ ’shd lky; SH margin ܐܟܘܬܟܝ ܠܟܝ ܡܢ ’šw’ lky = τί ἐξισώσω σοι;[83] T מה אסהד בך. The Versions may differ, but they represent different interpretations of the same consonantal text, cf. Schäfer (*BHQ*, 122*); see below.

MT כַּיָּם; so also P, V and T (in paraphrase); LXX ποτήριον. LXX *Vorlage* probably read כוס. MT is preferable.

* * *

The poet, who has painted a grim picture of the aftermath of 586 BCE and who has shown himself to be deeply moved by it all, continues in the same vein in this verse. However, here he addresses Zion for the first time. While the text is difficult, the author seems to be saying that Zion's experience of destruction is incomparable: it is an open question whether she can be restored.

---

[83] In the crowded margin of SH this reading appears to be an alternative rendering. It is followed by a reading attributed to Sym, ܐܟܘܬܟܝ ܠܟܝ ܐܕܡܐ ܕܐܕܡܝܟܝ, attached to the first line but which belongs with the second line; see Schäfer (122*).

מָה־אֲעִידֵךְ—Although LXX, P and T appear to derive אֲעִידֵךְ from עוד (denominative verb from עֵד ['witness']) 'to testify', the sense that emerges is far from satisfactory in the context: 'What shall I testify to/for you?'[84] Meinhold (286) suggested the emendation[85] מָה אֶעֱרוֹךְ and translates 'was soll ich zur vergleichung oder zum Trost dir vorlegen?' or 'was soll ich dir Vergleichen?' It is true that ד and ר are sometimes misread by scribes in transmission, and it is also true that at Isa 40.18 and Ps 89.7 the verb דמה appears in parallel with ערך and that ערך can mean 'to liken, compare' in other passages—Ps 40.6; Job 28.17, 19. The weakness of Meinhold's conjecture, however, is that it does not account for the suffix. It might be argued (so Kelso, 30; BHK, BHS) that V read אערך, but in V the 2nd p. s. suffix is represented.[86] Daiches (189) rejects this emendation as unhelpful. He claims that the verb עוד (HALOT √עוד I 'to return'; cf. Arabic *ʿāda* IV 'restore') here has the same meaning as in יעודד Pss 146.9; 147.6, and in נתעודד Ps 20.9. In Pss 146 and 147, the Polel means 'to restore, relieve, give strength to', and Daiches submits that there is a verb עוד 'to encourage, restore' and that we have it in this passage: Qal (*Kethib*) or Hiphil (*Qere*).[87] His translation, 'How shall I relieve thee (by words of comfort, or give thee courage)?', then produces a parallel with וַאֲנַחֲמֵךְ, and Daiches declares that the verse is now 'more symmetrical'. Gordis (164), though he does not mention Daiches, claims that the 'key to our understanding of the passage lies in recognizing the chiasmus of the four verbs' by which he means that the 1st and 4th are parallel to each other, as are the 2nd and 3rd. Reading the *Qere*, he draws attention to the Hiphil of עוד at Ben Sira 4.11 (ותעיד) with the meaning 'strengthen, fortify'. Gottlieb (32) follows this explanation, as does NEB[88] 'How can I cheer you?'; cf. also Gottwald (11) and Rudolph 'aufrichten' (1962, 217). Kraus (36, 38), reading 'Wie soll ich dir zureden', argues that the Hiphil of the verb עוד 'repeat (words)' may be interpreted 'console'; and so a similar result is obtained. Ehrlich (37) refers to Jer 49.19,[89] where מִי יֹעִידֶנִּי (vocalised by the Masoretes as from √יעד) is parallel to מִי כָמוֹנִי,

---

[84] NRSV's 'What can I say for you?' is too weak a translation of the Hiphil of עוד to be convincing.

[85] In this he is followed by Simian-Yofre (1999, 512). Meinhold is followed by Hillers[2] (100), though the latter acknowledges V's contribution here; and JPS's footnote to the translation 'take as witness', namely, 'Emendation yields "compare"', probably conceals a preference for Meinhold's conjecture.

[86] In fact, it is not certain that Jerome had a text based on ערך. The latter verb occurs at Isa 40.18; Pss 40.6; 89.7; Job 28.17, 19, with the meaning 'compare/liken', but V does not employ the verb *comparari* in those passages.

[87] The *Kethib* (אעודך)–*Qere* (אעידך) to which Daiches refers appears in מקראות גדולות, though not in *BHQ*; see also NEB and Gordis (1971, 134) and compare Gottlieb (32) and Alexander (2008, 136).

[88] Brockington (217) indicates that they read אֲעֹדֵךְ.

[89] It is interesting that NEB translates Jer 49.19 'who is my equal?' (יֹעִידֶנִּי יְעִידֵנִי), parallel to 'who is like me?'; cf. Brockington (214). For a discussion on Jer 49.19 and Lam 2.13a, see Barthélemy (805-808).

and argues that מָה־אֲעִידֵךְ is synonymous with the following words מָה אֲדַמֶּה־לָּךְ. In this he is following V[90] but he is careful to point out that Jerome did not read ערוך. Albrektson (108) agrees '...for the original meaning of עוד Hiphil is "repeat", and it is most probable that it should here mean "repeat = produce yet another case of, name a parallel to"'. Gordis's chiasmus may be lost, but it is not at all obvious that a chiastic structure is intended here, and Renkema (277) may be right in pointing out that the triple repetition of what amounts to the same question serves to underline the fact that nothing can compare with Zion's situation. I am inclined to favour Ehrlich's interpretation here.

הַבַּת יְרוּשָׁלַםִ—On this, see on בת ציון (1.6). While בת can be either absolute or construct, the presence of the definite article ensures that we see it as absolute and the relationship between the words as apposition. On בְּתוּלַת בַּת־צִיּוֹן, see on 1.15.

מָה אַשְׁוֶה־לָּךְ וַאֲנַחֲמֵךְ—The poet declares by these questions that there is no equal to Zion's calamity (cf. 1.12). If he could identify a people or nation who had suffered like Zion he would name it, and that would bring some comfort to Zion. It is not clear why the discovery of a comparable plight would be of any comfort, but Rashi points out: 'when adversity hits a person, others say to him "This happened to such and such a person"; and these are comforts to him'. Kara comments: 'the questioner asks the questions so that he might be able to say "there is no people to whom it has happened as it has happened to you, that you might look at it and be comforted"'; and this is how Calvin understood the passage.

The statement of the שבר being great as the sea is ambiguous. Does it refer to the expanse of the ocean (NEB) or to its depth (NIV)? It is not clear, but the reference to the sea in Ps 104.25, which has to do with the vastness of the sea, would seem to favour the former. The poet, casting around for a simile to describe the destruction, can think of nothing bigger than the sea. Renkema (278f.) is inclined to read too much into this simile. There is nothing sinister here. Yahweh created the sea (Ps 95.5) and has control over it (Job 26.12). The Targumist perhaps sees here a play on words. The שבר, he assumes, alludes to the משברי ים 'the breakers of the sea' (Ps 93.4), and he translates 'your break is as great as the breakers of the great sea's waves in a storm'. Gordis (165), though not referring to T, sees the same connection: '...the poet has chosen the noun שבר for "destruction, calamity" out of the many available synonyms because it suggests the noun משבר (Ps 42.8; Jonah 2.4) "breaker, wave", which is particularly appropriate in this comparison to the sea.' The trouble with this interpretation

---

[90] Luther's translation, 'wem soll ich dich gleichen', may owe something to V's rendering and may have influenced Ehrlich here; cf. also Knox 'Might I confront thee with another as thyself?'

is that it is inclined to deflect from the image, which is linked to the severity of Zion's calamity. The choice of the word שֶׁבֶר is because the poet has used it in v. 11, and it is used in v. 11 because the phrase שֶׁבֶר בַּת עַמִּי or שֶׁבֶר עַמִּי was an acceptable or an established way of referring to the downfall of the people (Isa 30.26; Jer 8.21; Amos 6.6; cf. Lam 3.48; 4.10); and the choice of 'sea' was because the poet could think of nothing bigger (גָּדוֹל) than the sea.[91] The idea is that the sea (= the Great Sea, the Mediterranean, probably) is beyond imagining; and the final stich states, in effect, that Zion's ruin seems beyond repair.

The four rhetorical questions directed, as it were, at Jerusalem reflect the poet's grief, earlier alluded to at vv. 11f., and his astonishment at the scenario now before him. The impregnable Jerusalem was not meant to be like this. What he witnesses is staggering. His final question: 'Who can heal you?' means 'You are beyond healing/repair'. And yet the personal interrogative 'who?' must reflect the possibility in the poet's mind that Yahweh is probably the only hope in this regard: the very one who has caused the catastrophe.

2.14

Text and Versions

MT (*Kethib*) לְהָשִׁיב שְׁבוּתֵךְ; MT (*Qere*) לְהָשִׁיב שְׁבִיתֵךְ with several MSS[Ken]; LXX τοῦ ἐπιστρέψαι αἰχμαλωσίαν σου; V *ut te ad paenitentiam provocarent*; T לאהדרותיך בתיובתא; P ܕܬܬܘܒܝܢ ܘܗܦܟ ܫܒܝܬܟܝ *dttwbyn w'hpk šbytky*. Versions differ, and P's double rendering reflects uncertainty; *Qere* is preferred (see below). On this see Albrektson (111) and Schäfer (122f.*).

MT מַשְׂאוֹת; LXX λήμματα; SH ܫܩܠ̈ *šql'*; V *adsumptiones*; P ܢܒܘ̈ܬܐ *nbywt'*; T נבואת. Versions read the same consonantal text as the Masoretes.

* * *

The connection with the previous verse is the poet's reflection on the great ruin (vv. 11, 13). For the first time in this poem the author feels the need to offer an explanation for what has happened (cf. 1.5, 8, 18, 22). The reference to the people's guilt is, therefore, important. The ruin would not have happened if the people had not sinned. In this regard, the prophets are singled out for severe criticism here. Zion is told that the prophets could have averted the disaster. They had 'seen' false and fraudulent visions, and the implication here is that they could have had genuine visions from Yahweh, which, if accepted and delivered to the people, would have provided an opportunity for escape from the disaster. The prophets are being condemned for not uncovering the guilt of the people.

---

[91] Hillers[2] (106f.) notes that in a Ugaritic text (*CTA* 23 = *UT* 52, 33-35) El's hand is 'long as the sea'; and at Job 11.9 God's measure is said to be broader then the sea. One is reminded of many passages where 'sand' is used to emphasise great numbers: Judg 7.12 '...their camels were without number, as the sand by the sea side for multitude'; cf. Ps 139.18 etc.

At first sight this looks like a further indictment, but the poet may be implying that had the prophets been in genuine contact with Yahweh they would have focussed on Zion's guilt. That focus was wanting, for that was the reason for the fall of Jerusalem. The entire verse seems to be an attack on the prophets. But does the poet mean *all* the prophets? It would appear, from Jeremiah, that he, at least, strove to uncover the sin and guilt of the people and their rulers. If we took Jeremiah to be the author of this poem, we might interpret this verse as an attack on his opponents, the false prophets (Jer 27.9, 16; 29.8; 37.19)—those who say 'All is well' when all is not well (Jer 6.14; 8.11). Even if Jeremiah is not the author, this verse should be interpreted as referring to the same false prophets. The inviolability of Jerusalem, where Yahweh dwells, was a vibrant doctrine prior to 586 BCE. The official prophets adhered to it, and those who spoke against it or disregarded it (e.g. Jeremiah) were regarded as heretics and traitors; but the poet here is saying, in effect, that the heretics were the official prophets who had silenced/opposed figures like Jeremiah.

The reference to 'prophets', at v. 9, has to do with Zion's prophetic figures *after* the fall of the city, while the reference in v. 14 is to the situation before the disaster occurred (Müller, 23). The tense, therefore, is preterite, and the LXX employs the aorist. As in v. 9, the root for prophetic vision is חזה. But the prophets mentioned here are false prophets,[92] and T spells this out: נביאי שקרי דבבינך, as does MLT.

The term שוא 'emptiness, worthlessness' is found at Ezek 12.24 חזון שוא 'a worthless vision'. It is construed with דָּבָר at Pss 12.3; 41.7, where the combination may mean 'to lie'; and the two versions of the Decalogue indicate that עד שוא (Exod 20.16) is equivalent to עד שקר (Deut 5.20), cf. Sawyer (882f.). At Ezek 13.6, 7, 9, 23; 21.34; 22.28 the term שוא is used in connection with false prophets.

תָּפֵל—This is a rare word. There appear to be two roots: √תפל I the root underlying תִּפְלָה 'unseemliness' (Jer 23.13) and תָּפֵל 'tasteless' (Job 6.6), and √תפל II the root of תָּפֵל 'whitewash' (Ezek 13.10, 11, 14, 15). LXX ἀφροσύνην 'folly' is a weak attempt at translating תָּפֵל here, but Albrektson (110) has shown that the Hebrew roots were unfamiliar to LXX translators. V *stulta* may have been influenced by LXX here, but the T paraphrase '…there is no substance (מֹשׁשׁ) to their prophecy' clearly takes תָּפֵל to be from the first root. MR quotes Jer 23.13 'In the prophets of Samaria I have seen תִּפְלָה', which indicates that the rabbis understood the term in Lam 2.14 as equivalent to תִּפְלָה.[93] Rashi explains the entire phrase

---

[92] This is clear from what follows. Jeremiah refers to these figures: Jer 2.8; 5.12; 6.13f.; 8.10; 14.14f.; 23.32; 27.10, 15.
[93] Although it should be noted that MLT appears to link both roots: 'False prophets…were comforting you and healing you in a superficial way, as scripture says "they have healed…" (Jer 8.11); וְתָפֵל: They were smearing תפל "whitewash" by their words, as scripture says "…unto those who smear whitewash…" (Ezek 13.11)'.

שָׁוְא וְתָפֵל 'words in which there is no taste/discernment'; and he glosses this in French *aflestrimant* 'insipidity'. At Ezek 22.28, Rashi explains תפל as חסר 'want', and at Job 6.6 he explains it as צריך 'need'. IE[1] comments that תפל is like שוא, by which he may mean that both words have roughly the same meaning and that the second is stressing the first, or is epexegetical of the first. Calvin, though not entirely confident—his translation is *insulsitatem (vel, insipidum)*—goes on to indicate that he took the term from the first root, speaking about the insipidity of the false prophets who had opposed Jeremiah.

Rudolph (1962, 217, 220) claims that the meaning 'insipid' is too weak here and opts for 'Tünche' and is followed by Kaiser (327), Westermann (145) and Hillers[2] (100). Of modern translations, NIV 'worthless' has stayed with √תפל I; so also, it would seem JB 'tinsel things',[94] JPS, Renkema (281), while NEB 'painted shrines' and NJB 'deceptive whitewash' have opted for II√תפל. Of all commentators, Calvin stands out on the question of responsibility. He acknowledges the guilt of the false prophets but he insists that there is an indictment here of the people, who heard gladly the message of those prophets and refused to listen to someone like Jeremiah (cf. Mic 2.11; Jer 5.31).

וְלֹא־גִלּוּ עַל־עֲוֺנֵךְ—At Job 20.27 גלה is construed with a direct object, and that is how it is usually found. Yet in Lamentations, both here and at 4.22, גלה in the Piel is construed with על.[95] Albrektson (111) notes that the literalness of LXX is shown by its representing the Hebrew construction rigidly in both passages. 'Your prophets' is the subject of לא גלו. They are criticised here because they failed to fulfil the true prophet's task of exposing iniquity; cf. Hos 7.1; Mic 3.8. The awareness of sin could have led to repentance which might have averted punishment—Jer 18; Jonah 3.10. The poet is aware of this fact. He believed that, had the iniquity been revealed, the people could have changed their ways and averted the disaster which he was describing earlier; cf. Ezek 18.23. עון is found also at 4.6, 13, 22; 5.7. It can mean 'iniquity' or 'guilt' or, indeed, 'punishment of iniquity' (BDB 730f.).

לְהָשִׁיב שְׁבוּתֵךְ—Reading the *Qere*, in line with Jer 32.44 (אָשִׁיב אֶת־שְׁבוּתָם). The word שבות occurs six times in the Hebrew Bible as *Qere* (for שבית), while שבית occurs four times as *Qere* (for שבות). Although the Versions almost always derive שבות from שבה 'to take captive' and hence the phrase השיב שבות (or שוב שבות)[96] as meaning 'to bring back the captivity', the evidence from Job 42.10—וַיהוָה שָׁב אֶת־שְׁבוּת אִיּוֹב—calls in question that derivation. AV 'And the Lord turned the captivity of Job' does not make sense in the context. Clearly, the phrase does not refer to 'captivity' but

---

[94] However, JB's footnote, 'Lit. whitewash and roughcast', indicates that the translators take the view that there is only one תפל root.
[95] The construction גלה על is found only in Lamentations—here and at 4.22.
[96] On Qal transitive, see BDB 998.

(based on a derivation from √שוב) 'to bring about change'; cf. *HALOT*. The precise meaning of להשיב שבותך will depend on the context. If one takes the passage as referring to the prophets in the midst of calamity (Provan, 74), dishing out platitudes and failing to expose the sins of the people, then the meaning may be 'to restore you to your former state' (cf. Ps 126.1). However, in the light of v. 9, where the present prophets were not receiving visions, the more likely scenario[97] is of the pre-exilic false prophets who failed in their duty to discern the people's state of moral health.

The final line poses several problems. There is the question of whether the poet is repeating the sentiments of line 1; there is the question as to whether the final three words are in a construct chain; and there is the meaning of the *hapax legomenon* מדוחים. There is a degree of repetition (of line 1) in this third line. חזה appears again, as do לך and שוא. The effect of this is to emphasise the theme of the misleading prophetic figures in the pre-exilic period. It could be argued that the manner in which the poet does so is a bit clumsy, but there is no doubt that the third line drives home the point made earlier. Syntactically, lines 2 and 3 are harmonious. Line 2 deals with what the prophets did not do (but should have done), while the third line describes what they did.

מַשְׂאוֹת—This term occurs only here in Lamentations. Most scholars interpret this noun[98] (מַשָּׂא II) as from קול נשא 'to raise the voice', i.e. 'utterance, pronouncement', as in Prov 30.1; 31.1. Here we have the pl. const. of מַשָּׂא 'utterance, oracle' (pl. abs. = מַשָּׂאוֹת). It is construed with חזה at Hab 1.1 and Isa 13.1, as well as here; and the meaning is 'to perceive an oracle' (as a prophet). That we are dealing here with prophetic utterances/oracles is clear from the context, and a glance at the Versions confirms this interpretation. IE[1] glosses the term with נבואות. The phrase מַשְׂאוֹת שָׁוְא וּמַדּוּחִים, which constitutes the object of ויחזו, is considered suspect by a number of commentators—who feel that the 3:2 rhythm is violated. Yet there are some who, with Bickell (110) and Budde,[99] are concerned about the violation of the metre, and disagree as to the solution to the problem. Budde (1898a, 89) merely vocalises מַשְׂאוֹת and considers the final two words to be in apposition (so also *BHK*, cf. *BHS*); but Rudolph (1962, 220), following Perles (1922, 41, 102) argues for a re-pointing—מַשְׁאוֹת from √נשא (Hiphil 'to deceive'). This is to introduce a *hapax legomenon*, though at Pss 73.18; 74.3 we do have the term מַשּׁוּאוֹת, meaning 'deceptions'. NEB 'delusions' follows Rudolph in this pointing and understanding of the term; cf. Brockington (217). Albrektson (112) rightly cautions against arguments from metre; so also Hillers[2] (100) who stresses that the construction is quite acceptable Hebrew.

---

[97] Dobbs-Allsopp (97) favours the former but considers it possible that *both* meanings are intended!
[98] As opposed to מַשָּׂא I = 'burden', though see de Boer (197-214).
[99] Cf. also Kraus (38), Wiesmann (153).

מַדּוּחִים—On the form, see BL 494g; another *hapax legomenon*, the meaning of which is uncertain. LXX and V 'expellings' take it to be from נדח√ I 'impel, banish', while P 'enticements' and T 'misleading words' appear to derive from one of the meanings of the Hiphil of the same root, *viz.* 'to seduce' (BDB 623).[100] Rashi, IE[1] and Kara all take this line. Scholars are divided. The meaning 'banishments, expellings' is surely to be interpreted as 'things causing banishment', so Calvin, Luther, AV (causes of banishments). Keil (503) draws attention to Jer 27.10, 15 which have to do with false prophets who speak lies leading to the people's expulsion from the land; and this is how it is understood by Löhr (1906, 13), Budde (1898ᵃ, 89), Nägelsbach (86) and, more recently, Rudolph (1962, 217), cf. NEB footnote. Those who follow P, T, Rashi etc. are Kaiser (327), Kraus (37), Hillers[2] (95), Westermann (142), Gottwald (11), Renkema (288), NEB, NIV, JB, JPS. The latter interpretation fits better with what has preceded.

2.15

Text and Versions
MT כְּלִילַת יֹפִי; LXX στέφανος δόξης; P ܓܡܝܪܬ ܫܘܦܪܐ *gmyrt šwpr*ʾ; V *perfecti decoris*; Aq τελεία κάλλει; T גמירת נואי ושופרא. Versions read the same text as MT.
The final line is unusually long. Bickell (110f.) wishes to delete הָעִיר, Budde (1898ᵃ, 89f.) deletes הָעִיר שֶׁיֹּאמְרוּ, Gordis (165) removes שֶׁיֹּאמְרוּ, while Rudolph (1938, 108) favours the deletion of לְכָל־הָאָרֶץ. BHK and BHS suggest deleting either שֶׁיֹּאמְרוּ or מָשׂוֹשׂ לְכָל־הָאָרֶץ to make the line conform to the usual pattern in the poem. The Versions substantially support MT, and Schäfer (*BHQ*, 123*) notes that, there being no textual evidence of a shorter text, such emendations seem arbitrary. It is *possible* that the poet originally constructed a line which ended with כְּלִילַת יֹפִי, to which has been added, in the course of transmission, משוש לכל הארץ. On the other hand, it may be that the poet allowed himself a bit of flexibility and deliberately lengthened the line.

* * *

The poet continues to address Zion in this verse, but, whereas v. 14 looked back at the period before 586 BCE, the situation now appears to be the present. The sight of the ruined city evokes responses from the outsiders. At 1.12 the phrase 'All you who pass by' is in the mouth of Zion. Here the poet imagines, perhaps, the same scene but, whereas in 1.12 the passers-by are not given a voice nor is their reaction noted, here the emphasis is on those, supposed, reactions; and the poet appears to stress that they are horrified at what they witness. With the final line's reference to Zion's former glory, the poet captures the contrast motif characteristic of the

---

[100] Kelso (31): 'Es ist beinahe unmöglich, zu entscheiden, ob diese Versionen diesem Worte eine sekundäre Bedeutung zugeschrieben, oder eine andere Lesart gehabt haben'. The LXX and V translators may have envisaged oracles leading to the banishment/exile of the people.

lament for the dead. The superlatives which are employed hark back to the good old days of prosperity and vigour which are in stark contrast to the scene before him and observed by the passers-by.

The interpretation of this verse poses problems. Do the actions of the passers-by consist of scorn/mockery? Or do they reflect shock? Or is there something more mysterious afoot? Köhler (136f.), arguing that the ancients believed that deserted towns were inhabited or haunted by demons and spirits, says that in such cases men would go past quickly, whistling and waving their hands to keep these phenomena at bay or to exorcise them. Citing Isa 13.20ff., he refers also to 1 Kgs 9.8; Jer 19.8; Lam 2.15; Zeph 2.13ff. in this regard. He is followed by Rudolph (1962, 225), Jahnow (187), Kaiser (339f.), JPS footnote. Renkema (291), however, rightly points out that we are not dealing with a deserted city, that Jerusalem '…was still substantially inhabited and was hardly the place one would expect to find ghosts'. The comments of IE[2] show that he feels that Zion is being mocked by these gestures; and this is substantially the view taken by several scholars—Keil (503), Hillers[2] (107), Provan (74f.), Kraus (47), cf. NEB, NIV.[101] Rashi, commenting on שרק 'hiss, whistle', says, 'It is usual for someone who sees an important thing ruined to do this', and this is basically the interpretation reflected in MLT ('…when a man sees his companion changed from what he was, he claps his hands at him and whistles and shakes his head') and by Kara. The latter cites Jer 19.8, which envisages the astonished horror of those who will witness the ruin of Jerusalem.[102] Calvin also concludes that abhorrence is the occasion and inspiration for these gestures.[103]

שֶׁיֹּאמְרוּ—The relative particle; שֶׁ (= אֲשֶׁר BDB 979f.; GK 36) occurs four times in Lamentations (2.15, 16; 4.9; 5.18). The form יֹאמְרוּ (Qal impf.) may be taken to mean 'they say, call' or 'it is said, called'; cf. Eccl 1.10 where the same construction and meaning occur.[104] The Masoretes have punctuated so that there are two epithets attributed to Jerusalem. LXX, however, without the Masoretic markings, runs them both together—'the crown of glory of joy of all the earth'.[105] P, V, T and Aq rightly keep them separate. They appear separately at Pss 48.2 and 50.3. Schleusner (22)

---

[101] On בַּת יְרוּשָׁלָ͏ִם, see on בַּת צִיּוֹן (1.6).
[102] McKane (1986, 453), on Jer 19.8, comments 'The horrific wounds inflicted on Jerusalem will appal those who see them, and a sharp expelling of the breath, indicative of the terror which the sight inspires, will issue as a kind of whistling. It is this which is intended by שְׁרֵקָה and שָׁרַק, and not, as some have supposed, a whistle of derision'.
[103] Renkema (291) takes the view that the gestures should be interpreted merely as shock at the sight of the city. He argues, rightly, that the gestures in themselves do not imply contempt and that the context must drive the interpretation in every case.
[104] On the impersonal subject, see JM 155b.
[105] εὐφροσύνης is the reading of most MSS, including B and A; but the editions rightly read εὐφροσύνη with Sinaiticus.

observed that LXX στέφανος for כלילה appears to have taken the Hebrew in its Aramaic (כלילא) meaning, 'crown' (cf. also Arabic *iklīl* 'crown' and Akk. *kilīlu* 'wreath').[106] The other Versions (including Aq) understand the form to mean 'perfection'—in this case, f. constr., with יְפִי (in pause, for יָפִי) 'beauty'; cf. GK 128x. Rashi's comment 'all beauty was hers' steers us also in this direction. In Ezek 27.3, the king of Tyre says of himself אֲנִי כְּלִילַת יֹפִי, and at 28.12 it is said that he is כְּלִיל יֹפִי. At Ps 50.2, Zion is described as מִכְלַל־יֹפִי. While מִכְלָל is a *hapax legomenon*, it is close enough to כלילה as to derivation and application that its meaning cannot be very different. Indeed, the occurrence of מִכְלַל־יֹפִי probably confirms the meaning 'perfection' (rather than 'crown') in this passage.

מָשׂוֹשׂ לְכָל־הָאָרֶץ—This is an epithet applied to Zion at Ps 48.3 where the phrase is מְשׂוֹשׂ כָּל־הָאָרֶץ. כָּל־הָאָרֶץ may refer to the whole land (of Palestine) but, in the light of Jer 51.41 where Babylon is described as תְּהִלַּת כָּל־הָאָרֶץ, it would seem to mean 'all the earth'.

As the poet considers those who may be in the vicinity of the ruined city of Jerusalem he notices their body language, which suggests that they are stunned and horrified at the sight, and he imagines them contrasting the scene with Zion in her heyday. The epithets, in the mouths of the passers-by, appear also in Psalms (48.3; 50.2) and are probably self-congratulatory phrases[107] reflecting not so much the thinking of others as Jerusalemites themselves. The tragic reversal element comes through strongly here, and we are reminded of the first verse of ch. 1 where other epithets—fine descriptions of the once great city—are set over against her present lowly state.

2.16

Text and Versions
On the question of the alphabetic order, see *Introduction*. Whereas at 1.16-17 the sequence reflects the accepted order of the alphabet (פ–ע), here (and in chs. 3–4) the order is ע–פ. To reverse the order in ch. 2 would do violence to the context. MT order is followed by LXX,[108] V and T. P changes the order of the verses to conform to that in ch. 1 and maintains this order in chs. 3–4, and four MSS[Ken] and one MS[de Ros] follow this order. MT order should be maintained.

---

[106] LXX made the same identification at Ezek 28.12. In fact, this is how it is taken by Ewald (335) and Driver (1950, 144f.). The phrase כְּלִילַת יֹפִי is then rendered 'beauteous crown', and the image will be of Jerusalem, which may have seemed crown-like from its surrounding valleys. Cf. Alexander (2008, 138 n. 54).
[107] Cf. 'The Athens of the North' of Edinburgh, and 'The Big Apple' of New York City.
[108] It should be noted that the person who placed the Ἄλεφ, Βήθ etc. above the units in the LXX is unlikely to have been the translator, for Ἄιν has been placed above the פ verse, and Φή above the ע verse in these three chapters, though this has been corrected in some MSS.

CHAPTER 2   161

MT בְּלָעֲנוּ—so also V and T; LXX κατεπίομεν αὐτήν—so also P and OL. On the basis of LXX, Dyserinck (369) suggests reading בִּלְעָנוּהָ; and he is followed by Budde (1898ª, 90), Kelso (32) and *BHK*; but note the renderings of AV, Luther, RSV, NIV, NJB, JPS etc., which translate MT as having an implied object. The same thing occurs in the final line where LXX (cf. also OL) translates מָצָאנוּ with εὕρομεν αὐτήν, and where OL translates רָאִינוּ with *vidimus eam*. There is no need to emend.

* * *

In this verse the poet turns his focus on the enemies of Zion, not to be confused with the passers-by of v. 15. He is still, as it were, addressing his remarks to Zion. Whereas in v. 15 the passers-by were horror-struck at what they saw, here Zion's enemies are in a triumphant and gloating frame of mind. The connection with the previous verse includes the idea of reaction, from the outside, to Zion's plight. There is also the introduction, in each case, of direct speech, giving vividness to the picture; furthermore, there are gestures which overlap to some extent with those described in v. 15. Just as in other cultures, whistling may be construed differently according to context, so in v. 15 whistling accompanies the horror/shock felt by the passers-by, while in v. 16 it is employed to emphasise the hostility of the enemies of Zion.

כָּל־אוֹיְבַיִךְ—While the expression 'all your enemies' is part of the hyperbole of the poem, there is no doubt that these will have included the Ammonites (Ezek 25.3, 6), Philistines (Ezek 25.15), Edomites (Ezek 35.12, 15; Obad 1f.) and, probably, Moabites.

פָּצוּ עָלַיִךְ פִּיהֶם—The exegesis of this phrase and the interpretation of the gestures which follow are informed by the direct speech of the enemies in the second half of the verse. There it is clear that the enemies are triumphant and are gloating over the downfall of Judah. The construction פָּצוּ פִּיהֶם occurs several times in the Hebrew Bible. In Gen 4.11; Num 16.30; Deut 11.6 the ground opens its mouth to eat. At Ezek 2.8 the meaning, again, is to open the mouth with a view to eating. At Job 35.16 the meaning appears to be 'to speak'; and at Ps 66.14 the verb is used in parallel with דָּבָר. The preposition עַל probably means 'against'. The combination here may, therefore, mean 'to abuse verbally', cf. RSV 'rail against'. Whistling may have had its origins in the dirge, cf. Renkema (296). While it was employed by the horror-struck passers-by in v. 15, here it takes its meaning from the other gestures—פצה פה and חרק שן and the direct speech which follows. That is to say, whistling is caught up with the triumphant derision of the enemies. It is a sound or gesture which accompanied other unambiguous gestures.

וַיַּחַרְקוּ־שֵׁן—The act of gnashing the teeth, in Western cultures, conveys the idea of anger or pain. The weeping and gnashing of teeth in the New Testament picture of hell (Matt 8.12; 13.42 etc.) indicates that the gesture was bound up with the notion of pain in New Testament Palestine. In this context, however, it can hardly have the meaning of pain in that the exclamations which follow are those of pleasure, relief, celebration and gloating. If we examine the other passages in the Hebrew Bible where the verb חרק occurs—Pss 35.16; 37.12; 112.10; Job 16.9—we see that grinding of/with the teeth is used of different emotions. It is associated with mocking in Ps 35.16, with aggression in Ps 37.12 and Job 16.9, and with annoyance in Ps 112.10; indeed, hostility appears to underlie all these passages. This fits in with v. 16, where 'enemies' is the subject. The enemies show their hostility towards Zion as they celebrate her downfall. It raises the question of the nature of the gnashing/grinding, which, as we may understand the words, are not very obvious gestures. It may be that the phrase envisages the baring or clacking of the teeth, not unlike a hostile and angry dog; and in this regard we may note that Luther translates 'blecken die Zähne'.

אָמְרוּ בִּלָּעְנוּ—We have already encountered the verb בלע (in the Piel) at vv. 2, 5 (twice) and 8, where Yahweh was the subject and Zion/Israel the object. In the light of the following verse, one may see that the poet realises that to say the enemy is triumphant may be misunderstood: Yahweh is the one who has organised the destruction. Not convinced that 'we have destroyed' is quite appropriate in the mouths of the enemies, Albrektson (114f.) argues that we are dealing here with another √בלע, cognate with Arabic *balaġa* 'to reach, attain'.[109] 'The meaning "reach", which is the primary sense of the Arabic word, makes בלענו in Lam 2.16b perfectly parallel with the two verbs in 16c, and we get three almost synonymous words which all express the enemies' triumphant exclamation: "we have reached", "we have attained", "we have seen"'. Militating against Albrektson here is the fact that the verb בלע 'swallow, engulf, destroy' has been used by the poet in vv. 2, 5 and 8, and it would seem strange to introduce another, obscure, root at this point; besides, the meaning 'destroy' fits very well here. As Hillers[2] (107) observes, 'Their (the enemies') "We have consumed" echoes "The Lord consumed" of vv 2 and 5'. While Gottlieb (33f.) merely rejects Albrektson's suggestion, Schüpphaus (136-39) rejects the idea that a root בלע = 'to reach' exists in the Hebrew Bible; and the tendency among commentators is to remain with the traditional interpretation.[110] The Masoretes, in vocalising Piel, were clearly of the opinion that the poet was picking up the occurrences of the verb בלע at vv. 2, 5 and 8. It might seem inappropriate for the expression בלענו to be in the mouths of the enemies, in that it is Yahweh who is the subject in vv. 2 and 5, but the poet imagines how the pagan

---

[109] The argument for this root is found in Jacob (1912, 287), Driver (1932, 40f.) and KBL (135). The identification with this root lies behind NEB's rendering 'Here we are'; cf. Brockington (217) who merely indicates that the Qal, rather then the Piel, should be read. Cf. also Fuerst (229).

[110] Cf. Barthélemy (886), Provan (75), NRSV etc.

enemies would feel at Zion's destruction. They would give themselves credit for what had happened; and that is why he goes on to explain, in v. 17, Yahweh's dominant role.

אַךְ זֶה הַיּוֹם שֶׁקִּוִּינֻהוּ מָצָאנוּ רָאִינוּ—The particle אַךְ is represented in the Versions and functions as an adverb emphasising what follows; cf. 1 Sam 16.6 (BDB 36); hence, Calvin *utique*, AV 'certainly', Wiesmann (154) 'Ja', Berlin (64) 'indeed'. The rendering 'ah' (RSV, NRSV, JPS, ESV) is inadequate. Hillers[2] (107) thinks that the mention of 'the day' here alludes to v. 1 where it is 'the day of Yahweh's anger', and he may be right; on the other hand, it may have been a disinterested choice on the part of the poet. The speech of the enemies continues with two verbs juxtaposed in the second stich of the third line. The effect, quite apart from confirming the 3:2 rhythm, is of exclamation. The verbs, together with קִוִּינֻהוּ, constitute an asyndeton which is maintained in LXX, V and T. P and Sym, however, add the copula.

מָצָאנוּ—The sense is similar to that in Gen 26.12; Num 31.50; Judg 5.30; Lam 2.9, *viz* 'obtain, achieve'—'we have achieved (it)'; cf. Sym κατελάβομεν.

רָאִינוּ—The sense is 'we have experienced (it)' or 'we have witnessed (it)', as in Est 9.26. The impression given by the full line is that the enemies (or some of them) have long waited for the time when Zion would fall. Judah had survived the Assyrian invasion of the west in the eighth century BCE when the northern kingdom was eclipsed. On a purely human level, there is always the desire to see the champion (cf. רַבָּתִי בַגּוֹיִם, 1.1) or the unbeaten team meet its match and be toppled, but Judah's relationship with its neighbours will have been problematic since the days of the expansion of the Davidic kingdom and, more recently, will have been aggravated by the territorial ambitions and actions of Josiah in the wake of the Assyrian demise.

The first person plurals are important for the poet here. He deliberately sets these two exclamations on top of בִּלַּעֲנוּ...קִוִּינֻהוּ, and the entire verse combines the gestures with the triumphant claims of the enemies, 'we' being repeated four times. But the poet has been active in other ways, too. Two plosives in the first line are followed by a clause which is heavy with echoing consonants—ק, ר, שׁ: שׁן שׁרקו ויחרקו.

The two verses (vv. 15 and 16) are cleverly combined by the repetition of שׁרקו, the phrase עליך, the description of gestures by outsiders and by the direct speech quotations, but whereas v. 15 refers to the passers-by being shocked at the sight of Zion, v. 16 has to do with the gloating of Zion's enemies at the same scene. It is possible that the poet imagines cries of triumph and gloating emanating from a variety of parties—Babylon, 'We have destroyed her'; one local enemy 'This is the day we have waited for'; another local enemy, 'We have achieved it'; and yet another, 'We have witnessed it'.

Up to v. 14 the author has focussed on Yahweh's devastating assault on Zion and on its effects—on the city, on her people and on the poet's own response. In these two verses (vv. 15f.) the poet challenges Jerusalem to take note of external factors: casual passers-by are stunned at the sight of you (v. 15), and your enemies are delighted with the same scenario, exclaiming in celebratory mood that this is what they had always hoped for (v. 16). Both verses are similarly constructed. The subject in each verse is named only in the second stich, probably due to the alphabetic requirements of the acrostic; and the hyperbole 'all' provides emphasis in each case. The actions and body language are highlighted; and this is followed by direct speech—imagined quotations from passers-by and enemies.

2.17

Text and Versions

MT אִמְרָתוֹ—so also P, V, OL and T; LXX ῥήματα αὐτοῦ. The LXX *Vorlage* may have been אמרתיו or it may be (so Albrektson, 115) that the translator vocalised אִמְרֹתָיו. It is possible that the translator allowed himself a little freedom with the term, which is, after all, a collective noun.[111]

* * *

The message of this verse coheres with that of the preceding verse in particular but also with what has gone before in the poem. The poet, having taken the standpoint of the observer—watching and listening to passers-by (v. 15) and listening to reports of enemy rejoicing (v. 16)—lifts the discussion back onto the theological plane. It may have seemed that the enemies were the perpetrators, but this was not the case: as was mentioned in vv. 1-9 (cf. especially v. 8), it was Yahweh who was at work on the demolition of Zion, and the enemies were just the means to that end. The author also wants to stress that the destruction of Zion was planned by Yahweh on the basis of his ancient word. Furthermore, even the smiles on the faces of Zion's enemies were put there by Yahweh. Hence, v. 17, besides offering a correction to the claim of the enemies in v. 16, confirms what has been said before, *viz* that Yahweh is to be credited with what has happened.

עָשָׂה יְהוָה אֲשֶׁר זָמָם—Although this idea has already been implied in vv. 1-8, the poet wishes to emphasise that the enemy boasting in v. 16 has no validity in fact.[112] Furthermore, Yahweh did what he had planned (זָמָם).[113]

---

[111] N.B. at Prov 17.27 LXX translates a plural אמרי with a singular ῥῆμα.

[112] As Renkema (300) puts it: 'While the enemy do indeed witness the downfall of Jerusalem, they do not observe true reality as the poets do from their theological perspective. Judah's devastation at the hands of her enemies is merely the visible effect of YHWH's own plans.'

As in v. 8, the point is that Yahweh acted not in the heat of the moment but in the cool hour: he planned it all. Consequently, we may translate in the pluperfect: 'Yahweh has done what he had planned'.[114]

בִּצַּע אֶמְרָתוֹ—Rudolph (1938, 109) points out that several MSS read אִמְרָתוֹ, which is what we expect (BDB 57). The sense is not affected. The noun אמרה is used of human (Ps 17.6; Isa 29.4) or divine speech (Deut 33.9; Isa 5.24). The verb בִּצַּע (Qal = 'cut, sever') is unusual. The Versions all testify to the meaning 'fulfil', though the verb does not elsewhere carry this precise meaning. MLT explains the phrase בִּצַּע אֶמְרָתוֹ by השלים דברו 'he fulfilled his word/promise' and cites Lev 26.31 where God says 'I will make your sanctuaries desolate'. Rashi glosses the passage with כלה גזרתו 'he completed his decree', quoting Job 6.9 where the verb occurs and where the meaning may be 'finish off'. IE[1] follows Rashi in using כלה and in his reference to Job. IE[2] comments 'For God had fulfilled (מלא) what he had spoken through his servants the ancient prophets'; and Kara, who also alludes to Moses in Lev 26.31, cites Isa 10.12 which deploys the verb in the sense of 'to complete'. It is clear that in the history of Jewish exegesis the notion of the fulfilment of the prophetic word of Yahweh is very important. This is further reflected in the Targum's paraphrase, which is probably focussing on the Leviticus passage and refers to God carrying out (גמר) his word commanded to Moses long ago.[115]

Although בִּצַּע אֶמְרָתוֹ is explained as 'fulfilled his word', the uniqueness of the phrase may be significant. The poet could have used more conventional language which would have tied the 'word of Yahweh' to that spoken by those pre-exilic prophets who had warned of Yahweh's intention to destroy Jerusalem, but the construction בִּצַּע אֶמְרָתוֹ coupled with the reference to מִימֵי־קֶדֶם suggests that the poet is reaching back to the distant past, to threats which pertain to the essence of Yahweh's relationship with his people and which under-girded the pre-exilic prophets' utterances. The latter announced the דבר יהוה, but Yahweh's אמרה may be seen here as an inclusive term. Renkema (301) may exaggerate rather the implications of the uses of this word, but he is right when he says '...the present text constitutes an explicit recognition of a distinct prophetic voice. The words of former prophets, who were once despised and oppressed, have been proven right in contrast to the words of Lady Jerusalem's prophets. The failure of the latter serves to canonise the prophetic words of the former which foresaw this disaster now confronting Judah.'

---

[113] זָמָם is in pause (for זָמַם) with $R^e\underline{b}îa^c$ accent; cf. GK 29i, and 15f.
[114] For the same combination of זמם and עשׂה, see Jer 51.12; Zech 1.6.
[115] It may be wondered why the Midrashim, T, Rashi and Kara focus on the warnings of Moses in Leviticus as the origin of Yahweh's planning. Why no allusion to Deuteronomy nor the pre-exilic prophetic word? Even IE[2], who differs from Rashi, Kara, T and Midrash in not mentioning Moses, speaks of עבדיו הנביאים הקדמונים, which hardly refers to prophetic figures like Micah or Jeremiah.

The verb בִּצַּע remains difficult. Renkema (301) translates 'consummated' (cf. OL *consumavit*), pointing out that 'fulfilled' is usually conveyed by the roots מלא, שלם and קום. There is a finality about בצע, and at Isa 10.12, again with Yahweh as subject, it has the meaning 'completed'. The poet in this verse (17), therefore, views the demolition of Zion as evidence that Yahweh's אמרה has finally been realised.[116]

אֲשֶׁר צִוָּה מִימֵי־קֶדֶם—The relative pronoun is probably related to the preceding noun אמרה, and the entire clause locates that word of Yahweh in the distant past. This is how the vast majority of scholars have understood the passage.[117] The other possibility is that אשר could have the force of כאשר— see *HALOT ad loc* B (e), i.e. 'just as', cf. Exod 34.18; Jer 48.4.

הָרַס וְלֹא חָמָל—The language of this cryptic sentence echoes that of v. 2 where the phrase ולא חמל (*Qere*) and the verb הרס appear. The fact that no object is mentioned led P to add the suffix 'her' (= Zion). NIV has also felt the need to supply an object in translation: 'you'. The phrase ולא חמל is adverbial (cf. on v. 2) and may be translated 'mercilessly'. The entire clause, therefore, emphasises the single-mindedness of Yahweh in his demolition of Zion.

וַיְשַׂמַּח עָלַיִךְ אוֹיֵב הֵרִים קֶרֶן צָרָיִךְ—The final statements continue the theme of Yahweh as the author of Zion's devastation. The poet had offered a theological explanation of the fall of Zion; now he offers a theological explanation of the high spirits of the enemies: Yahweh has caused your enemy to rejoice over you! On the term קרן, see on v. 3 where the image is cutting down of Israel's horn. The enemy's strength may now be apparent to all observers, but it is Yahweh who is behind this too: Yahweh has actually built up the enemy's might!

Before the poet turns to advise Zion he wants her to be certain that the true theological explanation of the scenario he has been describing is out in the open. The demolition of Judah and Jerusalem is not only the work of Yahweh: it is the result of planning. It amounts to the fulfilment of a threat made long ago; and his actions were without mercy. The poet also wants to rule out any harbouring of the notion that the enemies had ultimate control; even their rejoicings and apparent show of strength is the work of Yahweh.

---

[116] Hillers[2] (107) appears to interpret lines 1 and 2a as an assertion that Yahweh had always in mind to destroy Israel.

[117] Blayney (316) believed the meaning of אשר is 'that which' (cf. *DCH*, I, 429 3b) and that the referent is (הָרַס וְלֹא חָמָל). He translates 'What he constituted in days of old, he hath destroyed'. And Gordis (165f.), without reference to Blayney, follows a similar line and interprets it as a reference to 'the Temple, the building of which God commanded'; but cf. Gottlieb (34).

2.18

Text and Versions
MT צָעַק לִבָּם—so also LXX, OL, P, V and T; early corruption of Hebrew text which should read the imperative f. s. צַעֲקִי (see below).
MT חוֹמַת בַּת־צִיּוֹן; LXX τείχη Σιων; OL *muri filiae Sion*; V *super muros filiae Sion*; P ܠܘܬ ܡܪܝܐ ܕܫܘܪܐ ܕܒܪܬ ܨܗܝܘܢ (*lwt mry'*) *dšwr' dbrt ṣhywn*; T שׁוּרָא דְקַרְתָּא דְצִיּוֹן. It is clear that the Versions found this passage puzzling. LXX, OL, V and P vocalise חוֹמֹת (pl.) but they and T (s.) had the same consonantal text. The LXX omission of בת is probably due to haplography (cf. preceding חומת). MT is preferred.
MT הוֹרִידִי so also P, V and T; LXX καταγάγετε. LXX pl. is the result of the Greek translator vocalising חומת earlier in the verse, the final י being taken as a ו. MT is preferred.
MT בַּת־עֵינֵךְ; P ܒܒܬ ܥܝܢܟܝ *bbt 'ynky*; V *pupilla oculi tui*—so also OL; LXX θύγατερ ὁ ὀφθαλμός σου mistakenly took בת to be vocative. MT is preferred (see below).

* * *

In vv. 18f. the poet calls on Zion to address Yahweh in prayer accompanied by constant and intense weeping. This approach is on behalf of Zion's children, though this is not disclosed until the end of v. 19. The two verses are held together by the imperatives and prohibitions addressing Zion in 2nd p. f. s.

צָעַק לִבָּם אֶל־אֲדֹנָי חוֹמַת בַּת־צִיּוֹן—The entire first line of this verse has always been seen as difficult, and many textual and exegetical suggestions have been made throughout the history of interpretation; cf. Albrektson (116-18), Barthélemy (887-89).[118] On the phrase בַּת־צִיּוֹן, see on 1.6.

צָעַק לִבָּם—If we attempt to understand MT we are immediately in trouble. The subject of צעק must be לבם 'their heart cried out', but the referent of the suffix remains a mystery; and it is unusual for צעק to have לב as a subject. Again, since the Masoretes have placed an *athnaḥ* at אדני, it seems that they may have understood the following words חוֹמַת בַּת־צִיּוֹן as vocative (Michaelis 1773–88, 421), which means that 'they' address the wall of Zion; and that constitutes another problem.[119] The 3rd p. m. pl. suffix has often been taken to refer to the people of Jerusalem—MLT, Kara, Calvin, Keil (504), NIV, Provan (75)—or Israel (T). IE² takes the suffix to refer to the foes mentioned in the previous verse (צוֹעֵק לֵב צָרֵיךְ) and appears to understand the passage as a continuation of the speech addressed to Zion. Blayney (131) seems to take the suffix to refer to the passers-by of v. 15, while Renkema (308) believes the reference is 'to the

---

[118] In addition, Michaelis (1773–88, 422) suggested reading אֲדָנֵי for אֲדֹנָי and renders *clamat cor illorum ob fundamenta murorum Sionis*, but this has not commanded support.
[119] The Masoretes' placing of the *athnaḥ* at אדני (the only occasion in Lamentations where *athnaḥ* appears in the middle of the first line of a three-line verse) means that they regarded the first stich as somehow complete in itself.

heart of Lady Jerusalem's languishing children'. Albrektson (116f.) also takes the referent to be the enemies, though he emends the text at the same time (see below).

While none of the above are impossible, none of them is easy. What drives those who suggest emendations is the structure of the context in which line 1 appears. The poet has been addressing Zion since v. 13 (2nd p. f. s.) and, in vv. 18bc and 19, these 2nd p. f. s. forms continue in the form of imperatives. If the first stich of line one (MT) is original, it is quite intrusive. Furthermore, it does not make a positive or meaningful contribution. What IE² felt instinctively (in his use of the 2nd p. f. s. form (צָרַיִךְ) was that the Zion address should continue; and many scholars, though differing in detail, offer suggestions in terms of 2nd p. f. s. As far back as 1866,[120] Ewald (335f.) suggested reading (צַעֲקִי לִבֵּךְ). Most scholars accept the imperative as a restoration of the original Hebrew, but while Ewald suggested לבך (which he translates 'schreie deines Herzens' or 'unverdrossen schreie') for לבם and was followed by Dyserinck (369) and Kelso (33), Bickell (111) opted for לך and is followed by Budde (1898ᵃ, 90). Löhr (1906, 14) read קוֹלֵךְ (translated 'schreie unverdrossen') and Rudolph (1938, 109) לָךְ מָלֵא, all of which give good sense, though Rudolph's is graphically rather remote. Gordis (166), who clearly rejects MT, suggests that we read צְקִי לִבֵּךְ 'pour out your heart', but the proximity to v. 19b שִׁפְכִי לבך must reduce the likelihood of this emendation. Driver (1964, 92) takes לבם to be an abbreviation = לֵב מָלֵא 'with a full heart' which is the basis for NEB (Brockington, 218), but this has not won support, partly because the idiom does not otherwise exist and, like Rudolph's proposal, is graphically remote. Albrektson (116f.), who accepts Ewald's suggestion of צעקי, puts forward the suggestion[121] that לבם should read לבהם. The word לִבָּה is found at Ezek 16.30 with the meaning[122] 'rage', related to the rare Aramaic[123] לבתא 'anger' and Akkad. *libbātū* 'rage'. Albrektson translates 'cry out about their rage to the Lord', the suffix referring to 'your foes'.[124] McDaniel (203f.) offers an interesting solution which involves less in the way of emendation than most other proposals. Accepting Ewald's צעקי, he reckons that the *mem* of לבם is not a pronominal suffix but adverbial (cf. יומם later in the verse, and see GK 100g). Drawing attention to Hos 7.14 where זעק occurs with the adverbial phrase בלבם, and to Ps 142.2 where the adverbial accusative קולי occurs with the

---

[120] Schleusner (1783, 23) had proposed an imperative צְעַק here, though he did not account for לבם.
[121] Cf. Driver (1931, 366).
[122] Cf. Driver (1928, 393).
[123] Cf. Cowley (134, 140).
[124] However, Gottlieb (36) argues 'The objection can be made to this view that the noun לבה in Hebrew and Aramaic otherwise occurs in the expression לבה מלא with an objective genitive, so that לבהם should mean "wrath against them". It is a more substantial objection that a summons to lament over the wrath of the *enemies* fits particularly badly in the context in Lam. 2, where it is the consistent theme…that misfortune is to be ascribed exclusively to the wrath of *Yahweh*.'

same verb, McDaniel (204) sees לבם as functioning 'much like the adverbial accusative of Ps 142.2'; and he translates 'Cry out unto the Lord (from) the heart...' This proposal has found favour with REB and Hillers[2] (101)[125] and appears to suit the context.

חוֹמַת בַּת־צִיּוֹן—The Hebrew is difficult, and RSV deletes חוֹמַת. Gottwald (11), ignoring the Masoretic punctuation, takes חוֹמַת as an expression for 'Lord', i.e. to be in apposition to אדני—'...to the Lord, the Wall of the daughter of Zion!' In support of his position, Gottwald cites Zech 2.9 (Eng. 5) where Yahweh says he will be a wall of fire around Jerusalem; and Provan (76) agrees: 'That God himself should be described as "the wall of daughter Zion" in this context is...most natural. Those who pray approach him in the realization that it is only through him, and not by means of physical structures that there can be real protection for Jerusalem.' 'Wall' has also been taken as standing for Zion itself, and this would accord with the placing of the *athnaḥ* at אדני. This is how LXX (cf. also T) seems to have taken it, i.e. as a vocative, and addressed by the imperatives that follow; cf. also Calvin. At v. 8c it is said that 'rampart and wall (חומה) languish together', so that it is not impossible that the wall of Zion is personified here.[126] This interpretation has been followed by NRSV, NEB, NIV, JPS, NJB, Gordis (167), Dobbs-Allsopp (98). Finally, 'wall' has been understood in its plain sense. V *super muros* (vocalising חוֹמֹת) has taken the term to be adverbial of place (GK 118d), cf. also P (see above), Douai 'upon the walls' and REB 'at the wall of the daughter of Zion', a rendering which may owe something to the practice of Jews at the 'Western Wall' in Jerusalem!

Again, emendations have been suggested by several commentators who find MT too problematic. Houbigant (479), in the 18th century, proposed reading בתולת בת ציון, though he leaves the first stich unaltered; and his suggestion was followed by Bickell (111), Löhr (1906, 14) and is entertained in *BHK*. Budde (1898a, 90) thinks that the original reading may have been the imperative הֱמִי from √המה 'roar, growl, groan', which provides a good parallel to צעקי. This suggestion is followed by Kraus (38), Haller (102), Westermann (146), Kaiser (327), JB, *BHS*.[127] Albrektson (117) suggests that חומת בת ציון is a corruption of an original הבת ציון = vocative with the article, and points to 2.13 where הבת ירושלם 'O (daughter

---

[125] Yet another proposal, which has not found favour but which Gottlieb (37) says should not be ruled out, is that of Thenius (149), *viz* that צְעַק לִבָּם אֶל־אֲדֹנָי is a gloss which has replaced the original Hebrew. This would have to be understood as a description of what takes place in the verse, and it would identify the speaker in the verse as the people of Zion.

[126] Keil (504) refers to Isa 14.31, הֵילִילִי שַׁעַר זַעֲקִי־עִיר, where gate is parallel to city and urged to howl and cry out; and Berlin (75) draws attention, in this regard, to the Lamentation over the Destruction of Ur (*ANET*, 456, ll. 48ff.): 'O Thou brickwork of Ur...'

[127] Those who espouse this emendation might find support from Ps 55.18, where המה is parallel to שיח, and where evening and morning are mentioned (as in this verse), and where there is an expectation of an answer from Yahweh.

of) Jerusalem' occurs. RSV 'O daughter of Zion' seems to have obtained the same result by merely deleting חוֹמַת. McDaniel (204) suggests reading הוֹמַת (i.e. ה for ח) = f. s. participle of √המה which can mean 'be tumultuous' (BDB 242), with the old f. ending ת֗ retained, as in פּוּגַת later in the verse (see GK 80f). He translates 'O tumultuous one, daughter Zion'. But Zion's state is not aptly described by this terminology. Finally, Hillers[2] (101) suggests reading the Niphal f. s. participle from נחם *viz* נֶחָמַת. He translates 'O remorseful Zion'.

The suggested emendations in v. 18a are mainly context-driven. Verse 18b through to v. 19c comprises a series of imperatives and prohibitions where Zion is addressed. If v. 18aα could be seen as an aside or an interruption which made sense, as at 1.9c, 11c, then accommodation could be made for these words, but it is difficult to see how they might fit the context. The arguments for the retention of MT as original are unconvincing, doctrinaire and tortuous (especially Renkema, 307-12). It is true, the Versions strongly support MT, though not entirely, but this may simply mean that the alleged corruption of the text had taken place before any translation, represented by the Versions, was made (as in the first stich); and the Versions, as noted earlier, show signs of being baffled by the text before them.

We should note that the poet was required, by his acrostic pattern, to begin with a צ. Familiar with the language and grammar of Hos 7.14; Pss 3.5; 66.17; 119.145; 142.2, he addresses Zion in f. s. imperative צעקי. He understands that Yahweh did not listen to Israel's cry in Hosea because it was not uttered from the heart, and he knows the construction קרא קול 'cry with the voice' in Ps 3.5 (cf. Ps 66.17). The original text was probably צעקי לבם. Subsequently, a scribe omitted a י, resulting in the indicative clause = MT. While the LXX translator was in receipt of the tradition which took חומת בת ציון as vocative, those of P and V were not, hence the confusion in these Versions.[128] The Masoretes, by their positioning of the *athnaḥ*, persisted with the 'vocative' tradition; and T knew it also.

It is *possible* that the second stich originally read בת ציון or הבת ציון, which degenerated into חומת בת ציון through a dittography of בת (Albrektson, 117f.) and was then made to conform to v. 8aβ, but we must allow for the author's propensity for poetic diction. He had coined the phrase 'wall of the daughter of Zion' earlier in the poem when he had used חומה to refer to a physical structure in v. 8a (*pars pro toto* = walls); but, in the same verse (v. 8c) he personifies חומה as the poet in him views the wall and rampart as languishing. Here, at v. 18, where, in the midst of his addressing Zion he uses the terms הבת ירושלם and בתולת בת ציון, he now varies it again with חומת בת ציון; but just as we did not distinguish between הבת ירושלם (v. 13a) and בתולת בת ציון (v. 13b), so we should, perhaps, allow that at v. 18a this new figure has a similar force.

---

[128] V '...to the Lord upon the walls of the daughter of Zion', P '...to the Lord of the walls...'

הוֹרִידִי כַנַּחַל דִּמְעָה יוֹמָם וָלַיְלָה—The command to bring down tears like a torrent is part of the hyperbole indulged in by the poet. The intensity is further heightened by several imperatives and prohibitions over vv. 18f. and by the language and posture of plaintive lament in these two verses, and by the reference to its extent—night and day, without respite.[129] There can be no doubt that the poet is here calling on Zion to bring her case before Yahweh, after the manner of the plaintive laments of the book of Psalms. There is the hint that the more tears that can be mustered and shed the more likely that Yahweh will hear and respond, cf. Pss 6.6-8; 39.13; 56.9. Furthermore, the tears that are called for are not the natural outpouring of grief on Zion's part. While not exactly false, they are, to some extent, to order; for the poet is calling to Zion to plead with Yahweh and to make sure that that pleading is accompanied with the maximum amount of tears. This reflects the custom of ancient professional lamenters who performed for effect.

אַל־תִּתְּנִי פוּגַת לָךְ—פוּגַת is a *hapax legomenon*. It is probably an example of a form which retains the old feminine ending (cf. GK 80f, BL 510v).[130] The word may derive from √פוג 'to cool off, grow weary'. The clause will mean: 'Allow yourself no let up' and it reinforces the previous words regarding weeping day and night.

אַל־תִּדֹּם בַּת־עֵינֵךְ—The subject of this prohibition is בַּת־עֵינֵךְ which P translates as 'apple of your eye'; cf. also V *pupilla oculi tui*, Rashi, Vermigli (100).[131] At Ps 17.8 we have the phrase כְּאִישׁוֹן בַּת־עָיִן which is usually translated 'as the apple of the eye' and considered a compound concept (Kraus 1993, I, 144). Blayney (316) had considered בַּת־עֵינֵךְ to mean the issue from the eye, i.e. 'tear'; and Robertson (59), who makes no reference to Blayney, argues for the same meaning—'Let not the tear-drop cease'. While many translations try to maintain something of the poetic language and render 'apple of your eye'—AV, Luther, Calvin, Keil (380), Wiesmann (157), Rudolph (1962, 217)—many prefer their own poetic renderings: 'Let your tears never cease' (NEB), 'Give your eyes no rest' (NJB).

The mood has changed somewhat. The poet wants to stress the importance of Zion crying out to Yahweh from the depths of her disastrous situation. The appeal to Yahweh must have all the marks of sincerity as well as intensity. It must be accompanied by copious weeping, day and night. She should not consider any let up, any break from this activity.

[129] Renkema (313) draws attention to 'the unique image of a ravine (נחל), which, after heavy rainfall, guides the water downwards with enormous intensity'.
[130] Other examples are found at Gen 26.26 and 2 Kgs 9.17. IE¹ takes it as construct, and Kaiser (327 n 30) identifies the term as the construct state (before a preposition) of פוּגָה, cf. JM (129 n).
[131] Rudolph (1962, 220) draws attention to Zech 2.12 where we get בְּבָבַת עֵינוֹ, which, if original, presupposes a noun בָּבָה (BDB 93); he prefers to read בָּבַת here.

2.19

Text and Versions
MT רֹנִּי; LXX ἀγαλλίασαι; Aq αἴνεσον; V *lauda*; P ܫܒܚܝ *šbḥy*; OL *expergiscere*; Sym ἀδολέσχησον; T עסוקי במשנה. It is difficult to understand where the OL and Sym renderings come from, and T seems not to be related to the Hebrew text,[132] but the *Vorlagen* of the other Versions seem to have been identical with MT.
MT (*Kethib*) בַּלַּיְל MT (*Qere*) בַּלַּיְלָה—so also many MSS[Ken]. Although *Qere* agrees with the vast majority of occurrences, the *Kethib* form is poetic and found in Isa 16.3.
MT לְרֹאשׁ אַשְׁמֻרוֹת; LXX εἰς ἀρχὰς φυλακῆς σου; OL *in principio vigilae tuae*; P ܒܪܝܫ ܡܛܪܬܐ *bryš mṭrtʾ*; V *in principio vigiliarum*; T בשירוי מטרת שפרפרא; BHK maintains that the *Vorlage* of LXX was לראשי אשמרתך. The fact that this translator is meticulous in his handling of his *Vorlage* means that it is possible that he did have a different Hebrew text before him, though Rudolph (1938, 109) argues that the Greek merely reflects style. OL 'corrects' the first word to a singular but otherwise follows LXX. P and T have singulars throughout, and only V matches MT. It is, however, possible that the consonantal text of MT lies behind all the Versions and that what appears, to be variations consist of attempts to understand the passage.
MT הָעֲטוּפִים בְּרָעָב בְּרֹאשׁ כָּל־חוּצוֹת—additional gloss (see below).

* * *

The intensity of v. 18 continues into this verse with four more imperatives. The poet, in calling on Zion to plead with Yahweh, urges her to make maximum effort throughout the night hours. It is as if the phrase 'day and night' (v. 18) was not strong enough or needed emphasis.

קוּמִי רֹנִּי בַלַּיְל—The hyperbole continues. Zion is urged to put on an irresistible display of weeping and wailing, which involves activity during the night. The letter ק is required by the acrostic, and the verb קוּם fits beautifully with the context. Zion is to break her night's sleep so that the intensity of the display is maintained. The basic meaning of the verb רנן is 'to give a ringing cry' and may be onomatopoeic. While רנן is usually found in a context of joy and triumph,[133] here it is quite different, and IE[1] (cf. also Kara) points out that the verb means raising the voice in song or

---

[132] The OL rendering may be due to a parallel passage like Isa 51.17. Kelso (33) notes that the Sym verb ἀδολέσχησον translates שׂוח in LXX, suggesting that Sym may have had a different *Vorlage*. It may be, though, that Sym was casting around for something more plausible to do 'in the night' and thought of Ps 77.7, where LXX uses ἀδολέσχεω. T 'busy yourself in Mishnah' is homiletically driven. On the latter, see Alexander (2008, 140 n. 68).
[133] LXX ἀγαλλίασαι 'rejoice' has taken the verb in its usual sense, and so have P, V and Aq. (OL 'awaken' and Sym 'chatter' have each chosen a different path.) It may have been felt by the LXX, P, V and Aq translators that even if one intended to plead with God one should preface one's petition with praise. It should be noted that, although he was not a Hebraist and was dependent on the V, Coverdale renders this passage: 'Stonde up and make thy prayer...', while Douay 'Arise, give praise...' and Knox '...raise thy song...' are tied to Jerome's rendering *consurge lauda*.

in lamentation.¹³⁴ The verb may have been chosen because it stresses a high pitch to the cry which would have been particularly appropriate in the normally quiet night. The two imperatives without the copula add poignancy to this line.

לְרֹאשׁ אַשְׁמֻרוֹת—Note the distributive *lamed* (GK 123d) and the related use of the plural (GK 124), cf. Judg 12.7; Isa 50.4; Job 3.16; 40.29. The correct meaning of the phrase is not immediately obvious. Is Zion being called to cry out when the watches start (RSV, NRSV, JPS, NIV)? Is it a call to cry out at the beginning of every watch (Keil, 504; Hillers², 95; Gordis, 168; NEB, REB, NJB)? Or is it a poetic way of urging Zion to cry out *throughout* the night: an explication of the phrase 'in the night' in the previous stich? The term אשמורה (or אשמורת) is not a common one in the Hebrew Bible. The occurrences are Exod 14.24; Judg 7.19; 1 Sam 11.11; Pss 63.7; 90.4; 119.148 and here. At Judg 7.19 we get the phrase רֹאשׁ הָאַשְׁמֹרֶת הַתִּיכוֹנָה, which must mean 'the beginning of the middle watch', the implication being that there were three watches, as in Mesopotamia. In the New Testament (Matt 14.25) there is reference to the fourth watch, which accords with Roman custom. On the basis of the Judges passage, the term רֹאשׁ cannot surely mean 'first' (contra Renkema, 314); hence the poet enjoins Zion to cry out regularly throughout the night.

שִׁפְכִי כַמַּיִם לִבֵּךְ—Lest crying out in the night be misunderstood as putting on a *show* of grief, the writer urges Zion to pour out her heart before God. This combination occurs at Ps 62.9, 'O people, pour out your heart before him', where the context is one of trust in Yahweh. The poet may have had this passage in mind. For him, the only hope for Zion was if she could, in sincerity and trust, be entirely honest about her feelings of betrayal as well as guilt. The similar construction at 1 Sam 1.15 וָאֶשְׁפֹּךְ אֶת־נַפְשִׁי לִפְנֵי יְהוָה probably carries the same meaning. The phrase כמים echoes כנחל of the previous verse, both part of the hyperbole of the passage. It is associated with the verb שפך at Deut 12.16, 24; 15.23; Ps 79.3; Hos 5.10.

נֹכַח פְּנֵי יְהוָה—'before Yahweh', the equivalent of לפני יהוה. The word נֹכַח used as a preposition, 'opposite', and probably chosen to fill out the stich. The 'crying out' must be directed at God and not as a mere wailing as in a קינה. T, which sees the passage addressed to the congregation of Israel in exile (cf. also MLT), takes the phrase to imply that the prayer must be made in the synagogue.

שְׂאִי אֵלָיו כַּפַּיִךְ—The final imperative in this passage urges Zion to plead with Yahweh. The lifting up of the hands (יד), in the Hebrew Bible, may imply blessing (Ps 134.2), supplication (Ps 28.2) or the making of an oath (Deut 32.40); but the combination of נשא with כף (Ps 63.5; 141.2) appears

---

¹³⁴ The noun רִנָּה is found at Pss 17.1; 61.2; 88.3; Jer 7.16 in a context of lament.

to imply entreaty and supplication. The word כַּף usually means the palm of the hand, and the raising of the up-turned hands—probably the gesture of the beggar—suggests, in itself, pleading and entreaty.[135]

עַל־נֶפֶשׁ עוֹלָלָיִךְ—The poet, it seems, has called on Zion to engage in this fervent prayer on behalf of her young children (mentioned already at v. 11) in desperate straits. Why the author confines his words to this single category is uncertain. He may mean Zion's entire population, though this would conflict with our understanding of vv. 11f. Perhaps he focuses on the עוללים as the most vulnerable citizens, with the idea that Yahweh could hardly resist a plea on their behalf. On נפשׁ 'life', see on v. 12.

הָעֲטוּפִים בְּרָעָב בְּרֹאשׁ כָּל־חוּצוֹת—This phrase is descriptive of the עוללים. The definite article serves as a relative pronoun (GK 138i). We had already encountered the root עטף III in vv. 11f. in a similar context. Here we have the adjective[136] עָטוּף 'weak, feeble' from the same root—'who are weak with hunger'. The phrase בְּרֹאשׁ כָּל־חוּצוֹת is often translated 'at the head of every street' (NRSV) or 'at every street corner' (JPS, REB), but this conjures up the structure of a modern town. The expression, which also occurs at Nah 3.10, is describing the public places: whenever one enters a public place one encounters these starving children: 'at every public corner'.

This verse has eight stichs instead of the usual six. Bickell (111) suggested that the words לְרֹאשׁ אַשְׁמֻרוֹת שִׁפְכִי כַמַּיִם לִבֵּךְ were a later addition and, although his suggestion was not followed, other commentators have wrestled with the anomaly. Ewald (336) regarded the fourth line as a gloss, based on vv. 11f. and 4.1, and in this he has been followed by several scholars: Dyserinck (370), Budde (1898a, 90), Kraus (38), Rudolph (1938, 109), Gottlieb (37), *BHK*, *BHS*, Gordis (168), Wiesmann (157), Westermann (146), Hillers² (101), Albrektson (119), JB, NJB, NEB. Meek (22) identifies the second line as a variant of the first and argues that this accounts for the excess material, but Albrektson points out that the second line does not begin with a ק. Keil (398) considered Ewald's suggestion arbitrary and simply accepts the irregularity, and this position is followed by Barthélemy (866f.), Provan (77), Renkema (317), Berlin (65), House (371), RSV, NRSV, NIV, REB, JPS.

If any material is to be sacrificed it can only be the fourth line. This is not only because it appears to explain the third line—and so might be seen as a gloss on that line—but because it is the most prosaic of the lines. Should it be deleted on the simple basis of being a fourth line (cf. 1.7)?[137]

---

[135] IE² takes the injunction to mean 'complain (about)'—ותתאוננו—but this misses the import of the language here.
[136] BL 471 u. BDB (742) takes it to be the passive participle (= 'weakened, made faint').
[137] Schäfer (*BHQ*, 123*) '...it should be noted that there is no textual evidence that would indicate an addition, i.e. the "addition" belongs to the development of the text prior to the state that can be reached by textual criticism'.

The poet may have thought that he needed to remove the ambiguity of עֹלְלָיִךְ, although it was to spoil the symmetry. However, the fourth line does not have the 3:2 rhythm of the other lines, and this, together with its prosaic nature, makes it suspect.

These two verses (vv. 18f.) contain no fewer than eight imperatives/ jussives directed at Zion urging her to plead with Yahweh with all guns blazing—loudly, weepingly, constantly, without let-up, especially at night—remembering the lives of her children.

2.20

Text and Versions

MT פֶּרְיָם—so also V; LXX καρπὸν κοιλίας αὐτῶν; P ܦܐܪ̈ܝܗܘܢ *p'ryhn* (some MSS) ܒܢܝܗܘܢ *bnyhn* (some MSS including 7a1); T פירי בטניהון. Kelso (34) and *BHK* suggest that LXX and T may have read a Hebrew text פרי בטנם; and Blayney (317) feels that the original text was פרי רחם. However, the variations in the Syriac MSS probably show that LXX and T are explicatory, and the plural in P is natural in the light of the plural נָשִׁים.[138] MT is preferred.

MT עֹלֲלֵי טִפֻּחִים; LXX ἐπιφυλλίδα ἐποίησεν μάγειρος· φονευθήσονται νήπια θηλάζοντα μαστούς; V *parvulos ad mensuram palmae*; Aq βρέφη παλαιστῆς P ܥܘ̈ܠܝܡܐ ܪܓܝܓܬܐ ܕܗܘܘ ܡܬܠܦܦܝܢ *ylwd' dmštqpyn*; T עולימיא רגיגתא דהוו מתלפפין בסדינין דמילתין. MT may be difficult but the variations arise from the meaning of the text rather than the text itself; see *BHQ* (124*) and below.

* * *

The previous imperatives of vv. 18f., addressed to Zion, now bear fruit, in that Zion, for the first time in this poem, now cries out to Yahweh. The terms employed are exactly the same as at 1.11c (cf. 1.9c, 20; 5.1). It is the language of the one who pleads in prayer, as in Pss 80.15; 84.9; Isa 63.15; cf. Ps 13.4; 25.18; 74.20. Zion turns to the one who can make a difference, the one who, depicted earlier in the poem, is responsible for her tragic circumstances. The allusion to extreme famine here is echoed at 4.10 where women are depicted as eating their own children. At Lev 26.29, in the context of Yahweh predicting punishment for sin, the eating of children is envisaged; cf. also Deut 28.53, 56, 58. The prayer of Zion confronts Yahweh with the situation which he has caused by presenting him with the outcome of his actions: famine and desecration. Famine is represented by the picture of starving and desperate women eating their little children, and desecration by the picture of priests and prophets being murdered by the enemy in the very temple of Yahweh. But while the prayer is confronting Yahweh it is not until v. 21c that it gets intense; and Zion's language, in v. 20bc, appears tentative, almost as though she was

---

[138] Albrektson (120) rightly recognises the reading ܒܢܝܗܘܢ *bnyhn* as 'an attempt to explain the meaning of the literal (and probably original) ܦܐܪ̈ܝܗܘܢ *p'ryhn* in most MSS, possibly with reference to 4.10'. Ewald (336) follows LXX.

reporting a situation in a court of law; and she resumes in this vein in v. 21ab and again in v. 22.

רְאֵה יְהוָה וְהַבִּיטָה—See on 1.11c. The poet picks up the language of 1.9c and 1.11c but, whereas in the latter passages the words did not lead into sustained argument, here the words are at the head of a prayer which continues to the end of v. 22.

לְמִי עוֹלַלְתָּ כֹּה—'Whom have you treated in this way?'[139] Does this question imply a covenantal relationship between Zion and Yahweh? Is Zion saying: 'Should you have treated your covenant people thus?'? Although T, MR and MLT do not appear to interpret in this way, by Calvin's time this view was extant and is espoused by him. He paraphrases: 'O Lord, hadst thou thus cruelly raged against strangers, there would have been nothing so wonderful; but since we are thine heritage, and the blessed seed of Abraham, since thou hast been pleased to choose us as thy peculiar people, what can this mean, that thou treatest us with so much severity?' We find it also in Nägelsbach (95), Keil (398), Westermann (146) and Rudolph (1962, 226). Gottwald (99) is almost persuaded but is aware that the argument is weak. Ehrlich (38), however, maintains that the opening words רְאֵה יְהוָה וְהַבִּיטָה do not lead in, syntactically, to the words that follow but constitute an interjection, and that לְמִי עוֹלַלְתָּ כֹּה is an independent clause meaning, simply, 'wenn sonst hast du solches angetan?' He is followed by Albrektson (119f.), Kaiser (328) and Renkema (319f.). The poet, then, has Zion asking Yahweh if he has treated anyone in the following way.[140] 'Whom have you ever treated like this' (NIV). The question echoes 1.12 where Zion asks the passers-by: 'Look and see (הַבִּיטוּ וּרְאוּ) if there is any pain like mine which the Lord has dealt out to me (עוֹלַל לִי)...' The idea is that the treatment is unprecedented as well as severe.

The voice in v. 19 urged Zion to cry out for the life of her children (עוֹלָלִים), and Zion in v. 20 appears to comply in that the first element in her prayer concerns עֹלְלֵי טִפֻּחִים. There may be, as Renkema (319) argues, a word-play[141] here between the verb עלל and the noun עוֹלֵל but, in any case, Yahweh, the author of Zion's disasters, is now inextricably linked with the horrific effects of his actions against Jerusalem. Zion lays before Yahweh the facts that women were eating their own children and that priests and prophets were slain in Yahweh's own sanctuary. It is not clear why the reference to famine comes before that of slaughter here. Both are shocking; but perhaps the idea of women eating their offspring conjures up the more horrendous picture of devastation. In any case, the reference to children appears to be in response to the call שְׂאִי אֵלָיו כַּפַּיִךְ עַל־נֶפֶשׁ עוֹלָלָיִךְ in v. 19.

---

[139] On the verb עלל, see on 1.12.
[140] The word כֹּה 'thus' refers forward to the contents of the next two lines. The interrogative mood is carried on by אִם...אִם. See GK 150c.
[141] Dobbs-Allsopp (99) describes it as 'a horrific pun'.

אִם־תֹּאכַלְנָה נָשִׁים פִּרְיָם—The unusual פרים (lit. 'their fruit') means 'their offspring'. The form פִּרְיָמוֹ is used at Ps 21.11 with the same meaning, as can be deduced from the parallel וְזַרְעָם in the same line. The suffix (m.), when we might have expected the feminine פְרִין, is a frequent anomaly in the Hebrew Bible (e.g. Gen 31.9; GK 135o). IE² interprets בניהן (and 'corrects' the suffix!). By speaking of 'their fruit' the poet means to shock: eating one's fruit (= fruit that one acquires—apples, figs etc.) is normal, eating one's own issue is quite another matter.¹⁴²

עֹלְלֵי טִפֻּחִים—The final words of the second line are meant to be epexegetical (of פרים). The noun עוֹלָל, employed by the voice of v. 19, is picked up again by Zion as she confronts Yahweh. Far from being explanatory, however, the word טפחים is a *hapax legomenon* and has been problematic since the time of the Versions. LXX produces a double translation (*BHK*, *BHQ*). The first, ἐπιφυλλίδα ἐποίησεν μάγειρος (cf. LXX on 1.22), appears to be a rough translation of עלל טבח, where the translator must have had a text which differed from MT and where he misunderstood the root עלל. The rare טִפֻּחִים will not have helped, but the meaning 'the butcher has made a gleaning' is quite out of line with the context. The second, φονευθήσονται νήπια θηλάζοντα μαστούς 'shall infants sucking the breast be slain?' is another attempt (possibly not by the same translator) at making sense.¹⁴³ This translator understands עוֹלָל but guesses at the meaning of טפחים. It is usually thought that LXX translates יהרג twice, but Albrektson (121) may be correct in thinking that the 'glossator' took טפחים to be a form from √טבח 'to slaughter, slay'.¹⁴⁴ P translates 'children which are laid low (prostrated)'; again, the *hapax legomenon* seems to have baffled the translator. At v. 22 where another, related, *hapax legomenon* occurs, namely טפחתי, P renders ܫܩܠܬ *šqlt* 'I have carried', and Kelso (34f.) wonders if, at v. 20, we should read ܕܡܫܬܩܠܝܢ *dmštqlyn* '(children) who are carried'; cf. Abelesz (8), Albrektson (121) and Rudolph (1938, 109). Aq 'infants of a span' seems, perhaps, to have vocalised the Hebrew טְפָחִים (from the rare טֶפַח 'span, handbreadth'); and V 'children of a span long' (AV, Douai) may have been influenced by this. It is not clear how T understood טפחים. The paraphrase 'desirable children wrapped in linen cloths' (cf. T's rendering of טפחתי at v. 22) suggests that √טפח has been understood as 'to wrap'; cf. Jastrow (546) 'to close carefully'. Rashi interprets 'tender children who are still growing by the pampering (cf. Alcalay, 882f.) of their mothers (בטפוחי אמותם)'. IE¹ comments: 'As is the custom of women with little children who are asleep', but his meaning is not clear. It is possible that he has in mind children in arms patted by the mother. Calvin's *parvulos educationis*

---

¹⁴² Cf. the question in Mic 6.7, הַאֶתֵּן בְּכוֹרִי פִּשְׁעִי פְּרִי בִטְנִי חַטַּאת נַפְשִׁי, where similar allusions are operating.
¹⁴³ Albrektson (121) thinks that these words are a gloss, meant to correct the passage, which was incorporated into the text at a later date.
¹⁴⁴ Indeed, Döderlein (199) suggested that the translator read עֹלֵל יְטַבַּח.

'children of rearing/nursing' and Luther's 'die Kindlein, die man auf Händen trägt' may be guessing. Blayney (317), relying on 'handbreadth', takes the phrase to mean 'children of palms', meaning 'such as are of an age or size to be so carried about'. Driver (1950, 138f.), although acknowledging that Aq and V 'approach the sense of the original words', points out that V cannot 'mean that the children are literally the measure of the palm of a man's hand; for new-born children are some three times that size', but we must keep in mind that this is poetry and, if the songwriter can speak of a newborn baby as 'tiny as a peanut', we must allow for similar exaggeration here. Driver, however, wonders if the term (along with טפחתי in v. 22) is related to the Arabic *ṭafaḥa* 'to bring forth fully formed children',[145] and that עֹלֲלֵי טִפֻּחִים 'may be paraphrased "children whom they have nurtured" or the like'. NEB, following Driver, renders rather prosaically 'the children they have brought safely to birth'.[146] Better than NEB is JPS 'their new-born babes'.

אִם־יֵהָרֵג בְּמִקְדַּשׁ אֲדֹנָי כֹּהֵן וְנָבִיא—In 1.10 the author regards the very entry of the enemy into Yahweh's sanctuary[147] as horrifying. Here, the picture is even worse. The temple is profaned in the extreme by the slaughter of human beings in it, and especially so in that the victims are prophets and priests, the cultic personnel and the servants of Yahweh himself.

Although it was argued at v. 20a that the question לְמִי עוֹלַלְתָּ כֹּה carried no covenantal overtones, this final line does. Children being eaten by mothers may be a violation of the moral order of God's world, but the slaughter of priests and prophets in the temple comes close to being a violation of the covenant between Yahweh and his people (cf. Keil, 399).

This is the first of three verses which constitute the prayer that the poet urges Zion to make. The words are the poet's and not Zion's; and he is urging his audience/readers/commemorators to adopt his stance regarding Yahweh. Our poet is distressed about the devastation all around him, the destruction and the slaughter, the cannibalism, the infanticide and the sacrilege. He is convinced that Yahweh is the perpetrator and feels that Yahweh should be confronted with what he has done; and he puts the words in the mouth of the stricken city. By referring to the desperate situation the women and children find themselves in, he hopes to appeal to Yahweh's compassion; and by the reference to the violation of the temple and the cultic personnel he appeals to Yahweh's self-respect!

---

[145] Cf. also Akk. *ṭuppû* 'raise children'. *HALOT* and *DCH* ('children of birth') have followed Driver's philology here.
[146] Note that the revision of NEB (= REB) has rejected this position, rendering 'the children they have held in their arms'.
[147] The term מקדש clearly means the Jerusalem temple, as it does at 1.10 and 2.7. One might have expected מקדשך in a speech addressed to Yahweh (cf. Pss 68.36; 74.7; Dan 9.17), and indeed, OL reads here *sanctuario tuo*, but the apparent anomaly is common enough in the Hebrew Bible (cf. Amos 4.11).

2.21

Text and Versions
MT שָׁכְבוּ לָאָרֶץ חוּצוֹת; LXX ἐκοιμήθησαν εἰς τὴν ἔξοδον; V *iacuerunt in terra foris*; P ܐܚܕܐ ܒܓܐܐ ܒܚܒܐ *škbw ʾl ʾrʿ ʾ bšwqʾ*. LXX is thought to be a scribal error (for εἰς γῆν ἐξόδων)—so Ziegler (479), cf. *BHK*, Rudolph (1938, 109). MT is supported by V and P and is preferred.

MT נַעַר וְזָקֵן—so also LXX and V. The fact that P and T render in the plural does not mean that their *Vorlagen* were different from MT; cf. English translations of RSV, JB, NEB. Bickell (112) suggested, on the basis of Ps 76.7, that the original was נְעָרַי וְזָקֵן, but MT is grammatically quite acceptable and is supported by the Versions. Budde (1892, 271) suggested that the original may have been נערי וזקני, presumably in line with the following בְּתוּלֹתַי וּבַחוּרָי, which have suffixes, but this is unwarranted and has no Versional support.

MT בְּתוּלֹתַי וּבַחוּרַי נָפְלוּ בֶחָרֶב—so also V, P; T קטלין בחרבא נפלו וריביי ובתולתי; LXX παρθένοι μου καὶ νεανίσκοι μου ἐπορεύθησαν ἐν αἰχμαλωσίᾳ ἐν ῥομφαίᾳ καὶ ἐν λιμῷ (ἀπέκτεινας); SH (margin) ܘܒܟܦܢܐ *nplw bsypʾ*. Ziegler (479) ignores the strong LXX MSS tradition and prints ἐπεσαν ἐν ῥομφαίᾳ, which he bases on the SH marginal note. Rudolph (1938, 109f.) considers that the wording from 1.18c was a marginal note which replaced the original ἐπεσαν ἐν ῥομφαίᾳ. It is quite possible that a scribe felt that the maidens and young men had already been consigned to exile (1.18c) and that 2.21b was, therefore, in error. Rudolph may be right, but there remains the additional material in LXX—καὶ ἐν λιμῷ—and the fact that the verb הרגת (ἀπέκτεινας) has been construed (in LXX) with the previous line: 'You have slain (them) by sword and famine'. Metric considerations would require הרגת to be taken with the remainder of v. 21; and this underlines the corruption in the LXX text. It is passing strange that NEB should, therefore, regard וברעב as original (Brockington, 218). It is not found in any Version except LXX (and not in all MSS) and, from the point of view of metre, it overloads the line. The explanation[148] by Albrektson (123) seems best: 'The addition ἐν λιμῷ is probably rightly explained as a reminiscence from 4.9 and especially from Jer., where the combination ἐν ῥομφαίᾳ καὶ ἐν λιμῷ occurs frequently in the second half of the book…: 45 (38).2; 49 (42).22; 51 (44).12, 18, 27; cf. also 49 (42).17.'

MT לֹא חָמָלְתָּ—so also LXX; P ܘܠܐ ܚܣܬ *wlʾ ḥst*—so also SH, T and several MSS[Ken].[149] MT is preferred.

* * *

The speech of accusation begins in the same style as v. 20bc, as it were, reporting further atrocities, but the verse ends by direct accusation of Yahweh; he is accused of merciless slaughter. As though casting around for hyperbole, Zion snatches at terminology which includes her whole population—devastated and killed by the enemy; but Yahweh is the main culprit.

שָׁכְבוּ לָאָרֶץ חוּצוֹת—'They lie upon the ground in the streets'. שכב ל is equivalent to שכב על (cf. Gen 28.13; Job 20.11; 21.26 and Job 7.21). If

---
[148] Cf. also Barthélemy (889f.), Schäfer (*BHQ* 124*).
[149] That V *nec* testifies to ולא is not certain (contra *BHK*, *BHS*). At 3.43 לֹא חָמָלְתָּ is rendered by V *nec pepercisiti*; and for 2 Chron 36.17 ולא חמל V reads *non est misertus*.

Ziegler's 'restoration' of LXX is correct (see above), it follows that the Greek translator interpreted the unvocalised ארץ as in construct with חוצות. Clearly, the pointing by the Masoretes suggests that חוצות has been understood as an adverbial accusative (contra Dyserinck, 370); and this is how V and P[150] read it. Kraus (37), who reads 'in den Staub der Gassen', and Westermann (143) *appear* to follow LXX, as do RSV and NIV, and Haller (102) spells out his preference; but Kaiser (328), Hillers[2] (96) and Plöger (141) see no need to read anything other than MT. Gordis (168) thinks that MT is a conflation of two readings—שכבו לארץ and שכבו (ב)חוצות, but his argument is based on too rigid a view of metre.

נַעַר וְזָקֵן—By referring to young and old, the poet alludes to the fact that the devastation and horror affected everyone. It appears, from what was said at v. 19, that young and old may be lying languishing in public, but this is another category—the boys and old men are dead. The alphabetic acrostic forces the poet to use a שׁ at this point, but although the verb שכב is ambiguous, it can sometimes mean to lie dead[151] (e.g. Isa 43.17; Ezek 31.18; Job 7.21; 14.12; 21.26), and this interpretation is confirmed when we recognise the chiastic structure of the first two lines of this verse, where שָׁכְבוּ לָאָרֶץ חוּצוֹת parallels נָפְלוּ בֶחָרֶב. On בְּיוֹם אַפֶּךָ, see on 1.12; 2.1, 3, 6; and cf. 3.43, 66; 4.11, 20.

טָבַחְתָּ—'You have slaughtered'. LXX ἐμαγείρευσας 'You have butchered'. This is the only occurrence of √טבח in Lamentations. We have seen, above (v. 20), that the LXX translator appears to have read a form of טבח for טפח. But his translation here is ambiguous.[152] The meaning of טבח is 'to butcher, slaughter'—BDB (370), *DCH* (III, 339)—and the poet employs the term as a parallel to הרג in order to emphasise the brutality of the killing experienced by the people of Jerusalem. It may be that the poet had in mind only the young men and women, but this is unlikely. His use of הרג, which was used of the enemy killing priests and prophets (v. 20), suggests that he now has in mind Yahweh's responsibility for *all* the slaughter—the death of the children, prophets, priests, boys, old men, young men and women: it can all be laid at Yahweh's door. Renkema (326) is probably right to see assonance in the use of טבח and טפח in adjoining verses (vv. 20, 21, 22).

---

[150] *BHK* wrongly assumes that P read בחוצות. The T tradition is ambiguous (see Levine, 42).
[151] IE[1] is aware of the ambiguity and points, in explanation, to Gen 47.30 וְשָׁכַבְתִּי עִם־אֲבֹתַי. And IE[2] explains further—מתו נערים וזקנים בתולות ובחורים.
[152] LXX has trouble elsewhere with this root. At Jer 52.12 (cf. Gen 41.10) the Babylonian official, Nebuzaradan, has the title רב טבחים which LXX translates ὁ ἀρχιμάγειρος 'the chief cook', though V, P and T get the (military) sense of the term; cf. McKane (1996, 1367). We should note, however, that at Isa 65.12 the translator got it right (σφαγῇ); cf. also Exod 21.37; Jer 11.19; 32.34.

לֹא חָמָלְתָּ—Yahweh has already been described as having no pity, in two other passages in the poem: vv. 2, 17. The meaning in each case has been taken adverbially 'without mercy', and we may interpret it similarly here. On the other hand, the bold assertion of the poet, turning on Yahweh, as it were, and accusing him of blatant slaughter, receives a certain sharpness if we take these three 2nd p. m. s. verbs as delivering three separate accusations: 'You killed, you butchered, you did not spare'.

The mood in v. 20 and v. 21ab is one of anguished pleading, while at v. 21c Zion accuses Yahweh directly and confronts him head on with what he has done. She knows (v. 14) that the destruction is punishment for her guilt, so she is clearly confronting the one who has dealt logically with her sins. But Zion's guilt is not mentioned here and, in keeping with the rest of the poem, the terrible effects are centre-stage.

2.22

Text and Versions

MT תִּקְרָא—so also P, V, T and LXX^Q (ἐκάλεσας); LXX^{B,A} ἐκάλεσεν. It is likely that ἐκάλεσεν is the original reading and that ἐκάλεσας is a later correction on the basis of the Hebrew. ἐκάλεσεν may have arisen through haplography in the *Vorlage* (note חמלת at the end of v. 21), cf. Rudolph (1938, 110), *BHQ*. It is also possible that, because Yahweh is referred to in the third person later in the verse, the translator opted for consistency. MT is preferred.

MT מְגוּרַי מִסָּבִיב; LXX παροικίας μου κυκλόθεν; V *qui terrerent me de circuitu*; P ܒܕܠܒܒܝ ܡܢ ܚܕܪܝ *bʻldbby mn ḥdry*.[153] It is best to emend to מְגִירַי.

MT אֲשֶׁר־טִפַּחְתִּי וְרִבִּיתִי so also P, V and T; LXX ὡς ἐπεκράτησα καὶ ἐπλήθυνα; Aq οὓς ἐπαλαίστωσα καὶ ἐπλήθυνα. LXX has misunderstood construction. MT is preferred.

MT אֹיְבַי כִּלָּם—so also V; LXX ἐχθρούς μου πάντας; Aq οἱ ἐχθροί μου συνετέλεσαν αὐτούς; P ܒܕܠܒܒܝ ܓܡܪܘ ܐܢܘܢ *bʻldbby gmrw ʼnwn* so also T; LXX vocalises incorrectly, Aq, P and T have perhaps vocalised אֹיְבַי כֻּלָּם. MT is not in question.

* * *

The final verse is the third in the prayer to Yahweh though it lacks the punch and intensity of vv. 20f. After the third line of v. 21, in which Zion accuses Yahweh of merciless slaughter, it is as though she has now expressed the ultimate in accusation and, although she continues in v. 22a to address Yahweh, she lapses into a sad reflection on the sorry state she is in (v. 22bc) and the effects of Yahweh's assaults.

תִּקְרָא—Although the other verbs in this prayer have been either in the imperative or the perfect, this is in the imperfect. The acrostic demanded an initial ת and, though the poet could call upon several verbs in Hebrew which begin with ת, he knew that coming after the perfects, he could employ an imperfect which could express the past (GK 107h). P and V

---

[153] On T's paraphrase here, see Alexander (2008, 142 n. 77).

interpret the Hebrew as referring to the past, as do Luther, Calvin, AV, RSV, Rudolph (1962, 218), Kraus (37), NEB, NIV, JPS.[154] Berlin (65) 'You invite' seems to follow Rashi's observation, though she may be thinking here in terms of a frequentative. At 1.15 Zion describes Yahweh as having called (קרא) a מועד against her. Here the object of the verb is not the מועד but מגורי מסביב. The thought is similar, but here Yahweh is actually addressed. Yahweh is in control of Zion's destiny. He can and did summon מגורי מסביב. This must be brought out into the open. Zion may blame her circumstances or she may attribute her terrible devastation to the invader, but, ultimately, it is Yahweh who is the author and instigator of it all.

מְגוּרַי מִסָּבִיב—Translators and commentators have struggled with this phrase. The second element מִסָּבִיב is straightforward: prep. מִן (see BDB 578, 1 c) plus סביב—either 'from every side' or 'on every side/round-about'. Clearly, the difficulty is with מְגוּרַי. There are three roots: גור I 'to dwell, sojourn', גור II 'to provoke, attack', and גור III 'to fear, be afraid'. If we go with גור I, we are in the company of LXX translator 'my sojourners round about', MR and Rashi 'my evil neighbours'; cf. also JPS. On this interpretation the meaning will be that Yahweh had arranged for Zion's hostile[155] neighbours—Edom, Moab etc.—to close in on her; and there were so many that it was like the pilgrim crowds at festival time. Relying on the same root, Ewald (336f.) takes a different line. He translates 'meine Weiler ringsum' by which he means the settlements and villages around Jerusalem, which would expect protection from the city, during the siege, but which would end up sharing the disaster with Zion's inhabitants. This interpretation, though followed by Löhr[156] (1894, 11), has not commanded support—see Keil (400), Rudolph (1962, 221). As Provan (78f.) comments: 'Comparison with 1:15, however, where it was claimed that God had "summoned (Heb *qārāʾ*) an assembly (Heb *môʿēd*) against" Zion, suggests that *mᵉgûray* here is a reference to hostile forces rather than Judaeans, and that the imagery of the gathering of people for a religious festival is once more being used to describe the convergence of these forces upon Zion'.

The most common interpretation is based on גור III 'to fear'. This was adopted by V 'who terrify me'.[157] Many translators and commentators

---

[154] Rashi, in a cryptic note, observes that תקרא is like קראה; and he adds that it refers to the present tense. IE² interprets כאילו קראת. T takes it as a future 'You will proclaim...' but goes off in midrashic fashion and does not do justice to the prayer of anguish. Kara appears to take תקרא as both future and past: 'You will summon an appointed time against the nations...like the day you summoned against me...'

[155] Rashi's comment is שכני הרעים להאסף עלי להשחית.

[156] 'Die Leute aus den umliegen Dörfern und Weilern strömten wie an einem Festtage in die Stadt schutzsuchend; aber da gab kein Entrinnen.'

[157] The accusative suffix suggests that Jerome might have read the Polel participle, *viz* מְגוֹרְרַי—so *BHK*, *BHS*, Rudolph (1938, 110)—but he may have been translating freely (Albrektson, 125) or instinctively.

relate the expression to that found several times in Jeremiah (6.25; 20.3, 10; 46.5; 49.29) and in Ps 31.14—מָגוֹר מִסָּבִיב, which is usually translated 'terror[158] (is) on every side', cf. McKane (1986, 151-53), i.e. מָגוֹר is viewed as a noun from גור III 'to fear'. In this verse we find a plural noun with suffix, and this is translated 'my terrors on every side'; so Calvin, Vermigli (105), AV, RV, RSV, NIV, Gottwald (12), Haller (102), House (370), cf. JB, Albrektson (124), Pham (101). IE[1], quoting Job 19.29, takes the same line, though he admits that others take it from גור 'to dwell'.[159] He is followed by Kara. P 'my enemies', using the same word as in the final line, *may* have been a free translation based on גור III 'to fear; so also Luther, NEB, REB, but it draws attention to a problem with the 'my terrors' rendering, for the idea of summoning terrors seems strange even though we are dealing with a poet. Hillers[2] (102) comments that 'to have 'terrors' invited to a festival would involve a mixture of metaphors not typical of Hebrew poetry'. McDaniel (42f.), Gottlieb (38) and Berlin (66) think along the same lines, and I think that they are right. We may be dealing here with גור II 'to provoke, attack' (cf. Isa 54.15; Ps 59.4), in which case the original reading may have been the Hiphil participle of this root—מְגוּרַי—'my attackers' or 'men to attack me' (cf. 1.17). This is graphically very close to MT, and the corruption may have occurred because of the phrase in Jer 6.25 etc. *HALOT* and *DCH* both advocate reading the Polel participle of גור III—'those that frighten me'.

פָּלִיט וְשָׂרִיד—The perfect tense is resumed in v. 22b. The two words, which are almost synonyms, serve to heighten the hyperbole in Zion's prayer. The idea that no one escaped is scarcely true, however, if the poet, for one, was there to witness events described elsewhere (cf. v. 10); but no one was unaffected.

The phrase (בְּיוֹם אַף(־)יְהוָה) is a common one in the Hebrew Bible and especially in this poem—vv. 1, 21; cf. also 1.12; Ezek 7.19; Zeph 1.18; 2.3; Isa 13.13. The fact that Zion is addressing Yahweh in prayer leads *BHK* to suggest emending MT (though without textual support) to אַפֶּךָ (cf. v. 21), but see v. 20 where the same phenomenon occurs. Apart from the possibility of poetic freedom here, we should note, with Westermann (146), that we have a fixed expression here.

אֲשֶׁר־טִפַּחְתִּי וְרִבִּיתִי—The LXX translator did not understand the function of אשׁר here, introducing the objective clause (cf. GK 157c) possibly because the verb which governs the clause comes at the end of the line. As a result he misunderstands the entire line, 'whereas I have strengthened and multiplied all my enemies', making no sense in the context.

---

[158] At Jer 6.25, Rashi glosses מגור with יראה ('fear'); and Kimḥi employs פחד ('dread').
[159] Looking at the syntax of the passage, IE[2] comments: 'it is as if you summoned all my objects of dread (פחדים) and gathered them around me'.

טִפַּחְתִּי—A *hapax legomenon* and, as such, proved difficult for the Versions and subsequent commentators (see also v. 20). The accompanying verb רִבִּיתִי (√רבה in Piel) probably has the same meaning[160] as in Ezek 19.2 which speaks of the rearing of lion cubs, i.e. 'to rear/train'; and it was deemed reasonable to find a meaning for √טפח that fitted with 'rear'. The known noun טֶפַח 'handbreadth' had further influence,[161] and this is seen in Aq οὓς ἐπαλαίστωσα, P ܕܫܩܠܬ *dšqlt*, Luther 'Die ich auf den Händen getragen (und erzogen) habe', AV 'those that I have swaddled...', RV 'those that I have dandled...', Knox 'all I fondled...', JB 'those whom I had nursed...', REB 'All whom I have held in my arms...', ESV 'those whom I held...' All appear to sense that the first of the two verbs concerns the early stage in the lives of children.[162] As mentioned at v. 20, Driver (1950, 138f.) suggests that √טפח may be related to the Arabic *ṭafaḥa* 'to bring forth fully formed children', and this has been adopted by *HALOT* and *DCH* ('give birth') and followed by Kaiser (328) 'Die ich heil gebar...', NEB 'All whom I brought safely to birth...',[163] JPS/NRSV 'those whom I bore...' While this is the case, the final line may also refer to the whole population of Zion: all those she had borne and reared.

אֹיְבִי כִלָּם—'My enemy has destroyed them', i.e. the Piel of כלה plus 3rd p. m. pl. (accusative) suffix. P has vocalised אֹיְבַי כִלָּם. NEB 'All whom I brought safely to birth and reared were destroyed by my enemies' is explained by Brockington (218) as the vocalisation אֹיְבַי כָּלָּם, but the latter reading precludes any verb for the line! NEB[164] seems to want כלם to do double duty—כִלָּם and כָּלָם. Brockington claims support in P, but P (see above) = 'my enemies have destroyed them'.

In this final verse of ch. 2, the poet interweaves two ways of viewing the assault on Jerusalem and its dire effects. He continues with his theological interpretation of events, accusing Yahweh of summoning the attack on Jerusalem in fulfilment of his day of wrath; and he regards the facts on the ground, as it were, albeit with customary hyperbole, as also true: the bottom line is that the enemy has destroyed Zion's cherished children.

---

[160] It could mean 'I multiplied' and it is taken this way by LXX and Aq.
[161] It is interesting to note Jerome's ambivalence as to the root. At v. 20 he rendered עֹלְלֵי טִפֻּחִים as *parvulos ad mensuram palmae*, but here, at v. 22, אֲשֶׁר־טִפַּחְתִּי is rendered *quos educavi*!
[162] IE² clearly indicates that the first verb refers to small children, and רִבִּיתִי to bigger children. MLT's reference here to young men and maidens, however, would suggest that not all commentators viewed אֲשֶׁר־טִפַּחְתִּי as referring to small children.
[163] Although following Driver's philology, NEB seems to have ignored his suggested rendering, 'whom I have nurtured', and gone for a translation which is anything but poetic.
[164] Fuerst (231f.), commenting on the NEB, does not notice this and he is misleading on מְגוּרַי מִסָּבִיב.

CHAPTER 3

Introductory

Chapter 3 resembles chs. 1 and 2 in that it is of the same length (66 lines), like chs. 1, 2 and 4 it is written in the same poetic rhythm and is an alphabetic acrostic and, as in chs. 2 and 4, the alphabetic order is ע-פ. But it differs in that the acrostic is much more intensive—three lines begin with *aleph*, three with *beth*, and so on;[1] and, unlike chs. 1, 2 and 4, it does not begin with the dirge-like 'Alas!' Indeed, the mood is also different. We do not encounter the names of Jerusalem, Zion, Judah or Israel, and there is little to suggest the actual aftermath of 586 BCE.[2] It is likely that it was composed at a later date; cf. Westermann (193). The composition may be divided: vv. 1-25, 26-39, 40-47, 48-66.

One of the main problems of interpretation in this chapter is the identification of 'the man' (v. 1).[3] During the early history of interpretation, when most commentators were of the opinion that Jeremiah[4] was the author of all the poems, identification was not an issue: the man was Jeremiah.[5] This view was even maintained by some who subsequently denied Jeremian authorship.[6] With the advent of critical scholarship the identification of 'the man' went in two different directions: (a) the view that we are dealing with an individual sufferer, and (b) the view that the singular should be viewed as a collective. The first group divides further. There are those who identify the man with a known figure—several claim Jeremiah (see above), Hardt opts for Meshach, Gurewicz (22) and Porteous (244f.) argue for Jehoiachin, and, more recently, Saebø (301-304) for

---

[1] This feature led to the Masoretic division into 66 verses (22×3).
[2] Speaking of ch. 3, Westermann (71) declares 'This particular text, if heard on its own terms, deals unambiguously with the catastrophe of the year 587 BCE in not a single one of its clauses'.
[3] For a short survey of opinions, see House (405-407).
[4] Ibn Ezra, in his opening remarks on ch. 3, appears uncertain: 'Our fathers of blessed memory said that Jeremiah wrote this scroll. If so, he may be the one who utters 'I am the man'; or any Israelite may be speaking. But this comment was a voice in the interpretative wilderness.
[5] Applying Gematria (Hebrew גימטריה, Greek γεοματρία)—a (later) system where numerical value is linked to the Hebrew alphabet—we discover that the opening words of ch. 3, 'I am the man' (אני הגבר) is equivalent (271) to 'Jeremiah' (ירמיהו)!
[6] Budde (1898a, 91-93), Löhr (1904a), and more recently Meek (23) and Rudolph (1962, 227-45). The latter sees here an idealised Jeremiah standing for a paradigm (*Vorbild*) of suffering.

Zedekiah, though the tendency among modern scholars is to shy away from such precise identifications. More popular is the position where scholars opt for an unknown individual—a devout man (Renkema, 348), a soldier (Lanahan, 45f.) or a strong man (O'Connor, 1046). Hillers[2] (122f.), taking his cue from Ewald (324) and Keil (403), argues, 'He is an "Everyman", a figure who represents what any man may feel when it seems that God is against him. Through this representative sufferer the poet points the way to the nation, as he shows the man who has been through trouble moving into, then out of, near despair to patient faith and patience, thus becoming a model for the nation.'

The identification is, I think, facilitated by reading through to the end of the chapter. The poem ends as it began with first person singular forms. The passage vv. 40-47, where first person plural forms predominate, may be explained as the poet showing his hand, revealing that his piece is communal in intent;[7] and we must conclude that the same person is speaking throughout.[8] The author, who was responsible for the alphabetic acrostic form, must have envisaged that the figure who describes the misery which he has experienced, in the first few verses, is the figure who pleads with Yahweh for vengeance on the enemy in the final section. We have to keep in mind not only that we are dealing with poetry but also the fact that the positioning of this poem (whether by the author or some other redactor) with the other four, all of which are communal in nature, is a factor in the identification of 'the man', a factor which points in the direction of a collective interpretation. That the singular may stand for the plural is well established. In Deuteronomy, Israel is often addressed in the singular as well as in the plural. Judah, addressed by Isaiah, is sometimes singular and sometimes plural, and in the Psalms there is often movement between the singular and the plural.[9] Those who favour this interpretation are not all in agreement. Some may think that the community is Zion, others Judah or all the people of Israel, or just the exilic community. Among these are Ehrlich (39f.),[10] Gottwald (38-42), Streane (359), Dhorme (1489), Albrektson (127-29), Berlin (84f.); cf. Gerstenberger (493). My own position is that the figure in this poem represents the people who commemorate the awful tragedy which began with the fall of Jerusalem and who still experience its effects.

The author does not mention the city or its fall at all, but he does identify with the suffering of that time and with the hardship that followed. But whereas the previous compositions captured the tragic reversal

---

[7] Eissfeldt (503) observes '...the change over to "*We*" (vv. 40-7) can only be understood if the poet had from the outset a plural entity in mind, Jerusalem or Judah...' And Simon (185) thinks that Ibn Ezra, at 3.1, was suggesting this.
[8] Contra Hillers[2] (123).
[9] Gordis (1967–68, 14-18) speaks of 'fluid personality' and invokes the (singular/plural) problem of the servant songs; cf. also Smend (62 n. 3), H. W. Robinson (1936, 49ff.).
[10] It is Ehrlich's instinct to interpret the figure collectively but he resorts to a conjectural emendation to bolster his case (see commentary).

and bemoaned the fact, the intent of the author of ch. 3 is to change that atmosphere and to give a different emphasis. There is no doubt that the other authors were men who had not abandoned Yahwism, as many of their fellow Judahites will have done—the fact that they created these poems demonstrates this—but ch. 3's author sees in the other poems too much that is inward-looking, too much concentration on what has happened and not enough on what can happen. He does not want to denigrate or trivialise the suffering. In this, his contribution to the liturgy, he wants to lift the commemorating community out of the slough of despond where one limits oneself with bemoaning one's fate and calling for disaster to fall on the enemy. This author, unlike the others, has a message for his community. There is a way out of the ignominy and suffering and it lies in making contact with Yahweh who has been punishing us, 'for rejection by Yahweh is not for ever; even if he has afflicted he will have compassion in line with his great kindness; for he does not willingly afflict or grieve any mortal' (vv. 31-33).

Verses 1-25: The poem begins with a long section, reminiscent of an individual lament in the book of Psalms and which has some affinities with Ps 56. The speaker describes in vivid terms adversity at the hands of Yahweh. Although he is not mentioned by name until the end of v. 18, Yahweh is the protagonist throughout these verses, and the speaker the victim. There is nothing systematic about the progress of this piece; indeed, the poet seems bent on describing his distress and misery in every conceivable way, pulling metaphor and imagery from every walk of life, giving the impression that he is trying to convey, albeit in poetic language, that Yahweh's onslaught was as complete and as multifaceted as could be. The fact that he attributes his misery to Yahweh suggests that he has been a Yahweh worshipper, that he still believed that Yahweh was in control; but he indicates that the physical and mental violence which he has experienced has led him to despair and to abandon hope in his God. The figure of Job comes to mind (vv. 1-18). This passage is followed (after a short reflection, vv. 19-20) by a surprising piece in which the same voice declares that he will wait patiently because he has faith that Yahweh's love is still operating and that he is good to those who trust in him and seek him. Some of these statements sound personal in nature, while others, although not recognisable quotations,[11] seem to be statements from a formal, communal setting (vv. 21-25).

Verses 26-39: Already, vv. 1-25 differ markedly from the rest of Lamentations, but at v. 26 we have another unusual development. The passage picks up the avowal of trust in vv. 21-25 and proceeds, wisdom-like, to give explanation and instruction on trusting and waiting patiently for Yahweh on the basis that Yahweh does not reject permanently: he may punish, yet he will have compassion for he does not afflict in a capricious

---

[11] The demands of the alphabetic acrostic may have had something to do with the wording here.

manner. The speaker then, on the basis of the foregoing, rejects the practice of complaint (vv. 26-39). The author juxtaposes extreme adversity at the hands of Yahweh (vv. 1-18) with doctrine from the past, which he believes, or wants to believe. He seems to say: It may be that we have suffered beyond all imagining, but these things are true too; and if they are true we must turn to Yahweh: there is nowhere else to go, for he is the one with whom we have to do, and we must face this fact. He is in charge of our world, and we have no right to complain about any punishment meted out to us (v. 39).

Verses 40-47: Let us, therefore, examine ourselves and let us return to Yahweh (vv. 40-41). The speaker emphasises a radical return and in sincerity. He couches it in first person plural[12] terminology which reminds us of part of a communal lament in the Psalms. The exhortation (vv. 40f.) is followed by the prayer. That Yahweh is being addressed is clear enough, though his name is not in evidence, merely the 2nd p. s. forms and suffixes; but the 1st p. pl. forms also continue, so that this is unmistakeably a prayer of the people. Although the 1st p. pl. forms give way to 1st p. s. (v. 48), we should probably interpret the prayer as continuing to the end of the chapter. The prayer begins with confession,[13] (v. 42a) but this is followed by a sharp accusation (v. 42b), and the latter continues to v. 47. Conditions are such that it would seem that Yahweh had not taken note or had not responded to the confession.

Verses 48-66: The poet reverts to 1st p. s. but, as Hillers[2] (131) notes, 'one may think of this 'I' passage as a continuation and completion of the collective prayer'. The first few verses appear to be an aside, within the prayer, vowing to maintain weeping until Yahweh responds (vv. 48-51). The prayer resumes at v. 52, praising Yahweh for a past experience when, in distress, he had been invoked and *had* responded (vv. 52-58); and, on the basis of this positive experience (and, presumably, Yahweh's character as in vv. 22-33), the prayer proceeds to plead for present deliverance. There is an urgency about the final verses, and Yahweh is invoked by name three times. The ignominy experienced by the people and the mocking by the enemy prompts an urgent call on Yahweh to bring a curse upon the enemy and to wipe them off the face of the earth (vv. 59-66).

Translation

1. I am the man who has experienced affliction by the rod of his wrath.
2. He led and guided me into darkness and not light.
3. Indeed, he has repeatedly shown hostility towards me all day long.

---

[12] The move to the 1st p. pl. may have been sparked off by the acrostic need, at this point, to employ the letter *nun* as the opening letter for vv. 40-42.
[13] Unlike some of the prayers in the Psalms, there is no hint of innocence, nor that the punishment has been unjust.

4. He has worn away my flesh and my skin, he has broken my bones.
5. He besieged me and surrounded me with bitterness and hardship.
6. He has made me sit in darkness like those long dead.

7. He hemmed me in and I cannot escape, he weighed me down with chains.
8. Also, when I call out and cry for help, he shuts out my prayer.
9. He blocks my paths with hewn stone, he distorts my ways.

10. He is a bear lying in wait for me, a lion in hiding;
11. He put briars on my paths and lamed me, leaving me wretched;
12. He readied his bow and made me the target of his arrows;

13. Into my innards he shot the contents of his quiver.
14. I have become a joke to all nations,[14] the butt of their song all day long;
15. He has filled me with bitter herbs, sated me with wormwood.

16. He has crushed my teeth with gravel and has pressed me into ashes.
17. My soul has been shut out from peace, I have forgotten prosperity.
18. And I thought: My future and my hope from Yahweh have gone,

19. Remembering my affliction and my trouble is wormwood and gall.
20. My soul well remembers and is bowed down within me.
21. But this I call to mind and therefore I have hope:

22. Yahweh's kindnesses have not ceased,[15] his compassions are not spent.
23. They are new every morning; great is your faithfulness!
24. My very being declares: Yahweh is all I have, therefore I will hope in him.

25. Yahweh is good to those who look to him, to all those who seek him.
26. It is good that one should wait quietly for Yahweh's deliverance.
27. It is good for a man to bear a yoke when young;

28. He should sit alone and be silent for he has laid it upon him.
29. He should put his mouth in the dust—there may yet be hope;
30. He should offer his cheek to the smiter, he should suffer reproach in full measure.

31. For rejection by Yahweh is not for ever;
32. Even if he has afflicted he will have compassion in line with his great kindness;
33. For he does not willingly afflict or grieve any mortal.

34. To the crushing underfoot of any prisoner on earth,
35. The denying of rights to a man in the face of the Most High,
36. The depriving a man of justice in court—Yahweh pays no attention!

37. Who has spoken and it came to pass? Has not Yahweh commanded it?
38. Do not both bad and good proceed from the mouth of the Most High?
39. Why should a man alive complain, a man about his punishment?

40. Let us examine our ways and test them, and let us return to Yahweh;
41. Let us raise up our hearts with our hands to God in heaven!
42. We have transgressed and rebelled, but you have not forgiven.

---

[14] *Nations*, prb. rdg. Heb. *my people.*
[15] *Have not ceased*, prb. rdg. Cf. P and T; Heb. reads *we are not consumed.*

190   LAMENTATIONS

43. You have covered us in anger and pursued us, you have slain without mercy.
44. You have covered yourself with cloud so that our prayer cannot get through.
45. You have made us filth and refuse among the nations—
46. All our enemies openly rail against us;
47. Panic and pitfall, calamity and collapse have come upon us!
48. My eyes shed streams of water because of my people's ruin;
49. My eyes shall flow without ceasing, without respite,
50. Until Yahweh looks down from heaven and pays attention;
51. My eyes cause me pain more than all the daughters of my city.

52. My enemies hunted me down like a bird, gratuitously;
53. They silenced me in a pit and threw stones at me.
54. Waters flowed over my head; I thought, 'I am lost!'

55. From the depths of the pit I called on your name, Yahweh.
56. You heard my cry 'Do not hide your ear from my gasping[16]!'
57. You were near when I called you, you said, 'Do not fear!'

58. You championed my cause,[17] you redeemed my life.
59. O Yahweh, you have seen the wrong done to me, judge my case!
60. You have seen all their vengeance, all their plots against me,

61. You have heard their reproach, O Yahweh, all their plots against me,
62. What my assailants say and murmur against me all day long.
63. Look, I am their taunt-song whatever their activity!

64. O Yahweh, pay them back what they deserve, for what they have done!
65. Give them derangement of mind. Your curse be upon them!
66. Pursue them in anger and destroy them from under the heavens of Yahweh.

Commentary

3.1

Text and Versions

MT אֲנִי הַגֶּבֶר—so also LXX, V and T; P ܐ ܓܒܪܐ *'yl gnbr'*. MT is preferred.

MT רָאָה עֳנִי, followed by T; LXX ὁ βλέπων πτωχείαν; Sym κάκωσίν μου— followed by a few MSS[Ken and de Ros] עָנְיִי; SH margin ܡܣܟܢܘܬ ܕܝܠܝ *msknwt' dyly*; V *videns paupertatem meam*; P ܚܙܝ ܚܫܥܒܕܝ, *ḥzy ḥšw'bdy*; Scholars generally agree that MT preserves the best text here, but there is evidence that the *Vorlagen* of the Versions may have varied in one or two places. LXX, though perceiving the suppressed relative,[18] points רֹאֶה (so also V), while V either had a text reading עָנְיִי or imagined עָנִי to be a suffixed form[19] (so also P, SH margin and Sym). P pointed רְאֵה, an imperative. It is likely that the Syriac translator

---

[16] *My gasping*, prb. rdg. Heb. adds *to my relief.*
[17] *My cause*, prb. rdg. Heb. adds *O Lord.*
[18] The suppressed relative is not universally recognised. In MR, a certain R. Samuel bar Nahman is quoted: 'The congregation of Israel said: "When he saw me poor (עניה) in (the performance of.) commandments and good deeds, he brought upon me the rod of his wrath"'.
[19] LXX[B] ends the verse with ἐπ' ἐμέ, which, though probably not original—see Ziegler (480), Albrektson (129)—but an inner Greek error coming from v. 2, developed naturally, as did the first person suffixes of P, V, Sym; cf. *BHQ*.

had an unclear Hebrew text before him, at least for the opening words, cf. Abelesz (36f.), Wiesmann (172), Kraus (52). The following words struck him as reminiscent of Lam 1.9, ראה יהוה את עניי, so he vocalised accordingly, viz רְאֵה. He may also have been influenced by a number of passages where ראה and עני are combined and where the idea is not *experiencing* affliction but looking sympathetically upon affliction (Pss 9.14; 25.18; 31.8; 119.153; Job 10.15; Neh 7.9). Having decided that ראה was an imperative, he interpreted עני as 'my affliction' and cast around for a vocative in the opening words. He may then have decided that his text was a corruption of אל גבור (Isa 9.5; 10.21; Jer 32.18; Neh 9.32)—'O Mighty God'. Having made this decision, he was forced to understand the final suffix as referring to the enemy (2.22).

* * *

The first three verses begin with an א, the second three with a ב, and so on. The alphabetic acrostic, barely noticeable in the first two poems, is now much more in the face of the reader. This first verse is unusual in that it begins in the 1st p. s. The identity of the speaker, who claims to have suffered at the hands of Yahweh, is not revealed. The other unusual feature is the 3rd p. m. s. suffix on the final word, a suffix which has no apparent referent.

The opening 'I am the man' is arresting. Gerstenberger (492f.) notes 'The present introduction has not been caused by acrostic considerations; it would have been easy to start, e.g., an invocation of God with the letter *aleph*. The composer consciously chose descriptive affirmations to begin the complaint, perhaps in line with the "narrational" openings of Lamentations 1, 2 and 4, after the opening shouts. The question arises, too, why the wailing shout *'êkāh*, "alas", is missing in ch. 3. We may surmise that the self-presentation...at the time was seen as an adequate introduction to a mourning rite.' The fact that 'alas' is missing may simply mean that the author did not regard his piece to be in the same category as chs. 1, 2 and 4. We should note that at Eccl 1.12 a passage begins 'I, Qoheleth, was king...' and that the Mesha inscription begins 'I am Mesha, son of Chemosh [...], king of Moab'; and Dobbs-Allsopp (108f.) has drawn attention to similar style in self-presentation in other royal inscriptions.

Good sense can be obtained for MT as it stands. The NRSV translation 'I am one who...' has been criticized by O'Connor (1046), cf. also Dobbs-Allsopp (106f.), Berlin (84f.). O'Connor suggests that the speaker here is a strong man or a soldier. There may be some significance in the author's choice of term here,[20] but the noun גבר can be equivalent to איש or אדם; cf. Ps 1.1 אשרי האיש; Ps 40.5 אשרי הגבר, and note its occurrence in Pss 94.12; 128.4 and Jer 17.7 (see Lundbom, 782). Furthermore, the term, which is

---

[20] Perhaps, coming to the commemoration corpus where Zion is construed as feminine (for example, 1.1), he wanted to slant his piece in favour of the community: those (from city and outlying districts) who would be commemorating the fall of Jerusalem and the resultant suffering, i.e. the people (עם = m.; cf. v. 48) and those who would subsequently identify with them.

used in Lamentations only in ch. 3 (vv. 1, 27, 35, 39) is not employed in a military context (cf. NRSV readings there); indeed, at v. 39 גבר is simply parallel with אדם. So the NRSV translators are thinking along these lines. However one interprets הגבר, one may note that the speaker introduces himself in this first verse as someone who has experienced affliction, the relative pronoun אשר having been suppressed before ראה (cf. GK 144p) and the verb ראה taken in the sense of knowing by experience (BDB 907), cf. Jer 5.12; Job 11.11. Furthermore, the suffix with which the verse ends may, in the present context, be taken to refer back to Yahweh (2.22); and the entire line functions as an introduction to the passage vv. 1-18 which elaborates on the specifics of the affliction.

The occurrence of עני after אני leads Nägelsbach (103) to suggest that the author juxtaposed these two similar-sounding words for poetic effect; cf. also Watson (1984, 243; cf. also Ps 88.16; Lam 1.13). The term עני can mean 'affliction' or 'poverty'. LXX, V and SH margin translate 'poverty', while P, T and Sym render 'affliction'. In the light of the subsequent verses, 'affliction' would appear to be the better choice; so AV, RV, NEB, NRSV, JPS, Rudolph (1962, 227).

בשבט עברתו—The referent of the final suffix is not exactly clear. While LXX and V transmit the ambiguity, T takes it to be Yahweh, as do MR, MLT, Rashi, Kara, Vermigli (107), Calvin, Keil (403). NRSV 'under the rod of God's wrath' and JPS 'under the rod of His wrath' remove the ambiguity. IE[1] (cf. IE[2]) argues that the suffix refers to the enemy (2.22), though he is aware of the other (prevailing) view that the reference is to Yahweh. The term שבט sometimes refers to the sceptre of a king (Pss 45.7; 125.3), or even the rod/club of a shepherd (Ps 23.4; Mic 7.14),[21] but it may also refer to a rod for punishment (Prov 22.15; cf. also Job 21.9; 37.13; Isa 11.4). The phrase שבט אפי is found at Isa 10.5 where Yahweh describes Assyria as 'the rod of my anger'. It is possible that the present poet had this passage in mind. The fact that the poet employs the suffix may mean that he composed his piece to fit after 2.22, in which case the referent is probably יהוה. However, it may be that he thought that, in the context of commemoration (for which he was writing), the referent would be obvious, regardless of the location of the poem. It is clear that it was his intention to construct the long passage (vv. 1-18), maintaining anonymity as to the subject of the verbs and using only 3rd p. s. pronouns and suffixes until the end of v. 18.

Although the history of exegesis betrays some misgivings with both the text and the interpretation of the passage, most scholars are content to comment on MT. Not so Ehrlich (39f.). He is unhappy with the construction ראה עני where ראה has to mean 'know/experience', and he offers a

---

[21] Some scholars fix on this aspect of 'rod', seeing a link in the following verse with the words 'lead' and 'guide', and so an ironic reference to what one might expect from Yahweh.

conjecture based on Mic 7.14 (רעה עמך בשבטך), namely, רעני בשבט עברתו 'He (the Lord) has shepherded me by the rod of his wrath'. In the light of this, he conjectures that הגבר should read הָעֵדֶר 'the herd/flock'. The full reconstruction results in: 'I am the herd which the Lord, with the rod of his fury, shepherds'.[22]

3.2

Text and Versions
No significant material.

* * *

The subject of the verbs in this verse is the same as in v. 1, *viz* Yahweh, although he is still not specifically mentioned. By using the verbs 'guide/ lead' the poet seeks to make a contrast between what one might expect from Yahweh and the present reality.

נהג—The verb נהג may be ambiguous. It may carry an aggressive tone and mean 'drive', as in Gen 31.18, but the meaning is often of a more pastoral nature 'lead', 'care for', as in Ps 80.2; Exod 3.1 and Isa 11.6; indeed, at Exod 10.13; Deut 4.27; 28.37; Isa 63.14, where the verb is construed with Yahweh as subject, the sense is 'leading/guiding'. It is, perhaps, a little unusual for LXX to render נהג by παρέλαβεν. As Albrektson (129) remarks, we would probably have expected ἄγω or the compounds ἀπάγω or ἐπάγω. However, as Albrektson goes on to observe, ἀπάγω is 'used to render Hiphil of הלך (which is usual in LXX), and this is probably the reason why the more unusual rendering παραλαμβάνω was chosen for נהג. The Greek rendering probably means 'lead', for it is found also at Song 8.2 and 2 Chron 25.11, translating נהג and where that must be the meaning. P renders ܕܒܪ *dbr*, the verb used also at Song 8.2 and 2 Chron 25.11, and we may conclude that 'lead' is meant here also. V *minavit* 'he drove' takes נהג in its more aggressive sense, while T דבר may mean 'drive' (so Levine, 68) or 'lead'.[23] Vermigli (109) and Calvin *deduxit* emphasise the leading rather than driving and they are followed by AV, RV, Keil (400), Hillers[2] (109), Rudolph (1962, 227), NJB and NEB.

וַיֹּלֵךְ (= וַיֵּלֶךְ)—On the form, see GK 53n; BL 46, cf. also 3.5 (וַיִּקַּח). The author virtually repeats the concept introduced by נהג. Indeed, Vermigli (107) translates with only one verb. הלך in the Hiphil, with Yahweh as subject, is found also at Deut 8.2; 28.36; Jer 2.6, 17. It is likely, therefore,

---

[22] While no subsequent commentator has embraced Ehrlich's suggestion, a footnote in JPS shows an affinity with it *[Emendation yields 'whom the Lord has shepherded with']*.
[23] Whether the more aggressive meaning is to be preferred, following the harshness of v. 1, is debatable. Renkema (353f.) 'he drives me forth' understands it this way; cf. also JPS, NRSV, Haller (102), Wiesmann (174), Kaiser 342, Berlin (77).

that the author, in using these two verbal forms, was associating them with Yahweh's care of Israel in the past.[24] If so, then there is a touch of irony here, for the remainder of the line is not what one expects from Yahweh's leading and guiding.

חֹשֶׁךְ—Bickell (112) suggests reading לחֹשֶׁךְ and is followed by Kelso (37). Neither offer an explanation but, presumably, the ל ensures that חֹשֶׁךְ is read as accusative 'into darknes...', whereas MT may be read as adverbial accusative 'in darkness...' But the emendation is unnecessary. LXX εἰς σκότος and P ܒܚܫܘܟܐ *bḥšwkʾ* interpreted MT as accusative of direction (GK 118d); cf. Wiesmann (172).

חֹשֶׁךְ ולֹא אוֹר—The phrase is found at Amos 5.18 and Job 12.25. Does the author mean 'into darkness and not into light'? This is how V, P and T render the phrase, while LXX εἰς σκότος καὶ οὐ φῶς is slightly ambiguous, though probably means the same. This is how Vermigli (107) takes it, as do Calvin, Luther, AV, Nägelsbach (103). Although MLT's comments sit lightly to the text, the phrase ולֹא אוֹר is explained as בלֹא תורה 'without Torah' (cf. Licht, 21), and some interpret our phrase similarly, *viz* 'without light'. This is the thinking behind RSV, NRSV 'without any light', NEB 'where no light is'; cf. Prov 10.9. Note also Wiesmann (174) 'in lichtlos Finsternis', Berlin (77) 'with no light', Westermann (160) 'into unilluminated darkness'. Rudolph (1962, 230) points out that 'לֹא gehört nicht zum Verb, sondern verneint אוֹר'; cf. GK 152a, d.

Because he takes the subject of the verbs to be the enemy, IE² interprets the verse to refer to the deportation into exile, but if we understand Yahweh to be the subject we should probably interpret in more general terms of adversity; cf. Blayney (320).

3.3

Text and Versions
MT יָשֻׁב יַהֲפֹךְ; LXX ἐπέστρεψεν; SH ܘܐܗܦܟ ܦܢܐ *pnʾ wʾhpk*; Sym ἐπιστρέφει καὶ μεταβάλλει; V *vertit et convertit*; P ܘܗܦܟ ܢܬܘܒ *ntwb wnhpk*; T יתוב יגלגל; LXX represents only one verb here, and *BHK* concludes that the Greek translator's *Vorlage* had only יָשֻׁב. Rudolph (1938, 110) argues that the LXX text is the result of haplography (so also *BHQ*), the original being ἐπέστρεψεν καὶ ἔστρεψε, cf. Albrektson (130).

* * *

The aggression of Yahweh towards the speaker continues in this verse. Whereas v. 2 alludes to the general negative situation, v. 3 emphasises the ongoing nature of that experience, employing an image of constant attack on the part of Yahweh. This is achieved by the use of the imperfect tense and an adverbial phrase.

---

[24] An observation which perhaps lends support to the 'collective' interpretation of הנבר.

אַךְ—This particle can mean 'surely/indeed', 'howbeit' or 'only'. The Versions mostly transmit this ambiguity, though V is specific: *tantum* = 'only'. This is how Rashi understands it; and Kara points out that while other nations sin, Israel *alone* is singled out by God for punishment.[25] This is followed by NRSV, JPS, NJB, REB, Berlin (77), Kraus (51), Keil (400), Blayney (320). This interpretation implies that the גבר has been singled out for treatment. MR seems to interpret אַךְ as 'indeed, surely', and this is how Vermigli (109) takes it, as do Calvin, AV, NIV, Nägelsbach (103), Renkema (354), Westermann (160), Kaiser (342), Provan (85), Gottwald (12). This latter interpretation sees the גבר emphasising that the action is towards himself (cf. the earlier emphasis אני הגבר, v. 1, and אותי, v. 2), but not necessarily to the exclusion of others.

יָשֻׁב—This form (of שׁוּב) is also found at Ps 146.4. Most MSS[Ken] read ישוב. It is, clearly, 3rd p. m. s. impf. Qal of שׁוב. This verb is frequently used as an auxiliary, denoting repetition (e.g. Gen 26.18; Num 11.4; Isa 3.5). While the mode is usually that of finite verb plus infinitive construct, there are a few instances where both auxiliary and main verb are imperfects without copula (Ps 71.20; Mic 7.19). Hence, יָשֻׁב יהפך means 'he repeatedly turns (his hand)'; cf. GK 120d, g. T is the only Version not to insert a copula here; the others do not recognise the auxiliary nature of ישׁ.

The author depicts Yahweh[26] as 'turning his hand against me'. The construction 'to turn the hand' occurs elsewhere only in contexts of wheeling round the chariot (1 Kgs 22.34; 2 Kgs 9.23; 2 Chron 18.33), and Fitzgerald (1967, 368f.) argues that יד here derives from the root ידד, means 'love' and that the translation should read 'Alas, he ceases to favour me'. Gottlieb (39), however, points to the expressions השיב ידו על (Ps 81.5; Isa 1.25; Amos 1.8; Zech 13.7), היתה יד ב (Exod 9.3;[27] Deut 2.15; Judg 2.15; 1 Sam 7.13; 2 Sam 24.17), and עוד ידו נטויה (Isa 5.25; 9.11, 16, 20; 10.4). הפך יד ב may have originally denoted a change of horse direction, but possibly came also to mean 'to attack'. Rashi, IE¹, MLT interpret the construction in terms of a repetition of blows; cf. T מחתיה. Curiously, although the Versions are elsewhere acquainted with the auxiliary function of שוב, LXX, P, V and T translate the verbs separately; and this is echoed by Vermigli, AV, RV, Luther, Calvin.

כָּל־הַיּוֹם—Found also at 3.14, 62 and at 1.3, כל־היום means 'all the day' or 'continually, always'. The combination of this phrase, the auxiliary verb and the imperfect tenses convey to the reader/hearer a situation where the speaker is constantly experiencing the hostility of Yahweh.

---

[25] Clearly, Kara believes that the גבר is the nation of Israel!
[26] It is interesting to note that IE¹, who had claimed (v. 1) that the suffix on עֶבְרָתוֹ referred to the enemy (2.22), here reminds commentators who had interpreted it as referring to God that they ought to interpret the suffix on ידו similarly, citing Exod 9.3. It is as if he were beginning to have doubts as to the line he took at v. 1!
[27] Also cited by IE¹.

3.4

Text and Versions
LXX follows MT in the first stich but reverses the word order in the second, while P and V both reverse the order of 'flesh and skin' in the first stich. T, in paraphrase, follows MT order throughout. MT is preferred.

* * *

The poet produces another in the sequence of vignettes depicting the affliction suffered by the speaker at the hands of Yahweh. If the latter's actions in v. 3 were aggressive, then the author wishes to emphasise its violent nature.

IE[2], like T, sees a link between the two verses, 'and from the many blows (v. 3) his flesh and his skin wore out and his bones were broken',[28] but it is likely that the poet has merely assembled a number of images which depict the afflicting Yahweh (cf. 2.2-8). The verb בלה in the Qal means 'become old/be worn out', often used of clothes (Deut 8.4; 29.5; Josh 9.13; Job 13.28; Neh 9.21). It is not used elsewhere in Lamentations. It is also employed of people and earth wasting away (Ps 102.26; Isa 50.9; 51.6) and of the human body (Ps 32.3). The Piel here is causative. The Piel (לְבַלּהֹ) occurs at 1 Chron 17.9, where the subject is evil-doers, the object 'Israel'. In the (earlier) parallel passage (2 Sam 7.10) the construction had been לְעַנּוֹתוֹ (ענה III 'to be afflicted', Piel 'to afflict, humble'), which may mean that the Chronicler (or a later scribe) regarded the verbal forms as parallel in meaning; indeed, the LXX translation is the same in in each passage, namely, τοῦ ταπεινῶσαι αὐτόν. The author here, though, was bound to begin the line with a ב. In this passage it is Yahweh who is the subject, and the speaker is the object of physical attack. It is not clear what the author has in mind here. On the surface it seems entirely physical, and Renkema (355) thinks that the wasting away of flesh and skin 'is a powerful reference to the emaciation brought on by famine', though when he (356) comes to שבר עצמותי he prefers a figurative interpretation. It is doubtful if the author of this passage was speaking literally in the first stich and figuratively in the second. The word עצם 'bone' occurs frequently in the Hebrew Bible. The word may denote individual bones (human or animal) or the physical frame (skeleton).[29] Since bones constitute a human's most basic element, the term is sometimes used to denote 'self', as in the phrase בעצם היום הזה 'on that very day' (Gen 7.13).[30] When flesh and bone appear together the emphasis may be on the physical elements (Exod 12.46; Ezek 24.6) or kinship (Judg 9.2; 2 Sam 19.12). In

---

[28] Cf. Reyburn (78).
[29] Beyse (305).
[30] Cf. Modern Hebrew עצמו 'himself', בעצם 'in itself/actually'.

our passage these two terms are combined with 'skin' (cf. Mic 3.3) and together appear to cover the basic elements of the human body; and it is possible to interpret the line as referring to a physical assault; cf. Westermann (171), Berlin (77).
But this verse must be taken in conjunction with other poetic passages—in particular Ps 51.10 'Let the bones you have broken rejoice'; cf. also Pss 38.3; 102.5; Job 33.21. We have to remember that this is poetry. Calvin cites Isa 38.23; Pss 51.10; 102.5 and admits that we are dealing with hyperbole in these passages. It is likely that hyperbole is operating here and in the first stich. The elements flesh, skin and bones constitute the whole person; and Yahweh is credited with attacking the speaker in such a way that he feels battered and bruised.

3.5

Text and Versions
MT ראש ותלאה; LXX κεφαλήν μου καὶ ἐμόχθησεν; Sym χολῇ καὶ μοχθῷ; V *felle et labore*; P ܡܪܕܐ ܘܚܘܪܒܐ *mrdʾ wḥwrbʾ*. MT is superior.

* * *

From LXX onwards, the text and exegesis of this verse have been in dispute. The main problem is with the second stich, but the cryptic nature of the first stich contributes to the obscurity. Not surprisingly, suggestions for emendations abound. This verse, then, portrays the speaker besieged not by weapons but hemmed in on every side by bitterness and hardship. He sees no way out, for Yahweh is the protagonist.

ראש ותלאה—LXX κεφαλήν μου καὶ ἐμόχθησεν leads *BHK* to suppose that the Greek translator's *Vorlage* was ראשי וילאה. While it is clear that LXX understood MT ראש as 'head' and the accusative of ויקף, and the final form as a *waw*-consecutive imperfect, Albrektson (131) may be right when he observes that 'μου may be an almost necessary addition and probably does not presuppose a suffix in the Hebrew *Vorlage*'. V appears to assume MT, but P, which characteristically adds a suffix 'me' to the translation of ויקף, renders 'rebellion and destruction'.[31] While Sym accords with MT, the Targum, although a paraphrase, agrees with LXX in that ראש has been understood as 'head' and ותלאה as a verbal form—ושלהיאונון 'and wearied them'.

The difficulties reflected in the Versions are evident also in later interpretations of the passage. Before Rashi offers his interpretation[32] of ראש as Nebuchadnezzar and תלאה as Nebuzaradan (cf. MR), he glosses the

---

[31] Albrektson (131) thinks that ܡܪܕܐ *mrdʾ* is an inner-Syriac corruption of ܡܪܪ *mrrʾ* 'bitterness' (cf. Kelso, 37), and that ܚܘܪܒܐ *ḥwrbʾ* is a free translation of תלאה.

[32] Rashi's comment suggests a 'collective' interpretation of גבר (v. 1).

two words with ראש ולענה, citing Deut 29.17.[33] IE[2] contemplates taking ראש as 'head', as does MLT. Vermigli (110f.) translates 'he surrounds my head with weariness' but acknowledges that others take ראש as 'with bitterness' or 'gall' and that either rendering is possible. Luther 'mit Galle und Mühe' and Calvin *felle et molestia* do not appear to be troubled by the combination of the concrete and the abstract nouns; cf. Hillers[2] (113).

Of the later commentators, Blayney (320), who reads 'He hath built upon me, and encompassed my head, so that it is weary', says he follows LXX ראשי and draws attention to one MS[Ken] which reads ראישי i.e. it preserves the י, though transposed. He also argues that ותלאה is verbal and that the feminine form may be explained in that ראש, as a part of the body, could be feminine as well as masculine. Bickell (112) wants to read ראשי with LXX. Löhr (1894, 12) emends to ראש ולענה,[34] though he changes his mind in his 1906 edition (17). Dyserinck (371) rearranges somewhat: בנה ויקף ראשי תלאה עלי, while Praetorius (326) suggests reading ויקף תלאה ויקף ראשי 'Er hat mein Haupt mit Mühsal umkreist', presumably allowing that the copula was originally the י of ראשי. This is followed by Gottlieb (40). Wutz (1930, 185-87) merely repoints רָאשׁ 'poverty' (from the root רוש 'be in want, poor'), an alternative spelling (see also Prov 30.8) for רֵישׁ (Prov 10.15) and רָאשׁ (Prov 28.19). This is followed by Gordis (1974[a], 176), Hillers[2] (113) and JPS.

Of the more recent translations, JB, NJB, NEB and REB show that scholarship has not settled the problems of this verse. JB 'He has made a yoke for me, has encircled my head with weariness' is based on the Dyserinck emendation בנה על ראשי תלאה, while NJB 'He has besieged me and made hardship a circlet round my head' goes back to Praetorius. NEB 'He has built up walls around me, behind and before' is based on a philological note by Guillaume[35] which explains תלאה in connection with the Arabic 'that which is behind', while REB '...bitterness and hardship' reverts to the more traditional understanding of the problem terms. There remains the suggestion of *BHS* that we read מִתְלָאָה ראשׁ.

The first stich is heavy with terminology belonging to the siege. The construction בנה על is found in contexts involving a siege wall—Deut 20.20; Ezek 4.2; Eccl 9.14—while the verb ויקף (Hiphil of נקף II 'to encircle, surround') is found (with על) at Pss 17.9; 88.18, carries the idea of hemming in and is also employed in siege situations—Josh 6.3; 2 Kgs 6.14. The preposition does double duty, then, for the two verbs (one in the perfect tense, the other, *waw*-consecutive with the imperfect), as in v. 2. It is natural to look to the second stich for the accusatives of these verbs and also to expect terms such as מצוד (Job 19.6; Eccl 9.14) or מצור (Deut 20.20); but this is poetry, and the poet skilfully combines here the physical

---

[33] This is a phrase, 'wormwood and gall', which occurs also at Lam 3.19. In a critical age one can imagine Rashi suggesting an emendation here!
[34] As in v. 19; so also *BHK*, Ehrlich (40).
[35] Guillaume (1963–64, 14).

and the abstract; and the abstract is in the adverbial accusative. The original meaning of ראש may be 'poisonous plant' but, as Barthélemy (891f.) observes, all the twelve occurrences of the word in the Hebrew Bible have a metaphorical import; cf. Keil (406).

תלאה—'Trouble, hardship'. Albrektson (130f.) notes that this word is often used of the tribulation of Israel (Exod 18.8; Num 20.14; Neh 9.32) and wonders if this signifies that the one who is suffering is Israel.

3.6
Text and Versions
There are no textual problems here. Kelso (38) notes that P has singular ܡܝܬ *myt'* instead of the plural. This is true also at Ps 143.3; but the difference is, orthographically, minimal, being the absence of *seyame*.

* * *

This verse in its entirety corresponds with the final words of Ps 143.3, except that the first two words are in a different order, probably due to the requirements of the acrostic.[36] Renkema (358) considers the psalmist to have borrowed from this passage. The poet offers another picture of his feeling of imprisonment at the hand of Yahweh.

במחשכים—The plural here (of מחשך) may be the plural of amplification[37] (GK 124e), other examples being מבטחים Isa 32.18, גבורות Job 41.4, רחמים Gen 43.14; perhaps 'deep darkness'. The poet may be thinking of Sheol, and the second stich does not persuade us otherwise. The speaker imagines himself isolated, cut off from others, from communication; and the image of the grave comes to mind. Yahweh has effected this. The image is similar to Ps 88 where Sheol is mentioned (v. 4), where isolation is explicitly described (vv. 6, 8) and where the same phrase במחשכים is in parallel with בבור תחתיות (v. 7).

T renders 'in a dark house of punishment' which accords with the traditional interpretation that this is a reference to the Exile (cf. Alexander 2008, 144). MLT specifically states 'This is the exile for it is darkness and gloom'. By the same token, in that the exile was not the end, MLT points out that the reading is כמתי not כמיתי; i.e. the midrash would vocalise כְּמָתֵי not כְּמֵתֵי: 'like men of the world'. כְּמָתֵי teaches that there is yet hope (whereas כְּמֵתֵי does not), as scripture says: 'And there is hope for your future...' (Jer 31.17). What the author means by כמתי עולם is not clear. Although it would be possible to vocalise מְתֵי and so assume the noun מת 'male, man', in m. pl. construct, a form which occurs in phrases like מתי שוא 'men of falsehood' (Job 11.11), מתי ישראל 'men of Israel' (Isa 41.14),

---
[36] LXX translates both passages identically.
[37] IE¹ puts it 'מחשך in the midst of מחשך'.

the meaning would be less satisfactory than MT. מְתֵי is Qal participle, m. pl. construct of מות 'to die', as in Isa 22.2. כמתי עולם may mean 'like the dead of ancient time' = 'those long dead'; cf. Isa 44.7 עם עולם 'ancient people' and Ps 24.7, 9 פתחי עולם 'ancient gates'. T 'like the dead who have gone to the other world (לעלמא אוחרן = the world to come) has taken עולם in the late sense of 'world'. I have followed this reading,[38] but a variant reading[39] is לעמא אוחרן 'to another people', an alteration in accordance with the interpretation that the exile is in mind here.

3.7

Text and Versions

MT נחשתי, followed by LXX and V; P ܐܣܘܪܝ 'swry; T כבלין דנחשא; Sym (βαρὺ ἐποίησε) τοῦ κλοιοῦ μου.[40] MT is preferred.

* * *

In this verse the speaker describes further action on the part of Yahweh. He depicts himself as walled-in to such an extent that escape was not possible and, just to enhance the image of the prisoner, he alludes to heavy fetters.

The LXX translation is literal in the extreme. The ו in ולא אצא introduces a final clause (GK 107q), yet LXX merely represents it (καὶ) without any attempt at conveying the meaning. The SH margin records the rendering of Aq and Sym as ܣܘܡ ܥܓܠܐ ܕܢܚܫܐ—a much superior rendering;[41] cf. Kelso (38).

נחשתי—LXX and V render in accordance with the Masoretic pointing. Both P and T have the plural. Budde (1898ª, 93) disagrees with the Masoretic vocalisation and points נְחֻשְׁתַּי, and he is followed by Rudolph (1962, 230). If the singular is original (and the meaning is 'fetters' or 'leg irons'), it is the only instance in the Hebrew Bible where the singular is used in this way. נחשת can mean 'copper/bronze' in general (Gen 4.22) and as armour (1 Sam 17.5, 6). When the meaning is 'fetters', the word is usually in the dual נְחֻשְׁתַּיִם (Judg 16.21; 2 Sam 3.34; 2 Kgs 25.7; Jer 39.7; 2 Chron 33.11; 36.6). Renkema (361f.) maintains that the singular is original but interprets it as a collective 'metal chains', citing Ps 107.10, but he also raises the possibility that a single chain, perhaps a neck-chain, is meant. There may be some support for the latter in the translation of Sym (see above) which alludes to a collar.

---

[38] See Heide (21*).
[39] See Levine (44, 126), Alexander (2008, 144 n. 12).
[40] So Field (754), translating SH ܓܠ ܕܢܚܫܐ ܣܘܡ ܥܓܠܐ ܠܡܥܒܕ ܥܣܩܐܝܬ yqyrʾ ʿbd lḥšlh dqwlrʾ dyly and having difficulty with ܥܓܠܐ. For the latter, Ziegler (481) suggests 'τὸν ζυγόν'. I think that Sym has in mind the construction of the collar—√ܫܠܚ 'to forge'.
[41] Cf. also V ut non egrediar and T בנין דלא אפוק מן טריקא.

AV 'he hath made my chain heavy' characteristically follows the Hebrew idiom; so also Vermigli (112), Löhr (1906, 18), Gottwald (12), Renkema (361). It is not that Yahweh has increased the weight of his chain but that he had put him in heavy fetters. Hence Rashi 'he made heavy fetters for my feet', Westermann (161), Rudolph (1962, 228). NEB 'weighed me down with fetters' captures the image; cf. also NIV, NJB, JPS.

3.8

Text and Versions

MT תפלתי שׂתם, followed by LXX, V and Sym; P ܐܠܗܐ ܨܠܘܬܝ ܠܐ *lʾ šmʿ ṣlwty*; T אסתחת בית צלותי. MT is not in question.

* * *

As in 3.44, the author draws attention to the futility of prayer to Yahweh in the situation he finds himself in. Although he cries out and pleads, it is all in vain.

The verse begins with גם 'moreover'. It is not as though there is a necessary connection with v. 7, but the acrostic demands that the author begins with a ג. It is interesting that vv. 7 and 9 both begin with the same verb, and it might be argued that if v. 8 followed v. 9 the passage would read more smoothly; cf. Wiesmann (174).

כי—The sense could be 'when' (GK 164d), as in Hos 11.1; Num 33.51 (see AV, NJB, JPS, NIV); or 'although' (GK 159bb), as in Hos 13.15; Pss 21.12; 23.4 (see RSV, NRSV); or 'if' (GK 159bb), as in Job 7.13; Num 5.20 (see IE²—אם). The two verbs אזעק ואשוע are in the imperfect, thus conveying continuity of action. These two verbs occur together also at Hab 1.2 and Job 35.9, while at Job 19.7 שוע is grouped with צעק. Renkema (362) notes that at 2.18 the verb צעק is used and wonders (because he believes the author of ch. 2 is also the author of ch. 3) why the difference occurs. He concludes that זעק is chosen here because it is grouped with שוע, the combination becoming a fixed expression, but he has not noticed that at Job 19.7 the combination is צעק and שוע. The difference may be explained on the basis of different authors or simply that both spellings were employed arbitrarily (cf. Hasel, 630), although the difference may have been dialectical; cf. Judg 12.6 (and see BL 28 v). This combination of זעק and שוע strongly emphasises the distress of the speaker.

The *hapax legomenon* שׂתם in the second stich has occasioned much debate. LXX, Sym, V and T have all understood it as a variant spelling of סתם 'to shut, obstruct'; and it should be noted that many MSS^Ken read סתם. Furthermore, Rashi, IE¹ and MLT are at pains to make this clear, IE¹ citing Hos 8.4 where, he suggests, a similar instance occurs—cf. Macintosh (1997, 298)—and MLT citing Num 22.2 (שתום העין). P 'he did not hear my prayer' is an attempt at understanding the sense of the passage (perhaps recalling Isa 1.15 'when you make many prayers I will not hear') and does not (contra *BHK*) indicate that the Syriac translator's *Vorlage* read לא שׁמע תפלתי; cf. Kelso (38), Abelesz (37) and Albrektson (132). Vermigli (112) and Calvin continue the tradition of taking שׂתם as סתם. Luther '...so stopfet er die Ohren zu vor meinem Gebet' offers a paraphrase and shows some unease with the concept of shutting out prayer; cf. Kakar (135). And Löhr (1894, 12) translates 'mein Gebet bleibt unerhört'. This unease with the image of God shutting out a prayer is probably already present in the rendering of T, where the verb is in the passive and the subject is בית צלותי: 'The house for my prayer was closed'; cf. Levine (127). Budde (1898a, 93) also finds the construction unsatisfactory and conjectures שׂתם מִתְפִלָּתִי 'er hat verstopft gegen [das Durchdringen] mein[es] Gebet[es]. Vgl. v. 44 מֵעֲבוֹר תְּפִלָּה'; and in this he is followed by Kaiser (343). And Ehrlich (40), too, citing Job 10.20 in support, suggests reading שָׁת מִתְּפִלָּה 'er wendet sich ab von meinem Gebete', while Rudolph (1962, 228, 230) senses a haplography here (שָׁתַם מִתְּפִלָּה) and renders 'verschloss er (sein Ohr) meinem Gebet', cf. Budde.

Of those who retain MT, many render 'he shuts out my prayer'; cf. AV, NRSV, JPS, NIV, Berlin (78). Barth (1893, 9) questioned the variant spelling theory and wondered whether the Arabic *šatama* lay behind our word. This was picked up by Driver (1950, 139) who suggests שׂתם really means 'reject'. Driver is followed by Gottwald (12), Albrektson (132), Renkema (363), Gottlieb (40), NEB, REB but not others.

The precise meaning is difficult to ascertain, but a glance at the context must surely point in the direction of the traditional understanding. The speaker had described that Yahweh had walled him in (v. 7) so that he cannot escape. In v. 9 the same verb גדר is used, thereby emphasising his negative plight. In between these two lines, as if to drive home the fact of his secure containment, comes v. 8 describing the continuous pleading of the victim and the repudiation of that by Yahweh. What we have here is a graphic allusion to Yahweh's refusal to listen, employing a term 'to block, stop' which echoes גדר.

3.9

Text and Versions

MT בגזית; so also Aq, Sym, V and T;[42] LXX ἐνέφραξεν; P ܒܚܨܒܐ *bkwbʾ*. Kelso (38) thinks that the LXX reading is connected with the previous verse 'Dieses griechische Wort überträgt gewöhnlich das Hi. oder Pi. von סתם und eine solche Lesart konnte sehr leicht von dem vorhergehenden Verse, wo שׂתם verkommt, übernommen werden'. *BHK* considers LXX to be a corruption of ἐν φράγμῳ (cf. Num 22.24; Pss 61.3; 79.12; Prov 24.46; Eccl 10.8 where φραγμός translates גדר), while Albrektson (132f.) imagines that LXX originally read ἐν φράξει 'with a barricade' and became a verbal form ἐνέφραξεν

---

[42] Some MSS read simply באבנים while others contain a gloss פסיל; cf. Levine (128f.) and Heide (21).

because of the accusative τρίβους μου which follows. P connects with no other Version. Kelso (38) suggests it translates an otherwise unknown reading, while Wiesmann (174) thinks it an alteration on the part of the Syriac translator.[43] MT is not in question.

MT עִוָּה; LXX ἐτάραξεν; Aq ἐκάλυψε;[44] V *subvertit*; P ܚܡܬ *'qm*; T סרך; *BHK*'s suggestion that Aq read עָוַר is strange, but MT is not in question.

* * *

There is no prison imagery in this verse, although freedom of movement is certainly not the theme. The poet, casting around for negative ways to express his negative experiences, imagines Yahweh actively engaged in frustrating his every movement.

The first thing we notice about this verse is that it begins with the same verb, גדר, as v. 7. In that context the speaker is describing the sense of imprisonment which Yahweh has caused and from which there was no escape. In v. 9 the speaker is not talking about imprisonment (N.B. 'paths/ways') but a feeling of being thwarted wherever he turns. Again, it is Yahweh who brings this about. Why the poet employs גדר twice is not clear. One can hardly accuse him of lacking imagination, but it may be that, for him, no other Hebrew verb beginning with ג seemed available. It is possible that in this ג triad (vv. 7-9) the author emphasises his isolation by placing his blocked prayer (v. 8) within two lines where blockage is the theme;[45] but it should be said that the poet is not averse to repeating words in his efforts to maintain the acrostic structure, cf. vv. 19f., 25ff., 31ff., 43f., 49/51, 59f.

גזית—This is not a common term in the Hebrew Bible. From the root גזה 'to cut', it is a feminine noun meaning 'ashlar' or 'dressed stone', often in the construction אבני גזית (1 Kgs 5.31; Ezek 40.42), but also without אבני, as in Exod 20.25; Amos 5.11; Isa 9.9. The speaker, therefore, by using the combination of גדר and גזית, wishes to emphasise his unfortunate condition by picturing Yahweh using hewn stones to block his paths. The emphasis here must be that progress is impossible.

The second stich parallels the first: 'he twisted my ways'. The term נתיבה (also found in masculine form נתיב) is often in parallel with דרך (Job 19.8; Ps 119.105). We should note that, although the primary (concrete) meaning of the noun דרך is an actual pathway, it is used more often in the Hebrew Bible in its secondary (abstract) meaning of 'way' = 'way of/in life, progress'.

---

[43] He may have had Hos 2.8 in mind, although the Peshitta in that passage employs another word for thorns—ܕܪܕܪܐ *drdr'*.
[44] Kelso (38) thinks that the *Vorlage* of Aq may have read כסה (cf. Hos 2.8).
[45] In his editing of Vermigli's commentary (114), Shute, who senses that Vermigli has noticed this, observes that '...the effect is positively claustrophobic... The structure of these verses imitates their meaning—rather like a Gerald Manley Hopkins poem. Martyr [= Vermigli] is a sharp commentator, and his insight here foreshadows so-called literary reading of Scripture.'

עוה—The Qal means 'to do wrong'. The Piel, here, 'to twist' is found elsewhere only at Isa 24.1 where Yahweh is depicted as twisting the face of the earth. Jeremiah (3.21) had accused the people of corrupting (Hiphil of עוה) their own way (of life), and Ps 146.9 speaks of Yahweh twisting (עוה) the way of the wicked. It is not clear what is meant here, but in parallel with the first stich it must mean that Yahweh thoroughly frustrates and confuses the speaker wherever he turns.[46]

3.10

Text and Versions

MT (*Kethib*) אריה; *Qere* ארי with many MSS[Ken]; Both *Kethib* and *Qere* are masculine nouns meaning 'lion'. Cf. 2 Sam 23.20 where the same *Kethib*/*Qere* appears. Bickell (113) suggests that בסכה has dropped out after ארב (cf. Ps 10.9; Jer 4.7; Job 38.40), and Kelso (39) thinks that this produces a better parallelism in the verse. But the verb ארב carries with it the idea of adopting a covert position from which to strike; besides, there is no textual support for this suggestion.

* * *

The poet offers another image of Yahweh, this time in terms of wild animals: the bear and the lion. Both animals are mentioned together at 1 Sam 17.34ff.; Prov 28.15; Isa 11.7; Hos 13.8; Amos 5.19 and represent the dangers of the countryside. They are also figurative of man's enemies as in Pss 10.19; 22.14; and in Isa 38.13 and Hos 13.8 God's angry treatment of his people is described in terms of a bear and a lion. In each stich the animal is depicted as lying in wait/lurking and ready to pounce.

ארב—The verb means 'to lie in ambush', cf. 4.19. The active participle is employed here giving the impression that Yahweh is constantly poised to attack.[47]

מסתר—במסתרים 'secret place' is nearly always in the plural, cf. Jer 13.17; 23.14; Pss 10.5f.; 64.5. With this phrase the second stich balances the first: both animals, dangerous in themselves, are depicted as ready to pounce. This is an important aspect of what the poet says—Yahweh is both dangerous and unpredictable.

3.11

Text and Versions

MT דְּרָכַי—followed by Aq, P, V and T; LXX κατεδίωξεν. MT is preferred.

---

[46] IE[1] understands נתיבות as 'known paths'.
[47] It should be noted here that this is the only passage where a bear is described as lying in wait. Indeed, IE[1] comments that a bear's habit is to call out loudly!

MT סֹרֵר; LXX ἀφεστηκότα; Aq ἐξέκλινε; P ܚܡܣ 'qm; V subvertit; Sym (SH) ܐܝܟ 'zy; T סראב; MT is not in question.
MT וַיְפַשְּׁחֵנִי; LXX καὶ κατέπαυσέν με; Aq καὶ ἐχώλανέ με; P ܦܫܚܢܝ pšḥny; V et confregit me; T ושסעיני. The Masoretic choice of diacritical point on ש is probably mistaken; we should read וַיְפַשְׂחֵנִי (see below).

* * *

The interpretation of this verse is hampered by the fact that it contains a *hapax legomenon* and a form where the philology is disputed. The poet has (vv. 1-10) alluded to negative experiences by means of various exaggerated images, but the latter are not always related to one another. Hence, although vv. 7 and 9 begin with the same verb, the experiences described are quite different. The previous line has depicted Yahweh as a wild animal lying in wait, and the following verse (v. 12) presents Yahweh as an archer with the speaker as the target. Here Yahweh is experienced as a saboteur.

Renkema (366) interprets the line as a continuation of the image begun in v. 10, *viz* 'the wild beast'. Having in mind the picture of the bear or lion ready to pounce, he translates (rather freely) 'I want to escape, but he rips me open; he destroys me'; cf. also Berlin (81f.) and Provan (86f.). We see this interpretation, too, in JPS and NIV. It should not be ruled out that the poet is continuing the imagery of v. 10; after all, v. 13 carries on the imagery of v. 12; but Hillers[2] (113) sounds a cautionary note to the effect that we cannot be certain about much of this verse. Since the earliest translations, this verse has presented difficulties. The first word in MT דְּרָכַי comes under the spotlight to begin with in that LXX begins with a verb 'he pursued'. LXX uses this verb (καταδιώκω) in the vast majority of cases to translate רדף, and Schleusner (29), Dyserinck (371), Kelso (39) and Wiesmann (176) think that this was the reading in the LXX *Vorlage*. Robinson (1933, 258, also *BHK*), noting that the acrostic demands a word beginning with a ד, suggests that LXX may have read דלק, a verb which can mean 'to set on fire' but also 'to pursue'; cf. Gen 31.36; 1 Sam 17.53; Ps 10.2; Lam 4.19. Driver (1934, 308) thinks that the Greek translator perhaps vocalised דֹּרְכַי, claiming the Arabic root *drk* 'pursue, overtake' in support, but Albrektson (135) rightly points out (cf. Jastrow, 323) that the Aramaic root דרך can also have this meaning. While this may explain the LXX rendering, it should be noted that Aq followed MT, as did P, V and T. דְּרָכַי can mean 'my paths' or 'my ways' in the sense of 'my activity'.

סֹרֵר—It is, perhaps, this second word which has caused some of the confusion in the exegesis of this stich. The LXX translator, having read a verbal form for דְּרָכַי, may have taken this to be the active participle of √סור, which can mean 'to turn aside'. Aq has taken it as a transitive verb, i.e. Polel of סור, which would be a unique form. P employs the same verb as for עוה (v. 9), giving the impression that the poet is almost repeating himself. V *subvertit* also employs the same verb as for עוה (v. 9).[48] The idea may be that Yahweh disturbed the activity of the speaker.

Rashi interprets סוֹרֵר as a denominative verb from סִיר 'thorn'—'to make thorny': 'he made (my ways) thorny';[49] and he is followed in this by Kara; cf. also Vermigli (114), *Le Glossaire de Leipzig*,[50] Broughton, Perles (1930, 111), Rudolph (1962, 230), Gordis (176f.), JB, Barthélemy (894). IE[1] mentions this view, quoting Hos 2.8 (הנני שך את דרכך בסירים), but rejects it and, instead, refers his readers to another passage in Hosea (4.16)—כִּי כְּפָרָה סֹרֵרָה סָרַר יִשְׂרָאֵל. In the latter passage the term סֹרֵרָה is usually taken as meaning 'stubborn', from √סרר 'be rebellious', but IE[1]'s commentary on that passage indicates that he took סֹרֵרָה to be from √סור. Vermigli (114f.) is aware of both interpretations but sides with Rashi, while Calvin understands סוֹרֵר as a transitive form from סור—*vias meas pervertit* 'God directs our ways when he blesses our counsels and our actions; so, on the other hand, he perverts them when all things turn out unsuccessfully…' AV follows Calvin, as does Michaelis (1773–88, 424f.), Keil (407), Löhr (1894, 12), Ehrlich (41), Westermann (161), Berlin (81f.), Kaiser (343), Gottwald (12), JPS, NIV, NRSV. The fact that JB follows Rashi, while NJB prefers סור 'to turn aside' shows continuing uncertainty. Driver (1950, 139f.) argues for the verb סרר 'was rebellious, stubborn' and translates 'he made my ways refractory'; and this—though it is not clear what Driver meant by this wording—unhappily found its way into NEB. However, the revision (i.e. REB) 'he has forced me aside' reverts to √סור. If דְּרָכַי alludes to ways/activity, the combination with סוֹרֵר may mean 'he disturbed my activity'. Glancing forward to the end of the line where the speaker ends up desolate at the hands of Yahweh, one begins to be sceptical of the view that v. 11 carries on the (wild beast) imagery of v. 10; and this scepticism is strengthened when one encounters the renderings of the next verbal element.

וַיְפַשְּׁחֵנִי—*Waw*-consecutive, 3rd p. m. s. imperf. Piel of the root פשח plus 1st p. s. suffix. The history of exegesis[51] shows that this *hapax legomenon* has always puzzled translators and commentators. BDB takes this to mean 'to tear in pieces', deriving it from the root in Aramaic/Syriac; cf. also *HALOT*. At 1 Sam 15.33 Samuel hewed שסף Agag in pieces, and T there translates[52] with פשח; and at Judg 14.6, where Samson tears apart (שסע) a lion, P uses ܦܫܚ *pšḥ*; and P uses the same verb here. LXX καὶ κατέπαυ-σέν με 'and he made me rest' or 'and he stopped me'. It is sometimes

---

[48] V has *subvertit* for the Hiphil of סור at Exod 14.25.
[49] Barthélemy (893) notes that this derivation did not originate with Rashi but previously appeared in the work of Ibn Ghayyath, and was followed by Menaḥem ben Saruq, Tanḥum Yerushalmi and others.
[50] Banitt (III, 1642f.).
[51] See Barthélemy, 892-94.
[52] IE[2] draws attention to this Targumic reading.

argued that the LXX translator had a text which read וישבחני or וישביתני (Dyserinck, 371; cf. also *BHK*), or that the LXX original read κατέσπασε; see Albrektson (135). Aq 'and he made me lame' which may mean that he read √פסח or √פשׂח for √פשׁח, though no causative form of פסח appears in the Hebrew Bible.[53] Michaelis (1773–88, 425) does not refer to Aquila when he conjectures ויפשׁחני, translating[54] *claudicare me fecit*; and this is followed by NEB,[55] Kraus (51f.), Wiesmann (177). REB 'he has thrown me down' may be a very free translation of this conjecture.

Rashi, who had envisaged paths strewn with thorns, thinks that the term refers to spreading/widening of the legs: 'for those who walk along uncleared paths must widen their stride'. This may be a guess on Rashi's part, as it is difficult to ascertain his philology here.[56] Kara glosses the term with בקע 'to split', a suggestion also found with MR and MLT, and based on the Aramaic understanding of the root פשׁה. Vermigli (111), also struggling with the verb, translated 'he cut me down', while Calvin, unsure of his ground, renders *et scidit me* (*vel, dissipavit, vel, laceravit*), and Luther has 'er hat mich zerfleischt'; cf. AV.

I refer again to the final words of the line where the speaker says that Yahweh left him desolate. If he has been pulled in pieces (AV) or torn in pieces (NRSV), 'desolate' is surely a non-sequitur;[57] and this observation should inform the exegesis of the earlier part of the line. It is natural to look for similarities with, or connections between consecutive verses, but, in the case of v. 11, this has led to exegetical error. Rashi saw the problem and stood his ground, interpreting v. 11 quite apart from v. 10, but some earlier exegetes were not so circumspect. The *hapax legomenon* ויפשׁחני was problematic. It was natural that the P and T translators interpreted in the light of the root פשׁה in Syriac and Aramaic (= to tear in pieces), and this would have encouraged interpreters to view v. 11 as continuing the wild beast imagery of v. 10. LXX is difficult but is quite different from P and T, and V employs a verb (*confregit*) that is used by Jerome elsewhere to translate שׁבר, which may mean that he shared a view which we find in MR and MLT, where בקע 'split' is used as a gloss on פשׁה. We must remind ourselves that the *Vorlagen* of the Versions would have lacked diacritical points as well as vowel points; hence all the translators would probably have encountered a text reading ויפשׁחני. Aq chose to 'pronounce' שׂ rather than שׁ, and his translation 'made me lame' fits very well with the scenario of the briar-strewn paths. It is clear that both 'pronunciations' existed at that time, and the Masoretes favoured שׁ, thereby influencing the subsequent history of the exegesis of this passage. The combination of

---

[53] On the question of ס and שׂ, see JM (28f.).
[54] In his (earlier) German translation he is more traditional—'und zerreist mich'.
[55] See Brockington (218).
[56] It may be that he felt that the verb was close to √פשׂק 'to open wide, straddle'.
[57] Cf. Barthélemy (893) 'il semble que שׁמני שׁממ soit un résultat trop modeste pour décrire l'état dans lequel une bête fauve laisse celui qu'elle vient de mettre en pièces'.

Rashi's understanding of סורר and Aquila's choice of the diacritical point results in a much less constipated and tortuous line: Yahweh scattered briars on my paths and, as a consequence, made me lame; he left me desolate.[58]

שָׁמֵנִי שֹׁמֵם—'He has made/left me desolate/wretched'. LXX ἠφανισμένην and V *desolatam* render שׁמם as though it was a feminine form, although it is the גבר who is still speaking.[59] שֹׁמֵם is the active participle Qal of √שׁמם; the root is found at 1.4, 13, 16; 4.5; 5.18. The meaning varies according to context but is always negative in the extreme; here, as a result of Yahweh's treatment, it may mean 'wretched'.

3.12

Text and Versions
No significant material.

* * *

In this verse the image of Yahweh as an archer is reminiscent of 2.4 where Yahweh represented the invader's archers. The speaker now sees himself as a target with Yahweh shooting at him; and the image continues into v. 13. The references in Kara and MLT to exile confirm that they interpret the speaker as representing the exiles in Babylon.

There is a play on the root דרך here.[60] On the idiom of treading the bow, see the comment on 2.4; cf. NEB 'he has strung his bow'. P ܡܠܐ ܩܫܬܐ *ml' qšth* (as at 2.4) may mean 'to draw the bow', cf. Payne Smith (1903, 274), but it may represent a stage further, *viz* the loading of the bow. The translation 'stretch/bend' is, therefore, ambiguous. Is the bending preparation (stringing) of the bow or the actual bending just prior to the discharge of the arrow? An examination of other passages where the idiom is found (Pss 7.13; 11.2; 37.14; Isa 5.28; 21.15; Zech 9.13) would indicate that it is the preparation of the bow that is in mind here.

וַיַּצִּיבֵנִי—√נצב (in the Niphal = 'to stand') in the Hiphil (*waw*-consecutive, 3rd p. m. s. + 1st p. s. suffix) can mean 'to place, set up' (memorial stone 1 Sam 15.12, boundaries Deut 32.8). He has set me up, put me in position as an archer uses a target for practice.

---

[58] Barthélemy (894), though following Rashi on סורר, follows MT thereafter, and renders 'il m'a déchiré', but the tearing is that of the briars; cf. JB 'and torn me'.
[59] Albrektson (136) attempts to explain this in the light of previous chapters where the speaker was feminine.
[60] In v. 11 we have the noun דרך: here it is the verb. It may be that the LXX translator (at v. 11) was influenced by the beginning of this verse.

מַטְרָא—כַּמַּטָּרָא is a variant spelling[61] of מטרה (1 Sam 20.20; Job 16.12). It is a feminine noun from נטר 'to watch, guard'.

3.13

Text and Versions

MT הֵבִיא—so also LXX, V and T; P ܡܐ ܐܥܠ *hʾ ʿl*. P 'Behold, he caused to enter' may point to a *Vorlage* beginning with הנה—so Abelesz (37); but as it is the only Version with such a reading, Albrektson (136) suggests that this extra word has arisen in the process of the transmission of Syriac MSS. MT is preferred.

MT בְּכִלְיוֹתָי—The first stich seems unusually short, and Budde (1882, 6; 1898ᵃ, 94) followed by Dyserinck (372), Haller (104), Wiesmann (176) suggest reading כֵּלָיו after בכליותי—a haplographical error. The passage would then read 'He shot his missiles into my kidneys, the contents of his quiver'. *BHK* notes this suggestion. While most modern commentators dismiss or ignore Budde's suggestion, the fact remains that the first stich is on the short side.

* * *

The picture of Yahweh as archer, begun in v. 12, continues into v. 13. The preparation for the attack on the speaker is stated in v. 12, and the attack itself is envisaged in v. 13.

הֵבִיא—The Hiphil of בוא 'to come, enter' is used (cf. Lev 26.36; Ezek 37.5) for the effective shooting of arrows: 'He caused to enter'. LXX and T follow MT closely. V *misit* 'sent' is the verb (*mittere*) used at 1 Sam 20.20; 2 Chron 26.15 for the shooting of arrows.

בְּכִלְיוֹתָי—The noun כליה occurs only in the plural (cf. Job 16.13), meaning 'kidneys' or 'vital parts'. It is not just the speaker's body in general that is being penetrated but the most sensitive and vulnerable part.

בְּנֵי אַשְׁפָּתוֹ—Literally, 'the sons of his quiver', a poetic expression[62] for 'his arrows'. For the use of בן for inanimate things, see GK128v. This is the only occurrence of the phrase, though the arrow is called בן קשׁת at Job 41.20. Indeed, P translates prosaically 'his arrows', and T 'the arrows of his quiver'.[63] LXX ἰούς 'venom', when we expect υἱούς 'sons', is explained as a scribal error by Schleusner (30); cf. also Kelso (39), Albrektson (137). Schleusner also observes that V reads *filias* for *filios*, and Rudolph (1938, 111) thinks that this is because the word for arrow in Latin is *sagitta*, i.e. feminine; cf. Wiesmann (176).

---

[61] So IE¹; BL (511x) regards the ending as influenced by Aramaic.
[62] IE¹ comments: He likens a quiver to a pregnant woman.
[63] Levine (131) thinks that T's rendering intentionally precludes two interpretations of בני, namely 'inhabitants of Jerusalem' and 'the enemy'. This ties in with the comments of Kara who is at pains to explain the phrase in terms of arrows.

The idea is that Yahweh discharged/shot the contents of his quiver into the vitals of the נבר. Because the kidneys are regarded as the seat of the emotions (cf. Job 19.27; Prov 23.16), some translations try to convey the psychological as well as the physical by rendering 'heart', thus RSV, NIV.

3.14

Text and Versions
MT עַמִּי—so also LXX, Sym and V; T לכל פריצי עמי; P ܥܡܡܐ '*mm*' followed by several MSS[Ken] עמים and *sebir*; four MSS[Ken] העמים. Preferred reading—עַמִּים—see below.

* * *

In this verse the speaker describes the ignominy of being mocked. This is the only verse in the first 16 where Yahweh is not depicted as actively at work, but the implication is that he has brought about this state of affairs. In the history of exegesis, the interpretations depend on the identity of the speaker. Is the individual voice complaining about his own folk deriding him; or does he himself represent the people who are being mocked by the nations? I favour the latter.

T's rendering of עמי is ambiguous. It could be translated 'to all the unbridled of my people' (Jastrow, 1227) or 'to all the bold of my people' (Brady, 161); but the term עמי is clear enough; so it looks as though the Targumist's *Vorlage* read עמי. The ambiguity of the paraphrase is reflected in MR where one may detect two interpretations, cf. Levine (131). P 'peoples/nations' seems to presuppose עמים, and there are many MSS which have this reading.[64] In addition, the Masoretic *sebir* is עמים. It is possible that the *sebir* was based on manuscript evidence, though it may simply reflect a preferred reading of the Masoretes.[65] Cappel (1006) considered that עַמִּי should be interpreted as standing for עַמִּים (cf. GK 87f.); and this is the view of Lowth (II, 133), Bickell (113), Ewald (338), cf. JPS.[66] It might be argued that the plural suffix of נגינתם would favour the plural עמים, though the collective noun עם is often the referent of this plural suffix, cf. Gen 11.6; Exod 3.7.

Among those who favour emending MT to עמים are Budde (1898[a], 94), Löhr (1894, 13), Perles (1930, 111), Kaiser (343), Albrektson (137f.), Provan (87f.), *BHK*, *BHS*, RSV, NEB,[67] REB. Those in favour of retaining

---

[64] Ehrlich (41), who favours the plural here, suggests that the original was עמין and that the ending was lost through haplography, but he does not account for the many Hebrew MSS reading עמים.
[65] Cf. Driver (1913[a], 90ff.), and note Frensdorff (1876, 143).
[66] A similar problem appears at Ps 144.2 where MT עמי must mean עמים (cf. Ps 18.48), though there is more Versional and manuscript evidence in support of this reading (Kraus 1993, II, 540); cf. also at Mic 6.16, discussed by McKane (1998, 206).
[67] See Brockington (218).

MT are JB, NJB, NIV, NRSV, Keil (408), Wiesmann (177), Gottwald (13), Meek (24), Hillers[2] (109), Rudolph (1962, 230), Gottlieb (40f.), Kraus (51), Westermann (161), O'Connor (2001, 1049), Berlin (82), Barthélemy (894f.), Renkema (369ff.), House (403).

At 3.1, IE[1] had been undecided as to the identity of the speaker. It is, therefore, not surprising that at 3.14 the same uncertainty is evident. He feels that more than one interpretation is possible. He translates 'to all my people mocking me' but goes on to say that it may mean 'to all the people who had been under my power',[68] citing in support Exod 17.13. He then gives another view, *viz* that 'the י is additional/superfluous (נוסף) and not as in 2 Sam 22.44[69]…where עמי is like עמים'. MLT (Greenup, 46) asks 'why is a מ missing? These are the Chaldeans who are more lowly than any other nation…' While it is not easy to follow the argument here, it is clear that MLT regards the mockers as the Babylonians and Israel the butt of their song.

נְגִינָתָם—The noun נגינה may refer to music generally (Pss 4.1; 6.1; 54.1; 55.1) or to a mocking song (Job 30.9; Ps 69.13; cf. Lam 3.63).

It is clear that where commentators interpret the passage, from v. 1 onwards, as a lament of an actual individual, the reading עמי = 'my people' is preferred. By the same token, those who see the speaker as representing Israel will favour reading עמי as a form of עמים or will argue that the original reading was עמים. Some object to the reading 'my people' on the grounds that the speaker's fellow countrymen will be suffering the same affliction as he is, and so to mock him would seem out of place. This is an important point. Renkema (370f.) tries to get around this problem by emphasising that it is not the speaker's affliction that they are mocking but 'his continued faith and trust in God… Those who ridicule him have clearly given up the struggle and have lost their faith in YHWH.' But there has been nothing in the previous verses to suggest that the speaker is a man of faith. The mocking is the mocking of those who look down on the downtrodden and the defeated, especially those they have conquered; cf. 2.16.

3.15

Text and Versions
No significant material.

* * *

In v. 14 the speaker was describing his state of mind vis-à-vis the mocking of his position. In v. 15 he reverts to the previous pattern/shape of

---

[68] This is probably a reference to the nations ruled by Israel in Davidic times.
[69] Kimḥi's comment here is simply עמי כמו עמים and referring also to Ps 144.2.

describing Yahweh's attack on him. Here he uses verbs normally found in positive statements to paint a further negative picture. Yahweh is depicted as 'satisfying' him with bitter herbs and 'sating' him with wormwood.[70]

The Hiphil of both שׂבע and רוה may be construed with or without a preposition; cf. Gibson (1994, 113f.). Here, השׂביע is construed with ב,[71] while הרוה is not. Löhr (1894, 13), followed by Dyserinck (372), on the basis of Job 9.18, emends to ממרורים, but as Budde (1898ᵃ, 94) observes, this is unnecessary: שׂבע is construed with ב at v. 30.

בַּמְּרוֹרִים—This term (מרורים) is usually translated with an abstract noun—LXX πικρίας, V *amaritudinibus*, Luther 'Bitterkeit', AV 'bitterness'; so also Calvin, Rudolph (1962, 228), Gottwald (13), Westermann (161), Haller (104). The singular (מרור) is not found, and the plural is understood as the plural of intensity (GK 124e). The noun is also used at Exod 12.8; Num 9.11 for the bitter herbs of the passover meal, and MR, Vermigli (118), Kaiser (343), NEB, REB, NIV are inclined to translate in this way. The argument is that the pericope has to do with physical affliction and that the speaker is forced to eat the least attractive edible material; and the same argument is applied to the parallel לענה, although the latter (wormwood, gall) is otherwise always used figuratively.[72]

לענה—Also at v. 19, לענה occurs elsewhere at Deut 29.17; Prov 5.4; Jer 9.14; 23.15; Amos 5.7; 6.12. Although normally used figuratively, of bitter hardship, the word originally applies to a plant—possibly *Artemesia absinthium*[73]—the juice of which was known to be extremely sour-tasting; and the word here may refer to that juice. If we take the passage to refer to the physical, we may note that the dire straits of the speaker are further emphasised here. It is as though he was in prison and that his daily rations were bitter herbs and wormwood. Yahweh, the prison warder, is the supplier, and the provision is lavish. The verbs (השׂביע and הרוה) imply feeding to the full and the supply of more than enough to drink. The irony is that the fare is the least attractive of all possible provisions. However, we cannot be certain that the latter interpretation is the only one: it may be that the physical and the figurative are *both* present. Berlin (91) draws attention to the similarity of the passage to Jer 9.14 and points out that in that passage the reference is to exile.[74]

---

[70] IE² comments to the point: תחת לחם ומים מרורים ולענה. This comment would suggest that he understood the words to be taken as physical rather than figurative.
[71] IE¹ regards the ב as supplementary and points to another example at Ps 80.6.
[72] Strangely, Renkema (372) translates this 'bitterness' having argued that we should interpret it as probably indicating the bitter sap of a plant.
[73] Cf. Tristram (493).
[74] MLT, which consistently interprets the speaker as the people of Israel, understands these two terms (מרורים and לענה) as referring to the first and second destructions of Jerusalem.

3.16

Text and Versions

MT וַיַּגְרֵס; LXX καὶ ἐξέβαλεν; Aq ἐξετίναξε (ψήφῳ ὀδόντας μου); Sym ἐξέβαλε (ψηφῖσι); P ܘܬܒܪ *wtbr*; V *et fregit*; T וּרְעַץ; MT is preferred.

MT הִכְפִּישַׁנִי בָּאֵפֶר; LXX ἐψώμισέν με σποδόν; Sym κατέχωσέ με σποδῷ; P ܘܦܠܢܝ ܒܩܛܡܐ *wplny bqṭmʾ*; V *cibavit me cinere*; T קְמָמָא כְּנִיעִיתְנִי.⁷⁵ Variations reflect difficulty with the Hebrew, but MT should be retained. See below.

* * *

The author, who has set himself the task of beginning each verse of the triad (vv. 16-18) with the letter *w*, settles for introducing each line with a *waw*-consecutive. In v. 16, he chooses to employ two verbs in the Hiphil, as he did in v. 15; and the pattern continues of Yahweh in aggressive action against the speaker.

The understanding of this verse has been hampered somewhat by ignorance of the two verbs גרס and כפש. גרס appears elsewhere only at Ps 119.20 (in the Qal), where its meaning is not certain, while כפש is a *hapax legomenon*. A comparison of two modern translations illustrates that continued uncertainty: RSV 'He has made my teeth grind on gravel and made me cower in ashes'; NEB 'He has broken my teeth on gravel; fed on ashes, I am wracked with pain'.

וַיַּגְרֵס—Hiphil (of גרס) meaning 'cause to grind' (*HALOT*). BDB (under √גרש) has 'and he hath crushed'; cf. also *DCH*. Kelso (40) suggests that LXX either guessed at the meaning of the verb or read ויגרש (√גרש 'to drive out'); and the image seems to be of Yahweh knocking out the teeth with stones.⁷⁶ P's decision not to use the Syriac verb ܓܪܣ *grs* 'to crush' is interesting. It may be that the *Vorlage* did not match MT; on the other hand, the P translator is not always precise in his renderings. V 'he broke'⁷⁷ accords with the Syriac; cf. also T.

בֶּחָצָץ—'With/in pebbles' or 'with/in gravel'.⁷⁸ Houbigant (480) suggested the emendation כחצץ 'like gravel'. The image, then, might be that the broken teeth were as gravel. But the parallel phrase in the second stich militates against this; and MT is supported by the Versions here.

---

⁷⁵ There are variations in the T MSS, see Barthélemy (896).
⁷⁶ Cf. Robinson (1933, 258); cf. *BHK*.
⁷⁷ Jerome uses this verb to translate the Hebrew שבר at Lev 22.22; Ezek 34.4; Dan 8.8.
⁷⁸ V *ad numerum*: Jerome understands חצץ in Prov 20.17 as gravel (*calculus*), so his rendering here is difficult to understand. 'And he has broken my teeth one and all'; so Knox; '…one by one' (Douai). It may be, as Wiesmann (176) suggests, that the translator interpreted from the basic meaning of the root חצץ, meaning 'to divide'. However, the parallel phrase in the second stich—בָּאֵפֶר with/in ashes—rules out V's interpretation here.

There are different images here. Yahweh is depicted as somehow crushing the speaker's teeth with gravel (so AV), or simply causing the speaker to crush/grind his teeth in gravel (so NRSV). Rashi glosses וַיַּגְרֵס with שׁבר, citing Lev 2.14 where גֶּרֶשׂ refers to (crushed) grain; and IE[1] glosses similarly—וישבר. The picture with these commentators may be of Yahweh knocking out teeth (cf. LXX), but it is perhaps more likely that the image is of Yahweh creating the conditions in which the teeth were destroyed/crushed. MR, MLT, Rashi and Kara all allude to the interpretation that the Israelites in exile had ignored God's message via Ezekiel (12.3), 'Pack what you need for going into exile'. Having to knead dough in pits, the gravel would enter the dough with the result that those who ate the bread destroyed their teeth; hence it could be said that Yahweh, in causing the exile, had crushed the teeth of the exiles.

הִכְפִּישַׁנִי (בָּאֵפֶר)—The *hapax legomenon* has long proved problematic for translators and commentators.[79] In addition to the variations in the Versions, we might compare two modern translations: NJB 'he has fed me on ashes'; JPS 'he has ground me into the dust'.

LXX 'he has fed me ashes' and V 'he has fed me with ashes' stand apart from the other Versions here. It is possible that their *Vorlagen* read האכילני. It is also possible that the Greek translator guessed the meaning from the context,[80] and that Jerome, baffled by the root, followed in his footsteps.

The rabbis also struggled with the term. Rashi employs the verb כפה 'to overturn' to explain the meaning: 'he overturns me in ashes like a vessel turned over on its mouth', while IE[1] says that it means גאלני 'he defiled/ contaminated me'. MLT (cf. Sym) defines it with הטביעני 'he has sunk me (in ashes)', suggesting that although not found elsewhere in scripture, the root is found in the Talmud (*Yeb.* 107b).[81]

Vermigli (119) appears to follow Rashi's interpretation. Calvin, guessing, translates *involvit* ('rolled/covered') but notes that it could be *foedavit* ('defiled') or *versavit* ('overturned'). Luther 'er wälzet mich' and Broughton 'he hath turned me on my face' reflect Rashi's comments, while AV 'he has covered me' picks up Calvin's first choice.

Not surprisingly, there are those who suspect corruption in the text and who propose emendation. Thus Haller (104) reads הֶאֱכִילַנִי which *BHK* considers as the possible *Vorlage* of LXX. Praetorius (1895, 326) suggests reading הִפְלִישַׁנִי—another unique form, but a root (פלשׁ) which, in the Hithpael, may mean 'to roll in dust' and which is construed with (ב)אֵפֶר at Job 6.26 and Ezek 27.30. Praetorius translates 'er hat mich gewälzt'.

---

[79] On the history of the exegesis, see Barthélemy (895ff.).
[80] Abelesz (21) (cf. also Albrektson, 138) thinks that the translator was thinking of the passage in Ps 102.10—כִּי־אֵפֶר כַּלֶּחֶם אָכָלְתִּי.
[81] The passage is unclear but the passive participle f. s. does appear in the phrase מדה כפושה. MLT may have taken this to mean a sunken measure.

Wutz (1933, 500), followed by Wiesmann (177), suggests 'restoring' to הִכְשִׁפַנִי 'sättigte mich' on the basis of Akkadian *kušapu*. The translations of NEB 'fed on ashes, I am wracked with pain' and REB 'wracked with pain, I am fed on ashes' appear to be based on some adjustment to the text, but Brockington (218) offers no explanation.
Peiser (1897, 350f.) identified the root as related to the Amarna *kapāšu/kabāšu*[82] 'to press or trample', and McDaniel (44), Dahood (1965, 331), Gordis (177) and others have accepted this; i.e. the root כפש is a variation of כבש which appears several times in Biblical Hebrew and can mean 'to subdue/trample'. It is an interpretation found in NIV and JPS. Yahweh is then depicted as humiliating the speaker by actually trampling him into ashes.

What, then, of the imagery here? Is the situation related to that of 4.5 where the once well-off are seen clinging to ash heaps, foraging for scraps and encountering gravel and ash (so Renkema, 373)? Or is it simply the continuation of v. 15 where Yahweh, as prison guard, provides the speaker with bitter herbs etc.? This latter seems to be in keeping with the pericope so far. The speaker exaggerates the conditions he endures so that even food, bitter and meagre, is mixed with gravel, and his foraging among the ashes appears as though thrust upon him by Yahweh.

3.17

Text and Versions

MT וַתִּזְנַח; LXX καὶ ἀπώσατο; P ܐܬܛܥܝܬ *w'tt'yt*; V *et repulsa est*; T וּקְצָת. While the *Vorlagen* of P,V and T are the same as MT, the reading וַתִּתְנַח is preferred, see below.

* * *

The bulk of the previous verses in ch. 3 (vv. 1-16) have described Yahweh, in the third person, attacking the speaker in a variety of ways. It is, perhaps, unexpected to find a change of subject (to first person) at v. 17. The poet has the speaker pausing after some graphic descriptions of adversity and reflecting on his state of mind. His present circumstances are so far from what he has known that he has virtually forgotten what it was like to live at ease.

וַתִּזְנַח—The form could be 3rd p. f. s. or 2nd p. m. s. (imperfect). If the Masoretes had second person in mind here, it is picked up by Salmon ben Yeruham and is present in AV 'And thou hast removed my soul far off from peace'; cf. RV, Nägelsbach (110), Rudolph (1962, 231), Westermann (161), Albrektson (138), Kraus (51), Gottwald (13), Gottlieb (42), Barthélemy (899). It is argued (Kraus) that the abrupt change of person

---

[82] N.B. the פ/ב permutation is found in Hebrew/Phoenician ברזל, Aramaic/Syriac פרזל. Barthélemy (896f.) notes that Saadya had drawn attention to this by noting the variation נֶשֶׁף (Isa 40.24) and נֶשֶׁב (Prov 9.3).

which this entails is found also at v. 23 where the second person suffix occurs just as suddenly. Barthélemy (899) points out that Yahweh is the subject of זנח in the other instances in the book, *viz* 2.7; 3.31. In the face of this ambiguity, Ehrlich (41) regards MT an error for וַתַּנַּח (Hiphil of נוח) which, when construed with מִן, he regards as having the same meaning as הרפה מן—'Hier ist gemeint das Aufgeben des Gedankens an Frieden'.

וַתִּזְנַח—LXX continues with the 3rd p. m. s. This latter may reflect an original ויזנח (*BHK*), but in the light of the other Versions it would seem that the LXX reading is the result of a translator or scribe *expecting* the third person; cf. Kraus (53), *BHQ*. P and V support the consonantal basis of MT but appear to have vocalised וַתִּזָּנַח, i.e. the Niphal, although the verb occurs only in the Qal and Hiphil in the Hebrew Bible; and the subject of the verb in P and V is נפשי, whereas, in LXX, it is Yahweh.[83] T's rendering shows that the translator understood MT as 3rd p. f. s. with נפשי as the subject. Since P and V, there has been a tendency to take נפשי as the subject and to vocalise וַתִּזְנַח. Thus Luther 'Meine Seele ist aus dem Frieden vertrieben'; Calvin *et remota fuit a pace anima mea*; cf. also Gerlach (90f.), Ewald (338), Keil (401), Wiesmann (177), Dobbs-Allsopp (114), Provan (89), Berlin (78), Renkema (374). The LXX reading will have been the basis for the early exegesis, but it does not seem to have commanded much support later in the history of exegesis, Dyserinck (372), Budde (1898[a], 94) and Kaiser (343) being lone voices.

The problem with ascertaining the meaning of the passage is the use and force of the verb זנח. In the Hebrew Bible it occurs 16 times in the Qal (Hos 8.3, 5; Zech 10.6; Pss 43.2; 44.10, 24; 60.3; 74.1; 77.8; 88.15; 89.39; 108.12; Lam 2.7; 3.17, 31) and three times in the Hiphil (1 Chron 28.9; 2 Chron 11.14; 29.19). Yaron (237) takes the root to be cognate with Akkadian *zenû* 'to be angry', but most scholars are inclined to see the link with Arabic *zanaḥa* 'be remote, repel'; cf. BDB, *HALOT* and Ringgren (105) hold to the meaning 'reject'. Certainly, 'to be angry' will not fit the present context, though Yaron (238) offers the translation: 'My soul has been in anger, far off from peace'.

Apart from Hos 8.3, where Israel is the subject (v. 5 is problematic), the verb in the Qal usually has God as subject and, especially in the Psalms, has to do with God's rejection of the speaker or the people. Later in the chapter (v. 31) the same force obtains. Consequently, it is natural to think of God as protagonist, especially since vv. 1-16 have described his hostile actions towards the speaker. The fact that Yahweh is actually addressed in this stich is unusual in that Yahweh's name has not yet been mentioned in the chapter. However, the 2nd p. m. s. suffix appears also at

---

[83] The Masoretic vocalisation may be construed as either 3rd p. f. s. or 2nd p. m. s. MLT incorporates both in its comments. It would also be possible to vocalise וַתַּזְנִחַ, i.e. the Hiphil.

v. 23, again in the midst of third person forms. If we interpret in this way, Yahweh is being accused of having expelled the speaker from the realm of שלום. The form נפשי stands for the personal pronoun 'me', as it does in vv. 24, 51, 58 (BDB 660). The second stich, in first person, will then be taken as a consequence of Yahweh's action. I forgot happiness.[84] Yahweh's hostility has been such that the poet cannot remember what well-being is. This is the only occurrence in Lamentations of the verb נשׁה.

If we read the Niphal (with P and V—and I think that they interpret correctly), then נפשי stands for the personal pronoun in the nominative (= I). This would fit well with נפשי of v. 24, and the parallelism is better in that both stichs (in 1st p. s.) appear to be describing the same experience—exclusion from prosperity—and blend with the 1st p. s. of the following verse.[85]

3.18

Text and Versions

MT נצחי; LXX νεῖκός μου; P ܢܨܚܢܝ *nṣḥny*; V *finis meus*; T תוקפי. The *Vorlagen* of the Versions are probably identical with MT.

* * *

This verse brings to an end the sustained pericope which began at v. 1. The poet began in the first person singular and although, for the most part, he describes Yahweh's hostile actions with verbs in the third person, those actions and their effect are always with the poet in mind: first person suffixes occur throughout the passage. In v. 17 he concludes that well-being is a thing of the past for he has well nigh forgotten what it was like to be at peace. In v. 18 we get the poet's summing up of his situation vis-à-vis Yahweh. Yahweh's name has not been mentioned until now, although the referent of the suffix in v. 1 and the subject of the 3rd p. s. verbs throughout is undoubtedly Yahweh.

The text of this verse is not in question. It is vouched for by P, V and T.[86] Verse 18 closes the ו stanza and, as with vv. 16f., begins with *waw*-consecutive.

---

[84] טובה should be taken as in parallel to שלום. It can mean 'prosperity' or 'happiness', BDB (375).
[85] McDaniel (201f.) draws attention to the מן in משלום and notes the difficulty in translating it with 'from'. Drawing on an observation of Hummel (105), he suggests reading the preposition as the enclitic מ—ותזנח-ם שלום נפשי-ם—'and my soul rejected peace'. McDaniel is followed only by Hillers[2] (114)—'I despaired of having peace', and House (400); but cf. Gottlieb (42) who is sceptical.
[86] LXX *may* have originally read καὶ ἀπώλετο (so *BHK*), though some MSS do have καὶ εἶπα ἀπώλετο; see Ziegler (482), Rudolph (1938, 111).

וָאֹמַר—The 1st p. s. imperfect of the Qal of אמר. It is not so much that the speaker uttered the words that follow but that he reflected, said to himself (Rashi), thought (NJB, JPS).

The main exegetical problem here centres on the term נצחי. LXX renders νεῖκός μου, which may be translated 'my victory, success'.[87] G. W. Anderson (1998, 533) notes that 'The LXX offers a bewildering variety of translations of נצח'. P has vocalised as a plural 'my glories', while T 'my strength' avoids the root נצח. These differences reflect uncertainty about the term. What V may have meant by *finis meus* is difficult to say,[88] and Michaelis (1773–88, 427) dismisses the effort with contempt. At 4.18, קִצֵּינוּ is translated by V as *finis noster*, which prompts *BHS* to wonder if V was translating קִצִּי here.

Rashi glosses with עוֹלָמִי, by which he could mean 'my world, existence, future'. IE[1], paraphrasing and citing Isa 63.3, where נצחם appears to mean 'life-blood',[89] seems to settle for the meaning 'life, existence'. Calvin translates *fortitudo mea*, without discussion, and this is followed by AV 'my strength'; cf. RV, Blayney (322), Keil (401), NEB, JPS, JB; but the early rendering of P has persisted: Luther 'mein Ruhm', Budde (1898a, 94), Kraus (51), RSV, NRSV, NIV 'my glory'.

Rudolph (1962, 231) suggests emending to רַחְצִי 'mein Vertrauen', based on the Aramaic verb 'to trust' (Dan 3.28; see Jastrow 1469). He cites Ps 60.10 where סִיר רחצי is rendered by LXX λέβης τῆς ἐλπίδος μου 'my cauldron of hope'. He is followed by Haller (104), and *HALOT* considers it worthy of mention. A similar meaning is claimed by Hoffmann (1931, 145) and Kopf (1958, 184f.) but without emendation!

It seems that the author's meaning has been guessed at from LXX onwards. BDB (664) gives the meaning 'enduring', and Anderson (1998, 531) points out that the term always refers to the future, never to the past.[90] This fact plus the context probably rules out the meaning 'my glory'. The poet is at rock-bottom at every level. His 'glory' has long since gone! In the previous verse, he says that he no longer experiences peace and prosperity. In such a condition he reflects on what is left and he concludes that all is lost.

The question remains of the force of the preposition מן. Is it a causative מן where Yahweh is depicted as the cause of loss experienced by the poet? Or is it a privative מן, where the emphasis is on the separation of the poet from Yahweh? The latter seems preferable in that the author has stated clearly throughout the previous verses that Yahweh is the cause of all his

---

[87] LXX may have interpreted as from the Aramaic verb נצח 'be victorious'; cf. Albrektson (139).
[88] Rudolph (1938, 111) notes that V's rendering echoes the regular LXX translation εἰς τέλος of the phrase לנצח.
[89] Cf. BDB נצח II. Ibn Ezra's suggestion of the relevance of Isa 63.3, though not acknowledged by later commentators, is in fact the basis of Gordis 'my vital spark' (1974a, 178) and Dahood 'my sap' (1975, 184).
[90] Cf. Kaiser (343n), Westermann (165), Berlin (78).

affliction. Dahood (184) translates 'without Yahweh'. Dobbs-Allsopp (2002, 114) wants to read both the causative and the privative; and this remains a possibility, especially since we are dealing here with poetry. That we have here a hendiadys, i.e. 'my enduring and my hope' = 'my lasting hope', is argued by Hillers² (114), cf. Dobbs-Allsopp (114), NJB, but Gordis (178) points out that a hendiadys would require the reverse order of nouns. The use of אבד in the singular does not support a hendiadys (GK 145o).

3.19

Text and Versions

MT זְכָר־עָנְיִי וּמְרוּדִי; LXX ἐμνήσθην ἀπο πτωχείας μου και ἐκ διωγμοῦ μου; Aq μνήσθητι κακουχίας μου καὶ ἀποστασίας μου (ἀψινθίου καὶ χολῆς); P ܐܬܕܟܪ ܥܘܒܕܝ ܘܡܪܕܘܬܝ, 'tdkr šw'bdy wmrdwty, V recordare paupertatis et transgressionis meae. BHK suggests that the Vorlage of LXX, 'I remembered', may have been זכרתי; Hillers² (114), who takes his cue from LXX, supposes that the Vorlage read either זכרתי or זכור אני, i.e. the infinitive absolute plus pronoun. The LXX translator had further difficulties with the rest of the verse and it may be, as Albrektson (140) observes, that he was trying to make sense of a difficult passage.⁹¹ MT possibly underlies the various renderings and is preferred.

* * *

When the speaker reflects on the extent of his various afflictions and trouble, alluded to in the previous verses, it is equivalent to wormwood and gall.

The ז stanza (vv. 19-21) begins ambiguously. The Masoretes have vocalised זְכָר. This could be either an imperative or an infinitive construct. The consonants might also have been pointed as a noun,⁹² namely זֵכֶר. The traditional understanding is of an imperative and this is represented by Aq, P, V, T and in MR.⁹³

IE² interprets in terms of the speaker remembering (i.e. as an infinitive), as does Vermigli (122). Calvin discusses the ambiguity of MT but, while admitting that one may read an imperative, prefers to interpret the verse as a continuation of the previous verse, that it is the speaker who remembers. AV follows Calvin but records the imperative option in the margin, while Luther, possibly influenced by V, holds to the imperative. Michaelis (1773–88, 147) shows a preference for the imperative, as do RV (which records the infinitive in the margin), Löhr (1906, 19), Keil (401), Gottwald (13), Gordis (178), NJB, RSV, Berlin (78), Renkema (379). Others take it as an infinitive—Ehrlich (13), Westermann (165), NEB,

---

⁹¹ Dobbs-Allsopp (117) specifically follows LXX here; so also BHK; cf. NIV which does the same but without note.
⁹² Cf. Dyserinck (372), Budde (1898ª, 94), Rudolph (1938, 111), Haller (104).
⁹³ Cf. MLT which takes it as an infinitive.

REB, JPS, JB, NRSV. It is clear that scholars are divided on this issue which is inextricably linked to the immediate context and, with some commentators, to the book as a whole. The reluctance of commentators to read an imperative, addressing Yahweh, is based on the context. In vv. 1-18, Yahweh's acts against the speaker are alluded to in the third person. Yahweh is not addressed; indeed, Yahweh's name only appears at the end of v. 18. It has seemed to some commentators that addressing Yahweh at this point is too abrupt. Albrektson (140f.), in support of the imperative reading, draws attention to the literary style of Lamentations (especially ch. 3) and to that of the Psalms: 'Several instances can be adduced from such psalms, where a stichos begins with an imperative זכר as an exhortation to Yhwh'. Renkema (379), too, reading the imperative, points out that in Psalms (Pss 2.5, 6, 7; 74.2, 18, 22; 89.47, 51; 106.4; 119.49; 132.1; 137.7) the imperative זְכֹר always addresses Yahweh. While it is true that Yahweh is addressed in all these instances, it is also true that God's name appears in each passage; and in the only other passage in Lamentations (5.1) where זְכֹר occurs, it is followed by the name Yahweh. It is true that the suddenness with which the imperative comes on the scene is paralleled in 1.9c, 11c but in each case there is never any doubt as to the addressee: Yahweh.[94] It would seem, therefore, that the balance is in favour of reading the infinitive and that v. 19 continues the mood of v. 18 where the speaker is at his lowest ebb; indeed, the following verse (v. 20) extends the reflective mood further.

זְכָר־עָנְיִי וּמְרוּדִי—LXX may presuppose a Hebrew text which differs from MT. LXX has ἐμνήσθην ἀπὸ πτωχείας μου καὶ ἐκ διωγμοῦ μου which Robinson (1933, 258) thinks translates זָכַרְתִּי מֵעָנְיִי וּמְרָדְפִי but suggests that the *original* reading was זָכַרְתִּי מְעַנִּי וּמְרָדְפִי. Albrektson (140) sounds a note of caution here. He acknowledges that the LXX translator took the מ of ומרודי to be the preposition מן but counters the suggestion (also shared by Abelesz, 21) that the translator read a form of √רדף: 'Possibly he read MT but connected it with √רדה, which in Biblical Hebrew means "tread, rule" (Qal) but later also "drive, chase" (Piel)'. P and V reflect MT, but T's paraphrase suggests that the translator read a form of מרר; cf. Levine (135), RSV 'my bitterness'. P, V and Aq derive the form from the root מרד 'to rebel', taking the passage to be a confession of past sins. On the term מְרוּדִי, see commentary on 1.7.[95]

MR inherits the מרד derivation (וּמְרוּדֵי שְׁמַרְדְּתִי בָךְ), taking the verse to be a confession by Israel before Yahweh of former misdeeds (cf. also MLT, V and Aq). Rashi, who at 1.7 suggested the derivation from √ירד,

---

[94] The combination of זכר and עני is found also at 1.7 where it is Jerusalem that remembers affliction. We should note that the two terms—עני and מרוד—appear together in both passages.

[95] For detailed discussion, see Barthélemy (864ff.). The noun מרוד is considered by BDB and *HALOT* to derive from √רוד 'to wander restlessly, freely' and may have the meaning 'homelessness'; cf. NEB, NIV.

merely glosses the term here with the French *conplaynemant* ('lamentation') (cf. Banitt, 1644). If we assume that Rashi took זכר as an imperative, addressing Yahweh, we may infer that this is, for him, a confession to Yahweh. Vermigli (122) translates *aerumnae* 'trouble', but without comment; and Calvin prefers this rendering, though he notes that others translate variously. Meek (25), as at 1.7, takes the term to be an abstract noun from √רדד 'to oppress'—'my oppression'.

The phrase לענה וראש occurs at Deut 29.17, in the reverse order, but the two terms occur as parallels at Jer 9.14; 23.15; Amos 6.12 (cf. also 1QH 4.14). לענה also occurs at Prov 5.4; Lam 3.15; Amos 5.7; and ראש occurs also at Deut 32.32 (רוש); Ps 69.22; Jer 8.14; Lam 3.5 (cf. also CD 8.10-11 and 19.22-23). It is probable that the two terms were proverbially associated with one another; cf. Seybold (1997, 15).

As to syntax, AV took the phrase to be in apposition to עניי ומרודי, i.e. the accusative of זכר; so also NEB margin, NIV, Berlin (78), while Kaiser (343), Westermann (161), JPS regard the phrase as predicate: it is the remembering which is wormwood and poison.

3.20

Text and Versions

MT זְכוֹר תִּזְכּוֹר; LXX μνησθήσεται; P ܐܬܕܟܪ *'tdkr*; V *memoria memor ero*; T מדכר תדכר. The Versions vary as they did in v. 19 (q.v.), but MT may be the underlying text (see below).

MT (*Kethib*) וְתָשִׁיחַ MT (*Qere*) וְתָשׁוֹחַ—so many MSS[Ken]; LXX καὶ καταδολεσχήσει; Sym[96] κατακάμπτεται; P ܘܦܐ *wpn'* V *et tabescet*; T ותצלי. MT (*Qere*) is preferred (see below).

* * *

The speaker continues to reflect on his terrible circumstances and is depressed as a result. The exegesis of this verse was in trouble early in its history. Because the speaker declares in v. 21 that he now has hope, the change-over is variously discovered in v. 19 and in v. 20. The evidence for the confusion and disagreement is found in the Hebrew textual tradition, the Versions and early exegesis. LXX, for example, is at its most 'wayward' in these verses, and modern commentaries are equally divided.

MT's opening infinitive absolute followed by a finite verb (which could be either 2nd p. m. s. or 3rd p. f. s.) is rendered by a simple imperative by P (as at the beginning of v. 19) addressed to Yahweh, while V takes it as 3rd p. f. s. with נפש as subject, as does T. The LXX tradition also varies, the beginning of the verse seeming to construe with the end of v. 19 rather

---

[96] This reading is based on SH margin—ܡܬܟܦ *mtkpp'*—but Field (755) notes another reading attributed to Sym—(ἑαυτῇ) προσλαλήσει—more in line with MT (*Kethib*); cf. Barthélemy (900f.).

than with v. 20. In addition to what has been said above, we might conclude that the LXX translator either had difficulty with the Hebrew text, as we have it, or, more probably, had a somewhat mutilated *Vorlage*.[97] In translating καταδολεσχήσει, the translator read *Kethib* וְתָשִׁיחַ, i.e. with a שׂ (not שׁ as indicated by *BHK* and *BHS*). Both Sym and V seem to accord with *Qere*, but P seems to have read a Hiphil form of שׁוב, cf. Kelso (41), *BHK*. Barthélemy (900) points out that at 1.11, 16, 19, P translates השיב נפש in this way: 'Il est possible que le traducteur syriaque, ne sachant comment interpreter ici sa *Vorlage*, s'est rappelé cette tournure familière'. T ותצלי from צלי II (Jastrow, 1283), a root which corresponds to Biblical Hebrew נטה, taken by Levine (69) as 'pray', appears to follow the *Qere*.[98] Finally, as *BHK* indicates, a *Tiq. soph.* exists which suggests that נפשי originally read נפשך, the suffix referring to Yahweh, considered an offensive anthropomorphism by the scribes—cf. C. D. Ginsburg (1966, 361f.)—and so was altered to נפשי.

In addition to various readings, there has also been uncertainty as to the subject of the verbs here. P understands the entire verse to be addressed to Yahweh, with נפשי as the object, while for V and T, נפשי is the subject of both verbs.

Rashi and IE[1] agree with V and T as to the syntax but are aware of a tradition which takes the first stich as addressing Yahweh, while in the second נפשי is the subject of the verb—an interpretation also found in Kara, MR and MLT: 'I trust that you will, indeed, remember what the nations of the world have done to me, but until vengeance comes upon them, my soul is cast down'; cf. also Luther. The would-be exegete, therefore, is faced with a plethora of possibilities.

Having opted for זכר as infinitive in v. 19, recalling past affliction, it is natural to read the verbs of v. 20 as 3rd p. f. s. with the subject נפשי.[99] This is the preferred interpretation of Rashi and IE[1], of Vermigli (122), Calvin, Budde (1898[a], 94), AV, REB, JPS, NRSV, Berlin (82). Among the Versions, only P takes the verbs as 2nd p. m. s. (see above). Luther's translation 'Du wirst ja daran gedanken, denn meine Seele sagte mir's' takes the first stich as 2nd p. s., cf. Nägelsbach (113); but Gottwald (13), who had interpreted זכר v. 19 as imperative, translates both verbs as 2nd p. m. s., 'Thou wilt surely remember and bow down to me'. He is prompted to do this by adopting the reading נפשך, which is claimed to be one of the *Tiq. soph.* NEB's 'Remember, O remember and stoop down to me' is the only modern translation[100] which accepts the reading נפשך; cf.

---

[97] Verses 22-24 are not even represented in LXX.
[98] So Albrektson (142) and Barthélemy (900). Levine (135f.) argues that T did not decide between *Kethib* and *Qere* but combined שׂיח and נחח in his rendering.
[99] The author of ch. 3 used נפשי as equivalent to the 1st p. s. pronoun at vv. 17 and 24; indeed, V translates the opening phrase as if it were a first person form.
[100] Its revision (i.e. REB) rejects the entire exegesis 'I remember them indeed and am filled with despondency'.

Brockington (218). Barnes (1900, 401, 412f.) is doubtful as to the authenticity of this *tiqqun*, and McCarthy (1981, 120-23) has likewise questioned it, noting that it does not appear in the early lists of *tiqqunim* and is only partially attested in the Masoretic lists. Gottlieb (42-44) is also sceptical of its authority.[101] What he means is that in the tradition the *tiqqun* is sometimes נפשׁי for נפשׁך (or for נפשׁו); but sometimes it seems to be that the original text was עליך נפשׁי, cf. Barnes (401).

A decision must be made on *Kethib*[102]/*Qere*. The *Qere* וְתָשׁוּחַ is probably from שׁוח a by-form of שׁחח, שׁחה (*HALOT*) 'to sink/bow down/be bowed down'. If we take וְתָשׁוּחַ as 3rd p. s., with נפשׁי as subject, the meaning will be that the speaker (remembers and) is depressed (his soul is bowed down).[103]

3.21

Text and Versions
MT זֹאת אָשִׁיב אֶל לִבִּי; LXX ταύτην τάξω εἰς τὴν καρδίαν μου; Sym ταύτην (*or* τοῦτο cf. SH ܗܕܐ *hd*ʾ) μνησθήσομαι ἐν τῇ καρδίᾳ μου; P ܗܕܐ ܐܗܦܟ ܒܠ ܠܒܝ *hd*ʾ *ʾtyb ʿl lby*; V *hoc recolens in corde meo*; T דא נחמתא אתיב על לבי. Versions substantially support MT.

* * *

After what looks like a solid basis for utter despair, the speaker begins to introduce grounds for hope, and the clouds begin to lift. We may recall the passage in Isa 60.2: 'For darkness shall cover the earth, and thick darkness the peoples; but the LORD will arise upon you…'

The text of this verse is not really in question, although LXX τάξω is a strange translation of אָשִׁיב, and Kelso (41), followed by *BHK, BHS, BHQ*, Rudolph (1938, 112), suggests that the LXX translator may have read אשׂים.[104] Albrektson (143) raises the possibility that the *Vorlage* read אשׁית (cf. LXX of Jer 2.15; 3.19; Hos 2.5; Job 14.13).

The construction השׁיב אל לב (found also at Deut 4.39; 1 Kgs 8.47; Isa 44.19; 46.8) means 'to bring to mind/take to heart/consider'.

---

[101] 'In general one should be particularly cautious in ascribing significance for textual criticism to the *tiqqune sopherim*, especially when, as here, the tradition is not supported by the witness of the Versions.'
[102] Some doubt exists as to the precise reading of *Kethib*. MT preserves the form ותשׁיח but because the *Qere* vowels are superimposed on the *Kethib*, we cannot be certain if *Kethib* had a שׂ or a שׁ. Some scholars (*BHK, BHS*) read *Kethib* as ותשׁח from שׁיח 'melt away', but, beginning with LXX, we detect that *Kethib* may have been ותשׂיח from שׂיח—Luther, Bickell (113), Albrektson (142f.), Gottlieb (43), Rudolph (1938, 112), Wiesmann (179f.) 'to ponder, consider, muse'; and Albrektson points out that זכר and שׂיח occur in parallel at Ps 77.4.
[103] On עלי = 'within me', see Pss 142.4; 143.4, cf. Ps 42.6, 7 where the mood is the same.
[104] This may be another instance of the state of the *Vorlage*.

זֹאת—'This' is usually taken to refer to what follows in vv. 22f. This is in accordance with normal practice: Ezek 20.27; 36.37; Isa 66.2; and this is how it is understood by Rashi, IE¹, Kara, MLT, Vermigli (123), Calvin, Michaelis (1773–88, 428), Ehrlich (41), Budde (1898ª, 94), Kaiser (344), Renkema (382f.). Gottwald (13) seems to understand 'this' to refer to what he regards as expressed hope in the previous verse, cf. also Westermann (162); and Albrektson (143ff.) also takes this line, arguing that על כן 'normally refers back to what precedes'; however, as Gottlieb (45) points out, על כן does refer back to זאת earlier in the verse. The speaker is about to announce something which is the basis for his composition in the first place; indeed, the basis for any of Israel's laments.

3.22

Text and Versions

MT תָמְנוּ; 1MS^Ken תמו; V *sumus consumpti*; OL *defecimus*; P ܠܠܡ *tlqnn*; T פסקו; Aq συνετελέσθημεν; Sym ἀναλώθημεν. I follow P and T, reading תַּמּוּ, see below.

* * *

The poet's hope finds its restoration in the love of Yahweh.

Verses 22-24 are not represented in LXX. We have noticed that the LXX translator usually reflects our MT but that, in vv. 19-21, there have been signs either that the translator had a faulty Hebrew text from which to work, or he was uncharacteristically lax. The absence of the three verses—the ח stanza—might confirm the suspicion that there was a substantial lacuna in his *Vorlage*. However, as Albrektson (145) notes, v. 24b is almost identical to v. 21b, and this similarity probably led to the lacuna through *homoioteleuton*. It may be, therefore, that LXX's 'waywardness' reflects tired or unfocussed scribal activity, cf. Barthélemy (902).

This verse is unusually long, and this feature plus the sudden appearance of a 1st p. pl. form תָמְנוּ has led to various suggestions. Thus, for example, Bickell (113) seems to omit כי twice and emends תמנו to תמו. While the length of line has exercised modern critical study, it was not an overt consideration among ancient translators and commentators. What did concern the ancients, however, was the term תמנו. What looks like a 1st p. pl. form (from √תמם) is rendered by P¹⁰⁵ and T as 3rd p. pl.,¹⁰⁶ though as 1st p. pl. by OL, V, Aq and Sym. Certainly, the parallelism of the verse כי לא כלו//כי לא תמנו and רחמיו//חסדי יהוה suggests a 3rd p. pl., and this may have influenced P and T in their renderings. Furthermore, the sudden appearance of an isolated¹⁰⁷ and unsustained 1st p. pl., after 21 lines, is

---

[105] Albrektson (145) is not convinced that P's *Vorlage* read תמו, but *BHK* and *BHS* assume this.

[106] According to GK 67e, תָּמְנוּ is for תַּמּוֹנוּ in Num 17.28; Ps 64.7; cf. Alexander (2008, 149 n. 36).

[107] 1st p. pl. forms are found in a sustained passage later in this poem (vv. 40-47).

enough to raise questions as to the verb in question. Rashi's comments are interesting here: כי לא תמנו כמו כי לא תמו. This seems to be his preferred interpretation, though he does go on to mention other interpreters who take תמנו as 1st p. pl. IE[1] also gives both meanings, explaining the reasoning behind the 3rd p. pl. as the נ standing for the doubled מ. Kara espouses only the 1st p. pl., interpreting the reference as the failure of Nebuchadnezzar and the exile to wipe out the people of God. MR appears to interpret as third person, but MLT incorporates both interpretations. Luther reads first person, while Calvin, although giving both meanings, comes down on the side of third person, arguing that in the context this is more suitable. Pagnini (1556, 264) translates in first person but, in his notes, seems to prefer third person.[108] AV renders 'It is of the Lord's mercies that we are not consumed...'; and this is how it is taken by Nägelsbach (115), Keil (413f.) and, more recently, Albrektson (145), Dahood (185), Renkema (385), NIV. But the majority of commentators are inclined to read the 3rd p. pl.: Blayney (322), Bickell (113), Ewald (338), Dyserinck (372), Rudolph (162, 231), GK 20o, Meek (25), Wiesmann (179), Kraus (53), Gottwald (13), Gottlieb (46), Berlin (83), RSV, NEB,[109] JPS, JB, NRSV. By following this emendation, the chiastic structure of the line is maintained, cf. Watson (1984, 203).

As to syntax, it is best to view כי as asseverative, cf. McDaniel (212), Gordis (179), Hillers[2] (115), NEB, NJB, NRSV, not causative. Gottlieb (45) suggests taking כי as explicative, stemming from זאת in v. 21. The position of חסדי at the beginning of the verse is due to the alphabetic demands of the strophe, although the emphasis which this position affords is very convenient for the poet, cf. Isa 63.7.

חַסְדֵי יְהוָה—The term חסד occurs over 200 times in the Hebrew Bible. It occurs only twice in Lamentations, both in this chapter (v. 22 and v. 32). It is normally found in the singular, the plural being found only 18 times. In v. 22 it is in the plural; and in v. 32, *Qere* reads plural. The actual phrase חסדי יהוה occurs elsewhere at Isa 63.7; Pss 89.2; 107.43. חסד is a difficult word to translate. Zobel (1986[a], 51) says 'the most appropriate translation of *hesed* is "goodness", "grace", or "kindness"'; and Jepsen (1961, 266) emphasises that it always designates not just an attitude but also the act that arises from that attitude. Zobel has shown that the term was linked to the covenant between Yahweh and his people comparatively late, hence it is perhaps reading too much into this passage to assume that the poet was thinking of the covenant, contra Provan (93). As Renkema (385) observes '...the גבר does not build his hopes on covenant obligations but rather on the expressions of YHWH's goodness to which he has no obligation, acts of kindness which he continues to reveal nevertheless'. The phrase חסדי יהוה is here parallel to רחמיו 'his compassion', an abstract

---

[108] '*In hac lectione* תממו תמנו *ponitur*, נ *loco* מ *litterae geminandae*'.
[109] Brockington (218).

plural (of רֶחֶם) which does not occur in the singular in the Hebrew Bible. This pairing occurs elsewhere at Pss 25.6; 40.12; 51.3; 69.16; 103.4; Isa 63.7; Jer 16.5; Dan 1.9; Hos 2.21; Zech 7.9, but only at Isa 63.7 and Ps 25.6 is חסד in the plural, as here. It may be that we should, with Meek (25), regard the plural here as an abstract plural, in which case we may translate 'mercy of Yahweh...his compassion', or it may be that the plural is chosen to balance the plural רחמיו at the end of the line, and that the poet is thinking in terms of plurals, i.e. evidences of Yahweh's kindness and mercy.

The speaker, having suffered at the hands of Yahweh (vv. 1-20) and having been at a very low ebb, clings to a belief in Yahweh's nature which lifts his spirits. He remembers what he has been taught about Yahweh's mercy. There have been many examples/proofs of that kindness and compassion both in his life and in the life of his community, and his faith, which was almost gone (v. 18), pushes through. His only hope is in the belief that that compassion is not at an end but is on-going: it is for ever (לעולם), cf. Pss 25.6; 100.5.

3.23

Text and Versions

MT חֲדָשִׁים לַבְּקָרִים רַבָּה אֱמוּנָתֶךָ; V *Novi diluculo, multa est fides tua*; P ܚܕܬܐ ܒܨܦܪܐ ܘܣܓܝܐܐ ܗܝܡܢܘܬܟ *bḥwdt' dṣpr' sgy" hymnwtk mry'*; Sym καινή (SH ܚܕܬ' *ḥdt'*) πάσης πρωίας; OL *Renovabit illas sicut lux matutina: multi sunt gemitus mei, et cor meum defecit*, T נסין חדתין מרחיש בצפריא סגיאה היא הימנותך. We probably should insert הֵם after חֲדָשִׁים (see below); otherwise MT is preferred.

* * *

The speaker is trying to instil or rekindle his faith in the midst of despair. It is not that he *notices* or experiences Yahweh's mercies—in fact, he has suffered the very opposite—but he is recalling the old beliefs and certainties. Surely they are still true!

The text of this verse is not usually questioned and, as it stands, makes good sense. But while the Hebrew MS tradition is stable and, along with V, testifies to MT, there are some divergences among the Versions; in particular, OL reflects quite a different tradition.[110] P is probably a free rendering of a text close to MT. The translator takes רחמיו (or חסדי) of the previous verse as being further described, and fills out the second stich—which seemed a bit abrupt with the sudden appearance of the second person suffix—by the addition of 'O Lord', although the latter may have been transposed from v. 24, where it is a minus in P. The Targumist does not

---

[110] 'He has renewed them just as the light of the morning; many are my sighs, and my heart he sets free.'

regard חדשים as qualifying רחמיו (or חסדי). In the first stich he depicts God as bringing forth new things every morning, while his translation of the second stich is in accord with MT and V. Kelso (42) thinks that Sym is a translation of חדש כל בקרים and that the confusion of a כ and a מ, especially in the ancient script, might easily be made.[111]

The differences (from MT) in P and T probably arise from the abrupt nature of the Hebrew text. Budde (1898ª, 94f.) had suggested transposing רחמיו from v. 22 to follow חדשים—so also Blayney (322) and Wiesmann (180), cf. BHK—but this ruins the symmetry of v. 22. Bickell (113) reads חדשים לבקרים חסדיו and in the second stich suggests reading אמונתו 'his faithfulness', cf. also Wiesmann (180), Haller (104), NEB, REB, NJB. Löhr (1894, 15) suggested חסדך חדש לבקרים.

These latter suggestions are partly occasioned by the shortness of the first stich. The simplest remedy is a suggestion in *BHS*: inserting הֵם after חדשים lengthens the first stich, makes it clear that the first word חדשים refers back to רחמיו (and/or חסדי) of v. 22, and is easily explained as having dropped out through haplography. The second person suffix is certainly abrupt, and the verse would read more smoothly if the suffix was 3rd p. s. but, as Provan (94) points out, Hebrew style seems to accommodate changes in address. The ל in לבקרים is distributive (= every morning), cf. GK 119r. The phrase is found in Ps 73.14 and Isa 33.2. The terms חסד and אמונה are associated elsewhere at Pss 36.6; 40.11; 88.12; 89.2, 3, 25, 34, 50; 92.3; 98.3; 100.5. The form אמונתך 'your faithfulness' is found eleven times, all in the book of Psalms, at Pss 36.6; 40.11; 88.12; 89.2, 3, 6, 9, 50; 92.3; 119.90; 143.1. רבה אמונתך may not be an exact quotation from any known psalm, but the 2nd p. s. suffix suggests that the poet was influenced by liturgical experience, cf. 1.9c, 11c, 17.

It is the manifestations of Yahweh's love and compassion which bring about the expression of the second stich: 'your faithfulness is great', cf. Pss 36.6; 100.5.

3.24

Text and Versions

MT חֶלְקִי יְהוָה אָמְרָה נַפְשִׁי, followed by V and T; OL *Sors mea Dominus, dixi*; P ܐܡܪܬ ܢܦܫܝ ܡܢܬܝ ܗܘ 'mrt npšy mnty hw. The P translator, having utilised יהוה as addressee in v. 23, continues to translate freely. He does not represent יהוה except by the pronoun ܗܘ hw and he rearranges the wording somewhat. V and T follow MT precisely. On the basis of OL, *BHK* advocates reading אמרתי, probably for metric reasons, cf. also Haller (104); but it is difficult to see how אמרתי could have expanded into אמרה נפשי. It is much more likely that the Latin translator gave the sense of the passage. MT is preferred.

* * *

---

[111] He is referring to the similarity of these two letters *kaph* and *mem*, say, the Siloam script. If the words in the *Vorlage* were written close together, then the preposition ל might have been associated with the מ (= כ) at the end of חדשים.

The speaker continues expressing his confidence in Yahweh. He has been at rock bottom, and the beliefs he grew up with now come to his aid.

חֶלְקִי יְהוָה—The term חלק is often used in the Hebrew Bible for a piece of land apportioned by the community to a particular clan or family and to the division within that property.[112] As Renkema (390) notes, 'Such land ownership constituted the very basis of human survival', cf. Dobbs-Allsopp (118). It follows that when a man experienced the loss of his חלק, he felt adrift from the community; his very existence was under threat. Levites could not possess land but they are told that Yahweh was their חלק (Num 18.20; Deut 10.9), and from this idea sprang the notion that Yahweh himself was the portion of the landless,[113] that the latter could count on Yahweh as their basis for survival. The fact that the poet here exclaims 'Yahweh is my portion' does not mean *ipso facto* that he was a Levite. The name Hilkiah (חלקיהו)—2 Kgs 18.18; Isa 22.20; Jer 1.1; 29.3—means 'Yahweh is my portion'; and the sentiment occurs also at Pss 16.5; 73.26; 119.57; 142.6. The poet, then, was familiar with this phrase as he was with 'Yahweh is my shepherd' (Ps 23.1), 'my cup' (Ps 16.5) and 'my refuge' (Ps 73.28) and he employs it here because the end of his tether, described in vv. 1-18, has been reached. He may have blamed Yahweh for the adversity and suffering which he has endured but he knows that his fate is in the hands of Yahweh: his only hope, cf. NEB, NJB 'all that I have'. That is why the verse ends 'therefore I will hope in him'. The second stich is almost identical with the second stich of v. 21. (In v. 24 there is the additional לי.) The poet looks ahead to v. 22 where the mercies of Yahweh are mentioned. That (זאת) is what instils hope in him. Here in v. 24 he becomes more specific. It is Yahweh who is the object of his hope.

אמרה נפשי may be equivalent to אמרתי, cf. the Vulgate of v. 20 where Jerome renders ותשיח עלי נפשי by *et tabescet in me anima mea*. But the poet may be alluding to inner reflection, cf. IE[1] who simply adds לי after the lemma אמרה—'my soul said to me' = 'I said to myself'. Calvin explains: 'This then is the reason why the Prophet ascribes what he says to his soul, as though he had said, that he did not boast, like hypocrites, that God was his portion, but that of this he had a thorough conviction. My soul has said, that is, I am fully convinced that God is my portion'. The concern about אמרה נפשי arises from the length of the line, which appears too long; cf. Budde (1898[a], 95). Bickell (113) suggests reading יה for יהוה, and Budde proposed אמרתי, though without reference to OL, suggesting that נפש had slipped into v. 24 from the following verse. Wiesmann (180)

---

[112] Since Yahweh was the owner of the land (Deut 12.10), whoever gets a portion of the land has a portion in Yahweh's property. The term is often in parallel to נחלה 'inheritance' (Deut 18.1; 32.9; Jer 10.16; cf. Lam 5.2).
[113] Those who take the גבר as a collective might argue that the landless are in fact the exiles!

deletes נפשׁי and points אָמְרָה, arguing that this is a better parallel to אוֹחִיל in the second stich. Gordis (179f.) sees no need to shorten the line: 'The basic principle of Hebrew metrics—one beat per thought unit—is strikingly exhibited here. אמרה נפשׁ which corresponds in meaning to אמרתי receives one beat, so that the verse is in 3:2 rhythm.'

3.25

Text and Versions

MT (*Kethib*) לקוו (= לְקוָו) is followed by P; MT (*Qere*) לְקוָיו is attested by several MSS[Ken] and followed by LXX, OL, V and T. The *Kethib* is to be preferred to *Qere*—so Luther, Bickell (114), Blayney (322), Löhr (1906, 20), Meek (25), Wiesmann (181), Westermann (166), Gottwald (13), Kaiser (344), Kraus (53), Albrektson (146), Gottlieb (46), *BHQ*. The singular offers a better parallel to the singular in the second stich and, indeed, throughout the strophe. The sense is not affected. *Qere* is followed by Calvin, Keil (401).

* * *

The poet continues with statements of faith, which should be sufficient for hoping in Yahweh. The poet is making general statements: the singular in the second stich (and in vv. 26f.) does not refer to a particular individual but to 'everyone who seeks'; that is, the singular is used distributively, so that we may translate with NEB 'to all who seek him', cf. NJB.

The root קוה is in the same semantic field as יחל (vv. 21, 24, 26). In the Hebrew Bible יחל emphasises more the idea of 'waiting', and קוה more the idea of 'hoping', cf. Waschke (567), Westermann (1997, 541), but the distinction should probably not be pressed. The statement that Yahweh is good is found at Pss 25.8; 34.9; 86.5; 100.5; 106.1; 107.1; 118.1, 29; 119.68; 135.3; 136.1. This goodness is towards those who trust in him (Ps 34.9), who call upon him (Ps 86.5). It consists in being merciful and supportive (Pss 106.1; 107.1; 118.1, 29; 136.1).

דרשׁ—Although this root in late Hebrew has the meaning 'interpret, study' (Ezra 7.10), in the Hebrew Bible it generally means 'seek, ask' and is often parallel to בקשׁ (Deut 4.29; Judg 6.29; 1 Chron 16.11; 1 Sam 28.7; Prov 11.27; Isa 65.1; Jer 29.13). While there are many examples of the verb being used in a general sense—seek a person (Jud 6.29), seek justice (Isa 1.17)—its theological use is more prevalent, cf. Wagner (1978, 307); and this is how it is used here vis-à-vis Yahweh. It is also used in connection with gods other than Yahweh (2 Chron 17.3). There is evidence that דרשׁ may, at times, imply an approach to Yahweh (or to another god) in a cultic setting[114] (e.g. Ps 24.6) or at least with a prophet, a mediator,

---

[114] Renkema (394) rules out the cultic here because he assumes that ch. 3 was written at the same time as ch. 2, i.e. shortly after the destruction of the Temple and the formal worship of Yahweh in Jerusalem.

present (1 Sam 9.9; 2 Kgs 3.11; 8.8), but there are many passages where neither a cultic setting nor a mediator need be assumed and where it appears to denote repentance and faith (Hos 10.12; Amos 5.4-6; Jer 29.12f.; Isa 9.12).

טוב does double duty here for both stichs, the relative pronoun אשר before תדרשנו is suppressed (GK 155f-m), and נפש is used in the sense of 'anyone' (Exod 12.16; Lev 7.27).

The poet, then, is virtually quoting the language of the faith of Israel. He is not himself confident but he recalls and parades old dictums from his knowledge of the doctrines of his day, cf. Gerstenberger (2001, 494).

3.26

Text and Versions

MT טוֹב וְיָחִיל וְדוּמָם; 13 MSS^Ken read ויחל and one reads ודמם; LXX (ἀγαθόν)[115] καὶ ὑπομενεῖ καὶ ἡσυχάσει; V *bonum est praestolari cum silentio*; OL *bonum est sustinere et sperare*; P ܠܗ ܕܡܣܒܪ ܒܩܘܫܬܐ *ṭb lmn dmsbr bqwšt'*; Aq ...ὑπομένειν καὶ ἡσυχάζειν...; Sym ...τῷ ἀναμένοντι μετὰ σιγῆς (εἰς τὸ σωτήριον...); T טב לאורכא ולמשתק. Read טוֹב יוֹחִיל וְדוּמָם.

* * *

The speaker—perhaps recalling old adages from the past in order to boost his faith—reflects on the best way to handle adversity. If one's being is crying out for Yahweh's deliverance, then one should be quietly patient.

It is difficult to make precise sense of the first stich. GK 107q offers the translation of the first two words—'it is good and let him hope, i.e. that he should hope', and Keil (401) suggests translating 'It is good that [one] should wait and that in silence', cf. also Schäfer (127*); but many scholars feel that the text is corrupt and propose emendations. The history of translation and exegesis shows that the text of the first stich was problematic. The LXX *Vorlage* may not have had the same consonantal text as MT. In any case, the Masoretes vocalised וְיָחִיל, i.e. an adjective 'waiting', from the root יחל 'to wait', and דוּמָם the adverb 'silently', while the LXX rendering has two finite verbs 'and he will wait and he will remain quiet'.[116] Aq has two infinitives 'to wait and to be silent' which might presuppose the infinitives of √יחל and √דמם, i.e. הוֹחִיל וְדָמוֹם; and Sym's translation may be of a *Vorlage* reading לְיָחֵל וְדֹמֵם. P 'to the one who waits in truth' is puzzling, but Abelesz (9) is probably correct in surmising that

---

[115] Some LXX witnesses have ἀγαθόν at the end of v. 25 (see Swete III, 370; cf. Field, 755), though SH and OL follow the MT order which is desiderated in the interests of the alphabetic acrostic; and Ziegler (483) follows suit.
[116] *BHK* suggests that LXX read וְיָחֵל וְדָמַם.

ܒܫܬܩܐ is a scribal error for ܒܫܬܩܐ *bšwtq'* 'in silence', cf. Albrektson (148) and Robinson (1933, 258). That all three Greek Versions read a different Hebrew text is *possible*, but it is more likely that the translators were each making the best of a difficult passage; cf. Schäfer (127*). OL seems to tally with Aq, while V looks like a mixture of Aq and Sym; and T, although expanding the passage in the second stich, has two infinitives, as in Aq. It is not surprising that many scholars, even Renkema (395), reject MT and put forward suggestions as to the original reading. Syntactically, the structure טוב followed by ו...ו has been seen as problematic. Rashi notes that the first ו is superfluous,[117] as in the passage ואיה וענהו (Gen 36.24). His explication is: טוב שיחיל אדם וידום. The unpointed Rashi text seems to suggest that he took the verb to be from √חיל, but the fact that the poet has already, and in the same context, used the root √יחל makes it likely that this is the root that he is employing again.[118] Bickell (114) suggests reading יְיַחֵל—a Piel imperfect. The suggestion by Budde (1898a, 95) assumes that the second ו was wrongly attached to דומם and the first had, in transmission, changed places with the י: יוֹחִילוּ. He translates 'Gut ists, dass sie [קוּן] schweigend harren'. The suggestion has the advantage of accommodating all the consonants of MT. It is adopted by Haller (104) and *BHK*. Renkema (395) is unhappy with a plural verb because the plural of v. 25 is not, in his view, original. Gordis (180), who misquotes Haller, follows the suggestion that the second ו has become detached from the verb ויחילו. He translates 'It is good that men wait expectantly'. Hillers[1] (57), in despair of MT, claims that כ has fallen out of the first stich through haplography (similarity of כ to ב of טוב) and suggests that the original may have read טוב כי יָחִיל דוּמָם. In his second edition (1992, 115) he suggests טוב כי יָחִיל דוּמָם. His translation is: 'It is good that a man hope in quiet...' It is true, we might expect כי after טוב, cf. Job 10.3; 13.9; Ps 119.71, but if טוב is followed by an infinitive (with or without a ל), the same sense may be obtained, cf. Ps 92.2; Prov 18.5; 24.23; 25.27; 28.21; Eccl 5.17. This brings us to an observation by Delitzsch (1920, 120 §132b) that the letters וי are sometimes an error for the letter ה (cf. 1 Kgs 15.13 ויסרה with the parallel in 2 Chron 15.16 הסירה). He suggests reading הָחֵיל—Hiphil infinitive construct of יחל. Albrektson (146ff.) embraces this suggestion and goes on to suggest that another infinitive follows on; that is to say, in place of ודומם we should read וְדֹמֹם. By this Albrektson maintains the Hiphil of יחל (used by the poet at vv. 18, 21, 24) and the verb דמם (used also at v. 28).

Although the general sense of the passage is not really in question, there continue to be other suggestions as to the text here.[119] Furthermore,

---

[117] IE[1] is also exercised by this ו, but his brief comment: 'The ו is like the פ"ה רפה in Arabic' is not self-evident. Presumably he would agree with Rashi's rendering.
[118] Besides, many grammarians are not convinced of the existence of a root חיל with the meaning 'wait'; cf. Rudolph (1938, 112), Kraus (53), though see Gordis (180) and Gesenius (1949, 228).
[119] Thus, Perles (1930, 112) reads טוּבוֹ יָחִיל וְדָמַם, and *BHS* suggests וְדָמַם חַסְדּוֹ.

there are those, albeit in the minority, who take טוב to refer to Yahweh, as at v. 25.[120] It seems to me that the form following טוב must be verbal, hence the text must have suffered early in transmission, causing problems for the Versions. If we read יוֹחִיל for וְיָחִיל we have the Hiphil impf. 3rd p. m. s. of √יחל, and the passage may read: 'it is good that one (referring to the נפש of v. 25) waits…' וְדוּמָם is not a problem. דוּמָם means 'silently', cf. Isa 47.5, and the ו, while perhaps unnecessary and may be ignored in translation (cf. P, V and Sym), is not obtrusive. It is not that these Versions did not encounter a ו but that, in translation, it was more idiomatic to omit it, hence JPS 'It is good to wait patiently', cf. NJB, NIV.

3.27

Text and Versions

MT עֹל בִּנְעוּרָיו; LXX ζυγὸν ἐν νεότητι αὐτοῦ; P ܢܝܪܟ ܒܛܠܝܘܬܗ *nyrk bṭlywth*; V *iugum ab adulescentia sua*; OL *iugum grave a juventute sua*. The text of this verse is not seriously in question. P has 'your yoke' (as though addressing Yahweh [cf. v. 20] who has imposed the yoke), but the other Versions[121] follow MT. Many Hebrew MSS[Ken] read *plene* עוֹל, and several read מנעוריו for בנעוריו, corresponding to the readings of V and OL (cf. also JB, NJB, REB), but MT is to be preferred, cf. Budde (1898a, 95), Rudolph (1962, 231), Provan (96). The reading probably arises from scribes/translators familiar with passages such as Gen 8.21; 1 Sam 17.33; Isa 47. 12, 15; Jer 3.24; Zech 13.5; Pss 71.5, 17; 129.1, 2; cf. Matt 19.20; Acts 26.4.[122]

* * *

בִּנְעוּרָיו—Apart from anything else, the construction with the preposition מן implies that the yoke has been borne continually throughout life, whereas the idea here seems to be the early bearing of the yoke with the prospect of relief later; but see Alexander (2008, 151 n. 42).

Originally designed to control or harness animals, a form of yoke came to be used for the discipline of humans, especially prisoners or slaves. According to Tyer (1026f.), it became a symbol of the owner–owned relationship. It is often used in a transferred sense—of discipline, usually of a severe kind, cf. 1 Kgs 12.11. It was thought that discipline was important for the young (Prov 23.13; cf. 13.24; 29.15), and this may be the thought in this passage.[123] Calvin notes that it could mean 'instruction' or 'punishment' in the context of a relationship with God. The verse sounds proverbial, perhaps even a quotation which the poet employs to support what he is now going to say in v. 28.

---

[120] Hence, Ehrlich (42) who reads טוֹב לִמְיַחֲלֵי דוּמָם; cf. also Gottlieb (47) and Renkema (394f.).
[121] The Targumist interprets yoke to refer to the commandments (פקודיא), while MR equates it with Torah, matrimony and an occupation.
[122] Schäfer (127*) thinks that the variant 'probably emerges from the idea that the Torah is the yoke which one has to carry from childhood'; cf. the preceding note.
[123] IE[1] glosses על with מוסר 'instruction/chastisement', cf. Prov 1.8.

3.28

Text and Versions
No significant material.

* * *

The problems in this verse are the meaning of וְיִדֹּם and נָטַל and the subject of the second stich.

יֵשֵׁב בָּדָד וְיִדֹּם—There is an echo here of 1.1 where the phrase יָשְׁבָה בָדָד is used of Jerusalem.[124] The construction is also found at Lev 13.46; Jer 15.17. The imperfect of v. 27 (יִשָּׂא) is picked up in the jussives of v. 28 (יֵשֵׁב and יִדֹּם), v. 29 (יִתֵּן) and v. 30 (יִתֵּן and יִשְׂבַּע), having the same subject (גֶּבֶר). 'It is good that a man...; let him...' That בָדָד means 'alone' (Rashi גלמוד), see on 1.1.[125] The verb דמם occurs also at 2.10, 18, and at 2.10 it is construed with יָשַׁב, as here.

The root נטל is uncommon in Biblical Hebrew, occurring only five times (2 Sam 24.112; Isa 40.15; 63.9; Prov 27.3; Lam 3.28), though more frequent in post-Biblical Hebrew and in Aramaic. LXX translates ἦρεν. Since the translator has used the same verb to translate √נשא in v. 27 (cf. also at 2.19) where the subject is גבר, it follows that, for the Greek translator, the subject is the same here. The yoke is shouldered by the גבר.

While BDB classifies this verb as a rare synonym of נשא—and it occurs at Qumran with this meaning (CD 11:10)—*HALOT* indicates that another meaning may be 'to be heavy', as at Isa 40.15 where the context mentions 'scales', cf. Elliger (1978, 42); Thomas (1968, 218). In support we might cite the forms נֵטֶל meaning 'burden' (Prov 27.3), and נְטִילַי meaning 'laden?' (Zeph 1.11). If we were to adopt this meaning, the subject would then be the yoke (v. 27). This is how it is taken by NEB, NJB, Hillers[2] (116) and OL, though in the latter case there is also the suggestion that OL read עַל for עָלָיו.[126]

In Syriac, the root means 'to be weighty', but the P translator avoids using it because he believes that נטל in this passage means 'to bear, carry', and he uses ܣܒܠ *sbl*; again, the subject is גבר. The Syriac translator, however, feels the need to supply 'your yoke'. *BHK* implies that P read עליו עלך, but it is likely that P is translating freely here, maintaining his exegesis of v. 27 (cf. *BHQ*). It is clear that here, too, the subject is the patient man. T has a lengthy paraphrase, and Levine (141) claims that the

---

[124] The author of ch. 3, writing for the same commemoration as the poets in chs. 1, 2 and 4, occasionally uses similar vocabulary.
[125] McDaniel (40-42) questions this meaning, pointing out that we have a context of 'mourning' here, and that בדד is a synonym for דמם II 'mourn, moan'; but the context is more of resignation and submission. NEB translates דמם 'sigh', which may be following McDaniel, but the revision (REB) reverts to the meaning 'be silent', as in P, V and T.
[126] The words *jugu grave* are found in the Vulgate at 1 Kgs 12.11; 2 Chron 10.11, 14; Sir 40.1.

Targumist understood נטל as 'weigh heavily', but the argument is not persuasive. Levine may, however, be correct when he perceives, in the paraphrase, the Targumist 'alternately presenting the patient sufferer and God as the subject'.[127] Luther decided that the passage was ambiguous and so implies that the subject of נטל is God, cf. also Rashi, RSV, JPS, NIV, NRSV, Keil (401), Westermann (162), Berlin (79), Renkema (400); but Calvin rejects this exegesis as forced, translating *quia tulit super se*. However, Calvin does allow that the text may be corrupt: 'Were we to read עֻלּוֹ, *olu*, his yoke, it would be more appropriate, and a reason would be given for what goes before...' Gordis (142, 180) is confused, but at one point he wants to read עֻלּוֹ 'his yoke', attributing it to P, although P translates ܠܡܢܐ ܢܝܪܗ *'lwhy nyrk* here!

The advice offered here is to accept whatever comes upon one, sitting alone in silence. The reference to youth (v. 27) may seem out of place here, for the advice is general and not directed at youth in particular. It may be that we have another instance of the poet quoting a proverbial saying, as in v. 27.

The second stich appears to supply the reason for the advice to sit apart and be silent—because it is a divine imposition. LXX, P, V, OL, Sym all interpret כי as 'because', though the exegesis varies. Rashi and Kara are right in sensing that Yahweh is the subject of נטל, and IE¹ rightly explains that the object is the aforementioned yoke of v. 27. This necessitates taking נטל as 'lay upon, impose', cf. 2 Sam 24.12 where it has this meaning and is construed with על and where Yahweh is the subject. The absence of the name Yahweh is not a problem, for the poet is conscious that Yahweh is behind the adversity and in control of any deliverance, cf. v. 26 and v. 31f.

3.29

Text and Versions

MT אולי יש followed by V, T and OL; P ܡܛܠ ܕܐܝܬ *mtl d'yt*. MT is preferred. The verse is missing from LXX, again due to haplography: the beginnings of vv. 29 and 30 being identical: a case of homoioarcton, cf. Bickell (114), Albrektson (150). It has been 'restored' in the Hexaplaric and Lucianic recensions; and it is present in OL *Dabit in sepultura os suum, si tamen est spes patientiae*.

* * *

It is natural to interpret v. 29 along with vv. 28 and 30. The jussives ידם and ישב (v. 28) are followed by the jussive יתן. The advice continues; cf. Calvin. אולי יש is translated by P as 'because there is', giving quite a different twist to the clause.[128] It is unlikely that P read כי, as V, T and OL

---

[127] The uncertainty as to the subject is also found in Vermigli (129): '...the reason may be twofold depending on whether it can refer to God or to the man himself.'
[128] Cf. Job 11.18.

support MT. It may be that the Syriac translator felt that if אוּלַי 'perhaps'[129] was translated ܟܒܪ *kbr* it might convey too much by way of actual doubt, whereas the context seemed to him to stress the idea of faith in God: 'Let him put his mouth in the dust; perhaps there may be hope'.

To put one's mouth in the earth[130] was an ancient act of voluntary submission[131] before a superior (Ps 72.9; Mic 7.17). The superior here is Yahweh, as IE[1] עוֹשֵׂהוּ and MLT בוראו make clear; and Hillers[2] (129) suggests that Yahweh is probably also the identity of מכהו of v. 30.

3.30

Text and Versions

MT בְּחֶרְפָּה (singular) followed by P and T; LXX ὀνειδισμῶν followed by V and OL. The text is not really in question. What has occasioned the plural in LXX,[132] V and OL is the presence of the verb שׂבע 'be sated, filled, have in excess', cf. the translation of MT in RSV, NRSV 'and be filled with insults'.

* * *

בְּחֶרְפָּה—Greek and Latin do not need to represent the preposition בּ here (LXX and V), though we do find it in OL *in opprobriis*. P also omits it. IE[1] draws attention to the preposition and says that it is superfluous (as he did at v. 15 with במרורים). The sense would be the same without the preposition—with חרפה as adverbial accusative (GK 118q); and שׂבע sometimes takes the preposition, as in Pss 65.5; 88.4.

The copula in P and OL does not represent a different reading. It is natural for a translator or a scribe to add 'and' between the two clauses. Indeed, several MSS[Ken] read וישׂבע—and in a translation which does not claim to reproduce the poetry of the original, it is natural to supply it, cf. NEB, NRSV.

This verse continues to offer advice to the sufferer. The first stich suggests he should offer his cheek to anyone who would strike him. MR implies that God is the striker, and Levine (141) thinks that this is also the interpretation of T. It is true, Yahweh strikes the enemies of the psalmist (Ps 3.8) on the cheek, and the poet here has, in vv. 1-18, interpreted his adversity and suffering as coming from Yahweh; but the treatment alluded to in this verse (and in v. 29) is experienced at the hands of an enemy/ adversary, even if it is managed by Yahweh, cf. Provan (1991[a], 96).

---

[129] On אוּלַי, see Reimer (2003, 325-46).
[130] See Field (756) who cites Theodoret ἐν γῃ. IE[1], the putting of one's mouth in the earth is another way of saying יִשְׁתַּחֲוֶה.
[131] It also implies silence, in that the mouth, in the earth, cannot speak, cf. Keil (416).
[132] Albrektson (150) notes that the singular חרפתם in v. 6 is rendered by LXX τὸν ὀνειδισμὸν αὐτῶν, and at 5.1 חרפתנו is translated τὸν ὀνειδισμὸν ἡμῶν.

To strike someone on the cheek is to show disrespect and scorn for that person and demonstrates superiority (cf. 1 Kgs 22.24; Job 16.10; Ps 3.8; Mic 4.14). The sufferer is encouraged to suffer in silence, offering his cheek to the aggressor.

The second stich continues in the same vein. The advice is to be filled with reproach, i.e. to suffer reproach in full measure, cf. NEB '…and endure full measure of abuse'.

3.31

Text and Versions
MT may stand (see below).

* * *

In the next stanza the poet offers reasons for the hope which he has mentioned in v. 29. 'For the Lord will not ultimately reject. His abundant mercy ensures that he will have compassion, although he has caused grief. He does not willingly grieve anyone.'

Each of the three lines begins with כי (cf. vv. 25-27, all of which begin with טוב).

The textual problem here is based on the expected length of line. The second stich is unusually short, consisting only of אדני, itself a disputed reading (*BHK*). LXX, P, V and OL support MT with regard to the number of elements in the second stich,[133] though Albrektson (150) draws attention to the uncharacteristic word order in LXX. T is a paraphrase, but the translator 'supplies' an object for זנח, namely, עבדוהי. It does not follow that T's *Vorlage*[134] read עבדיו—a reading suggested by Lowth (1807, XL) and which NEB[135] opts for: 'For the Lord will not cast off his servants for ever'.

Bickell (1894, 114), who had earlier (1882, 117) suggested inserting עמו, imagines that a verbal element has dropped out of the original and supplies לא יטש before אדני. No one has followed these suggestions, but *BHK* and *BHS* (though not *BHQ*) indicate that a verb is missing. Löhr (1894, 15) holds that the phrase בני איש has dropped out in transmission (cf. v. 33). Budde wondered (1892, 272) if the original text had been ילדי אדם (deleting אדני), but later (1898a, 95) concluded that אדני gave rise to a haplography—אדם (cf. v. 36); and he is followed by Rudolph (1938, 112), Haller (104), Westermann (166), Meek (26) and Wiesmann (182). Kaiser (344) translates the second stich 'er wird noch freundlich sein', which is based on his reading עוד תרצה for אדני (cf. Ps 77.8). Kraus (53), while agreeing that a word is missing at the end of the line, considers the

---

[133] One cannot tell if these Versions read אדני or יהוה.
[134] We should note that the T traditions differ, cf. Barthélemy (905).
[135] Cf. Brockington (218); but note that the revision (= REB) follows MT.

various emendations risky. It is interesting to note that in translations which do not claim to emend MT we find an object supplied, e.g. JB 'For the Lord does not reject mankind for ever and ever', NJB 'For the Lord will not reject anyone for ever'; cf. NIV 'For men are not cast off by the Lord for ever'.

It would appear, at first sight, that something *has* dropped out in the second stich. If so, the suggestion by Budde—introducing אדם before אדני—might seem the most plausible, cf. v. 36. But length of line should not be pressed too strongly. Furthermore, there are similarities to the passage at Ps 77. 8 הַלְעוֹלָמִים יִזְנַח אֲדֹנָי וְלֹא־יֹסִיף לִרְצוֹת עוֹד where זנח in the first stich, with אדני as subject, does not have an object.

On the meaning of זנח, see on 3.17. The Versions generally take the verb to mean 'reject'. IE¹ glosses with מאס (as he did at 3.17), and IE² claims once more (cf. 3.17) that the verb is equivalent to שכח 'forget'. MR uses the Aramaic verb שבק 'abandon' by way of explication.

3.32

Text and Versions

MT (*Kethib*) חַסְדוֹ followed by MSS^Ken, LXX and T; MT (*Qere*) חֲסָדָיו followed by V and OL. *Kethib* is preferred. It is probable that the singular was original and that the plural arose in transcription because of the construction רב חסדו, since רב can be translated 'multitude, abundance' as well as 'greatness'; cf. Schäfer (127*).

* * *

The poet asserts—and this is the basis of his encouragement to be patient (v. 26)—that Yahweh's mercy underlies all his actions towards men. There may be hardship and devastation but compassion is ever present and will become evident.[136]

כִּי אִם־הוֹגָה—On כי אם, see GK 163c and on 5.22.[137] The sense is 'even if, although'. It is followed by the perfect Hiphil (of יגה) referring to the past—'Although he has caused grief...'—and this in turn is followed by ו consecutive + רִחַם, i.e. suggesting the future (or frequentative tense). Cf. Rashi and IE¹.

On יגה, see on 1.4.[138] The Hiphil means 'to cause grief' (1.5). 'Even if Yahweh has caused grief...' There is no question here of any doubt on the matter, for the poet has made clear throughout the earlier verses of the poem that Yahweh is behind the affliction and suffering.

---

[136] Kara and MR imply that, having caused grief, God *relents* and then has compassion; cf. also T ובתר כן יתוב וירחם, though Alexander (2008, 153 n. 47) interprets this 'he will again have mercy', contra Levine (70) and Brady (162).
[137] Cf. Salters (2003, 362-65).
[138] Cf. also Wagner (1986, 380-84).

וְרִחַם—The verb is denominative of רֶחֶם 'womb'. In the Piel it means 'to take pity on someone', often parallel with חנן (2 Kgs 13.23). It occurs only here in Lamentations, though the noun (רַחֲמָיו) appears in v. 22. On חַסְדּוֹ, see on v. 22.

3.33

Text and Versions

MT כִּי לֹא עִנָּה מִלִּבּוֹ; LXX ὅτι οὐκ ἀπεκρίθη ἀπὸ καρδίας αὐτοῦ; P ܕܠܐ ܗܘܐ ܡܛܠ ܕܠܐ ܐܢ ܡܢ ܠܒܗ; Aq ἐταπείνωσεν; V *non enim humiliavit ex corde suo*; OL *quia non humiliavit toto corde suo*. As Albrektson (150) notes, few LXX manuscripts represent the opening word of this verse—כי (cf. the rendering at v. 31: ὅτι). It has been restored (from SH) in the Ziegler edition; besides, the acrostic demands a beginning with a כ. The unvocalised *Vorlagen* of the Versions have led to variations in the interpretation of this verse. The LXX and P translators took ענה to be ענה I 'to answer', while Aq, V and OL agree in taking the verb to be ענה II 'be wretched' (Piel: 'to afflict'), in accordance with MT vocalisation. T's paraphrase offers a quite different exegesis, taking man as the subject of ענה, but the translator seems to have vocalised as in MT; cf. Levine (142f.).

MT וַיַּגֶּה; read probably וַיְגֶּה (see below).

* * *

The particle לֹא appears to do double duty in this verse, applying to both verbs: 'Yahweh neither afflicts nor grieves'.

וַיַּגֶּה—Several MSS^{Ken} read ויגא but this is probably a scribal error. Michaelis (1773–88, 429) observes that after a *waw*-consecutive one would not expect a ל"ה verb to retain the ה. He subsequently concludes that the reading should be וִיְגֶּה *et dolere facit*.[139] Dahood (1978, 186f.) claims (wrongly) that MT derived from נגה 'to shine'. It is, as GK 69u (cf. BL 443 k) observes, an apocopated Piel (for וַיְגֶּה); cf. also וַיַּדּוּ for וַיְיַדּוּ at v. 53. Because this would be the only instance of a Piel of √יגה in the Hebrew Bible, together with the fact that the poet in v. 32 had used the Hiphil הוגה, some scholars have suggested, correctly I think, that the Hiphil pointing וַיֹּגֶה should be adopted.[140] The Hiphil pointing is not, however, based on LXX.[141]

Rudolph (1938, 112) raises the possibility of the vocalisation being וַיַּגֶּה (from נגה 'to heal'), though he does not opt for this in his commentary (1962, 228). He indicates that this would provide a balance,[142] noted in v. 32—רחם : הוגה / נגה : ענה.

---

[139] Note that his German translation reads 'beschusst' (from נגה).
[140] So Budde (1898⁸, 95), *BHK, BHS*, Wiesmann (182), Dahood (186), Westermann (166).
[141] So *BHK* and Brockington (218); cf. Albrektson (150). *BHK* cites OL, in addition to LXX, but OL *neque repulit* (for ויגה) differs from the rendering of the Hiphil הוגה in v. 32, *humiliavit*. It is likely that *BHK* meant to cite V where *abjecit* is used for הוגה (v. 32) and for ויגה (v. 33).
[142] In this case, לֹא will only apply to the first verb.

בְּנֵי־אִישׁ—The actual expression is uncommon in the Hebrew Bible. It simply means 'men, mortals, people'.[143] Kraus (1993, I, 148) argues that at Ps 4.3 (and Pss 49.3; 62.10) the phrase is a term for respected and prominent people, cf. *HALOT*, Gerstenberger,[144] REB. However, in their commentaries (on Lamentations) both scholars translate the phrase in a general sense, *viz* 'Menschenkinder' (Kraus, 51) and 'human beings' (Gerstenberger 2001, 494). The context here requires the meaning 'men, people' in general, and not distinguished or mighty men.

מִלִּבּוֹ—Although the combination of לב with the preposition מן is found elsewhere (Num 16.28; Ps 31.12; Isa 59.13; Ezek 13.2, 17), the other contexts do not raise the same problem as here. What does it mean to say that Yahweh does not afflict 'from his heart'? With the exception of T, the Versions translate literally. T's paraphrase imagines two subjects in this verse,[145] man and God, and speaks of *man* not removing arrogance *from his heart*. Rashi, IE[1] and Kara gloss the phrase with מרצונו 'from his will', Rashi pointing out that the affliction comes because of iniquity; and Kara sees the phrase as applying to vv. 34 and 35 also. MLT cites Ezek 18.23 in this regard: 'Yahweh has no pleasure in the death of the wicked'; that is to say, the phrase is taken as adverbial—'willingly', cf. AV, REB. Vermigli (131ff.) is exercised by this meaning, as though God may do something unwillingly! Calvin, although translating literally—*ex corde suo*—admits that the expression is problematic, but points out 'it is enough to know that God derives no pleasure from the miseries of men'. In Jeremiah (7.31; 19.5; 32.35) Yahweh is depicted as distancing himself from idolatry in Judah—לא עלתה על לבי 'it did not come into my mind'. What the poet is saying here is that Yahweh is not a God of affliction: it is not in his nature to grieve human beings. The passage does not deny that Yahweh has afflicted and grieved—vv. 1-18 have made it quite clear that Yahweh is the author of terrible affliction—but that afflicting is not of the essence of Yahweh. That is why Renkema (409f.) introduces the concept of punishment. Yahweh's nature is such that he must punish iniquity, though he would rather not have needed to, cf. Keil 416.

---

[143] P translates ܒܢܝ ܓܒܪ̈ܐ *bny gbrʾ* 'sons of mighty men' or 'mighty men', where we might have expected ܒܢܝ ܐܢܫܐ *bny ʾnšʾ* (cf. at Ps 4.3). The other Versions support MT.

[144] Gerstenberger (1988, 55) notes that, while the phrase occurs only four times in the Hebrew Bible (Pss 4.3; 49.3; 62.10; Lam 3.33), the number of בני occurrences is about 2000, and the more general בני אדם occurs 62 times in Psalms alone. 'The scant evidence available…could therefore indicate that this designation may signify "nobleman, of noble descent"…just like *mār awilim* in some Old Babylonian texts (*AHw* I, 90)'.

[145] Alexander (2008, 153 n. 49) detects that T 'sees the first half of the verse as picking up the thought of vv. 28-30: humility will in the end turn away God's anger'.

3.34-36

Text and Versions

MT לֹא רָאָה—followed by P; LXX οὐκ εἶπεν followed by OL *non dixit*; V *ignoravit*; LXX (OL) is usually taken as an inner Greek error (for εἶδε), perhaps occasioned by the nearby εἶπεν in v. 37; cf. Schäfer (127f.*), Rudolph (1938, 113).

* * *

Some scholars find the syntax of this stanza impossible. Böttcher (1863, III, 205) resorts to emendation, reading רצה for ראה, and in this he is followed by Löhr (1894, 16), though Löhr (1906, 20) later changes his mind. Budde (1898ᵃ, 95) and Hillers² (116) note that ראה is not normally found with an infinitive with ל. Hillers, therefore, prefers to explain the infinitives as dependent on the parallel verbs in v. 33. Verse 36b is then seen as a circumstantial clause; but the resultant translation leaves a lot to be desired.

Although the text is not seriously in question throughout, the ambiguity of v. 36b has led translators and commentators to take up various exegetical positions. Would-be exegetes have long been puzzled by the stanza. Is it self-contained? In which case, what is the syntax? What relationship does it have with v. 33 or, indeed, v. 37?

As early as the LXX, translators have considered the three infinitives, with which each verse begins, to be an indication that the author understood each in the same way and that v. 36b amounted to the main clause in the passage vv. 34-36. Hence, although interpretations vary, one finds this followed in P, V, Luther, Calvin, AV, RV, NJB, NIV, NRSV. We may divide the latter into (a) those who take v. 36b as an indicative,[146] and (b) those who think it a rhetorical interrogative[147] (cf. GK 150a); but even within (a) and (b) interpretations vary. Quite apart from v. 36b, factors which may detain the exegete are the referent of the suffix 'his' (v. 34a), and the meaning of אֲסִירֵי אָרֶץ (v. 34b) and נֶגֶד פְּנֵי עֶלְיוֹן (v. 35b).

לֹא רָאָה—The second stich of v. 36 is problematic. T is the only Version that renders in the interrogative: 'Is it possible that this shall not be revealed before Yahweh?'[148] The other Versions translate in the indicative.

---

[146] LXX, V, P, AV, RSV, Gottwald (14), Meek (27), Douai, NEB, Gottlieb (50), Rudolph (1962, 232), Renkema (415), O'Connor (2001, 1052), Dobbs-Allsopp (2002, 121).

[147] T, Luther, Michaelis (1773–88, 430), Nägelsbach (120), Keil (401), NJB, NIV, Löhr (1906, 20), Haller (104), Kaiser (345), Kraus (51), Wiesmann (191), Westermann (166), Berlin (83).

[148] Several translators and exegetes have seen here a rhetorical question. It is true that a question need not be introduced by an interrogative particle (GK 150 a): context and natural emphasis may be enough to indicate that a question is present, e.g. Gen 27.24; 1 Sam 11.12; Jonah 4.11. It is, however, not at all certain that such conditions prevail here, and the exegete must choose the direction in which to go. The effect of the question at the end of v. 36 is to link the entire stanza with the preceding context in which the poet

It is just possible that V's *Vorlage* was לא ידע, though it is also possible that Jerome was just trying to make sense of לא ראה (and it may be that LXX's οὐκ εἶπεν was trying to do the same). V *ignoravit* is interesting. Jerome may have had Ps 73.11 and Isa 40.27 in mind here, or Ps 31.8 where ידע and ראה are in parallel (cf. 1 Sam 12.17; 14.38; Jer 2.19; Job 28.7). His translation suggests that he understood the passage vv. 34-36 as a statement of despair on the part of the poet. God does not pay attention to atrocity and injustice: he does not act, cf. Gen 20.10 which connects 'seeing' and 'acting'.[149] Rashi comments (on לא ראה) לא הוכשר בעיניו 'It did not seem right in his eyes'; and Kara follows this exactly.[150] The view that ראה can mean 'approve' is followed by AV, RV, Blayney (324), Nägelsbach (120), Ewald (339), Ehrlich (43), Gottwald (14), Gordis (143), Meek (27), McDaniel (38), NEB, cf. JPS 'choose'. Calvin is aware of several interpretations of the passage. His conclusion is that the passage reflects the unbelieving element in Israel: a complaint that God is not moved by cruelty and injustice, *Ad conterendum... Ad pervertendum (ad declinandum)... Ad pervertendum... Dominus non videt.* Rudolph (1962, 229, 232, cf. 240f.) also, taking the passage (vv. 34-36) as a whole, regards it as an objection (*Einwand*) of the author's fellow-countrymen in parenthesis and translates the final stich '...das hat den Herrn nicht gekümmert'. Gottlieb (49f.) roughly takes the same line except that he regards the objection as part of the poet's *own* fluctuating feelings of trust and despair, cf. vv. 21-24, 29, 31-33: 'There is nothing to prevent the man praying thereafter expressing his despair over the fact that Yahweh does not intervene in the concrete situation of distress. Verse 36b should be read as a statement in the indicative, as an expression of the fact that the man praying is conscious of being deserted by God.' Renkema (415-18) argues strongly along the same lines. He draws attention to the employment of ראה, addressing Yahweh, at 1.9c, 11c, 20a; 5.1. He regards it as a primary theme in the book, whether Yahweh will pay heed to his people's affliction, but here the scepticism prevails: 'This frequently repeated and urgent appeal to YHWH to look down and see his people's affliction implies, in fact, that he has not done so up to the present moment. It would appear that he does not want to see, that he has become estranged from his people.' Dobbs-Allsopp (2002, 121) agrees that v. 36b should be read 'as a straightforward declarative clause'; and he further observes: 'The hyperbolic claim that God does not see (3.36) serves to point up all the places in Lamentations where God is requested to see and look upon the destruction (1.9c, 20a; 2.20a; 3.59-60, 63; 5.1)'. The speaker, who has related his

---

is trying to restore faith in a merciful God. This effect has been sufficient reward for those who see a question here.

[149] We should note that the translations of V: Douai 'hath not approved' and Knox 'cannot overlook it' seem to be embarrassed with their *Vorlage*.

[150] MLT is almost the same but uses ראוי, a Mishnaic term (= appropriate), cf. רְאָיוֹת at Est 2.9.

own dire experiences at the hands of Yahweh, is not here complaining about that adversity. In vv. 31-33 he has trotted out statements which belong to his past upbringing which encourage him to hope for Yahweh's deliverance, statements which portray Yahweh in a better light. He does not say that that is his experience of Yahweh's dealings. In this passage he appears to juxtapose that high view of Yahweh with an observation that the same Yahweh pays no attention to severe cruelty in the world. Whether it is the observation of the unbelieving in Israel (Calvin) or the objection of his fellow countrymen (Rudolph) or a conclusion of his own (Gottlieb) is difficult to say. The examples he gives (of cruelty and injustice) do not seem to be personal experiences but rather general observations, so that Rudolph's interpretation may be the correct one. It is all very well to speak of Yahweh's great mercy etc., but what about the blatant, shameless injustice and cruelty in the world, which he seems to ignore?

תַּחַת רַגְלָיו—If there is a strong connection between v. 34 and v. 33, then the suffix may refer to Yahweh (v. 31), the subject of vv. 32f. and the referent of the suffixes there. Rashi, who links vv. 33 and 34, takes 'his feet' to be Yahweh's feet: 'God does not afflict willingly by crushing...'; and Kara takes the same line. But if, as seems likely, the stanza does not connect syntactically with v. 33, the suffix need not refer to Yahweh but to 'oppressors' or 'enemies'; and we may translate 'underfoot'—Gottwald (14), RSV, Gordis (142), Wiesmann (191), Berlin (79), NIV, NEB, NJB, NRSV, Westermann (162). The phrase is not to be taken literally. Elsewhere we find references to 'crushing the needy' (Amos 4.1) and 'crush my young men' (Lam 1.15) where the meaning must be 'severe subjugation' or 'abusive treatment'.

כָּל אֲסִירֵי אָרֶץ—The phrase is obscure. כל may be taken in the sense of 'all' or 'any'. The entire line conjures up extreme cruelty. At Pss 68.7 and 69.34, prisoners are the object of God's compassion, and one may associate God with hearing their groans, in Ps 102.21. Here, the action is of the oppressor paying no heed to the groans and to the situation of the vulnerable in society and actually increasing their misery. The phrase occurs only here. Kara explains it as 'those in correction' but later glosses it with 'those subdued with toil'. MLT thinks the meaning is equivalent to 'the sons of man' (v. 33). NEB's 'any prisoner in the land' seems to restrict the meaning to refer to Palestine, cf. Meek (26), Wiesmann (186), Rudolph (1962, 229), Kraus (51), Westermann (162), Renkema (412), Berlin (79), but REB 'prisoners anywhere on earth', cf. Luther, Calvin, AV, Vermigli (134), Gottwald (14), JPS, Kaiser (344), Gordis (142), Hillers[2] (111) takes a broader view. It seems that this line (v. 34) alludes to extreme cruelty on the part of the perpetrator. To crush the disadvantaged is bad enough, but to crush those who are already in custody, or bound in fetters (cf. IE[2]) is wicked; it is, we imagine, contrary to what God would do (Ps 68.7). That the speaker is referring to actual captives on the occasion of a particular event as, for example, the fall of Jerusalem, is unlikely.

לְהַטּוֹת מִשְׁפַּט־גָּבֶר—The Hiphil of נטה√ ('reach out') can mean 'to twist', and it is construed with מִשְׁפָּט at Exod 23.6; Deut 16.19; 24.17; 27.19; Prov 17.23. The author has in mind the distortion of justice, forbidden in Israel.

נֶגֶד פְּנֵי עֶלְיוֹן—The term עליון occurs also at v. 38, and it is likely that it means the same in both passages. Levine (143f.) thinks that T's rendering אפי עלאה is not a reference to the deity but to a powerful human litigant and, in support, draws attention to T's translation of גבר viz גבר מסכן 'a poor man'; that is, T sees here the situation where justice is denied to the poor man before the powerful. But Greenup (30), Brady (162) and Alexander (154) translate 'the Most High', and in v. 38 T clearly understands עליון as referring to God.[151] The author, then, is describing the practice of distorting justice; and he emphasises its blatancy by adding this phrase. The injustice is done 'in the very face of the Most High', i.e. shamelessly.

לְעַוֵּת אָדָם בְּרִיבוֹ—The first stich of v. 36 resembles that of v. 35; indeed, IE¹ comments: מלת הטה עם משפט כמו עוות. The verb עות (Piel) means 'to bend'. It is construed with מִשְׁפָּט at Job 8.3; 34.12. Here it is construed with רִיב 'lawsuit, legal process'. The idea is of legal subversion. LXX καταδικάσαι (OL *condemnandum*) and P ܠܡܚܝܒܘ *lmḥybw* may be a little strong. Robinson (1933, 258), who notes that LXX καταδικάσαι usually translates the Hiphil of רשע, thinks that the original may have been ἀδικῆσαι, which LXX uses for יְעַוֵּת at Job 8.3; cf. *BHK*.[152]

3.37

Text and Versions
No significant material.

* * *

The poet picks up on the divine responsibility for what happens on earth.

In this and in the following verse (38) we encounter rhetorical questions. Verse 37 begins with the interrogative מִי 'who?'. The combination מִי זֶה is emphatic. There is a suppressed relative pronoun אשר before אמר which is represented by V—*qui*.

---

[151] Although עליון occurs (22 times) in secular contexts to differentiate between something high and something lower (gate: 2 Kgs 15.35; courtyard: Jer 36.10; tower: Neh 3.25) and even to David's superiority as king (Ps 89.28), it is not used in the way Levine claims.
[152] The fact that P renders 'condemn' leads Kelso (44) to suspect P's dependence on LXX, but Albrektson (151) cautions against such a conclusion.

וַתֶּהִי—*Waw*-consecutive + apocopated form of 3rd p. f. s.[153] imperf. (תִּהְיֶה) of היה, and vocalised in pause, cf. Ps 33.9—כִּי הוּא אָמַר וַיֶּהִי. One is immediately struck by this vocabulary היה...אמר, echoing 'creation' passages in Genesis (1.3, 6, 7, 8, 9, 11, 24); and the combination of these two verbs with the verb צוה (second stich) is echoed in Ps 33.9, again a reference to creation; cf. Ps 148.5.

In the absence of a coordinating particle, the second stich looks like a statement, but it is probably to be taken as a rhetorical question (הֲלֹא = לֹא) given momentum from the first stich which was introduced by מִי. The second stich is usually interpreted as a conditional clause, so V, Luther, AV, Ewald (339), Ehrlich (43), Rudolph (1962, 229), JPS, NEB, NIV, NRSV, Nägelsbach (121), Wiesmann (186), Kraus (51), Westermann (163). However, Albrektson (152) points out that 'v. 37a must then refer to men, which is highly improbable'. It is better to see here a rhetorical question: 'Who spoke and it came to be? (followed by another) Has not the Lord commanded it?' McDaniel (208) takes another line. He understands לֹא as the emphatic particle[154] לְא and translates the second stich: 'Verily, the Lord has ordained it'; and Hillers[2] (117) adopts this.

3.38

Text and Versions

MT וְהַטּוֹב followed by LXX and T; LXX[L] τα ἀγαθα followed by SH margin, P and V; MS[Ken] והטובת. The accuracy of MT is not generally questioned. LXX follows MT exactly, though the Lucian recension, SH margin, P and V appear to favour the plural reading והטובות. Driver (1960, 115) regards והטוב as an abbreviation for הטובות, but his claim that he is supported by P, V and Budde is, perhaps, unfounded. All may be harmonising (so *BHQ*), and Budde (1898[a], 96) certainly is! It is true that the combination, as in MT, is unbalanced, and it may be that the variations of V, P etc. do not represent another Hebrew text but are attempts at balancing the second stich. It is interesting that the Targum, though a paraphrase, also maintains a balance, but with a *singular* in each case (בשתא...טובא). We may note that it is usually *translated* in a balanced manner, cf. AV, RV, Luther, Calvin, NIV, JPS, NJB, REB, NRSV.

* * *

Problems continue with this verse. Do we have another rhetorical question here, or is a statement being made? The early exegesis of this passage shows no signs of it having been regarded as a question. None of the Versions, including the paraphrastic T, betray any knowledge of an interrogative.[155] IE[2], Kara, MLT and MR all read the passage as a statement, clearing the Most High of causing evil. Calvin, on the other hand,

---

[153] The feminine form (cf. Ps 33.9 ויהי) is to be explained by the tendency to refer to the abstract with the feminine gender (GK 122 q). Thus Isa 7.7 לֹא תָקוּם וְלֹא תִהְיֶה.
[154] Cf. Haupt (1894, 107-108; 1905, 201; GK 143e).
[155] Douai, supposedly a translation of the Vulgate, does render in question form: 'Shall not both evil and good proceed out of the mouth of the Highest?'

although he presents two translations, rightly favours the rhetorical question, which he interprets to imply that both good and evil *do* proceed from the mouth of the Most High; and this is how most commentators and translators have taken it. Renkema (421ff.) takes an unusual line with this verse. He draws attention to the phrase מִפִּי עֶלְיוֹן and compares it with מִפִּי יְהוָה of Jer 23.16 which passage has to do with (false) prophecy. For him, הָרָעוֹת refers to evil words. He then takes the following *waw* as adversative. His translation is 'From the mouth of the Most High come not evil words, but the good.' Ehrlich (43f.) emends the text to read הָרַע אֶת הַטּוֹב. Gordis (183) follows this reading, declaring that the Hebrew is impossible and translating the whole line: 'Not from the mouth of the Most High issues (the decision) to bring suffering on the righteous man'.

3.39

Text and Versions

MT יִתְאוֹנֵן; LXX γογγύσει; P ܡܬܚܫܒ *mtḥšb*; V *murmuravit*. MT is preferred.

MT (*Kethib*) חֶטְאוֹ followed by LXX; MT (*Qere*) חֲטָאָיו followed by several Hebrew MSS[Ken], P, V and T. MT (*Kethib*) is preferred; see below.

* * *

There are a number of exegetical issues which arise in this verse. There is the meaning of the rare verb יתאונן; there is the unusual phrase אדם חי; there is the inclusion of the term גבר in the second stich; there is the meaning of חטאו (*Kethib*), חטאיו (*Qere*); and there is the question of whether the whole verse consists of one question or a question and an answer.

יִתְאוֹנֵן[156]—The root אנן occurs only in the Hithpoel in the Hebrew Bible (here and at Num 11.1 מִתְאוֹנְנִים), though it also occurs in Sir 10.25 (יתאונן). LXX translates 'murmur, grumble' (as at Num 11.1), as does V.[157] P translates 'consider, plan', although at Num 11.1 the rendering is ܪܛܢ *rṭnw* 'murmur'. It may be, as Rudolph (1938, 113) claims, that the Syriac translator read יתבונן, though Albrektson (153) puts the P reading down to unfamiliarity with the rare word.[158] None of the mediaeval rabbis dispute the meaning 'complain', but Calvin is aware of various renderings—Why should a man lie? Why should a man harden himself? Why should a man murmur? He rejects them all and takes the meaning to be: Why does a living man weary himself? However, it is Luther's translation 'murren' which the majority of subsequent scholars adopt; hence, Gesenius (1835, 126) *conquestus, quiritatus est*; cf. BDB (59).

---

[156] On the pointing of י (in מה יתאונן) with *dagesh forte conjunctivum*, see GK 20c-f; 37b.
[157] Why V translates in the past tense is strange. It may be that Jerome associated the complaining with that of the גבר of vv. 1-18, and so in the past; but the reading probably does not reflect a different *Vorlage*.
[158] Cf. Ehrlich (44) who adopts the reading יתבונן.

The term חי occurs at Ps 143.2 (in the phrase כל חי) with the meaning 'living person'. It would seem that it occurs here to emphasise אדם as a living human, a man who is alive, cf. Löhr (1894, 16: '...ein Mensch, solange er lebt'. Nägelsbach (120) says that 'it reminds us of the grammatical construction אל חי, Pss 42.3; 84.3...' The emphatic use of חי here is perhaps a reminder that many have perished in the adversity experienced by the poet; and Renkema (423) translates 'a survivor', cf. Provan (99).[159] The appearance of גבר in the second stich is considered strange, but the poet has employed אדם at v. 36 and גבר at v. 35, presumably for variety of expression—cf. Job 14.10; 16.21; 33.17; Prov 20.24; Jer 17.5. גבר is then just picking up the reference to אדם in the first stich; or we might take אדם as generic 'men' (cf. Luther 'die Leute') and גבר as 'a man'.

Scholars differ on the meaning of the final term in the line. The Versions are almost as obscure as MT. LXX, following *Kethib*, translates with ἁμαρτίας αὐτοῦ, a term (ἁμαρτία) which can only mean 'sin, fault'; so also P. V *pro peccatis suis* can bear the meaning 'sin' and 'punishment for sin' (cf. V at Num 32.23; Isa 53.12), while T's paraphrase is too remote to be helpful here. Gesenius (465) rightly understands this passage to mean *poena peccati*; so also BDB; *DCH*, III, 197; cf. AV, Löhr (1894, 16), NRSV, NIV, Gordis (184), Meek (27), Hillers[1] (111), Berlin (80), House (420). Others follow *Qere* and render 'his sins'—Budde (1898[a], 96), Kaiser (345), Keil (401), Gottwald (14), Kraus (52), Wiesmann (187), Rudolph (1962, 229), Westermann (163). The trouble with the latter meaning is that the line then appears to ask why a man should complain about (or against) his sins; and this does not seem to make good sense. Hence, we find in Rashi, Kara, MLT and MR the tendency to interpret as though two points were being made, the second being that a man *ought* to complain about his sins because they have brought trouble on him. But in order to interpret thus, one must not read the line as only comprising a rhetorical question: one must see here a question plus an answer. In MR the first stich is interpreted separately from the second. Thus, the first comment on 'Why should a living man complain?' is 'It is enough that he lives!' And R. Huna is quoted as saying: 'Let him stand up like a strong man, let him confess his sins and let him not complain'. It would seem that the Midrashists took the verse to be a question plus answer; and this is the structure perceived by Luther—'Wie murren denn die Leute im Leben also? Ein jeglicher murre wider seine Sünde!' cf. also Budde (1898[a], 96), Westermann (163), Rudolph (1962, 232), Gottlieb (52), Driver (1950, 140), Kaiser (345), JB, NJB, JPS. The latter reads: 'Of what shall a living man complain? Each one of his own sins!'

---

[159] Some scholars think that the phrase is simply equivalent to אדם: so Kaiser (345), Haller (104), Gottlieb (51), Hillers[2] (111), cf. JB, NJB. The problem is not solved by reading against the accent and connecting חי with גבר. This merely shifts the problem to the second stich and compounds it, in that the adjective חי is now in a problematic position vis-à-vis גבר.

Some scholars feel that the Hebrew will not yield such an interpretation without emendation. Thus Driver (1940, 140) suggests that a י has dropped out through haplography and that the text should be restored to יִגְבַּר עַל חֲטָאָיו 'let him be master of his sins'. *BHK* suggests that יהי be read for חי, which NJB adopts 'Better to be bold against one's sins'. Westermann (166) also adopts this, offering the (literal) rendering 'Let him become master over his sins'.[160] Not satisfied with the latter, Rudolph (1938, 113), again reading יהי, vocalises גְּבַר (as in Gen 27.29) but obtains the same sense; so also Haller (104), *BHS*.[161]

While it is possible that MT is corrupt, it should be said that it may be translated and understood satisfactorily. יתאונן may do double duty, functioning in the second stich as well as in the first. אדם חי may have the force simply of אדם, or the poet may have been alluding to those survivors of calamity. The use of גבר in the second stich can be seen to be picking up the subject of the first and may be an allusion to the figure of vv. 1-18 who had been complaining. If *Kethib* is preferred to *Qere*, חֶטְאוֹ can be interpreted as consequence for sin, i.e. punishment, and the entire line seen as the poet questioning a man's right to complain about his punishment in the light of the sovereignty of God (vv. 37f.).

3.40

Text and Versions

Text and syntax are straightforward. LXX misunderstands the first two cohortatives (which occur nowhere else in the Hebrew Bible) as Niphal perfects and either read דרכנו 'our way' or ignored the י in MT דרכינו (Kelso, 44) but took it as the subject of these verbs. When it came to ונשובה, the translator recognised the cohortative (there being no Niphal of שוב!), but it did not occur to him to reconsider the first two verbs in the context of the verse; cf. Albrektson (153f.). P, V and T read three cohortatives.

* * *

Punishment for sin now prompts the poet to reflect on the present circumstances and the suffering described earlier. Because his lament is on behalf of his community, he now employs 1st p. pl. verbal forms, the first in the poem so far; and this is sustained in verbal form and suffix until v. 47.

---

[160] Westermann (163) interprets this statement to mean 'Let us all master our own sins'.
[161] Though he does not adopt the suggestion—he regards it only as a possibility—Rudolph notes that חי גבר may be a corruption of חיו כרע (haplography of ע): 'Was murrt der Mensch über sein Leben? Er beuge die Knie wegen sein Sünde.' Dahood (187) offers yet another suggestion. He takes חי to be the target of the complaining: 'With עליון in the preceding verse it forms a composite divine title whose roots are also found in the Samaria Ostraca personal name yhw'ly, as well as in the parallel cola of Ps 30.4 and 71.20...' Repointing גְּבַר עַל, he translates 'Why does man complain about the Living God, if the malice of his sins runs its course?'

The two verbs חפש and חקר occur here together for the only time in the Hebrew Bible. They reinforce one another: חפש used in parallel with בקש at Prov 2.4, means 'search, test'; חקר has a similar and, perhaps, more intensive meaning—'explore'.[162] The poet, who now identifies himself with his community, realises that the adversity experienced by him and others is due to the misbehaviour of his people; and he advocates a thorough examination of the ways or practices which presently characterise his community before approaching Yahweh in repentance.

וְנָשׁוּבָה—'And let us return'. The verb does not always mean 'to return in repentance' (cf. at 3.3) but that is the meaning here. T, which is otherwise word for word with MT, feels the need to render ונתוב בתיובתא 'and let us return in repentance' (cf. T at Eccl 7.2). Albrektson (154) thinks that the expression שוב עד is stronger (and rarer) than שוב אל, but this is not demonstrated; and Hos 6.1 שוב אל and 14.2 שוב עד probably show that they are interchangeable. Wolff (1969, 260) thinks that שוב עד was primarily used for returning to Yahweh from worshipping foreign gods, but this too, as Renkema (429) notes, cannot be maintained. There is certainly no overt allusion to apostasy in the context. While the prophets, like Hosea, who called for a return to Yahweh, often had apostasy in mind, the sins of which they spoke—neglect of orphans and widows, heartless treatment of the poor—were also included; and the poet here has not mentioned and does not mention other deities.

3.41

Text and Versions
MT אֶל־כַּפָּיִם; LXX ἐπὶ χειρῶν; P ܠܐܝܕܝܢ 'l 'ydyn; V *cum manibus*; Sym σὺν. MT is not in question; see below.

* * *

The exhortation continues in this verse, with the poet urging his community to pray to Yahweh in sincerity.

The textual and exegetical issues here are the phrase אֶל־כַּפַּיִם and the form לְבָבֵנוּ. The line begins with another cohortative[163] נִשָּׂא. IE¹ makes a brief comment, citing Gen 43.34, which seems to warn against interpreting the verb too literally. Although MT reads 'our heart' (singular), LXX, P, V

---

[162] V *quaeramus* 'let us seek' seems to miss the mark here. Jerome usually translates חקר with *investigare* (Job 5.27; 8.8; 28.27; Pss 44.22; 139.1; Prov 18.17; Eccl 12.9). It may be, however, that he linked חקר more closely with the following verb (שוב), in which case he saw the seeking as part of the return to Yahweh.

[163] Albeit without the characteristic ending (GK 48c,d); cf. König (197 b); Rudolph (1962, 232).

and T render in the plural, as though the text before them read לבבינו: and many MSS^{Ken} concur.¹⁶⁴ The sense of the passage is not affected, and Albrektson (154) notes that the plural 'is very natural in the context'. In this regard, we might note that at Josh 2.11 and 1 Kgs 8.58, where לבבינו occurs in some MSS, AV translates לְבָבֵנוּ 'our hearts'; and at 1 Kgs 8.58, LXX renders in the plural. In fact, לבב hardly occurs in the plural (Nah 2.8 reads לְבָבֵהֶן while 1 Chron 28.9 reads לְבָבוֹת); hence it would seem likely that MT is original.

אֶל־כַּפָּיִם—This reading has long puzzled translators and exegetes. The translations of LXX and P have led some (e.g. BHK, BHS) to assume that in the *Vorlagen* the reading was על for אל, while V *cum* appears to differ again¹⁶⁵ and accords with Sym. It is likely that the Versions were confused as to the precise meaning here. Rashi paraphrases: 'When we lift up our hands to Heaven, let us also lift our heart with them'; and this corresponds with Kara who spells it out: 'The interpretation is עם כפים—Let us lift up our hands with our hearts (לבבינו)'. So also Luther 'Lasst uns unser Herz samt den Händen aufheben…' and Calvin *cum manibus*; cf. AV, Blayney (159), NJB, NIV, REB, JPS,¹⁶⁶ Hillers² (117), Renkema (429), Dobbs-Allsopp (123), Berlin (80), Schäfer (128*); cf. NRSV 'as well as'. Rashi alludes to another explanation: אל כפים can mean 'into the clouds', since כף may mean 'cloud' at Job 36.32, cf. also 1 Kgs 18.44; and Vermigli (138) looks favourably on this suggestion, citing also Exod 33.22.

Beginning with Goldziher (1911, 73),¹⁶⁷ followed to some extent, by Ehrlich (44) and Perles (1922, 26), some scholars prefer to emend the text, reading וְאַל כפים. This assumes haplography of ו. Driver (1950, 140) embraces this suggestion, reading נשא לבבינו (וְ)אַל כַּפֵּינוּ 'let us lift up our hearts (and) not our hands'. He cites Joel 2.13 וְקִרְעוּ לְבַבְכֶם וְאַל־בִּגְדֵיכֶם in support. This (without the ו) has been followed by NEB;¹⁶⁸ cf. also Gordis¹⁶⁹ (185), Gottwald (14), Kaiser (345), Kraus (53) and McKane (1974, 101). Keil (420) retains MT, claiming that the image is of the heart being lifted up to the hands (that are raised towards heaven). Albrektson (154f.) also retains MT. Citing Lev 18.18 וְאִשָּׁה אֶל אֲחֹתָהּ לֹא תִקָּח 'and you shall not take a woman in addition to her sister' and drawing attention to Lam 2.19 שְׂאִי אֵלָיו כַּפַּיִךְ, he argues that 'it is not so much a matter of lifting up the hearts *instead of* the hands as *in addition to* them'.

---

¹⁶⁴ This is the only occurrence of לבב in Lamentations; at 5.15, 17, the form is לבנו (from לב).
¹⁶⁵ BHK thinks that Jerome's *Vorlage* read עם.
¹⁶⁶ JPS does have a footnote: Lit. *'to'; emendation yields 'rather than'; cf. Joel 2.13.*
¹⁶⁷ Goldziher actually reads וְאַל כפינו.
¹⁶⁸ At least, Brockington (218) does not record it.
¹⁶⁹ Gordis's reading accords with Goldziher, and he points out that, at Josh 5.1, there has been a scribal confusion—נו Kethib ם Qere—and also at Ps 12.8 'where תִּצְּרֶנּוּ is parallel to תִּשְׁמְרֵם and obviously the same person is required in both suffixes'.

אֶל־אֵל בַּשָּׁמָיִם—This is the only occurrence of אֵל for God in Lamentations. 'In heaven', God's dwelling-place, has been occasioned by the movement of the hands upward in prayer; cf. Hillers[2] (111) 'to God above'.

All commentators are agreed that the poet is urging sincerity in his community in their approach to Yahweh. The custom in Ancient Israel was to raise the hands in prayer to God (Exod 9.29, 33; Ezra 9.5; Job 11.13; Pss 28.2; 44.20; 63.5; 119.48; 134.2; Isa 1.15), but like any liturgical act the attitude can become an empty gesture if the worshipper's heart is not in it. We are reminded of Hos 7.14 'they do not cry to me from the heart'. Our poet, then, before supplying the words of the prayer, encourages the people to make sure that the approach to God in heaven is sincere and genuine, and not empty ritual. He is not ruling out the lifting of the hands (which is what the emendation of Perles etc. seems to imply).

3.42

Text and Versions

MT נַחְנוּ—followed by P, V, T and SH; LXX does not represent נחנו, and Bickell (115) deletes it, though preserving the acrostic by reading וְנִפְשַׁעְנוּ. However, the Niphal of פשע occurs only dubiously at Prov 18.19 (see BDB 833), while the Qal (MT) fits well with the context.[170] LXX does not represent the copula[171] between the two verbs of the first stich, although it is found in P and V. T agrees with LXX. On the other hand, LXX has a copula introducing the second stich, as does P and T, whereas V agrees with MT[172]

* * *

Having urged his community to proceed in sincerity (v. 41), the poet appears to lead and to supply the words of the prayer to Yahweh. He begins with confession and moves quickly to accusation.

The form נחנו 'we' occurs only at Gen 42.11; Exod 16.7, 8; Num 32.32; 2 Sam 17.12 and here. Although אנחנו is more common in the Hebrew Bible, it is a later form, as is evident from Akkadian, Arabic and Ethiopic;[173] and IE[1] notes that the א is additional (נוסף). The demands of the acrostic influenced the poet here. In vv. 40f., the cohortatives (beginning with נ) served his purpose, but now he wants the people to join him in addressing Yahweh (v. 40) and confessing in the perfect tense. Because the poet employs the pronoun אתה in the second stich, we must see that he

---

[170] Cf. Albrektson (155f.) who excuses the LXX translator by claiming that the Greek verbal ending includes the pronoun, just as the non-representation of אתה in the second stich is seen to be included in the Greek ἱλάσθης. It should be noted that אתה is represented by SH.
[171] Possibly due to haplography; see Schäfer (128*).
[172] Cf. also variations in modern translations: JB, NEB, NJB, NIV, NRSV, JPS.
[173] See Moscati (1964, §13.1).

wishes to draw a contrast: 'We...you...'[174] Having requested sincerity (v. 41), the poet now supplies the words of the prayer (beginning at v. 42 and continuing at least as far as v. 47). Although the noun פֶּשַׁע occurs at 1.5, 14, 22, this is the only occurrence of the verb in Lamentations. It is usually translated 'to transgress' (AV) and carries the idea of deliberately crossing the boundaries. The verb מרה 'to rebel' occurs also at 1.18, 20 where the personified Jerusalem admits to having rebelled against Yahweh. The force of מרה is similar to פשע. Both are stronger than חטא 'to sin'.

Rashi regards the first stich as confession. He paraphrases: 'This is our way [perhaps with v. 40 in mind] because of the evil inclination'. He then appears to take the second stich as accusation, pointing out that forgiveness is God's way! Kara takes the same line: 'We have done what belongs to us...but you did not do what belongs to you'.[175] MLT quotes R Huna (in the name of R Joseph): 'We have sinned and rebelled honestly (באמונתינו). You have not forgiven honestly (באמונתך)', and MR quotes the same Rabbi with slightly different adverbial phrasing: 'according to our nature (כמדתינו)...according to your nature (כמדותיך)'. IE² has a different slant on the passage: 'Israel confesses that they did not return to God, therefore he did not forgive'; and this accords with the T paraphrase 'We have rebelled and disobeyed and, since we did not return to you, you have not forgiven'.[176] Vermigli (139), too, sees in the second stich a further confession 'one of the praise of divine justice. In the same way that they confess that they have sinned, so they attribute justice to God, who punished them in this way.' Calvin is aware that there are views on this passage other then his own: 'The faithful do not here expostulate with God, but on the contrary acknowledge that God's severity was just. That God then had dealt with them severely, they ascribe to their own sins. This is the substance of what is said'; cf. also Luther's translation of the second stich: '...darum hast du nicht vergeben'; cf. Keil (421).

But Rashi's instinct is probably correct: there is accusation here. The confession of sin is thorough—the poet uses two verbs which cover all eventualities vis-à-vis Yahweh. The ball is now in Yahweh's court. The poet had been brought up to believe that sin and rebellion provoked God's anger; and he had also been taught that confession/repentance brought about divine forgiveness (Pss 32.5; 86.5). The latter, however, has not been forthcoming. Yahweh has not kept his side of the bargain, as it were. The use of the pronouns is important here: אתה is surely to be translated 'but you...'; cf. Dobbs-Allsopp (123).

---

[174] The poet uses personal pronouns only here and at v. 1 and v. 63.
[175] The idea that forgiveness belongs to God may arise from the fact that in the Hebrew Bible the verb סלח is used only of God forgiving, never of humans forgiving one another; cf. Hausmann (1999, 259). At Pss 86.5; 103.3; 130.4 forgiveness is referred to as a characteristic of Yahweh.
[176] Cf. also V *idcirco tu inexorabilis es*.

3.43

Text and Versions

MT לֹא—so also LXX; many MSS^Ken ולא—so also P, V, SH, T; We note that elsewhere in Lamentations, practice varies. Thus at 2.17 we get ולא חמל, but at 2.21 and here it is חמל לא; and at 2.2, *Kethib* is לא חמל while *Qere* is ולא חמל. The absence of the ו gives the construction an adverbial force 'without mercy', cf. NRSV, NJB, NIV, NEB at 2.21 and here. *BHQ* implies that the inclusion of the ו is spontaneous. Calvin renders *et non pepercisti*, and Luther reads 'und ohne Erbarmen'.[177] MT is preferred.

MT בָּאַף—so also LXX, V and T; P ܒܪܘܓܙܟ. MT is preferred (see below).

* * *

The accusation continues with this verse, which is remarkable for its having four (finite) verbal forms. The plethora of verbs, coming after 'you did not forgive'(v. 42), gives the impression of an accuser bursting forth with pent-up emotions, as though he had been waiting for this opportunity.

The text is not generally thought to be in doubt. According to *BHK*, P read בְּאַפְּךָ, but, as Albrektson (156f.) points out, the Syriac translator is inclined to make minor additions in translation, cf. v. 42 where he also added the same (explanatory) suffix (*BHQ*, Kelso, 45).

סַכֹּתָה—The main problem in this verse is the meaning of סַכֹּתָה, a form with which v. 44 also begins. The fact that there is more then one root סכך in the Hebrew Bible (BDB and Jastrow show two, and *HALOT*, three) increases grounds for disagreement among scholars. Ehrlich (44), while accepting the form in v. 44, finds סַכֹּתָה unacceptable here and emends to סַבֹּתָה (from סבב): 'du hast dich umgewendet'. NEB follows this suggestion: 'in anger thou hast turned',[178] as does Wiesmann (188), though he takes סַבֹּתָה as transitive, with 'us' as object: 'im Zorne hast du uns umstellt...' While in v. 44 סַכֹּתָה is constructed with the preposition לְ, giving a reflexive sense, here it is not. The question is—can √סכך (in the Qal) have a reflexive meaning? Kronholm (1999, 239f.) notes that the dozen occurrences of the Qal of √סכך I usually express the covering function of the cherubim associated with the ark in Jerusalem; but none of these occurrences portray the verb in a reflexive mood. It is only the context of 3.43 and the proximity of v. 44 which raises that possibility. BDB (697) tentatively suggests it is reflexive here, but many translators and commentators are not convinced. LXX ἐπεσκέπασας (so also at v. 44) 'covered', P ܛܠܠܬ (so also at v. 44) 'covered', V *operuisti* 'covered', do not carry a reflexive meaning, while T טללתא עלנא 'covered over us' clearly shows that the Targumist took סכך to be a transitive verb, taking the object as the accusative suffix in the following ותרדפנו.

---

[177] We may note that AV translates 2.21 'and not pitied' but 3.43 'thou hast not pitied'.
[178] See Brockington (218).

We may conclude that all the Versions took סכתה as transitive, and that the object was 'us' as in the accusative suffix of the following verb.

Rashi's understanding of the passage is not clear. He paraphrases: 'You have separated off (חצצת) anger to be a barrier between you and us and you pursued us with it', taking 'anger' as the object of the verb. There is just a hint of the reflexive here. IE[2] 'You have placed a covering of anger over us' and Vermigli (140) 'You have covered us by your anger' appear to follow the Versions, as do Calvin, AV, RV, Kaiser (345), Hillers[2] (117), Provan (101), Gottlieb (53), NJB, REB. Many scholars have chosen to squeeze a reflexive sense out of סכתה—RV margin, Keil (421), Gottwald (14), Kraus (52), Haller (106), Meek (27), NIV, JPS, Renkema (433), Berlin (96), O'Connor (2001, 1054). Budde (1898[a], 96f.) is of the opinion that סכתה is not reflexive and suggests reading פָּנֶיךָ for בָאַף—'You have covered your face'. Rudolph (1938, 113), admitting that if MT is followed, the object of the verb must be the same as the suffix of the second verb, *viz* 'us', is unhappy with the text as it stands. He suggests reading אַפֶּיךָ (for בָאַף) and translates 'du hülltest dein Angesicht'. Hillers[2] (117), in adhering to MT, draws attention to 3.2, 5, 66 for shared objects and translates 'You have enveloped us in anger...'; cf. Levine (149) and Gottlieb (53).

It is *possible* that the text is corrupt and that the original reading has been replaced by סַכֹּתָה under the influence of v. 44; but this has taken place before the early translations of LXX etc. It is also possible that the poet has a play on words here: a transitive verb (v. 43) followed by a reflexive construction (v. 44) but with similar sound/appearance. He may have meant to stretch the connotation of the verb (normally meaning 'to cover' in a protective way) by using it in two different ways: one to cover in an aggressive fashion (v. 43), the other (v. 44), 'to cover' in the sense of 'shut out'; cf. Berlin (96).

The verbal form וַתִּרְדְּפֵנוּ 'and you pursued us' is followed by LXX, P, and T, the latter adding 'in exile'. V *et percussisti nos* 'and you struck us' is strange. This verb usually translates the Hiphil of √נכה 'strike (fatal) blow'. It may be that Jerome thought that the image of Yahweh chasing his people was inappropriate and took his cue from the verb that follows (הרג). Although רדף may mean both 'to pursue' and 'to persecute', most commentators translate this with 'pursue'; so Hillers[2] (111), Westermann (163), Berlin (80), NJB, NIV, NEB, JPS, NRSV.

3.44

Text and Versions

MT בְּעָנָן—so also LXX and V; P ܚܒܒܢ *b'nnk*; T דילך יקרא בעננא. MT is preferred (see below).

MT מֵעֲבוֹר followed by V, OL, T and Sym; LXX εἵνεκεν; P ܕܬܬܪܐ ܓܠܝ *w*ˣ*brt ṣlwtn*. MT is preferred (see below).

* * *

This verse is closely connected to the previous one, continuing the accusatory tone and beginning with the same word.[179] The terrible accusations of vv. 42f., that Yahweh has been their adversary in the extreme, are given further emphasis by the accusation that Yahweh has cut off all communication. Prayer cannot get through. This state of affairs, considered unfair by the poet, is a theme of the laments in the Psalms, cf. also v. 8.

While in v. 43 the object is supplied in the following verbal form, here there is no following verb. The ל is used here either as an object marker, as in Aramaic (GK 117n), or (more likely) as *dativus ethicus* (GK 119s). The effect is to turn a transitive verb into a reflexive: 'You have covered yourself'.

בֶּעָנָן—P 'with your cloud' and T 'with your clouds of glory' have understood the לך as further defining ענן. the Targumist also supplies the object of סכותה, namely 'the heavens'.

מֵעֲבוֹר—מִן + infin. const. of √עבר 'to pass by, through' (GK 119x). LXX 'for the sake of' apparently either misinterpreted מעבור or read בעבור. P 'and you have made our prayer pass by' has paraphrased his *Vorlage*, unless he read תעביר (so Kelso, 45) or מעביר (so Albrektson, 157). The presence of the first person suffix 'our prayer', found in P and OL, is natural and does not reflect different Hebrew text; cf. AV, NEB, *BHQ*.

3.45

Text and Versions
MT סְחִי וּמָאוֹס; LXX καμμύσαι με καὶ ἀπωσθῆναι; V *eradicationem et abiectionem*; P ܩܝܪ̈ܐ ܘܡܣܠܝܐ '*qyr' wmsly'*; Aq λαλιὰν καὶ ἀτιμίαν (ἔθηκας); Sym κοπρίαν καὶ κιβδηλείαν[180]... (SH ܕܚܠܐܠܐܗܐ ܘܚܣ ܙܒܠ *zbl' wtslwt'*); T שלטולין ורטישין. The text of LXX appears to be corrupt.[181] As it stands it would seem that the translator regarded the ׳ as the first person singular suffix; Ziegler (458) suggests that the original Greek was καμψαι, which is a retranslation of the marginal note in SH, *viz.* ܠܡܟܦ *lmkp*; but MT is to be preferred.

MT תְּשִׂימֵנוּ—so also LXX, P and T; V *posuisti me*. In the midst of a context of 1st p. pl. forms, this seems to have been a lapse in concentration on the part of the translator rather than a *Vorlage* which had תשימני.

* * *

This line, reminiscent of sentiments found in Psalms (cf. the passage Ps 79.4 'we have become...' with this 'you have made us...'), continues the accusation begun in v. 42. The plight of the poet's community is the work of Yahweh.

---

[179] סכותה is written *plene* here.
[180] κιβδηλειαν is Ziegler's (485) rendering of the SH; Field (756) guesses *rejectmentum*.
[181] Cf. Kelso (45f.), Rudolph (1938, 113f.), Albrektson (157f.). The Greek verb is generally employed in LXX for עצם.

סְחִי וּמָאוֹס—This verse begins with two unique forms. The meaning of the second of these, from the root מאס 'to reject', found also at 5.22, is not in doubt; the infin. abs. as substantive (GK 113d, Rudolph, 232) means 'rubbish/refuse'. The first term[182] סחי may be related to the verb סחה (IE[1]), which occurs only at Ezek 26.1 where it seems to mean 'to scrape off, clear away'; hence BDB, AV, NEB 'offscouring'; NRSV, JPS, ESV 'filth'.[183] Ibn Ezra (cf. also IE[2]) thinks that the reference here is to exile or homelessness (טלטול). Kara cites Deut 28.63 'You shall be forcibly removed (ונסחתם = Niphal of √נסח 'to tear away') from the land...', and also suggests that homelessness or exile is in mind here. Rashi makes no attempt at derivation but believes that the two terms are equivalent to the Mishnaic (BK 3b) phrase 'phlegm and mucus'; and he offers a vivid description of the latter's journey from lung and throat! The P translator 'uprooted' may have derived it from √נסח. He renders both terms in the plural, which suggests he envisaged a plurality of those driven from their homeland. V's translation also points in the same direction. T 'wanderers (and banished)', like P, translates in the plural and has a strong flavour of the exile about it.[184]

בְּקֶרֶב הָעַמִּים—The final phrase is important for the interpretation of the verse. Is it equivalent to בגוים at 2.9, which has to do with those living abroad, or is it as in 1.1, which seems to refer to Jerusalem's reputation abroad—what they think of us? The answer to this question depends to some extent on the date of the poem and on the standpoint of the poet. Is the latter referring to the nations in Palestine such as Moab, Ammon etc., or is he thinking on a broader canvas and including nations further afield, such as Babylonia? Does the 'us' (in the first stich) refer to those in Judah or does it include those who fled to Egypt, Moab etc. or those deported at the fall of Jerusalem? A glance at v. 46 would suggest that the poet is thinking of the people of Yahweh in Palestine who are hated and despised by other entities in the immediate vicinity, but exegetes who have interpreted the context as depicting the harsh conditions of the deported Judahites, post-586 BCE, interpret the phrase as 'in Babylonia'.

3.46

Text and Versions
The acrostic in this chapter follows the alphabetic order of chs. 2 and 4. Two MSS[Ken] and five MSS[de Ros] place vv. 46-48 after vv. 49-51, thereby achieving the alphabetic order

---

[182] On this, see Schäfer (128*).
[183] Calvin comments: 'Whatever is cleaned off by sweeping or scouring, that is the filth of the house or the floor is called סחי'; cf. also Luther 'Kehrricht und Unrat'.
[184] Cf. MR's gloss is מאסיוא פסילאייא 'loathsome outcasts'; see Jastrow, 722. 1195. MLT interprets as a reference specifically to the diaspora; cf. also Alexander (2008, 156f. n. 63).

found in ch. 1. This alteration is also found in SH and P. That it is not the original order is clear from the context: vv. 40-47 are in 1st p. pl., while v. 48 begins the section in 1st p. s.[185]

* * *

The wording of this verse is very close to that of 2.16a. Whereas at 2.16 Jerusalem is being addressed, here we have part of a prayer to Yahweh, and the 1st p. pl. suffixes refer to the speaker and his fellow-sufferers.

3.47

Text and Versions

MT פַּחַד; LXX[B,A] θυμὸς; LXX[L] τρόμος; LXX[Mss] θάμβος; SH ܬܘܗܬ‎ *twht*ʾ; P ܕܚܠܬܐ *zwʿtʾ*; V *laqueus*; T עציו. Schleusner (39) plausibly suggested that LXX θυμὸς is an error for βόθυνος (cf. at Isa 24.17 and Jer 48.43 where LXX translates פַּחַד by βόθυνος), and this is adopted by Ziegler (485); but see Schäfer (*BHQ* 129*) who observes that there is no textual evidence for this reading. Nevertheless, the fact that the Versions had no difficulty with the term in the Isaiah and Jeremiah passages but struggle in this passage is surprising. Robinson (1933, 258) may be right that a desire, on the part of the translators, for a synonym might account for the alternative Greek readings and for the Syriac. MT is preferred.

MT הַשֵּׁאת; LXX ἔπαρσις, so also Aq; V *vaticinatio*; P ܓܘܡܨܐ *gwmṣʾ*; T רתיתא. One may account for LXX 'pride' and V 'prophecy' in that the translators have derived the unpointed השאת as from נשא 'to lift'; cf. Calvin, Kelso (46), Schäfer (*BHQ*). P 'pit' may be explained as having read הַשַּׁחַת: cf. Abelesz (39) but see Schäfer (*BHQ* 129*). T 'trembling' may be a guess from the context. The fact that the poet employs the definite article with the second word-pair and not with the first is interesting, and Delitzsch (1920, 75a) suggests we read here Niphal infin. abs.—וְהִשָּׁבֵר הִשָּׁאוֹת; cf. also Rudolph (1962, 232) and Meek (28). We should note that LXX does not represent the definite article in either of the final two words (cf. v. 38).

* * *

The poet, in summing up the effects of Yahweh's lack of forgiveness and response to prayer, and the subsequent abuse by the enemies, employs terminology that was probably proverbial in his day (Hillers[2], 132). This final line is charged with alliteration and assonance:[186] the first two terms beginning with *pah* and the final two beginning with *hašš*. Obscurity in terminology and groupings has led to translators and commentators guessing and differing as to the precise meaning of the passage, which concludes the 1st p. pl. section begun at v. 40. Verse 47a is reminiscent of two other passages—Isa 24.17-18 and Jer 48.43-44. In the latter two passages the assonance is more obvious in that *three* words begin with *pah*.

---

[185] The Syriac translator (or copyist), in placing the פ stanza after the ע stanza, altered the plural to singular to make it blend with the new context.

[186] Attempts have been made to reproduce this in English translation, thus JPS (panic and pitfall...death and destruction); cf. also RSV, NRSV, Hillers[2] (111), Gordis (143), Berlin (80) and Knox (1252 n. 2).

פַּחַת occurs infrequently in the Hebrew Bible (2 Sam 17.9; 18.17; Isa 24.17f.; Jer 48.43f., 28) and has the meaning 'pit/trapping pit' or 'hole'. V *laqueus* 'snare, trap' is the only Version that comes near this. The word-pair, together with פַּח 'snare' (in Isaiah and Jeremiah passages) conjure up the idea of the hunt (cf. McKane 1996, 1195f.); and NEB conveys this in the rendering 'hunter's scare and pit'.[187] While this may be the original application of the terminology, the meaning in our passage must surely be figurative of calamity; cf. BDB, *HALOT*. The *hapax legomenon* הַשֵּׁאת continued to baffle would-be translators. Rashi explains it with another *hapax legomenon*—שְׁאִיָּה (Isa 24.12) 'ruin, desolation'; IE[1] says that the meaning is שׁוֹאָה 'destruction',[188] while Kara, citing Isa 6.11 and Zeph 1.15, follows suit. Then Vermigli (141), following Münster, *seductio*, appears to deduce it from נשׁא Hiphil 'to deceive'. Luther 'Schrecken' may be a guess, but Calvin, although he does not offer any derivation, settles for *destructio*.[189] The construction היה ל may denote possession (cf. JPS), or, more likely, may be rendered 'happened to/come upon', cf. LXX, V, AV, NRSV.

3.48

Text and Versions

MT תֵּרַד עֵינִי; LXX κατάξει ὁ ὀφθαλμός μου; P ܐܪܕܝ, ܚܡܪ ܐܪܕܝ ʾrdy ʿyny. The fact that P has the plural here probably does not reflect a different reading. LXX, V and T all have the singular. P has the Aphel of ܐܪܕܝ *rdy* '(my eyes) shed', while LXX κατάξει 'bring down' may mean that these Versions read Hiphil (cf. 2.18) of ירד (cf. Albrektson, 159), but it may be that the translators were simply not at ease with the construction.

* * *

In this line the poet appears to return to the lament prior to v. 40. Having identified himself with his suffering people, he speaks now of his own feelings, not for himself this time, but for his people. The occurrence of שֶׁבֶר 'destruction' in the previous line leads him to dwell on it for the next three verses. 'It is as if the corporate attempt to rehearse the disaster before God has proved too much for him. It has overwhelmed him emotionally…'[190]

תֵּרַד—The normal form is תֵּרֵד (3rd p. f. s. Qal impf. of √ירד 'go down', used figuratively 'flow'), cf. Ps 119.136; Jer 9.17; 13.17; Lam 1.16 of water/tears; Ps 133.2 of oil. The form occurring here appears also at Jer 13.17.

---

[187] This is clearer at Isa 24.17f. and Jer 48.43f. *paḥad* is taken (NEB) as the hunter's device which produces terror (= hunter's scare) rather than general fear in the animal; cf. Müller (2001, 518).
[188] Ibn Ezra points out that the א is a root letter, that is, he takes the term from שׁאה.
[189] Calvin is aware of other views and, indeed, mentions *deceptio* as a possibility.
[190] Provan 1991[a], 102.

פַלְגֵי־מָיִם—'Streams of water'. The idea is of the eye flowing *with* floods of tears (GK 117z), cf. 1.16. The poet uses hyperbole here to emphasise his grief. On the phrase עַל־שֶׁבֶר בַּת־עַמִּי, see on 2.11.

3.49

Text and Versions

MT נִגְּרָה; LXX κατεπόθη; SH ܐܬܦܩܥܬ *'tpḥt*; Sym ἐπέμεινεν; P ܕܡܥܐ *dm^ᶜ*; V *adflictus est*; OL *absorptus est*; T זלגת דמעין. The variations probably reflect difficulty with the Hebrew. Schleusner (40) thinks that LXX read נגרע (from גרע II = 'to drip?'),[191] while Kelso (46) is sure that the *Vorlage* was נבלע; and OL might support Kelso here.[192] Ziegler (485), on the basis of SH, has adopted the reading κατεπονήθη (for κατεπόθη). However, Albrektson (160) points out that LXX elsewhere renders the root in various ways, which probably suggests that there was considerable uncertainty as to meaning. V 'my eye is afflicted' hardly fits the context,[193] P is almost certainly a guess, but T, although a paraphrase, supports MT.

MT וְלֹא תִדְמֶה followed by V, P and Sym; LXX καὶ οὐ σιγήσομαι; SH ܘܠܐ ܬܫܬܠܐ *wlʾ tšlʾ*. Dyserinck (374) and Kelso (47) think that the LXX *Vorlage* was אדמה, while *BHK* suggests that אֲדֹם (root דמם) lies behind the Greek rendering. Schleusner (40) thought that the LXX reading was due to the translator finding it difficult to speak of the eye being silent! Cf. *BHQ* 129*. There is something in what Schleusner observes, though Albrektson (160f.) thinks that a scribe altered an original σιγήσεται. MT, however, is superior.

* * *

The intensity of the language of v. 48 continues in this verse. While there is little doubt as to the general meaning of the passage, the language employed has occasioned some difficulty. This is seen already in the Versions.

נִגְּרָה—Niphal perf. (from √נגר 'pour, run'). The use of the Niphal may emphasise the reflexive nature of the weeping—the eyes pour themselves out (GK 51c). The use of the perfect here may suggest the certainty of the action (cf. Meek, 28): 'shall flow'.

וְלֹא תִדְמֶה—An adverbial phrase 'without ceasing' (lit. and does not cease), cf. Jer 14.17. T's 'and does not cease from crying' gets the sense of the passage.

מֵאֵין הֲפֻגוֹת—The presence of the *hapax legomenon* has led to variations in interpretation here, and this is compounded by the ambiguous function of the מִן; cf. at 1.3. The passage has echoes of 2.18 where Jerusalem is addressed and where we have the form פּוּגַת, another *hapax legomenon*.

---

[191] The root occurs only at Job 36.27 in the Piel.
[192] Cf. V at Ps 69.16.
[193] Jerome uses *adflictus* for the root רעע on two occasions (Ps 106.2; Jonah 4.1) but also for נגש (1 Sam 13.6) and דרך (Ps 38.9).

The latter is from √פוג 'grow numb' and is probably a noun with archaic ending (GK 80 f.), with the meaning 'rest, relief'. הַפֻּגוֹת must be related to פוּגַת and many commentators and translators regard it as plural of הַפָּנָה with the same meaning. There are, however, those who, because of the strange initial ה, resort to emendation.[194] IE[1], aware of the unusual form, explains the ה as a nominal prefix (GK 85 r) like the ת in תרומה. The early Versions struggle with the meaning of the מן. LXX 'so that there shall be no rest' took it to have a final sense (GK 119 y; Job 23.21; 28.11), while P, V and T took it as causal (GK 119z; 1 Kgs 8.5). Rashi senses that the meaning of מֵאֵין is as in Isa 5.9, 'without respite' (cf. GK 152y), and Vermigli (143) seems to prefer this meaning, though in his actual translation (142) he seems to take the מן as causal (*eo quod non*). Calvin *ut non sint intermissiones* is following the interpretation of LXX; and Luther *denn es ist kein Aufhören da* follows V. AV 'without any intermission' follows Rashi; and this is how most scholars have taken it since: Wiesmann (189), Westermann (163), Albrektson (161), RSV, Provan (103), Gordis (144), Hillers[2] (111), though Keil (402, 423) interprets as LXX. By adding this phrase, the speaker wishes to rule out any possible break in the weeping.

3.50

Text and Versions
MT is intelligible as it stands. Bickell (115) inserts בי before מִשָּׁמַיִם, presumably to lengthen the line; Budde (97) prefers to lengthen עד to עד כי (cf. Gen 41.49). *BHK* suggests reading עַל פִּי 'according to' for עַד, but Rudolph (1938, 114) finds this suggestion unintelligible.

* * *

The need for Yahweh to 'see' the ruin and misery experienced by the poets of Lamentations and their people, is alluded to at 1.9, 11; 2.20; 5.1. The implication is that Yahweh is paying no attention (see on v. 36, cf. 1.9); and the ploy of weeping copiously and without a break is designed to engage with Yahweh, who is the author of the situation. If he can be persuaded to look down, the poet assumes that this will lead to Yahweh showing the mercy and compassion referred to at vv. 22f.

יַשְׁקִיף—√שקף in Hiphil is construed here with the verb √ראה (as at 2 Sam 24.20, cf. Ps 14.2) and means 'to look down'. The (anthropomorphic) image is of Yahweh in the heavens looking out and down on the situation described by the poet. IE[1] says the picture is as if there is a heavenly window through which God may look. MLT draws attention to a similar image in Ps 102.20f. LXX translates with διακύπτω 'bend down to see',

---

[194] E.g. BDB (806) would prefer to read פוּגֹת.

as at 2 Sam 24.20 and Ps 14.2, capturing the imagery of the Hebrew, while P ܢܕܝܩ *ndyq* 'gaze upon' is less graphic. The jussive form וְיֵרֶא, rather than the impf. וְיִרְאֶה, is explained as due to rhythm and the *zaqeph qaton*, cf. GK 109k; Rudolph (1962, 233), however, thinks that the reason is to denote a final sense; cf. GK 109f. T adds an accusative here, namely עולבני 'my affliction'—exegetical expansion—but NEB's 'while the Lord in heaven looks down and watches my affliction' is the result of emendation[195]—transposing עיני of v. 51 to v. 50 and emending to עָנְיִי.

עד 'until' followed by the impf. (BDB 725, cf. 1 Sam 1.22). The weeping will continue to this point. NEB translates עד 'while' which is possible but less likely. The purpose of the weeping is to get Yahweh to 'see', i.e. to act regarding the misery. If translated 'while', then Yahweh is depicted as merely observing the misery, and the purpose of the weeping is removed.

3.51

Text and Versions
No significant material.

* * *

In this verse the poet exaggerates the effect that weeping has on his inner being—it is greater than the effect the city's keening women would have.

The majority of translators and commentators, from the Versions to the present day, have had problems with this verse. As a result, apart from various exegeses of MT, there have been several suggestions as to emendation. MT may be difficult (Gordis, 185), but proposed emendations remain unattractive. Bickell (1882, 117) originally read בכות for בנות, but then (1894, 115) accepted MT. Dyserinck (375) reads בָּכוֹת (i.e. Piel infin. const.). The assumption that בנות is an error for בכות is picked up by Rudolph (1962, 232), Haller (106), Kaiser (346), Kraus (53) and Westermann (167), but see Schäfer (129*). NEB's translation 'while the LORD torments me with the fate of all the daughters of my city' rests on an emendation by Perles (1930, 114), *viz.* עוֹלֵל יהוה for עוֹלְלָה (i.e. ה is taken as an abbreviation for יהוה).[196] Hillers[2] (118) has re-written the entire line: עֳנִי עוֹלֵל לְנַפְשִׁי מִכָּלֶּה בְנוֹת עֵינָי 'The affliction done to me has consumed my eyes', where 'daughters of my eyes' = 'my eyes' (cf. 2.18).

עוֹלְלָה—On the verb עלל, see on 1.12. The root עלל construed with the preposition ל occurs five times in Lamentations (1.12, 22 [*twice*]; 2.20; 3.51). On each occasion, LXX employs the verb ἐπιφυλλίζω 'to gather',

---

[195] See Brockington (218); cf. Wiesmann (189), JPS footnote.
[196] Cf. Driver (1960, 119f.); see Brockington (218).

i.e. the translator took עלל to be the denominative verb עלל 'to glean', but the result is a very opaque rendering.[197] P employs ܥܒܕ *ʿbd* at 1.12; 2.20 but ܛܪܦ *ṭrp* at 1.22 (*twice*) and 3.51. Here the translator seems to take עוללה as the Poal, i.e. the passive conjugation—'my eye is agitated (or worn out)'. Having done that, he takes the preposition ל to be equivalent to על—'my eye is agitated because of my soul'—and the result is also obscure. V *depraedatus est animam meam* 'has ravaged my soul' uses quite a different verb from the other instances of עלל in Lamentations; and, again, the meaning is not clear. The meaning of MT could be that the speaker imagines that his 'eye', i.e. what he sees (cf. Gottwald, 14) has an adverse effect on his soul: What I see pains my inner soul; or—and this is more likely—that his eyes (constantly weeping, v. 49) have had an adverse effect on his inner being.

Problems in the second stich begin with the function of מִן. Is it causative (GK 119z), as understood by LXX, V, T, AV, Luther, Vermigli (142), Keil (402), REB, Kaiser (346), Westermann (163), Renkema (443)? If we are dealing here with a causative מִן, the meaning of the verse may be that the poet is grieved/pained because of the plight or fate of the women in his city. This could refer to the vulnerability and the abuse of women at the hands of soldiers and/or overlords; and this is how it is taken by several commentators. Another exegesis based on the causative מִן has been suggested by interpreting 'daughters of my city' to be the villages and settlements around Jerusalem. Jerome renders מִכֹּל בְּנוֹת עִירִי *in cunctis filiabus urbis meae*, which makes better sense if 'daughters' are taken figuratively. P ܩܘܪܝܐ ܕܝܠܝ *qwryʾ dyly* has the plural 'my cities' which *may* reflect a similar interpretation; and T's paraphrase (cf. also MLT) refers to פילכי עמי, 'districts of my people' which probably has the figurative interpretation lying behind it.[198] Vermigli (143) notes this as a possible interpretation, and it is adopted by Ewald (340), Blayney (326) and Löhr (1894, 17). But 'daughters of my city' is not used elsewhere for outlying districts and villages, and that, in itself, makes it suspect.

Exegesis based on the comparative[99] מִן (GK 133a) puts a very different complexion on the verse but should be considered. Rashi's comments are not altogether clear, but what *is* clear is that he interprets מִן as comparative: 'my family has more to cry for than all the families of the city…' He does not allude to a causative approach. IE[1] and Kara do not feel the need to engage in debate on this particular issue, but IE[2] spells it out: 'My eye affects my soul with weeping more than all the daughters of my city where it is the custom of women to weep'. Vermigli (143f.) certainly regards the comparative מִן with some respect, and Calvin prefers it to the

---

[197] See on 1.22, cf. Albrektson (161).
[198] The Targumist follows this with a literal interpretation 'and the humiliation of the daughters of Jerusalem, my city'; cf. Alexander (2008, 158 n. 69).
[199] Although we cannot be certain, it is possible that P, whose translation of the first stich is unusual (see above), interprets this way.

causative, which he says is how it is usually taken, Luther being in the latter company. The tendency nowadays is to take the 'causative' line and to see this as a reference to the plight of the women of the city; cf. JPS, NRSV, Westermann (163), Barthélemy (906), House (424f.).

The phrase 'daughters of my city' is found nowhere else in the Hebrew Bible. We do find 'daughters of Israel' (2 Sam 1.24), 'daughters of Judah' (Ps 48.12),[200] 'daughters of the nations' (Ezek 32.16), 'daughters of Rabbah' (Jer 49.3), 'daughters of Zion' (Song 3.11). In nearly all of these passages the reference is either to rejoicing or to weeping, reflecting the custom in the ancient world of women being involved in the rituals of celebration and tragedy. When David returns from his encounter with Goliath (1 Sam 18.6) it is the women who come out to greet him and to celebrate; when the psalmist calls on Zion to rejoice, the parallel line is 'let the daughters of Judah be glad' (Ps 48.12). In the lament for Saul and Jonathan, David fears that the news will cause the Philistine women to rejoice (2 Sam 1.20). Tragedy called forth weeping and wailing, mainly by women. David calls on the 'daughters of Israel' to weep for Saul (2 Sam 1.24), Ezek 32.16 speaks of the 'daughters of the nations' weeping for Egypt, and Jer 49.3 calls on the 'daughters of Rabbah' to cry out. Jeremiah 9.16-19 refers to the mourning women (מקוננות) and to the teaching of the art to their daughters.[201] In the New Testament (Luke 23.27f.), Jesus instructs the 'daughters of Jerusalem', already weeping for him, to weep for themselves and for their children.

Hence, while the phrase 'daughters of my city' is only found here, it is a distinct possibility, especially in the context of eyes running with water, that these 'daughters' are the professional mourners. While it is not conclusive, it should be noted that, in the combination of מן with כל, מן is comparative in the vast majority of cases, though the partitive מן is also found. The causative מן is found only at Mic 7.16.

The purpose of the professional mourners was to effect an atmosphere of sadness and feelings of sorrow and to induce weeping which would be appropriate in any tragic situation. The poet, then, is saying that all the professional wailing of the day has less effect on him than his own eyes have because of all the continuous weeping they have done. The Hebrew may not be elegant, in our eyes, but that is what the text is saying.[202]

3.52

Text and Versions
No significant material.

* * *

---

[200] Cf. NRSV and REB which translate this 'towns of Judah'.
[201] Cf. de Vaux (1965, 60f.).
[202] Cf. Moskowitz (27 n. 38) and Berlin (97).

The poet continues in 1st p. s. but here he looks back at what he has experienced at the hand of his enemies. The raw adversity was like the experience of a bird being hunted down.

The verb צוד 'to hunt' is found also at 4.16, but hunting imagery is found at 1.3, 6; 3.43, 66; 4.19 employing the verb רדף 'pursue'.[203] The poet emphasises his statement here in two ways:[204] (a) by the employment of the infin. abs. (GK 113l), and (b) by the adverbial phrase חִנָּם 'without cause'. The latter phrase is slightly ambiguous. Does it (a) apply to the *action* of the enemies—uncalled for, unprovoked (NJB), or (b) is it a reference to those who were enemies for no reason (NEB)? On the basis of Ps 119.161 (רדפוני חנם), we could interpret as (a)—so LXX, V, P, MLT, Berlin (80); but in the light of Ps 69.5 (שֹׂנְאַי חִנָּם) we may interpret as (b)—so IE[1], Westermann (163), Hillers[2] (112), Kaiser (346), Keil (424). The (a) option is to be preferred. The poet wishes to stress the wanton nature of the hostility. It is not that the enemies have no reason to be enemies, but that their wanton attacks are gratuitous; cf. Renkema (446).

The idea of being hunted like a bird is found at Ps 124.7, as MLT points out. There, the image is of Israel, escaping from the snare of the fowler; and Albrektson (162) draws attention to this passage as possible support for the collective interpretation of the 1st p. s. here.

3.53

Text and Versions

MT צָמְתוּ; LXX ἐθανάτωσαν; OL *mortificaverunt*; SH ܐܡܝܬܘ *w'mytw*; Sym καὶ κατεσιώπησαν; P ܫܬܩܘ *štqw*; V *lapsa est*; T עברו. That V had a different *Vorlage*—a form of √צמת?—is possible. The copula in SH and Sym is ruled out by the demands of the acrostic, but MT is not in question.

* * *

Although the text of this verse is not usually questioned, attempts at understanding the Hebrew are varied. The combination of two unusual verbs contributes to the uncertainty, as does the ambiguity of the words 'pit' and 'stone'. The adversity experienced is depicted in terms of a victim cornered and set upon.

צָמְתוּ—The root צמת occurs 15 times in the Hebrew Bible, only once (here) in Qal. In the Hiphil it means 'to exterminate', in the Niphal 'to disappear', and in the Piel 'to put an end to/to silence'.[205] In Syriac (Pael) it

---

[203] This root is a lot more common, but the poet must begin this stanza with the letter צ.
[204] The poet indulges in assonance here—צוֹד צָדוּנִי—and that too increases the emphasis. On hunting methods, see Renkema (445).
[205] Gesenius III, 1174 takes Qal and Piel as *siluit, tacuit*.

means 'to silence'; and in Ugaritic and Ethiopic 'to wipe out'. In Aramaic it may mean 'to detain' or 'to meet'.[206] LXX (OL) 'They put my life to death in a pit'[207] is somewhat strong, even acknowledging hyperbole, given that the speaker utters an exclamation in the next verse. The Targumist, faced with the root צמת, which may have meant, to him, 'to meet', decided that the subject of the plural verb was the plural form חַיַּי 'my life'[208] and guessed the meaning 'my life passed into a pit'. Likewise, Jerome took 'my life' as the subject of the verb: 'my life has fallen into a pit'. V does not have much difficulty with the root צמת elsewhere in the Hebrew Bible, but here, having decided that 'my life' was the subject and that 'in(to) the pit' was close by, he made a stab at making sense of the stich. Rashi refers to Song 4.1 (לְצַמָּתֵךְ) but explains צמתו with אסרו 'they bound',[209] perhaps thinking in terms of צמדו. IE² explains צמתו with הושמתי 'I was made desolate', thus revealing the uncertainty among the mediaeval commentators. Calvin, too, struggles: *Succiderunt (vel potius, constrinxerunt*[210]*) in puteo...=* 'They have cut off...or they have bound...', while Luther 'Sie haben mein Leben in einer Grübe umgebracht...' is close to LXX. Vermigli (144ff.), although translating 'they closed up my life...', is influenced in his comments by Rashi. He imagines that Jeremiah is speaking and that the scenario is connected with Jer 38.6 where ropes are mentioned.[211] He comments: 'Not only did they throw him in, they also bound him'. Michaelis's translation is 'Ich bin lebendig in die tiefe Stille der Grube gewarfen...'

בַבּוֹר—Either 'in' or 'into' (V, T) 'the pit'. בּוֹר can mean a cistern, for water or grain (Jer 2.13), or grave (Prov 28.17), or prison (Gen 37.20-22). Judging from the second stich, the poet has a form of prison in mind.[212]

וַיַּדּוּ—This is *waw*-consecutive, impf., 3rd p. pl. Piel, for וַיְיַדּוּ (see GK 69u, and cf. v. 33) of √ידה I 'to throw/cast'. It is a rare word and found at Jer 50.14 and Zech 2.4 (Piel). LXX καὶ ἐπέθηκαν 'placed, laid' may be a guess by the translator[213] who has already, by his rendering of צמת, envisaged a more final scenario. V *posuerunt* (= OL) 'put, placed' is in line with LXX.[214]

---

[206] Cf. Jastrow (1290).
[207] That OL has *in lacum* for LXX ἐν λάκκῳ (i.e. 'into' rather than 'in') probably shows some uncertainty on the part of the Latin translator as to the meaning of the entire stich.
[208] The poet balances חַיַּי in the first stich with בִּ in the second: it is tantamount to saying 'they silenced *me*'; cf. NJB.
[209] He further glosses in Old French *estreyture* 'tightening'. Banitt (1650) records a similar gloss in *Le Glossaire de Leipzig*: *étraindrènt* = ils ont serré.
[210] Perhaps influenced by Rashi here.
[211] This is usually interpreted as the employment of ropes to lower the prisoner into the pit.
[212] Rashi takes the pit to mean prison, בית הכלא.
[213] Cf. at Jer 50.14 where the Greek translator uses τοξεύω.
[214] Jerome, at Jer 50.14, uses *debellate*, which may indicate that he was uncertain of the meaning of the verb.

In the case of LXX, OL and V, the accusative is 'a stone (over me)' for אֶבֶן בִּי. The image here is of a large stone over the entrance to the pit. The idea of placing a stone over the pit's entrance is probably entertained in MR, where attention is drawn to Daniel (6.18). Rashi, too, speaks of the stone over the mouth of the pit and refers to Daniel.[215] But √ידה will hardly bear such an interpretation.

P and T 'they hurled stones at me' conjure up the image of the victim down in the pit and being pelted with stones. אבן has rightly been taken as a collective (cf. Lev 20.2, 27; 1 Kgs 12.18) and is accepted as such by MLT (אחד אחד), Luther, RSV, Gordis (144), Westermann (164), Rudolph (1962, 233), Wiesmann (196), Hillers[2] (112). Furthermore, 1 Kgs 12.18 shows that the preposition ב should be translated 'at/against' rather than 'over'.[216]

We note that the hunting imagery of v. 52 is not continued in this verse; nor is it present in v. 54. The poet appears to be operating as he was in vv. 1-18, describing adversity with a variety of images. Thus, in this verse, while the 3rd p. pl. verbs have as their subject the enemies of v. 52, the imagery changes to that of a prisoner dumped in a cistern. We cannot be certain as to the meaning of the first verb. The poet, though given to hyperbole, cannot be saying that the enemies have put him to death in a pit and placed a stone over him—LXX lacks imagination! Whether we take חַיָּי to be 'my life' or 'me alive', it is clear that the image is of the victim alive in the pit. NIV has taken the first stich to mean that they *intended* to end the speaker's life in the pit—'They tried to end my life in the pit…'[217]

Some translations appear to be guesses from the context; hence, RSV 'They flung me alive…', JB 'they tumbled my life into a pit…' The reading in NEB, 'They thrust me alive into the silent pit…', is trying to preserve the meaning 'to silence', but is otherwise guessing. The same may be said for Rashi's 'they bound'.

The idea that אֶבֶן refers to a slab or boulder placed over the mouth of the pit to prevent escape is found as early as LXX and V, in Rashi and Calvin and as late as NEB and Berlin (81).

The picture, then, is of the prisoner down in the pit being pelted with stones. He is not just imprisoned: he gets further hostile treatment.

---

[215] Strangely, Rashi at Jer 50.14, while citing the Lamentations passage, seems to understand the verb ידה to mean 'throw' זרק; and Kimḥi glosses it with השליכו 'throw'.

[216] Nägelsbach (131f.) points out that if the action were the placing of a stone over the pit the preposition would be על.

[217] This is probably based on the observation by Keil (424) that the construction 'must be understood *de conatu* 'they sought to destroy my life when they hurled me down into the pit…'

3.54

Text and Versions

MT נִגְזָרְתִּי; LXX ἀπῶσμαι; Sym ἐξεκόπην; P ܐܬܛܒܥܬ 'trḥqt; V perii; T מן אתגזרית עלמא. According to *BHK*, the *Vorlage* of LXX was נדחתי, but Albrektson (162f.) points out that LXX employs ἀπωθέω at Ps 87(88).6 to translate the Niphal of √גזר and that there is no standard rendering of this root in LXX; cf. also Rudolph (1938, 114f.). P 'I am cast far off' is not precise, though it does not follow that P had a *Vorlage* involving the root רחק; but it may be noted that had the Syriac translator employed the root ܓܙܪ, especially in the Ethpeel, the result might have been interpreted 'I am circumcised'!

* * *

The speaker continues in this verse to describe adversity. In itself, the imagery is simple: water flows over his head, and he considers that his end has come (cf. NEB).

The picture is similar to that in Jonah 2.4f. In the latter passage, the exclamation is introduced by the same verb, אָמַרְתִּי = 'I thought/said to myself/reckoned'. Rashi suggests that the waters flowing is a reference to the heathen—probably an allusion to the exile; and this is echoed in MLT and MR, and so a collective interpretation of the 1st p. s. Calvin, who refers to this verse as a third comparison, thereby implying that vv. 52f. contained independent images of adversity, observes that in the following verse the speaker invokes God. He explains: 'When, therefore, the Prophet says that in his own judgment he was lost, he does not mean that his faith was so extinguished that he ceased to pray to God; for in the next verse he shews that he persevered in prayer'.

3.55

Text and Versions
No significant material.

* * *

Scholars and commentators are divided on the tenses in vv. 55-62. Some take the view that the perfects refer to the past, i.e. they are preterites and allude to a past call and answer to/from Yahweh; others understand the perfects to refer to the present (cf. GK 106g-h). Some scholars see here what are called precative perfects.[218]

קָרָאתִי שִׁמְךָ—The Versions translate קָרָאתִי as referring to the past. To call out to God is usually קרא plus the preposition לְ or אֶל, but occasionally the verb is construed with the accusative (יהוה) (Pss 17.6; 18.4) or, as here,

---

[218] See the discussions by Provan (1991b), Hillers² (118), Joyce (531), Dobbs-Allsopp (126f.), Berlin (97).

with שֵׁם (cf. Ps 99.6 for both constructions). More frequently the construction is קרא בשם יהוה (Gen 4.26).

תַּחְתִּי—מִבּוֹר תַּחְתִּיּוֹת, adj. and subst. (see BL 501x), 'lower, lowest (place)'. The expression, found also at Ps 88.7, may signify the lowest place of the pit.

3.56

Text and Versions

MT אָזְנְךָ—followed by P, V and T; LXX τὰ ὦτά σου; LXX 'your ears' does not necessarily imply that the *Vorlage* read אָזְנֶיךָ. It is likely that the Greek translator rendered in natural fashion; cf. *BHQ*, Albrektson (164).

MT לְרַוְחָתִי לְשַׁוְעָתִי; LXX εἰς τὴν δέησίν μου (v. 57 begins: εἰς τὴν βοήθειάν μου); P ܐܠܐ ܐܪܘܚ ܠܝ ܘܦܪܘܩܝܢܝ 'l 'rwḥ ly wprwqyny; Sym εἰς τὸ ἀναψῦξαί με καὶ σῶσαι; V *a singultu meo et clamoribus*. The variety here probably reflects the difficulty facing translator and transmitter. The displacement in LXX is probably not original but due to faulty transmission.[219] Delete לְשַׁוְעָתִי as an explanatory gloss.

* * *

The connection with v. 55 is clear. The speaker recalls the actual words of his successful plea to Yahweh.

Apart from the argument on tenses (see on v. 55), there are some problems with this verse. There is the unusual combination of the verb √עלם 'hide' with the noun אֹזֶן 'ear'; and the second stich is unusually long. The extra-long second stich is usually explained as due to the final form לְשַׁוְעָתִי being a gloss on the penultimate, rare לְרַוְחָתִי;[220] but others[221] regard לְרַוְחָתִי as the intruder and delete accordingly, while *BHS* suggests we delete one or the other. P 'but relieve me and save me', Sym 'to refresh me and to redeem', V 'from my sobs and cries' all appear to be struggling with the Hebrew text as we have it and interpreting according to context.[222] Those who retain MT vary in their exegesis.

The final words of the second stich are problematic. רוחה occurs elsewhere only at Exod 8.11 where it must mean 'relief, respite' (from √רוח 'be wide, spacious'. The plea might then be for Yahweh not to hide his ear regarding the speaker's ease/relief. The plea is extended to the speaker's cry for help (שועה 'cry', from √שוע Piel 'to cry for help'). The combination, at first sight, does not give a satisfactory sense: 'Do not hide your ear with respect to my relief, to my cry', even if we supply a copula, as do

---

[219] The alphabetic acrostic rules out the possibility that the following verse (57) can have begun with לְשַׁוְעָתִי; besides, the first stich in LXX (v. 57) is overloaded.
[220] So Ewald (341), Budde (1898ᵃ, 98), Löhr (1906, 22), *BHK*, Rudolph (1962, 233), Kraus (53), Kaiser (346) Gottlieb (53f.), Albrektson (163f.), Westermann (167).
[221] Bickell (115f.), Ehrlich (45), Wiesmann (194).
[222] *BHK* surmises that P may have had a different *Vorlage* here, but this is doubtful.

several MSS[Ken], Sym, V; cf. Calvin, Luther, Gottwald (14), Renkema (453). RSV 'to my cry for help' (with footnote *Heb uncertain*), NIV, ESV *may* have understood the two forms as constituting a hendiadys, cf. Berlin (83) who certainly does, but a hendiadys is defined as two nouns joined by 'and' in one concept, and that is not what we have here.

Jerome had translated לְרַוְחָתִי 'from my sobs/gasping', which may mean that he derived the noun from a √רוח[223] 'to breathe'; cf. also Calvin (*ad respirationem meam*), Luther, AV, Vermigli (146f.), JPS, Gordis (186), Renkema (453).

Those who regard לְשַׁוְעָתִי to be a gloss on לְרַוְחָתִי are in the difficult position of explaining how the former could explain the latter. Furthermore, if לְרַוְחָתִי was the original wording, then the hiding/closing of the ear to relief is too obscure. Of course, if we translate לְרַוְחָתִי 'to my sobs' or 'to my groan' (JPS), the result is quite intelligible. The gloss theory can only stand if the ultimate form throws light on the penultimate form (or vice versa).

Quite apart from the gloss theory, there have been several attempts at emendation. Cappel (626) had concluded that LXX had read לְצַוְחָתִי לִתְשֻׁעָתִי, i.e. the latter being a noun from √ישע Hiphil 'to deliver' and the former being a noun from √צוח 'to cry aloud'; and Houbigant (481) accepts this with the adjustment of the second form to לִישׁוּעָתִי (so also Perles 1930, 115) and argues that this was the original Hebrew. He also thinks that V read לִצְוחָתִי; and *BHK* thinks that the latter (or לְרִנָּתִי) plus לִתְשֻׁעָתִי lies behind LXX. Bickell (1894, 115f.) suggested reading קוֹלִי לְשֻׁוְעָתִי, i.e. deleting לרוחתי as an unfortunate variant of לשׁועתי and moving אָזְנְךָ to the first stich where it becomes the subject of תעלם. שמעת then stands alone, assuming an ellipsis of עֵינֶיךָ or פָּנֶיךָ: 'Your ear heard my voice; hide not (your eyes/face) from my cry'. Bickell is the point of departure for Driver (1950, 140). Driver deletes אָזְנְךָ, which he regards as a gloss, citing Ps 10.1 where the verb תַּעְלִים is elliptical. His reasons for deletion, 'it is hardly suitable to the verb and spoils the rhythmical balance of the verse', may command sympathy, but if אָזְנְךָ is not suitable he has to assume that the scribal addition (meant, we assume, to be explanatory and helpful) was clumsy and *un*helpful. Driver goes on to suggest emending לְשַׁוְעָתִי to לִישׁוּעָתִי, following Houbigant, and claiming LXX and Sym in support. He is, however, not altogether convinced by his own reconstruction (which he translates 'hide not from my relief [and] from my salvation') and offers an alternative reading, reversing the order of the final two words, and translating 'at my crying "To my relief!"'[224]

It is clear that confusion existed at an early stage of the transmission of the passage. The Versions are in disarray, and it can hardly be that transmission in that field is to blame in every instance. The fact that the line is

---

[223] Syriac has a root ܢܦܫ 'to breathe'; cf. BDB (924) and *HALOT*.
[224] NEB 'when I cry, "Come to my relief"' is based on this latter suggestion of Driver, but Brockington (218) makes no mention of it.

over-long should make us consider the possibility of additional elements; and the formal similarity of the final two words (preposition + noun with 1st p. s. suffix, with no copula) should make us suspicious. Ewald (341) had made the suggestion, followed by Löhr (1894, 17) and Budde (1898ᵃ, 98), that לשועתי should be omitted as a gloss on לצוחתי (the emendation which originated with Cappel). This has the advantage of shortening the long second stich and helping us to see how לשועתי *could* be an explanatory gloss. However, Cappel's emendation may not be necessary. The reading לצוחתי is clear enough and does not need explaining, while the obscure לרוחתי is more likely to have attracted an explanatory gloss. If רוחה is seen as a noun from √רוח 'to breathe' with the meaning 'gasp, groan', cf. V *a singultu meo*, then this unusual word was seen, early on in the transmission of the text, to need some explanation; cf. also the translations of Calvin, Luther, AV, Vermigli (146f.), JPS, Gordis (186), Renkema (453). The attempts by modern translators and commentators[225] to retain the reading לרוחתי לשועתי are unwarranted and unsuccessful, as seen, for example, in NRSV '...Do not close your ear to my cry for help, but give me relief!' Construed with תַּעְלֵם, the *lameds* of the final stich must be understood as 'with respect to/vis-à-vis'.

3.57

Text and Versions
The text of this verse is not in question. The addition μοι in LXX, found also in P, does not imply a different Hebrew text (as claimed by *BHK*), but is a natural, value-added touch, cf. *BHQ*, Albrektson (165f.), Gordis (144). The copula in P ܘܐܡܪܬ *wʾmrt* is a common addition in this Version.

* * *

Continuing to look back on previous positive prayerful experiences with the divine, the speaker remembers that Yahweh made his presence felt. Yahweh's words, 'Do not be afraid', were reassuring.

בְּיוֹם אֶקְרָאֶךָ—The imperfect here has frequentative force (GK 107e). Whereas the perfect קָרַבְתָּ: expresses the poet's experience of God in the past, the imperfect specifies that Yahweh's comforting presence was experienced every time he invoked him. אֶקְרָאֶךָ, has the *nun energicum* (GK 58i-l). The poet associates that divine presence with the words 'Do not be afraid'. Yahweh had drawn near and had confirmed his presence and his intention to help with the words 'Do not be afraid'. This injunction is found in several places in the Hebrew Bible and in various contexts—Gen 15.1; 21.17; 26.24; 46.3; Deut 20.3; 31.6; Josh 8.1; Judg 6.23; 11.6; 2 Kgs 6.16. It is found in non-religious contexts where one person reassures another in the face of a problem. A midwife comforts Rachel

---

[225] So Provan, Renkema, Berlin, House, NJB, REB, NIV, Barthélemy (907).

(Gen 35.17), Joseph reassures his brothers (Gen 50.21), Boaz encourages Ruth (Ruth 3.11). The words are found frequently in the context of war, especially just before a battle (Exod 14.13; Deut 1.21, 29; 3.22); indeed, it has been argued[226] that the *Sitz im Leben* of the phrase is in this battle context. Fuhs (1990, 305), on the other hand, senses that the formula may have its origin 'in the so-called priestly oracle of salvation', thereby agreeing with Gressmann (1914, 254-59): 'in the name of the deity, the priest addresses the suppliant with the "fear not" formula, followed by the self-predication of the deity ("I am...") introducing the oracle'.[227] Whatever its origin, the poet employs it here out of his own positive experience of Yahweh's care and protection and of Yahweh's ability to intervene in history. It is on the basis of his *past* experience that he can call on Yahweh for help and encouragement.

3.58

Text and Versions
MT רִיבֵי followed by LXX and T; V *causam*; P ܕܝܢ‍ *dyn'*. The rare plural רִיבֵי is found also at 2 Sam 22.44 (= Ps 18.44).[228] As Albrektson (166) notes, 'The fact that a form is rare is not sufficient reason for emendation'—cf. also Gottlieb (54)—but the latter possibility is raised by those scholars who feel that the first stich is over long, cf. Wiesmann (195). The fact that P and V translate with the singular, though LXX has the plural, suggests to some that their *Vorlage* was רִיב; so Kelso (48), *BHK*, *BHS*.[229] אֲדֹנָי is thought by some to be the intruder—Budde (1898ᵃ, 98), Haller (106)—while Kaiser (346), Rudolph (1938, 115) and Meek (29) argue for deleting נַפְשִׁי and reading רִיבִי, and Westermann (167), who reads the singular רִיב, also considers deleting רִיבִי and reading רַבְתָּ אֲדֹנָי נַפְשִׁי. Deleting אֲדֹנָי is, perhaps, the least violent.[230] אֲדֹנָי may well be a gloss on יהוה of v. 59, incorporated into the text in transmission, though at an early stage since all the Versions testify to it. The first stich would then be less clumsy, and nothing would be lost.

* * *

Again, the poet looks back at the support and backing that Yahweh has provided in the past.

רַבְתָּ—From √רִיב 'to plead someone's (legal) cause' (Jer 50.34; 51.36; Mic 7.9; Prov 22.23; Ps 74.22), the only occurrence of the verb in Lamentations. It is construed with the cognate noun רִיב (which does occur at v. 36). The parallel verb in the second stich גָּאַלְתָּ is from √גאל I 'to redeem, buy back, ransom'. It is often used of Yahweh in Deutero-Isaiah (41.14; 43.14; 44.6, 24; 47.4; 48.17; 49.7, 26; 54.5, 8), passages which speak of deliverance from the power of Babylon; and it is linked with √רִיב elsewhere at Ps 119.154; Prov 23.11; Jer 50.34. The latter passage has to

---

[226] Derousseaux (97).
[227] Fuhs (305).
[228] A f. pl. form רִיבוֹת appears at Deut 17.8 and Job 13.6.
[229] *BHS* suggests reading the singular, while *BHK* offers either to delete אֲדֹנָי or to read רִיב. Robinson (1933, 258) prefers the latter.
[230] נפשׁי of the first stich balances חיי in the second.

do with deliverance from Babylon. If MT רִיבֵי נַפְשִׁי is retained, the plural may refer to several instances of divine support, equivalent to the frequentative (imperfect) tense in the previous verse. The speaker, then, has experienced Yahweh's positive intervention in his life, and for this he is grateful. Those who advocate a collective interpretation of the 1st p. s. here may detect an allusion to the deliverance of the captives in exile.

3.59

Text and Versions

MT עֻוָּתִי followed by V, P and T; LXX τὰς ταραχάς μου; Sym ἃ ἠδικήθην. The difference here is a matter of vocalisation. LXX and Sym vocalised עֻוֹּתִי.

MT שָׁפְטָה followed by Aq, V and T; LXX ἔκρινας; P ܕܢܬ wdnt. The *lectio difficilior* i.e. the imperative שָׁפְטָה is preferred; cf. Schäfer (130*) (see below).

* * *

Now, under the Babylonian yoke, can the deliverance be repeated? On the basis of past experience and because he feels that Yahweh knows his situation, the speaker pleads with Yahweh to judge in his favour.

רָאִיתָה—The full form (GK 44g) of the 2nd p. m. perfect Qal of √ראה is found also in the next line. The *hapax legomenon* עֻוָּתָה [אֶעֱוָתָה] from √עות 'to be bent, crooked', appearing mostly in the Piel 'to falsify, subvert', as at Job 19.6; Eccl 7.13; Lam 3.36; Amos 8.5. The noun must mean 'subversion/deprivation of justice', i.e. the opposite of מִשְׁפָּט (BDB 736). With the 1st p. s. suffix, the meaning must be 'the injustice done to me', as rendered by Jerome: *iniquitatem adversum me* and as spelt out by Rashi, IE[1], Kara and Calvin.[231]

The main problem in this verse is in the second stich. Do we have an imperative 'judge my cause' (MT, V, T and Aq), or should we read, with LXX and P, the indicative, 2nd p. s. perfect, as in the first stich: 'you judged my cause'—a reference to past experience? The Masoretes vocalised שפטה as the lengthened (with paragogic ה) form of the imperative (GK 48i). Cappel (254), Schleusner (42), *BHK* and Haller (106) think that the *Vorlage* of LXX and P must have been שָׁפַטְתָּ, while NEB (see Brockington, 218) explains LXX as having vocalised שָׁפְטָה (for שְׁפַטְתָּה); cf. also Rudolph (1962, 233) and Kraus (53). Most translations and scholars follow MT[232] and explain LXX and P as being influenced by the context of 2nd p. m. forms, cf. *BHQ*, Albrektson (166f.). The imperative of MT may seem somewhat inappropriate in the context, and this may explain the

---

[231] Calvin is aware that others render this *iniquitatem meam*; and Schute (147 n. 196) draws attention to Pagnini's 'my perversity', but neither of these renderings appear to discern the objective nature of the suffix.
[232] AV, Luther, Calvin, JPS, NRSV, NIV, Keil (402), Wiesmann (196), Hillers[2] (112), Renkema (457), Berlin (81), House (427).

readings of LXX and P as perfect, either in transmission or by translator initiative (though, in the case of the slavish LXX, this is unlikely), but it should be noted that the pattern of perfect followed by imperative/ prohibition is found at v. 56. The speaker may be recounting past experience in order to launch his plea to Yahweh for present intervention.

In previous verses, the speaker has related the positive interventions of Yahweh in his life. Now he confronts Yahweh with the present situation vis-à-vis the enemies (v. 46); and this is his theme until the end of the poem. It is significant that the poet uses the verb ראה here (and in v. 60).[233] At v. 50 the speaker vows to plead with Yahweh until he pays attention (ראה). Here he puts it to Yahweh that, on the basis of the speaker's past experience, Yahweh has indeed noticed the many wrongs done to him, and he cries out to the judge of all the earth (Gen 18.25; Ps 94.2) for present justice. The fact that the poet uses the longer form of the 2nd p. s. (רָאִיתָה) may be due to stylistic considerations, for it would not be noticed in oral presentation of the passage. Visually, however, and combined with the imperative (with paragogic ה)[234] the effect is surely to raise the urgency level of the prayer. This is further enhanced by the degree of assonance in שָׁפְטָה מִשְׁפָּטִי.

3.60

Text and Versions

MT נִקְמָתָם—followed by LXX, P and T; Sym τὴν μῆνιν; V *furorem*. MT is not seriously in question. V does not represent the 3rd p. m. pl. suffix in the first stich, though it *is* translated in the second stich. The other Versions support MT here, so it may be that Jerome considered his suffix *eorem* was doing double duty. The same might, perhaps, be said of Sym here.

MT כָּל־מַחְשְׁבֹתָם—followed by V and T; LXX[BA] εἰς πάντας διαλογισμοὺς αὐτῶν; P ܘܟܠ ܕܬܚܫܒܘ *wkl d'thšbw*. The unusual rendering of LXX is interesting. Ziegler's edition omits εἰς on the basis of one MS and SH, agreeing with MT. But other MSS have καί in place of εἰς. The copula is not surprising—P often adds it—but εἰς is another matter. Rudolph (1938, 115) regards it as a scribal error for καί. We may explain the latter on the same grounds as we would explain the copula in P, *viz.* as natural expansion,[235] cf. *BHQ*. It may be that a copyist felt that some help was needed to interpret the combination of the verb 'to see' with מַחְשְׁבֹתָם. The scribe understood the passage as having insight *into* (εἰς) inner machinations. P translates freely; MT is preferred.

MT לִי; LXX ἐν ἐμοί; P ܥܠܝ *'ly*, also T; V *adversum me*. Albrektson (167) draws attention to the similarity between v. 60b and v. 61b. The only difference is that in v. 61b the final form is עָלַי. Some Hebrew MSS have לִי in both verses. LXX preserves the variation of MT (though some Greek MSS have ἐπ' ἐμοί in v. 60b), while P, V and T have the same in both passages. Meaning is not really at stake, and MT is preferred.

* * *

---

[233] It is not just a matter of fact: it is almost accusatory.
[234] JM (143) notes that the imperative with paragogic ה is emphatic in origin, though the nuance is not always evident; cf. GK 48i,k.
[235] Note that Luther, AV, RV, Douai all add the copula in translation.

Harking back to 'all our enemies' of v. 46, the speaker picks up the wrongs referred to in the previous verse, explicating them in terms of genre, though not in specifics. 'You have seen' is repeated as Yahweh continues to be addressed, to stress that Yahweh is witness and that the ball is in his court.

The noun נִקְמָה does not occur elsewhere in Lamentations. It has the meaning 'revenge' or 'retribution', cf. Lipiński (1999, 1). The 3rd p. pl. suffix (in both stichs) has no immediate referent but it must surely refer to the enemies of v. 46. As nothing has been said about the *reason* for revenge,[236] the question arises as to the identification of the enemies. Clearly, 'our enemies' of v. 46 are the enemies of the people of Yahweh, but it can hardly be said that the Babylonian conquest amounted to revenge. Renkema (458f.) suggests that the author has the Edomites in mind here. Relations between Israel and Edom left a lot to be desired from the early monarchic period onward, cf. 2 Sam 8.13f.; 1 Kgs 11.14-16, 25; and Edom is depicted as co-operating with Babylon in the destruction of Judah (Ps 137.7; Obad 11, 13f.). The latter could be said to amount to revenge; and Ezek 25.12-17 refers to Israel's vengeful enemies, in particular Edom's revenge (√נקם) against Judah (v. 12). As Edom is the only enemy named in Lamentations (4.21-22), there may be something in Renkema's suggestion. The poet is, however, writing much later than Renkema believes, hence we must think of this revenge as continuing long after the fall of Jerusalem.

כָּל־מַחְשְׁבֹתָם—The word מַחֲשָׁבָה from √חשב can mean 'thought' or 'plan'. It can have a positive slant (Ps 40.6) or it may refer to evil intention (Ps 33.10). The context here suggests that the author has the evil plots of the enemy in mind. IE[1] sees in this verse a contrast between the vengeful acts (כָּל־נִקְמָתָם) done in public and the further unspecified, clandestine plans (כָּל־מַחְשְׁבֹתָם) of the enemy. Yahweh has witnessed the former and sees/knows the latter.

3.61

Text and Versions
MT יְהוָה—followed by V, P, T, OL, SH; LXX omits. The omission of the Tetragammaton in LXX must be the result of a scribal error. Apart from the fact that it is present in all the other Versions, its absence affects the rhythm of the line in that the first stich is too short.

* * *

The author continues to remind Yahweh that he is witness, that he has heard the insults and the planning of the enemies. For IE[1], the scenario is the exile.

---

[236] Perhaps that is why Sym and V translate this 'wrath, anger'.

This verse resembles v. 60 in structure and in vocabulary. The second stich is almost identical with v. 60b, and the verb (שָׁמַעְתָּ) again governs both stichs. Rudolph (1962, 233) regards the second stich as corrupt since it is almost a repeat of v. 60b. He proposes מַלְשְׁנֻתָם 'ihr Verleumden' from the denominative verb לשׁן 'to insult' (Ps 101.5; Prov 30.10). This is certainly a good parallel to חֶרְפָּתָם in the first stich, but Rudolph has produced a *hapax legomenon*. The repeat phrase may offend our sensibilities but may have been quite acceptable in Hebrew verse, cf. Eccl 4.1. Wiesmann (196) follows Rudolph here.

3.62

Text and Versions

MT שִׂפְתֵי קָמַי—so also LXX, V, OL; P ܣܦܘܬܐ ܕܩܝܡܝܢ *spwtʾ dqymn*. P struggled and rendered freely, cf. Albrektson (168).

MT וְהֶגְיוֹנָם; LXX καὶ μελέτας αὐτῶν; V *et meditationes eorum*; P ܘܪܢܝܢ *wrnyn*. The text of this verse is not in question. The word הגיון 'utterance, musing' occurs only in the singular in Biblical Hebrew (Pss 9.17; 19.15; 92.4) but may be taken as a collective (especially following the plural שִׂפְתֵי קָמַי) as has been done in the translations of LXX, OL, P and V, which render in the plural, cf. Kelso (49). P, which translates freely, seems to have avoided the Syriac ܗܓܝܢ *hgynʾ* 'meditation', probably because it always appears in a positive sense, while this passage has to do with negative thinking/expressions.

* * *

The speaker adds further to what Yahweh has heard and witnessed.

שִׂפְתֵי—Plural constr. of שָׂפָה f. noun 'lip, utterance'—a poetic reference to a plethora of utterances; cf. Job 11.2 אִישׁ שְׂפָתַיִם 'one full of talk' (NRSV).

קָמַי—Qal part. m. pl. from √קוּם with accusative suffix 1st p. s.: literally 'those who rise against me', i.e. 'my assailants' (NRSV). The reference is probably the same as the 3rd p. pl. suffix in vv. 60f. (GK 116i).

וְהֶגְיוֹנָם—The translations of LXX, OL, V almost give the impression that the enemies are engaged in audible study. עָלַי is ambiguous but in the context must mean 'against me'; and the combination is best understood as 'murmurings against me'; cf. IE[1], who makes the cryptic comment לְרָעָתִי 'to my hurt'; cf. also LXX, V, MLT, Keil (402). It is not clear if v. 62 continues the accusatives of the √verb שמעת in v. 61 or is a free-standing statement. LXX, OL, P and V follow the former,[237] while T prefers the latter.[238] Whichever way it is taken, the meaning is not greatly affected.

---

[237] Cf. also AV, Calvin, Luther, Vermigli (148), NEB, JPS, NJB, NIV, Rudolph (1962, 230), Renkema (462).
[238] Cf. also Gordis (145), Kraus (52), Kaiser (346), NRSV, Hillers[2] (112), Berlin (81), ESV.

כָּל־הַיּוֹם—MLT cites Ps 44.23 'Because of you we are being killed all the day', which cannot simply mean 'all the day', and suggests that this phrase should be taken in a transferred sense, meaning 'generation after generation'. Clearly, the midrash interprets the 1st p. s. as collective, referring to the people of Yahweh in general. In this passage the phrase is poetic for 'constantly'.

3.63

Text and Versions

MT הַבִּיטָה—followed by LXX, V, OL, T; P ܐܣܬܟܠ ’stklt. Albrektson (168) explains P's 1st p. s. perfect as due to the translator's general misunderstanding of the line plus the presence of the pronoun אֲנִי. The suggestions of Kelso (49), that P's *Vorlage* read אביטה, or of Rudolph (1938, 116), that the *Vorlage* was הביני, are unnecessary.

MT מַנְגִּינָתָם; LXX^B ἐπ᾽ ὀφθαλμοὺς αὐτῶν; OL *in oculos eorum*; V *psalmus eorum*; P ܡܢ ܪܢܝܗܘܢ *mn rnyhwn*; Aq ᾆσμα; Sym ψαλμός; T זמריהון. The *hapax legomenon* is probably the reason for the variations in the Versions. The Masoretes vocalised מַנְגִּינָתָם—a f. s. noun with 3rd p. m. pl. suffix, interpreting it like נְגִינָתָם in 3.14 (q.v.) 'their mocking song'.[239] It would seem that P mistook the *mem* for the preposition מִן but otherwise is in accord with MT (Albrektson, 169). The consonantal text may be read as singular (מַנְגִּינָתָם) or plural (מַנְגִּינֹתָם), and T took the plural option, while P, V, Aq and Sym render in the singular. LXX 'upon their eyes' does not make sense, and this is the result of faulty transmission. The fact that, at 3.14, LXX rendered נגינתם by ψαλμὸς αὐτῶν leads us to conclude that LXX originally had ψαλμὸς (or ψαλμοὺς, cf. SH ܐܢܐ ܡܢ ܙܡܝܪܬܐ ܕܝܠܗܘܢ *’n’ mn zmyrt’ dylhwn*) and not ὀφθαλμούς. Hence Ziegler (486f.), following Döderlein (1780, 204), adopts ἐγὼ ψαλμὸς αὐτῶν. Robinson (1933, 258; *BHK*) suggests that LXX originally had ἐγὼ ἀπὸ ψαλμοῦ αὐτῶν. This could then be explained as the translator understanding the *hapax* as נְגִינָתָם plus the preposition מִן.[240]

* * *

The speaker draws Yahweh's attention to the fact that the enemies continually taunt him with mocking songs.

הַבִּיטָה—Hiphil imper. of √נבט with paragogic ה; cf. v. 59 and see on 1.11; 2.20 and 5.1. In this verse the suffixes have the same referent as those in v. 62. The form שִׁבְתָּם is Qal infin. constr. from √ישׁב with suffix. The form קִימָתָם, another *hapax legomenon*, is a f. noun, קִימָה (cf. קִינָה, see BL 452 q), with suffix[241] from √קום. The pair together are probably meant to

---

[239] MLT suggests that the word is to be understood as a variant spelling of מרנינתם from √רנן 'to murmur'—נ is in place of ר: כמו נאסר ראצר שהם רוגנים עלי. The reference is to the variation in the spelling of Nebuchadnezzar/Nebuchadrezzar (Jer 21.7; 29.1). But MLT has produced another *hapax legomenon*! IE¹ equates it with נְגִינָתָם, citing Job 30.9, adding, simply, that *mem* is an additional letter; cf. Rössler (1962, 128) who understands the latter to be an enclitic *mem*: 'besser ⁿnı-ma nᵉgînātām'.

[240] By the time of the LXX and P translations, the present form then existed, in that they misinterpret the initial *mem*, but it is *possible* that V, T, Aq and Sym read נְגִינָתָם.

[241] McDaniel (204f.) has suggested that the final *mem* in שִׁבְתָּם and קִימָתָם is an adverbial *mem* and not a pronominal suffix, but in view of the several instances of 3rd p. m. pl.

convey total activity—see Ps 139.2, שִׁבְתִּי וְקוּמִי, and cf. Deut 6.7; 11.19; Isa 37.28; hence Hillers² (112) 'in everything they do'.

On the syntax of the line there is some disagreement. Because of the (transitive) imperative,²⁴² הַבִּיטָה, which addresses Yahweh and which is located in the first stich, the first two forms are often taken as the object of that imperative. This is what we find in LXX, V, OL, AV, Calvin, Vermigli (150), Gottwald (15), RSV, Nägelsbach (137), Keil (402), Renkema (463). But it is best to take the opening phrase²⁴³ as adverbial, so IE² (תמיד), Michaelis (1773–88, 148), Löhr (1894, 18), Ewald (341), Wiesmann (196), Dyserinck (375), Meek (29), Provan (108), Westermann (167), Berlin (81). T's rendering maintains the ambiguity of the Hebrew. Levine (71) takes the phrase as adverbial, while Brady (164) translates 'Look at their sitting and rising!'

3.64

Text and Versions
MT גְּמוּל—followed by LXX, V, OL; P ܦܘܪܥܢܗܘܢ pwr'nhwn followed by one MS^(de Ros); T גמולא בישא. The suffix in P (also in MS^(de Ros)) is the result of the translator (or scribe) adding value to his text; cf. Albrektson (169) and *BHQ*.

MT כְּמַעֲשֵׂה יְדֵיהֶם—followed by P; LXX κατὰ τὰ ἔργα τῶν χειρῶν αὐτῶν followed by V, OL, T.

It is also unlikely that LXX, V, OL and T read מעשי (so *BHK*). It may be that these translators understood מעשה as a collective (Kelso, 49). Albrektson (170) and *BHQ* explain the pl. as an error due to the sound of the s. and pl. being the same.²⁴⁴

* * *

The speaker, having reiterated the evil actions of the enemy, now pleads with Yahweh to intervene on his behalf; and this continues to the end of the poem.

As the three lines of the final stanza must begin with the letter ת, the poet elects to employ the imperfect 2nd p. m. s. of three verbs with the force of the imperative; cf. Isa 18.3 (GK 107n). The ending is typical of communal and individual laments where Yahweh is called upon to bring retribution on the enemy aggressors. In this verse there is a plea that the enemies should receive what they deserve 'according to their deeds'. The question arises as to responsibility. Yahweh has brought punishment, and

---

suffixes in these verses this is not likely; besides, as Ehrlich (45) observes, the phrase itself is in the adverbial accusative of time.
²⁴² The observation made by Meek (29), that RSV's 'behold' has no basis in the original, is incorrect.
²⁴³ The acrostic structure has influenced the position of the phrase.
²⁴⁴ It should be noted that at Pss 28.4 and 62.13 the same inconsistency occurs. LXX renders the singular by the plural, though V here maintains the singular, while P follows singular in Ps 28.4 but the plural in Ps 62.13.

the enemies have been his instruments. According to Renkema (465f.), the guilt of the enemies hangs on their having gone beyond the mandate received from Yahweh, but there is nothing in the text to suggest that the speaker has made this judgment.

גְּמוּל—'Recompense' is construed with שׁוּב at 2 Chron 32.25; Ps 28.4; Prov 12.14; Joel 4.4, 7. It can have a positive meaning, the meaning depending on the context. At Ps 103.2 and 2 Chron 32.25 it means 'benefit', but more often it has the force of 'requital'; hence, the Targumist renders 'evil recompense'.

3.65

Text and Versions

MT מְגִנַּת־לֵב; LXX ὑπερασπισμὸν καρδίας; P ܬܕܐ ܕܠܒܐ *krywtʾ dlbʾ*; V *scutum cordis*; T תבירות לבא. MT is preferred.

MT תַּאֲלָתְךָ לָהֶם; LXX μόχθον σου αὐτοῖς; P ܘܡܚܘܬܟ ܠܗܘܢ *wmḥwtk lhwn*; V *laborem tuum*; T ושלהיאותך ישלהי להון. MT is not in question. The non-representation of the second לָהֶם in V is not significant. Jerome may have felt that *eis* in the first stich did double-duty (cf. on v. 60), especially since he translates the second stich in the accusative, so understanding it as in apposition to מְגִנַּת־לֵב. It is represented in the other Versions.

* * *

The invective continues to build up, cf. 1.21f.; 2.21f.

Two *hapax legomena* in this verse have made elucidation difficult and have occasioned a variety of translations and exegesis from earliest times to the present day. Compare, for example, V's rendering with NEB: V *dabis eis scutum cordis laborem tuum* = 'You shall give them a heart shield, your work'; NEB 'Show them how hard thy heart can be, how little concern thou hast for them'.

מְגִנַּת־לֵב—מְגִנַּת is vocalised by the Masoretes as if from √גנן 'to cover, defend'. LXX, in characteristically literal fashion, renders 'a shielding (of heart)', deriving it from the same root but preserving the obscurity. So also V— Jerome understood מְגִנַּת to be a variant of מָגֵן 'shield', but his translation is opaque.[245] Although Syriac has a word meaning 'shield', P does not employ it. He translates 'sadness/anxiety of heart'. Either he had a different Hebrew text or he thought that the context demanded something more negative than shield. T's 'heartbreak, grief' may also be a similar guess. It is difficult to identify any other philological background to either P or T.[246] The trouble with LXX and V is that one expects the speaker to plead for something more aggressive to fall on his enemies; and

---

[245] We should note that, in the SH margin, the term is glossed by ܣܒܪܐ *sbrʾ* 'shield'.
[246] Schleusner (43) concludes that P (and T) did not know the meaning of מגנה.

a shielding of the heart/mind does not fall into that category. That is probably why P and T opt for a more suitable sentiment. MLT explains the term as meaning 'madness' (טירוף הדעת) and claims that this is based on Greek, but this is difficult to verify; cf. Delitzsch (1867, 343). MR refers to two opinions: the first, based on Gen 14.20, is identical with T; the second, based on Deut 33.29, takes it to mean עזיזות ליבא 'hard of heart' or 'obduracy' (Jastrow, 1061). Rashi glosses שבר לב, citing Hos 11.8 and Gen 14.20, and seems to follow T (so also Kara), though he is aware of other views.[247] IE[1] is of a different opinion, though in citing Isa 31.5 (גַּנּוֹן) his precise meaning is not clear, except that he takes it from √גנן. Calvin translates *impedimentum cordis (alii, obstinationem)*, commenting that the author '…no doubt meant blindness of heart, and at the same time included stupidity'. Luther 'das Herz erschrecken' = '(let) their heart be frightened' may suit the context but appears to be a mere guess. AV 'sorrow of heart' may be following T (or P). Keil (428f.) thinks that the expression is analogous to κάλυμμα ἐπὶ τὴν καρδίαν at 2 Cor 3.15; and he translates 'blindness of heart'; but, again, this seems to be guesswork.

Not many emendations have been suggested. Torczyner (1912, 403) thought that the original text read גְּמוּלָם but, as Rudolph (1962, 234) observes, this is too close to the sentiments of v. 64. Perles (1930, 116), citing Ezek 21.20 (לְמוּג לֵב), suggests reading מִיגַת לב, i.e. a f. s. noun (which would be another *hapax legomenon*) מִיגָה from √מוג 'to melt'. But the sense of מְגִנַּת־לֵב eludes us. It is possible that an early scribal error is to blame and that MT is a corruption of מגפת לב 'plague of the mind'—a נ and a פ are very similar in the palaeo script (*nun* and *pe*). The word does occur in the construct at Zech 14.15; and at Zech 14.12 we are told that this plague shall strike all the nations that wage war against Jerusalem, i.e. enemies of Jerusalem.

Attempts have been made to discern another philology behind the term. Meek (30) suggests translating 'derangement of mind' (cf. MLT above) on the basis of an Arabic cognate, which he does not specify (possibly *janna*), but which is supplied by *HALOT majannat* 'insanity'; cf. also Gordis (187f.).

In the second stich, the second *hapax legomenon* also occasions some difficulty and this, combined with uncertainty as to syntax, leaves the would-be exegete in the dark.

תַּאֲלָתְךָ—'your curse' from √אלה II 'to curse, swear' (BDB 46). Although a *hapax legomenon*, the form is recognisable, with ת as nominal prefix (GK 85p-r; BL 495m). The syntax of the second stich is unclear. V takes

---

[247] In citing the Hosea and Genesis verses Rashi seems to be saying that these passages share the same meaning (or same root) as this passage. In his commentaries on Hos 11.8 and Gen 14.20, however, Rashi glosses אמנך with מסר (so also Kimḥi) and מגן with הסגיר!

it as in apposition to מִגְנַת־לֵב in the first stich, as do Calvin, AV, RV, Rudolph (1962, 234), Hillers[2] (112), Renkema (469), whereas most other translators/scholars—Luther, RSV, NIV, JPS, NRSV, Westermann (164), Gordis (145), Kraus (52), Gottwald (15), Haller (106), Kaiser (346), Berlin (81)—see it as a separate statement/wish, i.e. as a shortened form of תְּהִי תַאֲלָתְךָ לָהֶם 'may your curse be on them'. It is more appropriate to take it as a further wish, assuming a suppressed jussive תְּהִי, than as the object of תִּתֵּן of the first stich; cf. Keil (429). None of the Versions[248] translate 'curse', though it is recognised by IE[1] and MLT.

Rudolph (1938, 116) questions MT on the basis of haplography and wonders if the original should be אָתָת אֶלְתְךָ (= 3rd p. f. s. perf. Qal of √אתה 'to come' (see GK 75m) which he translates (1962, 230) 'dein Fluch kam über sie'.[249] The apparent difficulty (evident in *BHK*, KBL and Provan), in presenting the variant renderings/readings discussion, not only indicates the possibility that the *Vorlagen* of LXX, V and T read תלאתך, but also that the translators may have misread their texts.[250] In this connection, we may note Kara's comment on the word: 'As though to say, "All the troubles (תלאות) that you brought upon me bring on them…"'

A marginal note in SH reads ܐܘܠܝܬ ܕܡܢܟ ܠܗܘܢ *'wlyt' dmnk lhwn* 'your wailing (i.e. wailing from you) upon them',[251] which takes תַאֲלָתְךָ as from √אלה III 'to wail' (BDB 46).

3.66

Text and Versions

MT תִּרְדֹּף בְּאַף וְתַשְׁמִידֵם; LXX καταδιώξεις ἐν ὀργῇ καὶ ἐξαναλώσεις αὐτούς; P ܬܪܕܘܦ) ܬܪܕܘܦ ܘܒܪܘܓܙܟ ܬܘܒܕ ܐܢܘܢ (*trdwp*) *wbrwgzk twbd 'nwn*; V *persequeris in furore et conteres eos*; T תדלוקנון ברוגזא ותשיצנון. T represents an accusative suffix[252] on תִּרְדֹּף. It is natural to supply such an accusative here; see among translations Luther, RV, NIV, NRSV, NJB, JPS, NEB, Gordis (145), Westermann (164), Berlin (81), Renkema (471),

---

[248] LXX and V 'trouble, work', P 'scourge', T 'weariness'; cf. Kelso (49f.) and Levine (161) who draw attention to the apparent metathesis of א and ל, producing תלאתך.
[249] *HALOT* translates Rudolph incorrectly: 'your curse came over you'. *BHS* gives, as a propositum, אָתָא אֶלְתְךָ which seems to be a clumsy, inaccurate attempt at reproducing Rudolph. *BHK* mistakenly reckons that LXX and V read תַאֲלָתְךָ, when it should read תלאתך (corrected in *BHS* and *BHQ*); and Provan (109) makes the same mistake in the very sentence where he discusses the early confusion of the order of the consonants! *HALOT* also makes this mistake!
[250] At 3.5, T translates תְּלָאָה with the same term (Jastrow, 1578). T's 'your weariness' is probably based on a form from √לאה; P 'your affliction' may also be based on this root but we cannot be certain, cf. *BHQ* and Albrektson (171), while Schleusner (43) thinks that P could be a weak translation of MT.
[251] Ziegler (487) and Schäfer (*BHQ*) attribute this to Sym, but there is no indication of authorship in SH; cf. Field (758).
[252] *BHK* and *BHS* claim that LXX read תרדפם, but this is probably not so; see Ziegler (487), Rudolph (1938, 116), Schäfer (*BHQ*, 130*).

all of which supply the accusative without adopting a different Hebrew text; and Douai supplies it although V does not represent it! P adds a 2nd p. m. s. suffix to בְּאַף, though LXX and T follow MT. Again, it may be natural to fill out the expressions, as P is certainly inclined to do—he did it in 3.43—and we find it in Dahood (189) and Gordis (145).

MT מִתַּחַת שְׁמֵי יְהוָה; LXX ὑποκάτω τοῦ οὐρανοῦ κύριε; V *sub caelis Domine*; P ܡܢ ܬܚܝܬ ܫܡܝܟ ܡܪܝܐ *mn thyt šmyk mry*; T מתחות שמי מרומא דיי. MT is not in question (see below).

* * *

The imagery in this verse is from the hunt. Yahweh is urged to hunt down the enemies of Israel and to wipe them out. MLT suggests that the very memory of the enemy is to be obliterated from the world. The sovereignty of Yahweh is caught in the phrase 'heavens of Yahweh', and the poet exults in the certainty of the exercise.

מִתַּחַת שְׁמֵי יְהוָה—T is the only Version that follows MT (though it adds an adjective after שְׁמֵי). LXX, P and V all take יְהוָה as vocative. LXX and V render שְׁמֵי as absolute (the heavens), while P adds a suffix (*your* heavens). The ancient translators were probably faced with the same text as the Masoretes but were troubled by the fact that the two verbs address יְהוָה, yet in that address Yahweh seems oddly to appear in the third person. The fact that יְהוָה was in the vocative at the beginning of the final stanza (v. 64) led them to take the final יְהוָה as vocative also and, subsequently, to make sense of the stich. Change of person within a sentence is not unknown in the Hebrew Bible. IE[1] comments: 'it is like שְׁמֵיך, like (Exod 24.1): And God said unto Moses, "Go up to the Lord..."'; cf. also Amos 4.11f. where the third person ('God') is found in a speech of Yahweh. In support of MT, see AV, NRSV, JPS, Löhr (1906, 22), Ewald (341), Gordis (145), Renkema (473), Westermann (168), Kaiser (346), Gottlieb (56), Schäfer (*BHQ*, 130*).

However, several commentators opt for an emendation here. Perhaps the mildest is that of Ehrlich (45) who suggests vocalising שָׁמַי 'my (= the speaker's) heavens' and taking יְהוָה as vocative, the consonantal text remaining the same as in MT. Gottlieb (55f.) points out that the expression 'my heavens' nowhere appears on the lips of Israel, but Deut 28.23 speaks of your (= Israel's) heavens...shall be brass', and Albrektson (172) points out that at Lev 26.19 and Deut 33.28 the suffix on 'heavens' refers to Israel, so that if Israel is speaking here, the phrase 'under my heavens' could mean 'the land I live in'.

The reading השמים יהוה 'the heavens, O Yahweh', claimed by Kelso (50) to underlie LXX, is favoured by Dyserinck (376) and House (402), while several translations and commentators have adopted the reading שמיך יהוה 'your heavens, O Yahweh', claiming P in support—RSV, Wiesmann (196), Rudolph (1962, 234), Kraus (52), Meek (30), Gottwald (15), NEB.[253] A variation of this is reading שמיך and deleting יהוה, probably

---

[253] There is no reference to this emendation in Brockington (218).

originating with Budde (1892, 272), and it is followed by Löhr (1894, 18), Plöger (148), Haller (106), JB, NJB. The thinking behind this is (a) the stich is over-long, and b) the phrase שְׁמֵי יְהוָה is an explication of שָׁמֶיךָ. The latter appears in an address to Yahweh at Pss 8.3 and 144.5. While 'your heavens' allows for a shorter and so more typical stich, we should not press the metre argument too far, especially since we are at the conclusion of the poem. The poet may be ending with a flourish.

CHAPTER 4

Introductory

This chapter has some affinities with chs. 1 and 2. It begins in the same way: Alas! It, too, is an alphabetic acrostic, and the poetic rhythm is the same. These features show that the style which we first encountered in ch. 1 was considered appropriate and attractive to someone contributing to the commemoration process. Another similarity to the first two chapters is the use of different voices; and the order of the alphabet in this chapter agrees with that adopted in ch. 2. There are differences, and we should note that it is shorter than chs. 1 and 2: although there are 22 verses, corresponding to the letters of the alphabet, there are only two lines to each verse, while chs. 1 and 2 had three lines to a verse. Other important differences, though on the level of content, are that Yahweh, though mentioned in vv. 11 and 16, is not addressed at all; and the poem ends with a threat to local enemy, Edom. The chapter may be divided thus: vv. 1-16, 17-20, and 21-22.

Verses 1-16: These verses amount to a list of observations on the suffering of the population. The poem begins (vv. 1-2) as though the author was trying to put in a nutshell and in figurative language the scene after the fall of Jerusalem. The people of Zion, whom he regards as more precious than gold, have been treated like mere pottery. Thus the dirge-like theme of tragic reversal sets the scene for the remainder of this section. The author then proceeds to dwell on the dire effects of the famine which began with the siege of Jerusalem. He observes that sucklings are deprived of sustenance, and children lack food of any kind. (vv. 3-4). This is not surprising in that those who had been wealthy and well-to-do are reduced to foraging in dunghills (v. 5). At v. 6 the poet pauses to reflect on the situation, for this is worse than that experienced by Sodom. The hyperbole is marked here. The reference to the fine aspect of the nobles prior to the siege, compared to their present appearance, is in exaggerated language (vv. 7-8). A related reflection is that those who died by the sword were better off than those who survived (v. 9). Then the ultimate horror of the famine—women cooking their own children (v. 10)—leads the author to reflect theologically: We must acknowledge that it was Yahweh's anger that has destroyed Zion (v. 11), for everyone, even foreigners, had believed that Jerusalem was impregnable (v. 12). That old dictum had gone! And Zion's demise can be linked to wrongdoing (cf. v. 6), in particular, the sins of the prophets and priests (cf. 2.14), accused here of murder (v. 13). The final three stanzas of this section are obscure and, perhaps, corrupt, but they appear to continue to describe the effect of the aforementioned blood-shedding and resultant defilement (vv. 14-16; see commentary).

Verses 17-20: The voice changes, or rather the speaker (in vv. 1-16) begins (by using first person plural verbs etc.) to speak as for the entire community. He looks back at the scenario which obtained before the conditions he has just been describing and laments the fact that help from Egypt had not materialised (v. 17). Turning back to the scene he had been describing, he alludes to the effects of the enemy's dominance and ruthlessness, involving restricted movement, which prompts him to conclude that the end was upon the people of Yahweh. He indulges in further hyperbole in his description of the prowess of the enemy hunting down the would-be escapees (vv. 18-19). Then, as though the last hope lay with the Davidic dynasty, the poet alludes to the capture of their king (v. 20).

Verses 21-22: The final verses are unique in Lamentations. A prophetic voice—the nearest we get to the divine voice—issues a threat to the Edomites who have infiltrated the land, and at the same time, an oracle to Zion which comes close to predicting an end to adversity.

Translation

1. Alas, gold is grown dim, fine gold is changed; precious stones lie scattered at the head of every public place.

2. Alas, the precious people of Zion, more precious than fine gold, are now reckoned as earthenware, the handiwork of a potter!

3. Even jackals offer the teat, they suckle their cubs: but my people are become cruel, like ostriches in the desert.

4. Sucklings' tongues stick to their palates with thirst; children beg for bread but no one gives them a crumb.

5. Those who ate dainties are desolate in the streets, those brought up in scarlet now cling to dunghills.

6. The punishment of my people is greater than that of Sodom, which was overthrown suddenly without a hand being laid on her.

7. Her nobles had been brighter than snow, more dazzling than milk; in body they were ruddier than coral, their hair (shone) like sapphire.

8. Now they look darker than soot, not recognised in the streets; their skin shrivels on their bones, become dry as wood.

9. Better off were those slain by the sword than those slain by famine, who pined away pierced for lack of food from the field.

10. Hands of compassionate women have boiled their own children; they became their food when my people were destroyed.

11. Yahweh has carried out his wrath, poured out his anger; he started a fire in Zion, and it consumed her foundations.

12. Neither the kings of the earth nor any of the world's inhabitants believed that adversary or foe could ever enter the gates of Jerusalem.

13. It was for the sins of her prophets and the iniquities of her priests who, in her midst, had shed the blood of the just.

14. They wandered blindly in public, defiled with blood,
    So that no one could touch their garments.

15. Away! Unclean![1] Away! Away! Do not touch!
    When they fled, they also wandered;[2] they should stay here no longer.

16. Yahweh himself scattered them, he no longer regards them.
    The priests are shown no respect, the elders no favour.

17. Still, our eyes failed looking for our vain help;
    From our towers we watched for a nation powerless to save.

18. Our movement is restricted[3] so that we cannot walk in public;
    Our end is close! Our days are numbered! For our end is come.

19. Our pursuers were swifter than the eagles in the sky;
    They pursued us hotly in the hills, they ambushed us in the desert.

20. The breath of our nostrils, Yahweh's anointed was caught in their traps,
    Of whom we had thought: 'In his shadow we shall live among the nations'.

21. Rejoice and be glad, O Edom, dwelling in the land;[4]
    But to you, too, the cup will pass; you will get drunk and strip naked!

22. Your guilt, O Zion, has run its course, it will not cause you further deportation.
    He will punish your iniquity, O Edom, he will uncover your sins!

Commentary

4.1

Text and Versions

MT יוּעַם—so also LXX, V and T; P ܡܣܬܠ *mstlʾ*; Aq ἀμαυροῦται—so also Sym. MT is preferred.

MT יִשְׁנֶא; several MSS^Ken ישנה; LXX ἀλλοιωθήσεται; P ܘܫܢܐ *wšnʾ*; T אשתני. MT is preferred (see below).

MT הַכֶּתֶם הַטּוֹב; LXX τὸ ἀργύριον τὸ ἀγαθόν; P ܕܗܒܐ ܛܒܐ *ṣwbʿ špyrʾ*; V *mutatus est color optimus*; Aq βάμμα. Versions probably read the same text as MT.

MT אַבְנֵי־קֹדֶשׁ; LXX λίθοι ἅγιοι—so also P; Aq ἡγιασμένοι; V *lapides sanctuarii*; T מרגלאוון קדישין. Differences not due to different underlying text (see below); it may be that קדש should receive a different pointing—קָדֵשׁ?

* * *

---

[1] *Unclean!* prb. rdg. Heb. adds *they called to them*.
[2] *Wandered* prb. rdg. Heb. adds *they said among the nations*.
[3] *Our movement is restricted* prb. rdg. Heb. reads *They hunted our steps*.
[4] *In the land* so Sept. Heb. reads *in the land of Uz*.

The poem begins (אֵיכָה) as in chs. 1 and 2. In the first verse the author announces his reversal theme in poetic fashion, and the verse serves as a thematic heading (cf. Gerstenberger, 498). On אֵיכָה, see on 1.1.

יוּעַם—Another unusual form, usually taken as Hophal of √עמם II 'darken, be dim'. LXX ἀμαυρωθήσεται is another example of the Greek translator's strict adherence to his *Vorlage*, in that he represents the Hebrew imperfect with a future tense. The imperfects here, however, are not futures but describe a state of affairs (GK 107b) which the poet witnesses. P translates 'rejected, thrown away'. Albrektson (172f., cf. Abelesz, 23) is probably correct when he observes that the Syriac translator 'did not know the verb but tried to find a suitable rendering guided by the context'.[5] T (עמא) and V (*obscuratum est*) are in agreement with the LXX interpretation. MLT represents יועם with החשיך; Rashi cites Lev 13.6 where the Targum of כהה is עמיא; IE[1] indicates that there has been some debate about the form יועם. He, too, cites Lev 13.6 and the Targum there. He also cites Ezek 31.8 for another appearance of the root עמם, and Isa 28.28 where the Hophal of √דקק is יודק. He points out that some say עמם is like חשך; and Kara glosses יועם with the Hophal of חשך, citing also Ezek 28.3; 31.8, the only other occurrences of the root עמם.

יִשְׁנֶא—Although the Versions testify to its presence, ישנא has been considered a gloss (Budde 1892, 273; Löhr 1894, 18). From the point of view of rhythm, v. 1a scans better without it; and the Masoretic punctuation (where *zaqeph qaton* comes after זהב) would appear more natural. If it was an explanatory gloss (on the form יועם), the original text would have יועם doing double duty (for כתם as well as זהב), and this is a possibility. Bickell (1894, 116) suggests that ישנא is a corruption of ישן (cf. *BHK*) and translates 'altes Gold' giving a good parallel to כתם טוב; but on the basis of *difficilior lectio*, ישנא should not be so readily dismissed. Several MSS read ישנה, reflecting the variation in spelling of this ל"ה verb (cf. GK 75rr). LXX ἀλλοιωθήσεται shows that again the Greek translator has taken the Hebrew imperfect as a future. He understood ישנא to be from שנה 'to change' and he translated in the passive, that is, he may have vocalised יִשָּׁנֵא.[6] Rashi glosses ישנא with ישתנה, i.e. he senses that the verb has this passive meaning, cf. *HALOT*; cf. also Kara. IE[1] stresses that ישנא comes from the same root as שנים, i.e. √שנה.

הַכֶּתֶם הַטּוֹב—The subject of the verb ישנא has also caused some difficulty among translators and commentators. In the Hebrew Bible כֶּתֶם appears to mean 'gold' and is used as a parallel to זהב (Job 31.24) and פז (Isa 13.12).

---

[5] Hillers[2] (137f.), on the basis of his interpretation (96f.) of יָעִיב (2.1), emends the text to read יֻעַב, which he translates 'is despised', partly because, as he points out, 'Gold does not tarnish or grow dark in any striking way'. However, as Dobbs-Allsopp (130) notes, 'the occurrence of the impossible pointedly underscores the severity of the situation'. Hillers goes on to read יִשָּׂנֵא 'is hated' in the second stich.
[6] Cf. the note by Löhr (1894, 18) where this pointing is attributed to Nöldeke.

LXX ἀργύριον 'money, silver' is a strange rendering if only because LXX usually reserves this term for כסף; indeed, this is the only example of the term being employed for anything other than כסף. Consequently, *BHK* suggests that the *Vorlage* of LXX read הכסף. Rudolph (1938, 116), however, argues that 'ἀργύριον setzt keinen anderen Text voraus, sondern dient der Abwechslung im Ausdruck'; and Albrektson (173) agrees, pointing out that LXX is inclined to be free in its translation of כתם (cf. Job 31.24). P 'beautiful colour' seems, at first, to be a dubious translation of MT. Albrektson (173) excuses the Syriac translator by pointing out that there is no other word in Syriac for 'gold', that the P translator was rendering freely, and that ܫܦܝܪ *špyr'* for טוב is because P had already used ܛܒ *tb'* earlier in the line. Albrektson may well be right (especially regarding ܛܒ), but if the Syriac translator knew that כתם meant 'gold', ܨܘܒܥ *ṣwb'* is a strange term to employ as a synonym. It is more likely that he did not know the meaning of כתם and linked it with the root כתם *ktm* 'defile, stain'. T's paraphrase does not permit deductions as to how the translator understood כתם, but V 'the finest colour is changed' suggests that Jerome took it in the same way as P. The fact that Aq, at Isa 13.12, translates כתם with σπίλωμα 'defilement, filth',[7] even in the face of the parallel פז, and that here he renders 'dye' suggests that כתם meaning 'gold' was not universally known. MR seems to interpret כתם as אבן טובה ומרגליות 'precious stone and pearls' (cf. also MLT). Rashi has הכתם. קביצת כלי נוי הזהב שהם לעדי קרוי כתם; and this is the first mention of 'gold' in comments on כתם. IE[1] does not attempt to define כתם, while Kara glosses הכתם הטוב with אוצר, i.e. 'treasure', but there is no mention of gold. The word, which occurs in parallel with זהב at Job 31.24; Prov 25.12 and here, and which occurs in several other passages—Job 28.19; Ps 45.10; Song 5.1; 1QHa 26.8—is probably an Egyptian loan word[8] and was not known among the translators of the Versions on Lamentations.

אַבְנֵי־קֹדֶשׁ—LXX, P and T translate 'holy stones', cf. also RSV, NJB, NRSV. V 'stones of the sanctuary' takes a different line. Although there is no trace in either MR or MLT of this interpretation (that the poured out stones were the rubble of the fallen Temple), it is followed by Luther ('die Steine des Heiligtums') and Calvin and found its way into AV, RV, NEB and REB.[9] It is interesting to note that Rashi, IE[1] or Kara show no knowledge of V's interpretation. However, the absence of the definite article makes V's interpretation unlikely—stones of the sanctuary would probably be אַבְנֵי־הַקֹּדֶשׁ, cf. Ehrlich (45f.). But the translation 'holy/sacred stones' is unclear. The Targumist ('sacred jewels'), who understood the aforementioned reference to gold as that of the temple (cf. also Calvin), seems to take the phrase as denoting temple treasure; cf. Vermigli (152), Meek (30). Michaelis (1793, 435f.) took the term to be a reference

---

[7] Reider (1966, 287) argues that Aq derived the term from late Hebrew כֶּתֶם 'stain'.
[8] Lambdin (151f.) thinks that the Egyptian *ktm.t* = 'gold' may be a Sumerian loan word.
[9] The meaning of this phrase may not always be the same.

to jewels on the high priest's robe, part of his holy garments (בגדי קדש), while Löhr (1906, 24) suggests that the holy stones are jewels used in amulets, a view which Rudolph (1938, 116) embraces. Rashi's comment is interesting: אבני קדש. בנים המאירים כאבנים טובות. Schleusner says nothing of Rashi,[10] but notes the commentary by Michaelis (1773–88, 436)—'Ego in universum *lapides pretiosos* intelligere mallem'—which may have been a hunch, since he does not offer an explanation for the rendering, but this is an interpretation that seems to fit well in the context; indeed, Budde (1898[a], 99), without any reference to Schleusner, emends the text to read אַבְנֵי־יְקָר. Emerton (233-36) is of the same opinion as Schleusner, but his conclusions are philologically based. He notices that Arabic *qadīsun* means 'precious stone', that Aramaic קְדָשָׁא and Syriac ܩܕܫܐ *qdš*' have the meaning 'ear-ring' (in none of these cases is 'holy' involved, though we cannot rule out the possibility that these items served as amulets). He cites Brockelmann (649) who links the Syriac word with the Babylonian *qudāšu* (which occurs in a list of precious objects), and he thinks the latter word may derive from the root *qdš* 'be pure, bright' in Akkadian. The latter root lies behind the adjective *quddušu* 'brilliant/shining', and *qudāšu* may well be related. Emerton (236) renders 'precious stones' and this meaning is found in footnotes on NEB, REB; cf. also JPS.

בְּרֹאשׁ כָּל־חוּצוֹת—This phrase occurs at 2.19, and בחוצות occurs elsewhere in ch. 4 (vv. 5, 14). The scene is Jerusalem, and the phrase expresses the widespread nature of what is described by תשתפכנה אבני קדש. The poet is not speaking of actual gold or precious gems nor of the stones used to build the Temple. As v. 2 indicates, the references to gold etc. are to be understood figuratively (cf. Gottlieb, 61).

4.2

Text and Versions
The *BHS* suggestion of אַבְנֵי for MT בְּנֵי must be a misprint.[11] A ב is required for the acrostic sequence; besides, there is no support for it in the Versions or elsewhere.
MT הַמְסֻלָּאִים בַּפָּז; LXX οἱ ἐπηρμένοι ἐν χρυσίῳ;[12] P ܕܡܛܪܝܢ ܗܘܘ ܡܢ ܟܐܦ ܛܒܬܐ *dmtryn hww mn k'p' tbt*'; Sym οἱ ἐκλεκτοὶ ὑπὲρ χρυσίον πρωτεῖον; V *et amicti auro primo*; T דמתילין איקוניהון לדהב טב. The Versions' source was probably the same as MT.
MT מַעֲשֵׂה—so also P and V; LXX ἔργα; T עובדי. There is no need to assume (*BHK*, Schäfer, 130*) a plural construct מעשי in the *Vorlage* of LXX (cf. note on 3.64). The LXX often renders the term in the plural—Gen 5.29; Exod 18.20; 34.10.[13]

* * *

[10] And it must be said that Rashi is not specifically *defining* our phrase with אבנים טובות.
[11] Footnote (a) is also attached to נִבְלֵי־חֶרֶשׂ later in the verse, where it is also out of place.
[12] SH has a marginal note on the word for gold—ܣܘܡܩܐ *swmq*' 'red, reddish'.
[13] Albrektson (170) may be right in surmising that the variation may have resulted from the translator repeating the phrase to himself and then rendering the similar sounding plural form. Although the LXX translator is normally very careful, he may have been influenced by the fact that the referent, *viz.* בני ציון is plural; and the same consideration may have obtained with T.

The 'alas' of v. 1 is echoed in this verse as the poet tries to make sense of the terrible situation in which he finds himself: 'All is changed, changed utterly'.

It may be unusual, in the book of Lamentations, to find איכה repeated after v. 1, but there is no need to treat it with suspicion (cf. Kelso, 52). The exegesis of v. 1 is supplied by v. 2: the אַבְנֵי־קֹדֶשׁ are indeed the precious people of Zion who are 'worth their weight in finest gold' (REB). The poet, wishing to contrast the awful present with the glorious past, further emphasises this by the repetition of איכה; and his choice of language and imagery is intended to shock the reader: the beautiful expensive jewellery is now treated like pottery work (cf. Eccl 10.7). A radical upheaval in society is described by Ecclesiastes as 'slaves riding horses while princes walk on the ground', and the prayer of Lam 5.8 speaks of 'slaves ruling over us', but the author of ch. 4 expresses the astounding turnaround in the fortunes of his people by couching it in vivid poetic language. We thought very highly of Jerusalemites: they were the *crème de la crème*, but now they are become quite ordinary.

בְּנֵי צִיּוֹן הַיְקָרִים—'The precious people of Zion'. There is, clearly, a play on the word אבן here (v. 1a). Of the 71 instances of the adjective יקר in the Hebrew Bible, 18 of them occur qualifying the noun אבן. The pun is also present, but not so clearly, at Jer 31.20; indeed, this passage may have been in the poet's mind here.

הַמְסֻלָּאִים—The *hapax legomenon* (vocalised Pual participle, m. pl. from the root סלא 'to weigh') was puzzling for some early translators. The LXX translator: 'who were lifted (in value) with gold' was struggling. Some think that this translation is based on √סלל.[14] However, the Greek verb ἐπαίρω never renders the Hebrew סלל in LXX. We should note that that verb translates the Hebrew נשל 'to lift' in a context regarding comparative weight (Isa 40.15). The poet was probably thinking of the comparative (ב of comparison—see *HALOT* ב [14] and the renderings of P and Sym) value of the 'precious sons' vis-à-vis 'gold', but LXX is so literal that the sense is virtually lost. P's rendering 'who were better than precious stones' is a free translation or a guess (Albrektson, 174) and echoes Sym 'who were preferred to (better than) best gold'. V 'and clothed in best gold' is a guess, as is T 'whose appearance is like fine gold'. Albrektson (174) is probably correct when he claims that MT may be explained as a variant spelling of √סלה II 'weigh, balance'. The latter root (BDB 699), also in the Pual, is found at Job 28.16, 19, also with the construction ב and in similar context. There is, therefore, no need to emend the text, as does Rudolph (1938, 117), supposing the original to have been הַמְמֻלָּאִים.[15]

---

[14] Cf. Schleusner (46), Blayney (327), Kelso (52).
[15] Rudolph (1962, 245) renders 'die in Feingold gefasten'.

The poet uses a third word for gold—פָז—often translated 'pure/fine gold', found parallel with זהב at Pss 19.11; 119.127; Job 28.17 and with כתם at Isa 13.12. The effect is to emphasise the already hyperbolic descriptions of the people of Zion (cf. the titles given to Jerusalem at 1.1) and so draw attention to the contrast with the present state of affairs.

נֶחְשְׁבוּ לְנִבְלֵי־חֶרֶשׂ—The word חֶרֶשׂ can mean 'potsherd' (Isa 45.9) or 'earthenware' (Jer 19.1). Construed with the pl. constr. of נֵבֶל I 'jar', the meaning is 'earthenware vessels';[16] and the contrast with gold is further emphasized by the final phrase 'the work of the hands of a potter'. The construction נֶחְשְׁבוּ plus preposition לְ (cf. Job 41.19) has to do with evaluation—they are counted as earthenware vessels.

4.3

Text and Versions

MT (*Kethib*) תַּנִּין; MT (*Qere*) תַּנִּים—so also three MSS[Ken]; LXX δράκοντες; P ܝܪܘܪܐ *yrwr*ʾ; V *lamiae*; T חורמנא; Sym σειρῆνες. MT (*Kethib*) is preferred, see below and cf. Schäfer (130f*).

MT הֵינִיקוּ גוּרֵיהֶן—so also P and V; LXX ἐθήλασαν σκύμνοι αὐτῶν. MT is preferred, see below.

MT בַּת־עַמִּי followed by P and V; LXX θυγατέρες λαοῦ μου.[17] MT is preferred. MT לְאַכְזָר; LXX εἰς ἀνίατον; P ܠܡܚܘܝܘ ܕܠܝܬ ܠܗ ܐܣܘܬܐ *lmḥwtʾ dlyt lh ʾsywtʾ*; V *crudelis*. MT is preferred.

MT (*Kethib*) כִּי עֵנִים; MT (*Qere*) כַּיְעֵנִים + many MSS[Ken]; LXX ὡς στρουθίον; P ܐܝܟ ܢܥܡܐ *wʾyk nʿmʾ*; V *quasi strutio*; T כנעמיא; MT (*Qere*) is preferred. Albrektson (175) notes that P renders כ by ܐܝܟ *ʾyk* 'like', and this results in a very different meaning: 'like jackals, they uncover their breasts…'; but there is no referent for ܓܠܝ *gly* in the preceding verses, and the point of the verse is lost.[18]

* * *

The author employs two images from nature to introduce his description of his people: they do not measure up to jackals in their provision for their young and are more like the cruel ostriches.

תַּנִּין—תַּנִּים. MT (*Kethib*) has an Aramaising plural (GK 87c; cf. Lam 1.4); the form is usually תַּנִּים (Mic 1.8; Jer 9.10; 10.22). תַּן = jackal (BDB, KBL, Bodenheimer, 110f.). The plural is confusingly similar to the singular noun תַּנִּין meaning 'serpent, dragon, sea-monster' (e.g. Gen 1.21; Jer 51.34). LXX 'dragons' makes this mistake[19] but also renders it in the

---

[16] Cf. Honeyman (1939, 84f.). *BHS* entertains the possibility of reading אַבְנֵי חֶרֶשׂ 'stones of earthenware', but, quite apart from not being supported by Version or MS, this does not make good sense.

[17] The reading of Codex B—θυγατέρας—must be a scribal error.

[18] P may have tried, in translation, to maintain the acrostic at vv. 1-6 (cf. vv. 8f. and the *sound* of the beginning of v. 10, and spasmodically throughout), and ܓܠܝ may reflect this.

[19] Albrektson (174) notes that the same mistake by LXX is found at Mic 1.8; Jer 9.10.

plural! According to SH margin, Sym also translated with the plural—'sirens'.[20] P translates 'jackals', but V makes use of an unusual word, *lamiae* (= λάμια), which seems to refer to a fabulous monster or shark (LSJ, 1027). It is used by Jerome to translate לילית at Isa 34.14. And T, though very paraphrastic and bizarre, appears to understand the term as 'sea-monster'—חורמנא.[21] Clearly, LXX, V and T suspect that the poet is alluding to quite unusual creatures with which to compare בת עמי. MR interprets the term ירודתא, a term which Jastrow (594) notes is used in T to Mic 1.8 (for תנים)

The mediaeval exegetes, Rashi, Ibn Ezra and Kara, are not concerned with the exact meaning of the term. Luther reads 'Schakale' (= jackals), while Calvin has *serpentes* (= serpents), the latter probably accounting for AV 'sea monsters'. It is clear that there is a great deal of uncertainty as to the meaning here, and the *Kethib/Qere* readings may represent the same uncertainty: some felt that תן in the plural—either תנין or תנים—was the subject of the plural verb חלצו, while the form תנין reminded some of the sea-monster (Gen 1.21); and תנין was seen as a collective which might account for the plural verb. That uncertainty still dogs our steps; cf. Renkema (499f.). 'Jackals' is the preferred translation among most modern commentators—Westermann (194), Rudolph (247), Kaiser (360), Hillers[2] (138), Berlin (101), House (431); cf. RV, RSV, JB, NIV, JPS, NRSV. NEB, REB translate 'whales', though this is based on the emendation תַּנִּינִים. If we translate 'whale/sea-monster', we are in the realm of the fabulous, in that the activity of these creatures vis-à-vis their young is speculative; whereas if we choose 'jackals', we may imagine the poet appealing to known facts. It may be that the author had in mind the passages in Jer 9.11 and 10.22, where the prediction is that Jerusalem would become 'a den of jackals'. It could be that the poet had observed how jackals could carry on as normal among the city ruins. If 'sea-monsters' is meant, then the poet alludes to *stories* of the activity of such creatures. Even these monsters nourish their young. The point of the passage is that even in the realm of animals the young are nursed, but this is not the case in Zion. We might compare this with the passage at Isa 1.2 where Yahweh points to the instincts of the ass and the ox which are absent in his people. The poet wishes to stress here and in the following verse that the situation in Zion is desperate and that normal human activity has been severely disrupted. גם 'even' emphasises the comparison between jackals and the women of Zion (Calvin).

---

[20] Siren may denote some kind of wild bird noted for its singing sound (Muraoka 1993, 213); cf. also *KlPauly* 5, 79f. The uncertainty on the part of the SH translator is shown by his referring to the Hebrew (although he was translating from the Greek) thus: ܚܒ. ܐܪܢܒ.

[21] So WT; YT reads תנינא, which, according to Jastrow (1682), denotes a sea monster; cf. Alexander (2008, 165).

חָלְצוּ שַׁד—On the use of the perfect, see on 1.1. The jackals are depicted as women who draw out their breasts to suckle their young (cf. Calvin, Hillers[2], 139). By representing the animals in this way, the poet sharpens the contrast he wishes to make. Even those wild creatures who have begun to inhabit the city ruins (cf. 5.18) gently nourish their young. חָלְצוּ—The verb is used of drawing off the shoe in Deut 25.9, 10; Isa 20.2. IE[2] notices that the term תנין or תנים is m. pl. and yet גּוּרֵיהֶן has f. pl. suffix. Since the verbs are common plural, he deduces that the males take hold of the breasts of the females and feed the young of the females![22]

הֵינִיקוּ גּוּרֵיהֶן—LXX σκύμνοι, being nominative, is the subject of ἐθήλασαν, while גוריהן is the *object* of היניקו. Albrektson (175) notes that θηλάζω can mean both 'suckle' and 'suck' and that this may be the reason why some readings have the accusative σκύμνους. היניקו, however, can only be transitive; and MT, which is followed by P and V, is the superior reading.

בַּת־עַמִּי—As LXX renders בת עמי elsewhere (2.11; 3.48; 4.6, 10) with the singular, it would seem that the translator's *Vorlage* may have read בנות. T does have בנאתא דישׂראל but the entire verse is handled in such a midrashic fashion that one cannot deduce what the *Vorlage* was. Indeed, the plural in LXX (and T) is explainable 'as a more or less conscious, tendentious correction, in which the copyist has been guided by the understanding that in the context it is the individual mothers, not the nation as a whole, that have failed the children' (Gottlieb, 61). A number of scholars emend the Hebrew text and read בנות on the basis of LXX—Bickell (117), Budde (1898a, 99), Rudolph[23] (1938, 117), Kraus (72); so also JB. NEB and REB 'daughters' appears merely to be an interpretation of MT. Renkema (502) cautions against interpreting the analogy with sucking animals too strictly, in that the population as a whole is meant by בַּת־עַמִּי: 'The poets clearly have more than inadequately lactating mothers in mind; their reference is to the lack of parental care of the entire population'. The contrast between בת עמי and the תנין is not signalled by any particle, nor do any of the Versions introduce a contrasting element, cf. also Calvin, AV, RV. IE[2] highlights the contrast by his paraphrase ובת עמי לא עשתה כן. Kara, too, introduces the contrast thus אבל בת עמי, as does Luther 'aber die Tochter meines Volks', and most modern translations.

לְאַכְזָר—The adjective אכזר (cf. also אכזרי, see BDB 470) is an uncommon term[24] in the Hebrew Bible (Deut 32.33; Job 30.21) meaning 'cruel,

---

[22] He does note that others understand that it is the females who suckle their young.
[23] Rudolph (1962, 247) feels that the plural fits the context better in that the poet is referring to individuals, not the people as a whole.
[24] The formation with א (from √כזר, cf. GK 85b—note also אכזב 'deceitful' from √כזב 'to lie') may be related to the Arabic *elative* form, used for comparative and superlative purposes in Arabic, though this is not the case in Hebrew (cf. GK 133a[1]).

fierce'. The presence of the ל is attested in LXX, P and T, though the exegesis is different in each case. V does not represent the ל (in translation) but this may be because Jerome, although encountering it, felt that it introduced the predicate much like the passage at Dan 9.16; indeed, P introduces the verb 'to be' (ܗܘܐ *hwt*) to facilitate this. *BHK* and Westermann (196) wonder if היתה should be added after עמי; but P, as we have seen, is prone, occasionally, to introduce elements which may enhance understanding, so that we cannot assume that the Syriac translator's *Vorlage* contained היתה. Albrektson (176) is inclined to view the ל in the same light as in לנידה 1.8, though without a verb; and this is how several translators and commentators have understood the passage.[25] Eitan (1928, 202) suggests that ל functions here as an emphatic particle,[26] and he has been followed by Rudolph (1962, 245) 'fürwahr grausam', Gordis (189), Kraus (72), Hillers[2] (135, 139) 'truly cruel', Renkema (502f.), Gottlieb (61). Whether or not אכזר was a common term in ancient times is impossible to say, but the point that the poet wishes to make is that the people of Jerusalem are unusually (and unnaturally) cruel; and he does this by resorting to further animal imagery. LXX εἰς ἀνίατον 'incurable' is a strange rendering of לאכזר and makes little sense in the verse as a whole. As Albrektson (176) notes, LXX translates similarly at Isa 13.9 (MT אכזרי). P 'for which there is no cure' tallies with LXX here. It would seem that P is leaning upon LXX in both instances (cf. Kelso, 53f.).[27]

MT (*Kethib*) כִּי עֵנִים makes no sense in the context. It appears to begin a further reasoning, but even if we detect a m. pl. participle from, say, ענה III 'be afflicted', it is difficult to squeeze good sense from it; and MT (*Qere*) is usually accepted. יענים would be a unique form from [יָעֵן] 'ostrich' (BDB, *HALOT*), though the form יענה occurs a number of times. Whatever the meaning of יענים, the author believed, or was in the receipt of a tradition, that these creatures were characterised by their cruelty. In Job 39.13-18, reference is made to רננים, which Driver (1921, 317) thinks may be a poetic name for the ostrich. Indeed, several scholars (cf. *BHK*) emend MT there to יענים. The Versions differ as to the identification of this term, but V renders *strutio* 'ostrich' in the Job passage as well as in Lam 4.3. In the description of the רננים the passage depicts the female as neglectful of her eggs and harsh in her treatment of her chicks. Driver (1955, 137f.), who explains the term יענים as deriving from the reputation of the ostrich being greedy (Syriac ܝܥܢ *yʿnʾ* 'greedy'), takes the view that the bird's actions are misinterpreted, that it is, in fact, quite caring of its young. Whatever the facts, it is clear from our passage that the poet thinks otherwise and assumes that his readers will take his point.

---

[25] Cf. Berlin (101).
[26] Cf. Haupt (1894, 107-108), McDaniel (206-207).
[27] For a fuller discussion on this phenomenon, see Albrektson (176f.).

4.4

Text and Versions
No significant material.

* * *

The verse continues to develop the theme of starvation, hinted at in v. 3.[28] (The idea of starving children was also treated at 2.11f.) In the first half of the verse the poet depicts suckling children so deprived of moisture that their tongues are sticking to the roofs of their mouths. The implication here is that the mothers are themselves no longer able to produce milk, in that they themselves are so undernourished. The other half of the verse deals with the severe lack of food for the young (weaned) children (see 1.5; 2.11, 19, 20). Naturally, they ask for food (cf. 2.12), but the response is such that they go without.

לְשׁוֹן—This noun is usually feminine but here (as in Job 7.21) it is construed as masculine.

פֹּרֵשׂ אֵין לָהֶם—The form פרשׂ may be a variant spelling of פרס 'to break, divide' (BDB, *HALOT*)[29] as in Mic 3.3. This is taken for granted by MR which cites as parallels Jer 16.7 and Isa 58.7.[30] That LXX ὁ διακλῶν and V *qui frangeret* had *Vorlagen* reading פרס is doubtful (contra Kelso, 54). P uses ܩܨܐ *qṣ'* and adds the verb ܝܗܒ *yhb* by way of explanation (so Albrektson, 178): 'no one breaks[31] and gives to them'. T מושיט לית להום 'no one hands it to them', on the other hand, appears to take the verb to be פרשׂ 'to spread, extend'.

4.5

Text and Versions
No significant material.

* * *

Those who had been accustomed to living well are depicted as experiencing a devastating reversal to the point that they resort to dung heaps or rubbish pits—whether for scraps of food or for a measure of warmth generated there.

---

[28] Rashi interprets vv. 3f. together: 'They see their children crying out for bread, but no one gives/breaks off (פורס) to them, because their own lives come before that of their children on account of the famine'.
[29] IE¹ points out that פרשׂ is to be understood as פרס, as in Isa 58.7. He further comments that the meaning is 'a morsel of broken bread'—והוא פת לחם פתותה; cf. JPS, REB. Kara glosses it with בצע 'break off'.
[30] So also MLT, which refers to the cruelty of v. 3 as the context for this state of affairs.
[31] P avoids employing ܦܪܣ *prs* 'to spread, to extend; also to divide' in favour of ܩܨܐ *qṣ'* which means 'to break (bread)'

This verse continues the dirge-like observations, contrasting the present state of affairs with the good old days of the past. The poet finds the greatest contrast in the change of fortunes of the well-to-do. How that has changed! Provan (112) wonders if the poet refers to the nobility as a whole or only the children from a privileged background. If the latter, the link with v. 4 is more apparent, but it may be that the sight of starving children leads the poet to consider further horrifying reverses in city life. Perhaps he is saying that the calamity has hit not only the children of the common people but also those of the nobility (cf. Calvin).

הָאֹכְלִים—The active participle here conveys the idea of customary activity (GK 116a), i.e. 'eating', not the present tense; LXX οἱ ἔσθοντες is a case of the Greek translator taking a very mechanical approach to his task. P ܗܢܘܢ ܕܐܟܠܝ ܗܘܘ *hnwn dʾklyn hww* 'those who fed (were eating)' and T דהוו רגילין למיכל 'those who were accustomed to eat' capture the meaning, as does V *qui vescebantur* 'who were feeding'.[32]

לְמַעֲדַנִּים—The ל introduces the accusative, as in Aramaic (GK 117n) and is recognised as such by LXX, P and T. The word מעדנים occurs at Gen 49.20 and Prov 29.17 and appears to be related to עֶדֶן 'luxury, dainty'. LXX, P and T all agree that 'delicacies' is the meaning here, while V *voluptuose*, although an adverb, conveys a similar sense. MR attempts to give substance to the term with its gloss נחוסקין וחמר עתוק 'superior olives and old wine'. IE[1] merely interprets the phrase with שיתעדנו 'who indulge in luxury', while Kara comments הגדולים שהיו נהוגים לאכול למעדנים 'the important who were accustomed to eat dainties'.

נָשַׁמּוּ—Niphal of √שמם. On the use of the perfect, see 1.1. The root appears at 1.4, 13, 16; 3.11; 5.18, though this is the only occurrence of the Niphal. The meaning of the verb is not clear. The Versions are imprecise: LXX (ἀφανίζειν—aorist passive indicative) could mean 'desolated' or 'perished'. P ܗ̱ ܣܝܡܝܢ *hʾ symyn* may be corrupt (see Albrektson, 178), and T אשתוממו merely repeats MT's ambiguity. V *interierunt* 'died' is the most negative translation. If the poet wished to convey a startling reversal of fortune, then perhaps V's rendering provides the sharpest contrast, but one wonders if V is reading too much into נשמו. MLT interprets 'swollen with hunger' (cf. JPS 'lie famished'). Luther 'verschmachten' = 'pine away, die' may have been influenced by V, cf. also NJB 'now lie dying', NRSV 'perish'. According to Keil (434), נשמו בחוצות has the idea of sitting in a troubled state of mind on the streets, while Kaiser (360) translates 'liegen erstarrt auf den Strassen'. The Niphal of שמם occurs 25 times in the Hebrew Bible. Where the subject of the verb is human, the sense seems to be 'be astonished, appalled', cf. Jer 4.9 (where נשמו is in parallel with יתמהו); Job 18.20; 21.5. The meaning here, therefore, ought to approximate

---

[32] Cf. also MLT שהיו אוכלים and modern translations, such as NJB 'who used to eat'.

to the meaning in these passages. The latter speak of devastated individuals because of the dire circumstances. Those who had been used to luxury are publicly devastated.[33]

הָאֱמֻנִים עֲלֵי תוֹלָע—The entire phrase is parallel to הָאֹכְלִים לְמַעֲדַנִּים of the first line, and is meant to convey the notion of former privilege. The basic meaning of the root אמן is 'be firm, trustworthy; to support'. Most biblical instances of the Qal (Num 11.12; Ruth 4.16; 2 Sam 4.4; 2 Kgs 10.1, 5; Est 2.7; Isa 49.23) have to do with the upbringing or nursing of children; and this is how LXX, P, V and T have taken the passive participle here. MLT has taken the phrase as meaning 'who were clothed in pleasant garments and all kinds of colours and crimson yarns'.[34] The poet is saying that those who, all their lives, have lived off the fat of the land are now at the other extreme. As for תוֹלָע 'scarlet',[35] it seems that red was considered a startling and impressive colour in the ancient Near East and much sought after; cf. Nah 2.4 where the impressive warriors are wearing scarlet.

חִבְּקוּ אַשְׁפַּתּוֹת—P ܗ̇ܘ ܕܕܡܟܝܢ ܒܩܘܠܬܐ. ܗ̇ܘ *h' dmkyn bqwlt'* has added the particle ܗ̇ܘ, possibly to highlight the contrasting circumstances, but then translates חבק as 'to sleep'. Kelso (54) notes 'Das hebräische Verbum bedeutet "umarmen" und zu sagen, dass sie einen Felsen oder Düngerhaufen umarmt haben, ist gleichbedeutend mit, dass sie darauf liegen. Obgleich die P nicht wörtlich übersetzt, gibt sie doch den genauen Sinn des Urtextes.' Cf. also Albrektson (178). It should be noted that P, at Eccl 3.5 and Job 24.8, translates חבק literally.

The picture that Rashi envisages is that these notables now lie upon dunghills in the street; cf. also Kara who explains that this is because dunghills provide warmth. IE[2] reads 'because they are cast there like dung, and there is no one to bury them'; that is to say, he takes the phrase to refer to the situation after the death of those who once fared well; cf. V's interpretation of נשמו above. The passage echoes Job 24.8, where the destitute are said to cling to the rock for shelter.

4.6

Text and Versions
MT חָלוּ; LXX ἐπόνεσαν; P ܠܝ *l'y*; V *ceperunt*; Sym ἔτρωσαν. The differences in the Versions are to be traced to different interpretations of חלו (see below).

* * *

---

[33] Kinnear Wilson (1962, 178f.) suggests that שמם be interpreted through the Akk. *ḥamāmu* 'to gather up', *ḥummumu* 'to pick up (litter, scraps)', but this has not convinced other commentators.
[34] Cf. KBL 'wearing'.
[35] On colour in the Hebrew Bible, see Gradwohl (1963).

As the poet reflects on the horrors of his people's plight, he compares it with the archetype of devastation, namely, the overthrow of Sodom (Deut 29.23; Isa 1.9; Jer 50.40; Amos 4.11) and he concludes that the sins of his people must have been worse than those of Sodom.

This verse does not, thematically, connect with the previous verses, nor to the words which follow, although בת עמי appears in v. 3 as well as here; and the verse is formally linked to v. 5 by the *waw*-consecutive of ויגדל.[36] One of the difficulties in this verse is the force of עון and חטאת. Do they carry the meaning of punishment as a consequence of iniquity/sin, or is the poet referring merely to the sins themselves? The answer to this question depends, to some extent, on the meaning of the final stich which in turn hinges on the verb there.

LXX translates both words with ἀνομία 'lawlessness'; and P translates עון by ܥܘܠܐ *ʿwlʾ* 'iniquity' and חטאת by ܚܛܝܬܐ *ḥṭytʾ* 'sin'. Neither in Greek nor in Syriac do these have the meaning 'punishment for sin'. V employs *iniquitas* for עון and *peccatum* for חטאת. While *peccatum* can have the transferred meaning 'punishment for sin', it is not often used that way, but *iniquitas* does *not* carry that secondary meaning. This suggests that the translator must have had the primary meaning in mind. T employs חובה 'sin, guilt' for both words'.[37] Although the Hebrew words can have the meaning 'punishment for sin', the passages Gen 18.20; Ezek 9.9; 16.49 where the words *must* mean 'sin/iniquity' would support the view that this is what was in the mind of the poet. MR, quoting Gen 18.20 and Ezek 9.9, does not comment on the actual words, but the very quotations suggest the primary sense is in mind. MLT, however, alludes to the view that the secondary meaning is meant נקמה...נקמה. Rashi comments 'Their punishment פורענותם proves that their iniquity was greater than that of Sodom', which suggests that he considered that the author had 'sin' and not 'punishment' in mind. Kara also takes a firm stand for the primary meaning by quoting Gen 18.20 and Ezek 9.9; but IE², citing Gen 4.13; 15.16; 1 Sam 28.10, where עון must mean 'punishment', is clearly arguing that the passage is about punishment for sin. Luther 'Die Missethat…die Sünde…' is in the Rashi-Kara camp, while Calvin takes the other view, albeit cautiously. His translation begins: 'Et major fuit poena filiae populi mei poena Sodomae (*ad verbum est*, iniquitas filiae populi mei peccato *vel* scelere Sodomae)'. He comments: 'The Prophet says first that the punishment of his people was heavier than that of Sodom. If any one prefers the other version, I will not contend, for it is not unsuitable.' Since Calvin, many exegetes have sided with his position, cf. AV, RSV, NIV, REB, NRSV, Gordis (189),

---

[36] The acrostic demands a ו. The authors of chs. 1, 2 and 3 employ the *waw*-onsecutive whenever the ו is required.

[37] Levine (167) acknowledges that the Targumist's choice of word means that 'punishment for sin' was not in mind, but when he (Levine, 72) comes to translate his text, he renders 'the punishment…the punishment'; Brady (2003, 164) translates T 'sin…sin'.

Löhr (1894, 19). Others follow Luther, cf. Nägelsbach (154), Keil (429), Löhr (1906, 24), Budde (100), Kraus (71), Kaiser (360), Meek (31), Hillers[2] (135), Westermann (194), Renkema (508), RV, JB, JPS, though footnotes often indicate a certain ambivalence.

The tension between the primary and secondary sense of עון and חטאת will have been in the mind of the poet, but it cannot be conveyed in English translation. He is of the opinion that there is a correlation between sin and punishment, but his concern is not primarily with comparing the sins of Jerusalem and Sodom but with the present outcome of sin. Furthermore, as Calvin argues, the words which follow suggest that the severity of the judgment is in the poet's mind when he hints that the suddenness of Sodom's overthrow was preferable to Jerusalem's drawn-out agony (cf. v. 9).

כְּמוֹ־רָגַע—In prose we get כרגע (Num 16.21; 17.10) 'in a moment', and even in poetry (Ps 73.19). כמו is a poetic form of the preposition כ (BDB 455f.). The destruction of Sodom is depicted as being sudden.

וְלֹא־חָלוּ בָהּ יָדָיִם—This clause has long puzzled translators and exegetes (cf. Albrektson, 179f.) mainly because of the verb חלו.[38] LXX ἐπόνεσαν may have derived חלו from √חלה 'be weak' (cf. HR 1186, Albrektson, 180), although πονέω is employed by LXX to translate √חול at Jer 5.3; 28(51).29; 1 Chron 10.3; cf. Kelso (54). P 'were weary', probably derived from √חלה, though *BHK* wonders if P's *Vorlage* read לאו. V *ceperunt* 'and hands captured nothing in her' is difficult to relate to MT and may be a guess on the translator's part. That Jerome read לקחו (*BHK*) is speculative.[39] Sym 'have wounded' has derived from √חלל I, while T's paraphrase bears little relation to MT.

MLT is pointing out that Sodom was not handed over to the power of an enemy who rejoiced in her, but the Holy One himself took revenge on her. ידים is interpreted as the hands of the enemies, and although חלו is not commented upon as such, it is likely that the midrash understands it as from √חול 'to dance/turn/writhe'. Rashi also identifies ידים as 'the hands of the enemy' but, apart from attributing Sodom's fall to the work of angels, does not develop his understanding of חלו. IE[1] says that חלו is from חול/חיל but cites the opinion of others that the sense is found in Jer 30.23 על ראש רשעים יחול. The trouble with this is that the latter passage is not clear either: 'it shall fall with pain upon the head of the wicked' (AV), 'it

---

[38] The Masoretic reading—the stress on the first syllable—indicates that the verb חול is meant, but the *Vorlagen* of the Versions would be ambiguous, leaving it open to being either חול or חלה or even חלל.

[39] It is more likely that *ceperunt* would translate לכדו. If V should read *coeperunt*—read by Cappel (362), Michaelis (1773-88, 436f.), Schleusner (48) and Kelso (54)—the derivation may have been from √חלל III, which in the Hiphil can mean 'begin'; cf. Schäfer (131*).

circles over the heads of the wicked' (McKane, 771).⁴⁰ Kara, somewhat indulging in midrashic interpretations, quotes R. Tanḥuma, who appears to take חלו as from √חלה 'be weak' (reading against the Masoretes who indicate √חול), and to interpret the clause 'the hands in her (Jerusalem) were weak', alluding to the fact that Sodomites did not stretch out their hands to (do) the commandments. But Kara goes on: 'According to the plain sense—the iniquity of the daughter of my people was greater than the sin of Sodom which was overthrown as in a moment. The angels who were sent to overthrow Sodom overthrew her in a moment and did not leave in her a place that was not overthrown. This is what was written... חלו is like (the verb) in 2 Sam 3.29.'⁴¹ Because of the difficulties, scholars have resorted to emendation. Bickell (117), followed by Löhr (1894, 20), Budde (100), deletes בה on grounds of metre, though without any further argument and with doubtful effect. Rudolph (1938, 117) reads ילדים for ידים (cf. *BHS*) and, deriving חלו from √חלה 'be weak, ill', translates: 'ohne dass Kinder darin leiden mussten'. Although there may be slight support (from P) here for the derivation, the reading ילדים does not offer such obvious relief from the undoubted problems. More recent scholarship has been content to remain with MT. The main division lies in the derivation of חלו. Those who think that the root is חלה 'be weak, ill'⁴² do not convince. Nägelsbach (154f.) 'and no hands became slack thereby' is difficult to accommodate, and Rudolph (cf. also Haller, 108) (see above) is not any better, given that he also resorts to emendation. Fitzgerald (1967, 373f.) is close to Rudolph, though his exegesis is based on repointing יָדִים 'dear ones'. However, if we opt for חול we are still left with a difficult exegetical problem. If חול means 'turn, twist, writhe' and if 'hands' is the subject of חלו, the sense may be, as Thenius (167) argues, 'nicht rangen darin Hände', though as Keil (435) points out, it is doubtful if the association of חול and ידים could yield this meaning. This exegesis is more or less followed in JB, NEB, REB, although, as Provan (113f.) points out, these renderings are not all saying the same thing. The hands, according to this exegesis, are those of the Sodomites, בה meaning 'in her'.

חול is, however, employed at 2 Sam 3.29; Jer 23.19; Hos 11.6 with a meaning which is relevant here. The verb is construed with על in the Samuel and Jeremiah passages, and with ב (as here) in Hosea; but in all three texts the meaning appears to be 'to turn upon/against'. In this passage the translation might then be 'and hands turned not against her', (elucidating כמו רגע) in which 'hands' are those of the enemy (cf. Michaelis 1773–88, 436). Sodom was suddenly overthrown without physical onslaught (cf. Dan 2.34, 45). The comparison with Jerusalem is made

---

⁴⁰ This may mean that IE¹ sees another root חול here.
⁴¹ The Samuel passage is not easy either. Rashi glosses יהלו with ינוחו 'may it (the blood of Abner) rest'. Kimḥi also takes the subject to be the blood of Abner and interprets יהלו 'let it fall (נפל) and settle (חנה) upon...'; and he quotes Jer 30.23 in support. Kimḥi appears to be deriving יהלו from √חול II 'be firm' (BDB 298).
⁴² Perhaps taking their cue from P.

sharper. It is clear from v. 9 that the poet felt that Sodom's fate was preferable to that of Jerusalem, and the latter's greater sin would account for it.[43] Several scholars opt for this interpretation, among whom are Kaiser (360), Gottlieb (61f.), Westermann (194), Ehrlich (46f.), Meek (31), cf. NJB, JPS, NRSV.[44]

4.7

Text and Versions

MT אָדְמוּ עֶצֶם מִפְּנִינִים; 5QLam א[דמו עצם מפנינים; LXX ἐπυρρώθησαν ὑπὲρ λίθους; V *rubicundiores ebore antiquo*; ܣܡܩܘ ܓܪ̈ܡܝܗܘܢ ܡܢ ܣܪ̈ܕܘܢ smqw grmyhwn mn srdwn; Sym πυρρόρεροι τὴν ἕξιν ὑπὲρ τὰ περίβλεπτα; T סמיקו חיזו יתיר מזהורין מזהורין. It cannot be said for certain that the LXX *Vorlage* included עצם, but the fact that the other Versions seem to have struggled with some form of עצם might suggest that the LXX translator could not accommodate it in his rendering, or perhaps considered it included in the finite verb—ἐπυρρώθησαν. MT is preferred (see below).

MT סַפִּיר גִּזְרָתָם; LXX σαπφείρου τὸ ἀπόσπασμα αὐτῶν; V *sapphyro pulchriores*; P ܘܡܢ ܣܦܝ̈ܠܐ ܓܘܫܡܝܗܘܢ wmn spyl’ gwšmhwn; Sym σάπφειρος τὰ μέλη αὐτῶν. MT is preferred (see below).

* * *

Verses 7f. comprise a unit. The poet bursts forth in hyperbole to make his point: he recalls the refined beauty of the nobles and contrasts it with what he now observes; so changed are they (cf. v. 1f.) that they are unrecognisable. All beauty is gone.

The perfect tenses of the verbs in v. 7 are in contrast with those of v. 8. In v. 7 זכו, צחו and אדמו refer to the state of affairs before disaster struck, while חשך, נכרו, צפד and יבש, declarative perfects, describe the situation as witnessed by the poet.

נְזִירֶיהָ—'Her nobles' are the focus of attention in vv. 7 and 8 (the suffix refers back to בת עמי of v. 6, cf. Rashi). That the author is referring here to the Nazirites seems unlikely. The passages which allude to Nazirites (Num 6.2-8, 13, 18-21; Judg 13.5-7; 16.17; Amos 2.11f.) never speak of their beauty but only of their abstinence from wine, their avoidance of corpses and their vows to allow their hair to grow freely. It is just possible that the hair-growing was an attractive feature of the Nazirites;[45] in any event, the Versions, LXX, P, V, T and Sym all translate 'Nazirites'. Cohen's translation of MR *ad loc* 'princes' may be mistaken. After the lemma, the comment is 'for they used to drink snow…'; and this comment probably arose from the knowledge that Nazirites were supposed to

---

[43] Support for this exegesis is found at Qumran, where the phrase יחלו ידם appears in the War Scroll (1QM 9.1; 16.8; cf. 17.4), possibly meaning 'to attack'; cf. McDaniel (45ff.).
[44] NIV 'without a hand turned to help her', while deriving from חול 'to turn', has supposed a meaning which not only is otherwise unsupportable but does not fit well in the context.
[45] Cf. Rashi.

abstain from drinking wine. MLT, however, while repeating MR, goes on to cite other views (ס'א) which take נזיריה to mean 'her princes' (שׂריה) who were separated מונזרים from the rest of the people with regard to wealth etc., and quotes Nah 3.17 מנזריך 'your princes' in support.[46] Rashi *begins* his comments by glossing נזיריה with שׂריה (= MLT). He then goes on in such a way as to suggest that his initial remarks amounted to the citing of a current opinion: 'But I say that the meaning is actual Nazirites who had long hair and were of fine appearance'. IE[2] does not comment on the term itself but simply notes that the verb זכו refers to the past 'in the days of plenty', emphasising the contrast with the scene confronting the author. Kara, on the basis of Jer 7.29, where נזרך is taken to mean 'your hair' (cf. LXX, P, V, Kimḥi, AV, REB, BDB 634; McKane, 176f.), though Sym takes it to mean 'Nazirites' there), argues that נזיריה means 'her hair' and understands this passage to be referring to the way someone's hair becomes white when one is ill. Kara, therefore, understands the verb זכו to be a declarative perfect, describing not the past, but the present. Calvin does not appear to hesitate here, translating *Nazaraei* and referring to Num 6. Calvin's explanation is that the Nazirites, who abstained from drinking wine, would become pale as a result.[47] While AV, Douai, Hillers[2] (135), House (432) retain 'Nazirites', Luther ('Ihre Fürsten…'), following MLT, is in a long line of scholars who prefer[48] 'nobles, princes'—RV, RSV, NRSV, JPS, NIV, NEB, Westermann (196), Kaiser (360), Renkema (511), Berlin (99).

Ehrlich (47) was the first to suggest an emendation here, reading נְעָרֶיהָ, which he translated 'children', not 'youths' (cf. Exod 2.6), and this reading is supported by Rudolph (1938, 117f.) who argues that the error was occasioned by the ז of זכו! Rudolph, however, renders the emended text 'ihre jungen Männer', pointing out that the very young are dealt with earlier (v. 4). The suggestion is entertained by *BHK*, *BHS*, Kraus (72), Haller (108), while JB 'young men' and NJB 'young people' *appear* to adopt Ehrlich's emendation and Rudolph's interpretation. Albrektson (180), cf. also Renkema (512), rejects this emendation as unnecessary and trivial, citing Gen 49.26 and Deut 33.16 where the meaning of נזיר is probably 'prince'.[49] With regard to the choice of words here, Renkema points out that 'the poets…were unable to use שָׂרִים 'princes' because they had already been driven from the city (1.6), carried into exile (2.9) or even hanged (5.12); but this begs the question of the unity of the book. It is best, perhaps, to understand נזיריה as referring not necessarily to 'princes' but to 'nobles', cf. Keil (435), Berlin (99), Schäfer (131*).

זַכּוּ—As vocalised by the Masoretes, the verb is √זכך, a by-form of √זכה (*HALOT*), meaning 'be clean, pure, bright', and is construed parallel to

---

[46] This is translated *custodes tui* by V.
[47] This is a view also taken by Michaelis (1773–88, 437).
[48] Occasionally, some are in doubt, hence margin of RV and NEB, and see Hillers (140).
[49] Cf. LXX in both passages, though V translates *nazarei* each time.

√צדק in Ps 51.6; Job 15.14; 25.4, i.e. morally pure. Since in this context the parallel verb is √צחח (with which there is a certain assonance) and since the poet goes on to employ the verbs √אדם 'be red' and √חשׁך 'be dark', all in the description of נזיריה, it is unlikely that it is their moral cleanness that is being alluded to here; rather, it is the brightness/whiteness of the nobles; cf. Brenner (29f.), who argues '…צחו and זכו become— or function as—parallels to לבן when associated with שׁלג and/or חלב, which are known to function as specifications of לבן elsewhere (Ps 51.9; Is 1.18; Gen 49.12)'. That the whiteness refers to clothing (Eccl 9.8) is unlikely (Keil, 435) in that the passage goes on to speak of the body. The poet's fondness for hyperbole is to the fore here: the skin of someone living in Palestine is likely to be a shade of olive, but it is possible that the paler the skin the more refined a p]erson was thought to be. The second stich repeats the idea of the first.

צַחוּ—This is from √צחח 'be dazzling' and confirms our interpretation (contra JPS, cf. REB) that זכו here does not mean 'morally pure', cf. LXX ἔλαμψαν 'they shone (more than milk)', and P ܘܚܘܪܘ *wḥwrw* 'and they were whiter (than milk)'.[50]

אָדְמוּ עֶצֶם מִפְּנִינִים סַפִּיר גִּזְרָתָם—The second half of v. 7 is difficult, and this is reflected in the Versions. To begin with, עצם is not represented in LXX, though the other Versions (P, V, Sym and T) show that their *Vorlagen* included it (or some form of it). As the text stands, עצם is an adverbial accusative (GK 118m, n) and may mean 'in body' (AV, cf. Ehrlich, 47; Albrektson, 181; Kraus, 72), though Gottlieb (62f.) thinks this rendering is forced. The fact that P, V and T all take a different line raises the question of its function and even its originality. P 'their bones' either took it in the usual sense 'bone' or, since Syriac ܓܪܡ *grm* has a metaphorical application, 'self', but the translator understood the term to be the subject of אדמו and so rendered it by a plural (possibly taking it as a collective) to agree with the plural verb, supplying, in addition, the suffix (3rd p. m. pl.) 'their bones'. I think that P meant 'they themselves'. V 'than old ivory' does not[51] omit עצם, but Jerome struggles with the final stich. T 'appearance' is a free rendering of עצם. Rashi, who leaves the precise definition of עצם until v. 8, takes it to mean 'appearance' מראה, quoting Exod 24.10, and then he glosses with the French *couleur* which shows that he possibly means 'complexion'; but one gets the impression that Rashi was struggling here.

---

[50] While the additional copula is characteristic of the Syriac translator, the further addition ܒܡܪܥܝܬܗܘܢ *bmrʿythwn* 'in their flocks/congregations' is more difficult to understand. Kelso (55) considers it as due to the paraphrasing tendency of the translator, but this is not a paraphrase. It is more likely to be a gloss by a later hand, cf. Abelesz (9), Albrektson (181).
[51] Contra Houbigant (482).

Various emendations have been suggested. Bickell (1894, 117) suggests reading אדמו מעצי פנים, and Löhr (1894, 20)[52] suggested reading אדם עורם 'their skin was rosier than coral', cf. also *BHK* and Rudolph (1962, 248). Dyserinck (377) merely deletes עצם, on the basis of LXX. Robinson (1933, 259) points out that the general colour of the skin must be implied in the first line, *viz*. white. His conjecture אדמה שפתהם—'their lip(s)'—gives good sense but is graphically quite far removed from MT; and Driver's (1950, 140f.) suggestion מעצם פנינים, which he translates 'they were more ruddy than the bone of (red) corals', i.e. than the coral itself, requires us to accept the displacement of the preposition.[53] Westermann (196f.) emends to עצמיהם 'their bones, bodies' which becomes the subject of אדמו. Gottlieb (63) appears to adopt Driver's suggestion, arguing that it explains why LXX does not represent עצם. He further draws attention to the phrase בעצם היום הזה which we find in Gen 7.12; Exod 12.17, 51; Lev 23.31; Deut 32.48; Josh 5.11; Ezek 40.1. In the latter passages LXX does not represent עצם.

פנינים—BDB suggests the meaning 'corals', while *HALOT* has 'pearls of corals'. Although a similar word exists in Greek (πίνη), LXX translates simply[54] (ὑπὲρ) λίθους. P 'than sard' (a shining red stone); T 'than sparkling gems'; V 'than old ivory'.[55] While the Versions appear to struggle with this term, and we cannot be certain as to its denotation, the verb √אדם 'be ruddy' controls the exegesis to some extent.

The remainder of the verse is also problematic. גזרתם (= גזרה + 3rd p. m. pl. suffix) is a rare word, occurring at Ezek 41.12-15; 42.1, 10, 13, where it denotes 'a separated room or forecourt'. The suffix probably refers back to נזירים of the first line, but the word cannot have the meaning it has in Ezekiel. LXX τὸ ἀπόσπασμα αὐτῶν 'their pieces' is unclear. It seems that the translator was content to lean upon the root גזר, though whether αὐτῶν refers back to the nobles or to λίθους is not certain. P 'their body' and Sym 'their limbs' may just be attempts at squeezing a meaning out of the obscure word. T 'their faces' represents another attempt at interpretation, while V *pulchriores* 'more fair' resorts to a free rendering. Rashi does not betray any problem with the term, but Kara glosses it with מצוחצח 'their *shining* was like sapphire'. Calvin translates *excisio ipsorum* but does not elaborate. Luther's translation is 'ihr Ansehen war wie Saphir'. That גזרתם refers to 'their form' is followed by RSV, Keil (436), Rudolph (1962, 245). Since vv. 7f. are concerned with the drastic change in the circumstances of the נזירים and since the contrasts are couched in terms of colour—white and red—there are some who see in the term 'sapphire' a

---

[52] Löhr (1906, 25) returned to reading MT.
[53] This is the emendation behind NEB, REB, see Brockington (219).
[54] Cf. also LXX at Prov 3.15; 8.11; 31.10 where פנינים is rendered λίθοι πολυτελεῖς.
[55] *BHK* thinks that V read מלפנים.

reference to the colour blue. Hence, Blayney (328) 'their veining was the sapphire: נזר signifies to *divide* or *intersect*, as the blue veins do on the surface of the body'. This line is taken by NEB 'lapis lazuli', cf. NIV, NRSV margin, Renkema (513) 'as azure', Bickell (117) and Haller (108) 'saphirblau'. However, those who regard סַפִּיר as indicating colour are divided: as well as those who see it as referring to the veins shining through the skin, there are those who take it to refer to the hair of the head. It might seem strange that prominent blue veins would have been a focus of admiration. That the hair of the head could be described as blue is not so strange as it may seem. In praising the beauty of the bride in Song 7.5, the bridegroom says: 'the locks of your head are like אַרְגָּמָן'—AV, NRSV 'purple', REB 'lustrous black'; and in an Egyptian description of Re we are told 'his bones were of silver, his flesh of gold, and his hair of genuine lapis lazuli'.[56] It is, perhaps, unlikely that anyone's hair in the ancient Near East was anything but black, but healthy lustrous black hair may/does reflect the blue sky (the healthier, the bluer) and gives the impression of being blue or purple; cf. Salters (1979, 251). Because of the difficulties, Löhr (1894, 21) suggested the emendation נזרתם (from נֵזֶר in Jer 7.29), which he translates 'ein Saphir glänzte ihr Haupthaar'.[57] The problem of נזרתם, however, remains unsolved. Hillers[2] (135) translates 'their beards', a guess. His argument is simply that the term must refer to some part of the body that can be compared to a dark blue substance, and he finds references to lapis lazuli vis-à-vis the beard, the hair and eyebrows in Sumerian and Egyptian literature.[58] There is no consensus: their shining/ polishing, their form, their countenance, their limbs, their veins, their hair, their beards, their hue have all been suggested; and ספיר is variously understood in terms of its colour or its form.

4.8

Text and Versions

MT צָפַד; LXX ἐπάγη; P ܡܦܗ[59] *qpwd*; V *adhesit*; T אדק. Versions do not reflect a different reading.

* * *

The picture of beauty and health painted in v. 7 is contrasted with the situation now encountered by the poet. The human mind likes contrasts to be vivid (rags/riches; black/white), and this poet who has been eloquently extravagant in v. 7 tries to paint the opposite extreme. The nobles who had

---

[56] See Hillers[2] (140f.), who points out that ancient sculptors often represent hair on carved heads by inlaid lapis lazuli.
[57] Budde (1898ᵃ, 100) considers this rather forced. Kimḥi takes נֵזֶר in Jer 7.29 as head of hair, cf. McKane (1986, 177), Lundbom (1999, 490).
[58] See Hillers 140f. for references.
[59] An old form of the preterite according to Payne Smith (1903, 512).

been fine specimens in every sense are now unrecognisably emaciated and unattractive.[60] The background to the sentiments of these verses is the famine in Judah following the collapse of Jerusalem. Verses 2 and 5 allude to the reversed circumstances of the elite, and vv. 7f. are in the same mould. It is not that the tables are turned in any form of revolution—the suckling and the small child also starve (v. 4)—but famine becomes the great leveller: the elite cannot now be distinguished from the ordinary citizen. The point is made by resorting to exaggerated imagery.

In contrast to v. 7, the exegesis of v. 8 is relatively clear, and this is reflected in the ease with which the Versions render. There is nothing in the syntax which suggests 'then' and 'now': all verbs are in the perfect; but note that translations[61] introduce words to achieve the contrast which the poet undoubtedly had in mind.

הָאָרֶם—The subject of the first stich. The suffix refers back to the nobles of v. 7 (תאר 'appearance'). At 1 Sam 16.18 David is said to be איש תאר REB 'handsome', i.e. the word may refer to the facial features as well as to the general appearance. (See also Gen 39.6 where Joseph is described as יפה תאר ויפה מראה.) LXX renders εἶδος αὐτῶν which retains the ambiguity of the Hebrew; and P and T are in the same category. V *facies eorum* is more explicit, perhaps being influenced by the second stich which speaks of recognition, something usually associated with facial features; cf. Banitt *leur fayture* = face.

מִשְׁחוֹר—The noun שחור is a *hapax legomenon*.[62] LXX translates ὑπὲρ ἀσβόλην 'than soot'; V *super carbones* 'than coals'. Rashi glosses the word with פחם 'soot/coal'. Like the other comparisons in vv. 7f., this is an exaggeration to enhance the point being made (cf. Brenner, 80). IE² notes that the reason for this darkness of skin is famine. The nobles could maintain a healthy glow when times were good and food plentiful, but famine brought even them to the point of starvation and it showed in their skin condition. They became unrecognisable in the streets where, before, they stood out and were easily identified.

צפד—This is another *hapax legomenon*. BDB and *HALOT* give the meaning 'contract, shrivel', cf. Arabic *ṣafada* 'to bind', Syriac/Aramaic (Payne Smith 1901, 3429: *constrinxit*; Jastrow, 1295: 'cleave, contract'). LXX

---

[60] In vv. 7f. there are a number of words which occur only here in Lamentations: זכך, נזיר, שלג, צחה חלב, ספיר, פנינים, גזרה, אדם (as a verb), שחור, תאר, נכר, צפד, יבש.
[61] So, Kara עכשיו, Renkema, JPS, NRSV, NEB ('once/but/now').
[62] That שחור might mean 'dawn' is unlikely. Blayney (328), who translates 'duskier than the dawn', argues 'when it is neither light nor dark, but between both, at which time objects are not easily distinguished'. But this would be an odd comparison and would probably require an emendation to שַׁחַר.

'fastened', V and T 'stuck', P 'shrivelled'. Rashi glosses with נקמט ונתחבר 'shrivelled and adhered', while IE¹ explains it with דבק; cf. Banitt *froncer* 'wrinkle'. The subject of this verb is עורם. T's plural משכיהון probably does not indicate a different reading, but rather the recognition of the Hebrew as a collective. The same is probably true of עצמם—the plurals of LXX, P and T do not indicate the reading עצמיהם as suggested by *BHK*. Albrektson (182f.) comments: 'The plural readily suggests itself in this context and is found also in modern translations: AV for instance has "their bones"'; cf. also Kelso (57). The effect of the severe famine not only affects the colour of the skin, which is now dark and dull, but also its texture and elasticity, giving the impression that it is close to the bone.

יָבֵשׁ הָיָה כָעֵץ—The subject of these verbs is עורם of the previous stich. LXX has both verbs in the plural[63] which probably means that the subject (for the translator) was 'their bones' (so Kelso, 57). Albrektson (183) thinks it is probably ναζιραῖοι of v. 7. The construction יבש היה כעץ is a little clumsy; indeed, Budde (1898ᵃ, 100) regards היה as superfluous (also Haller, 108), and *BHS* suggests deleting on grounds of metre, while Wiesmann (224) thinks that the intruder here is יבש. The Versions all testify to the presence of a form of the verb 'to be', and most modern commentators are reluctant to emend the text. T read יבש as an adjective—'it has become dry like wood'—which is how some translators have taken it: NJB, JPS, RSV, NRSV, NEB.

4.9

Text and Versions
MT יָזוּבוּ; LXX ἐπορεύθησαν; P דבו *dbw*; V *extabuerunt*; OL *abierunt*; T דייבן. MT is preferred (see below).

* * *

The poet, continuing with the theme of famine and its dire effects, makes a comparison between those who suffered death by the sword and those who died of starvation. The latter was a slow and distressing process, and the author reckoned that to be killed by the sword, although horrific, was preferable to death by starvation.[64] In the following verse (v. 10) he produces an illustration—a horrific scene of human activity *in extremis*.

---

[63] *BHK* suggests that the LXX *Vorlage* read יבשו היו, but see Albrektson (183): 'the change of number is simply due to another understanding of the connection between the words in Hebrew'.
[64] RV translates as though it were a dictum, but the poet is thinking of the specific—commenting on the fall of Jerusalem.

The meaning of the first line is straightforward: those killed by the sword were more fortunate than those killed by famine. The double use of חללי in MT is confirmed by LXX, OL, P and T. V's *occisis gladio quam interfectis fame* probably reflects the translator's wish to vary the wording, the meaning being unaffected.

Cohen (1910, 190f.) raises the question of the interpretation of חללי רעב. Since חלל is used elsewhere to refer to death (or wounding) by a weapon, he feels that 'killed by famine' is incorrect. Pointing to v. 10 where women 'kill' their own children because of famine, he translates 'slain by reason of famine', i.e. slain in order to provide food. But this suggestion insults the poet and ignores his creativity. He is using a term literally in the first stich and creating a secondary sense in the next stich. The skill of the poet must be admired here.[65] Note also a certain assonance between the phrases חללי חרב and חללי רעב.

The second line of v. 9 is obscure, and this is reflected in the Versions and the history of exegesis.[66] The fact that the passage contains three rare words does not help, but the syntax is also problematic.

שֶׁהֵם—In theory, the referent could be either those killed by the sword or those killed by famine. The latter is, perhaps, more natural and is how it is usually understood. The particle שׁ (see also at 2.15f.; 5.18) is usually a relative pronoun (= אשר GK 36) but may also serve as a conjunction (Song 5.2; Eccl 2.16; 8.17; GK 104). In this passage it is usually taken as a relative, in which case it is more natural to take the referent of הם to be חללי רעב. If taken as a conjunction, it is more natural to find חללי חרב as the referent; cf. T.

יָזוּבוּ—This verb √זוב usually has the meaning 'flow, drip', often of water (Pss 78.20; 105.41; Isa 48.21). LXX, which does not represent שהם, translates ἐπορεύθησαν, a verb (πορεύω) which normally translates הלך. It is unlikely that the LXX *Vorlage* read ילכו (or יזלו, so Wiesmann, 224). The translator decided that זוב here means 'to expire', and both הלך and πορεύω can carry this figurative meaning.[67] V 'pass away' (cf. OL *abierunt*) is in the same vein.[68] Jerome knew the verb √זוב (cf. Jer 49.4 where he translates *defluxit* 'ebb away') and decided that a figurative sense was called for here.

P 'waste away' is similar. However, P otherwise diverges from MT and LXX and renders 'as those who are wounded and thrown in the field'. Attempts to understand P's ܘܫܕܝܢ *wšdyn* 'and thrown' (Abelesz, 40;

---

[65] The same objection applies to Guillaume (47f.), who takes חללי רעב as 'wasted away from hunger' on the basis of Arabic *ḥalla* 'was emaciated'.

[66] *BHK* and *BHS* indulge in reconstructions, and Robinson (259) thinks the line 'hopelessly corrupt'.

[67] Driver (1934, 308) thinks that the LXX translator may have taken the Hebrew to be from זבב.

[68] Contra Robinson (259) who thinks V read רקבו 'to rot'.

Albrektson, 184f.) are unconvincing, and Kelso (57f.) may be correct in suspecting that P's *Vorlage* differed from MT. In the light of the other Versions, however, P may simply reflect a genuine struggle with the same text as confronted LXX.[69] These Versions, it seems, struggled to find a suitable translation, in their respective languages, for an unusual expression, but there is scant evidence for a different Hebrew text. The mediaeval commentators were also at a loss to know the meaning of the text. Rashi, who regards the line as referring to victims of famine, interprets יזובו as referring to body fluids oozing from bodies split (מדקרים) by hunger and aggravated by the smell of (enemies) cooking outside the city wall, and by eating roots and grasses of the field.[70] IE² takes the line to allude to those killed by the sword, יזובו referring to those shedding blood after being pierced (מדקרים). Those who had fallen by the sword had (earlier) been satisfied by eating the fruits of the field. Calvin, who sees a connection with v. 6 where the sudden fate of Sodom was preferable because of its suddenness, does admit that the verse is obscure. His interpretation is that those suffering death by famine were cut off from the fruits of the field and pined away as though pierced. Luther's 'die verschmacteten und umgebracht werden vom Mangel der Früchte des Ackers' is substantially the same as AV.

The majority of commentaries not only accept MT but interpret as AV, though some renderings are somewhat surprising.[71] *BHK* makes no attempt at emendation for שהם יזובו, but proposes מוּקָדִים כִּתְנוּבַת ('burnt[72] like the fruits [of the field]') for מדקרים מתנובת. *BHK* considers another possibility, namely reading כתלאובות for מתנובת, i.e. 'like drought', a suggestion which originates with Ewald (1866, 343), '…wie von des feldes dürre.'

Perhaps the most radical suggestion comes from Rudolph (1962, 248) who reconstructs the entire line, שֶׁהֵם יַזּוּ בִמְקוֹר דָּמָם מֵתוּ בְחָשׁ, and translates 'weil jene den Quell ihres Blutes verspritzten, eilends starben'.[73] Other conjectures[74] need not detain us.

Gordis (190f.) explains MT with reference to ellipsis. Citing Isa 66.3c where the passage מעלה מנחה דם חזיר must mean 'the one who offers a cereal offering is like one who offers swine's blood', and pointing out that זוב is a term meaning 'blood flow', he translates: 'they whose blood flowed, being stabbed, than those who perished for lack of the fruits of the field'.

---

[69] Albrektson (184) wonders how P's ܐܕܝܢ *šdyn* could possibly translate MT מתנובת, but the Syriac is surely to be explained in relation to שׂדי, although P does also represent שׂדי by ܚܩܠ *ḥqlʾ*.
[70] MR and Kara have similar interpretations.
[71] E.g. JB 'spent and sinking, deprived of the fruits of the field'.
[72] Wiesmann (224) reckons that מוּקָדִים lies behind V *consumpti*; cf. also Dyserinck (377).
[73] *BHS* appears to reproduce Rudolph's conjecture but prints יָדוּ for יַזּוּ.
[74] Houbigant (482), Ehrlich (47), Meek (32), Driver (1950, 141), Cohen (1910, 191); cf. also *BHQ*.

I am inclined to agree with Provan (115f.) and Renkema (517f.) that MT should stand. It is possible that the poet considered that he had, with the first line, produced a fine turn of phrase, and wanted to continue in poetic vein with an equally clever second line. His figurative use of (the second) חלל in the first line is paralleled by the figurative use of דקר in the second. This latter verb normally applies to physical piercing, as in Jer 51.4 (where חלל and דקר also appear together) but, having spoken of those 'pierced/slain' by famine—and this is the point of the verse as a whole—the poet sees no reason why, similarly, he may not coin or extend the application of the verb דקר. Again, the verb זוב√, normally 'flow, flow away', is used metaphorically to refer to the ebbing away of the lives of the starving and, because they are dying of starvation, they can be said to have been 'pierced' through lack of the produce of the land (cf. Deut 32.13). The preposition מן, in the phrase מתנובת שדי, is the privative מן, as in Gen 27.39 (see BDB 578, 7b).

4.10

Text and Versions
MT לְבָרוֹת; LXX εἰς βρῶσιν—so also V, P and T. The consonantal text underlying the Versions is the same as that of MT, but we read with the Versions—לְבָרוּת.

* * *

The theme of famine and its physical effects reaches its climax in this verse. The poet has painted a picture of horror where the world has been turned upside-down. Starvation has been the great leveller, for whereas one would expect the weak and the vulnerable to suffer in the face of famine, the experience has been that even the world of the rich has plummeted to the very depths, the severe suffering evoking the cry that those killed by the sword were better off. Finally, the poet points to the lowest level in the community's experience—women cooking their children for food. It cannot get worse than this.

The wording of the first line is interesting. The subject of בשלו is 'the hands of the women'. Elsewhere in the Hebrew Bible the verb takes a human subject. It may be that the constraints of the alphabetic acrostic have pressed the poet into this unusual construction, but it could be that the picture that the poet wishes to convey is of the inevitability of this horrendous scene. Since mothers would be the last people to cook their children, the construction suggests that it was not the will of the mothers to do this.[75] This may be further emphasised by the adjective רחמניות 'tenderhearted, compassionate'.[76] As Provan (116) notes, 'That it was the

---

[75] Cf. Gottwald (59), Renkema (519).
[76] רחמניות is a *hapax legomenon*, and is an adjective derived from the noun רחמים 'compassion', which appears many times in parallel to חסד.

nature of these women to be compassionate simply brings home the horror of it all, for it is when evil appears in such close proximity to good that it is most shocking'. The verb בשל may mean 'cook' or 'boil'. MR does not take the verse literally, but MLT does, though it is clear that 'compassionate' should be seen as describing the women *prior* to the crisis.[77] Rosenberg (54) cites Beer Moshe which offers another interpretation of the passage: because of the famine, the compassionate women allowed their children to cut off their hands to cook them—'hands' taken as the object not the subject of בשלו; presumably, 'hands' were seen as the subject of היו. It is interesting that the noun ילד 'child' occurs only here in Lamentations. The young are otherwise referred to by עלל, יונק and בן.

לְבָרוֹת—This is a unique form. ל + infin. const. Piel of ברה 'to eat'. The Versions (LXX, P, V and T) have all translated 'for food', i.e. they appear to have vocalised לברות = ל + בָּרוּת a noun meaning 'food' which occurs at Ps 69.22; cf. 2 Sam 12.17. *BHS* suggests reading לְבָרוּת. Perles (85f.) suggested that the expression is to be explained with reference to an Akkadian vampire Labartu,[78] and this was seized on by Gordis (1967–68, 30f.) who proceeded to translate 'They (i.e. the compassionate women) became vampires to them (their own children)'. In his later commentary (1974a, 191f.), he repeats this interpretation enthusiastically but then, surprisingly, abandons it (p. 192), and in his translation (p. 147) he appears to settle for the vocalisation as in LXX etc. No other modern commentator has followed Perles.

לָמוֹ—Poetic form of להם; see on 1.22; 4.15 and GK 103f. The masculine form, referring to the women, while imprecise, is not unusual, see GK 135o, 144 a, 145p, t, u; cf. Job 39.3 where the suffixes on חבליהם and ילדיהן have the same referent.[79] Ehrlich (48) thinks that the unusual terminology calls for a more specialised term and, citing 2 Sam 3.35, suggests that we are dealing with such a grave and extreme situation that ברות refers to 'Trauer- oder Kondolenzmahl'; and his suggestion is adopted by Haller (108), Rudolph (1962, 246), Kraus (71f.) and Renkema (520) 'food of solace'. There is something to be said for this understanding of ברות in that it has something of this flavour at Ps 69.22. While Luther translates MT 'zu essen', AV follows the Versions, and this is how most moderns read the text (JB, RSV, NEB, JPS, NIV). On בְּשֶׁבֶר בַּת־עַמִּי, see on 2.11 and 3.48. The final stich seems abrupt in the list of horrendous vignettes in vv. 1-10, but the poet means to put the entire passage in the context of the fall of Zion.

[77] It seems that this term was thought to be out of place in describing women who would cook their own children. IE² notes that the compassionate women were turned into cruel women, and Kara is careful to explain that the adjective refers to the past. Cf. Calvin.
[78] *BHK* entertains this as a possibility.
[79] Löhr (1894, 21) tried to accommodate the masculine למו by taking it to refer to the children, but this has not been accepted.

4.11

Text and Versions
No significant material.

* * *

Verse 11 appears to begin a new section in the poem; at least the poet no longer dwells on the terrible *effects* of the famine but begins to focus on other aspects of the catastrophe. Yahweh was not mentioned in vv. 1-10 but now, in v. 11, he is the subject and he is depicted as having wrought havoc; and one is reminded of the passage 2.1-8.[80]

The verb √כלה occurs in Lamentations at 2.11 (Qal), 2.22 (Piel), 3.22 (Qal), 4.11 (Piel), 4.17 (Qal). In the Qal it can mean 'to come to an end', 'be finished', 'perish', 'fade'. In the Piel it may mean 'to complete' or 'to destroy'. Helfmeyer (159f.) argues that the emphasis is not so much on stopping as bringing to an appropriate conclusion or goal. The poet, perhaps, draws on traditional language here in that in the ambiguous passage Isa 10.25 we meet the combination זעם and כלה; and, in his use of the Piel, he may reflect the language of Ezekiel (cf. 6.12; 7.8; 13.15; 20.8; 20.21). The concept of bringing anger to completion is related to Yahweh's characteristic reaction to his people's sin and to their transgression of his commands: anger, on Yahweh's part, is considered appropriate. He therefore responds in full measure. The aforementioned passages in Ezekiel demonstrate this. Lamentations 4.11 does not mention sin, but vv. 6 and 13 reveal the links. Understanding this concept is one thing—translating it is another. LXX employs the verb συντέλεω (here and in the Ezekiel passages), which captures the meaning to some extent but which requires comment. The P translator, sensitive to the idea, employs the Shaphel of ܡܠܐ *ml'* 'to fulfill', and V *complevit* also shows that Jerome was aware of the meaning of the Hebrew; but T סף 'finish' lacks something of the original. MLT refers to Deut 32.23 in its explanation of √כלה, but then cites another opinion which points out that while Zion was destroyed, Israel was not, an observation also found in MR. T also appears to be thinking of this distinction.[81] Luther 'vollbracht', Westermann (1990, 161) 'vollstreckt' capture the sense of the passage, and AV 'accomplished' approximates to this, but translations such as 'vented all his fury' (JPS, NRSV) or 'indulged his fury' (JB, cf. REB) miss the mark. It is not the case that Yahweh is going over the top in his anger or that he was acting in an unrestrained manner. As the author of the first poem says (1.18), 'Yahweh was in the right, for I rebelled against his command'. The

---

[80] Indeed, the term אף 'anger', referring to Yahweh's anger, is concentrated (in Lamentations) in ch. 2 (vv. 1, 3, 6, 21, 22); and שפך and חמה are also found at 2.4.
[81] Cf. Levine (169).

anger is appropriate to the situation. Calvin *complevit* reproduces V, but his explanation 'the meaning is that he (God) had executed his extreme judgment' goes beyond the force of the Hebrew.

שָׁפַךְ חֲרוֹן אַפּוֹ—The phrase חרון אפו 'his hot anger' occurs some thirty times in the Hebrew Bible (e.g. Exod 32.12; Num 25.4), and there is no need to delete חרון (Budde, 101). It always refers to Yahweh's anger, delivered or promised, in punishment for wrong-doing. By using the phrase here, the poet accepts that what has been experienced in the fall of Jerusalem and its aftermath is punishment for sin. The verb שׁפך is often employed in connection with anger, cf. Ezek 7.8; Zeph 3.8.

וַיַּצֶּת־אֵשׁ וַתֹּאכַל יְסוֹדֹתֶיהָ—On the verb יצת, see GK 71. The construction of Hiphil with אשׁ + ב means 'to set fire to'. The phraseology is reminiscent of Amos 1.3–2.5 and Jer 21.14, where Yahweh, in (יום יהוה) punishment, is the source of exterminating fire. The *waw*-consecutives may stress the point that the known threat has been realized. However, the language is hyperbolic and poetic in that, in actual fact, foundations would not have been consumed. The poet may have in mind an aspect of the catastrophe as described in 2 Kgs 25.8-10 where Nebuchadnezzar set fire to the temple, the palaces and all the houses in the city. If this is so, then the author wants to emphasise that that destruction was the work, not of Nebuchadnezzar, but of Yahweh. Nevertheless, since 'fire' is used as a metaphor for the wrath of Yahweh—IE[1] comments briefly דמה האף לאש—it is likely (following the reference to Yahweh's anger in the first line) that this is what the poet is thinking of; one is reminded of Deut 32.22 'For a fire is kindled by my anger, and burns to the depths of Sheol; it devours the earth and its increase, and sets on fire the foundations of the mountains'.

4.12

Text and Versions
MT (*Kethib*) וְכֹל—so also P, V and T; MT (*Qere*) כֹל—so also 13 MSS[Ken] and LXX. *Qere* is preferred.
MT כִּי יָבֹא—so also LXX, V and T; P ܕܐܬܐ ܒܗܘܢ *d'ṭ wʿl*. MT is preferred.

* * *

The connection with the previous verse is not immediately obvious. In v. 11 an angry Yahweh is the subject and a destroyed Zion the object; in v. 12 the poet reflects that the fall of Zion could not have been envisaged by anyone. Perhaps he is emphasizing that the conquest must have been divinely inspired and managed.

The text of this verse is straightforward. P begins the verse with the copula, but this reflects the translator's lack of precision; besides, the acrostic precludes beginning with anything other than a ל. His expansion of the phrase כי יבא is typical. The Syriac verb ܐܬܐ ʾtʾ 'to come' is not an exact equivalent of the Hebrew בוא, and the Syriac translator may have felt that the sense was obtained by supplementing with ܠ ʿl the verb 'to enter', cf. Albrektson (185). T paraphrases and draws on MR, in that Nebuchadnezzar and Nebuzaradan are mentioned as entering Jerusalem, while MLT observes that the kings of the earth were incredulous because Sennacherib had not succeeded in entering the city. The phrase 'kings of the earth' is found in Pss 2.2; 76.13; 89.28; 148.11.

יֹשְׁבֵי תֵבֵל—The word תבל (always without the article) occurs over forty times in the Hebrew Bible and is a poetic synonym of ארץ when the latter denotes the whole world (cf. Ps 24.1). The phrase occurs at Ps 33.8; Isa 18.3; 26.9, 18. Cross and Freedman (1955, 248f.) raise the possibility of another interpretation of the phrase. On the basis of Amos 1.5, 8 (cf. Zech 9.5, 6), where תומך שבט is parallel with יושב מבקעת און, they conclude that יושב can carry the meaning 'throne-sitter' and that the translation might therefore be 'rulers of the world', balancing 'kings of the earth'. But Ps 33.8 and Isa 18.3 militate against this viewpoint, which has not been adopted by other commentators. The poet declares that the very invasion of Jerusalem had been quite unexpected, even among the heathen; indeed, it had been thought to be impossible. On 'believe' (האמינו), Renkema (525) draws attention to Gen 45.26 where 'Jacob cannot believe (likewise Hiphil of √אמן + לא) that Joseph is still alive let alone that he is ruler over the entire land of Egypt. Such a thing could not be possible.' Whether or not the gates of Jerusalem had ever been entered by an invading army is not important here, and Nägelsbach (162) wastes time delving into the history of the city, citing 1 Kgs 14.26; 2 Kgs 14.13, 14; 23.33-35; 2 Chron 33.11 as instances when Jerusalem *had* been captured.[82] When the poet uses these phrases 'kings of the earth' and 'inhabitants of the world' he is not divulging the result of a contemporary opinion poll or survey. This is hyperbole. The tradition that Yahweh had chosen Jerusalem as his dwelling-place (Ps 132.13f.) may have been influenced by the strategic position of the city, which, because of location and fortifications, would present major problems for an attacker; and the belief was strengthened by the failure of Sennacherib to take the city in the 8th century BCE. A combination, therefore, of the formidable fortress and Yahweh's choice and protection gave rise to the belief that Jerusalem could not be taken; see Roberts (108). This belief, which was now shattered, will hardly have been shared (or even known) by foreign kings, let alone all the inhabitants of the world, but Jerusalem's reputation as an impregnable fortress may well have held true among her neighbours. The fall of the city will have dismayed the people of Judah, and other states may have been surprised, but the poet treats this surprise as though it were universal and comprehensive.

---

[82] It is doubtful, in spite of what Nägelsbach maintains, that heathen enemies ever actually marched through the city gates.

Ewald (344) links vv. 12 and 13 (cf. also Kara) because of the causative מִן with which v. 13 begins, but, as Keil (437) points out, this serves to distort the meaning of both verses: 'Verse 12 contains an exclamation over the incredible event that has happened, and verse 13 assigns the cause of it.'

4.13

Text and Versions

MT מֵחַטֹּאת נְבִיאֶיהָ—so also P and V; probably read הִיא מֵחַטֹּאת נְבִיאֶיהָ (see below).

MT בְּקִרְבָּהּ דַּם צַדִּיקִים—so also P, V and T; LXX αἷμα δίκαιον ἐν μέσῳ αὐτῆς. MT is preferred (see below).

* * *

The poet reflects on the reasons for the tragic fall of Jerusalem—it was the fault of the prophets and the priests who were guilty of the murder of innocent folk.

The verse, as Wiesmann (226) notes, does not make sense in itself. The link with v. 12 is not entirely clear. The astonishing fall of Jerusalem should be explained with reference to sin: the sins of the prophets and the iniquities of the priests. The author is, perhaps, concerned that the reason for the fall of the city should not be in terms of logistics, tactics or the might of the enemy. Only a theological explanation will do; hence the link with v. 11 becomes clear, and v. 12 comes as an aside or as parenthesis. This link between sin and punishment, while not overplayed, is clearly drawn in all the poems of Lamentations.[83] The abrupt manner in which this verse begins[84]—the causative מִן (GK 119z)—is probably to be explained by the demands of the acrostic (cf. Löhr 1906, 26). Textual variations are not significant. P's additional copula (*and* the iniquities of the priests) is almost par for the course, and the fact that a singular appears for the MT plural is not to be explained by a different *Vorlage*. Of the many instances of the plural of עָוֹן in the Hebrew Bible, nearly half are translated by the singular in P.[85] However, some commentators have been unhappy with the text as it stands. Following a remark by Bickell (118) on the length of v. 13a, Budde (1898ª, 101) wonders if באו has fallen out following נביאיה, the subject presumably being the enemies of v. 12. However, he goes on to suggest that the 'missing' word might be זאת. A more attractive solution to the problem of the short first stich is that suggested by Rudolph (1938, 119), namely that היה or היא should be 'restored' after נביאיה. The insertion of היא is adopted by Haller (108). The translation obtained by the latter emendation is similar to that offered by Luther 'Es ist aber geschehen...';

---

[83] Cf. Salters (2003, 347-69).
[84] See Gordis (148) who connects the verse with v. 14.
[85] At 2.14; 4.22, P has the plural for MT's singular.

cf. also RV, JPS, NIV, NRSV, NEB, Kraus (71), Kaiser (361), Westermann (197), the latter claiming that 'It happened' is in the text by implication.

בְּקִרְבָּהּ דַּם צַדִּיקִים—The word order in LXX differs[86] from that of MT (which is followed by P, V and T) and LXX has the singular δίκαιον for צדיקים. Kelso (58) suggests that LXX may have read צדיק, but Albrektson (186) is probably correct in seeing here an inner Greek corruption. MSS and Versional evidence support MT, and Ziegler (489) has printed δικαίων, an emendation 'supported' by an Ethiopic MS. This is the only occurrence of the phrase דם צדיקים in the Hebrew Bible. The usual phrase is דם נקי 'innocent blood' (Deut 19.10; Isa 59.7 etc.) or דם נקים (Jer 19.4)[87] T's paraphrase describes the prophets as having uttered false prophecy and the priests as having burned incense to idols and appears to link this behaviour with the resultant shedding of innocent blood. That is to say, the irresponsible behaviour led to the downfall of the city and the slaughter of its inhabitants which included innocent people. MLT, while taking the view that it was the false prophets and priests that are referred to here, goes on to note another interpretation which attributes the sins and iniquities to the people, who actually murdered the prophets and priests. Rashi notes simply that false prophets are being blamed here for the evil, i.e. the catastrophe. IE[1] comments only on דם צדיקים, which he says means 'the blood of every just man'. IE[2] paraphrases 'because of the sins of the prophets of Baal and the priests of the high places, the holy ones (החסידים) were killed, according to the words of Asaph'.[88] He seems to have understood חסידים to mean 'just people', and the blood to have been shed by apostate prophets and priests. Calvin argues that the attack on the prophets and priests in no way exonerated the people who had been led astray, but that the origin of the evil lay with the prophets and priests. The latter 'had no doubt led the people astray in other things, for they flattered their vices, and gave loose reins to licentiousness; but the Prophet here fixed on one particular sin, the most grievous; for they had not only, by their errors and false doctrines and flatteries, led away the people from the fear of God, but had also obstinately defended their impiety, and by force and cruelty repressed their faithful teachers, and put to death the witnesses of God'. Calvin argues that the sin mentioned—the murder of the just—was the worst, in that it involved God's witnesses, i.e. the true prophets. Although the poet has already alluded to the sins of the people as a whole (v. 6), in this verse he lays the blame for the fall of Jerusalem on the prophets and priests. If he had concluded with this statement, we might have interpreted him as referring to the false and wayward leadership which the prophets

---

[86] This order might be explained as being preferable in Greek. Cf. AV, NRSV.
[87] The phrase דם הרשע occurs at Ps 58.11.
[88] Probably an allusion to Ps 79 (מזמור לאסף v. 1), which speaks of the heathen entering the Temple and committing murder (of חסידים v. 2).

and priests had offered; and this would tally with the author of 2.14 who blames (false) prophets for leading the people astray. It would also have fitted in with Jeremiah's dismissal of prophets and priests as 'godless' (Jer 23.11) or 'frauds' (Jer 6.13). But the final line, 'who shed the blood of the just in her midst', raises the question of the actual involvement of the prophets and priests in the murder of innocent and just people. Jeremiah and Ezekiel condemn leaders and people for the killing of innocent people (Jer 7.6; 19.4; 22.3, 17; Ezek 22.27)—and we must assume pre-exilic Jerusalem as being fraught with violence and injustice—but nowhere in the Hebrew Bible do prophets and priests engage in actual murder. However, at Jer 26.7-24 it is at the instigation of prophet and priest that Jeremiah himself was threatened with death, and the passage, vv. 20-24, goes on to note the murder of Uriah, another prophet who had opposed the status quo.

4.14

Text and Versions
MT עִוְרִים—so also V, Sym and T; LXX ἐγρήγοροι αὐτῆς; LXX^{Luc} νεανίσκοι αὐτης; P ܚܘܖܒܢܝܗ rwrbnyh; 5QLam^a ם[. MT is preferred (see below).

MT בְּלֹא—so also LXX; P ܘܠܐ wl'; V non; T ועל דלא; Sym ὥστε μὴ; 5QLam^a בל. MT is preferred (see below).

* * *

The passage vv. 14-16 is fraught with problems, not least because the subject of the various verbs is not clear, though even if the subject was beyond doubt, the content of these verses is not uncomplicated.

Westermann (202) argues, 'The conceptually meaningful sequence of the verses has been disrupted here under the constraint of the alphabetic arrangement. Consequently it is up to the interpreter to read as a unit the material that belongs together.'[89] Others detect corruption in the transmission of the text and proceed to emend and reconstruct, though it should be said that the ambiguity of MT is often preferable to some scholars' conjectures! It should be noted, by way of contrast, that in vv. 1-13 the subject of the verbs is always clear; and vv. 17-22 are, for the most part, similarly clear. The proximity of צדיקים (v. 13) led Kraus (79f.) to view 'the righteous' as the subject of the verbs. Keil (438) thinks that 'the priests' are the subject, while Westermann (202), Renkema (530f.), Berlin (109) and House (444f.) think 'prophets and priests' are in that role; and Hillers[2] (149f.) and Provan (117f.) are of the opinion that the poet is

---

[89] While the construction of the acrostic may have had an adverse effect on style and sense, it should be noted that vv. 1-13 and 17-22 are comparatively free of the ambiguity and anomaly we find here, yet the poet was similarly constrained in those verses. Westermann thinks that v. 16b originally preceded vv. 14-15.

talking about the people as a whole. Westermann (202) may be right in seeing vv. 14-16 as the continuation of the description of misery which is found in vv. 1-10. Various groups are represented in the latter—children, the elite, nobles, mothers—all of whom had experienced extreme reversal of fortune. It is natural, therefore, to think of the prophets and priests (or simply the priests), referred to in v. 13, as the subject of the plural verbs in vv. 14-16.

עִוְרִים—The LXX and P translators were either baffled by עורים or their *Vorlagen* were slightly different, but they understood the word to be the subject of נעו. So, too, T, MR (contra Cohen's translation) and Rashi: 'when the blind walked in the street they would stagger and their feet would slip on the blood of the slain—those killed by the wicked in her midst'. LXX 'her watchers' is explained by Kelso (59) and Albrektson (186) as the result of the Greek translator having a text which read עירים (for עורים) from √עור 'awake'; and the αὐτῆς may be due to the final ם being read as a ה. LXX^Luc νεανίσκοι αὐτης, according to Michaelis (1773–88, 438), presupposes the reading בחוריהם, while Rudolph (1938, 119) reckons that it may be translating the word נערים. P 'her nobles/ princes': Kelso (59) claims that this 'ist eine Auslegung der LXX und nicht eine Übersetzung des MT', while Abelesz (40) thinks that P may have read שׂרים (cf. Albrektson, 186f.). BHK wonders if P read נגידיה, and Rudolph (1938, 119) thinks the *Vorlage* was חרים or נגדים. The suffix in P may be due to the translator's tendency to expand, as he adds the same suffix to the following בחוצות. While Sym, V and T translate MT 'blind', it is not clear if V *caeci* is the subject or if it stands as an adverbial accusative (GK 118r), i.e. 'they wandered as blind men' (cf. the renderings of V in Douay and Knox); probably the latter. MLT כמו עורים clearly takes עורים as adverbial accusative, as does IE¹ who cites Deut 4.24 אש אוכלה הוא in support of this interpretation. Calvin '*errarunt caeci (subaudienda est nota similitudinis*, sicut)...', Luther 'Sie gingen hin und her...wie die Blinden' are in the same vein; and AV, JPS, NIV, NRSV, REB and JB interpret in this way. Löhr, who in his first edition (1894, 22) was sceptical of the originality of עורים, suggests (1906, 26) that the word was an old gloss; but if we delete עורים the stich is too short, and we are left with another problem.⁹⁰ Ehrlich (49) regards עורים as a corruption of עֲרוּמִּים 'naked', and Driver (141) picks up on this suggestion, modifying it to עָרוֹם (cf. *BHS*) and pointing out that the word occurs in Job 24.7 with a plural verb and that the form does not necessitate any essential alteration of the consonantal text. Rudolph (1962, 249) sees here a dittography of עו (נעו) and suggests reading דָוִם (plural of דָוֶה 1.13; 5.17; cf. *BHS*). He translates (246) 'Elend schwanken sie...'⁹¹ The majority of scholars retain MT

---

⁹⁰ *BHK* considers deleting עורים.
⁹¹ Of all the conjectures, Rudolph's is the most reasonable, though we are not quite persuaded.

and translate 'They wandered as blind men/blindly...', though not all agree as to the subject of נָעוּ. Is the author referring back to the prophets or the priests, or to both (v. 13), or to the righteous (also v. 13), or to the people as a whole? That the subject of the first stich is 'the righteous' (Kraus, 79f.) is questioned by Renkema (530), who observes that the construction שָׁפֵךְ דָּם implies death,[92] so that the righteous are no more; but Renkema should allow for hyperbole here—the poet was not speaking of the wiping out of all righteous people; nevertheless, most scholars look elsewhere for the subject.

נְגֹאֲלוּ—The unusual vocalisation (from √גאל II 'defile') is found also at Isa 59.3. GK 51h describes it as a *forma mixta*, in the sense that the punctuators intended to combine two optional readings: נִגְאֲלוּ perfect Niphal, and גֹּאֲלוּ perfect Pual'.[93] Again, the subject of this verb is in doubt. Löhr (1906, 26) takes v. 14a to refer to the prophets and priests, and v. 14b to the other inhabitants of Jerusalem. Gordis (192) translates: 'they (the prophets) now wander blind through the streets; they (the priests) are defiled by blood...'; but most scholars take נעו and נגאלו as having the same subject: 'They are polluted with blood', presumably the blood of those slain (T and IE²).

בְּלֹא יוּכְלוּ יִגְּעוּ בִּלְבֻשֵׁיהֶם—On בלא see BDB (520). It is found also at Job 18.1; Prov 16.8; 18.1; Isa 55.1 (twice); Jer 2.11; 22.13; Lam 1.6; Ezek 22.29. BDB translates 'without (that) men are able to touch...' On asyndeton, see GK 120g. P *may* represent another reading, but it is likely that the translator was struggling to find a satisfactory exegesis. The history of the interpretation of this line demonstrates that there has been no consensus as to what the author was trying to say.[94] T, which seems to take 'blind' literally, interprets יוכלו as referring to this lack of sight: 'because they could not see, they touched their garments'. Levine (171) notes that the Masoretes' placing of *zaqeph qaton* after יוכלו supports T's interpretation, and he sees here an echo of the LXX interpretation. While the LXX, for the most part, supports MT, the variant 'her watchers' continues to be the subject of the verbs, and the idea there is that the watchers were polluted with blood. Verse 14b in LXX is ἐν τῷ μὴ δύνασθαι αὐτοὺς ἥψαντο ἐνδυμάτων αὐτῶν, which may be translated 'in their weakness they touched their clothes'. The idea seems to be that the watchers could not avoid pollution. V *cumque non possent tenuerunt lacinias suas*, while probably not indicating a different *Vorlage*, suggests that Jerome struggled

---

[92] *HALOT*: 'When used of people שָׁפֵךְ דָּם is not a neutral word for to kill but it implies a considered judgement about the action; it is a deliberate act of killing and (with the exception of acceptable acts of vengeance, as Gen 9.6) is a criminal act'.
[93] Cf. IE¹ already: מלה מורכבת מבנין נפעל ובנין שנא נקרא שם פועלו. This is explained by Odeberg (178) as intending 'to avoid the homonymity with נגאלו = "are redeemed"'.
[94] Indeed, Hillers² (142) concludes that MT '...is really not possible'.

with the meaning here.⁹⁵ The idea seems to be that the holding up of their skirts was to avoid further pollution. Those who retain MT usually translate with P 'so that no one could touch their garments', cf. GK 120g, Luther, AV, NEB, NRSV, JPS, NIV.

Meek (33) points out that if ב introduces a result clause, it would be unique in Hebrew literature. He argues 'It is better to take ב as introducing a clause that is the object of יִגְּעוּ, a verb which regularly takes its object with ב; the subject of the verbs (both imperfect) would be the same as in the first line and not indefinite. Translate accordingly, "Those whom they should not, they kept touching with their clothes"', i.e., they were ceremonially unclean because of the bloodshed and should not communicate their uncleanness to others, but in their heedlessness and general lack of responsibility they did.' Albrektson (187) points out that if read in this way the emphasis is still on reversal: 'in v. 14a the point is that the priests, who had shed the blood of the righteous, are now the bloodstained victims, and in b that those who had been anxious to keep all the cultic rules of purity cannot avoid contact with unclean things'.

The background to the sentiments expressed here (and in v. 15) is to be found in strict ancient taboos among primitive peoples. With regard to blood which, in Israel, was thought to be the seat of life (Lev 17.11; Deut 12.23), the fear of pollution by contact with it was strong (Deut 22.8).

4.15

Text and Versions

The two lines of v. 15 are particularly long. As all Versions appear to have encountered a form of all the elements, any supposed additions must have been made early in the transmission of the text. The lines may be shortened by deleting קָרְאוּ לָמוֹ (in the first line) and אָמְרוּ בַּגּוֹיִם (in the second) and regarding them as exegetical glosses.

MT סוּרוּ טָמֵא—5QLamᵃ טמאו; LXX ἀπόστητε ἀκαθάρτων; P ܐܬܦܪܩܘ ܡܢܗܘܢ ܛܡܐܐ *prwšw mnhwn wṭmʾ*; V *recedite polluti*. MT is preferred (see below).

MT קָרְאוּ לָמוֹ—so also V; 5QLamᵃ קראו למו; LXX καλέσατε αὐτούς—so also P. MT is superior to LXX but is a gloss: a marginal comment attempting to indicate who was speaking to whom and later incorporated into the text.

MT אָמְרוּ בַּגּוֹיִם—so also P and V; LXX εἴπατε ἐν τοῖς ἔθνεσιν. MT is superior to LXX but is a gloss: a marginal comment designed to encourage the reader to interpret the passage as a reference to the exile.

* * *

The ambiguity and lack of clarity continue in this verse. Who are the speakers and who is being targeted? Do the 3rd p. pl. verbs share the same subject as those in v. 14? Both lines in this verse are exceptionally long, and the Masoretic punctuation reflects problems in understanding the sense of the passage. In addition the Versions offer limited help in that

---

⁹⁵ It is interesting that *lacinia* does not translate לְבוּשׁ elsewhere in V.

they appear to have had difficulties with the Hebrew—etymology, orthography, vocalisation. *BHK* suggests five emendations, *BHS* three. Scholars and modern translations pull in different directions. It is hard not to conclude that the text is corrupt in some way. The history of the interpretation of this verse shows no consensus as to the speakers or the addressees or, indeed, the circumstances alluded to.

סוּרוּ טָמֵא—The passage begins with a plural imperative vouched for by all the Versions: depart! The second word, the adjective[96] 'unclean', is singular in MT, hence the AV '*It is* unclean',[97] while RV 'Unclean!' accommodates the anomalous singular by rendering it as an exclamation;[98] cf. JB, JPS, REB, ESV.

That the original Hebrew was the plural טמאים is a possibility. LXX, P and V either read a plural or felt forced to render in the plural. It should be noted that 5QLam[a] reads טמאו (see Baillet, 175), though this reading does not lie behind the renderings of the Versions. It may simply represent a levelling on the part of a scribe who noticed that the other finite verbs in the verse were plural. Indeed, the plurals of LXX, P and V may have originated in the same circumstances. T, however, reads the singular.[99] LXX ἀπόστητε ἀκαθάρτων may be translated 'depart from the unclean ones', which may just presuppose the reading מטמא. More serious is P 'depart from them and call them unclean', but while this reading has affinities with LXX, the Syriac certainly does not presuppose מטמאים. V *recedite polluti* takes טמא (or טמאים) as vocative. Hence already in the Versions we have evidence that interpreters and translators were unclear as to the identity of the speakers and the addressees. Whether the text behind the Versions was the same as MT is not certain; it may be that it was and that each Version was trying to make sense. Rashi, like V, takes טמא as vocative, 'depart from us, you unclean people (אתם הטמאים)' who are polluted with blood', and *interprets* as plural. IE[2] says that the speakers are addressing each other, 'Keep away from us' (cf. Lev 13.45), but he notes, in frustration, that the actual callers are not identified. The Targumist, however, does identify the callers—the peoples (עממיא)—while those addressed appear to be the people of Judah, possibly in exile. MLT agrees with T in identifying the callers (as האומות), and they are addressing one another regarding the men of Jerusalem: 'Do not touch these filthy people'. Keil (439), who suggests that the singular טמא may be accounted for by the allusion to Lev 13.45, where the leper is enjoined to call out

---

[96] The Masoretic vocalisation could be interpreted as Qal 3rd p. m. s. of the verb 'become unclean'.
[97] AV margin gives an alternative: 'ye polluted' (cf. NIV), though this surely implies a plural of some sort.
[98] The singular can be understood as arising from Lev 13.45 where טמא טמא means 'Get out of the way! Here comes an unclean person!'
[99] T's reading is זורו ממסאבא 'turn away from the unclean'.

'Unclean, unclean!' (טמא טמא יקרא), points out that in *that* passage the cry was not addressed to the unclean, but 'the call here is addressed to the priests, who are staggering towards them with blood-stained garments. They must get out of the way and not touch those they meet.'

קְרְאוּ לָמוֹ—The unpointed Hebrew was vocalised by LXX and P as imperative, while V and T translators took it as indicative; and this is further evidence that the meaning of the passage was problematic. *BHK* appears to be in favour of the LXX/P pointing, but *BHS* is inclined, rightly, to delete the entire phrase.

The second line, which begins as though offering the reason for the imperatives and the prohibition of the first line, does not assist us in our understanding of the first. The fact that the Masoretes placed an *athnaḥ* after נעו probably indicates that they struggled with the sense of the passage.

כִּי נָצוּ גַם־נָעוּ—נָצוּ is another *hapax legomenon*. BDB tentatively suggests that it is from √נצה, related to √נצא 'to fly', while *HALOT* accepts Driver's (378) suggestion that it is from √נוץ, related to the Arabic *nwṣ* 'to flee'. LXX ἀνήφθησαν is a rendering which represents the first recorded struggle with meaning. Although the verb has a wide semantic range, ἀνάπτω is employed elsewhere in the LXX to translate verbs such as נשק, יצת, בער, להט, יצא, עלה: in every context, fire or burning is involved. It is possible, therefore, that in this passage the Greek has a meaning such as 'they are on fire'. Since LXX at v. 11 renders ויצת with καὶ ἀνῆψε, it is possible that the translator's *Vorlage* read נצתו (cf. Kelso, 59, *BHK*, Robinson, 259). Another possibility is that the translator guessed at the meaning; and Albrektson (189) notes that at Jer 21.12 and 48.9 'forms of יצא have been rendered by ἀνάπτω, as if the Hebrew text read יצת'. One is almost persuaded by Albrektson except that, if the translator made a mistaken derivation, it is strange that, in the context, נצו would suggest to him יצת and not יצא. 'They are on fire' seems out of place in a passage dealing with blood pollution. P ܐܪܓܙܘ *'rgzw* 'they caused provocation' raises the possibility that the translator read נאצו (cf. P on Pss 10.13; 74.10, 18). There is also the possibility that, although faced with נצו, he *derived* it from √נאץ or from √נצה II; V *iurgati quippe sunt* and T ארום אתקוטטו 'for they quarrelled' are in the same category.[100] Rashi seems to take the basic meaning of נצו as 'stench and filth' (סרחין ולכלוך), citing Lev 1.16 where בנוצתה is translated by T as באוכליה (אוכלא) 'excrements', Jastrow, 25). IE¹ comments on נצו: 'They have feathers (נוצה) like a bird', citing נצא תצא Jer 48.9 in support.[101] He, therefore, connects נצו with a root נצה 'to fly' (BDB 663). Cf. also Kara, citing Jer 48.9 and glossing with the verb עוף

---

[100] This interpretation is also found in MR and MLT, but it seems out of place here; cf. Keil (439f.).

[101] On the problems connected with this phrase, see McKane (1996, 1163ff.).

'to fly, flutter'. Kara interprets נצו as 'they fled/departed from the ways of God'. Vermigli (174) 'When they flew away', Luther 'Wenn sie flohen', Calvin 'quia evolarunt (*aut*, festinarunt)' and AV 'When they fled away' set the pattern for future translations—RSV, NEB, NRSV 'So they became fugitives'.[102]

לֹא יוֹסִיפוּ לָגוּר—The Masoretes punctuated as though the final stich consisted of an utterance among the nations. Some, including Hillers[2] (143) and Gordis (192f.), interpret as though אָמְרוּ should receive the *zaqeph qaton*, introducing the statement 'among the nations they shall stay no longer'. We have deleted אָמְרוּ בַגּוֹיִם as a gloss; cf. *BHK* לָגוּר—preposition ל + infin. abs. of the verb √גור 'to stay as an alien'. This must be understood (in conjunction with the two verbs נָצוּ and נָעוּ as alluding to the peregrinations of the prophets and priests of v. 13. They will be always on the move. Albrektson (190f.) suggests taking it as from √גור II 'to attack'. He translates: 'Yea, they flee, they stagger; they will no more (be able to) assail'; and he adds 'God has put an end to their attacks upon the righteous'; but this has not had backing among scholars.

These verses began their life describing the fate of some wicked prophets and priests—outcasts in Zion's public places, fleeing and wandering with no fixed abode—but the passage has been hijacked by an early scribe who took advantage of the ambiguity to impose an interpretation which points in the direction of the exile of the people as a whole.

4.16

Text and Versions

MT פְּנֵי יְהוָה—followed by LXX, P and V; Aq νεῦσον κύριε. MT is preferred.

MT חִלְּקָם—followed by P and V; LXX μερὶς αὐτῶν; Aq διαμέρισον αὐτούς; T אתפליגו; the LXX translator[103] vocalised חֶלְקָם, i.e. as a noun (חֵלֶק = portion, share) with 3rd p. pl. suffix, whereas the Masoretes vocalised as a verb √חלק I (Piel) 'to divide' (3rd p. m. s.) with accusative suffix. Aq seems to have taken it as Piel imperative (Field, 759 n. 32), while T, although probably reading the same text as MT, has put the verb in the passive in order to avoid the combination of the divine name and an active verb. MT is preferred.[104]

MT נָשָׂאוּ—followed by LXX, P and T; V *erubuerunt*; Sym κατησχύνθησαν; *BHK* suggests that the *Vorlagen* of V and Sym read בּוֹשׁוּ. It is true that both these Versions are close in meaning; however, where the idiom נשׂא פנים occurs in the Hebrew Bible Jerome does seem at ease in translating, e.g. Gen 32.21; Num 6.26; Job 22.26; 42.9; Mal 1.8.

---

[102] Calvin thinks that the exile of the people is meant here; so also Michaelis (1773–88, 439) and Houbigant (482).

[103] In vocalizing חֶלְקָם, the translator possibly thought that the passage was concerned with the lofty role of prophet and priest whose portion was (the face of) Yahweh (cf. Num 18.20; Pss 73.26; 119.57; 142.6) and he viewed the second stich as indicating the contrast, the reversal—cut off.

[104] Contra Ehrlich (51) and Meek (33f.).

Consequently, it is possible that he was influenced in his rendering here by Sym, although the idea 'the faces of the priests were not ashamed' hardly fits the context. MT is preferred.

MT (*Kethib*) זְקֵנִים—so also LXX and T; MT (*Qere*) וזקנים—followed by many MSS[Ken], P and V. The copula may be a natural addition by a scribe; on the other hand the ו of נשאו might have been originally attached to זקנים and copied in error to form נשאי; it might then have happened that a scribe added a ו to חנן to bring that verb into line with נשאו (Wiesmann, 229); MT (*Kethib*) is preferred.

The פ verse precedes the ע as in chs. 2 and 3, though five MSS[Ken] have the reverse order which is found also in P;[105] 5QLam[a] follows MT order (cf. Schäfer, 133*).

* * *

In the final reference to prophets and priests, the poet interprets their fate as evidence that Yahweh has abandoned them; and he follows this up with the observation that priest and elder lack honour and respect.

פְּנֵי יְהוָה—This phrase is rendered by Aq 'turn, O Lord', which may presuppose a *Vorlage* פנה יהוה, but apart from the witness of other Versions, an imperative and vocative here merely adds to the problems of this passage and should be viewed as a clumsy attempt at making sense of the text. The phrase פני יהוה is the subject of the verb √חלק. Although פני is plural in form, and the verb is singular, GK 146a notes that in these cases 'the predicate sometimes agrees in gender and number, not with the nomen regens, but with the genitive, when this represents the principal idea of the compound subject', cf. Lev 13.9; Job 15.20; Isa 2.11. Literally, 'the face of Yahweh' is often used in a positive sense (Exod 33.14f.; Num 6.24-26), but in Lev 20.3, 6; 26.17; Pss 34.17; 80.17 and here it represents Yahweh in angry mood.[106] While this is not spelt out in any of the Versions, Rashi פנים של זעם מאת הקב"ה and IE[2] אף השם and some later translations do make this clear; e.g. Luther 'Des Herrn Zorn', AV, RV 'The anger of the Lord'. Others leave the interpretation to the reader (as with LXX, P and V), rendering ambiguously 'the face of Yahweh' (JB, NJB), 'countenance of Yahweh' (Renkema, 542; cf. JPS).[107]

חִלְּקָם—Those who vocalise חלקם as a verb are divided as to its meaning here. BDB (323) gives the meaning of √חלק I 'to divide, share', Piel 'to apportion, distribute', and suggests 'scatter' for this passage and for Gen 49.7. The meaning in the latter passage is confirmed by the use of √פוץ (Hiphil) in parallel. Dahood (1963, 548) translates 'the fury of the Lord destroyed them'. Dahood bases his rendering on Ugaritic *ḥlq* and

---

[105] Cf. Salters (1994, 88).
[106] פני יהוה is really equivalent to Yahweh himself, as is implied by Kara and argued by Budde (102), Kraus (71), Rudolph (1962, 246), Wiesmann (228f.), Westermann (197), Gerstenberger (498); cf. also RSV, NIV, NEB, NRSV. The wording is occasioned by the demands of the acrostic.
[107] N.B. Hillers[2] (136): 'the splendor of the Lord'.

Akkadian *ḫalāqu* 'destroy'. His suggestion is followed by McDaniel (48), Hillers[2] (143), Levine (172), NJB and has been adopted by *HALOT* as √חלק III. Whatever the referent of the suffix (which we take to be the prophets and priests), the meaning 'destroy' seems too fierce in the context and, in the light of the fact that חלק does not unequivocally have this meaning anywhere else in the Hebrew Bible, it seems best to stay with the traditional[108] 'scatter, disperse'. As Gottlieb (67) observes, 'The chapter is concerned to a very small degree with the slain, but dwells the whole time on the fate of the survivors', cf. also Rudolph (1962, 249). Löhr (1894, 22) who had removed אמרו בגוים from v. 15b, adds בגוים after חלקם (cf. also Wiesmann, 228) and represents the view that חלק refers to the dispersion of the exile.

לֹא יוֹסִיף לְהַבִּיטָם—'He no longer[109] regards them'—Yahweh himself (פני יהוה) being the subject. He has withdrawn his link with them.

פְּנֵי כֹהֲנִים לֹא נָשָׂאוּ—The construction נשא פנים means 'to respect, be gracious unto, honour'. The poet deliberately uses the term פני כהנים, perhaps for assonance, to echo פני יהוה of line 1, though the construction and meaning are quite different. The verb חנן 'be gracious, favour' parallels נשא פנים at the beginning of the line; cf. 2 Kgs 3.14. The second line of this verse is problematic in that the verbs, again lacking a specified subject, are in the plural, whereas in the first line the verbs are in the singular and Yahweh is the subject.[110] The Versions support the plurals of MT, though it should be noted that there are no other examples of 3rd p. pl. perfect Qal of חנן in the Hebrew Bible.[111] It is, however, possible to take these plurals as expressing an indefinite subject (GK 144g) and to be rendered as passives; cf. Job 4.19; 6.2; Ps 63.11; Prov 2.22 (where יִסְחוּ is parallel with יְכָרְתוּ). Understood in this way, the passage is seen as part of the description of misery and reversal which now concludes with a statement that even the (normally respected) priests and elders[112] no longer have any standing in the community. Whether this is an allusion to their status under the enemy rule or to the community of survivors is not clear.

---

[108] Apart from the Versions, MLT understands חלק to mean 'scatter' (פזר) and takes this to be a reference to exile, adding בגוים; cf. also Rashi and IE².

[109] On the auxiliary use of the verb יסף, cf. BDB (415). It occurs in Lam 4.15, 16, 22.

[110] Some, e.g. *BHK*, suggest that the singular verbs in the first line should be read as plurals, viz יוֹסִיפוּ...חלקום; others, e.g. Bickell (118), Dyserinck (378), Löhr (1894, 22), Budde (1898ª, 102) and Kelso (60), think that the verbs in the second line should be read as singulars.

[111] While I have followed MT (*Kethib*), accepting the plural verbs in the second line, others—Bickell (118), Budde (1898ª, 102), Wiesmann (229), NEB, REB—read singular verbs (see above): לֹא נשא וזקנים לֹא חנן. This has the effect of making Yahweh the subject in the verse as a whole; and it removes the awkward and abrupt change of subject.

[112] One expects the text to read 'priests...prophets' at this point, and this is the reading of some LXX codices and OL, and followed by Moffat and JB (though not NJB!); however, this is usually regarded as levelling (on the basis of v. 13) and not original.

4.17

Text and Versions

MT (K^(Occ)) עוֹדֵינָה supported by 5QLam^b; MT (K^(Or)) עוֹדֵינוּ is followed by *Qere*, several MSS^(Ken), LXX, P and V; both readings are possible (Rudolph 1938, 120): The f. pl. suffix may be seen as anticipating 'eyes'; the suffix of *Qere* may anticipate the suffix 'our (eyes)'; cf. BDB. It is possible that the variant has occurred under the influence of the other 1st p. pl. suffixes in the rest of the verse. עוֹדֵינָה is to be preferred, cf. Haller (110), Renkema (546). There is no advantage in the various conjectures of עֵד (Bickell, 118), עד מה (Dyserinck, 378), עדנה or עד הנה (*BHK*); and Budde's (1898^a, 102) description of MT as a monstrosity (cf. also Nägelsbach, 165) is simply pedantic and ill-informed; cf. BL 634 v; GK 100o. Hillers² (144) suggests an emendation ערנו from עור 'to watch': 'we watched' and adds a conjunction before תכלינה; but this is unnecessarily clumsy and overloads the verse with verbs of watching.

MT בְּצִפִּיָּתֵנוּ צִפִּינוּ; LXX ἀποσκοπευόντων ἡμῶν ἀπεσκοπεύσαμεν; P ܗܡ ܗܦܟ *dqw dwqyn*; V *cum respiceremus adtenti*; T בסכיתנא. MT is preferred (see below).

* * *

This verse depicts a desperate, frantic hope on the part of the people of Judah/Jerusalem for some rescuing nation during the run up to (and during) the siege of Jerusalem. It was a hope that was ill-founded, for no help was forthcoming.

Although there are several allusions to 'enemies' or 'nations' in the book, this passage (vv. 17-20) comes closest to securing Lamentations, or at least ch. 4, to a specific period. It is true that, in the reference to expectation of help and the nation that could not save, no people or nation is actually named—it is not even certain who 'we' refers to—but exegetes have been quick to identify and specify here. For MR, the people of Judah were expecting help from Neco of Egypt. Reference is made to a story which grew up around the failure of Egypt to show up, in which the Egyptians recall the fact that their ancestors drowned while pursuing the rebellious ancestors of Judah, so they turned back and did not provide help. Jeremiah 37.7 is quoted as the scripture which underlies this verse. MLT, which recounts an even fuller version of the same story, quotes Isa 30.3-8 as evidence that Egyptian help was worthless; and Rashi too alludes to the story, acknowledging the midrash as his source and quoting Jer 37.7 and Isa 30.7.

Although coming after descriptions of dire circumstances in the aftermath of the fall of Jerusalem in 586 BCE, this verse harks back to earlier days, the period during the siege, when Jerusalem's survival probably depended on external help. Of the surrounding nations, Egypt was the obvious one, with sufficient military muscle. It was also in the interests of Egypt to stop the advance of the Babylonian army in Palestine, so preventing it following up the defeat of Judah with an attack on Egyptian borders. In a few words, the poet describes the intense desire for military aid and the Egyptian failure to provide it. Jeremiah 37.5 describes how the

Babylonian siege was almost abandoned at the news of an approaching Egyptian army; and Jer 37.7 reveals that the same army had turned back. The writer here, speaking for the besieged people, recalls this faith in the Egyptians. This was in spite of the warnings in Isa 30.2-7.

תִּכְלֶינָה עֵינֵינוּ—The combination of 'eyes' with the verb 'to be finished' occurs at 2.11 (q.v.); Jer 14.16; Ps 69.4; Job 11.20; 17.5. As at Lam 2.11, the Versions struggle to capture the sense here. LXX ἐξέλιπον (as at 2.11) 'failed' is ambiguous. P ܚܣܟ hšk (a singular verb with a plural subject) seems to mean 'became dim'. V *defecerunt* 'became weary'. T (paraphrasing) ספאן לאסתכלא 'fail to look for'.

The idea seems to be that the eyes were exhausted scanning the horizon for a sign of approaching help. We should note that LXX, P and V interpret the imperfect תכלינה to be referring to the past, to the expectation of help *before* the fall of Jerusalem.[113] This is the view of most commentators. Some scholars, however, feel that the passage should not be interpreted in such a restricted manner. Keil (441f.) thinks that the imperfect תכלינה is used with the meaning of the participle here and because, in vv. 18-20, Judah is completely in the power of Babylon, the words of v. 17 must refer to the search for help *after* the enemy had already taken Jerusalem. This exegesis is echoed by Streane (387), in Renkema (546f.) and may be behind translations such as AV, RV, NEB, JPS.

עֶזְרָתֵנוּ הָבֶל—Isa 30.7[114] speaks of the Egyptians offering help described as הבל וריק, hence we should probably take the phrase to mean 'our vain help', cf. Vermigli (178), Luther, Calvin, AV, Ewald (345) 'unserer eitlen hülfe'. The idea is that the eyes strained as they looked towards empty assistance. It was like chasing after wind (Eccl 1.14). Most commentators take הבל adverbially, reading 'in vain, vainly', cf. Renkema (546), NIV, NEB, NJB, JPS.

בְּצִפִּיָתֵנוּ צִפִּינוּ—As pointed, we have another *hapax legomenon*: צפיה a feminine noun from √צפה 'to watch'. *HALOT* gives the meaning 'observation point'. Hence we get translations 'from our towers we watched' (NIV, JB), cf. Dahood (1970, 403), Hillers² (136, 144). LXX ἀποσκοπευόντων ἡμῶν ἀπεσκοπεύσαμεν (= 'when we were looking') does not actually represent the preposition ב and has a verbal form rather than a noun.[115] Rudolph (1938, 120) thinks that LXX read בְּצַפּוֹתֵנוּ, i.e. the Piel

---

[113] T seems to be describing a later period, a time when the Romans could have been a possible help.
[114] It is the combination of הבל and עזר which points clearly to Egypt as the nation alluded to in this verse.
[115] T paraphrases, but its בסכיתנא witnesses to the ב and a noun 'lookout 'or 'hope' (Jastrow, 989; Brady, 165).

infinitive construct,[116] which, unpointed, is very close to MT. While P is a free rendering, V *cum respiceremus adtenti* may have judged בצפיתנו to function almost as an infinitive absolute. Scholars are divided as to the meaning of בצפיתנו צפינו. IE¹ comments on בצפיתנו: 'It has no significance', as though to say, the following finite verb carries the sense here; cf. Luther 'und wir warteten auf ein Volk'.

אֶל־גּוֹי לֹא יוֹשִׁעַ—We assume a suppressed relative (אשר) after גוי. LXX εἰς ἔθνος οὐ σῷζον renders the imperfect with a participle, giving the sense of a 'non-saving nation', and V *ad gentem quae salvare non poterat* captures the poet's intention here. AV 'for a nation that could not save us' also gets the sense of MT; cf. NIV, NJB, JPS, NRSV and NEB 'for a nation powerless to save us'.

4.18

Text and Versions

MT צָדוּ צְעָדֵינוּ; so also 5QLam^b; one MS^{Ken} צרו; LXX ἐθηρεύσαμεν μικροὺς ἡμῶν; P ܨܕܘ ܠܕܩܕܩܝܢ *ṣdw lddqdqyn*; Aq ἠρημώθησαν τὰ διαβήματα ἡμῶν ἀπὸ τῆς πορείας; Sym ἐθήρευσαν τὰ διαβήματα ἡμῶν; V *lubricaverunt vestigia nostra*; T הנון צדאן שבילנא. Read צָרוּ צְעָדֵינוּ (see below).

MT כִּי; so also P, V and T; LXX omits. MT is preferred.

* * *

The first person plurals of v. 17 continue in this verse, but the unreliable nation has disappeared. It would seem that the passage may refer to a period after the capture of Jerusalem by the Babylonians, i.e. a period subsequent to that of v. 17 where the poet recalled the time when the people hoped for deliverance.

The subject of the first verb is not specified, and the Versions do not help in this regard. Even T, which had referred to Romans and Edomites in the previous verse, makes no attempt to identify the subject. The verse reads like a description of misery and persecution and is not unlike 5.1-18. Rashi identifies the subject as 'our enemies' and, though MR, MLT, IE¹ and Kara do not mention a specific subject, it is likely that all are in agreement. Calvin refers to those who apply this verse to the Egyptians, but he interprets it vis-à-vis the Babylonians (cf. 1.5f.). Ewald (345) is one who continues the Egyptian interpretation, arguing that an Egyptian king has issued an edict prohibiting refugees from Judah from carrying on trade with Palestine, but Nägelsbach (166) points out that this is pure speculation on the part of Ewald. Keil (442f.), too, regards the subject as the Babylonians.

---

[116] Bickell (119), in his reconstruction of the verse, had earlier suggested this form, but without reference to LXX.

צָדוּ צְעָדֵינוּ—The poet, who has set himself the task of following the alphabet, which now demands a צ, chooses, for reasons of assonance,[117] another word beginning with the same letter. The assonance is enhanced by both words ending with the same sound/letter—וּ. Nevertheless, the opening clause is difficult. LXX's *Vorlage* may have read צדנו צעירינו (suggested in *BHK*), but 'we have hunted for our little ones' makes little sense in the context. In P 'they hunted the common people', the verb agrees with MT while the second word may reveal an affinity with LXX in that ܢܕܩܡܐ *dqdq'* comes from the adjective ܕܩܡܐ *dqdq* meaning 'small, minute'. *BHK* and *BHS* think that V may have read מעדו for צדו, but of the seven instances of that verb (מעד) in the Hebrew Bible, not one is translated in V with *lubrico*.[118] 'They hunted our steps' is awkward[119] if only because the subject is unspecified,[120] and this—as well as the fact that the first stich is rather short—has led to the conjecture that צרינו 'our foes' has fallen out (haplography) after צדו; see Dyserinck (378), Budde (1898a, 103), *BHS*. If this suggestion is adopted, the problem of the short stich disappears, although the exegetical awkwardness is not entirely removed. Another measure which may relieve the tension somewhat is to consider the form צָדוּ. The Masoretic accent, as Rudolph (1962, 249) and Schäfer (133*) observe, suggests the verb is √צדה I, although LXX, P, Aq and Sym all took the verb to be √צוד 'to hunt'.[121] Rashi's rephrasing of the first two words אויבינו ארבו את צעדינו, 'our enemies ambushed our steps', shows that he took צדו to be from √צדה I 'to lie in wait' and not √צוד 'to hunt'.[122] On the basis of Ugaritic *ṣd* 'wander, range', Dahood (1962, 71-72) translates 'our feet have ranged far (without coming into our squares)'; so also McDaniel (49). Gottlieb (68) also finds this suggestion attractive, although he points out that 'the noun צעד is never otherwise used in the Old Testament as the subject of a verb which signifies a movement'. NEB, REB 'When we go out, we take to byways to avoid the public streets' is a paraphrase based on the conjecture צָדוּ (Brockington, 219), i.e. from √צדד 'to shun'; but this has not commanded support. *BHS* notes that one MS[123] reads צרו. Although Ehrlich (52) does not refer to this MS, he does suggest reading צָרוּ (from √צרר I 'to bind, be restricted') and cites Prov 4.12 in

---

[117] Noted by Vermigli (181).
[118] Kelso (61) attempts to explain V: 'Vulg, *lubricaverunt* mag eine andere Lesart gehabt haben, doch ist es wahrscheinlicher, dass sie eine Auslegung des Originals gegeben hat. Die Wurzel צוד bedeutet "zu jagen", und die Vulg. gibt den Sinn von einem schlüpfrigen Pfade und somit die Idee eines Falles.'
[119] IE[1] sees the problem. We may judge from his comment 'As if they hunted our steps' that he takes the statement to be hyperbole or poetic language.
[120] Although it might be argued (Provan, 122) that the poet supplies the subject in v. 19, 'our pursuers'.
[121] T 'they prowled' follows the Masoretic hint.
[122] None of the commentators who have taken this line, e.g. Albrektson (192), Kraus (71, 81), Rudolph (1962, 249), seem to acknowledge Rashi in this.
[123] In fact, this is the only variant in MSS[Ken].

support. The latter passage reads בלכתך לא יצר צעדך. It should be noted that in this passage the verb צרר is construed with צעד and the infinitive of הלך, as here. The combination of צעד and צרר is also found at Job 19.7. In the light of this, and in view of the confusion on display among the Versions, this would seem to be the best suggestion.[124] The problem of there being no subject of the verb, together with the awkward notion of 'hunting our steps', are removed. What the poet is saying is that our movements were restricted in our own streets—literally 'our steps were restrained from walking in our streets. The background is occupied Jerusalem. On the meaning of the preposition מן, see GK 119x. Other examples may be found in 1 Sam 15.26; Isa 24.10.[125]

The second line of this verse gives the impression of being overcrowded, and this, together with the repetition of קִצֵּינוּ, has led scholars to suggest emendations. Renkema (552) defends MT on the grounds that this style and terminology are frequently found in the prophetic announcement of the Day of Yahweh.

קִצֵּינוּ...קִצֵּינוּ—The spelling here is strange in that the word (plural of קֵץ), on both occurrences, is construed as a singular, and we expect קִצֵּנוּ 'our end'. LXX ὁ καιρὸς ἡμῶν does not reflect a different Hebrew text. This is how LXX translates in Gen 6.13; 2 Chron 21.19; Jer 50.26. The Greek translator interprets in terms of time: the end of our time draws near. The poet reflects on the circumstances he has been describing and perhaps concludes that, if a people cannot move around freely in their own city, the end must be close. There is a certain amount of hyperbole here. Some scholars are unhappy about the fact that קרב קצינו is followed by בא קצינו, and in a line that seems on the long side. Bickell (119) deleted the first קצינו and translated 'genaht ist, dass unsere Tage sich erfüllen (zu Ende gehen)', but this was rejected by Budde (1898a, 103) in favour of a suggestion by Löhr (1894, 23) that combines קרב and קצינו in קצרו 'kurz sind'; cf. also BHK, Haller (110). The JB translators who had 'restored' צרינו to the first line, delete כי בא קצינו from the second. The NEB translators ('our days are all but finished, our end has come') have shortened the line by deleting the first קצינו and making קרב plural—קרבו; see Brockington (219). ימינו is then served by two verbs.

What we have in this second line is the poet recalling cries of despair from the people, cries with which he is in sympathy: 'our end is close' and 'our days are numbered' wring from the poet the conclusion 'for our end has come'. MT can stand[126] and, read this way, is superior to the several reconstructions mentioned above. The repetition of 'our end' is deliberate and functions as a bell-toll announcing the ultimate reversal.

[124] Cf. also Gordis (1974a, 194), Kaiser (362), Wiesmann (231).
[125] P ܠܕܡܚܠܟܝܢ ldmhlkyn did not identify this construction, apparently reading the Piel participle of הלך rather than מן with the infinitive construct; cf. Albrektson (193).
[126] Most modern translations retain MT: NIV, NRSV, NJB, JPS.

4.19

Text and Versions
MT דְּלָקֻנוּ; LXX^B ἐξέπτησαν (probably inner Greek error[127] for ἐξήφθησαν); OL *accensi sunt*; P ܪܕܦܘܢ *rdpwn*; V *persecuti sunt nos*; T אדלקו יתנא. MT is preferred.
MT אָרְבוּ—so also LXX, P, V and T; OL *insidiatus est*. MT is preferred.

* * *

Again, the first person plurals, begun at v. 17 and maintained through v. 18, continue in this verse. The vignette here is probably of the period when Judahites were hounded by the Babylonians during the siege of Jerusalem as well as after the capture of the city. The poet indulges in hyperbole in his description of the occupying power—their speed in pursuit of us outshines the speed of the eagles of the sky—though the subsequent clauses, describing chase and ambush, may be close to the facts. The comparison with eagles is found also at Deut 28.49; Jer 4.13; 48.40. It is likely that the poet simply meant that they did not waste any time, much as we might say, 'they were as quick as lightning'.

דְּלָקֻנוּ—The verb √דלק has two meanings—(a) a primary sense 'to set on fire' (Obad 18), and (b) a secondary sense 'to pursue hotly' (1 Sam 17.53). The LXX translator here took the primary meaning, which makes no sense in this passage, but the other Versions understood the verb as referring to the hot pursuit by the enemy. Albrektson (193) observes that the suffix in MT is not translated in either LXX or P, unless the translators included this in ἡμᾶς and ܠ (for MT's לנו) at the end of the line. Certainly the two Versions are related, though P can hardly be accused of following LXX in that the two translators have understood the root דלק quite differently. It may be that the *Vorlage* of LXX and of P simply read דלקו, but V and T both witness to the 1st p. pl. suffix on the verb. Wiesmann's suggestion that we restore a ו (lost through haplography) to במדבר, though unnecessary and without support, raises again the question of the original; cf. v. 16 *Qere*. Since במדבר begins a second action in the line it would not be inappropriate, though not essential, if it started with the copula, as Wiesmann envisages. If the ו got separated in transmission and became attached to דלקו, a subsequent scribe might have 'restored' the text to דלקנו, the obvious accusative in the context and parallel with לנו at the end of the line. Bickell's (119) suggestion that לנו be deleted, on metric grounds, has no support.

The scenario envisaged in v. 19 is not necessarily the same as in the following verse. It is a reflection on what happened around the time of the fall of Jerusalem, perhaps before the actual fall, when the Babylonian

---

[127] See Wiesmann (232), Rudolph (1938, 120); cf. Field (760).

army was mopping up the countryside;[128] but many will have perished at the hands of the enemy. Kara notes that pursuers normally chase their quarry on the plains or in settled areas and will not usually tire themselves out by pursuing them into the hills or the desert, but these people (= Babylonian soldiers) were prepared to hunt in the hills and ambush in desert areas. Kara recognises the thoroughness and intensity of the chase which the poet is trying to highlight here.

4.20

Text and Versions

MT רוּחַ אַפֵּינוּ—so also P, Aq, Sym; LXX πνεῦμα προσώπου ἡμῶν;[129] OL *spiritus ante faciem nostram*; V *spiritus oris nostri*. MT is preferred.

MT מְשִׁיחַ יְהוָה—so also P and T; LXX χριστὸς κυρίος—so also OL and V *Christus Dominus*; LXX (plus OL and V) is, as Rudolph (1938, 120) observes, a Christian correction (for χριστὸς κυρίου). Although T paraphrases, the genitive construction is still clear enough.[130] MT is preferred.

MT בִּשְׁחִיתוֹתָם; LXX ἐν ταῖς διαφθοραῖς αὐτῶν; LXX^Q ἐν ταῖς διαφθοραῖς ἡμῶν; P ܒܓܘܡܨܗܘܢ *bgwmṣhwn*; V *in peccatis nostris*; OL *in interitu nostro*. MT is not in question (see below).

* * *

In this verse the poet waxes lyrical as he alludes to the capture of the king and the hope that had attached to him.

רוּחַ אַפֵּינוּ—The phrase in apposition to מְשִׁיחַ יְהוָה. The combination of רוּחַ and אַף is found at Ps 18.16 (רוּחַ אַפֶּךָ), Job 4.9 (רוּחַ אַפּוֹ), Exod 15.8 (רוּחַ אַפֶּיךָ), all with a flavour of violent aggression; indeed, V translates Ps 18.16 *spiritus furoris tui*, Job 4.9 *in spiritu irae eius*, and Exod 15.8 *in spiritu furoris tui*. In apposition to מְשִׁיחַ יְהוָה, this aggressive meaning will simply not fit, and this may have prompted Jerome to translate אַף with *os* 'mouth'; cf. V at Ezek 16.12.

Although the majority of scholars are convinced that the disasters behind the book of Lamentations are to be associated with the fall of Jerusalem in 586 BCE, the authors of the poems never mention an individual by name

---

[128] At 2 Kgs 24, after the Jehoiakim rebellion against Babylon, Nebuchadnezzar sent in raiding parties from Babylon, Syria, Moab and Ammon. This may also have happened after Zedekiah's rebellion. The account of the fall of Jerusalem says nothing about the outlying districts and villages of Judah, but it is likely that they suffered devastation either before or during the siege of the city (cf. Lachish Letter No. 4 [*ANET*, 322]); and many of the occupants of the towns and settlements will have attempted to escape from their homes into the desert areas and the hill country. The attempt at escape will have had mixed results. Some would-be escapees found refuge beyond the borders of Judah, but many will have perished at the hands of the enemy.

[129] LXX προσώπου ἡμῶν does not reflect a *Vorlage* פָּנֵינוּ. As Kelso (62) notes, this is how LXX translates אַף in many passages, e.g. Gen 2.7; 3.19; Num 32.31.

[130] On T's rendering, see Alexander (2008, 173 n. 49).

and seldom supply sufficient information with which to identify someone from the life and history of Israel. This verse comes as close as any. The individual of whom the author speaks here would seem to be a king (the Lord's Anointed). If one is convinced of Jeremianic authorship then one would identify the individual as a Davidic king in Jeremiah's day (cf. Salters 1999, 206) and since the author appears to view the figure in a favourable light, the identification is, perhaps, straightforward, *viz* Josiah. The Targum's paraphrase is clear: 'King Josiah, who was as dear to us as the breath of our nostrils...'; and this is how it is interpreted in the Talmud (*b. Taan.* 22b). But while many of the early interpreters held this position—MLT gives the impression that it was a widely held view—there were others who felt that it did not suit the context, and MLT seems to favour the identification with Zedekiah, who was 'captured/taken' (Jer 39.7). This is also the view of IE[2] who argues that all the distress occurred after the death of Josiah and yet here it says, 'the punishment of your (Zion's) iniquity is complete' (v. 22); hence Zedekiah is the person alluded to here. The debate was not over, however, for Kara weighed in with yet another suggestion. He is aware of the Josiah interpretation but says nothing of Zedekiah. He argues for Gedaliah, son of Ahikam, who was appointed by the king of Babylon (Jer 41.18). He points out that in Josiah's day the tribes of Judah and Benjamin had not yet gone into exile, but in Gedaliah's day one could envisage 'living under his shadow among the nations'. That the author alludes to Zedekiah is most likely. He could be termed 'the Lord's anointed', while Gedaliah could not, and he was captured (not killed, as were Josiah and Gedaliah); and the phrase 'in their pits' could be poetic language for that capture (Jer 52.7-11). This is the position taken by Vermigli (184), by Calvin[131] and by most commentators since: Blayney (330), Nägelsbach (167), Rudolph (1962, 254), Kaiser (371), Renkema (558). If, as seems likely, the poet speaks about Zedekiah in this verse, the language is noticeably different from that of 2.6, 9 where the monarch is simply referred to as מלך. Either this is a different poet speaking, or it is the same poet who now wants to emphasise something important about the king (and his capture). 'Our life's breath'—what gives us life (cf. Gen 2.7; Ps 104.29), is a highly charged phrase. It is as though the writer considered the monarchy, the Davidic monarchy, to be essential to the continued existence of the community. It is not so much praise of Zedekiah as praise of the office of king. The words of Seneca (*De Clementia* 1.4) come to mind here: 'He (the Emperor) is the breath of life which these many thousands draw'. The same idea of the king as the breath of the people is found in the Amarna letters (*ANET*, 484); and Rameses II of Egypt is referred to as 'the breath of our nostrils' in an inscription from Abydos (de Savignac, 82). Hence, although the language is highly charged, the idea of the king being the breath of life is not unique to Israel. It seems to have been shared with other peoples and in other locations. It is, of course, hyperbole. On this, see Hillers[2] (151f.).

---

[131] Calvin argues 'this passage cannot be understood except of King Zedekiah'.

מְשִׁיחַ יְהוָה—'Yahweh's anointed'. The phrase is also found at 1 Sam 24.7, 11; 26.9, 11, 16, 23; 2 Sam 1.14, 16; 19.22, where it refers to the reigning king.¹³² By juxtaposing these two phrases, the poet highlights the subject of this passage and raises the stakes for what is to follow in this verse. Westermann (204f.) draws attention to the contrast-motif and the dirge-like quality here: 'Even the king, "our breath of life", was snatched away in the collapse'. We may think that the phrase נלכד בשחיתותם 'captured in/by their traps' merely refers to 2 Kgs 25.3-7 when Zedekiah failed to escape (cf. also Ezek 12.13), but the author wants to highlight the final nail in the nation's coffin, the graphic description of 'our end' (v. 18). The Davidic monarchy had not always been untroubled but it had not previously been brought to an end completely. Even Athaliah, daughter of Ahab, who took the throne in Jerusalem for a short time (2 Kgs 11.1), failed to wipe out the dynasty; and when Nebuchadnezzar occupied the city in 597 BCE he replaced Jehoiachin with Zedekiah, who, although a vassal, was of the house of David and was king of Judah. But his capture by the Babylonians meant, for this poet, something important. It may be that the author was unaware of the continued existence of Jehoiachin in Babylon (2 Kgs 25.27-30) or, if he did know, it was irrelevant in the circumstances. Practically speaking, Zedekiah had been the people's last hope.

בִּשְׁחִיתוֹתָם—This is the only form in the verse which is in dispute among commentators. LXX 'in their destructions' does not presuppose a different Hebrew text. Albrektson (193f.) observes that LXX translates in the same way at Ps 107.20. BDB (cf. BL 604 c; *HALOT*) derives the word שחית from √שחח 'to bow down', but the LXX translator derived it from √שחת 'to ruin' (Piel); cf. Kelso (62). P seems to presuppose a singular בשחתם and, although a paraphrase describing Josiah's capture 'in the corrupting pit of the Egyptians', T also testifies to a singular. The fact that שחית is a rare word and that P, T, and OL testify to a singular, has led some scholars to suggest the emendation בשחתם; so Budde (103), *BHK*, cf. Ezek 19.4, 8; but most translations and commentators follow MT.¹³³ The sense is probably not seriously at stake here. שחית may mean 'pit' or some other humiliating trap. Rashi makes it clear that, for him, the שחית was something dug. In Ezek 12.12f., where the capture of Zedekiah is described, the phrase is נתפש במצודתי 'caught in my snare'. The latter passage is in prose, but the

---

¹³² The depiction of Cyrus of Persia as Yahweh's anointed (Isa 45.1) is a later and unique application of the title to a non-Davidic king who was Yahweh's instrument of deliverance to the exiles; cf. Seybold (1998, 52f.). This may have led Kara to think also of Gedaliah in his comments on this verse.

¹³³ V 'in our sins' is due to the Christological rendering of מְשִׁיחַ יהוה and, perhaps, the moral use of שחת (Piel and Hiphil), which saw the passage as an allusion to the crucifixion. The reading does not constitute a serious claim to originality. The 1st p. pl. suffix (also found in OL and LXX^Q) makes no sense in the context and, again, has originated in the Christological interpretation of the passage.

Lamentations poet is alluding to the same event about which probably little was known. The relative particle אֲשֶׁר refers back to the captured 'Yahweh's anointed', and there is a certain wistfulness in the words that follow.

אָמַרְנוּ—'We had thought', i.e. the pluperfect (GK 106f.), as in NEB, JPS. The thought itself is separated from אֲשֶׁר אמרנו by the *zaqeph qaton* (serving as a colon introducing the content of the thought), which creates a certain unevenness in the final line.

The image of God as shadow (i.e. protection[134]) is found at Isa 49.2; Pss 17.8; 91.1; 121.5. This is the only passage which speaks of the king as protector. Hillers[2] (151) draws attention to the use of this imagery, in Egyptian and Mesopotamian texts, for the protection offered by the king. The hope, now dashed, had been that Zedekiah, albeit the vassal of Nebuchadnezzar, the Babylonian king, would have offered protection (and continued existence) to the people of Yahweh. 'Among the nations' might here simply mean 'in Palestine', or may allude to a national entity (Blayney, 330); cf. on 1.3.

4.21

Text and Versions

MT (*Kethib*) יוֹשַׁבְתִּי; MT (*Qere*) יוֹשֶׁבֶת; the archaic paragogic י (GK 90l-n) has been 'corrected' in MT (*Qere*), as in Jer 10.17; Ezek 27.3 (cf. also Jer 22.23) but MT (*Kethib*), as *lectio difficilior*, is preferred (JM 93 o; Schäfer 134*).[135]

MT בְּאֶרֶץ עוּץ—so also P, V and SH; LXX^B ἐπὶ γῆς; LXX^{AQ} ἐπὶ τῆς γῆς; OL *in Geth*; T בארע ארמוניה. Read with LXX^{AQ}—בָּאָרֶץ. MT is the result of early dittography of ע (see below), cf. Salters (2007, 331-34).

MT כּוֹס—so also 5QLam^a, P, V and OL; LXX ποτήριον κυρίου—so also SH; T כס דלוט. MT is preferred.

MT וְתִתְעָרִי—so also V; LXX καὶ ἀποχεεῖς; P ܘܬܫܬܪܦܝܢ *wtštrpyn*; Sym καὶ ἀσχημονήσεις; OL (*bibes,*) *et inebriaberis adhuc*; T ותתרוקני; on P's reading, see Albrektson (195f.). MT is preferred (see below).

* * *

Verses 21f. comprise a unit in which Edom and Zion are addressed. The poet attacks Edom, predicting disaster, while Zion is given a measure of assurance. Verse 21 is concerned only with Edom.

שִׂישִׂי וְשִׂמְחִי—The verse begins like a salvation oracle. The verbs 'rejoice' and 'be glad' often reinforce one another in the Hebrew Bible, and these two verbs √שׂושׂ and √שׂמח are construed together at Pss 40.17; 68.4; 70.5;

---

[134] The image has its origin in the protection from the sun in the branches of a tree, cf. Renkema (558f.).

[135] REB's rendering 'daughters of Edom, dwellers in the land of Uz' would suggest that the translators read בנות אדום יושבות בארץ עוץ, but there is no explanatory footnote.

Job 3.22; Isa 66.10. The call to Edom to rejoice[136] is ironic, for soon she will experience punishment. The poet is saying: 'Rejoice for all you are worth but you will not escape punishment'.

In the communal psalms of lament there is a tendency to call on God for vengeance on the enemy (Pss 74.22f.; 79.12), and we have noticed this element at Lam 1.21f and 3.64ff. Although Yahweh is not addressed here,[137] the prediction that Edom will be punished echoes the call of the communal lament for punishment to fall upon the enemy. The fact that Edom is mentioned by name is somewhat surprising in that the authors of Lamentations are otherwise inclined to refer to enemies by the terms אויב(ים) (1.2, 5, 9; 2.3, 4, 5; 3.46; 4.12); צר(ים) (1.5, 7, 10; 2.4, 17; 4.12; נכרים (5.2); זרים (5.2).[138] Not even the Babylonians get a specific mention. This has led to the surmise that the reference to Edom here simply means 'enemies', and this interpretation is probably based on the fact that Edom had been a traditional enemy of Israel.[139] However, it has to be said that if this is in the mind of the poet it is the only passage in the Hebrew Bible where the term אדום or בת אדום is so used. Another, related, view is that Edom is an oblique reference to Rome.[140] However, the world known to the author of this poem did not include Rome, and the first references to Rome (2nd century BCE) do not depict them as enemies but as allies.[141] We must, therefore, interpret Edom as the historical Edom and we must ask why the animosity should surface in this way. The prose accounts of the fall of Jerusalem (2 Kgs 25; Jer 52) speak of the Babylonians, and if the author had burst forth with an attack on Babylon by name it would have been understandable; and if, as I have argued elsewhere,[142] he had attacked 'the enemy', it would have been natural to have interpreted this as a reference to the Babylonians. It would seem, therefore, that the poet who knew that his readers would take a reference to 'enemies' to mean Babylon, and the unreliable nation (v. 17) to mean Egypt, had something specific to say about the Edomites.[143]

בְּאֶרֶץ עוּץ—The fact that the (very literal) LXX does not represent עוץ raises the question of the authenticity of MT, though P, V, SH all follow MT.[144] I have argued (2007, 332f.) that on the basis of LXX usage the

---

[136] Cf. 1.21 and 2.17.

[137] In contrast to poems 1, 2, 3 and 5, Yahweh is not addressed anywhere in this poem.

[138] The specific mention of Egypt and Assyria at 5.6 is in a different category: they are merely nations with whom Israel had traded.

[139] The references to Edom in the Hebrew Bible often give the impression that a particular hostility existed between the two nations (Ps 137.7; Ezek 25.12-14; Obad 1, 8).

[140] We find this in the Targum's paraphrase, in Rashi's commentary, in MR and in MLT. IE[1] and Kara, however, speak of the historical Edom.

[141] Vermes (215f.).

[142] Salters (2007, 331).

[143] On the expressions בת אדום and בת ציון in these verses, see on 1.6.

[144] In OL it is represented with *in Geth*, while T's paraphrase has 'in Armenia', suggesting, perhaps, that something followed בארץ in the *Vorlage*.

phrase בארץ עוץ is likely to have been translated ἐν γῇ Ως. The fact that LXX reads ἐπὶ τῆς γῆς would not lead one to assume that a word had dropped out after γῆς.[145] There is some concern about the length of the second stich,[146] and Haller (110) suggests reading simply בעוץ, a suggestion which has not received support. But there is another factor here which has a bearing on MT. The addressee in MT is said to be dwelling 'in the land of Uz'. This is surely strange.[147] If the text had read 'Bozra in the land of Edom' it would have been less problematic. Can Edom be said to be living in any land other than Edom? We do not know if Edomites ever occupied the land of Uz; if they had, it would have been irrelevant in this context. We do know that the Edomites, whose territory lay east of the Wadi Arabah, expanded and moved west, encroaching on Judah's southern borders.[148] If the poet had this in mind he is accusing the old enemy of infiltration and of taking advantage of Judah's demise at the hands of the Babylonians (cf. Ps 137.7). Now, if we are correct in reading בָּאָרֶץ, the reference is to the land of promise (cf. Gen 12.6; 1 Kgs 4.19; 9.18; 2 Kgs 3.27; Isa 37.18; Hos 1.2). The emendation shortens the second stich and gives a better balance, and it also explains why Edom receives unusual and specific attention. It is interesting to note that the LXX rendering of בת אדום is Θύγατερ Ἰδουμαίας. The Greek translator may have been thinking of the time when the southern territory was occupied and called Idumea.

גַּם־עָלַיִךְ תַּעֲבָר־כּוֹס—The preposition על sometimes has the force of אל, as here (JM 133 b); in addition, the verb √עבר is construed with על at Exod 30.13, 14; Isa 45.14 with the meaning 'to pass over to' (BDB 755; *HALOT*, על [6]). גם is used here because the poet is aware that the punishment he promises to Edom has already been experienced by Zion. The contents of the cup are still unspecified, and Edom is encouraged to indulge to the full. The image of the cup being passed around has its origin in joyous occasions but, as part of the ironic call to rejoice, the cup will amount to a cup of punishment. The cup of wrath[149] motif is found at Jer 25.15-29 (cf. also Ps 75.9; Isa 51.17, 22; Jer 49.12; 51.7; Ezek 23.31-34). The LXX reads 'cup of the Lord'. It is unusual for the LXX translator to expand in this way and it may be that his *Vorlage* read כוס יהוה. Such a reading would overload the first stich of this line, hence it must be regarded as a scribal explanatory addition, based probably on Jer 25.17 where we find the words הַכּוֹס מִיַּד יְהוָה.

---

[145] Contra Albrektson (194), Rudolph (1962, 249), Schäfer (134*).
[146] Cf. S. R. Driver (1921 xxviii), Wiesmann (234), Kraus (72).
[147] Hence Ehrlich (52) proposes reading בְּאֶרֶץ עוֹד; Buhl (1893, 73) prefers בְּאֶרֶץ יהוה; Budde (1898ᵃ, 103) proposes בְּאַרְצֵנוּ.
[148] See Bartlett (143).
[149] The T paraphrase renders the term 'cup' as כס דלוט 'the accursed cup'. In the Yemenite MSS the reading is כס פורענותא 'the cup of punishment'; see Heide (35*).

תִּשְׁכְּרִי וְתִתְעָרִי—The two imperfects (2nd p. f.), corresponding to the two imperatives with which the verse began, address Edom further. What you thought was the cup of merriment will end, as in Zion's case, in shame! The verb √שכר here means 'to become drunk' (cf. Gen 9.21: שְׁתה וַיִּשְׁכָּר). The verb √ערה, a parallel form of √ערר II 'to strip oneself', can also mean 'to pour out' (BDB 788), and this is how LXX understood it, and perhaps T.[150] This association of drunkenness and nakedness is found also at Gen 9.21 and Hab 2.15, the nakedness itself being a source of shame. The Piel of √ערה means 'to strip bare' hence the Hithpael 'to expose oneself' may refer to the bravado of the drunk who has abandoned his sense of decency and his judgment. In receiving the cup that Zion has drunk from, Edom will end up in shame just like Zion.

4.22

Text and Versions

MT תַּם־עֲוֺנֵךְ, so also LXX, V and T; P ܐܬܦܩܕܘ ܚܘܒܝܟܝ *'tpqdw ḥwbyky*. MT is preferred, see Albrektson (196).

* * *

In this verse, which clearly belongs with v. 21, attention turns first to Zion, who, in the first line, is accorded muted comfort, and then, by contrast, to Edom where the poet explicates the threat of the cup.

Scholars have struggled with the meaning of the first line and many have concluded that this is a prophetic voice announcing the end of Zion's punishment, so vividly described earlier in the chapter (cf. translations such as NEB, REB, JPS, NJB). Renkema (564-69) objects to this interpretation, pointing out that there is no evidence that Zion's punishment is at an end (note the endings of chs. 1, 2, 3 and the entire final poem), and he points out that confusion in this first stich has led to misunderstanding of the second.

תַּם־עֲוֺנֵךְ—This is the only place in the Hebrew Bible where the verb √תמם is construed with the noun עון. As we noted at v. 6, עון can mean 'iniquity' or 'punishment for iniquity'. It is not clear what the LXX translator 'your sin has come to an end' had in mind. What *is* clear is that he does not understand עון as punishment; and the other Versions—P, V, OL and T[151]—appear to be in agreement, that is, the words they use to render עון

---

[150] The Greek translator may have thought that this was a reference to vomiting; cf. Rashi whose comment is 'like כדה ותער' (Gen 24.20). Levine (73 and 175) seems undecided! Cf. this sequence at Jer 25.27 שְׁתוּ וְשִׁכְרוּ וּקְיוּ. Alexander (176) translates T 'you shall become drunken and depopulated'.

[151] Levine (73) wrongly translates T 'your punishment shall be concluded'; cf. Brady (166) and Jastrow (1049), and see Alexander (2008, 176), who renders 'your iniquity shall be expiated'.

do not carry the meaning 'punishment'. It would seem, therefore, that the preference for translating עָוֹן as 'punishment' is at odds with the Versions, although it is not always clear what those translations mean exactly. This is partly because of the added difficulty of the verb תמם√ (3rd p. m. s. perfect Qal)—BDB (1070) gives the meaning 'be finished, come to an end' (cf. also *HALOT*). I have argued[152] that the poet probably means that Zion's iniquity/guilt has run its course/come to fruition. Zion's iniquity had attracted the attention of Yahweh, and she had drunk from the aforementioned cup. In Gen 15.16, where עָוֹן is construed with the adjective שָׁלֵם—לֹא־שָׁלֵם עֲוֹן הָאֱמֹרִי עַד־הֵנָּה—the meaning is 'the guilt of the Amorite has not yet run its course'. The poet was obliged, because of his commitment to the alphabetic acrostic, to employ a word with initial ת (at the beginning of the verse), though he may have been thinking more in terms of שלם√.[153] Our translation would then be 'Your guilt, O Zion, has run its course'. It is not that Zion's miseries are over—this is, clearly, not the case—it is that her iniquity has come to fruition in the disaster promised by the pre-exilic prophets.[154]

לֹא יוֹסִיף לְהַגְלוֹתֵךְ—The verb יסף√ 'to add' (Hiphil impf. 3rd p. m. s.) acts as an auxiliary verb[155] and is construed with the infinitive to stress either repetition or continuity of the action. The interpretation that Zion's punishment is over, which may have originated in MR, has led many commentators to identify the subject of the second stich as Yahweh, the punisher; but if we translate as above, it allows us, more naturally, to take the subject of the second stich as that of the first, *viz* 'your iniquity'[156]: 'it will not cause you further deportation'. Kraus (83) may be correct in thinking that there is an allusion here to Jer 52.28-30, which speaks of several deportations by the Babylonians. The statement that there is to be no further deportation may refer specifically to the one carried out by Nebuzaradan in 581 BCE.

פָּקַד עֲוֺנֵךְ בַּת־אֱדוֹם—In the second line the concentration is on Edom's iniquity/sins and Yahweh's punishment thereof. The words עֲוֺנֵךְ and חַטֹּאתָיִךְ are in parallel and both should be taken in their primary sense. It is only in conjunction with the verbs פקד and גלה that the idea of 'punishment' is

---

[152] Salters (2007, 335f.).
[153] The root שלם has a slightly wider semantic range than תמם. It is interesting to note that, although the root תמם exists in Aramaic, T translates with שלם.
[154] Translations such as JPS 'your iniquity…is expiated', and NJB 'your wickedness is atoned for…' demand too much from the verb תמם√. NIV (cf. also Provan, 123) '…your punishment will end' has taken the verb תם to be a prophetic perfect (GK 106n) balancing the imperfect of the second stich; and this remains a possibility, especially since the verbs in the second line are probably of this nature.
[155] Cf. Waltke and O'Connor (39.3.1b).
[156] IE[1] is uncertain here as to whether the subject is 'your iniquity' or 'God', but he does entertain the former as a possibility; cf. Salters (2007, 336 n. 35).

arrived at.[157] The construction פקד עון occurs only here in Lamentations but is common in the Hebrew Bible (Exod 20.5; 34.7; Lev 18.25; Jer 36.31 etc). The verb must be taken as a prophetic perfect (as must the parallel verb גלה in the second stich): 'he will punish your iniquity, Edom'. Although Yahweh's name is not mentioned there can be no doubt that Yahweh is the subject of these two verbs. The poet believes that Yahweh was behind the fall of Jerusalem and the affliction of the people and that he will deal out similar treatment to Edom. She will drink of the cup that Zion has drunk from.

גִּלָּה עַל־חַטֹּאתָיִךְ—The verb √גלה in the Piel means 'to expose, disclose'. The exposure of sins (Lam 2.14; cf. Hos 2.12) leads to punishment for those sins. The second stich, in parallel with the first, predicts and promises punishment. The construction גִּלָּה עַל־חַטֹּאתָיִךְ is unusual (and P does not represent עַל), but it is also found at 2.14 וְלֹא־גִלּוּ עַל־עֲוֺנֵךְ (cf. also Jer 51.47, 52 where we get פקד על). There is a certain wordplay here—גִּלָּה echoes the form לְהַגְלוֹתֵךְ in the first line, but whereas the latter is part of a positive note to Zion, this final stich carries an entirely negative message for Edom. The question arises as to the nature of Edom's sins.[158] We have taken the view (v. 21) that it was Edom's expansion into southern Judah (בארץ) that occasioned this outburst by the poet in these two verses; and Renkema (571) draws attention to archaeological research which confirms that Edom did invade southern Judah and took possession of land there. Renkema also points to 1 Esd 4.45, which depicts the Edomites as setting fire to the temple in Jerusalem. While 2 Kgs 25.8f. attributes this to Nebuzaradan, Renkema wonders if the actual task was given to the Edomites because the Babylonians did not want to incur the wrath of the god who was being worshipped there. In any case, Obadiah and Ps 137.7 confirm Edom's military involvement in the fall of the city, and this, together with the subsequent occupation of Judah's territory, will have incurred the wrath of those in Judah who survived the Babylonian conquest.

This final unit (vv. 21f.) combines promise and threat. Edom is threatened with punishment, and Zion is shown a faint light at the end of the tunnel. Renkema is correct in drawing attention to the continued affliction in all five poems, but he does not adequately acknowledge that the present passage is designed to raise the morale of the people of Yahweh. The negative prediction (ironic call to rejoice, the cup and the threat) is not intended for the rulers of Edom to read/hear and be fearful and downcast: it is meant for home consumption alone—for the people of Zion, who are meant to receive it and to take heart. And the snippet about Zion, though not a full-blooded oracle of salvation, will have been meant to raise the spirits of the suffering Judahites.

---

[157] This fact reinforces the decision to translate עֲוֺנֵךְ in the first line as 'iniquity' and not 'punishment'. The poet is unlikely to have used the term עון in two different senses in the same passage.

[158] On this, see Renkema (570-72).

CHAPTER 5

Introductory

The final poem in the collection is quite different from the others. It is not an acrostic,[1] though it is alphabetical in that it consists of twenty-two lines, the number of the letters of the Hebrew alphabet. The poetic rhythm differs from the other four chapters, consisting of balanced stichs, akin to other Hebrew poetry. Finally, unlike the other poems, the composition closely resembles the communal lament in the book of Psalms (Pss 44, 60, 74, 79, 80) where God is addressed throughout and where the community is represented by the use of the first person plural forms. In early interpretations, this poem is sometimes entitled 'The Prayer of Jeremiah' (see *Introduction*). Like other communal laments it contains a description of misery and an appeal to Yahweh for help. The latter is remarkably short, while the former is uniquely long. The length of the description of misery may be due to the poet extending an earlier version to produce an 'alphabetic' unit of twenty-two lines.[2] There is no allusion to the actual fall of Jerusalem here, hence it is likely that the poet is describing the ongoing misery under the Babylonian yoke.[3] The poet appears to pick up terminology from chs. 1, 2 and 4, so it is probable that the composition dates after those poems but before ch. 3.

Verse 1: In this first verse Yahweh is invoked and urgently requested to remember, look and see. The request is made from a position of adversity (what has happened to us).

Verses 2-18: This passage, which may be sub-divided, lays before Yahweh what is troubling the community and is an elaboration of 'our disgrace' in v. 1. First person plural forms dominate in vv. 2-10, 15-18; in between is a section which describes in the third person the fortunes of various social groupings; women, princes, elders, young men (vv. 11-14). But whether in first person or third person these verses constitute the heartfelt prayer of the community which includes a confession of guilt

---

[1] Bergler (317) claims that there is an acrostic here. He reads the first letter of each line (deleting *ʿl zh* in v. 17 and *ʿl hr* in v. 18) and produces the following sentence: *zōnîm ʿam ʾāʿîb ʿōnēš bûz šānāhāh ʾlōhêkā*, translating 'the apostates, the people I despise, punishing them with disdain, as your God is lamenting'; but this need not detain us. Cf. Gerstenberger (2001, 501).

[2] Cf. Kaiser (376-78). Berlin (116f.) points out, in this regard, that Pss 33 and 103 have 22 verses, and Pss 38 and 49 contain 23 and 21 verses.

[3] The reference at v. 18 to the desolate hill of Zion ties it all to the period between 586 and 520 BCE.

(vv. 6, 16). A sadness hangs over this passage as the poet describes the various aspects of hardship experienced by a subjugated people. It ends with a poignant glance at the place where the temple stood—now the haunt of jackals (v. 18).

Verses 19-22: This passage, which constitutes the lament's petition, is prefaced with a brief element of praise to Yahweh, referring to his everlastingness and his superiority (v. 19). But this is linked to the accusatory and poignant question: Why do you forget us...for so long? (v. 20). The prayer then concludes with the actual petition, pleading for restoration in the face of the stark fact that, in his anger, Yahweh has rejected them.

Translation

1. O Yahweh, remember what has happened to us;
   Look, and see our disgrace!

2. Our heritage is turned over to strangers,
   Our houses to aliens.

3. We have become orphans, fatherless;
   Our mothers are like widows.

4. We must pay for the water we drink;
   Our firewood comes at a price.

5. The yoke is on our necks, we are harassed;[4]
   Exhausted, we are allowed no rest.

6. We submitted to Egypt and to Assyria
   To get enough bread;

7. Our fathers sinned; they are no more;
   We bear their punishment.

8. Slaves rule over us;
   There is no one to rescue us from their power.

9. We get our food at the risk of our lives
   Because of the sword of the desert.

10. Our skin is become wrinkled as in an oven
    Because of the ravages of famine.

11. They have raped women in Zion,
    Maidens in the towns of Judah.

12. Princes have been hung up by their hands,
    Elders are shown no respect.

13. Young men take up the millstone,
    And boys stagger under bundles of wood.

---

[4] *The yoke is on our necks, we are harassed* prb. rdg. Heb. reads *Upon our necks we are pursued*.

14. The elders have gone from the gate,
    The young men from their music-making.

15. Gone is the joy of our hearts;
    Our dancing has turned to mourning.

16. The crown has fallen from our head;
    Woe to us, for we have sinned.

17. For this, our heart has become sad;
    For these things, our eyes have become dim.

18. For the hill of Zion which lies desolate—
    The haunt of jackals.

19. But you, O Yahweh, remain for ever;
    Your throne endures to all generations!

20. Why do you forget us continually?
    Why do you abandon us for so long?

21. O Yahweh, restore us to yourself, and we shall return;
    Renew our days as of old,

22. Even though you have truly rejected us
    And been very angry with us.

Commentary

5.1

Text and Versions

LXX (Title): προσευχή (some MSS + SH), προσευχὴ Ἰερεμίου (some MSS), προσευχὴ Ἰερεμίου προφήτου (a few MSS); V (Title): *oratio ieremiae prophetae* with a few V[Mss]; P (Title) ܨܠܘܬܐ ܕܐܪܡܝܐ *ṣlwth dʾrmy*'; MT (untitled) is preferred.

MT (*Kethib*) הַבִּיט with a few MSS[Ken]; MT (*Qere*) הַבִּיטָה with many MSS[Ken] + 5QLam[a]; MT (*Kethib*) is preferred, cf. Keil (447), NEB (on which see Brockington, 219), Bickell (120), BL (366 t) and *BHQ*. MT (*Qere*) may have arisen due to 1.11; 2.20.

MT חֶרְפָּתֵנוּ; so also LXX, P, V, T; 5QLam[a] חרפותינו with several MSS[Ken] + LXX[Ms]. MT is preferred. The two imperatives (from √נבט and √ראה) occur also at 1.11, 12; 2.20. Bickell (120) deletes וראה, presumably because the line is longer than its companions, but the Versions support MT.

* * *

The three imperatives which dominate this verse set the tone for the entire prayer to Yahweh, which ends at v. 22. The imperatives are picked up again at v. 21. Yahweh is specifically addressed only at v. 1 and vv. 19-22, but the entire prayer is to Yahweh. The author speaks, as it were, for all the people—1st p. pl. appearing at vv. 1-10, 15-17, 19-22.

זְכֹר—The combination of Yahweh and the imperative 'remember' occurs nowhere else in Lamentations. We find it in Pss 74.18; 132.1; 137.17. The verb √זכר in the Hebrew Bible does not mean merely 'to call to mind'. While there is always an implied reference to the past, the emphasis is often on the present. Furthermore, the reference to the present often involves action in the present. Hence, when the poet calls on Yahweh to remember, he is not simply prodding Yahweh to recall, but is requesting action on Yahweh's part. No particular action is specified until v. 21, but what the three imperatives of v. 1 request is that Yahweh considers and pays attention to the condition of the people. The poet picks up the wording of 1.11f. and 2.20 (q.v.) and prefaces it with the call 'remember'. It may be argued that the previous instances of addressing Yahweh in the book hint strongly that, in spite of everything, the authors still clung to the idea that they were the people of Yahweh. The first word in ch. 5 confirms this. Although 'remember' is calling on Yahweh to 'consider' what has happened, the element of the past, which is always included in זכר, is based on the former and traditional relationship of the people to Yahweh. When God 'remembers' in the Hebrew Bible the meaning depends very much on the context: he may 'remember' with blessing (Gen 8.1) or he may 'remember' with punishment (Hos 9.9; Ps 137.7); that is to say, Yahweh's nature is such that certain situations call for blessing while others call for punishment. The parallel accusations in this verse, namely 'what has happened to us' and 'our reproach', are in general terms and lack specification.[5] However, the accusations of v. 1 are spelt out in vv. 2-18, an unusually long 'description of misery'. The author draws Yahweh's attention to 'what has happened to us'. Read in the light of the fall of Jerusalem and the aftermath, this phrase must refer to the actual conquest of Judah and to the ensuing hardships.[6]

חֶרְפָּתֵנוּ—The meaning of this word depends on context. It may mean 'taunt' (Ezek 21.33; Ps 22.7) or 'shame, disgrace', as here (cf. also 1 Sam 25.39; Isa 30.5, where it is parallel with בשׁת 'shame'). In Jer 29.18 it appears in a list of negatives 'I will pursue them with the sword, with famine, and with pestilence, and will make them a horror to all the kingdoms of the earth, to be an object of cursing, and horror, and hissing, and a derision (חרפה) among all the nations where I have driven them' (NRSV). Hillers[2] (162) comments 'Ancient Israelites possessed a keen sense of honor and of the proper order of things, so that when trouble came they would complain as often and as bitterly of the shame as of the physical loss or pain'; cf. also Dobbs-Allsopp (2002, 143). One could say that in this first verse the phrases 'what has come upon us' and 'our humiliation' are an introduction in general terms of what is about to be elaborated upon in the following verses.

---

[5] In the communal laments in the book of Psalms, the complaints are often left unspecified (cf. Ps 79.4).
[6] IE[1] seems to make a distinction between the context of the first stich and that of the second: the former refers to experiences before the exile, while the latter has to do with the present suffering.

5.2

Text and Versions
MT נַחֲלָתֵנוּ; several MSS[Ken] נחלתינו. MT is preferred.
MT בָּתֵּינוּ; T ביתנא; two MSS[Ken] בתנו. MT is preferred.
MT לְנָכְרִים; 5QLam[a] [לנו]כריאם; cf. Schäfer (135*) and DJD III, 175. MT is preferred.

* * *

The author gives expression to the pain and ignominy of having been dispossessed and living in occupied territory—strangers in their own country.

The verse reads smoothly and can stand without emendation; but there have been suggestions. Based on the observation that the metre of ch. 5 (3+3) differs from that (3+2) of chs. 1–4, it is noted that this verse (3+2) appears to have a short second stich. Budde (105) adds נתנו after בתינו; and this is followed in *BHK*, and by Wiesmann (247), Haller (110) and Westermann (210). In MT, נהפכה does double duty for נחלתנו and בתינו and, syntactically, may be said to be at odds with the plural. T 'our house' is probably due to the interpretation by the Targumist that 'our heritage' refers to the Temple.

נַחֲלָתֵנוּ—'Our heritage'. The word נחלה is very common in the Hebrew Bible—over 200 instances—although this is the only occurrence of the word in Lamentations. The form with the 1st p. pl. suffix occurs only here, and at Num 32.19, 32; Ps 47.5. The term נחלה comes from the legal language of the Northwest Semites (Lipiński, 320). It has to do with the portion of the patriarchal estate received by succession; hence it is often in parallel with the term *ḥlq* ('share, portion', e.g. at Gen 31.14; Deut 10.9; 12.12), although, strictly speaking, *ḥlq* need not necessarily be a share of patriarchal property.

Israel believed that Yahweh had given the land to his people (1 Kgs 8.36). The idea of Yahweh as the father of Israel lies behind this belief and is reflected at Deut 32.6 and Hos 11.1; and the land as Yahweh's heritage is a common theme (cf. Ps 135.12; Jer 2.7; 17.4). The notion of *the people* as Yahweh's heritage is also found (Deut 4.20; 9.26, 29; Joel 3.2). Lipiński (331) notes that the term נחלה continues, at Qumran, to denote both land (1QM 12.12) and people (1QH 6.8). The term, then, lies at the heart of Israel's existence, and it is not without significance that it appears at the head of the poet's list here (Renkema, 590). The people's *raison d'être* is at stake. But there is another dimension which is not articulated here but which comes to light at the end of the prayer, namely Yahweh's relationship to his people. Verse 2 seems to imply that that relationship is called into question. The poet, in 'telling' Yahweh that the land has been handed over to aliens, is raising that very issue. Although he says '*our* heritage' and not '*your* heritage' (Ps 79.1), the very term 'heritage' (rather than simply 'land') is meant to highlight the people's position vis-à-vis

Yahweh and to confront Yahweh with that very relationship.[7] *Midrash Rabbah* (and MLT) identify 'our heritage' with the Solomonic temple, referring to Ps 79.1 where, it is claimed, 'your heritage' alludes to the Temple. It may be that T has the same interpretation; probably, the rendering 'our house' (singular) in the second stich is due to the interpretation by the Targumist that 'our heritage' refers to the Temple.[8] IE[1] interprets נחלה as 'fields and vineyards',[9] while Calvin takes it to be a general reference to the land (cf. also Keil, 447).

נֶהֶפְכָה—Niphal perf. 3rd p. f. s. from √הפך 'to turn, overturn'. The statement that the heritage is turned over to strangers formally conceals the fact that it is Yahweh who has done the turning over: the poet is confronting God with his handiwork and so is complaining. The passive voice reflects the powerlessness of the Judahites, and the theme of reversal is heard again. The reference to 'our houses' in the second stich seems at first to contradict Jer 52.13 and 2 Kgs 25.9, where it is said that all the houses of Jerusalem had been burned down (cf. also v. 18), but these passages describe the city of Jerusalem only, while the poet here—with his reference to heritage—must be thinking of Judah as a whole.[10]

זָרִים—This word can have the meaning 'illegitimate' (Hos 5.7), but more often it refers to non-Israelites (Ezek 7.21; Obad 11).

נָכְרִים—The adjective נכרי is used as a substantive 'alien, stranger'. The term often appears in parallel with זָרִים (Deut 14.21; Obad 11; Prov 20.16). The two terms allude to the invading Babylonians who took over Judah and Jerusalem in 586 BCE.

5.3

Text and Versions
MT (*Kethib*) אֵין אָב—followed by LXX, V, Sym, P, T; MT (*Qere*) וְאֵין אָב is supported by many MSS[Ken]; most commentators (+ *BHK*, *BHQ*[11]) prefer *Kethib*.[12] As Ehrlich (52) notes, 'Das *Kethib* אין ist vorzuziehen, denn besonders bei epexegetischen Sätzen mit dieser Negation an der Spitze fehlt die Konjunktion...'; he cites Gen 11.30; Exod 21.11.

---

[7] In Pss 79.1 the poet places before Yahweh the fact of the enemy invasion in such a way that he must see it as an invasion of his own property.
[8] MLT regards the plural 'houses' as a reference to the pre-exilic and post-exilic Temples.
[9] The IE[2] commentary of ch. 5 is technically missing in *Mikraoth Gedoloth*. In a private communication, Professor Ulrich Simon argues that IE[2] has replaced IE[1] there; cf. also Shute (1995, 35).
[10] Renkema (592) sees 'our houses' as synonymous with 'our heritage', citing Jer 12.7, where 'my house' and 'my heritage' both refer to Yahweh's people, and Hos 8.1; 9.15, where 'house' seems to mean 'land'. But in the present verse the term is 'our houses'. The poet has in mind actual dwelling places and is not using the term in a secondary sense.
[11] *BHS* is misleading here. It is interesting that at 5.5 and 5.7 too the *Qere* has a ו while *Kethib* has not. Budde (105) notes this, preferring the forms without the ו in each case.
[12] Of modern scholars, only Dyserinck (379), Haller (110) prefer *Qere*; cf. also NIV

MT אִמֹּתֵינוּ כְּאַלְמָנוֹת—so also Versions; the suggestion by Rudolph (1962, 257, 260) that we should emend the text to read the singular: אמנו כאלמנה = 'unsere Mutter einer Witwe gleich' on the basis of 1.1 is unnecessary (Wiesmann, 247), and is not followed by other commentators.

* * *

The loss of houses (v. 2) prompts the poet to think of the former occupants of these houses, i.e. the people who have been ousted by the aliens. We cannot be certain as to the meaning here. The poet may be thinking of actual orphans whose fathers had either been killed by the Babylonians or been taken off to Babylonia in exile and, as a result, left the mothers as though they were widows. As not all males were killed or deported, the author would be using hyperbole here.[13] Or is this a poetic way of describing the vulnerability of the population in the light of v. 2? IE[1], whose comments show that he links both verses, says: 'Furthermore, we have become a people of wretched sojourners, as though we had become orphans with no father…' MLT interprets in a similar way—'like orphans who have no helper', cf. NEB. The suggestion by Dobbs-Allsopp (2002, 145) that 'fatherless' may secondarily allude to the absence of God (Jer 31.9) is going too far down the homiletical road. The comment of Renkema (598) that, in addition to the plain sense, there may be an oblique note to the effect that in this final poem the alphabetic acrostic has been abandoned (*no aleph–beth*), is too midrashic to take seriously. Orphans and widows are grouped together in the Hebrew Bible, representing the most vulnerable in society. Even in peaceful times the prophets plead for the consideration of their rights—Isa 1.17, 23; Jer 7.6; Ezek 22.7; Zech 7.10; cf. Exod 22.21; Ps 68.6; how much more would these groups be vulnerable in circumstances where the normally secure are disenfranchised. The poet, then—and it must be stressed that this is poetry—may be speaking of the entire population of Judah who have suffered such loss of status that they may be described as orphans and widows. The poet uses the traditional language of vulnerability to emphasise the dire need of the people as a whole; and he addresses Yahweh, the traditional protector of the needy (cf. Provan 1991, 126).

5.4

Text and Versions

MT מִיָּמֵינוּ; LXX ἐξ ἡμερῶν ἡμῶν. The Greek translator, who had the same consonantal text as in MT and witnessed to by P, OL, V and T, vocalised מִיָּמֵינוּ; later corrected in LXX[L].

MT בְּכֶסֶף שָׁתִינוּ is a minus in LXX, though witnessed to by P, V, OL and T.

MT עֵצֵינוּ—so also LXX, OL, V; P ܘܩܝܣܝܢ *wqysyn*; Sym τὰ δένδρα ἡμῶν (τιμῆς ἐτρυγῶμεν). MT is preferred.

---

[13] Cf. Meek (35), Gordis (195), Kaiser (374), who would translate 'our mothers are (indeed) widows', taking the preposition כ as *kaph veritatis*; cf. GK 118x.

MT יְבֹאוּ—so also P; LXX ἦλθεν; V *comparavimus*; OL *accepimus*; T אתון. Kelso (64) assumes that V's *Vorlage* read נביא for יבאו, but the difference may be explained by the awkwardness of the Hebrew construction. It is probable that MT lies behind the Versions.[14]

* * *

Having depicted the people as vulnerable as orphans and widows, the poet goes on to deal with the basics of living, whether or not they possessed land, notwithstanding their status.

The author, in this verse, conveys how the displacement (v. 2) and the reduced status (v. 3) shows itself in the practical problems of survival. Water is essential for living (cf. 1 Kgs 17.10) and it is often associated with wood (in the sense of firewood) in the Hebrew Bible (Josh 9.21, 23, 27). While the word עצים can mean trees (so Sym), the wood referred to here is firewood for cooking, as in 1 Kgs 17.10. The displacement of the community, the loss of נחלה, meant that ownership of anything was called in question. That is emphasised here. It was bad enough to have to buy the essentials: it was bitter to have to fork out money for water and firewood, previously taken for granted and rightly theirs. The poet's use of the 1st p. pl. 'our water' and 'our wood' is significant here, as Kara observes: 'It is not the water of others but our own water…not the wood of others but even our own wood'.

בְּכֶסֶף—The preposition ב in בכסף and במחיר is *beth pretii* (GK 119p) = 'in exchange for'.

יְבֹאוּ—The verb can have the meaning 'come, enter, appear, arrive' (cf. v. 9): 'Our wood arrives at a price'. The sense is found at Lev 25.22, cf. 1 Kgs 10.14. The unusual construction is difficult to translate, hence the variety of renderings.

The situation here is post-586 BCE when the Babylonians were in control in Judah, although IE[1] imagines the scenario while the city was under siege. Rashi comments that the people were afraid to take water from the river because of the enemy.

5.5

Text and Versions

MT עַל צַוָּארֵנוּ—so also LXX, P and T; V *cervicibus nostris*; OL *in cervices nostras*; Sym ζυγὸς κατὰ τοῦ τραχήλου ἡμῶν. Read with Sym: עַל עַל—one על has been lost through haplography.

---

[14] Compare the variety in translations such as RSV, JB, JPS and NEB—all based on MT.

MT (*Kethib*) לֹא הוּנַֽח־לָֽנוּ—followed by LXX and V; MT (*Qere*) וְלֹא הוּנַֽח־לָֽנוּ followed by P and T. MT (*Kethib*) is followed by most scholars, as in v. 3.

* * *

In keeping with the previous verses which allude to several forms of hardship, this verse adds another image of the exploitation of the people by the occupying Babylonians. The status of the people is at rock bottom.

The main textual problem is at the beginning of this verse. Although LXX and P agree with MT (עַל), OL and V probably presuppose it and even the paraphrastic T interprets as עַל, Sym appears to have read an extra word עֹל ('yoke') at the beginning of the line. If the original reading was עֹל עַל, one עַל could have been lost in transmission (haplography). As neck and yoke are often associated (Isa 10.27; Jer 27.8, 11, 12; 28.10, 12, 14; 30.8; Lam 1.14), this has proved an attractive emendation to many commentators, though it should be said that the terms are never in a construct relation.[15] It should also be said that MT has occasioned much heart-searching in the history of exegesis.[16] Hence T takes עַל צוּארנו to mean 'upon our necks', while MR and MLT imply that עַל צוּארנו means 'because of our necks'.[17] V *cervicibus nostris minabamur*, 'by our necks we were driven', is interesting. Almost every occurrence of this verb V corresponds to the Hebrew √נהג 'lead, drive' (cf. 1 Sam 30.20; Ps 78.52; Lam 3.2; Neh 2.7). This is the only time that Jerome employs it for √רדף. It may be that he imagined that the poet was alluding to slavery where slaves were led by the neck. Driver (1950, 142) may be right in discerning that we may have here a weakened sense of √רדף corresponding to Syriac ܪܕܦ *rdp*.[18] Other emendations vary. Some simply re-point the consonantal text עֹל 'yoke'—so Blayney (331), Budde (105), Kraus (85), Kaiser (374), Dahood (193f.), Westermann (210), Gottlieb (69), but most scholars go for the reading suggested by Sym, namely עֹל עַל צוּארנו—Michaelis (1773–88, 441), Dyserinck (379), Driver (1950, 142), Meek (35), RSV, JB, NEB. A variation of the latter is suggested by Hillers[2] (157), who supposes that *two* words have fallen out through homoioarcton, deletes נִרְדָּפְנוּ as a doublet, and 'restores' עֻלָּה עַל עַל 'A yoke has been set on our neck'. Ehrlich (53) finds the corruption elsewhere. For him, צוּארנו is the

---

[15] Gottlieb, 69. We should note that Rashi comments on the first three words 'because of the yoke of hard service'. Rashi was not in the business of textual criticism or emendation, hence his reference to 'yoke' does not arise from his acquaintance with Sym, but is probably due to the association of 'neck' and 'yoke' in the Hebrew Bible.

[16] Apart from the fact that P connects v. 4 with first words of v. 5. IE[1] does something similar in that he links both verses in his comments: 'And if we bring water and wood on our necks we are persecuted.'

[17] MLT: '…because they saw the youth of Israel—lovely, tall and with handsome necks, and they were envious of them and brought them and loaded them…'

[18] *BHK* notes another reading—נִרְדָּפְנוּ—and alludes to V *minabamur*, but Jerome does not translate הדף ('to push, drive') with *mino*.

unacceptable element which he emends to אָרְצֵנוּ 'In unserem eigenen Lande werden wir verfolgt'; and this is followed by Rudolph (257), Wiesmann (248) and *BHS*. *BHK* suggests reading נִיר טפנו for נִרדפנו, but this has not commanded the attention of scholars. There remain those who retain MT: Löhr (1906, 29), Albrektson (197f.), Provan (127), Gottwald (17), Gordis (195), (Renkema (600f.), Berlin (119), NIV, though it has to be said that the translations offered are not always convincing.[19] It may be that we encounter here an idiom that was in vogue in 6th-century BCE Hebrew. Whatever the precise meaning of v. 5a, the picture presented appears to be one of subjugation.

יָגַעְנוּ—The second stich is more straightforward. יגענו from √יגע I 'to be weary, toil', describes the result of the ill-treatment, and the rest of the line emphasises the low ebb of the people. The slightly awkward construction יגענו לא הונח לנו is rendered freely by V.[20]

5.6

Text and Versions

MT מִצְרַיִם נָתַנּוּ; P ܡܨܪܝܐ ܝܗܒܘ *mṣry' yhbw* vocalised מִצְרַיִם נָתְנוּ; LXX ἔδωκεν is probably a translational adjustment to the singular Αἴγυπτος (so Albrektson, 198, Schäfer, 135*) and does not reflect a Hebrew text נתן (contra Kelso, 64).

MT לָחֶם—so also P, V, T, SH, Sym; LXX αὐτῶν; OL *ipsis*. the LXX may have had a *Vorlage* which read להם (so *BHK*, Kelso, 65), but Rudolph (1938, 121; see also Ziegler's LXX, 492) is probably correct in discerning here an inner-Greek corruption for ἄρτων; see Albrektson (199) who is undecided.

* * *

This verse and the next amount to confession to Yahweh that in the period before the fall of the city the nation had made overtures to Egypt and Assyria, although prophets had condemned it (Hos 7.11). This had led to the fall of Jerusalem and the subsequent plight now being faced.

On this verse, Provan (1991, 128) concludes '...nothing is clear about the interpretation of this verse'; cf. Budde (105). It is true that the line is theoretically open to more than one interpretation, but the poet's meaning can surely be narrowed down. Early uncertainty is reflected in the Versions in that LXX and P took Egypt/Egyptians to be the *subject* of the verb, but the Masoretic[21] pointing נתנו confirmed Jerome's reading, namely that 'Egypt' (and 'Assyria') are in the accusative (of direction), cf. 1 Kgs

---

[19] If MT is preferred, the supposed *Vorlage* of Sym would have to be explained as (the result of) a dittography על על.
[20] Kelso (64) thinks that V's *Vorlage* read יגעים לא הונח.
[21] The fact that Rashi, IE[1] and Kara all draw attention to the *dagesh* in the *nun* suggests that they had encountered exegesis which ran counter to the Masoretic interpretation.

2.26 for the position of the accusative before the verb, and Josh 6.24 where נתן is employed with a following accusative.[22]

The construction נתן יד is not without ambiguity. At Jer 50.15 it appears to mean 'surrender' (cf. Fabry, 95; McKane, 1266f.). This may also be the meaning at Ezek 17.18 and 2 Chron 20.8. At 2 Kgs 10.15 and Ezra 10.19, however, the meaning seems to be 'to signal a pact', and this might be the meaning here. Translations can also be ambiguous: 'We have given the hand to the Egyptians' (AV), 'We made a pact with Egypt' (NJB), 'We hold out a hand to Egypt' (JB, JPS), 'We came to terms now with Egypt...' (NEB). Rashi takes the meaning as 'to supplicate'—'It is the practice of one who is falling but wishing to stand, to stretch out a hand to someone close by for help', cf. Calvin. IE[1], on the other hand, interprets it as a sign of an oath, citing Ezek 17.18 in support. Kara takes this idea further in that he sees the construction as indicating subordination and obedience; that is to say, he probably accepts IE[1]'s view that it is a handshake, but that the relationship is one of superior/inferior, cf. Keil (449). He quotes Isa 20.6, 'and he fled there (to Assyria) for help', as a related passage. For Kara, the implication is that Israel had made compromising overtures to Egypt and Assyria for the purpose of securing food. MLT, in citing Isa 31.1, 'Woe to those who go down to Egypt for help', and Hos 5.13, 'When Ephraim saw his sickness, and Judah his wound, then Ephraim went to Assyria...', appears to treat this verse as a confession of having been disloyal to Yahweh. These comments almost all interpret the action of the verse in pre-exilic times. They look back at attempts by Israel/Judah to secure food by political links with Egypt and Assyria—alliances condemned as showing disloyalty to Yahweh (Hos 5.13; 7.11). On this interpretation, we need to acknowledge that this verse does not continue the list of vv. 2-5 but, along with v. 7, is in fact a confession of wrongdoing on the part of the forefathers, wrongdoing which had its consequences. This idea then is carried on into v. 7, where the link between sin and subsequent adversity is highlighted. An expectation that the list of vv. 2-5 continues into v. 6 undergirds the exegesis of some scholars. Understanding it as referring to the same period, some argue that the people of Judah were desperately trying to make contact with old enemies for the purpose of staying alive. The objection that Assyria no longer existed when Jerusalem fell in 586 BCE is brushed aside by taking 'Assyria' to be 'a generic reference to Mesopotamia' (Berlin, 119; cf. NJB note), or by interpreting the terms 'Egypt' and 'Assyria' as meaning 'east' and 'west' (so Grossberg, 96; cf. Meek, 36). In this connection, one might point out that the people of Judah (or what was left of the people of Judah) were not in any position to make contact with *any* state for the simple reason that they were now an enslaved entity in occupied territory. Gedaliah may have been appointed as governor (2 Kgs 25.22), but Judah was now a province of Babylonia. One of the many deprivations was lack

---

[22] Cf. GK 118d, f; see also Keil (449).

of freedom. Hence, we must not think of Judah making a pact with either Egypt or Assyria post-586 BCE; and it does not make sense to speak of making a pact with east and west. Unless we understand נתן יד 'to make a humble request', the non-literal interpretation of 'Egypt' and 'Assyria' collapses.

The poet pauses (for two verses) in his sketch of tragic circumstances which he is presenting before Yahweh, because he needs to connect these circumstances with the past. They have not simply appeared out of the blue: they have a theological explanation.

5.7

Text and Versions
MT (*Kethib*) אֵינָם—so also LXX; MT (*Qere*) וְאֵינָם so also several MSS[Ken], SH, OL, P, V and T. The asyndetic construction represented by MT (*Kethib*) is preferred.

MT (*Kethib*) אֲנַחְנוּ—so also LXX, SH; MT (*Qere*) וַאֲנַחְנוּ—so also several MSS[Ken], OL, P, V and T. Again, MT (*Kethib*) as the *lectio difficilior* is preferred. In each case, *BHQ* prefers MT (*Kethib*) as the *lectio difficilior*. Rudolph (258) prefers MT (*Qere*). Westermann (210) follows *Kethib* in the first case and *Qere* in the second. The sense is not affected.

* * *

The poet continues in confessional mood here, though it should be noted that in neither verse (vv. 6 or 7) is there a reference to present responsibility. Verse 6 had alluded to the mistaken efforts of past generations to procure food from the heathen, and this verse speaks of 'our fathers' having sinned.[23] The author, then, believes that previous generations are bound up with present generations in such a way that sins committed in a previous generation may be punished later; and he identifies the tragic events of his day as punishment by Yahweh for the sins of the past. At v. 16 the poet refers to the part played by the *present* generation's sins, which may seem to call this passage into question, but the received tradition was not that *all* sins were punished in a later generation. Jeremiah 3.25, '…we have sinned against the Lord, our God, both we and our fathers from our early days until now…', expresses something very similar. AV 'our fathers have sinned' gives the impression that the sins were committed in the immediate past, while NRSV 'our ancestors sinned' appears to push the sins much further back in time.

אֵינָם—Literally 'they are not', i.e. 'they are no more'. T 'and they are not in the world'; cf. Gen 5.24 'Enoch walked with God, and he was not (וְאֵינֶנּוּ), for God took him'. There is a certain sharpness in the Hebrew construction without the copula.

---

[23] IE[1] notes the relationship of this passage with Exod 20.5 where Yahweh promises to punish the children for the sins of the parents.

סְבָלְנוּ—The verb √סבל, which occurs generally in the Semitic languages, means 'to carry' (Gen 49.15; Isa 46.7). It is also used in a figurative sense, as in Isa 46.4 (in parallel with נשא), meaning 'to support'. The sense here (v. 7) is of 'bearing punishment', a meaning also found at Isa 53.11. Indeed, at Isa 53.11, the construction וַעֲוֹנֹתָם הוּא יִסְבֹּל is similar to that in this verse.

עֲוֹנֹתֵיהֶם—The noun עָוֹן (though m., the plural is often f.) has been discussed at 4.6. It can mean 'misdeed, sin' (Isa 11.10) or 'guilt' (Num 30.16) or even 'punishment' (Gen 4.13). It has this latter meaning here: the adversity experienced by the people represented by the poet is associated with the punishment for the sins of the fathers. Among those taken into exile in Babylon there existed some who were inclined to take refuge in a self-justifying saying: 'Parents eat sour grapes, and their children's teeth are set on edge' (Jer 31.29; Ezek 18.2; cf. Exod 20.5), believing that the suffering of 586 and the forced exile were the result of the sins of *previous* generations. But our author—and here we must take the confession 'we have sinned' (v. 16) into consideration—distances himself from those sentiments. Taken with v. 16, the poet is saying that the suffering we now endure is not to be attributed to ourselves alone but to the sins of our forefathers as well.[24]

5.8

Text and Versions

There are no significant differences here. OL *et non est qui redimat de manibus eorum* raises the possibility of ופרק for פרק and מידיהם for מידם. P is similar to OL and adds an extra ܠ *ln*. T, although paraphrastic, does not represent a copula, but among the MSS (see Levine, 185) both the singular מידהון and the plural מידהום appear. As these additions/differences are natural, MT is to be preferred.

* * *

עֲבָדִים—The term עֶבֶד occurs over 800 times in the Hebrew Bible, though this is the only occurrence in Lamentations. Its meaning varies according to context but it always applies to the subordination of one person or entity to another. Hence 'slave' (Exod 21.7), 'official' (Jer 22.2), 'vassal king' (2 Sam 10.19), 'worshipper' (Num 14.24). The precise meaning here is uncertain. The LXX translates with δοῦλος, which has a much narrower semantic range; and the same is true of P, namely ܥܒܕܐ *ʿbdʾ*. MR, in identifying the term as the Egyptians, appears to have lost sight of the background of ch. 5.[25] T, too, refers to the sons of Ham. What the Targumist meant is difficult to say, but Vermigli (201) claims that T understood

---

[24] Cf. Keil (450).
[25] Cohen (1939, 239) explains that this is based on Gen 9.25; 10.6, where the descendants of Ham are declared to be slaves; cf. Alexander (2008, 182 n. 14).

the term to refer to Babylon. Although T does not refer to any specific nation, Gen 10.10 states that the Hamite Nimrod founded Babylon, and that would mean that the Babylonians would be the servants of the Shemites. MLT, more attuned to the context, takes the reference to be to Nebuzaradan and his like. Nebuzaradan is mentioned 15 times in the Hebrew Bible, always as 'captain of the guard'. He is also described as 'a servant (עבד) of the king of Babylon' (2 Kgs 25.8). A more natural interpretation comes from IE[1], who takes the term to refer to people who were formerly subject to Israel 'like Edom'. Certainly, those in ultimate control of Judah post-586 BCE were the Babylonians, who could hardly be described as mere slaves. It is possible that the king of Babylon, who had employed mercenaries from Aram, Moab and Ammon in the attack on Jerusalem (2 Kgs 24.2), employed some of the same to lord it over Judah.[26] That the poet refers simply to the officers of Babylonia (so Rudolph, 261; Hillers[2], 164; Meek, 36; Berlin, 121) is unlikely. Are we not dealing here with the tragic circumstances in which the people find themselves, and is not the author reflecting on the tragic reversal, characteristic of the dirge and of which we get many examples in chs. 1, 2 and 4? The world is now topsy-turvy.[27]

מָשְׁלוּ—The verb √משׁל construed with preposition ב means 'to rule over'. The perfect is a declarative perfect. It is followed by an active participle, cf. 1.17. The final stich is circumstantial, highlighting the ignominy, in that the poet does not see any hope of rescue. The verb √פרק means 'to tear away'. Here, as in Ps 136.24, where it is construed with the preposition מן—וַיִּפְרְקֵנוּ מִצָּרֵינוּ—it means 'to rescue'.

The poet presents these facts also before Yahweh in his plea. He may be yearning for the return of the Davidic house or, perhaps as Kraus (89) notes, the rule of Yahweh (Judg 8.23).

5.9

Text and Versions
MT בְּנָפְשֵׁנוּ—so also P; LXX ἐν ταῖς ψυχαῖς ἡμῶν; so also many MSS[Ken] (בנפשינו); SH, Sym, OL and V. In Hebrew, נפשׁ (singular) is often used with the plural meaning (cf. Ps 124. 4, 5, 7) but it is natural to translate in the plural (cf. REB, NRSV). Besides, the plural of נפשׁ is נפשׁות, hence one might say that the form underlying might have been נפשׁותינו. MT is preferred.
MT לְחָמֵנוּ—so also LXX, OL, V and T; several MSS[Ken] read לחמינו; P ܠܚܡܗ *lḥm'* without the suffix, but this probably does not suggest a different *Vorlage* (as suggested by BHK; but see Albrektson, 199; cf. our water, our wood in v. 4). MT is preferred.

---

[26] Cf. also Neh 2.10, 19 where Tobiah the Ammonite is designated עבד.
[27] Qoheleth (Eccl 10.7) laments 'I have seen slaves on horses and princes walking on the ground like slaves'. Cf. Prov 30.21f.

הַמִּדְבָּר MT—so also LXX; V *in deserto*; P ܕܒܡܕܒܪܐ *dbmdbrʾ*. Kelso (65) thinks that this suggests a *Vorlage* בְּמִדְבָּר, but it is likely that the translators rendered freely (cf. NRSV) because of the ambiguity of the text; note also OL's *et solitudinis*.

* * *

בְּנַפְשֵׁנוּ—It is not clear from LXX, P and V how the translators understood the ב in this construction: they merely represent the preposition. T, however, with בסכנת נפשנא 'at the risk of our lives' has rightly understood it as ב *pretii* (GK 119p). This too is the interpretation of Rashi, IE¹ and MLT.[28]

מִפְּנֵי חֶרֶב הַמִּדְבָּר—That this phrase puzzled interpreters is clear from the renderings of the Versions. What is meant by 'the sword of the desert'? Rashi imagines the people taking their lives in their hands by attempting to bring in food from the field[29] because of the sword of the desert. He does not explain it and neither does IE¹. Calvin asks what the sword has to do with the desert. He concludes that חרב can meant 'drought': 'As the prophet is speaking of famine and the desert, I have no doubt but that dryness or drought is what the word means here; and I wonder that the word "sword" had occurred to any; they could not have regarded the context'. Luther's translation 'vor dem Schwert in der Wüste' follows the traditional understanding, and so do many subsequent translations: AV, NJB, NIV. At 1.20 (q.v.), חֶרֶב is used metonymically and if we retain MT this is probably how we should understand it here. The reference would then be to violence which would be encountered in the desert (cf. P's rendering: 'which is in the desert'). The poet could be thinking of the presence of Babylonian soldiers in and around Judah who would be brutally punitive on those Judahites who strayed from their base. More likely is that he is referring to marauding bands of Bedouin who would set upon those bringing back food to their homes in Judah, and who would rob them and, possibly, kill them (Keil, 451;[30] Blayney, 332; Meek, 36; Löhr, 1906, 30; Kraus, 89; Rudolph, 261; Kaiser, 381; Gottlieb, 70). Calvin's question has led some scholars either to accept that חרב may mean 'dryness, drought'[31] (Zech 11.17; cf. Gordis, 195; Berlin, 121), or to vocalise חֹרֶב 'waste, desert' (Gen 31.40; Isa 4.6; cf. Dyserinck, 379; Löhr 1894, 25;[32] Kelso, 65; *BHK*, NEB, REB; Brockington, 219). Further

---

[28] IE¹ cites 1 Chron 11.19 in support; but he begins his comments with what must have been a currently held opinion and one respected by him: 'Formerly, our servants would have brought our food but now we ourselves (בעצמנו)'.
[29] He uses the term שדה ('open country') and may be thinking of Jer 6.25, where the people of Jerusalem are advised not to go out to the שדה because of the sword of the enemy.
[30] Cf. Moffatt's translation 'from Arabs of the desert'.
[31] Support for the meaning 'dryness, drought' is often sought in the ambiguous passage Deut 28.22, where 'sword' is reckoned out of place and is rendered by V and IE¹ as 'drought'; see also Tigay (1996, 396 n. 32).
[32] In his second edition (1906, 30), Löhr changes his mind.

emendations are suggested: Beer (285) suggests that הַמִּדְבָּר should read וּמִדֶּבֶר '(because of the sword) and of the pestilence'. Dahood (1964, 401) wants to read it as הַמְדַבֵּר as Piel participle from the verb דבר√ 'to follow, pursue'—'the sword of the pursuer'; and this is accepted by McDaniel (51f.).

There is, however, no need to emend the text (Gottlieb, 70; Wiesmann, 254; Renkema, 607). The poet is thinking of the danger of foraging for food.[33] It is because of hostile elements in desert areas.

5.10

Text and Versions

MT עוֹרֵנוּ followed by LXX, OL, V, T; many MSS[Ken] read עורינו but, as Albrektson (200) observes, the plural of עוֹר is עוֹרוֹת, which makes the form suspicious (cf. נפשׁ in v. 9). P ܡܫܟܝܢ *mškyn* also has the plural.

MT נִכְמָרוּ—so also 5QLam[a]; LXX ἐπελειώθη συνεσπάσθησαν; P ܐܬܟܡܪܘ ܐܬܟܡܣ *'tqpdw wqn'w*; V *exusta est*; OL *livida facta est*; T אתקדרו; Aq ἐξεκαύθη. MT is preferred.

There is, clearly, a relationship between the LXX and P here,[34] though the word order is different. The lack of congruence (singular/plural) may be explained by the influence of the plural suffix on עורנו leading to the plural form נכמרו (cf. Albrektson, 200; Kaiser, 374), or taking the term עורנו as a collective (Renkema 607f.), or simply as an anomaly, cf. Meek (36), Wernberg-Møller (109).

* * *

נִכְמָרוּ—The meaning of the verb is crucial to the understanding of this verse. It is Niphal 3rd p. pl. of the root כמר, which appears only in the Niphal and which, according to BDB means 'to grow warm, hot' (*HALOT* 'to grow excited or to grow hot'). The verb occurs four times in the Hebrew Bible: the other passages are Gen 43.30; 1 Kgs 3.26; Hos 11.8, where the subject is either רחמים or נחומים.

The Versions show signs of struggling to translate. LXX translates *twice*, first with a verb in the singular and then with a verb in the plural:[35] (1) ἐπελειώθη 'is blackened', which assumes another root BDB כמר√ II, which may occur in Job 3.5 and which is found in Syriac ܟܡܝܪ *kmyr* 'black', ܟܡܪ *kmr* 'be gloomy'; (2) συνεσπάσθησαν 'are shrivelled up'. These words occur only once in the LXX. P also translates twice: (1) ܐܬܟܡܣ 'are shrivelled, shrunk'; (2) ܐܬܟܡܪܘ *wqn'w* 'and are become livid' (cf. Nöldeke, *Syriac Grammar* §172 c). Both verbs are in the plural. Rashi, who cites Gen 43.30, glosses with נתחממו (Nithpael of חמם) 'are become heated, inflamed'. IE[1], also citing Gen 43.30, explains in terms of

---

[33] לחם should be understood as basic food, sustenance, as in Ps 136.25; Prov 6.8; Job 24.5.
[34] Cf. Albrektson, 201.
[35] Robinson (1933, 259, cf. *BHK*) considers also the possibility that the LXX *Vorlage* may have contained סמרו as a doublet of נכמרו.

the verbs √בער and √יקד 'to burn'. Kara is a little more colourful. He takes כתנור to mean 'as if burned in a fiery oven', but נכמרו, for him, means 'shrunk and wrinkled'; and MLT hints at much the same thing, cf. MR. Vermigli (203) and Calvin both take the passage to refer to the skin being blackened (cf. also AV, NRSV, NEB, Hillers[2] 158; Dahood, 194), while Luther 'ist verbrannt' is followed by Keil (445), JB, RSV, NIV. Rudolph (256) 'schrumpft' is followed by Kaiser (381) and Renkema (607f.). The history of exegesis reveals that interpreters/translators have supported all the aforementioned positions. The meaning eludes us. Driver (1950, 143), who observes that tradition and philology together speak with an uncertain voice, resorts to a medical opinion. Starvation, mentioned in the second stich, does not produce a burning sensation in the skin, and the discoloration is not significant: 'the skin, however, does become wrinkled and flakes off...so that the Hebrew נכמר[36] must have the sense..."shrivelled" and here mean "wrinkled", as one of the translations of the LXX and that of the Pesh. suggest'.

כְּתַנּוּר—The preposition כ may mean 'as, like' (GK 102c) or in certain pregnant situations it may mean 'as in' (GK 118s-w). It might be expected that a glance at the second stich would help in the elucidation of the first, but here, too, we have an unusual term; and the history of exegesis sheds little by way of clarity.

זַלְעֲפוֹת—The word occurs once in the singular at Ps 119.53, and in the plural (vocalised זַלְעָפוֹת) at Ps 11.6. BDB takes it to mean 'raging heat', while *HALOT* defines it as 'agitations'; and *DCH*, III, 115 has 'raging'. Translators have struggled with the term. LXX καταιγίδων 'storms', Sym (SH) ܣܥܝ *sʿyʾ* 'attack', P ܬܘܪܦܐ *twrpʾ* 'trouble', V *tempestatum* 'storms, violence', OL *plagarum* 'blows', T ממפ 'exhaustion'.[37] The impression is given of translators guessing the meaning of the word, and this continues: Luther '...greulichen (Hunger)', AV '...terrible (famine)', RSV '...burning heat (of famine)', JPS '...fever (of famine)', NRSV '...scorching heat (of famine)'. Rudolph (256) '...Qualen (des Hungers)', so also Kraus (85), NEB '...ravages (of starvation)', must be nearer the mark.

In the preceding verses the poet has given several sketches of harsh existence after the fall of Jerusalem, with a theological reflection in vv. 6f. Verse 10 is yet another item in this presentation before Yahweh (invoked at v. 1). Reference has been made to the hazards of procuring food from desert areas, but the poet wants to stress that even if the people are not cut down as they forage for food, the pickings are so meagre that starvation stares them in the face, and this is evident from their cracked and wrinkled skin.

[36] Driver follows LXX, which has a singular verb.
[37] So Alexander (2008, 182); Levine (74) renders 'inflammation'; Brady (166) translates 'despair'.

5.11

Text and Versions
No significant material.

* * *

Up to now the poet has provided a picture of hardship and distress for the people in general, associating himself with them by employing the 1st p. pl. In vv. 11-14 the first person is absent, and the poet singles out specific groups and how they have experienced adversity. The order: women/ maidens, princes/elders, young men/boys, old men may be random, but the violation of women may come first because of women's vulnerability in the aftermath of war. O'Connor (2002, 76) seems to imply that the rape of women was an insult to the *men* folk and that the actual pain of women is not implied. This is unwarranted exegesis. One might just as well say that the torture of princes (v. 12) is purely an example of national ignominy and has nothing to do with suffering on the part of the princes. Furthermore, the fact that the poet has just left off using the first person plural suffixes points rather in the opposite direction. Also wrongheaded is the observation of Ehrlich (53) that the rape of women was in the capital city and that of the maidens took place in the other settlements of Judah. As Hillers[1] (98f.) points out, this is a clear case of Hebrew parallelism: women and maidens were raped throughout Judah. T's fanciful exegesis also disregards the parallelism: 'Women who had been married to husbands in Zion were raped by Romans, and maidens in the cities of Judah by Chaldaeans'.[38]

עִנּוּ—The Masoretes have vocalised as Piel, 3rd p. pl. The root is (BDB) √ענה III 'be afflicted'; Piel = 'to humble, rape' (Gen 34.2; Judg 19.24; 2 Sam 13.12; Ezek 22.10, 11). It is possible to translate 'they raped women in Zion...', and this is how LXX and V (?P) render. So also IE[1], Luther, Calvin, AV, Löhr (1906, 30), JPS, Rudolph (256), Hillers[2] (155), Kaiser (374), Renkema (609).[39] However, OL *humiliatae sunt*, T אתעניאו 'were raped' either vocalised Pual עֻנּוּ (so Wiesmann, 256) or understood the active form to carry the passive meaning (GK 144g). Other examples of this are Job 7.3; 18.18; Ezek 32.25; Prov 2.21; and this is how it is translated by Michaelis (1773–88, 151), Gordis (151), Berlin (115), NJB, NEB, NRSV.

---

[38] See Alexander (2008, 183 n. 19), Levine (187).
[39] IE[1] comments, 'not enough the distress of famine, the slaves (referring to v. 8!) raped our women...' JPS, 'They have ravished women...', maintains the active voice, with a footnote to the effect that the subject is the slaves of v. 8; cf. Ibn Ezra.

5.12

Text and Versions

MT בְּיָדָם; LXX ἐν χερσὶν αὐτῶν; OL *in manibus eorum*; V *manu*; P ܒܐܝܕܝܗܘܢ *b'ydyhwn*; T בִידֵיהוֹן. LXX, OL, P and T read as though translating בִּידֵיהֶם; however, Albrektson (201) rightly notes that the plural is natural in the context (cf. Levine, 187). V maintains the singular 'by the hand' without representing the suffix. MT is preferred.

MT פְּנֵי זְקֵנִים; LXX πρεσβύτεροι LXX[40] does not represent פְּנֵי. Since LXX is normally very literal, Albrektson (201) wonders if the minus is due to a scribal error in the transmission of the Greek text; P ܐܦܝ *w'py* adds the copula, as in v. 11. MT is preferred.

MT לֹא נֶהְדָּרוּ—so also LXX; V *non erubuerunt*; OL *non glorificaverunt*; P ܠܐ ܐܬܘ *l' yqrw*; T לָא סָבְרוּ. MT is preferred.

* * *

The poet, in his prayer to Yahweh, laments the collapse of accepted standards—values that had been commanded by Yahweh and even among enemies.

שָׂרִים—The term appears also at 1.6; 2.2, 9. The parallel term in this verse is זְקֵנִים, mentioned also at 1.19; 2.10, 21; 4.16; 5.14. The author, having described the ignominy of the women of Judah, moves on to what had been the upper echelons of society. Perhaps he thought that the dishonouring of women was almost a given in the context of conquest and occupation and that he needed to mention the shameful treatment of those from the top bracket. They, too, have become victims.

נִתְלוּ—The verb √תלה 'hang, hang up' is used of the hanging up of objects, e.g. Job 26.7; Ps 137.2; Song 4.4. It is also used at Gen 40.22; 41.13; Deut 21.23 etc. for killing by hanging. It is not clear what the author means to say here, and this ambiguity carries over into the Versions. The situation is further complicated by the phrase בְיָדָם. Does it allude to the manner of suspension, the suffix referring to the princes, or does the phrase pick up the reference in v. 8, מִיָּדָם, and refer to the oppressors, in which case the meaning will be slaughter by hanging at the hands of the oppressors. The Targumist employs the verb √צלב in the Ithpeel (= 'be hanged') which probably shows that he considered the action in the first stich to be the slaughter of the princes.[41] LXX and P maintain the ambiguity of MT, but V *manu suspensi sunt* seems to come down on the side of merely being hung up by the hand. MR, while not really engaging with the text, comments in such a way as to make it clear that תלה here means 'to kill by hanging'; MLT, on the other hand, indicates that hanging is torture for the extraction of money. IE[1], in linking this verse with the preceding, comments, 'We had no princes who could rescue our women because even

---

[40] The SH and Lucianic recensions have 'restored' according to MT.
[41] He could have used the Aramaic equivalent of תלה viz. תלא, but this would have continued the ambiguity; cf. Alexander (2008, 183 n. 20).

they had been hung up by their arms' It is clear that he understands בידם as indicating the manner of the suspension. He goes on to show that he is aware of other views, one of which is that the suffix on בידם is referring to the slaves mentioned in v. 8. Vermigli (204) is convinced that the verse speaks of death by hanging but he is unsure whether the princes hung themselves (by their *own* hands) or whether the hanging was done by the hands of the slaves (v. 8). Calvin believed that death is meant and that the hands of the princes were involved: 'I certainly do not doubt but that the Prophet says here that some of the princes had laid violent hands on themselves... [T]he princes were hung, not by enemies, for it was a common thing for the conquered to be slain by their enemies, and be also hung by way of reproach; but the Prophet, as it appears to me, meant to express something more atrocious...' Nägelsbach (185) dismisses Calvin's interpretation as incredible, citing Deut 21.23. He goes on to mention a view put forward by Ewald (347f.) who translates בידם as 'neben ihnen', implying that the hanging was done at the side of the cities mentioned in v. 11. He dismisses this too on the grounds that 'cities' is feminine while the suffix on בידם is masculine, and that the preposition would have to be ל for ב. He concludes that בידם must refer to the enemies.[42]

The view articulated by IE[1], namely, that the princes were hung up by their hands (he specifies 'arms'), does have some adherents—RSV, Berlin (123), NRSV; but some translations are unclear—NJB, Gottwald (17), Renkema (610), O'Connor (2002, 72).

Verses 11-14 contain descriptions of hardship, cruelty, exploitation and frustration. While the exegesis of one stich should not dictate that of its companion, as it were, we should note that the import of the second stich in v. 12 has to do with dishonouring elders. It would be more natural to find in the first stich a reference to ignominy experienced by the princes, rather than the execution of the same. A better balance, therefore, is struck by interpreting בידם as referring to the manner in which the princes were hung up, and to take the action to be cruel and degrading treatment.

פְּנֵי זְקֵנִים לֹא נֶהְדָּרוּ—On פני, see note at 4.16. The author, in presenting this stich in the negative, may have had the injunction of Lev 19.32 in mind: 'You shall rise before the old man, *and you shall honour the elder* (והדרת פני זקן)'.[43] Respect for the elder was not confined to Israelite society but was common practice in the ancient world. In addition, the employment of two passive verbs in this verse convey the feeling that the subjects, princes and elders, are victims of the action. The *nuns* of the Niphals[44] echo the 1st p. pl. of vv. 1-10.

---

[42] This is the position adopted by, among others, AV, Keil (451), Kraus (89f.), Westermann (209), Hillers[2] (158), JPS, Gordis (151), JB.
[43] Cf. Deut 28.50.
[44] N.B. also that the Niphal of הדר occurs only here in the Hebrew Bible.

5.13

Text and Versions
MT נְשָׂאוּ טְחוֹן בַּחוּרִים; LXX ἐκλεκτοὶ κλαυθμὸν ἀνέλαβον; P ܓܕܘܕ̈ܐ ܐܟܠܘ ܠܥܠܝ̈ܡܐ *gdwd' ṭhnw rḥy'*; V *adulescentibus inpudice abusi sunt*; OL *potentes molis molebant*; Sym[45] νεανίσκους εἰς τὸ ἀλέσαι ἔλαβον; T רוּבִין רֵיחַיָּא נְטָלוּ. MT is preferred.

* * *

The poet draws Yahweh's attention to the young men and boys who are also mistreated and made to serve as slaves.

טְחוֹן—Although a *hapax legomenon*, the root ('to grind') is well known (Kelso, 66) and could never have the meaning κλαυθμὸν (LXX). The root is vouched for in P, V, OL, Sym and T. LXX may have had a different *Vorlage*,[46] or it may be that it is corrupt. Robinson (1933, 259; cf. *BHK*) thinks it is a corruption of ἀληθόμενον.

The verse describes two mini-scenes involving young men and boys (2.21). Already deprived because of the Babylonian subjugation of their families who find it difficult to survive and are lacking in dignity, the general impression is given of the exploitation of these young people. The precise meaning of both stichs is unclear. The parallelism of the verse נָשָׂאוּ // נְעָרִים // בַּחוּרִים is obvious, though the actual force of the verbs is subject to the predicate in each stich. In the first stich we are hampered by the *hapax legomenon* טְחוֹן. *qiṭāl* forms (BL 473 *hβ*) often denote tools and instruments, hence the translation 'mill' from the verb √טחן 'to grind' is plausible; cf. Albrektson (202), Driver (1950, 143). If we translate the first stich as 'young men carried the mill' the sense is obscure. T's 'young men carried millstones' is a little clearer. P circumvented the problem by translating freely, 'young men ground the mill' (cf. OL and Kraus, 85). The text of LXX is probably corrupt (see above). V *adulescentibus inpudice abusi sunt* stands alone here, drawing on an interpretation found in MR at 5.1 (also *Soṭah* 10a), which understands Samson 'grinding' in prison (Judg 16.21) as a euphemism for sexual practices (cf. also Job 31.10; Jastrow 528). Rashi understood the passage to refer to the enemy tiring the young men by placing millstones on their shoulders. IE[1], obviously struggling with the verse, suggests taking טְחוֹן as an infinitive, citing Isa 1.14 נִלְאֵיתִי נְשֹׂא in support: 'young men carry to grind' or 'young men bear grinding'. As mentioned above, MR includes an interpretation similar to that of V. A similar interpretation is given at Job 31.10 by V and T (cf. *HALOT*); that is to say, the young men were subjected to sexual abuse at the hands of their overseers. The trouble with this interpretation

---

[45] Field (761) suspects that the SH marginal note ܣܘܡ̄ ܀. should have read ܐܩܘܠ̄ ܀., i.e. Aq rather than Sym. Cf. Payne Smith (1901, 1456).
[46] Kelso (66) suggests they read בְּכִי—the construction נָשָׂא + בְּכִי occurs at Jer 9.9.

is that it does not offer a balance with the second stich, as Calvin notes (cf. also Nägelsbach, 186; Albrektson, 202; Hillers², 159). Calvin takes טחון as accusative—*adolescentes ad molam sumpserunt*—the subject presumably being the same as in v. 11. He points out that 'of all the servile works this was the lowest; for as they used asses to grind, so also they used slaves'. The AV, 'they took the young men to grind', is substantially that of Calvin (cf. also Ewald, 347; Rudolph, 256); but in such a short passage as v. 13 it is unlikely that the subject of the verb נשאו is anything other than בחורים, just as in the second stich the subject must be נערים (cf. Keil, 452). Blayney (333), though he does not notice it, is close to IE¹'s interpretation. He translates 'were made to grind', but adds 'bore grinding, as a hardship or task imposed on them'. RV 'the young men bare the mill' is the starting point for Driver's note (1950, 143f.). While he regards RV as 'a philologically justifiable translation…the sense must surely be that young men bare/endured the labour of grinding (the corn)'; and he supports his interpretation by noting that נשא takes an abstract accusative at Prov 19.19; Isa 53.4; Jer 31.19; Ezek 16.52, and pointing out that Sym had translated טחון as an abstract 'grinding'.

The second stich seems, at first, straightforward. The verb √כשל means 'to stumble, stagger'. It is construed with preposition ב, which may mean 'by means of' (Nah 3.3) or 'at' (Jer 6.21); hence, one may translate 'boys stagger under (loads of) wood' (cf. REB). T וטליא בצליבת קיסא תקלו 'and boys stagger under crosses'. The suffering envisaged here is either actually on crosses or bearing crosses (Levine, 189, but cf. discussion in Alexander, 184). OL *et juvenes ligno confixi sunt* takes a similar position. Rashi understands the passage as referring to the strength of the boys failing (he quotes 1.14 and Neh 4.4 in support) in having to carry wood. IE¹ also speaks of the strength of the boys failing, but it is as they moved the wood of the mill. What he means by this is unclear, but Vermigli (205) envisages the young men leaning on wood as they continuously push the millstones round and round;[47] but he does admit the other possible interpretation, namely, of boys stumbling under bundles of wood (cf. also Calvin, RSV, REB, NJB, JPS, NIV, NRSV). The work at the mill and the continuous carrying of wood was not only heavy and draining of energy: it was the work of slaves or women, and the young men and boys would have found it humiliating and degrading as well as difficult (Exod 11.5; Judg 16.21; Isa 47.2). Berlin (123) envisages the work of large rotary mills normally operated by animals and wood-carrying also done by donkeys. This heavy labour was now imposed on the young.

---

[47] Cf. Gordis (196).

5.14

Text and Versions

MT זְקֵנִים—so also P, V and T; LXX καὶ πρεσβῦται. Albrektson (203f.) holds that the LXX *Vorlage* read וזקנים. This may be the case, although the copula is not attested in any Hebrew MS. The ו of כשלו (v. 13) may have been written twice in the *Vorlage* of LXX; but MT is preferred.

MT מִשַּׁעַר—so also LXX, P and T; V *de portis*. Kelso (66) thinks that Jerome read משערים, but this is a quite natural interpretation of MT. The poet means not one gate but the gates of the cities of Judah and Jerusalem. SH has the plural, though LXX has the singular.[48] MT is preferred.

MT מִנְּגִינָתָם; LXX ἐκ ψαλμῶν αὐτῶν κατέπαυσαν; P ܡܢ ܗܕܘܬܗܘܢ *mn ḥdwthwn*; V *de choro psallentium*; OL *a psalmis suis*; T מן בית זמררהון. Kelso (67) observes that LXX has vocalised the word as plural מִנְּגִינֹתָם. His explanation of the verb κατέπαυσαν as having been transferred from the first half of the verse is wrong-headed. The double-duty of שבתו has been spelt out by the LXX translator. MT is preferred.

* * *

The last verse in the section vv. 11-14 differs from the previous three in that it does not have to do with physical exploitation of the people. It is, however, in keeping with the entire prayer to Yahweh, adding to the list of brief scenarios where the tragic reversal is in evidence.

In each stich of this verse an old cherished custom is seen to have come to an end. There is no indication that the latter is the direct result of enemy interference or threat; rather, it seems as though the cessation and changes of which the verse speaks have happened by default. There are two aspects to the activity referred to in the first stich. In normal circumstances the elders would gather at the city gates to socialise (Gen 19.1; Ps 69.13; Prov 24.7; 31.23, 31), but it was also the place where disputes were settled and business transacted (Ruth 4.1-12; 1 Kgs 21.11-13). When the pre-exilic prophets call for justice 'at the gate' they are referring to these sessions. When the poet here speaks of the elders ceasing from the gate, therefore, we have to assume not only that normal socialising had ceased but that the customary settling of disputes had come to a standstill or been severely disrupted. It is unlikely that the occupying forces who were ill-treating the people would take any interest in anything other than major issues. As to the reason for the elders' absence, we may surmise that it was dangerous for anyone to engage in any unauthorised activity. The latter may also be the reason for the cessation[49] of music-making by the young men, though the forced heavy labour involving these young men (v. 13) would probably preclude sufficient leisure for the playing of musical instruments. The poet, however, is conscious of the absence of music-making.

---

[48] IE¹, with MT before him, refers to the *gates* of Jerusalem.
[49] The verb שבתו in the first stich does double-duty, as IE¹ makes clear.

נְגִינָתָם—Here the feminine noun נְגִינַת takes 3 p. m. pl. suffix. At 3.14 (q.v.) it is parallel to שְׂחֹק 'laughter, derision'. Here it means 'music'. The plural is found in the superscription[50] of several psalms (Pss 4.1; 6.1; 54.1; 55.1; 67.1; 76.1). BDB gives the meaning: '1. Music (of stringed instruments); 2. Song (with stringed instruments?)'; cf. also *HALOT*. מִנְּגִינָתָם is rendered by LXX and OL 'from their songs', P 'from their joy', V *de choro psallentium*, 'from the choir of singers', T 'from their house of music/ music hall'. It is clear from the Versions that early translators were unsure of the term, though the majority contain the element of music. Stringed instruments may be implied—the verb behind the LXX rendering, ψάλλω, means 'to play on a stringed instrument', and this is the view taken by the NEB translators 'young men no longer pluck the strings'.[51] There is ample evidence in the Hebrew Bible that music played a significant part in worship (cf. Ps 150), but the music referred to here would seem to be of the secular variety—either of celebration or, more probably, of general entertainment (Vermigli, 206). The latter may have normally taken place 'at the gate' where the old men assembled (cf. Ps 69.13); but those social occasions were at an end.

5.15

Text and Versions
MT לִבֵּנוּ—some MSS[Ken] have לבינו, but MT is followed by LXX, P and V. The plural is found in T, but this is a natural rendering as evidenced in 'our hearts' of NEB, NJB, JPS and NRSV.
MT מְחֹלֵנוּ—several MSS[Ken] read מחולינו. The plural suffix may be accounted for as above; and the *plene* spelling is the result of scribal activity.

* * *

When the poet refers to joy ceasing from the hearts of the people and dancing turned into mourning, he continues the theme of tragic reversal. But does he have something specific in mind? The fact that he uses the verb √שבת in both verses (vv. 14 and 15) might lead us to think that this משוש is part of the merriment and music-making no longer heard among the young men. This is how Calvin understood it. IE[1] is more specific. He relates the cessation of joy to the fact that the sacrifices had been brought to an end (על קרבנות שנכרתו); and this view is found also in MLT and, most recently, with Berlin (124). The passages which give rise to this interpretation are Ps 48.3; Lam 2.15 and Ezek 24.25, where, it is agreed, משוש alludes to the Temple Mount. Renkema (615) also holds that משוש לבנו is 'the jubilation experienced during the liturgy in Zion'. There is no doubt

---

[50] LXX usually translates with ψαλμός (as here). AV always transliterates 'Neginoth'.
[51] Calvin, 'adolescentes a pulsatione sua (*vel* canticis musicis)', may have been undecided as to the nature of the music, but his first choice may suggest that rhythm was the dominant feature.

that dance was part of the means of praising Yahweh (Pss 149.3; 150.4), but it is not confined to the liturgy (cf. Jer 31.4, 13; Ps 30.12 and see Wiesmann, 259). מָשׂוֹשׂ is found some 17 times in the Hebrew Bible and in most of these passages the word is quite detached from cultic matters. Indeed, at Isa 24.8, where it is construed twice with שִׂמְחָה the context is merriment—'The merry beat of the tambourines is silenced...the joyful lyre is silent' (REB). Furthermore, in passages such as Jer 7.34; 16.9, the word is associated with שִׂמְחָה and in a setting quite apart from Temple worship. In the latter passages where Yahweh is the subject, he banishes (Hiphil of שָׁבַת) this מָשׂוֹשׂ and שִׂמְחָה from the land. The poet, then, by using שָׁבַת in both verses (vv. 14 and 15), continues his description of the cessation of social life, and there may be an allusion to the Jeremiah passages where it is Yahweh who is the author of it all.

The verb in the second stich (Niphal of √הָפַךְ) is also interesting in this regard. Yahweh is the subject of this verb at Jer 31.13 where he reverses the process—turning mourning into joy. The use of the passive here may be an allusion to the Jeremiah passage and so a hint at the identity of the real protagonist.

5.16

Text and Versions
MT רֹאשֵׁנוּ—many Heb MSS[Ken] read ראשינו but the singular is followed by the Versions and is in keeping with the singular in vv. 9, 15, 17.

* * *

While the 1 p. pls. continue in this verse, the latter differs from the foregoing in important respects. The poet has been alluding to the physical and social effects of the fall of Jerusalem, but in v. 16 we suddenly get a confession of sin preceded, in the first stich, by a statement which does not speak of the physical: 'The crown of our head has fallen'.

The word for crown (עֲטָרָה) occurs 24 times in the Old Testament. It can denote the crown of a monarch (1 Chr 20.2; Ezek 21.31) or high priest (Sir 45.12), but is often used metaphorically as in Prov 12.4 or Job 19.9 where it refers to honour status. IE[1] considers the phrase to be a reference to 'the Temple, the place of the Shechinah', while MLT interprets it as alluding to the Torah, now handed over to foreigners. Vermigli (207) is similar to IE[1]—'What is called the crown of that people...must be understood to be about the Temple, the Ark of the covenant and the Tabernacle'. Luther (*Notes*) cites Jer 13.18 where Jehoiachin and the queen mother are requested to take a lowly seat 'for your proud crowns are fallen from your heads' (REB);[52] that is to say, Luther regarded the

---

[52] Following vocalisation as reflected in LXX, V and P; see McKane (1986, 304).

phrase in 5.16 as reflecting the people's loss of status. Calvin comments, 'By the crown of the head he no doubt understands all those ornaments by which the people had been adorned. They had a kingdom and a priesthood, which were like two luminaries or two precious jewels... But a crown was not only taken for a diadem—it was a symbol of joy and honour; for not only kings then wore crowns, but men were crowned at weddings and feasts, at games also and theatres.' Ewald (348) regards the expression as figurative: '*die gefallene krone* kann nur bildich den ganzen jezt verlorenen ehrenstand des volkes bedeuten'.[53]

This is surely the meaning here. The poet, as he nears the end of his litany, is struck by the tragic transformation of the once great people. His vignettes add up to a people without statehood. As O'Connor (2002, 76) puts it, 'Once a proud nation, they now have neither monarchy nor independence'. Because of the proximity of v. 15 and the reference to joy and dance, it may be that the poet had the festivity aspect also in mind; cf. Gerstenberger (503) and NEB 'the garlands have fallen from our heads'. Nägelsbach (187) seems, wrongly, to limit the expression to Jerusalem itself: 'The crown on the head of Jerusalem had consisted in this, that she was *great among the nations, a princess among the provinces, and perfect in beauty, the joy of the whole earth*'. Dobbs-Allsopp (146f.) may be asking too much of the passage here. He understands v. 15 to allude to the personified city and interprets the first stich of v. 16 in the same way: 'Reference to the "crown" falling "from our head" is not simply symbolic language for honor and glory and festivity (Job 19.9; Song 3.11), but a metaphor for the broken and collapsed walls of Jerusalem. The crenellated walls of Palestinian cities were often likened to a great crown that adorns the head of the city. The mural crown is a common motif associated with the personified city in the Old Testament (Isa 28.1-5; 62.3; Jer 13.18; Ezek 16.12). Thus, the image of "fallen" personified Jerusalem inheres in the poet's metaphorical language (cf. Amos 5.2).'

The sudden confession in the second stich is unexpected, coming as it does after the description of misery. אוי occurs 24 times in the Hebrew Bible. It is sometimes associated with הוי (which occurs 51 times); indeed, LXX often translates both terms by the same word οὐαὶ (Zobel 1978, 359).[54] In the majority of instances אוי is followed by the preposition ל + suffix and followed by a motivating clause, the latter providing אוי with specific meaning (Zobel 1978, 360). In this passage אוי is construed with ל + 1st p. pl. suffix and, in addition, the emphatic particle נא (as in Jer 4.31; 45.3).[55] The unexpectedness may be the result of the first stich which, in turn, as we have noted, arose from the interpretation of the sheer weight of adversity being described. The poet, in recognising the sudden loss of status and statehood, is forced to interpret in terms of cause and

---

[53] So also Keil (453), Löhr (1906, 31), Budde (1898ª, 107).
[54] Wanke (1966, 215-18) has shown that the two terms differ syntactically.
[55] Bickell (121) wishes to delete נא, but for no good reason.

effect, namely, sin and punishment. At 5.7 the poet had reflected on the sins of the forefathers and had connected those sins with the present suffering. Here, the 1st p. pl. embraces not only the present community but Yahweh's people past and present. This emphatic confession of sin, construed with that of v. 7, functions as an important element in the people's approach to Yahweh. There is no protestation of innocence (cf. Pss 44 and 59). Yahweh is in the right, for we have sinned.

5.17

Text and Versions
MT הָיָה, so also LXX, V, OL, T; P ܗܘܐ...ܗܘܐ h'...h'. Albrektson (204) argues that the second ܗܘܐ presupposes the first and that P has misread MT היה as הנה. *BHK* considers deleting היה, but this would upset the balance of the perfect (חשׁך) in the second stich. MT is preferred.

MT דָּוֶה; LXX^B has ὀδύνη ὀδυνηρά, but most Greek MSS actually omit ὀδύνη. The Vaticanus reading looks like a clear case of dittography.[56]

* * *

This verse has long puzzled commentators. Do זה and אלה refer back to v. 16 and beyond or forward to v. 18? Rashi interprets in terms of the following verse, and Kara follows suit, pointing out that the destruction of the Temple was the most devastating of all the distressing things which happened to the people. MR and MLT do not formally explain the verse, but their comments regarding the Temple indicate that they are probably 'thinking' along the same lines. T's paraphrase also points forward: זה is interpreted as the Temple (= hill of Zion), and אלה, a plural, is taken rather tangentially to refer to those people who went into exile. The latter shows that the Targumist had difficulty identifying אלה with the prowling of foxes. Although Vermigli (207) had interpreted the 'crown' (v. 16) as Temple, Ark and Tabernacle (see above), his comment here suggests that he links v. 17 with the preceding verse: 'The principal cause of our sorrow is that we have sinned and that the glory of our head has been taken away'. Calvin is roughly of the same opinion: 'He connects sorrow here with the acknowledgement of sin... At the same time, the Prophet, no doubt, includes here all that we have already observed.' Keil (453), while taking vv. 17 and 18 as forming the transition to the request in vv. 19-22, regards על זה and על אלה to refer to what precedes—'yet not in such a way as that the former must be referred to the fact that sin has been committed, and the latter to the suffering'. Nägelsbach (187), Budde (1898a, 107), Löhr (1906, 31), Rudolph (258), Gerstenberger (503), Reyburn (142), Renkema (619) and Berlin (124) all take the view that the verses look forward to v. 18; cf. also translations such as RSV, JPS, NIV, NEB, NRSV, REB, where punctuation suggests that זה and אלה point forward.

---

[56] Cf. Kelso (67), Ziegler (493), Swete (377), and Rudolph (1938, 122).

Hillers[2] (159), however, rightly argues that the demonstrative pronoun זֶה following עַל at the beginning of a sentence usually refers to what precedes rather than what follows (cf. 1.16); and this view is maintained by Westermann (215), Provan (132), Dobbs-Allsopp (147), House (467f.), O'Connor (2002, 73).[57] זֶה likely refers to the confession of sin (v. 16b). אֵלֶּה refers back to the various calamities listed before Yahweh in vv. 2-16.

דָּוֶה—An adjective from √דוה 'be sad, miserable', may mean 'sick, sad, faint'. It is construed with לֵב at Jer 8.18 and Lam 1.22, and the combination seems to allude to depression or sorrow.

חָשְׁכוּ עֵינֵינוּ—The verb √חשׁך 'be dark' is construed with עַיִן at Ps 69.24. At Eccl 12.3 the words וְחָשְׁכוּ הָרֹאוֹת בָּאֲרֻבּוֹת must have the same meaning. In the latter passage it seems to be a poetic reference to failing vision, and the psalmist's call, תֶּחְשַׁכְנָה עֵינֵיהֶם מֵרְאוֹת, seems to request poor eyesight for the enemy. In the Psalm passage the call may be that the sparkle may fade from the eyes of the enemy, i.e. may their eyes be lifeless and express depression, not vitality. In our passage the author may be referring to the effect that constant weeping has had on the community (cf. Zion at 1.2): their vision seems to be impaired. The combination of the two organs, heart and eyes, here is worth noting. The author appears to allude to further physical effects of the hardships, but it possible that just as לֵב דָוָה is poetic for sadness/grief, so the darkened eyes may be a poetic allusion to loss of vitality/lack of vigour; cf. Provan (132).

5.18

Text and Versions
MT עַל; P ܡܛܠ *mṭl*; V *propter*; T עַל; Sym περὶ; LXX ἐπ'; OL *super*; see below.
MT שֶׁשָּׁמֵם followed by LXX, Sym, P, V, OL and T. Several MSS[Ken] read שׁהשׁממו and *BHK* notes that western Masoretes had the same.[58] MT is preferred.
MT בוֹ—so also OL (*per eum*), V, P and T; LXX ἐν αὐτῇ and one Hebrew MS[Ken] reads בה. But MT, referring back to the hill, is to be preferred. ἐν αὐτῇ = בה probably indicates a scribal reflection on Zion (construed as feminine at 1.17).

* * *

There is a sense in which the final scenario says it all. The other items are enough to make the people sad and depressed, but the sight of the desolate and jackal-infested Mt. Zion is the ultimate in tragic reversal.

---

[57] In addition to the passages cited by Hillers (Ps 32.6; Isa 57.6; 64.11; Jer 5.9, 29; 9.8; 31.26; Amos 8.8), he notes that עַל אֵלֶּה, a plural, does not fit well with the single condition described in v. 18. Plöger (160) considers the עַל at the beginning of each statement to point in both directions. The problem is made more complicated by v. 18 beginning with the same preposition.
[58] Rudolph (1938, 122) wonders whether שׁהשׁממו is an unusual Hophal form or the definite article plus שׁממו.

The poet reaches the end of his list of disastrous circumstances; and his final item is the climax of all that he has been describing. The once vibrant hill of Zion is desolate.[59] Although עַל, with which v. 18 begins, has been translated by LXX as 'upon', taking the verse as quite separate from the foregoing, the translations of Sym, P, V and T show that they interpreted עַל as having the same force as עַל in v. 17.[60] It does seem unlikely that the meaning of the third עַל in a series should diverge from the earlier two; besides, if עַל in v. 18 means 'upon', the prepositional phrase (בוֹ) with which the verse ends is redundant.[61] Vermigli (208) translates 'on account of'; and this is substantially the rendering of Calvin, Löhr (1906, 31), Rudolph (1962, 257), Wiesmann (259), Berlin (115), Westermann (209), Renkema (620), NEB, JPS, NIV, NRSV.

'Zion' occurs 15 times in Lamentations. It is applied variously in the Hebrew Bible—often to parts of the city of Jerusalem or to the inhabitants of Jerusalem. Here, the phrase 'hill of Zion, Zion hill' (cf. Ps 2.6 'Zion, my holy hill') is referring to the Temple Mount where Yahweh was thought to dwell (Pss 9.12; 76.2; Isa 8.18; 18.7; Joel 3.17). It is, perhaps, difficult to appreciate the feelings of the people of Jerusalem who had held to the doctrine of the inviolability of the city (cf. Ps 125.1), in that here, in a short line, the poet contemplates the desolation which now characterises that holy spot. Micah (3.12) in the eighth century had predicted that the hill (הַר הַבַּיִת) would become a wooded height (see also Jer 26.18), and Jeremiah (19.8) envisaged something similar (cf. Mic 6.13; see also Jer 7.12-14; 26.9). The poet, in contemplating the desolate vista which was Zion hill, probably recalls how prophets had warned the people of what was in store for them.

שֶׁשָּׁמֵם—Relative pronoun שֶׁ (GK 36) + adj. שָׁמֵם 'which is desolate'. LXX took שֶׁ as a conjunction and שָׁמֵם as a verb ἠφανίσθη = aorist passive, used elsewhere in Lamentations (4.5) to translate the Niphal of √שׁמם; so also OL, V, Sym. IE[1] is careful to emphasise that the form is a verb like אָהֵב (Gen 27.9, 14). P and T, however, appear to take שֶׁ as a relative and שָׁמֵם as an adjective (BL 464 a); so also AV, Calvin, Kraus (85), Westermann (210), Ewald (348), Berlin (115). The sense is not affected. The second stich completes the awful picture of ruin and devastation. Once a place of teeming pilgrims and fine buildings, the desolate hill of Zion is now the haunt of jackals.

---

[59] The comments in MR and MLT suggest that the desolation of Zion is paramount in the eyes of the poet.
[60] It does demonstrate that the passage was already problematic in the early history of exegesis.
[61] The LXX translation ἐπ', however, has found favour with Keil (446), Gottwald (18), Hillers[2] (156) and Provan (132).

שׁוּעָלִים—That שׁוּעָל means 'jackal' *canis aureus* rather than 'fox' *vulpes* (V and OL) seems probable. Foxes are solitary/family creatures, whereas jackals roam in groups; and this is what seems to be implied here—cf. Tristram (87), Margalith (226).

הִלְּכוּ—LXX translates with διῆλθον 'pass through' (OL *transierunt*). The Greek translator envisages jackals frequenting the area, having free range. IE[1], who believes that jackals are often found in ruins, is anxious to point out that the Piel is intransitive, although at Job 24.10 it appears to be transitive. He suggests that the Piel of הלך may carry the idea of continuous action—הליכה. Kara, who thinks the Piel of הלך means 'to trample', paints a similar picture of jackals coming and going.[62] Hillers[2] (159f.) quotes a passage from Mesopotamian lament literature (The Curse of Agade): 'In your fattening pens...may foxes that frequent ruined mounds sweep with their tails'. Wild animals, such as jackals, which are nowhere to be seen in crowded towns, are attracted to deserted ruins where broken-down structures afford some shelter and ready-made dens.

5.19

Text and Versions

MT אַתָּה—so also T; two MSS[Ken] ואתה and LXX σὺ δέ; P ܘܐܢܬ *w'nt*; V and OL *tu autem*. The Versions seem to point to the presence of ו. However, at 1.19 (q.v.) P and V again represent the copula where it is absent in MT.[63]

* * *

Although vv. 1-18 constitute part of the prayer to Yahweh, now the poet suddenly reverts to addressing Yahweh directly. He has spoken, in v. 18, of Yahweh's holy hill as desolate, implying that the Temple of Yahweh, his throne, is no more; but he cannot entertain the notion that this carries any implication as to Yahweh's power and permanence. He clings (in faith) to the familiar words of the liturgy (cf. Pss 9.8; 45.7 and especially 102.13) and, as Berlin (125) says, 'makes an important theological statement'. Yahweh is not confined to a temple. His power and his activity are transcendent. Although the fall of Zion will have been interpreted by

---

[62] Cf. Ehrlich (54): 'הִלְּכוּ heisst es, nicht הָלְכוּ, weil es hier nicht auf die Fortbewegung, sondern lediglich auf die Bewegung innerhalb des genannten Ortes ankommt'.

[63] In Lam 1.19, it is a case of antithesis which is implied in the text and which is sometimes expressed by the copula (Gen 17.21; 19.19; GK 154a), cf. the translation of Lam 1.19 in AV, Luther, NRSV, JPS and NIV. It may be that at 5.19 the poet contrasts the ruin of the people with Yahweh's permanence and power, and אתה serves almost as ואתה (cf. Pss 3.4; 22.4; 41.10; 59.5). On the other hand, the original reading may have been ואתה, and the ו dropped out through haplography. This is the view of Wiesmann (261); cf. also Blayney (333), *BHK*, *BHS*, Westermann (210), Rudolph (1938, 122), Kraus (85), Kaiser (375).

many as an indication of Yahweh's weakness in the face of the Babylonian deities, the poet does not betray such sentiments. Yahweh is the one who has brought about the disastrous circumstances described in vv. 2-18. He is still all-powerful, as of old, and he remains the God of the people whom the poet represents.

תֵּשֵׁב—The verb √יׁשב may mean 'to sit' or 'to remain' or 'to dwell'. It may be that the term 'throne' in the second stich suggests that the poet had thought of Yahweh sitting enthroned, though a comparison of the passage with the terminology of Ps 125.1 and Joel 4.20 would suggest that 'to remain' was uppermost in the poet's mind. The LXX translator, as Albrektson (205) notes, often translates יׁשב with κατοικέω (as here) meaning 'to dwell', while P translates ܘܐܢܬ ܡܪܝܐ ܠܥܠܡ ܐܝܬܝܟ *w'nt mry' l'lm 'ytyk* 'and you, O Lord, are for ever'. These Versions together with V *permanebis* and T את הוא יי לעלם seem to interpret תשב as 'remain';[64] and this is true of MLT also. IE[1] paraphrases 'We know that your kingdom will not pass away (לא תסור) and that you sit on the throne of the kingdom for generation after generation'. He, clearly, understands the passage to refer to the eternal nature of Yahweh;[65] and he is followed by Vermigli (208) 'you, God, abide to eternity', and Luther is in agreement 'Aber du, HERR, der du ewiglich bleibst'. Likewise Calvin, although he sees also in the verb תׁשב the suggestion of God sitting as governor of the world. Keil (454) takes the view that the second stich ('throne') supplies the clue to the meaning of the first and translates 'Thou, O Yahweh, art enthroned eternally'; and this is substantially the rendering of Ewald (348), Budde (107f.), Haller (112), Meek (37), Renkema (622), Berlin (115), House (454), JPS, NEB. Others maintain the view reflected from the Versions to Luther: AV, Dyserinck (380), Ehrlich (54), Gottwald (18), Kraus (85), Rudolph (257), Kaiser (375). I am of the opinion that the early interpreters were correct. The first stich has to do with Yahweh's eternal existence, the second about his rule over all generations.

The phrase לדר ודור is parallel to לעולם in the first stich and is a standard expression (Deut 32.7; Ps 102.13; Isa 13.20; 34.17; 58.12). Renkema (624) may be correct in thinking that the poet had in mind the next generation 'which must suffer under the present situation of need, although they had no part in its cause'. Westermann (216) is right when he says that 'this verse is not spoken with straightforward jubilation. One must hear this verse in conjunction with the accusation against God that follows in v. 20.'

---

[64] See, however, Alexander (2008, 185 n. 32) whose rendering of T is 'You are the Lord. Forever your dwelling-place…', though the discussion in n. 32 shows some uncertainty as to the Targumist's thinking on the Hebrew syntax.
[65] IE[1] may have understood תׁשב as doing double duty here.

5.20

Text and Versions
MT לָמָּה—so also LXX, V and T; P ܠܐ *l*ʾ; *BHK* maintains that P's *Vorlage* read לֹא. Rudolph (1938, 122) thinks that the P translator has taken למה in the Syriac meaning 'nicht etwa'. It should be noted that P has employed ܠܐ in rendering למה at Pss 44.24, 25; 49.6; 79.10. MT is preferred.

MT לָנֶצַח—so also P, V and T;[66] LXX εἰς νεῖκος (cf. at 3.18). The usual rendering in LXX is εἰς τέλος (Pss 9.7, 19; 10.11; 51.7), which is the reading of Sym here. MT is preferred.

MT תִּשְׁכָּחֵנוּ תַּעַזְבֵנוּ—so also LXX, V and T; the verbs are in a different order in P. According to Kelso (67), this is mere scribal carelessness, but it may reflect P's tendency to treat his task with freedom at times.[67] MT is preferred.

* * *

Although vv. 20f. are in question form, they continue the passage begun at v. 19, which is a statement. Indeed, these questions are based upon the previous verse's declaration of Yahweh's sovereignty, as Rashi and IE[1] are careful to point out. The familiar vocabulary also continues as though the poet was now anxious to clothe his important plea in the traditional language of the cult. The synonymous parallelism is clear.

While a lot has been said about Yahweh's action vis-à-vis his people, he has not actually been *accused* of either forgetting or abandoning them, though it should be noted that the present prayer begins (v. 1) with 'Remember, O Yahweh'; and this is the only passage where למה 'why?' is directed at Yahweh. The verbs √שכח and √עזב, though not synonymous, are often juxtaposed (Job 9.27; Prov 2.17; Isa 49.14; 65.11). They are in the imperfect (as in v. 19). The question put to Yahweh is not simply why did you forget/abandon us when the Babylonians besieged and then destroyed our cities, our Temple, our lives, but why do you continue to do so?[68]

The adverbial elements in vv. 19f. are all constructed from substantives plus ל (GK 100c). Though not quite equivalent to one another, they all have to do with duration. The form לנצח constructed with שכח at Pss 9.19; 10.11; 13.2 and 74.19, is equivalent to נצח (Amos 1.11) and נצח עד (Ps 49.20) and probably means 'endlessly',[69] while לארך ימים means 'for a long period' (Ps 23.6). The basic meaning of נצח here is 'endurance', as in Isa 34.10, where it is in parallel with מדור לדור. This is how P, V, T and Sym take it. LXX εἰς νεῖκος may also, perhaps, be translated 'for ever' (= εἰς νῖκος, cf. LSJ 1176), but OL *in contemptu* and SH ܠܚܪܝܢ *lḥryn*ʾ

---

[66] OL *in contemptu* is an attempt to render εἰς νεῖκος of LXX. SH renders ܠܚܪܝܢ *lḥryn*ʾ.
[67] TEV, without reference to P, renders 'Why have you abandoned us so long? Will you ever remember us again?'
[68] The poet has already acknowledged (vv. 7, 16) that sin brought about punishment.
[69] P translates ܠܥܠܡ *lʿlm* as in v. 19.

obviously thought otherwise. LXX may be rendered 'so completely', which is probably where Luther 'so gar' gets his understanding of the phrase, but this is not so appropriate in a line where the balancing element is concerned with 'time'. 'Extent' is the reading preferred also by NEB, JPS, NRSV, Dobbs-Allsopp (148), Gerstenberger (504), while the idea of 'endurance' is presupposed by Calvin, AV, NJB, NIV and most commentators.

לְאֹ֣רֶךְ יָמִֽים—The term אֹ֣רֶךְ יָמִֽים occurs at Deut 30.20; Job 12.12; Pss 21.5; 23.6; 91.16; 93.5; Prov 3.2. It has the sense of 'length of days'. It occurs with לְ in Pss 23.6; 93.5, where LXX translates εἰς μακρότητα ἡμερῶν 'for a very long time'.

'Why?', addressed to Yahweh, is common in the laments in Psalms (44.24; 74.1; 79.10; 80.13; 88.15). Based on the statement regarding Yahweh in the previous verse, the poet questions Yahweh's attitude to his people. Why, since he rules over all and for all time, does he ignore his people?[70] Rashi interprets thus: 'Have you not sworn to us by yourself?' This comes after Rashi's comments on v. 19 where he seems to link the two verses. He appears to say that Yahweh's oath/promise must still be in operation, so why does it seem that he forgets (cf. also Kara)? Vermigli (209) is similar—'Since you have so promised our fathers, it is fitting that your faithfulness be eternal. Although we have sinned, it is not right that your promises change. For as stable as that throne and kingdom of yours, so ought to be your covenant and pact.'

5.21

Text and Versions
MT (*Kethib*) וְנָשׁוּב; MT (*Qere*) וְנָשׁ֣וּבָה—so also many MSS[Ken]; the *Vorlagen* of LXX, P, V and T cannot be determined. Read with MT (*Qere*), cf. Jer 31.18. Bickell (121) deletes יהוה, while Budde (1898ª, 108) deletes אֵלֶ֑יךָ; *BHK* wants to delete one or the other; but the rhythm in this verse (4+3) is the same as in v. 1 and v. 19. MT is preferred, cf. Rudolph (1938, 122).

* * *

This verse, the crux of the prayer, is a fervent plea for restoration, for the renewal of the relationship with Yahweh.

הֲשִׁיבֵ֨נוּ יְהוָ֤ה ׀ אֵלֶ֨יךָ—The verb √שׁוּב + אֶל may mean to return to a place (Gen 8.9) or to a person (Gen 22.19). It is also used figuratively to return to God (1 Kgs 8.33, 48; Jer 3.7; Hos 14.2), and it is used of God returning to Zion (Zech 8.3) and to his people (Zech 1.3). The Hiphil of the verb, very

---

[70] As Renkema (624) notes, this idea of forgetting 'does not imply any loss of memory, it is a statement rather of the fact that YHWH has not intervened to bring the affliction to an end'.

frequent in the Hebrew Bible, may mean 'bring/take back' a person (2 Sam 3.26) or thing (Gen 29.3), either physically or spiritually (Jer 15.19); and it can mean 'to restore' Jerusalem (Dan 9.25) or the people (Ps 80.4, 8, 20). It must be said that the meaning of the first stich is not entirely clear. The construction הֲשִׁיבֵנוּ יְהוָה אֵלֶיךָ וְנָשׁוּבָה is similar to הֲשִׁיבֵנִי וְאָשׁוּבָה at Jer 31.18, but the meaning of the latter passage is disputed.[71] While it is difficult to be certain of the exegesis of the early Versions, LXX, V and P, the paraphrase of T, 'Restore us, O Lord, to yourself, and we shall return in complete repentance', shows that the translator understood the poet to be speaking of spiritual returning. IE[1], however, takes the first verb to refer to a plea for Yahweh to bring back the people 'to the city, the dwelling-place of your name'; and this is how MLT understands it. The assumption is that the people are in exile (cf. IE[1] on שׁוּבֵנוּ in Ps 85.5).

הֲשִׁיבֵנוּ יְהוָה אֵלֶיךָ וְנָשׁוּבָה—The cohortative coming after the imperative often expresses an intention or intended consequence (GK 108d). We may translate: 'O Yahweh, bring us back to yourself that we may return'. We can, I think, rule out IE[1]'s interpretation that the passage concerns return from exile.[72] What the author is calling for is a restored relationship with Yahweh. He had begun his prayer with a call to Yahweh to 'remember' (v. 1) and he has just referred to the fact that Yahweh had long forgotten/abandoned his people (v. 20). The relationship between Yahweh and his people is hardly discernible and needs to be restored. The author has acknowledged (vv. 7, 16) that the people, past and present, have broken the relationship and have brought about the disastrous circumstances in which they find themselves. They are now at rock bottom and helpless. The initiative must come from Yahweh who, it seems, has abandoned all interest in that relationship. As Renkema puts it (628), 'it is the people's very inability to restore their relationship with God under their own steam which is the point of confession... YHWH alone, therefore, can break the great silence between himself and his people and create a new beginning.' The final element in the first stich completes the 'plea and response' formula,[73] illustrated at Jer 17.14—רְפָאֵנִי יְהוָה וְאֵרָפֵא הוֹשִׁיעֵנִי וְאִוָּשֵׁעָה. The poet is saying: If Yahweh will take us back, we shall come back. The verb √שׁוב is used here as in Amos 4.6, 8; Hos 14.2. Such a return involves repentance, but the emphasis is on the restoration of the relationship (as אֵלֶיךָ emphasizes).

---

[71] Cf. McKane (1996, 800).
[72] It was natural that this interpretation should be placed on the words, especially by commentators far removed from the scene, as it were. The movement from exile to homeland was, indeed, a return, but this prayer is not in the mouths of exiles; cf. Keil (454) and Renkema (627).
[73] Cf. Watson (280 n. 31).

חַדֵּשׁ יָמֵינוּ כְּקֶדֶם—The second stich parallels the first, calling for a resumption of the good old days of the happy relationship; cf. Pss 14.7; 80.19. This need not allude specifically to the 'honeymoon' period (Jer 2.2; Hos 2.16-25; Mic 7.14-20) nor to the heyday of the Davidic empire, but the poet speaks of that part of the history of the Yahweh–Israel relationship when Yahweh was their God, and they were his people.

כְּקֶדֶם—'as (in) former times'; cf. Jer 50.9. The preposition ב is occasionally elided after כ; cf. also Isa 28.21 כהר פרזים = 'as (on) Mount Perazim'. See JM 133 h.

5.22

Text and Versions
MT כִּי אִם; six MSS[Ken] כִּי; V *sed*; T ארום אילהן; Sym εἰ δὲ; LXX ὅτι; P ܡܛܠ *mṭl d*; OL *quia*. LXX and P do not specifically represent אם. It is possible that their *Vorlagen* read only כי (cf. the reading of the six MSS). It is also possible that the translators took כי אם as having the same force as כי, or that they ignored the difficult אם. But V's 'but' and T's 'but rather' suggest to most scholars that אם was present in their *Vorlagen*, while Sym's 'but if' clearly points to the presence of אם. The reading כי, of the six MSS, prompts Houbigant (483) to look askance at אם, and he suggests that it is the result of a dittograph of the first two letters (מא) of the following word מאס and should be deleted. MT is preferred as the *lectio difficilior* (see below).

* * *

The final verse continues to address Yahweh and is part of the plea (vv. 21-22). The intensity of v. 21 is maintained as the author stresses that he and the people of Yahweh continue to feel that they are the object of his rejection and anger.

כִּי אִם—Although not the only problem in this passage, the explication of these words is crucial to the understanding of the entire verse. A glance at the Versions shows that from LXX onwards translators and exegetes have struggled with the meaning, and there is no consensus.[74] We do not have the full verse in Sym, but he, alone among the Versions, appears to begin to treat the verse as comprising protasis and apodosis. That is to say the words כי and אם are taken (not as a combination) as though retaining their separate sense 'for if'. This is how Rashi and IE[1] understood it, and it is followed by Ehrlich (54), Kaiser (375) and NEB. But, apart from the grammatical irregularity (the apodosis is usually introduced by הנה or ו; cf. JM 118 m, 176 b), the resultant translation is awkward and unsatisfactory.[75] A novel variation of this is proposed by Linafelt (2000, 60f.; 2001, 342f.). He translates 'for if truly you have rejected us, bitterly raged

---

[74] Cf. Hillers[2] (160f.) for a summary of several attempts.
[75] As Hillers[2] (160) observes 'the second colon does not really state the consequence of the first, but is rather a restatement of it'.

against us...', that is, he takes the entire verse to be the protasis of a conditional statement *lacking* an apodosis. 'The book is left opening out into the expectation of God's nonresponse'. But, while theoretically possible, this proposal suffers from the fact that it is without parallel in the Hebrew Bible; and Berlin (126) describes it as 'too modern'; cf. Salters (2003, 364). RSV translates as though the verse was comprised of two questions[76]: 'Or hast thou utterly rejected us? Art thou exceedingly angry with us?' This is a view that has been dismissed by several scholars.[77] Meek (38) notes that the translation of כי אם as 'or' is impossible, while Hillers[2] (160) observes that כי אם nowhere else introduces a question. The translation 'unless' is suggested by Calvin and is found in RV (margin), Nägelsbach (190), Rudolph (1962, 257f.), Moffat, NRSV, JB, NJB, NIV, Provan (133), ESV, O'Connor (2001, 1071). An objection to this interpretation may be that such a meaning usually comes only after a negative clause (GK 163; cf. Albrektson, 206). Another problem with this view is that the author's intensity, so evident in vv. 19-21, falls flat. He is pleading with Yahweh to restore relations and now (if כי אם = 'unless') he lets Yahweh off the hook, as it were, by indicating that it would be quite understandable and acceptable if Yahweh had other plans![78] This is probably why several translators and exegetes have taken a different line. They sense that the words in the verse (apart from כי אם) are describing the state in which the author and his people find themselves. They have experienced/are experiencing Yahweh's rejection and anger. I believe that the *Vorlagen* of the Versions read the same as MT and that the translators[79] eschewed the option of taking אם as 'if' and כי אם as 'unless' for the reason given above. LXX and P chose the rendering 'because',[80] and V and T chose 'but',[81] allowing the rest of the verse to underline the present reality.[82]

Calvin, although preferring to translate 'unless', alludes to a prevalent view which understands כי אם as meaning 'though, although'. Perles (1930, 123) does not refer to Calvin, but this is also his interpretation—אף על פי—though he does not argue the case. It is, however, Gordis (1974[b], 291ff.)—mentioning neither Calvin nor Perles—who spells out

---

[76] This seems to have originated with Grotius (558), who, though annotating the Vulgate, translates אם as *an* and renders *An enim omnino nos abiiceres, et irascereris contra nos sine modo?* Cf. also Ewald (348).
[77] Though it is found in Keil (446), Löhr (1906, 32), Kraus (85), TEV, Gottwald (18), Westermann (211), Renkema (630); cf. also Gerstenberger (504).
[78] As Gordis (1974[b], 290) puts it: 'The syntactic difficulty aside, the problem of meaning remains: a plea for divine favor is logically and psychologically incompatible with the idea of a possible total rejection by God'.
[79] Apart from Sym.
[80] Cf. also Blayney (333), JPS.
[81] MLT אף על פי כן 'nevertheless' is probably quite close to V and T; cf. also AV, RV, Albrektson (206), REB, Hillers[2] (160f.), Berlin (115).
[82] The reading of the six MSS[Ken] may also reflect scribal perception and preference rather than sloppy copying.

this viewpoint. Gordis stresses that vv. 21f. should be taken together as at Ps 89.51f., where a plea stretches over two verses—main clause (v. 51), subordinate clause (v. 52). He then draws attention to passages such as Isa 10.22; Jer 51.14; Amos 5.22 where כי אם is best translated 'even if, although'; and he translates: 'Turn us to yourself, O Lord, and we shall return; renew our days as of old, even though you had despised us greatly and were very angry with us'. My only problem with Gordis[83] is that he takes the two verbs in v. 22 as pluperfects. There is no need for this: the poet and his people are praying out of a situation where it is all too obvious that Yahweh has rejected/been very angry with them.

מָאֹס מְאַסְתָּנוּ—The verb מאס√ means 'to reject' or 'to despise'. Some scholars take it to indicate finality, a complete severance of the relationship between Yahweh and his people and so as the mutually exclusive alternative to the restoration requested in v. 21 (so MR, RSV, NIV etc.), but the verb need not necessarily imply such finality, even though construed with the infinitive absolute. Internal parallelism, in which also the infinitive absolute is balanced by the adverbial phrase עַד־מְאֹד, suggests that the first stich has to do with extreme contempt/despising. If the first stich has to do with complete (i.e. for ever) severance, the second (which speaks only of extreme anger) is somewhat redundant.

In Jewish liturgical practice there is the tradition of not ending the public reading of this book with v. 22 (because of the negative and sombre wording) but to repeat after it the words of v. 21. The same practice is followed at the end of Isaiah, the Book of the Twelve and Ecclesiastes, referred to in the Masoretic mnemonic יתקק: Isaiah (ישעיה) indicated by י, Book of the Twelve (תרי עשר) by ת and the double ק denoting Ecclesiastes (קהלת) and Lamentations (קינות).

---

[83] Gordis is followed by Gous (1990, 287) and House (470-72).